Colección Támesis

SERIE A: MONOGRAFÍAS, 260

A COMPANION TO
LOPE DE VEGA

A COMPANION TO LOPE DE VEGA

Edited by

Alexander Samson

and

Jonathan Thacker

TAMESIS

© Contributors 2008

First published 2008 by Tamesis, Woodbridge

ISBN 978-1-85566-168-4

Tamesis is an imprint of Boydell & Brewer Ltd
PO Box 9, Woodbridge, Suffolk IP12 3DF, UK
and of Boydell & Brewer Inc.
668 Mt Hope Avenue, Rochester, NY 14620, USA
website: www.boydellandbrewer.com

A CIP catalogue record for this book is available
from the British Library

Printed from camera-ready copy supplied by Alexander Samson

This publication is printed on acid-free paper

Printed in Great Britain by
CPI Antony Rowe, Chippenham, Wiltshire

CONTENTS

LIST OF ILLUSTRATIONS

The following are all found in the plate section between pp. 272 and 273.

LIST OF CONTRIBUTORS

Elaine Canning is Lecturer in Hispanic Studies at Swansea University. Author of *Lope de Vega's Comedias de tema religioso: Re-creations and Re-presentations* (2004), she specializes in research into Spain's Golden-Age theatre and Spanish cinema. In addition to her publications on Golden-Age theatre she has published on film adaptations of the plays of Lope de Vega and on the themes of destiny, theatricality and identity in contemporary European cinema. She is the coordinator of the MA in European Stage and Screen at Swansea and is co-director of the Centre for Research into Iberian Stage and Screen.

Geraldine Coates is University Lecturer in Medieval Spanish Literature at the University of Oxford and Tutor in Spanish at St Anne's College. She is the author of several articles on medieval epic and historiography, and is interested in the representation of collective identities in literary and historiographical writing from the Middle Ages to the Golden Age. She is currently preparing a monograph on treachery and the nation in the legends of Fernán González, Bernardo del Carpio and King Sancho II, from the Middle Ages to the Baroque.

Frederick A. de Armas is Andrew W. Mellon Professor in Humanities at the University of Chicago. He is also Chair of the Department of Romance Languages and Literatures. His books and edited volumes include: *The Invisible Mistress: Aspects of Feminism and Fantasy in the Golden Age* (1976); *The Return of Astraea: An Astral-Imperial Myth in Calderón* (1986); *The Prince in the Tower: Perceptions of "La vida es sueño"* (1993); *Heavenly Bodies: The Realms of "La estrella de Sevilla"* (1996); *A Star-Crossed Golden Age: Myth and the Spanish Comedia* (1998); *Cervantes, Raphael and the Classics* (1998); *European Literary Careers: The Author from Antiquity to the Renaissance* (2002); *Writing for the Eyes in the Spanish Golden Age* (2004); and *Ekphrasis in the Age of Cervantes* (2005). His latest book, *Quixotic Frescoes: Cervantes and Italian Renaissance Art* was published by the University of Toronto Press in 2006.

Victor Dixon, after six years at Cambridge, taught for three at the University of St Andrews and fourteen at the University of Manchester. From 1974 until his retirement in 1999 he was Professor of Spanish at Trinity College Dublin. In 2008 he was admitted to Membership of the Royal Irish Academy. His publications include critical editions of three plays by Lope de Vega, verse translations of two and some sixty articles on Lope and other Golden-Age dramatists, as well as nine on Antonio Buero Vallejo. He has also directed or acted in over twenty Spanish plays.

Geraint Evans has taught at the Universities of Nottingham, London and Cambridge, and is now at the University of Nottingham Ningbo, China. He has worked mainly on early modern Spanish theatre, specifically issues of gender, and recently published on tragicomic effects in the *comedia* and their relation to Christianity in Lope. He is currently working on representations of the body in Calderón de la Barca and Guillén de Castro, adaptations into Chinese of Hispanic literature and Chinese slash fiction.

Tyler Fisher is the Queen Sofía Research Fellow in Peninsular Spanish Literature and lecturer in Spanish at Exeter College, Oxford. His M.Phil. thesis on Lope's self-referential metaphors led to his present research on Early Modern metaliterary figures more generally and their theological implications. Tyler's publications include editions and translations of José Martí's *Ismaelillo* and *Flores del destierro*, both from Wings Press.

Edward H. Friedman is Chancellor's Professor of Spanish and Professor of Comparative Literature at Vanderbilt University. His primary field of research is early modern Spanish literature, with emphasis on the picaresque, Cervantes and the *comedia*. His research also covers contemporary narrative and drama. His books include *Cervantes in the Middle: Realism and Reality in the Spanish Novel* (2006). He is editor of the *Bulletin of the Comediantes* and past president of the Cervantes Society of America.

Alejandro García Reidy is at present finishing his Ph.D. at the Department of Spanish Philology of the Universidad de Valencia. As a researcher he has specialized in the life and works of Lope de Vega, and has published several articles on this author and on other topics related to Spanish Golden-Age theatre. He is also a member of two research groups from the Universidad de Valencia: DICAT, which is in the process of completing a *Diccionario biográfico de actores del teatro clásico español*, and ARTELOPE, which is developing a *Diccionario de argumentos del teatro de Lope de Vega*.

David Johnston is Professor of Hispanic Studies and Head of the School of Languages, Literatures and Performing Arts at Queen's University Belfast. He is internationally known for his work on the relationship between translation and performance, and has written and co-edited four books and over twenty articles on the subject. His translations of a number of Lope plays have been performed around the world, most notably *The Gentleman from Olmedo* and *The Great Pretenders* for the ground-breaking Gate Theatre season in the early 1990s and *The Dog in the Manger* for the RSC Spanish Golden-Age Season.

David McGrath completed his Ph.D. in 2003 at Queen Mary College, London, where he submitted his thesis on *The Representation of the American Indian in the Comedia.* He is now at the University of Manchester, engaged in post-doctoral research into the letters of Luisa de Carvajal, the intrepid *jesuitina* who pursued her mission in post-Gunpowder Plot London. As a Visiting Research Fellow at King's College, London, he has also been developing dramaturgical projects, most recently adaptations of *Cardenio* (a Jacobean drama based on two episodes from *Don Quijote*) and excerpts from Lope de Vega's *Arauco domado.*

Arantza Mayo is University Lecturer at the University of Cambridge and Fellow and Director of Studies at Corpus Christi College. She is the author of *La lírica sacra de Lope de Vega y José de Valdivielso* (2007) and of a series of articles on early modern Spanish literature and twentieth-century Bolivian poetry.

Barbara Mujica is Professor of Spanish at Georgetown University in Washington, D.C., President Emerita of The Association for Hispanic Classical Theater and editor-in-chief of *Comedia Performance,* a journal devoted to early modern Spanish theatre. Her latest books are *Sophia's Daughters: Women Writers of Early Modern Spain* (2004), *Teresa de Jesús: Espiritualidad y feminismo* (2006) and *Lettered Women: The Correspondence of Teresa de Avila* (forthcoming). She is currently working on a performance-based anthology of early modern Spanish theatre, to be published by Yale University Press. Barbara Mujica's novel, *Frida*, was an international bestseller and appeared in seventeen languages. Her most recent novel is *Sister Teresa.* Barbara Mujica is director of El Retablo, the Spanish-language theatre group of Georgetown University and a member of the board of directors of GALA Hispanic Theatre.

Ali Rizavi is a first-year doctoral student at the University of Oxford, working on the reception of Cervantes's *Don Quixote* in seventeenth-century France.

José María Ruano de la Haza is Professor of Spanish at the University of Ottawa. He is the author of some critical editions of Golden-Age plays and of many articles on diverse aspects of theatrical activity in seventeenth-century Spain. He is the author of, among other books, *La primera versión de La vida es sueño* (1992) and *La puesta en escena en los teatros comerciales* (2000). He has edited six collective volumes and has adapted *Celestina*, *Calderón enamorado* and *La mujer por fuerza* for the stage. He is presently completing an edition of the twelve plays in Calderón's *Parte V* for the Biblioteca Castro.

Alexander Samson is a lecturer in Spanish Golden-Age literature, culture and history at University College London. He is the editor of a volume on *The Spanish Match: Prince Charles's Journey to Madrid, 1623* (2006), as well as having published articles on the marriage of Philip II and Mary Tudor, historiography and royal chroniclers in sixteenth-century Spain, Lope de Vega, firearms, Diego Hurtado de Mendoza, Cervantes, maps and Anglo-Spanish literary and cultural relations. His first book *Mary Tudor and the Habsburg Marriage: England and Spain 1553–1557* is due in 2008.

Jonathan Thacker is Faculty Lecturer at the University of Oxford and Fellow and Tutor in Spanish at Merton College. He is the author of *A Companion to Spanish Golden Age Theatre* (2007) as well as a monograph and articles on early modern Spanish drama. In addition to teaching and writing about Spanish Golden-Age theatre, he has acted as adviser to the Royal Shakespeare Company, has translated works by Cervantes and Tirso de Molina into English and is Editor of the Aris and Phillips Hispanic Classics series.

Isabel Torres is a Senior Lecturer and Head of Spanish and Portuguese Studies at Queen's University Belfast. She is the author of *The Polyphemus Complex: Rereading the Baroque Mythological Fable* (*Bulletin of Hispanic Studies*, Monograph Issue, 83.2 [2006]), and editor of *Rewriting Classical Mythology in the Hispanic Baroque* (2007). She has published several articles on early modern Spanish poetry and drama and is currently completing a book on Golden-Age love poetry for the Tamesis *Companion* series.

Xavier Tubau is Doctor in Hispanic Philology (Universitat Autònoma de Barcelona) and Associate Professor of Literature at the Universitat Pompeu Fabra of Barcelona. He is author of *Una polémica literaria: Lope de Vega y Diego de Colmenares* (2007), editor of dramatic texts by Lope de Vega and co-editor (with José María Micó) of a forthcoming Spanish poetry anthology. He is coordinator of the collection 'Clásicos y Modernos' (Crítica) as well as of publications of the Prolope project directed by Alberto Blecua.

Duncan Wheeler is currently preparing to submit his doctoral thesis at Oxford University, where he also teaches. The thesis is titled 'The *comedia* on page, stage and screen: the performance and reception of Golden-Age drama in Spain (1939–2008)'. He has written various articles on contemporary Spanish culture and politics, cinema and popular music that have been published in Spain, the UK and the US in journals such as the *Bulletin of Hispanic Studies*, *Bulletin of the Comediantes*, *Cuestiones de género* and *Media History*. His translations of various Spanish texts from the early modern period will be published shortly.

FOREWORD

We would like to thank everyone who participated in and made the conference out of which this volume arose, *Metamorphosis and Transformation in the Life and Work of Lope de Vega* in the summer of 2006, such an enjoyable and successful experience. Any introduction to the life and work of a figure as mercurial and prolific across all major literary genres as Lope must confront the problem of combining coverage with depth. This volume reflects our own vision of the *Fénix* and its origins in a consideration of change. We hope, nevertheless, that it will be useful to undergraduate students and their teachers as a sourcebook as well as inspiring well-travelled *lopistas* to look again at particular themes and approaches or ponder other important questions.

Some of the contributions focus on providing a synthesis of what has been written on a particular text or area, introducing for an undergraduate audience the state of the field, whilst at the same time indicating where more detailed and in-depth considerations of these issues are to be found. Other contributors offer fresh insights or enriching perspectives on well-known material, whilst others again have taken this opportunity to bring centre stage less well-known and perhaps unjustly neglected aspects of his output. What is clear is that in the face of the myriad of possible texts and approaches to Lope, we hope this volume showcases at least some of the exciting new developments in Lope de Vega studies today and reflects the freshness and energy pervading the field.

We owe a huge debt of gratitude to Charles Davis for his extraordinarily careful readings and numerous suggestions for improvements, this volume's successes would not have been possible without him. Finally, it remains to thank Merton College, Oxford for providing a grant to help with the final stages of editing the volume and Ellie Ferguson, of Boydell and Brewer, for her assistance throughout.

Introduction: Lope's Life and Work

ALEXANDER SAMSON and JONATHAN THACKER

Pocas obras hay en ninguna literatura más personales que la de este genial romántico. Al margen de cada uno de estos tremendos episodios de su vida crece frondosa la poesía, índice de sus emociones, y aquí más que nunca «fermosa cobertura» de las frivolidades de aquel para quien todos los sentimientos eran familiares, salvo el de la responsabilidad moral de sus propios actos. La vida de Lope pendía de su impulsivo y anárquico temperamento. Pero seamos indulgentes: tal vez nadie, en la historia de las literaturas, ha sabido dejar tras de cada acción liviana una tan brillante e inmaculada estela de belleza.[1]

[There are few works in any literature more personal than those of this outstanding romantic. In the margins of each of those momentous episodes of his life poetry grows luxuriantly, an index of his emotions, and here more than ever it is 'the beautiful covering' of the frivolities of the man for whom all feelings were familiar, except that of moral responsibility for his own actions. The life of Lope hung from his impulsive and anarchic temperament. But, let us be indulgent: perhaps no-one, in the history of literature, has managed to leave behind each fickle action a wake of such shining and immaculate beauty.]

Lope Félix de Vega Carpio (1562–1635) was perhaps the most extraordinary writer to leave his mark on early modern Spain, the period that Spaniards have designated their artistic Golden Age. Beyond Spanish borders it tends to be Cervantes who possesses the highest cultural capital for his role in the creation of the novel; Velázquez is the painters' painter; Quevedo and Góngora are admired for their poetic brilliance; and only Calderón's theatre is typically assumed to come close to the power and philosophical reach of Shakespeare's. Within Spain Lope is better known, of course, but it is probably true to say that his popular renown stems in roughly equal measure from his exceptional productivity and his eventful life. The 'Lope myth' which has grown up around him presents the man as a flawed character possessed of a unique genius.

Artistically, Lope is best known as a playwright, indeed as the creator of a national drama usually called the *comedia nueva*. The generically mixed type of play that he was instrumental in developing in late sixteenth-century Spain — not dissimilar in many respects to plays performed in Shakespeare's England —

---

[1] Américo Castro & Hugo A. Rennert, *Vida de Lope de Vega (1562–1635)*, 2nd edn (Madrid: Anaya, 1968), p. 44.

remained popular for well over a hundred years and would be sufficient on its own to guarantee his immortality as a writer. Plays such as *Fuente Ovejuna*, *Peribáñez y el comendador de Ocaña*, *El caballero de Olmedo*, *El perro del hortelano* and *El castigo sin venganza* have assured Lope a place in the pantheon of world dramatists.[2] However, as we shall see, Lope is a fascinating figure not only because of the scenes he created, the worlds he so skilfully depicted on the boards of the early modern playhouses of Spain, but for a host of other reasons, narrowly literary, broadly cultural and historical, and pertaining to his personal life.

In his hagiographical account of his mentor's life, Lope de Vega's contemporary and disciple, Juan Pérez de Montalbán, describes the state of the private chapel in the playwright's house on Francos street in Madrid: after Lope's death his friends discovered 'en un aposento donde se retiraba salpicadas las paredes y teñida la disciplina con reciente sangre' [in a chamber to which he would retire the walls were spattered, and his scourge stained, with fresh blood].[3] The extremity of his mortifications of the flesh and penitential practices testifies to the profound piety of a man whose first biographer sought to present to posterity a saintly figure who died mouthing the sweet names of Jesus and Mary. Later biographers, however, have refused to whitewash his peccadilloes, unable to overlook the extramarital relationships and large brood of illegitimate children, some of whom were conceived even after he took holy orders in 1614. The religiosity underlined by Montalbán's description of his friend cannot, however, be easily dismissed as hypocrisy and, while the *Fama póstuma* cannot be taken at face value either, it does point to an essential aspect of Lope's biography that demands more serious attention than it has hitherto received. The modern Lope is largely the creation of Cayetano Alberto de la Barrera y Leirado and his monumental *Nueva biografía de Lope de Vega*. Although it was completed in 1864, the work did not appear uncensored until 1890 when the Real Academia Española brought it out as the first volume of Lope's complete works. Despite its winning a prize, the panel of the Biblioteca Nacional had suppressed La Barrera's biography, worried that 'podía contribuir a rebajar el valor moral del Fénix de los Ingenios, considerado como hombre y como sacerdote' [it could contribute to the lowering of the moral standing of the Phoenix of Wits, as a man and as a priest].[4]

La Barrera's biography constituted such a significant development in the understanding of Lope's life because of its incorporation of material from the collections of his letters discovered in the Altamira archive in April 1863.[5] Two of

---

[2] Translations of titles of works by Lope can be found at the back of this volume, listed by genre and in alphabetical order.

[3] Juan Pérez de Montalbán, *Fama póstuma a la vida y muerte del doctor frey Lope Félix de Vega Carpio y elogios panegíricos a la inmortalidad de su nombre*, ed. Enrico di Pastena (Pisa: Edizioni ETS, 2001), p. xx. The house, in which Lope lived for a quarter of a century, is today a museum in the street now called Calle Cervantes.

[4] Cited in Lope de Vega, *Epistolario de Lope de Vega Carpio*, ed. Agustín G. de Amezúa, 4 vols (Madrid: Aldus, 1935–43), II, p. 6.

[5] The 10th Duke of Sessa's daughter, who succeeded her father, married the Conde de Altamira, Marqués de Astorga, in 1731.

the five codices transcribed at the instigation of the then head of the Biblioteca Nacional in Madrid, the dramatist Juan Eugenio Hartzenbusch, have subsequently disappeared. Similarly, twenty-one of the letters originally in the codex now housed in the Museo Lázaro Galdiano, also in the Spanish capital, have gone missing in what is one of the most mysterious episodes in modern literary scholarship. The codices were labelled *Cartas de Belardo a Lucilo*, the former a pseudonym used by Lope in various works and the latter a reference to his most important and long-lived patron, the Duke de Sessa. (Lucilo – Lucilius – was a disciple of Seneca and addressee of his letters, the Epistulae morales ad Lucilium; the name also referes to the satirist Lucilius, who was born in Sessa, the duke's seat, near Naples, and its initial recalls his first name Luis.[6]) The survival of their correspondence is in part a tribute to both Sessa and Lope's awareness of literary fame, an attempt to live on through their epistolary life, cementing their posthumous reputations as patron and artist respectively. The edition of the *Epistolario* by Amezúa was supplemented in the 1980s by Nicolás Marín, who gathered, from a variety of printed and manuscript sources, another four letters not included in the earlier collection.[7] The discovery of archival documents relating to the dramatist's failed relationship with Elena Osorio, published by Cristóbal Pérez Pastor, along with a number of further papers (in the Archivo Histórico de Protocolos de Madrid) notably those drawn up before Lope's friend, the notary Juan de Piña, largely completes the documentary picture we have of the subject of this *Companion*.[8] All of these sources, amounting to over a thousand documents, have recently been united and published in a two-volume work by Krzysztof Sliwa.[9]

While the documentary record may be largely complete, some new discoveries are still being made. An unknown letter resurfaced recently,[10] and more material has been discovered in the Archivo Histórico de Protocolos de Madrid. The latter relates to the dowry of a hitherto unknown sister, Catalina (in addition to a brother, Francisco, and two further sisters, Isabel and Juliana), the payment of Lope's pension from the archbishopric of Santiago de Compostela and an

---

[6] Lope de Vega, *Cartas*, ed. Nicolás Marín (Madrid: Castalia, 1985), p. 48 and n. 78. In this sense Lope is implicitly casting himself as Seneca, comparing their correspondence with a classical paradigm of the epistolary genre.

[7] *Cartas*, ed. Marín, and see his 'Un volumen de cartas de Lope poco conocido', *Cuadernos Bibliográficos*, 32 (1975): 63–75.

[8] See A. Tomillo & C. Pérez Pastor, *Proceso de Lope de Vega por libelos contra unos cómicos* (Madrid: Fortanet, 1901) and Cristóbal Pérez Pastor, *Noticias y documentos relativos a la historia y literatura española*, 1 (Memorias de la Real Academia Española, X) (Madrid: Real Academia Española, 1910), pp. 274–88. There is also José Simón Díaz, *Ensayo de una bibliografía de las obras y artículos sobre la vida y escritos de Lope de Vega Carpio* (Madrid: Centro de Estudios sobre Lope de Vega, 1955).

[9] Krzysztof Sliwa, ed., *Cartas, documentos y escrituras del Dr. Frey Lope Félix de Vega Carpio (1562–1635)*, 2 vols (Newark, DE: Juan de la Cuesta, 2007).

[10] Private communication. See also Joaquín Entrambasaguas, 'Un códice de Lope de Vega autógrafo y desconocido', *Revista de Literatura*, 38 (1970): 5–117.

inheritance of his daughter Feliciana.[11] The two wills that the playwright left behind, along with the descriptions in Montalbán of his house, library, religious artefacts and art objects, including tapestries, paintings and icons, provide us with a further insight into his material environment, status, habits and daily life. Despite the fact that an inventory of his library has never been found, his alleged ownership of 1,500 books — even if an exaggerated figure — suggests his avid and voracious appetite for knowledge and culture. As Victor Dixon clearly demonstrates in the first chapter of this *Companion*, dedicated to Lope's learning, his broad intellectual interest in everything from Greek to Christian hagiography and medicine to natural history, apparent in many aspects of his literary output, puts paid to the pervasive notion of a lack of heavyweight thought in his works.[12]

Lope's role as a leading light in the emergence of commercial theatre, and his gradual realisation of the possibilities that his literary fame afforded him for disseminating his work in print, meant that by the turn of the seventeenth century he was famous and wealthy, able to charge 500 *reales* (later 800) for a *comedia*. Miguel de Cervantes, with whom there was no love lost, dubbed him a 'monstruo de la naturaleza' [prodigy of nature] who 'alzóse con la monarquía cómica' [usurped the kingdom of drama] in his prologue to his *Ocho comedias y ocho entremeses*.[13] The success and perceived capabilities of this effervescent genius were reflected in the succession of highly placed aristocratic patrons who coveted an association with him, from Pedro Dávila, 3rd Marqués de las Navas, Antonio Álvarez de Toledo y Beamonte, 5th Duque de Alba, and Francisco de Ribera Barroso, 2nd Marqués de Malpica, to the 4th Marqués de Sarria, Pedro Fernández de Castro Andrade y Portugal, later 7th Conde de Lemos, and the aforementioned Luis Fernández de Córdoba y Aragón, 6th Duque de Sessa. Whatever the demands made on him as a secretary and confidant, however, his literary output never appeared to flag.

The solid facts of Lope's biography are somewhat harder to come by than one might wish in spite of the documentation and the numerous volumes dedicated to uncovering the man and his personality. Frequent autobiographical allusions in his prose, poetry and drama have allowed myths and half-truths about Lope and his writings to flourish unchecked. As Victor Dixon explains, 'he depicted in his writing every aspect of his life; no author was ever, in the broadest sense, more autobiographical'.[14] And yet, as Xavier Tubau argues in his study of *La Dorotea*

---

[11] See the excellent introduction to Charles Davis, ed., *27 documentos de Lope de Vega en el Archivo Histórico de Protocolos de Madrid* (Madrid: Comunidad de Madrid, 2004), p. 15.

[12] On the frequently clichéd attitude to Lope the thinker, see Enrique García Santo-Tomás, *La creación del Fénix: recepción crítica y formación canónica del teatro de Lope de Vega* (Madrid: Gredos, 2000), esp. pp. 7–12.

[13] Miguel de Cervantes, *Entremeses*, ed. Nicholas Spadaccini, 4th edn (Madrid: Cátedra, 1987), p. 93.

[14] Victor Dixon, 'Lope Félix de Vega Carpio', in *The Cambridge History of Spanish Literature*, ed. David T. Gies (Cambridge: Cambridge University Press, 2004), pp. 251–64 (p. 252).

in this volume (chapter 18), Lope's re-writing of his life in his works is artistic: care must be taken to separate fact from art.[15]

Lope lived during the reigns of three monarchs: Philip II (1556–98), his son Philip III (1598–1621) and his grandson Philip IV (1621–65). He was the child of a couple from the north who moved to Madrid when that city was appointed Philip II's new capital (in 1561) and began to swell accordingly. His youth coincided, serendipitously, with the creation of the *corrales*, the urban playhouses built in yards, part of whose proceeds went to fund hospitals for the poor. The future playwright's father Félix de Vega was an embroiderer whose notable devotion and charity no doubt cast a permanent shadow over his son's religious life.[16] The surname 'Carpio', adopted by the dramatist from his mother Francisca Hernández Flores's side of the family, may suggest that despite largely humble origins he had some contact with more elevated social circles, including perhaps his uncle Miguel de Carpio, a Sevillian inquisitor with whom he had apparently lived as a child and whom he thanked in later life in a dedication to his play *La hermosa Esther*.[17] It also came to represent Lope's social aspirations, as he linked himself to the legendary soldier Bernardo del Carpio, whose coat of arms he adopted on the basis of the coincidence of surnames, an action (amongst others) that provoked the satirical mirth of one of his poetic foes, Luis de Góngora.

The incident about which we know most, thanks to the legal record, is one to which Lope returned obsessively in his work, culminating in the semi-autobiographical fictionalisation of *La Dorotea*. In the mid-1580s, Lope had been displaced as the lover of the beautiful, married actress Elena Osorio (often 'Filis' in his poetry) by, it has been suggested, one of the nephews of Charles V's chancellor, Antoine Perrenot Granvelle.[18] This rejection provoked him to pen a series of satirical poems attacking Elena's father, Jerónimo Velázquez, manager of an acting troupe that had enjoyed a monopoly on Lope's output while the relationship lasted, and other members of her family. These poems led to his arrest, successful prosecution for libel and exile from Madrid for ten years. The initial sentence had been doubled in response to his continuing the literary attacks on Velázquez even after he was incarcerated, although the latter personally petitioned (successfully) for its reduction seven years later in 1595. As he prepared to leave Madrid Lope was named in another lawsuit for the 'rapto' [abduction] of the twenty-one-year-old noblewoman doña Isabel de Urbina (poetically 'Belisa'), who became his first wife and with whom he had two daughters, Antonia and Teodora. Neither girl would survive infancy.

Before the mid-1580s, nothing is known about Lope's life other than through references in his work. He was educated by the Jesuits at what later became the

---

[15] See the exemplary approach to this subject in S. Griswold Morley, 'The Pseudonyms and Literary Disguises of Lope de Vega', *University of California Publications in Modern Philology*, 33.5 (1951): 421–84, and further discussion of this issue below.

[16] See Davis, ed., *27 documentos*, p. 16.

[17] Castro & Rennert, *Vida de Lope de Vega*, p. 17. See the dedication to the play in Lope's *Parte XV* (Madrid, 1621).

[18] Castro & Rennert, *Vida de Lope de Vega*, pp. 52–55.

Colegio Imperial and was apparently a precocious student, learning Latin when about five years old and writing his first play when still a schoolboy. Later he is likely to have attended the University of Alcalá.[19] Military service in the Azores in 1583 and, shortly after his sentencing, an alleged involvement in the Armada Invencible [Spanish Armada] in which his brother, Francisco probably, was killed, a period of residence in the theatrically lively city of Valencia, then a return to Toledo, and three years in the ducal court at Alba de Tormes as gentleman of the chamber or secretary all preceded his return to Madrid as a widower following Isabel's death in childbirth in 1594. Sexual offences soon saw Lope in legal difficulties again, as he was accused in 1596 of an illicit, adulterous relationship with a widow, Antonia de Trillo de Armenta. There was considerable inconsistency in the way in which his carnal offences were treated. Perhaps the crucial difference in this case was the that they actually cohabited. In later years, a sixteen-year-long affair with the married Marta de Nevares, whom he had met in 1616, led to no apparent censure, despite the furious reaction of her husband, Roque Hernández de Ayala. 'Amarilis' or 'Marcia Leonarda', as she was dubbed in his work, was the dedicatee of the four interpolated *novelas* published in his poetic works *La Filomena con otras diversas rimas, prosas y versos* (1621) and *La Circe con otras rimas y prosas* (1624).[20] By 1628, after bearing Lope a daughter, Antonia Clara, Marta was blind and bouts of insanity plagued her until she died in 1632.

In the mid- to late-1590s, Lope had become involved with another actress, Micaela de Luján ('Lucinda' in his poetry), with whom he eventually had seven children, two of whom came to live with him some time after her disappearance from the documentary record in 1608. In 1598 he had taken a second wife, Juana de Guardo, the daughter of a wealthy meat merchant. By Juana he had a further four children, a favourite son Carlos Félix and three daughters, Jacinta, Juana and Feliciana. Only the last survived into adulthood, eventually outliving her father and marrying Luis de Usátegui, an official of the Secretary of the Council of the Indies.[21] Lope's other surviving daughters were Marcela de San Félix, as she became, who professed in the convent of the Trinitarias Descalzas in 1623, and Antonia Clara, who was dishonoured and abandoned by the noble Cristóbal Tenorio shortly before her father's death, adding to the personal tragedies of his final years. There were also important affairs with a further two actresses, Jerónima de Burgos (often 'Gerarda' in his verses), from 1607 until at least 1614, and Lucía Salcedo 'La Loca' [the mad] in 1615–16, before he met Marta de Nevares, and there existed at least another illegitimate son from his time in

---

[19] On Lope's possible presence at Alcalá, see Felipe B. Pedraza Jiménez, *Lope de Vega* (Barcelona: Teide, 1990), pp. 7–8.

[20] See, in chapter 17, Ali Rizavi's discussion of these texts and their political context — the early part of Philip IV's reign and the government of his *valido* or favourite, the Conde-Duque de Olivares, Gaspar de Guzmán.

[21] See the fascinating details unearthed surrounding her inheritance and dowry from her mother's marriage to Lope in Davis, ed., *27 documentos*, pp. 43–4.

Valencia.[22] These details complete the picture of 'la agitada y poco edificante vida de Lope de Vega' [Lope de Vega's unsettled and unedifying life], as it has been described.[23]

It has been suggested that the Council of Castile's decision to limit the funeral celebrations planned by the city in Lope's honour after his death in 1635 was the result of the 'vida irregular que había llevado' [the irregular life that he had led], a life characterised as 'una sucesión de aventuras, una intensa crónica sentimental' [a succession of adventures, an intense emotional chronicle], that of an 'aventurero íntimo' [adventurer in intimacy] and 'notario lírico de sí mismo' [lyrical recorder of himself].[24] These epithets point us to the fundamental paradox and central problem of his biography: the very documentary riches available to us and the apparently abundant autobiographical material in his fictions render Lope more mysterious and intangible rather than less.

The confusion and conflation of Lope de Vega's life and art in his own work is systematic and deliberate, undermining the strong temptation to read his texts biographically or use his fiction to solve puzzles about his life. The most obsessively confessional and intensely personal writing is simultaneously the most anonymised, self-consciously distanced and rhetorical, a function of the projection of a specific writerly image. It is a subjectivity ultimately defined by absence; constituted as a series of masquerades, intersecting personae and acts of contingent self-creation, and it often, of course, has his own social advancement in mind.[25] While his alter egos from Pánfilo de Luján, Belardo, Jacinto, Zaide, Gazul and Antonio González to Tomé de Burguillos originate in an urge to display and tantalisingly uncover, the use of the personal was a well-worn poetic topos, and ultimately their effect is to obfuscate, as guises and disguises. Perhaps the culmination of this process comes in the last of these figures from the 1634 *Rimas humanas y divinas del licenciado Tomé de Burguillos*, in which: 'El acto de velarse y de desvelarse a través de múltiples máscaras deviene en el último ciclo (*de senectute*) en oraciones lúdicas y autoparódicas' y 'se exhibe y se remeda paródicamente toda una subjetividad y se establece la despersonalización de quien habla a modo de un ridículo ventrículo, ya a un paso de las claves más modernas de la lírica del siglo pasado' [The act of veiling and unveiling himself by use of multiple masks becomes in the last phase (of old age) a series of playful, self-parodying pronouncements [and] we can see the parodic exhibition and mimicry of a complete subjectivity and the depersonalisation of the poetic voice into the form of a ridiculous ventriloquist, already just a step away from the most

[22] Castro & Rennert, *Vida de Lope de Vega*, p. 220 and Donald McGrady, 'Notes on Jerónima de Burgos in the Life and Work of Lope de Vega', *Hispanic Review*, 40 (1972): 428–41.

[23] See José de Armas, *Cervantes y el duque de Sessa: nuevas observaciones sobre el Quijote de Avellaneda y su autor* (Habana: P. Fernández, 1909), p. 19.

[24] Pedraza Jiménez, *Lope de Vega*, pp. 3 and 23.

[25] On Lope's attempts to rise socially and the reasons for his failure, see Elizabeth R. Wright, *Pilgrimage to Patronage: Lope de Vega and the Court of Philip III (1598–1621)* (Lewisburg, PA: Bucknell University Press, 2001), for the reign of Philip III, and Juan Manuel Rozas, *Estudios sobre Lope de Vega*, ed. Jesús Cañas Murillo (Madrid: Cátedra, 1990), pp. 73–130, for the time of Philip IV.

modern characteristics of lyric poetry from the last century].[26] Recent work on this theme is substantially advanced by Isabel Torres's exploration in this volume (chapter 6) of the plurality and indeterminacy of the poetic voice that characterised Lope's lyric trajectory, its multiple-determinations in relation to imitation and tradition, private self and public image, a self-representation always threatened with erasure in the ambiguousness of an identity constructed in a borrowed and yet authorised language.[27] As Tyler Fisher demonstrates in a reading of the first sonnet of his *Rimas* (chapter 4), the depth of Lope's authorial self-consciousness and the complexity of his understanding of literary fame, the interplay between text, author and reader, allowed him to conceptualise how reception might change his 'progeny' so completely as to render them unrecognisable even to their own 'father'.

The most frequently consulted biography of Lope, by Hugo Rennert and Américo Castro, last reissued with additional notes by Fernando Lázaro Carreter in 1968 but originally published in 1919, is marked by this desire to go beyond the life through the work. In his 'Advertencia' to the first edition, Castro admitted that the book was 'en ocasiones algo más que una mera biografía' [at times more than mere biography], although unfortunately 'no llega a ser, ni remotamente, un estudio de la obra del autor' [it does not manage even remotely to constitute a study of the author's work].[28] While this biography calls on the reader's indulgence of its subject's weaknesses, it does not eschew moral judgement altogether, describing the Elena Osorio episode as 'censurable en sí mismo' [censurable in itself] and attributing motives for which there is no direct evidence, for example by suggesting Velázquez pardoned Lope in order to marry him off to his daughter and secure the services of the most prolific and popular playwright of his time.[29]

At least the combination of Rennert and Castro avoided the excesses to be found elsewhere.[30] One biographer, in a life aptly subtitled 'flaquezas y dolencias' [failings and afflictions], characterised Sessa as not simply a womanising aristocrat but 'un anormal histérico, apartado de la finalidad moral y normal de la vida', 'intersexual, con sexualidad indeferenciada' [an abnormal hysteric, averse to the normal and moral objects of life, intersexual, with an undifferentiated sexuality], which allowed him to enjoy 'contactos afectivos hetero y

---

[26] Antonio Carreño, '«De esta manera de escribir tan nueva»: Lope y Góngora', in *Lope en 1604*, ed. Xavier Tubau (Lleida: Editorial Milenio, 2005), pp. 43–59 (p. 57).

[27] The neglect of this area was first pointed out by Mark J. Mascia in 'To Live Vicariously Through Literature: Lope de Vega and his Alter-Ego in the Sonnets of the *Rimas humanas y divinas del licenciado Tomé de Burguillos*', *Romance Studies*, 19.1 (2001): 1–15, although a fine essay on the same theme appeared almost simultaneously: Enrique García Santo-Tomás, 'Lope, ventrílocuo de Lope: capital social, capital cultural y estrategia literaria en las *Rimas de Tomé de Burguillos* (1634)', *Bulletin of Hispanic Studies* (Glasgow), 77.4 (2000): 287–303.

[28] Castro & Rennert, *Vida de Lope de Vega*, pp. 7–8.

[29] Castro & Rennert, *Vida de Lope de Vega*, p. 44.

[30] The best of the subsequent biographies is probably Alonso Zamora Vicente's *Lope de Vega: su vida y su obra* (Madrid: Gredos, 1961). The biographical sections of Pedraza's general book on Lope provide an admirable summary of what is known of his life, *Lope de Vega*, esp. pp. 1–32.

homosexuales' [affective contacts both hetero- and homosexual], something shared by Lope, who displayed a similar 'intersexualidad psíquica' [psychic intersexuality].[31] More sober heads, although avoiding suggestions that the duke and his servant were lovers, have found it difficult to assimilate fully the revelations of the letters about Lope's active sexual life, with a number of different women outside marriage and whilst in holy orders. In his knowing and witty biography Luis Astrana Marín called for a focus on the artist's work. Nevertheless, he accepted that 'amó demasiadamente. Excedióse en todo. Se horrorizan ante las terribles confesiones de sus cartas al duque de Sessa. Merecen borrarse' [he loved too much. He went too far in everything. They are horrified at the terrible confessions in his letters to Sessa, which deserve to be wiped out].[32] New directions in Lope biography are emerging, informed by more sophisticated understandings of the aesthetic distance implicit in formulations of semi-, neo- or pseudo-autobiographical works. Nevertheless, there is a clear need for an authoritative new biography of Lope, in which the man can emerge disentangled from the web of his own creation, but also from the moral censure of his critics and the subsequent manipulation of his figure for political or aesthetic ends.[33]

While Lope's correspondence is an essential source of information, of both a personal and, less well exploited so far, political nature, its dating (with very few contextual clues) by Amezúa presents serious problems and errors. A note written on the same piece of paper, in the same ink, in Lope's hand as three other draft letters (to the Duque de Feria, Hortensio Paravicino and Elvira de Toledo y Avalos) in Codex V in the British Library is dated at least six months apart from the other items.[34] The exploitation of aspects of Lope biography relating to his career, friendships and enmities, political connections, the printers and publishers with whom he associated, theatre professionals (especially the *autores de comedias* to whom he sold his work), religiosity, reading and the socio-historical contexts of places from Valencia to Alba de Tormes, will undoubtedly yield significant new insights in the years to come. New emphases, perhaps on tragedy and melancholy rather than on love and sexuality, might emerge from a move beyond the moral discomfort characteristic of his lives so far. The willingness to view Lope as an early modern professional writer, with the implications that has in terms of his need to fashion himself through his work, is only beginning to be

---

[31] Carlos Rico-Avello, *Lope de Vega: flaquezas y dolencias* (Madrid: Aguilar, 1973), pp. 82, 85 and 212.

[32] Luis Astrana Marín, *Vida azarosa de Lope de Vega*, 2nd edn (Barcelona: Editorial Juventud, 1941), p. 7. Marín falls prey to the temptation to eschew historical fact in his attempt to gaze into Lope's soul, e.g. p. 13.

[33] García Santo-Tomás, in his *La creación del Fénix*, studies the reception of Lope, and another fine contribution to this area is Joan Oleza's 'Claves románticas para la primera interpretación moderna del teatro de Lope de Vega', *Anuario Lope de Vega*, 1 (1995): 119–35.

[34] British Library Additional Manuscript 28,438, fol. 117r–117v, Codex V, nos 170–73. See *Epistolario*, ed. Amezúa, IV, pp. 48 and 208–9. Sliwa follows Amezúa; see *Cartas, documentos y escrituras*, II, pp. 498–99 and 556.

seen.[35] Alejandro García Reidy, in chapter 3 of this volume, discusses the related matter of how Lope's reluctance to publish his plays, founded on a notion that the dead text only came alive in performance, ceded to a realisation of the potential of the printed page for self-promotion in the competitive world of noble literary patronage and as a means of securing his cultural legacy. His loss of a court case against Francisco de Ávila's publication of twenty-four of his plays in 1616 spurred him to take editorial control of his life in print and bring out *Parte IX* himself.[36]

The playwright's bald pronouncement to Sessa in one letter that 'yo me pego lindos çurriagazos todas las noches' [I beat myself with swingeing lashes every night][37] cannot be dismissed given what we know from Montalbán, his membership of the congregation of the Esclavos del Santísimo Sacramento in the Oratorio del Caballero de Gracia from 1609, the Oratorio de la calle del Olivar from 1610, the congregation of the Orden Tercera de San Francisco from 1611 and the congregation of San Pedro in 1625, eventual ordination and the ritual life and religious culture of early seventeenth-century Spain. A series of long religious poems stretching back to 1582 but that cluster around the period 1599–1614 testify to the creative energy he expended on religious themes, regardless of their critical reputation now.[38] His patron awarded him his first ecclesiastical benefice soon after ordination, in his gift as Duque de Baena, settled in Córdoba. After trying from as early as 1615, he became by 1627 a chaplain of San Segundo, Ávila cathedral, where a protector, Jerónimo Manrique de Lara, had been bishop. After 1624 he also received an income from Santiago de Compostela.[39] Very little is known about the Duque de Sessa or why Lope chose to back a losing horse, a marginal figure with financial difficulties who, despite his connections, never really managed to forge a successful court career.[40]

This *Companion* does not set out to shed new light on Lope's biography but limits itself to considerations of the literary output of the man who 'aspiró a

[35] Works such as *Las fiestas de Denia* (Valencia: Juan Mora, 1599), *La Dragontea* (Valencia: Pedro Patricio May, 1598) and *La hermosura de Angélica* (Madrid: Pedro Madrigal, 1602) are evidence of his trajectory as a serious court poet. See especially Elizabeth R. Wright, *Pilgrimage to Patronage*, who does not hesitate to compare Lope to Shakespeare in this regard.

[36] See Davis, ed., *27 documentos*, pp. 25–27, 110–13 and 114–21, and Victor Dixon, 'La intervención de Lope en la publicación de sus comedias', *Anuario Lope de Vega*, 2 (1996): 45–63.

[37] *Epistolario*, ed. Amezúa, III, p. 58.

[38] See Mayo's chapter (5) for discussion of Lope as a religious poet. Amongst his most important works in this genre were: *Cinco misterios* (1582), *El Isidro* (1599), *El peregrino* (1604), *Jerusalén conquistada* (1609), *Pastores de Belén* (1612), *Soliloquios* (1612, 1616, 1621, 1629) and *Rimas sacras* (1614).

[39] See Davis, ed., *27 documentos*, pp. 46–47.

[40] There is no biography of Sessa. The most detailed picture of him is found in *Epistolario*, ed. Amezúa, I. On his finances see Antonio Domínguez Ortiz, *Las clases privilegiadas en la España del Antiguo Régimen* (Madrid: Ediciones Istmo, 1973), pp. 94–95. Sessa's closeness to the young Philip IV had seen him exiled from court in 1611, and Patrick Williams suggests that this may also have had something to do with his kinship with the Countess de Valencia, in *The Great Favourite: The Duke of Lerma and the Court and Government of Philip III of Spain, 1598–1621* (Manchester: Manchester University Press, 2006), pp. 166–67.

alzarse con la monarquía absoluta del arte literario' [aspired to the absolute monarchy of literary art], and to his subsequent reception.[41] The essays in section 1 aim to contextualise Lope the writer, looking at his artistic background and learning, the world of the theatre in Madrid of his day and his growing awareness of literary fame and the power of the printing press, alluded to above. The three essays on his poetry in the second section provide a close reading of a defining sonnet, an overview of his religious verse and a discussion of his creation of poetic identities. As the creator of a national drama, the *comedia nueva*, Lope deserves particular attention, and the most substantial section of the *Companion* is dedicated to this area of his art. Nevertheless only a limited coverage is possible, thanks both to the variety of Lope's output and his astonishing levels of productivity.[42] After an assessment of Lope's dramatic art, which he outlined in a poem, the *Arte nuevo de hacer comedias en este tiempo*, read to a Madrid academy, a series of chapters both deals with some major sub-groupings within his dramatic oeuvre — comedies, religious plays, chronicle-legend plays — and analyses particular examples of dramas which shed light on some of his dramatic concerns and practice. The fourth section turns the spotlight on to some manifestations of Lope's prose writing, perhaps the most neglected area of his literary output. Chapters here deal with his short fictions, written in imitation of Cervantes, and two longer and more innovative works, *El peregrino en su patria*, and the semi-autobiographical prose 'play', *La Dorotea*. Finally, the fifth section of the *Companion* deals with three aspects of the reception of Lope: the adaptation of his drama to the silver screen, his pictorial representations and the translation of his plays into English. All three chapters testify to the enduring creativity and the transcendent appeal of the figure of Lope de Vega.

The *Companion*'s purpose is in part corrective. As editors we have never intended to be encyclopaedic, or to provide a full introduction to Lope's life and work. We aim rather to raise his profile in the English-speaking world, belatedly perhaps but deservedly, through this series of assessments of his figure, his output, his reception and his influence written by experts in the field of Lope de Vega studies. We are not the first to have become acutely conscious of the difficulties involved in doing justice, within a restricted space, to the breadth and richness of our protagonist. We are aware for example that areas as important as the poet's early, cathartic *romancero* [ballads], his letters, his literary friendships and battles, his epic poetry, his *autos sacramentales* [Corpus Christi plays] and some important prose fiction, are omitted or only touched upon in passing. Plays as significant as *El caballero de Olmedo* and *El perro del hortelano* probably deserve a chapter to themselves, and the emerging sense of Lope as a political

---

[41] Pedraza Jiménez, *Lope de Vega*, p. 36.

[42] In 1604, in an incomplete listing of his plays, Lope records the titles of some 220 plays, and in 1618 he adds a further 210 new plays to this list: see S. Griswold Morley, 'Lope de Vega's *Peregrino* Lists', *University of California Publications in Modern Philology*, 14.5 (1930): 345–66. Scholars generally agree that he wrote between 600 and 800 full-length plays, of which some 400 survive.

playwright is insufficiently reflected. Nevertheless, we provide suggestions for further reading which relate to these areas as well as those covered in more detail. We are reassured, too, by the calibre of the contributors and the extent and quality of their coverage of many important aspects of the man, the artist and approaches to him and his work, that much can be learned about Lope de Vega from these pages. 'Es de Lope' became a proverbial indication of quality in the seventeenth century, and we hope that although this volume is about rather than by Lope, some of his lustre might have rubbed off.

Part 1: The Man and his World

1

Lope's Knowledge

VICTOR DIXON

Pero mil dan a entender	[But heaps of folk imply
que apenas supe leer,	I barely learnt to read,
y es lo más cierto, a fe mía;	and that's quite true, I swear;
que como en gracia se lleva	for just as knowing how
danzar, cantar o tañer,	to dance, or sing, or play
yo sé escribir sin leer,	is only a happy gift,
que a fe que es gracia bien nueva.	I don't read but I can write
(*Peribáñez*, lines 2355–61.)	— a novel gift, I'm sure.]

Under his favourite pseudonym, Belardo, Lope was responding tongue in cheek to all who might doubt if as a writer he could claim to be truly learned. No one could deny of course the breadth of the knowledge he displayed over the range of his immense output, but doubt has indeed been expressed, from his own time to our own, as to whether that knowledge had any depth or was merely superficial. Though the question has been addressed, largely in general terms, by countless modern scholars,[1] it is still unresolved, and probably doomed to remain so, but in approaching it here I shall seek to be specific.

The doubt can be said to have been fuelled, in at least three ways, by Lope himself. Firstly, his intense activity throughout his life and his phenomenal output as a writer have led some to wonder if he can ever have had the time, energy or opportunity to acquire any true erudition. But another look at his biography gives reason to question that view. We can be sure, without taking literally what we are told by Montalbán, his first biographer, or by Fernando, his *alter ego* in *La Dorotea*, that his genius showed itself early. Having perhaps been taught initially by 'mi maestro' [my master] Vicente Espinel, he attended a Jesuit college (where he will have studied Latin grammar, composition and rhetoric, plus a range of Roman authors), and we need not doubt, though we cannot document, his repeated assertions that he studied (perhaps from his mid-teens) at the University of Alcalá. Unquestionably, moreover, his memory, which educators then set great

---

[1] Marcella Trambaioli, in her recent edition of Lope de Vega, *La hermosura de Angélica* (Madrid: Iberoamericana, 2005), pp. 93–94, n. 237, quoted the divergent opinions of seven.

store by exercising, was exceptionally retentive and ready, and it may well have
been assisted by maintaining, as many Humanists advised, a *codex excerptorius*.[2]

His lengthy life thereafter, apart from his various amours and incessant writing,
was certainly a full one. At twenty, for instance, he saw active service on an
expedition to the Azores (whether or not he actually sailed with the Armada in
1588). But after his exile in Valencia, then a hub of intellectual activity, he spent
some years from 1591 at the sophisticated court of the fifth Duke of Alba, near
Salamanca. There in particular (though also perhaps as the servant of various
other noblemen, or with the help of patrons like Juan de Arguijo), he probably had
considerable opportunity for study, as Amezúa and Jameson supposed.[3]
Especially once firmly established, moreover, in Spain's still relatively small
capital, he was always, as Portús has insisted, 'más o menos fiel a un grupo social
compuesto por literatos, artistas cualificados o profesionales liberales, de entre
cuyos miembros extrajo sus principales amigos y del cual nunca abjuró' [more or
less faithful to a social group composed of men of letters, skilful artists or liberal
professionals, from among whose members he drew his principal friends and
which he never abjured].[4] Apart from no doubt conversing constantly with these,
he contributed prologues or poems to many of their books, and acted as censor for
numerous others; he must have been abreast of everything published.[5]

He referred repeatedly too to a passion for reading, which he said in 1624 he
indulged very early each day.[6] His income, moreover, despite many complaints of
poverty, was by and large substantial, though clearly intermittent and not
infrequently misused,[7] so that we can almost believe the assertion by Montalbán
that 'gastaba en pinturas y libros sin reparar en el dinero' [he spent on paintings
and books regardless of the expense], especially in the light of the inventory that
accompanied his testament of 1627. As well as numerous art-works, it listed 'mil

---

[2] One of his detractors indeed referred (not necessarily of course with inside knowledge) to 'su
cartapacio viejo donde tiene el retal de los latines que encaja en sus prosas a troche [y] moche' [his
old notebook in which he keeps the bits and pieces of Latin he inserts haphazardly in his writings];
see Joaquín de Entrambasaguas, *Estudios sobre Lope de Vega*, 3 vols (Madrid: Consejo Superior
de Investigaciones Científicas, 1946–58), II, p. 482.

[3] Agustín G. de Amezúa, in Lope de Vega, *Epistolario de Lope de Vega*, 4 vols (Madrid:
Aldus, 1935–43), I, p. 247; A. K. Jameson, 'The Sources of Lope de Vega's Erudition', *Hispanic
Review*, 5.2 (1937): 124–39 (pp. 126–27).

[4] Javier Portús, *Pintura y pensamiento en la España de Lope de Vega* (Hondarribia: Nerea,
1999), p. 134.

[5] See especially Florentino Zamora Lucas, *Lope de Vega censor de libros* (Larache: Boscá,
1941); idem, *Lope de Vega: poesías preliminares de libros* (Madrid: Consejo Superior de
Investigaciones Científicas, 1961).

[6] 'Entre los libros me amanece el día, / hasta la hora que del alto cielo / Dios mismo baja a la
bajeza mía' [The break of day finds me among my books, / until the time at which from heaven on
high / my God himself descends to my base hands] (a reference of course to his celebrating Mass,
as he did at home, said Montalbán, almost every day), in his *Epístola* to his friend Antonio
Hurtado de Mendoza, in Lope de Vega, *Obras poéticas*, I, ed. José Manuel Blecua (Barcelona:
Planeta, 1969), p. 1199.

[7] See José María Díez Borque, *Sociedad y teatro en la España de Lope de Vega* (Barcelona:
Antoni Bosch, 1978), pp. 93–117.

y quinientos libros' [fifteen-hundred books].[8] That was surely a hyperbolic colloquialism; Lope claimed in both *La moza de cántaro* and his *Égloga a Claudio* to have penned 'mil y quinientas comedias', at least double the number he wrote. But it undermines his frequently-adopted pose as a Neostoic philosopher content with only 'dos libros, tres pinturas, cuatro flores' [a couple of books, three paintings, and four flowers].[9] On the other hand, much of his reading must have been less for pleasure than as 'research'. For all his capacity to invent, and to transmute his own experience, a large proportion of what he wrote required him to cover and to some extent absorb (though he often did little more than transcribe or versify what he had before him) a vast amount of material.

Secondly, he must have nevertheless been pleased to be labelled by Cervantes 'the prodigy of nature' (el monstruo de la naturaleza), for he boasted incessantly not only of his clarity and directness of expression, by contrast with the obscurity and convoluted language of Góngora and his followers,[10] but also of an innate spontaneity, fluency and originality. Thus Azorín for example was able to argue that Lope 'no tenía por qué ser intelectual' [had no reason to be an intellectual], that 'se da cuenta de que es grande, magnífico, originalísimo, sin necesidad de erudición, de lo que llamamos ahora cultura' [he realises he is great, magnificent, highly original, with no need of erudition, of what we now call culture], and apparently to take at face value lines 361–65 in Canto I of his epic *Isidro*, which praised the saintly ploughman for reading only the catechism.[11]

Thirdly, and by contrast, what Azorín went on to call his 'prurito de parecer sabio' [itch to seem learned] drove Lope to positively invite suspicions about the true depth of his knowledge by adding in the margins or indexes of several of his works, and including in the text of almost all, constant displays of erudition. The explanation is simple. He was driven throughout his life by two inextricably intertwined ambitions: to rise in his society, by winning favour with the nobility, court and king, and to be acclaimed not merely by 'el vulgo' [the mob] but by 'ingenios y señores' [intellectuals and gentry] as the foremost writer of his day, whether in drama, prose or verse. But according to doctrines universally accepted then and propounded by Lope himself, this required him to show a capacity, as

---

[8] See *27 documentos de Lope de Vega en el Archivo Histórico de Protocolos de Madrid*, transcribed, with an introduction, by Charles Davis (Madrid: Comunidad de Madrid, 2004), pp. 162–71.

[9] So ends the last sonnet in Lope's *Rimas humanas y divinas del licenciado Tomé de Burguillos*, ed. Juan Manuel Rozas & Jesús Cañas Murillo (Madrid: Castalia, 2004), p. 337, where he similarly concluded another, p. 325: 'Haced de la virtud secreto empleo, / que yo, en mi pobre hogar, con dos librillos, / ni murmuro, ni temo, ni deseo' [Contrive to practise virtue secretly, / for I, in my poor home, with two small books, / don't either backbite, fear, or wish for more].

[10] A typical example is the sonnet in which 'Responde a un poeta que le afeaba escribir con claridad, siendo como es la más excelente parte del que escribe' [He replies to a poet who decried the clarity of his writing, that being, as it is, a writer's most excellent attribute], although he claimed at its end, as often, that his verse not only had solid content but was carefully polished; Lope de Vega, *Rimas humanas y divinas*, pp. 317–18.

[11] Azorín, 'Lope en silueta', in his *Obras completas*, ed. A. Cruz Rueda, 9 vols (Madrid: Aguilar, 1948–63), V, pp. 624–25.

well as to entertain, to edify and instruct based on universal knowledge.[12] He knew therefore that he needed not only to be, but more importantly to be recognized as, the 'científico poeta' [learned poet] that he often proclaimed himself.

Very frequently, as a result, he 'doth protest too much'. Numerous scholars have been able to prove (a matter I shall dwell on later) that a great deal of what might seem to be first-hand knowledge was lifted from one or other of the many dictionaries, compendia and so forth published and republished from early in the sixteenth century.[13] It needs to be stressed, however, that recourse to such works was as normal and widespread in Lope's time as it is in our own, and (as I pointed out in a recent study) accusations that he lied about or concealed having used them, though justified in part, have often been pushed too far.[14]

Some of those scholars have argued, moreover, that Lope did not always work in quite the same way. Jameson for instance insisted on differentiating in his epics between those references to Classical writers which must have been present in his mind when he was writing them and those that could have been added later,[15] and Osuna distinguished in his *Arcadia* between the 'erudición sobrepuesta' [superimposed erudition] that he piled into his most pedantic passages and his indexes or annotations, and 'ese inmenso tesoro de datos que no son añadidos y retazos, sino precisamente [...] su bagaje de escritor' [that immense treasure of data that are not additions and snippets but precisely [...] his baggage as a writer].[16] Similarly Trueblood, though suggesting that the frequent use of works of reference may have influenced his habits of thought, added that they must have furnished his mind with 'a wide assortment of humanistic instances and details which his pen could call upon as needed'.[17]

In addition, studies of the sources of his knowledge in particular works have hitherto been concerned almost wholly with his most ambitious, pretentious writings (like his *Dorotea*, his lengthy poems and narratives, his prologues and his dedications), to the neglect of his more spontaneous (like most of his plays and short poems, his letters, his *Novelas* and his *Pastores de Belén*), and in my study I therefore attempted to gauge in a few of the latter how much of his knowledge of

---

[12] See for instance the disquisitions on literature by several shepherds in Book III of Lope de Vega, *Arcadia*, ed. Edwin S. Morby (Madrid: Castalia, 1975), pp. 267–68.

[13] See Víctor Infantes, 'De *Officinas* y *Polyantheas*: los diccionarios secretos del Siglo de Oro', in *Homenaje a Eugenio Asensio* (Madrid: Gredos, 1988), pp. 243–57; Sagrario López Poza, 'Florilegios, polyantheas, repertorios de sentencias y lugares comunes: aproximación bibliográfica', *Criticón*, no. 49 (1990): 61–76; Isaías Lerner, 'Misceláneas y polianteas del Siglo de Oro español', in *Actas del Congreso Internacional sobre Humanismo y Renacimento*, 2 vols (León: Universidad de León, 1998), II, pp. 71–82.

[14] See Victor Dixon, 'La huella en Lope de la tradición clásica: ¿honda o superficial?', *Anuario Lope de Vega*, 11 (2005): 83–96.

[15] A. K. Jameson, 'Lope de Vega's Knowledge of Classical Literature', *Bulletin Hispanique*, 38 (1936): 444–501 (pp. 496–97).

[16] Rafael Osuna, *La Arcadia de Lope de Vega: génesis, estructura y originalidad* (Madrid: Real Academia Española, 1972), pp. 192–93.

[17] Alan S. Trueblood, 'The *Officina* of Ravisius Textor in Lope de Vega's *Dorotea*', *Hispanic Review*, 26.2 (1958): 135–41 (p. 136).

the Classical tradition was merely superficial, and how much he had made his own. That attempt was of course conjectural, and to broaden here the focus to the whole of Lope's apparent knowledge and to his works in their entirety cannot but be more so, but I hope it may prove worthwhile. My approach will be conservative; aware of his fondness for dropping names, compiling impressive lists, and quoting, as if directly but in fact at second hand, I shall try to make a balanced assessment.

In respect of religion, his knowledge was certainly not confined, like his Isidro's, to 'un libro solo' [a single book], but 'that Lope's memory was extraordinarily retentive is proved beyond doubt', as Jameson said, 'by his acquaintance with the Bible' — presumably the Vulgate, including of course the Apocrypha.[18] Though only half a dozen of his plays are on biblical subjects, evidence abounds in almost all his works, and above all throughout his sacred verse; again and again for instance he alludes to the life of Christ and meditates on His Passion, influenced undoubtedly by St Ignatius Loyola's *Ejercicios espirituales* [*Spiritual Exercises*] and by other devotional works, like Fray Luis de Granada's *Libro de la oración y meditación* [*Book of Prayer and Meditation*] and Francisco de Osuna's *Tercer abecedario espiritual* [*Third Spiritual ABC*]. Vosters, moreover, was able to trace the appearance throughout Lope's *oeuvre* of biblical symbols associated with serpents, with the Virgin and with aspects of the story of David (with whom he clearly felt a personal affinity). That knowledge however was buttressed, Vosters found, by acquaintance with works by various Fathers of the Church, though very possibly most of these, except St Bernard, were known to Lope best via authors of his own era he rarely mentioned, who had written both in Spanish (Vosters instanced ten) and in Latin (he listed eight).[19] Lope's biblical plays, however, were heavily outnumbered by his *comedias de santos*, no doubt because most were probably commissioned.[20] He appears to have relied in general on the *Flos sanctorum* by Alonso de Villegas or that by Pedro de Ribadeneyra, but to have consulted other sources also for at least eleven. The saints he seems most to have admired and been best informed about are Jerome (*El cardenal de Belén*), Augustine (*El divino africano*) and Francis of Assisi (*El serafín humano* and other plays about his disciples).

He had much more than Shakespeare's 'small Latin'. He made between 1581 and 1585 a translation (now lost) of Claudian's *De raptu Proserpinae*, and claimed in 1632 (as Fernando) that at Alcalá he had often written 'en versos latinos o castellanos. Comencé a juntar libros de todas lenguas, que después de los principios de la griega y ejercicio grande de la latina, supe bien la toscana, y de la francesa tuve noticia' [in Latin or Castilian verse. I began to collect books in all

---

[18] Jameson, 'The Sources', p. 137.

[19] Simon A. Vosters, *Lope de Vega y la tradición occidental*, 2 vols ([Madrid]: Castalia, 1977), I (*El simbolismo bíblico de Lope de Vega: algunas de sus fuentes*), especially pp. 501–2.

[20] Robert R. Morrison, *Lope de Vega and the 'Comedia de Santos'* (New York: Peter Lang, 2000), pp. 321–27, following S. Griswold Morley & Courtney Bruerton, *Cronología de las comedias de Lope de Vega* (Madrid: Gredos, 1968), listed 21 certainly and 4 probably by Lope (plus 29 of doubtful authenticity and a further 29 'sometimes attributed').

literatures and languages, for after the rudiments of Greek and much exercise of Latin, I learnt Tuscan well and became acquainted with French].[21] In fact, as well as making a few other versions,[22] he very frequently quoted lines or phrases from Classical writers in Latin or in translation, composed in that language some short pieces of verse or prose,[23] and included in his plays, for comic effect, numerous scenes and passages in the macarronic style.[24] He had certainly 'less Greek', and in fact advised his son Lope in 1620 that though he should diligently study (without failing properly to learn and use his native Castilian) the 'reina de las lenguas [...] por ningún caso os acontezca aprender la griega' [the queen of languages [...] it should on no account occur to you to learn Greek], as some arrogant ignoramuses pretended they had.[25] Many of his Greek quotations, therefore, were surely culled from reference works. Nevertheless he was apparently acquainted, via Latin or vernacular versions or commentaries, with a range of well-known Greek writings: the epics of Homer, the fables of Aesop, several works by Plato, Aristotle and Ptolemy, medical treatises by Dioscorides and Galen, and histories by Herodotus, Josephus and Pausanias, as well as the *Aethiopica* [*Ethiopian History*] of Heliodorus, to which he repeatedly referred and whose influence is apparent in his *La hermosura de Angélica* and especially in *El peregrino en su patria*.

His Latin would have given him direct access to all the Roman writers, but among those who wrote in prose we can be sure only of Diodorus Siculus, Cicero, Livy, Tacitus, the elder Pliny and the younger Seneca, with some of whose plays (although surprisingly he seems to have to have known little directly of Plautus or Terence) he was also familiar.[26] Latin verse attracted him far more. He was acquainted with poems by Lucan, Martial, Juvenal, Statius, Ausonius and Claudian, but above all he admired and knew well the odes and epodes of

---

[21] Lope de Vega, *La Dorotea*, ed. Edwin S. Morby (Valencia: Castalia, 1958), p. 288. I shall consider below his knowledge of modern languages.

[22] See for instance Silva I, lines 341–46, of Lope de Vega, *Laurel de Apolo*, ed. Christian Giaffreda, with an introduction by Maria Grazia Profeti (Florence: Alinea, 2002), p. 113, and Entrambasaguas, *Estudios*, II, pp. 505–26.

[23] For example a number of epigrams (like one at the conclusion of his *La hermosura de Angélica*), a six-line epitaph added to Sonnet 178 in his *Rimas* and another in two *octavas* as stanzas 70–71 of Canto VI of his *Jerusalén*, 16 mottoes and a possible inscription for the tomb of Philip III, and a letter to Pope Urban VIII (see *Epistolario*, ed. Amezúa, IV, pp. 62–64 and 98–99). He may well also have composed the ten lines near the end of his *Arte Nuevo*, though some critics suppose he was helped.

[24] See Elvezio Canonica-de Rochemonteix, *El poliglotismo en el teatro de Lope de Vega* (Kassel: Reichenberger, 1991), pp. 33–106.

[25] In the dedication of *El verdadero amante*; see Thomas E. Case, *Las dedicatorias de Partes XIII–XX de Lope de Vega* (Chapel Hill, NC: University of North Carolina & Madrid: Castalia, 1975), p. 104.

[26] See for instance Victor Dixon & Isabel Torres, '*La madrastra enamorada*: ¿una tragedia de Séneca refundida por Lope de Vega?', *Revista Canadiense de Estudios Hispánicos*, 19.1 (1994): 39–60.

Horace,[27] the *Eclogues*, *Georgics* and *Aeneid* of Virgil,[28] and all the major poems of Ovid, whom he saw as a kindred spirit.

Lope's familiarity with the 'narigudo poeta' [big-nosed poet], and his central role in increasing at his time Ovid's long-powerful influence, documented a century ago in Rudolph Schevill's *Ovid and the Renaissance in Spain*, has been emphasized for instance in Osuna's study of the development of the theme of natural abundance, most importantly from the elaboration of Polyphemus's song to Galatea in Book 13, lines 789–868, of the *Metamorphoses*.[29] That poem more than any other gave Lope an unsurpassed knowledge of Classical mythology, which he displayed throughout his *oeuvre*, but especially in five long poems and in seven plays (though in these at least, as Martínez Berbel has shown, he made great use too of the version by Jorge de Bustamante).[30] Several others, moreover, are set in the Classical era, including one at least, *Las grandezas de Alejandro*, about Alexander the Great, to whom he referred almost obsessively, drawing mostly, as Jameson showed, on Quintus Curtius, 'a classical historian whom he certainly knew well'.[31]

What other ancient authors he knew at first hand is very hard to determine. In the dedication of *El cardenal de Belén* he claimed he had never believed that 'sólo es digno de fama lo que no vimos ni conocimos [...] antes bien me causan mayor admiración las obras de los ingenios que vi y traté, si los hallé dignos de alabanza, al igual de los antiguos' [only what we have not seen or known is worthy of repute [...] rather I have more greatly admired the works of the writers I have seen and had dealings with, if I have found them worthy of praise, on equal terms with those of old], and went on to praise a dozen of his contemporaries;[32] yet he paraded in such writings a host of Latin quotations (a dozen, ironically, in that same piece), and many of these were clearly culled from more recent publications, like the jurist Matteo Gribaldi's *De ratione studendi*, to which he referred in other dedications,[33] and via which he silently quoted some other authors.[34] Overall,

---

[27] For example he constantly echoed and repeatedly glossed the epode *Beatus ille*, and in Sonnet 112 of his *Rimas*, which consists of lines (in four languages) borrowed from a total of eight poets, each of the three in Latin comes from a different ode by Horace.

[28] Jameson, in 'Lope de Vega's Knowledge', referred for instance (p. 494) to six passages in his epics evidently based on similar passages in the *Aeneid*. He very often praised (as well as the version by Gonzalo Pérez of Homer's *Odyssey*) the translations of Virgil by Gregorio Hernández, but would not have needed the latter.

[29] See Rafael Osuna, *Polifemo y el tema de la abundancia natural en Lope de Vega y su tiempo* (Kassel: Reichenberger, 1996); he lists in an appendix 119 of Lope's works, and on p. 3 states: 'Es Lope, con mucho, quien más generoso se manifiesta en el cultivo del tema' [It is Lope who proves by far the most generous in the cultivation of the theme].

[30] Juan Antonio Martínez Berbel, *El mundo mitológico de Lope de Vega: siete comedias mitológicas de inspiración ovidiana* (Madrid: Fundación Universitaria Española, 2003).

[31] Jameson, 'The Sources', p. 131. Other more or less historical plays with Classical settings are *Las justas de Tebas*, *Los embustes de Fabia*, *Roma abrasada*, *El honrado hermano*, *El esclavo de Roma* and *Lo fingido verdadero*.

[32] Case, *Las dedicatorias*, pp. 63–65.

[33] Case, *Las dedicatorias,* pp. 73 and 121.

[34] Lope de Vega, *La Dorotea*, pp. 26, 322–23 and 435–36.

nevertheless, Jameson was no doubt right to say that 'Lope had a not inconsiderable acquaintance with Latin literature and a slight knowledge of the Greek historians and geographers [...] And even if he got much of it at second hand it still represents a knowledge of classical literature of quite a respectable size'.[35]

It is time now to consider those 'second-hand' works. Many of them he named in one place or another (which is mostly why they can be identified), but undoubtedly he did so far less frequently than he used them, in some cases not only paraphrasing closely but incorporating their references or quotations. Some could be seen essentially as dictionaries or encyclopedias. We know that he utilized Ambrogio Calepino's polyglot lexicon, the *Enchiridion* by Antonio Maria Spelta, the dictionary of proper names by Carolus Stephanus, and Stobaeus's anthology of Greek *Sententiae* latinized by Conrad Gesner,[36] and above all that he constantly turned (especially when compiling lists) to Ravisius Textor's *Officina*, as countless critics have shown.[37] But even when using this, as pointed out by Vosters, he also drew more often than has been noted on other sources, and 'tales imitaciones híbridas han de prevenirnos contra una sobreestimación de la importancia de la *Officina* para la obra de Lope de Vega' [such hybrid imitations should warn us against an overestimation of the importance of the *Officina* for the work of Lope de Vega].[38]

Others were miscellanies. He claimed, perhaps not falsely, that he had never seen 'la Poliantea' (presumably the most famous Latin one, by Nanus Mirabellius),[39] but he utilized Pero Mejía's *Silva de varia lección* and Antonio de Torquemada's *Coloquios satíricos*, probably knew the latter's *Jardín de flores curiosas* and Luis Zapata's *Miscelánea,* and certainly made much use of both *De honesta disciplina* by Petrus Crinitus and *Il sapere util' e dilettevole* by Constantino Castriota.[40] Others again were commentaries, like those on Terence by the fourth-century Donatus and on the *Poetics* of Aristotle and Horace by the sixteenth-century Robortello that he used in his *Arte nuevo*, or that on the *Symposium* of Plato by Marsilio Ficino, together with works by other Renaissance Neoplatonists — Pico della Mirandola and Juda Leon Abarbanel (León Hebreo) —, the *Syntaxeon artis mirabilis* by Petrus Gregorius and Cipriano Suárez's *De arte rhetorica*.

[35] Jameson, 'Lope de Vega's Knowledge', pp. 500–1.

[36] All of these were used (and all but Stephanus named) in *La Dorotea,* and Stephanus was the main (though not the only) source of the 'Exposición de los nombres poéticos' [Explanation of the poetic names] in Lope's *Arcadia*; see Osuna, *La Arcadia,* pp. 208–16. On his use, sometimes mistakenly, of Stobaeus, see Dixon, 'La huella', p. 99.

[37] See especially Trueblood, 'The *Officina*'; Simon A. Vosters, 'Lope de Vega y Juan Ravisio Textor: nuevos datos', *Iberoromania*, n.s., 2 (1975): 69–103; Aurora Egido, 'Lope de Vega, Ravisio Textor y la creación del mundo como obra de arte', in her *Fronteras de la poesía en el Barroco* (Barcelona: Crítica, 1990), pp. 198–215; and more recently Lope de Vega, *La hermosura*, pp. 95–97.

[38] Vosters, 'Lope de Vega y Juan Ravisio Textor', p. 98: see also Dixon 'La huella', p. 88.

[39] See also Dixon, 'La huella', pp. 86–87.

[40] See especially Edwin S. Morby, 'Constantino Castriota in the *Arcadia*', in *Homage to John M. Hill*, ed. Walter Poesse (Bloomington, IN: Indiana University, 1968), pp. 201–15.

For knowledge on scientific subjects, he turned to a range of manuals, like various works by Franz Titelmans, primarily his *Compendium naturalis historiae*; agreeing fundamentally with a previous study by Vosters, Morby wrote: 'I suspect that future investigations will [...] confirm Titelmans's position as a major authority for Lope's conception of the physical and biological world and the operation of the human mind and senses.'[41] Other works he certainly mined, however, were Leo Suabius's compendium of Paracelsus, and *Occulta naturae miracula* and *De astrologia* by Levinus Lemnius[42] and Trivero's *Universae medicinae ... methodus*, and his interest in more curious lore is shown by references to books like Giovan Battista della Porta's *De i miracoli ... dalla natura prodotti* and Alessio Piemontese's *De' secreti*. Lope's many and varied more or less historical works (disregarding for the moment his plays set in Spain) required of course a different range of reading matter. Jameson, focusing on his *Jerusalén*, decided that 'Lope had prepared himself thoroughly for the groundwork of his poem by careful reading' of four and possibly more of the sources he mentioned,[43] and went on to consider further historical and geographical works he may have employed in this and other epics.

Though he never visited Italy, reading its language presented no problem, and he referred to many of its authors; having claimed (in his role as Filomena) to have imitated 'cuantos poetas / claros celebra Italia' [all the famous poets Italy acclaims],[44] in *Laurel de Apolo* (canto IX, lines 220–40) he proceeded to praise twenty-six. But he probably knew really well a much smaller number; Dante for instance he mentioned surprisingly rarely. With Petrarch (and probably his commentator Daniello) Lope was by contrast very familiar; his *Rimas* in particular often echo the *Canzionere*, and he imitated the *Trionfi* in his *Triunfos divinos*. As well as poems by Serafino Aquilano, he possibly knew Boiardo's *Orlando* and certainly Ariosto's, which inspired his *La hermosura de Angélica* and some of his early plays. Similarly he may have known works by Bernardo Tasso, and sought to compete with Torquato's great epic in his own *Jerusalén*. He seems too to have been acquainted, no doubt via Barberini (Urban VIII), with his

---

[41] S. A. Vosters, 'Lope de Vega y Titelmans: cómo el Fénix se representaba el universo', *Revista de Literatura*, 21 (1962): 5–33, and 'Dos adiciones a mi artículo "Lope de Vega y Titelmans"', *Revista de Literatura*, 22 (1962): 90; Edwin S. Morby, 'Franz Titelmans in Lope's *Arcadia*', *MLN*, 82.2 (1967): 185–97 (p. 185). See also Morby's later study, 'Two Notes on *La Arcadia*', *Hispanic Review*, 36.2 (1968): 110–23, in which he showed that Lope borrowed too from a version of Ptolemy's *Geographica*.

[42] E. S. Morby, 'Levinus Lemnius and Leo Suabius in *La Dorotea*', *Hispanic Review*, 20.2 (1952): 108–22. See also Frank G. Halstead, 'The Attitude of Lope de Vega toward Astrology and Astronomy', *Hispanic Review*, 7.3 (1939): 205–19, on his early studies of, lifelong fascination with, and possible reading about those subjects.

[43] Jameson, 'The Sources', especially pp. 127–29. The four were *La gran conquista de Ultramar*, William of Tyre's *Historia Belli Sacri*, Paulus Aemilius's *Res gestae Francorum*, and Blondus's *Historia ab inclinatione Romanorum*; the others included Pero Mejía's *Historia imperial y cesárea*, which Lope also used in a number of his plays: *Lo fingido verdadero*, *Roma abrasada*, *La Imperial de Otón* and *El rey sin reino*.

[44] Lope de Vega, *Obras poéticas*, I, p. 653.

contemporaries Bracciolini, Preti and Ciampoli, and repeatedly praised Marino,[45] referring to him (alongside Stigliani) when attacking Góngora and his disciples.

His *Arcadia* reveals a close familiarity with Sannazaro's, to which as Morby remarked 'it owes a great deal, though less than might be thought in view of the title'.[46] Repeatedly too he plundered the *novellieri* in search of plots for his plays, mostly reading them in Italian; he borrowed in at least nine from Lionardo Salvati's 'bowdlerized' version of the *Decameron*,[47] seven from Giraldi Cintio,[48] and fifteen from Bandello.[49] He showed some capacity too to write in Italian. One finds for example in his *Rimas* (as well as, in sonnet 112, seven lines by Italian poets) four of his own in sonnet 195, and in his *Descripción de la Tapada* (lines 505–12) an *octava real*;[50] above all, he could pepper his works with Italian words and phrases, especially as 'local colour' in seventeen plays, and included bilingual scenes in no fewer than seven. In short, we can surely agree that 'La cultura general italiana de Lope es amplia y sabe sacar provecho de ella' [Lope's general Italian culture is ample and he knows how to use it to advantage].[51]

His acquaintance with French and French literature was more limited by far. In a thorough-going study, Vosters found in his works only a scattering of quotations and allusions (for instance to Ronsard, who heads a list of eleven French poets merely named in canto IX, lines 216–19, of *Laurel de Apolo*), though that scholar concluded nevertheless that Lope was 'el rey de los ciegos, es decir uno de los pocos españoles de la época que se atrevía sobre el camino hacia el Parnaso de la gran cultura hermana, teniendo por cicerones a varios amigos franceses' [the king of the blind, that is to say one of the few Spaniards of the time who ventured on the road towards the Parnassus of the great sister culture, having several French friends as guides].[52] Even so, he rarely tried to use French or other foreign languages in his plays. In ten, by contrast, he included comic scenes that mixed Castilian with Portuguese, which he no doubt regarded (like Catalan or Basque) as a variant of Spanish. Indeed he had his Dorotea call that language 'dulcísima, y

---

[45] Especially in *El jardín de Lope de Vega* (Lope de Vega, *Obras poéticas*, I, p. 830) and a sonnet I shall mention later, as well as dedicating to Marino his play *Virtud, pobreza y mujer*. On Marino's versions of 48 of his poems, and on their relationship, see Dámaso Alonso, *En torno a Lope* (Madrid: Gredos, 1972), pp. 31–94, and Juan Manuel Rozas, *Estudios sobre Lope de Vega* (Madrid: Cátedra, 1990), pp. 221–56.

[46] Lope de Vega, *Arcadia*, p. 29. For details of Lope's indebtedness, see Osuna, *La Arcadia*, pp. 224–30.

[47] See Victor Dixon, 'Lope de Vega no conocía el *Decamerón* de Boccaccio', in *El mundo del teatro español en su Siglo de Oro: ensayos dedicados a John E. Varey*, ed. J. M. Ruano de la Haza (Ottawa: Dovehouse Editions Canada, 1989), pp. 185–96.

[48] See Lope de Vega, *Servir a señor discreto*, ed. Frida Weber de Kurlat (Madrid: Castalia, 1975), pp. 30–32.

[49] See Charles H. Leighton, 'La fuente de *La quinta de Florencia*', *Nueva Revista de Filología Hispánica*, 10 (1956): 1–12, and an independent study by Gail Bradbury, 'Lope's Plays of Bandello Origin', *Forum for Modern Language Studies*, 16 (1980), pp. 53–65.

[50] Lope de Vega, *Obras poéticas*, I, p. 719.

[51] Canonica-de Rochemonteix, *El poliglotismo*, p. 114; see also pp. 279–80.

[52] Vosters, *Lope de Vega y la tradición*, II (*El manierismo de Lope de Vega y la literatura francesa*), especially p. 276.

para los versos la más suave' [very sweet, and the smoothest for verse], quoting two lines from a sonnet by Camoens,[53] whom Lope often cited and praised, for instance among more than a dozen Portuguese writers eulogized at length early in canto III of *Laurel de Apolo*.

Lope's knowledge of Spain and everything Spanish was immense, as is evidenced for instance by at least a hundred *comedias* based on its history and legends from Roman times to his own, whose sources Menéndez Pelayo sought a century ago to determine. For its early history, that scholar found, he relied on chronicles, in particular the final reworking of the *Crónica general*, the popular *Valerio de las historias eclesiásticas y de España*, and probably the *Historia general* by his friend Padre Juan de Mariana. But though he no doubt preferred to work from a single text, he can be shown in several cases to have drawn on more, and though adding much of his own invention would often almost transcribe them, whether for ease of composition or out of the genuine respect for history he professed.[54] For *comedias* set in less ancient times he clearly read specific works, but a number were journalistic accounts of recent events, for which he had to use *relaciones*, and at least a dozen, especially of the genealogical kind, were undoubtedly commissioned; for these (as for *La Dragontea*, *Isidro* and *El triunfo de la fe*) he would have been given materials and expected to study them closely.[55]

His awareness in general of his nation's culture, particularly that of his own lifetime, was no less broad and deep, though possibly patchy. He alluded knowledgeably in many works to huge numbers of contemporaries, not only the rich and powerful whose favour he sought but scholars, writers and artists of every kind, especially in Book IV of his *Peregrino*, *El jardín de Lope* and *La Dorotea* but above all in *Laurel de Apolo,* in which he praised almost 300 Spanish and Portuguese writers and artists (at least a sixth of them friends), and which Maria Grazia Profeti has rightly described as fundamental to our knowledge of Lope's culture, of his poetics, and of his relations with Spanish intellectual circles.[56]

He must have been aware of but made few specific allusions to the 'tres o cuatro' [three or four] Spanish dramatists he said had written plays before him, or indeed to those he could boast that his own had engendered, 'más poetas / que hay en los aires átomos sutiles' [more playwrights / than there are flimsy atoms in the air],[57] and his knowledge of Spanish prose literature before his day (apart from the works already mentioned) may not have been extensive. He referred for instance on a few occasions to *Lazarillo de Tormes*, but the only pastoral novels in Spanish

---

[53] Lope de Vega, *La Dorotea*, p. 135. See also p. 410, where Fernando quotes four lines from another.

[54] In his *Epístola* to don Fray Plácido de Tosantos he praised twelve Spanish historians, contrasting their works with those of slanderous foreigners; *Obras poéticas*, I, pp. 1206–7.

[55] See (especially on *Arauco domado*) Victor Dixon, 'Lope de Vega, Chile and a Propaganda Campaign', *Bulletin of Hispanic Studies*, 70.1 (1993): 79–95.

[56] Lope de Vega, *Laurel de Apolo*, p. 17.

[57] See lines 469–74 of his *Égloga a Claudio*, and his *Epístola* to don Antonio Hurtado de Mendoza, *Obras poéticas*, I, p. 1197.

of significant influence on his *Arcadia* were those by Montemayor and Gálvez de Montalvo. The one very clear exception to the rule must be the *Celestina*; Lope borrowed from it for instance in a number of early plays, based on its central figure the character of Gerarda in *La Dorotea*, and outclassed in *El caballero de Olmedo* every later adaptation of it for theatrical performance. By contrast, no Spaniard of his day knew more of Spanish verse. His plays, especially but by no means only those based on national history and legends, were full of quotations and recreations of traditional poetry of every kind. He lamented frequently the abandonment of native metrical forms, lauding Manrique, Mena and other *Cancionero* poets (many of whose verses he glossed) for their 'agudeza, gracia y gala' [wit, grace and elegance],[58] but he was even more entirely familiar with those who had adopted Italian forms, admiring above all Herrera and Garcilaso (whom he constantly quoted), but naming hordes of others in innumerable lists (though singling out those he could similarly praise as unlike the *gongoristas*).

We can judge (especially from his name-dropping) that he was conversant with other aspects of the intellectual climate and culture of his society. Frequent praise for its singers and other musicians, in particular Juan de Palomares, Juan Blas de Castro and Vicente Espinel, suggest a perhaps not expert but keen and characteristically patriotic interest in their art,[59] and his plays are notoriously full of popular songs and dances. He shows indeed an extreme familiarity with folk culture and with peasant life and language astonishing in one who lived primarily in cities.[60] This was one of the many sources too of his outstandingly extensive vocabulary. As Américo Castro declared, 'es probable que ningún escritor del mundo tenga más abundante léxico' [it is probable that no writer in the world has a more abundant lexicon],[61] and among the nearly 9 million words that Lope wrote in his probably authentic works Fernández Gómez was able to list over 21,000 different items.[62] Another, despite Lope's limited experience of sea travel, was the language of ships and sailors, his deliberate displays of which have often been remarked on, though his familiarity with such terminology should not be over-stressed; he made relatively little go a long way.

Far greater was his knowledge of terms related to painting, architecture and sculpture, which draws attention to a vitally important aspect of his culture: his lifelong love of art and association with artists. As Portús has shown, he is 'el

[58]   Lines 1065–73 of Part II of *La Filomena* (Lope de Vega, *Obras poéticas*, I, p. 649); see also his *Respuesta a un señor destos reinos* (ibid., pp. 872–88) but also three prologues: to his *Isidro*, his *Rimas*, and the *Justa poética* in honour of the beatification of San Isidro.

[59]   Dedicating *Carlos Quinto en Francia* to Gabriel Díaz, he wrote of 'la gracia que a los españoles en todo género de música vocal o instrumental ha dado el cielo' [the gift for every kind of vocal or instrumental music that Heaven has bestowed on the Spanish], Case, *Las dedicatorias*, pp. 230–32. The 1627 inventory of Lope's possessions includes 'dos ynstrumentos' [two instruments]; see Davis, *27 documentos*, pp. 170–71.

[60]   Note too the 153 proverbs in *La Dorotea* (listed by Morby in his edition, pp. 453–61), though almost all had figured in the collections by Juan de Mal Lara and Hernán Núñez.

[61]   Quoted for example in Osuna, *La Arcadia*, p. 193.

[62]   Carlos Fernández Gómez, *Vocabulario completo de Lope de Vega*, 3 vols (Madrid: Real Academia Española, 1971), I, pp. lxiv–lxvii.

escritor del Siglo de Oro que más frecuentemente alude en sus obras a pintores y pinturas' [the Spanish writer of the Golden Age who most frequently alludes in his works to painters and paintings].[63] He constantly returned to the topos of the affinity between the visual arts and poesy, nowhere more neatly than in the sonnet in which he called Marino 'gran pintor de los oídos' [a great painter to the ears] and Rubens 'gran poeta de los ojos' [a great poet to the eyes].[64] He referred at least four more times to that great Flemish painter, whom he may well have met in 1628; and also mentioned other foreign artists, like Bosch, Raphael, Michelangelo, and above all Titian (whom he alluded to fourteen times and brought on stage in *La santa liga*),[65] but his knowledge of his coevals in Spain was clearly far greater.

Related by birth and marriage to various visual artists of some distinction, he formed close connections with others; certainly with Liaño, Ribalta, Pacheco, Jáuregui and Carducho, and probably with several more, like Maíno and Juan van der Hamen. He made at least three specific declarations in defence of the nobility of their art, most notably one of 1628 in support of the exemption of their work from purchase tax, which was published the following year and referred to by Carducho in his *Diálogos* of 1633, together with a ninety-two-line *silva* in praise of painting also penned by Lope.[66] Several of his plays, which in general were conceived for the eye as well as the ear,[67] require moreover the display of paintings on stage, and in a number of his publications, by way of self-promotion, he included emblematic engravings, some probably by his own hand. Indeed he was clearly fascinated by hieroglyphs and emblems. He constantly mentioned Alciato, and was probably well acquainted with other emblematists he mentioned or apparently reflected, like Valeriano, Aneau, Coustau, Reusner, Camerarius, Horozco, Hernando de Soto and Sebastián de Covarrubias, but the influence on his work of such combinations of image and text has only begun to be researched.[68]

Much else undoubtedly remains to be discovered about the knowledge on which his writings were based, but in conclusion we must surely agree with Jameson that 'there is a good deal to be said for the opinion that Lope is to be reckoned among the learned poets as well as among the popular', and that 'his store of knowledge was considerable and his reading wide if casual and

---

[63] Portús, *Pintura y pensamiento*, p. 134; in a note (pp. 205–6) he lists forty-two modern painters Lope referred to. His final chapter is a mine of information on Lope's knowledge of art.

[64] Lope de Vega, *Rimas humanas y divinas*, p. 271.

[65] See Frederick A. de Armas, 'Lope de Vega and Titian', *Comparative Literature*, 30.4 (1978): 338–52, and his chapter in this *Companion*.

[66] Vicente Carducho, *Diálogos de la pintura*, ed. Francisco Calvo Serraller (Madrid: Turner, 1979), pp. 448–49 and 254–56.

[67] See for instance Victor Dixon, 'La comedia de corral de Lope como género visual', *Edad de Oro*, 5 (1986): 35–58.

[68] See for example Warren T. McCready, '*Empresas* in Lope de Vega's Works', *Hispanic Review*, 25.2 (1957): 79–104; Victor Dixon, '"Beatus ... nemo": *El villano en su rincón*, las "polianteas" y la literatura de emblemas', *Cuadernos de Filología* (Valencia), 3.1–2: *La génesis de la teatralidad barroca* (1981): 279–300; idem, 'The *Emblemas morales* of Sebastián de Covarrubias and the Plays of Lope de Vega', *Emblematica*, 6.1 (1992): 83–101.

miscellaneous',[69] but also with Osuna, who wrote of 'la fenomenal cultura de Lope, la mayor de su tiempo entre literatos, si por cultura no nos limitamos a entender la información, profunda o no, que se adquiría en las universidades; en este sentido, solo Quevedo le supera' [Lope's phenomenal culture, the greatest of his time in Spain among men of letters, if by culture we do not understand merely the information, profound or not, that was acquired in the universities; in this sense only Quevedo surpasses him].[70]

[69] Jameson, 'The Sources', pp. 138–39.
[70] Osuna, *La Arcadia*, p. 195.

2

Lope de Vega and the Theatre in Madrid

JOSÉ MARÍA RUANO DE LA HAZA

On 7 September 1610, Lope de Vega bought a two-storey house on Francos street, on the edge of the Madrid theatre district. The focal points of this district were the Church of St Sebastian — which in 1631 would house the actors' guild[1] — the *mentidero de los comediantes*, or actors' 'gossip shop', in León street; and the two public playhouses: the Corral del Príncipe and the Corral de la Cruz.

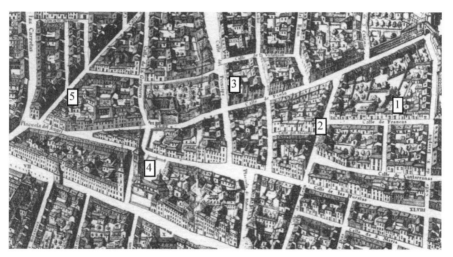

Texeira's 1656 map of Madrid (detail)
1. Lope de Vega's house; 2. *Mentidero de los comediantes*; 3. Corral del Príncipe; 4. Church of St Sebastian; 5. Corral de la Cruz

Lope paid 9,000 *reales* for the property, 5,000 as a down payment and the remainder in two instalments of 2,000 *reales* each payable in four and eight

---

[1] Known as the Cofradía de Nuestra Señora de la Novena. See José Subirá, *El gremio de representantes españoles y la Cofradía de Nuestra Señora de la Novena* (Madrid: Consejo Superior de Investigaciones Científicas, Instituto de Estudios Madrileños, 1960).

months.[2] Two years later, he applied for an exemption from the *Regalía del Real Aposento de Corte* [Royal Privilege on Private Dwellings], applicable since the time of Philip II to two-storey houses in Madrid. In accordance with this 'privilege', the owners of such houses, known as *casas de aposento*, were obliged to lodge (*aposentar*) a royal functionary and his family rent free on one of their two floors.[3] On 13 February 1613 the exemption was granted in perpetuity to Lope in return for an annual tax of 4,500 *maravedís* (132 *reales*), money which in theory would pay the rent of the functionary who would have occupied one-half of his house. In order to assess this annual tax, the house had to be properly measured. The length of the façade was found to be 53 Castilian feet and the depth of the property (including, one assumes, the backyard) 100 feet, giving a total of 5,300 square feet.[4]

The exact location of Lope's house was established in 1790 by José Antonio Álvarez de Baena in his *Hijos de Madrid ilustres* [*Illustrious Sons of Madrid*]. It was situated, past Niño street (present-day Quevedo street), on the left side of Francos street, as one enters it by the *mentidero*.[5] Years later, Mesoneros Romanos examined the original deeds of purchase and reconstructed the history of the property from the time it was endowed to the parish priest of the Church of the Holy Cross (c. 1570) to the building of the house (before 1587) and its purchase by Lope (1610) down to 1825, when it was bought by the father of the person who resided there at the time of his investigation.[6] Pedro Texeira's 1656 map of Madrid shows Lope's house as a small two-storey dwelling with only two windows on the first floor, a building very different from the one described by Mesonero Romanos in the nineteenth century and from its modern reconstruction. It is also much smaller: the façade of Lope's house in Texeira's map is about twenty-one feet shorter than the 1613 tax assessors had estimated. The most likely explanation for this discrepancy is that the depiction of private dwellings in Texeira's map is not always accurate. Although Texeira lived most of his life in Madrid, his map was actually printed in Amsterdam by Salomon Savry in 1656,

---

[2] The sale contract is reproduced and transcribed in *27 documentos de Lope de Vega en el Archivo Histórico de Protocolos de Madrid*, ed. Charles Davis (Madrid: Comunidad de Madrid, 2004), pp. 94–107. See also pp. 29–39 on this and other houses owned or occupied by Lope in Madrid.

[3] See Thomas Middleton, *The Urban and Architectural Environment of the 'Corrales' of Madrid: The Corral de la Cruz in 1600* (Ann Arbor, MI: University Microfilms International, 1976), pp. 47–52 for a useful overview of domestic architecture in Madrid.

[4] Cayetano Alberto de la Barrera, *Nueva biografía de Lope de Vega*, 2 vols, Biblioteca de Autores Españoles, 262–263 (Madrid: Atlas, 1973–74), p. 113n. A Castilian foot was about 28 cm long. In 1624, when his neighbours, who lived in the single-floor house to the right of his, were Alonso de Gastaneda and Juan Rodríguez de Matamoros, Lope's house was still exempt; José del Corral, *Las composiciones de aposento y las casas a la malicia* (Madrid: Instituto de Estudios Madrileños, 1982), p. 91.

[5] Juan Manuel González Martel, *Casa Museo Lope de Vega: guía y catálogo* (Madrid: Real Academia Española & Comunidad de Madrid, 1993), p. 33.

[6] Ramón Mesonero Romanos, *El antiguo Madrid* (1861), 2 vols (Madrid: Renacimiento, 1925), I, pp. 56–57.

presumably without his supervision.[7]

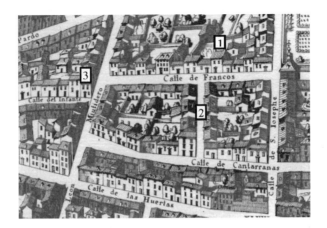

Texeira's 1656 map of Madrid (detail)
1. Lope de Vega's house; 2. Niño street; 3. Francisco Treviño's house

Lope de Vega's house-museum today

This accounts for its many misspellings ('Miutidero' for 'Mentidero') and omissions (the name of Niño street) as well as for the fact that, with the exception

---

[7] María Isabel Gea Ortigas, *El plano de Texeira* (Madrid: Ediciones La Librería, 1999), p. 17.

of a few landmark edifices — churches, the Royal Palace, the Retiro — other buildings, whose configuration and dimensions are known to us from different sources, are not always accurately depicted.[8] For example, according to a census taken in 1624 for the purpose of ascertaining the number and characteristics of the so-called *casas de malicia*,[9] the south-facing façade of the house owned by Francisco de Treviño, an actor by profession, on the corner of Infante and León streets (see above), measured 41 feet.[10] In Texeira's map that façade is no more than 28.5 feet long.

Lope lived in his house on Francos street until his death in 1635. Actors and *autores*[11] must have often visited him there. Some, like Francisco de Treviño,[12] were his neighbours. Pedro Maldonado and his first wife Magdalena de Chaves lived nearby in Cantarranas street.[13] Also in Cantarranas resided, at least in 1624, Sánchez, 'autor de comedias',[14] a man whose life may serve to illustrate the uneasy relationship that Lope sometimes had with certain members of the acting profession. The *Genealogía* (I, 883) says of him that he was a 'Representante antiguo, y fue autor, de quien se haze mención en el libro de sainetes de Luis Quiñones de Venauente en el folio 2, pero no emos podido aberiguar su propio nonbre' [an actor a long time ago (the *Genealogía* was compiled at the beginning of the eighteenth century), and he became an *autor*, mentioned on fol. 2 of Luis Quiñones de Benavente's book of short pieces, but we have not been able to

---

[8] For example, the two Madrid playhouses: see J. M. Ruano de la Haza & John J. Allen, *Los teatros comerciales del siglo XVII y la escenificación de la Comedia* (Madrid: Castalia, 1994).

[9] The *casas de malicia* were houses built in such a way that the owner would avoid having to comply with the *Regalía del Real Aposento de Corte*, from which Lope's house was exempted in 1613 (see Middleton, *The Urban and Architectural Environment*, pp. 47–48).

[10] Corral, *Las composiciones de aposento*, p. 76.

[11] The word 'autor' designates the actor-manager of a seventeenth-century company. The playwright was called the 'poeta'.

[12] Called Francisco Tribiño by the eighteenth-century compilers of the *Genealogía* (*Genealogía, origen y noticias de los comediantes de España*, ed. N. D. Shergold, & J. E. Varey, Fuentes para la Historia del Teatro en España, 2, London: Tamesis, 1985, I, 96), he was born in Valladolid and, on 17 September 1612, signed a two-year contract with the company of Juan de Morales, 'dándole cada día tres reales de ración y cinco reales por representación el primer año y seis el segundo' [giving him three reales per day for maintenance and five reales per performance in the first year and six in the second] (Francisco de B. San Román, *Lope de Vega, los cómicos toledanos y el poeta sastre*, Madrid: Imprenta Góngora, 1935, doc. 331, p. 176). In 1617 he was a member of the company of Pedro Llorente and in 1622 he worked for Cristóbal de Avendaño. In 1624 he rejoined Morales' company for the Madrid *autos* and in 1631 travelled to Italy with the company of Roque de Figueroa. He returned to Spain in 1638 and worked, first, for Lorenzo Hurtado, from whom in 1639 he demanded payment of 700 reales 'que se le debe de resto de raciones y representaciones del tiempo que asistió en su compañía' [which he is owed for the remainder of his maintenance and performance payments from the time when he belonged to his company] (Cristóbal Pérez Pastor, *Nuevos datos acerca del histrionismo español en los siglos XVI y XVII*, Madrid: Revista Española, 1901, p. 307) and then, in 1641, for Antonio Sierra (Luis Quiñones de Benavente, *Entremeses completos*, I: *Jocoseria*, ed. Ignacio Arellano, Juan M. Escudero & Abraham Madroñal, Madrid: Iberoamericana, 2001, p. 719).

[13] Pérez Pastor, *Nuevos datos*, pp. 124–25. By the time Maldonado died, in 1634, he was married to Jerónima Rodríguez (*Genealogía*, I, 105).

[14] Corral, *Las composiciones de aposento*, p. 76.

ascertain his Christian name]. The reference is to Quiñones's *Jocoseria*, published in 1645 in Madrid by Francisco García.[15] First in the volume is the *Loa con que empezó Lorenzo Hurtado en Madrid la segunda vez* [*Prologue with which Lorenzo Hurtado Opened in Madrid the Second Time*], and there, among many other famous *autores*, such as Cristóbal de Avendaño, Manuel Vallejo, Roque de Figueroa, Antonio de Prado, Juan Acacio and Andrés de la Vega, there is mention of a certain Sánchez.[16] His full name was Fernán or Hernán Sánchez de Vargas, and he was one of the twelve official *autores* named by the 1615 regulations.[17] According to Arellano, Escudero and Madroñal, he began his acting career in 1594 in the company of Diego de Santander, and then, after working for Baltasar Pinedo (1607) and Alonso Riquelme (1608), formed his own company in 1609.[18] In 1610 he bought Lope's *La hermosa Ester*, whose autograph manuscript is preserved in the British Library: he played the part of King Assuerus.[19] Late in 1611 or early in 1612 he must have been in Granada; in January 1612 an innkeeper from that city signed a promissory note agreeing to reimburse 200 *reales* to 'Fernán Sánchez de Vargas, autor de comedias, vecino de Madrid' [Fernán Sánchez de Vargas, *autor de comedias*, resident in Madrid].[20] For the 1612 Corpus Christi festivities, he was contracted to perform in the town of Esquivias (where Cervantes' in-laws lived) the same *autos* that he had already presented in Madrid, plus an unnamed play.[21] Sánchez Arjona claims that he favoured Andalusian playwrights, in particular Luis Vélez de Guevara, and that this earned him the enmity of Lope de Vega, who, in 1614, 'resentido de que no se hubiese limitado a representar sus obras únicamente se negó a escribir para él en Diciembre de 1614 un drama que le solicitó por conducto del Duque de Sessa' [upset that he had performed works by other dramatists, refused to write a play which Sánchez had requested through the Duke of Sessa].[22]

[15] See the recent edition by Arellano, Escudero and Madroñal (2001), cited above.

[16] Quiñones, *Entremeses*, ed. Arellano, Escudero and Madroñal, p. 127.

[17] J. E. Varey & N. D. Shergold, *Teatros y comedias en Madrid, 1600–1650: estudio y documentos*, Fuentes para la Historia del Teatro en España, 3 (London: Tamesis, 1971) (*Fuentes III*), doc. 6, p. 56.

[18] Quiñones, *Entremeses*, ed. Arellano, Escudero and Madroñal, p. 718.

[19] See Marco Presotto, *Le commedie autografe di Lope de Vega* (Kassel: Reichenberger, 2000), p. 250.

[20] Pérez Pastor, *Nuevos datos*, p. 127.

[21] Pérez Pastor, *Nuevos datos*, pp. 127–28. As Corpus Christi fell on Thursday 21 June in 1612, Sánchez must have performed in Esquivias on Tuesday 26 June. The *autos* must have been the ones he performed in Madrid the previous year, 1611, when he lost the *joya* (a prize worth one hundred ducats) to Tomás Fernández de Cabredo because 'sus dos Autos fueron mejores que los de Hernán Sánchez de Vargas' [his two autos were better than those of Hernán Sánchez de Vargas], Pérez Pastor, 'Nuevos datos acerca del histrionismo español en los siglos XVI y XVII (segunda serie)', *Bulletin Hispanique*, 9 (1907): 360–85 (p. 377).

[22] José Sánchez-Arjona, *Noticias referentes a los anales del teatro en Sevilla desde Lope de Rueda hasta fines del siglo XVII* (Sevilla: E. Rasco, 1898), p. 153. Lope wrote to the Duke: 'Sanchez trahe todas las comedias del Andaluzia, y tiene a Luis Velez y otros poetas que le acuden con los partos de sus yngenios [...] Sanchez me ha hecho a mí notables pesadumbres' [Sánchez gets all the plays from Andalusia, and he has Luis Vélez and other dramatists who bring him the fruits of their invention [...] Sánchez has seriously offended me], Lope de Vega, *Epistolario de*

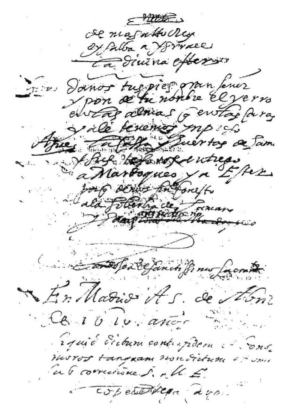

**Last page of the autograph manuscript of *La hermosa Ester*,
signed at the bottom by Lope de Vega in Madrid on 5 April 1610**

Lope's vindictiveness, not only towards some actors and *autores*, but also towards some fellow writers, is well known. His hostility towards Luis Vélez may have had something to do with the extended belief that he was fond of stealing other playwrights' plots.[23] This, however, did not prevent Lope, shortly after he moved to his house in Francos street, from founding with Vélez and other writers an academy, which Pedro Soto de Rojas, a second-rate poet friend of Lope's and enemy of Vélez's, wittily named *Academia Selvaje* because it met in the house of Francisco de Silva.[24] Lope's attacks on rival playwrights, such as the Mexican Juan Ruiz de Alarcón, and poets, particularly Góngora, are well documented.[25]

Lope de Vega Carpio, ed. Agustín G. de Amezúa, 4 vols (Madrid: Aldus, 1935–43), III, pp. 217–18.

[23] M. Romera-Navarro, 'Querellas y rivalidades en las Academias del siglo XVII', *Hispanic Review*, 9.4 (1941): 494–99 (pp. 496–97).

[24] Silva is the same as *selva*, jungle; hence, *selvaje* or *salvaje* [savage].

[25] See, for example, Hugo Albert Rennert, *The Life of Lope de Vega, 1562–1635* (1904) (New York: Benjamin Blom, 1968), chapters XI and XII.

Another possible 'enemy' was the young Calderón, perhaps as a result of an incident that took place near Lope's house in 1629.[26]

Fellow-poets, admirers, actors and *autores* who lived in the parish of St Sebastian must have been frequent visitors to Lope's house. Extant documentation shows that he had close ties with many members of the acting profession. He had a well-publicised and long-lasting love affair with Micaela Luján, who became the mother of five of his children and with whom he travelled extensively while she was performing,[27] as well as with, among others, Jerónima de Burgos, for whom he wrote *La dama boba*,[28] and Lucía Salcedo, 'the mad woman'. He also had many business dealings with *autores*, such as Pedro Jiménez de Valenzuela, who at one time owed him 400 *reales*;[29] Antonio de Granados, who bought from him three plays 'never before staged': *El cuerdo loco*, *Los esclavos libres* and *El príncipe despeñado*;[30] and Melchor de Villalba, for whom he composed *El maestro de danzar*: 'Hice esta comedia en Alba [de Tormes]' — says Lope on the last page of the manuscript — 'para Melchor de Villalva; y porque es verdad firmélo el mes que es mayor el yelo y el año que Dios nos salva 1594' [I wrote this comedy in Alba de Tormes for Melchor de Villalba, and because it is true I signed my name on the manuscript on the coldest month and in the year of our Lord 1594].[31]

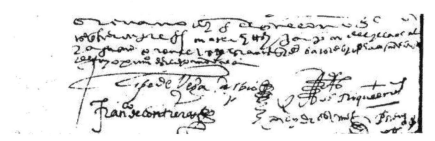

Lope de Vega's signature next to Alonso de Riquelme's

He appears as 'principal deudor y pagador' [main debtor and payer] for Alonso Riquelme in a contract by which the *autor de comedias* agreed to travel to the town of Oropesa,

con su conpañia [...] e que hara el dicho dia de señor san juan por la tarde en la dicha villa en la parte que le fuere señalado una comedia y el dia siguiente, que es domingo por la tarde otra, y el lunes siguiente por la mañana otra, y las comedias han de ser *El hombre de bien*, y *El secretario de si mismo*, y *La obediencia laureada*, bien fechas

[26] Emilio Cotarelo y Mori, *Ensayo sobre la vida y obras de D. Pedro Calderón de la Barca* (Madrid: Revista de Archivos, Bibliotecas y Museos, 1924), pp. 131–33.

[27] Ignacio Arellano, *Historia del teatro español del siglo XVII* (Madrid: Cátedra, 1995), p. 170.

[28] Sánchez-Arjona, *Noticias*, p. 146.

[29] Pérez Pastor, *Nuevos datos*, p. 351.

[30] San Román, *Lope de Vega*, doc. 129, p. 75.

[31] Sánchez-Arjona, *Noticias*, p. 95.

con sus adornos y entremeses y bailes.[32]

> [with his company [...] in order to perform in the afternoon of the said day of St John, and in a place to be designated, a play, and in the afternoon of the following day, which is Sunday, a second play, and in the morning of the following Monday a third play. And the plays shall be [Lope's] *The Good Man, His Own Secretary* and *Obedience Rewarded*. All three to be properly performed with their stage scenery and their interludes and dances.]

He must also have met many members of the acting profession — *autores*, actors, scribes, prompters, stage managers, other playwrights — in the *mentidero de los comediantes*, which was no more than 300 metres from his house in Francos street. No one knows exactly what it looked like. The more famous *mentidero* on the *gradas* of the disappeared Church of St Philip, which Lope also frequented, did not meet, as its name might suggest, on a flight of steps. Rather, as Mesonero Romanos showed, its members, among whom were some of the greatest writers and wits of the time, gathered on a raised promenade on the side of the church that ran alongside Calle Mayor [Main Street]:

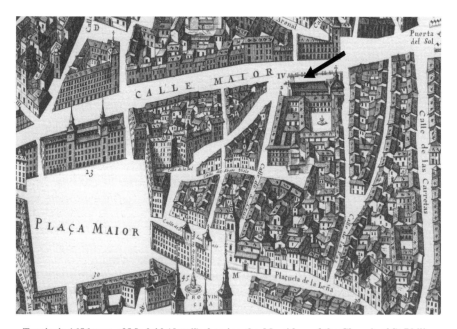

Texeira's 1656 map of Madrid (detail) showing the *Mentidero* of the Church of St Philip

[32] San Román, *Lope de Vega*, doc. 211, p. 126.

Church of St Philip showing the *Mentidero* promenade

It is likely that the more modest actors' *mentidero* was also some sort of promenade, for, as Texeira's map shows, León street does indeed widen just before the entrance to Francos street. Lope must have often dropped by the *mentidero* on his way to the centre of Madrid. There he would have met actors and *autores* spending time in Madrid between engagements, or during Lent, which was their enforced period of rest. He would have listened with interest to the latest gossip, such as the incident involving Luis de Toledo who slashed a woman's face in 1611, or, also in 1611, the arrest of Juan de Palacios (not mentioned in the *Genealogía* and probably not an actor), who was accused of stealing four 'new plays' from their owner, an unnamed *autor*.[33] He would have also learned about the formation of new companies, the failures and successes of actors and plays, and the issuing of ordinances and decrees aiming at controlling and regulating the acting profession. The most important of these were enacted on 14 March 1615, barely five years after Lope moved to Madrid. The document named twelve official companies and enjoined their *autores* to employ only persons of good morals and behaviour. Actors were forbidden to display lavish costumes prohibited by sumptuary laws outside the theatres; actresses were not allowed to perform dressed as men, nor play men's roles; men and boys were not permitted to play women's parts; lewd and dishonest dances, songs, gestures and movements were to be severely punished because they 'set a bad example'; male and female spectators were to be kept separate inside and in the vicinity of playhouses; no person, apart from performers, was allowed to enter the actors' dressing rooms (a rule often breached); companies were forbidden to put on plays

---

[33] Pérez Pastor, *Nuevos datos*, pp. 126–27.

in private houses without first obtaining a licence from the Council; performances were prohibited in churches, monasteries and convents as well as on Christmas Day, Easter Sunday and Whitsunday and from Ash Wednesday to Quasimodo Sunday; finally, playtexts were to be censored by a member of the Council, 'no permitiendo cosa lasciua, ni deshonesta, ni malsonante, ni en daño de otros, ni de materia que no conuenga que salga en publico' [not permitting anything that is lewd, dishonest, offensive, harmful to others, or which deals with matters to which an audience should not be exposed].[34] The fact that the Royal Ordinances made a point of outlawing all these practices surely implies that they must have been quite common, as indeed one may deduce from quite a few plays, among them Lope's *El galán de la Membrilla*, one of whose stage directions indicates that the part of young Prince Alfonso 'le puede hacer una mujer' [may be played by a woman].[35]

It is also likely that Lope was present at some rehearsals.[36] According to the 1615 regulations, rehearsals were to be conducted behind closed doors in the *autor*'s house.[37] Andrés Gil Enríquez's *entremés* of *El ensayo* does indeed take place in the house of the *autor*, Pedro de la Rosa, and his second wife, Antonia de Santiago, who is first shown knitting ('haciendo media'). The actors arrive one by one at the house. Two of the first to appear are Mariana Borja, who was a celebrated musician, and Luciana, probably her maid since she was not given a speaking part. They sit near Antonia de Santiago, herself an actress, and help her with her knitting. Next to enter is a certain Simón (Aguado?) who announces it is past 10 o'clock in the morning. Later on Gaspar enters carrying a lute, which he proceeds to tune whilst waiting for the rehearsal to begin. Two spectators (*mirones*) stand at one side to watch. The women sing. When they are ready to start the rehearsal they discover that the prompter is nowhere to be found. So Rosa decides to prompt himself. The stage direction is worth reproducing in full: '[Pedro de la] Rosa, seated on a low chair, takes on the role of prompter; on the other side [of the stage], the two women continue with their knitting. Those who are rehearsing stand before him, while he pretends to read to them'. At one point Mariana Romero forgets her cue and excuses herself by saying that she has not yet managed to learn her part. After hearing some particularly awful verses, Malaguilla fears that the audience will boo them ('Esto va tundido a silbos'). La Borja replies that what sounds awful in rehearsals is often well received on stage. Antonia, the *autor*'s wife, also forgets her lines and, upset, throws the manuscript at her husband's head. At that point they decide to postpone rehearsing until the

---

[34] *Fuentes III*, doc. 6, pp. 55–58.

[35] José María Ruano de la Haza, *La puesta en escena en los teatros comerciales del Siglo de Oro* (Madrid: Castalia, 2000), p. 99.

[36] Pérez Pastor shows that Calderón attended a rehearsal in 1659, but as a mere spectator, since the company in question, that of Diego Osorio, was learning a play by another playwright, Juan Bautista Diamante (*Documentos para la biografía de D. Pedro Calderón de la Barca*, Madrid: Fortanet, 1905, pp. 264–65). Josef Oehrlein emphasizes the importance accorded by actors and *autores* to daily rehearsals (*El actor en el teatro español del Siglo de Oro*, Madrid: Castalia, 1993, pp. 131–38).

[37] *Fuentes III*, doc. 6, p. 57.

following day. The playlet ends with Simón lamenting that 'Jamás / se hace ensayo con concierto' [there is no such thing as a problem-free rehearsal!].[38]

Rehearsals took place behind closed doors not only to prevent *mirones*, such as the two characters in Gil Enríquez's playlet, from ogling actresses, but also to discourage literary piracy. In the Prologue to the thirteenth volume of his collected plays (Madrid: Viuda de Alonso Martín, 1620), Lope complains about two literary pirates, 'que llama el vulgo, al uno *Memorilla* y al otro *Gran memoria*' [whom the populace has named Little Memory and Great Memory], because 'con algunos versos que aprenden mezclan infinitos suyos bárbaros, con que ganan la vida, vendiéndolas á los pueblos y autores extramuros' [they mix an infinite number of their own barbarous lines with just a few of his verses, which they had memorized, and they make a living selling these versions to village mayors and to *autores* outside Madrid]. At least two such piratical versions have so far been identified[39] and one of them, the Melbury House manuscript of Lope's *Peribáñez*, conforms exactly to Lope's description of such versions. But more common than memorizing a play (by watching it repeatedly at rehearsals or during performances) was stealing the original manuscript (as we saw Juan Palacios do in 1611) or, more often, an actor's partial copy. The original manuscript was sold by the poet to the *autor* who kept it under lock and key in the company's chest. One copy of the entire play was usually made for the prompter (and eventually ended in many cases in the hands of a printer) and partial copies were made for actors to help them learn their lines and cues. Occasionally, an actor who moved from one company to another would take with him his partial version, which was then used to reconstruct an illegal version of the play.[40]

The practice of keeping the poet's original manuscript in the company's chest after producing the prompter's copy helps to explain the survival of so many of Lope's autographs (as compared, say, with his contemporary, William Shakespeare). Marco Presotto has published a full list together with a detailed description of the contents of all thirty-six complete and nine partial extant autographs of Lope's plays. Among them are well known pieces such as *El bastardo Mudarra*, *Las bizarrías de Belisa*, *El Brasil restituido*, *El castigo sin venganza*, *La dama boba*, *El galán de la Membrilla*. They are preserved in Spain's National Library (22) and Royal Academy (3), The British Library (8), Melbury House Library (3), New York Public Library (1), Pennsylvania University Library (2), Boston Library (1) and Laurenziana Library (1). They

---

[38] Gil Enríquez, Andrés, *El ensayo*, in Hannah E. Bergman, ed., *Ramillete de entremeses y bailes* (Madrid: Castalia, 1970), pp. 337–46.

[39] See José María Ruano de la Haza, 'An Early Rehash of Lope's *Peribáñez*', *Bulletin of the Comediantes*, 35.1 (1983): 5–29; J. L. Canet Vallés, 'Las comedias manuscritas anónimas o de posibles "autores de comedias" como fuente documental para la reconstrucción del hecho teatral en el período áureo', in *Teatros y vida teatral en el Siglo de Oro a través de las fuentes documentales*, ed. Luciano García Lorenzo & J. E. Varey (London: Tamesis, 1991), pp. 273–83.

[40] José María Ruano de la Haza, 'La relación textual entre *El burlador de Sevilla* y *Tan largo me lo fiáis*', in *Tirso de Molina: del Siglo de Oro al siglo XX*, ed. Ignacio Arellano et al. (Madrid: Revista Estudios, 1995), pp. 283–95. Republished in *Hispanic Essays in Honor of Frank P. Casa*, ed. A. Robert Lauer & Henry W. Sullivan (New York: Peter Lang, 1997), pp. 173–86.

were bought by some of the best *autores* of his time, such as Baltasar de Pinedo, Antonio Granados, Alonso de Riquelme, Fernán Sánchez de Vargas, Domingo Balbín, Cristóbal Ortiz, Pedro de Valdés, Antonio de Prado, Juan Bautista Valenciano, Andrés de la Vega, Roque de Figueroa and Manuel Vallejo.[41] Some, such as the one reproduced below, contain cast lists in his own hand, evidence of the part he must have played in assigning the different roles in collaboration with the *autor*.

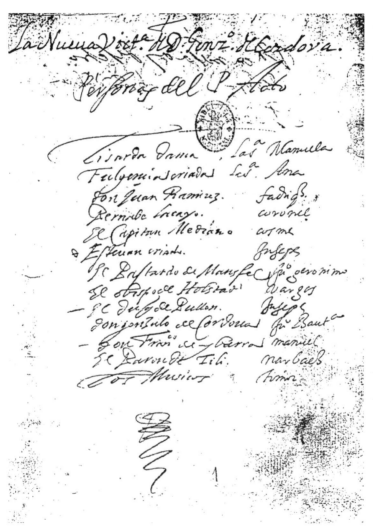

Autograph cast list for *La nueva victoria de Don Gonzalo de Córdoba*, dated in Madrid on 8 October 1622

---

[41] Presotto, *Le commedie autografe*, p. 44.

It goes without saying that, while in Madrid, Lope also regularly attended performances of his and other dramatists' plays.[42] In accordance with the Royal Ordinances of 1608,[43] the Madrid playhouses were to be open to the public at 12 noon, but performances began at 2 pm from 1 October to 31 March and at 4 pm during the remainder of the year. If Juan de Zabaleta, writing in the middle of the century, is to be trusted, women were the first spectators to enter the playhouses. Men, says the stern moralist, have an early lunch before heading for the theatre; women, on the other hand, tend to gather there even before lunch.[44] Men and women entered the playhouses through different doors and were kept strictly separated during the performance. This rule did not apply, however, to those spectators who hired an *aposento* or box in one of the houses adjacent to the playhouse. Some of these boxes, especially window boxes, were occasionally used by prostitutes.[45]

The physical configuration of the two Madrid playhouses was very similar.[46] Each consisted of a rectangular courtyard surrounded by four four-storey buildings covered by tiled roofs. Men stood in the patio, which on sunny days was covered by a canvas awning,[47] or sat on benches or tiers of seating (*gradas*) alongside its flanks. In the houses contiguous to the theatre, behind the rows of benches, rose three ranges of boxes (*aposentos*): windows on the first floor, balconies on the second and attic boxes on the top floor. On the side facing the stage was the entrance building, with two boxes (*alojeros*) on the ground floor, a large *cazuela* [stewpan] or women's enclosure on the first floor, boxes for the Madrid City Councillors and other dignitaries such as the President of the Council of Castile on the second, and, on the top floor, a smaller *cazuela*.

Opposite the main *cazuela* was a thrust stage, surrounded on three sides by spectators. The backstage consisted of a tiring house, which served as both the women's dressing room and the discovery space, and two galleries or corridors. All three were usually covered by curtains during the performance. The men's dressing room and the company's wardrobe were in the pit, under the stage platform. At the top of this structure, and hidden from view, was the *desván de los tornos* or stage-machine attic.

Lope composed most of his plays with this basic structure in mind. Often he wrote them to be performed on a bare stage platform. In Act I, scene 2 of *Barlaán y Josafat* [*Barlaam and Josaphat*], a play which, since the autograph manuscript

---

[42] In a letter to the Duke of Sessa in July 1611, Lope writes: 'Madrid is just as Your Excellency left it: Prado, carriages, women, heat, dust … *comedias* …' (Rennert, *The Life of Lope de Vega*, p. 197).

[43] *Fuentes III*, doc. 2, pp. 47–52.

[44] Juan de Zabaleta, *El día de fiesta por la mañana y por la tarde*, ed. Cristóbal Cuevas García (Madrid: Castalia, 1983), p. 317.

[45] José María Ruano de la Haza, 'Noticias para el gobierno de la Sala de Alcaldes de Casa y Corte', *Bulletin of the Comediantes*, 40.1 (1988): 67–74.

[46] This similarity, however, did not necessarily extend to other playhouses in the rest of Spain. See John J. Allen's survey of other theatres in the Iberian peninsula in chapter VI of Ruano & Allen, *Los teatros comerciales*, pp. 197–231.

[47] The awning must have also improved the acoustics in the theatre.

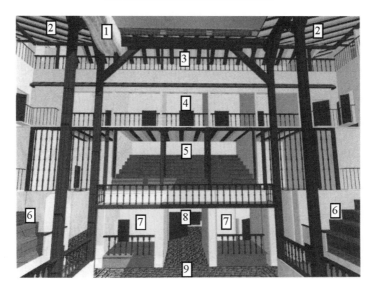

The *cazuela* of the Príncipe playhouse viewed from the stage

1. Canvas awning; 2. Roof over the *gradas*; 3. Upper *cazuela*; 4. Madrid City Council box; 5. Main *cazuela*; 6. Lateral *gradas*; 7. *Alojero* boxes; 8. Main entrance; 9. Patio

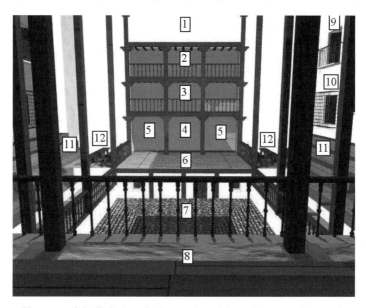

The stage of the Príncipe playhouse viewed from the women's *cazuela*

1. Stage-machines attic; 2. Second gallery (*lo alto*); 3. First gallery; 4. Discovery space; 5. Tiring house; 6. Thrust-stage platform; 7. Patio; 8. Main *cazuela*; 9. Balcony box; 10. Window box; 11. Lateral *gradas*; 12. Stage benches

is dated 1 February 1611,[48] Lope probably wrote in his house in Francos street, Josaphat conjures up the sights, smells, people, shops, buildings and streets of a whole city in the minds of the spectators, who only see in front of them an empty stage platform with a plain curtain as a backdrop. In other plays he utilizes the middle section of the tiring house as an 'inner stage'. Act III of *Las bizarrías de Belisa*, whose autograph manuscript, dated 24 May 1634, is preserved in the British Library, illustrates this stage convention:

FINEA.   ¿Escribir quieres agora?
BELISA.   Pon, Finea, en esa cuadra
           una bujía y papel,
           tinta y pluma.
FINEA.   Pienso que anda
           por esos aires tu seso.
BELISA.   ¡Corre esa cortina! ¡Acaba!

Corriendo una cortina, se descubre un aposento bien entapizado, un bufetillo de plata y otro con escritorios, una bujía y el Conde al lado.

BELISA.   ¡Jesús! ¿Qué hay aquí?
FINEA.   ¡Ay, señora!
           ¡Un hombre!
CONDE.   ¡Quedo! No hagas,
           Belisa, extremos. Yo soy.
BELISA.   ¿Vueseñoría en mi casa
           a tales horas? ¡Ay, Celia!
           ¡Buen cuidado, gentil guarda!
           ¿Tú pones en mi aposento
           al Conde y junto a mi cama?
           ¿Dónde se vio tal traición?

[FINEA.   Now you wish to write?
BELISA.   Please, Finea, bring to that room a lamp, some paper, ink and a pen.
FINEA.   I think you are out of your mind.
BELISA.   Draw that curtain! Hurry!

A curtain is drawn to reveal a room hung with tapestries, a small silver writing desk and another with writing implements, a lamp and the Count on one side.

BELISA.   Good heavens! What's this?
FINEA.   Ah, madam! It's a man!
COUNT.   Quiet, Belisa! Please, don't do anything foolish! It's only me.
BELISA.   Your Grace in my house and at this time of night? Ah, Celia! Is this the
           good care you take of me? You are indeed an excellent guardian! You
           have led the Count to my room, to my bed! Who ever saw such treason!]

[48] S. Griswold Morley & Courtney Bruerton, *Cronología de las comedias de Lope de Vega* (Madrid: Gredos, 1968), p. 89.

Two popular 'inner stages', conventionally used in dozens of plays by Lope and his contemporaries, were a private room, such as the one in which the Count is discovered in *Las bizarrías de Belisa*, and a garden. The following are two very plain and imperfect sketches of what must have been a very colourful display on a seventeenth-century stage:

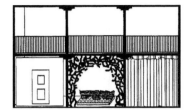

Two inner stages

The 'inner stage', then, was a small set at the back of the stage platform which served, among other things, to indicate, without having to resort to the spoken word, the location of the action of the play. This action, however, took place only minimally in the 'inner stage'. Actors still moved, acted and spoke their lines for the most part on the empty stage platform, which by means of the objects shown in the 'inner stage' had been transformed in the minds of the spectators into a garden, private room, throne room, drawing room and so forth.

A thrust stage has no wings; therefore all entrances and exits had to be done in Lope's time by the back curtains, which were often referred to as doors in contemporary stage directions. It also required that all stage 'sets', furniture, decorations, as well as *tableaux vivants* and 'discoveries', be shown behind the back curtains.[49] Mountain scenery was conventionally 'discovered' on the first gallery, as were windows (for example, the window from which Casilda speaks to the disguised Comendador in Act II of Lope's *Peribáñez*) and city walls, which were usually represented by a painted cloth thrown over the railings. For example, in Act III of Lope's *Las almenas de Toro*, King Sancho of Castile and his soldiers, among whom is the Cid, are on the stage platform when Nuño Velázquez and his soldiers enter the first gallery, which stood for the city walls. King Sancho gives orders to sound the call to arms and a stage direction says that '*Suben por las escalas, que han de estar puestas, con rodelas y espadas, defiéndense de arriba con alcancías y espadas*' [They (King Sancho's men), wielding swords and shields, climb the ladders, which must be in position, while those in the gallery try to repel the attack with swords and other weapons].[50] On the other hand, the top gallery (called *lo alto* in stage directions) was conventionally used to represent a tower, a high mountain peak or the 'heavens', the place from which angels and saints descended on stage machines to the stage platform. The most popular of

---

[49] For a full account of all these stage decorations, see my *La puesta en escena*.

[50] Fourteenth volume of Lope's collected plays (Madrid: Viuda de Fernando Correa Montenegro, 1621).

these stage machines was the *pescante* or canal, which, as shown in Sabbatini's drawing, consisted of a small platform (G) attached to a short upright (C-D) which moved up and down along a greased groove (E-F) by means of ropes and pulleys. When used for the ascent or descent of angels, saints, souls, devils and other supernatural creatures, the canal was usually covered by a cut-out piece of cardboard painted as a cloud (I):

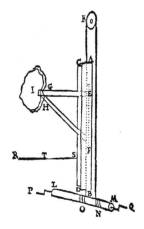

A cloud machine, Sabbatini, p. 109   **Ruano, *La puesta en escena*, illus. 8 showing the canal**

In the Prologue to the sixteenth volume of his plays (Madrid: Viuda de Alonso Martín, 1621), Lope included a short dialogue between the 'Theatre' and a 'Visitor' which gives a good idea of his views concerning the use and abuse of stage machinery in commercial theatres:

> TEATRO. ¡Ay, ay, ay!
> FORASTERO. ¿De que te quejas, Teatro?
> TEATRO. ¡Ay, ay, ay!
> FORASTERO. ¿Qué tienes? ¿Qué novedad es esta? ¿Estás enfermo, que parece tocador ese que tienes por la frente?
> TEATRO. No es sino una nube que estos días me han puesto los autores en la cabeza.
> FORASTERO. Pues ¿qué puede moverte a tales voces?
> TEATRO. ¿Es posible que no me ves herido, quebradas las piernas y los brazos, lleno de mil agujeros, de mil trampas y de mil clavos?
> FORASTERO. ¿Quién te ha puesto en estado tan miserable?
> TEATRO. Los carpinteros, por orden de los autores.
> FORASTERO. No tienen ellos la culpa, sino los poetas; que son para ti como los médicos y los barberos, que los unos mandan y los otros sangran.
> TEATRO. Yo he llegado a gran desdicha y presumo que tiene origen de una de tres causas: o por no haber buenos representantes, o por ser malos los poetas, o por faltar entendimiento a los oyentes; pues los autores se valen de las máquinas, los

poetas de los carpinteros y los oyentes de los ojos.

[THEATRE. Oh, oh, oh!

VISITOR. What's the matter with you? Why are you like this? Are you sick? You seem to be wearing a head dressing.

THEATRE. It's only one of those cloud machines that the *autores* like to place on my head these days.

VISITOR. But what can be the cause of such howling?

THEATRE. Can't you see the state I am in? I am wounded, my legs and arms broken; I am full of holes and trapdoors, with thousands of nails hammered into me.

VISITOR. Who has put you in such a pitiful state?

THEATRE. The carpenters, on the instructions of the *autores*.

VISITOR. They are not to blame. The poets are. They are the physicians and the *autores* mere barber-surgeons. The former prescribe the cure and the latter bleed you to death.

THEATRE. I find myself in a most sorrowful state and I suspect that this is due to one of three things: either there are no longer good actors, or the poets are all bad, or the audiences lack discernment. For *autores* think of nothing but stage-machines, poets think of nothing but carpenters and spectators think only with their eyes.]

1. Stairs; 2. Stage-machines attic; 3. The 'heavens'; 4. The balcony; 5. Women's dressing room; 6. Stage patform; 7. The pit, men's dressing room and wardrobe

Despite these assertions, Lope's plays, particularly his hagiographies, often required the use of elaborate stage machines. For example, *El cardenal de Belén*, which survives in an autograph manuscript dated 27 August 1610 (scarcely two weeks before he bought the house on Francos street), necessitates a large number of them, as well as several 'discoveries' and two 'mountains', which, unusually, had been sketched in the left-hand margin of the manuscript:

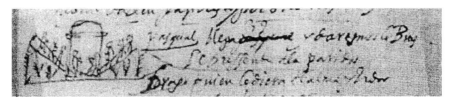

Autograph manuscript of *El cardenal de Belén* with mountains in left-hand margin

At first blush the staging of this play seems to fly in the face of Lope's own criticisms on the inordinate use of stage machinery. However, it is highly likely that *El cardenal de Belén*, which dramatizes the life of St Jerome and was licensed for performance in Madrid on 7 September 1610, Alcalá on 6 January 1612, Granada on 22 December 1613, Jaén on 17 June 1614 and Murcia on 22 December 1614,[51] was not a play destined for performance in a commercial playhouse, but rather in a public square and probably on carts. To begin with, the cast list has about three times as many speaking parts as that of a regular play: 43 characters (37 male and 6 female), even if some parts were doubled, plus an unspecified number of non-speaking parts, must have been impossible to accommodate even in a large playhouse like the Corral del Príncipe, let alone the one in Alcalá.[52] Difficult to fit too would have been the animals that must appear on stage. The lion which shows up in Act III is, of course, an actor in a lion's costume, but the donkey that the lion leads off stage ('Toma el león el cabestro y lleve el pollino') was in all likelihood a real donkey.[53] The number and complexity of some of the stage machines and 'discoveries' also suggest that *El cardenal de Belén* was meant to be staged in an open space and on a large stage platform, probably flanked by carts. For example, towards the end of Act I a stage direction requires that St Jerome be seized by the neck by some unspecified stage-machine and then carried aloft by an Angel, who holds him by his hair, to another part of the stage where a curtain will part to reveal a tribunal with four Angels and a Judge seated on a throne ('Asido por el cuello a una invención se descubra en ella un Ángel, que le lleve del cabello de la otra parte, donde se descubra un tribunal con cuatro Ángeles, y un Presidente, o Juez, con una vara, en una silla, o trono').

---

[51] Presotto, *Le commedie autografe*, pp. 135–36. The Jaén licence names the *autor* as Domingo de Balbín, an attribution corroborated on the title page of the thirteenth volume of Lope's plays (Madrid: Viuda de Alonso Martín, 1620).

[52] Even though there are serious doubts about their placement of the lateral boxes, the best description of the Corral de Alcalá is still Miguel Ángel Coso Marín, Mercedes Higuera Sánchez-Pardo & Juan Sanz Ballesteros, *El teatro Cervantes de Alcalá de Henares: 1602–1866. Estudio y documentos*, Fuentes para la Historia del Teatro en España, 18 (London: Tamesis, 1989).

[53] No donkey or horse could enter or be kept in the backstage area of the Príncipe or the Cruz, for it had no direct communication with the street. See Ruano, *La puesta en escena*, chapter 11.

**Niccolò Antonino Colantonio, *St Jerome and the Lion* (detail), c. 1445
Museo di Capodimonte, Naples**

Although not impossible to set up in a commercial playhouse, flights of this sort were much more easily carried out on a large stage erected for the purpose in a public square. The same holds true for the double 'discovery' that takes place towards the end of Act III: first, an Angel appears, presumably on a cloud machine; and then a curtain is drawn to reveal St Jerome with a very long white beard, dressed as a cardinal, writing seated at a desk, with a lion lying next to him ('Corra el Ángel una cortina, y véase una mesa, y San Jerónimo con una barba blanca muy larga, vestido de Cardenal, escribiendo, el león echado a un lado').

At the end of the scene, the Angel sounds a trumpet and a curtain opens on the top gallery to reveal a half arch, in the middle of which is a Judge; at one of his sides, a Hell's Mouth with some souls visible inside it; and on the other side, St Michael with the scales ('Tóquele un Ángel una trompeta al oído y véase arriba un medio arco en el medio del cual esté un Juez; una boca de infierno a un lado con algunas almas; y en la otra, San Miguel con un peso'). The sketch of two stage 'mountains' that we saw above is also evidence pointing to a performance in a large public square. Whoever was responsible for this sketch saw the need to draw it precisely because this was not the usual position for the 'mountains' on a commercial stage.[54]

Finally, the expense of building such stage machines and 'discoveries' would have made the play prohibitively expensive for a regular lessee or *autor*. Only the King, the Church or perhaps a grandee would have been able to finance a grand spectacle such as the one required for the staging of *El cardenal de Belén*. The unusual fact that some of the licences were issued by Church officials[55] hints at the involvement of the Church. In short, this hagiographical play — many of whose characters are allegorical (The World, Rome, The Devil, St Mercury [*sic*], Spain, etc.) and others historical (St Augustin, St Damasius, Emperor Julian) — is, like the Yepes version of Calderón's *El mágico prodigioso* [*The Wonder-Working Magician*] which was performed on carts,[56] closer to an *auto sacramental* than to a *comedia de corral* and may not, therefore, be used as evidence of Lope's fondness for elaborate stage machines in commercial theatres.[57]

More typical of the sort of spectacular play that was regularly performed in commercial playhouses was Lope's *Las paces de los reyes y judía de Toledo*, first published in 1617 in Madrid by the Viuda de Alonso Martín. Unlike *El cardenal de Belén*, which according to David Castillejo is among the top 5 plays (out of 400) in the number of characters,[58] *Las paces de los reyes* has as many speaking parts as, for example, *Peribáñez*. Part of Act I takes place on or near to Toledo's city walls and requires the use of the first gallery and the 'discovery' of an image of St James on horseback on an altar. Act II has a 'fishing scene', which was done by means of a trap door (misspelled as *costillon* for *escotillón* in the *princeps*) festooned with blades of grass on the stage platform: Raquel and Alfonso sit next to it, fishing rods in hand, and the king 'catches' a child's skull and an olive branch. In Act III an Angel appears on a stage machine ('Suena música y aparece en una tramoya un Ángel'), speaks eighteen lines and then exits; a second 'discovery', this time of the Virgin Mary, probably used the same altar-set where St James on horseback appeared in Act I. What differentiates 'spectacular plays' destined for performance in commercial theatres from those performed in open spaces is precisely their simplicity as well as the relatively small number of characters, stage machines, special effects and 'discoveries' involved in their staging.

Lope's move to Francos street in 1610 marks the beginning of his most important and productive period as a dramatist. At least until the arrival of

---

[54] See Ruano, *La puesta en escena*, pp. 192–99. It is always risky to use a single piece of evidence such as this drawing to generalize about the staging of plays in commercial theatres in the seventeenth century, which is unfortunately what Patricia Kenworthy does in her article 'Lope de Vega's Drawing of the *Monte* Stage Set', *Bulletin of the Comediantes*, 54.2 (2002): 271–85.

[55] See Presotto, *Le commedie autografe*, pp. 135–36.

[56] Melveena McKendrick, *Theatre in Spain: 1490–1700* (Cambridge: Cambridge University Press, 1989), p. 159.

[57] For a fuller treatment of spectacular plays in the commercial playhouses, see my *La puesta en escena*.

[58] David Castillejo, *Las cuatrocientas comedias de Lope: catálogo crítico* (Madrid: Teatro Clásico Español, 1984).

Calderón in the late 1620s, he reigned supreme and unchallenged over the Spanish stage for nearly two decades. In his house on Francos street, a short walk from the *mentidero*, the Church of St Sebastian, the two playhouses and the taverns and inns frequented by actors, at the very centre of theatrical activity in Spain, Lope composed some of his greatest masterpieces, plays that are still performed in theatres and studied in classrooms to this day: *Fuenteovejuna* (c. 1612–14), *La dama boba* (1613), *El perro del hortelano* (c. 1613–15), *El mejor alcalde, el rey* (c. 1620–23), *El caballero de Olmedo* (c. 1620–25), and *El castigo sin venganza* (1631).[59] There, in the midst of adulation and rivalry, surrounded by theatre professionals, working, drinking and eating with them, watching them rehearse and perform, aware of their successes and their financial woes, he found himself truly in his element.

---

[59] These are the approximate dates suggested by Morley and Bruerton.

3

From Stage to Page:
Editorial History and Literary Promotion in Lope de Vega's
Partes de comedias

ALEJANDRO GARCÍA REIDY

It is a revealing coincidence that printing presses were established in several cities in Spain roughly at the same time as theatre started to develop in the peninsula. It did not take too long for the paths of these two novelties to cross.[1] During the first half of the sixteenth century, poets who wrote plays to be performed by amateur actors during specific celebrations for religious or noble patrons saw print as a way to promote their dramatic work and try to obtain further patronage. Some of these authors printed their plays as part of larger collections of literary works. An early dramatist such as Juan del Encina, for example, included his plays in his *Cancionero* [*Songbook*], first published in Salamanca in 1496 and augmented with new poems and plays in successive editions. On the other hand, Lucas Fernández, who was master of music at the cathedral of Salamanca, published in 1514 a book entitled *Farsas y églogas* [*Farces and Eclogues*], which was devoted exclusively to his dramatic work. The plays of other authors, such as Gil Vicente or Diego Sánchez de Badajoz, remained unprinted during their lifetimes, but their drama was collected and published posthumously by their relatives.[2]

The development of commercial theatre during the second half of the century and the increase in the number of plays that were written by playwrights and performed by the first companies of professional actors did not modify this situation initially. The social, cultural and economic network that developed with the emergence of professional companies in the 1560s and was consolidated by the late 1570s and 1580s did not encourage the printing of plays. These companies formed by professional actors needed constantly to renew their repertoires with new plays to satisfy the ever-increasing audience in cities, towns and villages and

---

[1] This contribution is related to my current research, which is funded by an FPU scholarship from the Spanish Ministerio de Educación y Ciencia (AP2003-4900), and to the research projects *Diccionario de actores del teatro clásico español (difusión y actualización de la base de datos)* (HUM2005-00560/FILO) and *Diccionario de argumentos del teatro de Lope de Vega* (BFF 2003-06390).
[2] Miguel M. García-Bermejo Giner, 'Transmisión y recepción de la obra teatral en el siglo XVI', in *Historia del teatro español*, ed. Javier Huerta Calvo, 2 vols (Madrid: Gredos, 2003), I, pp. 527–48.

relied on buying the texts from poets. Playwrights would sell the original manuscripts of the plays they wrote to the directors of companies, who became the sole legal owners of the texts they bought (playwrights did not even keep a copy of the text for themselves). Playing companies, for their part, were not interested in seeing the plays they owned in print, especially the most successful ones, because it would have diminished the value of their repertoire. Joan Timoneda, who was not only a playwright but also a book-seller and a printer, did publish several of the plays he wrote, but Lope de Rueda, the most famous actor of the first generation of professional companies, never intended to transfer his plays to the printed page and it was only after his death that they were compiled and published by Timoneda. Another rare case within the second half of the century is Juan de la Cueva, who published his comedies and tragedies in two volumes (in 1588) some years after they had been performed by professional actors. Even so, these are special cases within the theatrical scene of the time: plays were conceived mainly to be sold to actors for a respectable amount of money, not to be printed like other literary works.

Lope de Vega participated in this socio-literary system when he began to write plays for the professional stage during the 1580s. He wrote his plays for companies such as those of Gaspar de Porres or Jerónimo Velázquez, who paid him well for his services and who, by performing them in the public playhouses of Madrid and other important cities, made Lope the most famous and successful playwright in Spain by the 1590s.[3] At the same time, Lope also became famous as a lyric poet and at the end of the century he developed a more ambitious career as a writer by devoting his pen to more culturally appreciated genres, such as narrative or epic poetry. In this sense, Lope was aware of the possibilities the printing press offered him as a way to shape his social image as a learned and courtly writer and promote himself through his cultural production in political circles. The publication, starting in 1598, of his great epic poems, of his lyrical *canzionere* or *Rimas*, of Byzantine and pastoral novels and of religious poems was not only meant to provide him with literary fame, but also to consolidate his position on the Spanish Parnassus and pursue the royal patronage of King Philip III. At the same time as Lope developed this side of his career, he continued to sell plays to professional companies, an activity that was his main source of income and served his literary aspirations by spreading his fame through the actors' performances on stages across the country. Under these circumstances, Lope had no need to consider print as a way for his plays to circulate: they served their purpose perfectly well without being published. His fame as an innovative playwright who was central to the development of a new style of writing plays (the *Comedia nueva*) was founded on performances, and therefore his efforts to publish were directed to the other literary genres he cultivated. As Miguel de

---

[3] Sturgis E. Leavitt, 'Spanish *Comedias* as Pot Boilers', *PMLA*, 82 (1967): 178–84; José María Díez Borque, '¿De qué vivía Lope de Vega? Actitud de un escritor en su vida y ante su obra', *Segismundo*, 8 (1972): 65–90; Noël Salomon, 'Algunos problemas de sociología de las literaturas de lengua española', in *Creación y público en la literatura española*, ed. J. F. Botrel & S. Salaün (Madrid: Castalia, 1974), pp. 15–39.

Cervantes acknowledged in wonder in 1615, 'pasan de diez mil pliegos los que tiene escritos, y todas [sus comedias], que es una de las mayores cosas que puede decirse, las ha visto representar u oído decir por lo menos que se han representado' [he has written more than ten thousand sheets, and he has seen all his plays performed — which is the most incredible thing that can be said — or at least heard that they have been performed].[4]

Theatre enthusiasts could, however, secure manuscript copies of plays for their own private enjoyment. One of these play-readers, none other than the Count of Gondomar, collected dozens of plays at the end of the century, which he had bound and kept in his private library.[5] By the turn of the century the huge success of the plays at public theatres caused people to show interest not only in attending performances at the playhouses, but also in being able to read plays by the most popular playwrights in the privacy of their homes. Furthermore, by the beginning of the seventeenth century companies owned a number of old plays which had lost their commercial value since they had already been performed in the main cities, and the revival of such plays did not attract the paying public to the theatres (plays seem to have had an active lifespan on stage of five to ten years). Therefore, selling copies of them for print now caused no harm to the actors' economic and professional interests. In 1603 Pedro Crasbeeck, a Lisbon-based printer, tried to exploit this market by publishing a volume of plays entitled *Seis comedias de Lope de Vega y de otros autores* [*Six Plays by Lope de Vega and Other Authors*], a misleading title as only one of the plays included in the collection, *Carlos el perseguido*, was an authentic play by Lope (the other five were published anonymously). Lope's reaction to this edition was quick and vigorous. A few months after its release he devoted the entire prologue of his Byzantine novel *El peregrino en su patria* to this matter. In his prologue Lope attacked Crasbeeck's edition for publishing one of his plays without authorization and for using his name in order to sell more by attributing to him plays that were not his. The Spanish playwright also offered a list of the 262 plays he had written up to then as a way to claim authorial possession of his work and prevent others from attributing to him plays he had never written, and warned readers that such plays could be textually corrupt: 'algunas [comedias] he visto que de ninguna manera las conozco' [I have seen some (plays) that I do not recognize at all].[6] Such harsh criticism implies that in 1603 Lope did not conceive of his plays as being for publication, but rather for performance and — at most — to circulate as manuscripts afterwards.[7]

---

[4] Miguel de Cervantes Saavedra, *Entremeses*, ed. Nicholas Spadaccini (Madrid: Cátedra, 1998), p. 93.

[5] Stefano Arata, 'Teatro y coleccionismo teatral a finales del siglo XVI (el conde de Gondomar y Lope de Vega)', *Anuario Lope de Vega*, 2 (1996): 7–23.

[6] Lope de Vega, *El peregrino en su patria*, ed. Juan Bautista Avalle-Arce (Madrid: Castalia, 1973), p. 63.

[7] Luigi Giuliani, 'El prólogo, el catálogo y sus lectores: una perspectiva de las listas de *El peregrino en su patria*', in *Lope en 1604*, ed. Xavier Tubau (Lleida: Milenio & Universitat Autònoma de Barcelona, 2004), pp. 123–36.

In spite of Lope's furious attack, the publication of plays by Spain's most famous playwright was an attractive prospect for publishers and bookselling entrepreneurs eager to exploit the emerging market. At the same time that Lope was writing this prologue condemning the unauthorized publication of his plays, Crasbeek's edition was being reprinted in Madrid, while another printer, Angelo Tavanno, was printing another volume of Lope plays collected by Bernardo Grassa. This edition, published in Zaragoza in early 1604, included twelve original plays by Lope and bore the title *Las comedias del famoso poeta Lope de Vega Carpio* [*The Plays of the Famous Poet Lope de Vega Carpio*]. This book ultimately set what would become the standard for the majority of printed play collections of the seventeenth century regarding the number of plays it included (twelve, plus some minor works such as *loas* and *entremeses*). Tavanno's edition did not refer to Crasbeeck's previous book and presented itself as a novelty (since it was the first book containing plays which were actually all by Lope), and similar play-books were promised in the prologue if this editorial adventure was profitable. The success of this volume was enormous: seven editions were printed in six different Spanish and European cities in just five years.[8] In 1609 a second volume of twelve plays by Lope saw the light of day, also followed by a great number of editions during the subsequent years. Prepared by bookseller Alonso Pérez and entitled *Segunda parte de comedias compuestas por Lope de Vega* [*Second Part of Plays Written by Lope de Vega*], it consolidated the series initiated by Grassa and Tavanno and also sold thousands of copies. The third *parte* in the series, though presented as being printed in Barcelona in 1612, was really printed in Seville, and returned to the practice of including only a couple of authentic plays by Lope among works by other authors, a fact that did not prevent it from being successful.[9] It was obvious that readers were eager to buy plays which they could read peacefully in their homes, especially if they were plays written by the most famous playwright of the time.

Despite the success of these editions during the first two decades of the seventeenth century, Lope proved to be unenthusiastic about the idea of publishing his plays and was more concerned about others taking advantage of his work and fame and harming his reputation as a playwright by publishing faulty texts or by attributing mediocre plays to him. When Lope finally decided to involve himself in the publication of some of his own plays he did not do so openly and still displayed a negative attitude towards this editorial practice. *Parte IV*, published in 1614, was paid for by the bookseller Miguel de Siles, although it was the *autor de comedias* (company director) Gaspar de Porres who obtained the legal approval, the privilege and the *tasa* (the official set price), and most, if not all, of the plays included in this volume came from his repertoire. The most interesting aspect of this *parte* lies in the fact that Lope had a hand in its publication: the dedication to the Duke of Sessa included in the volume is under

---

[8] See Lope de Vega, *Comedias de Lope de Vega. Parte I*, coord. Alberto Blecua and Guillermo Serés (Lleida: Milenio & Universitat Autònoma de Barcelona, 1997–), pp. 20–24.

[9] Jaime Moll, 'La *Tercera parte de las comedias de Lope de Vega y otros auctores*, falsificación sevillana', *Revista de Archivos, Bibliotecas y Museos*, 77 (1974): 619–26

Porres' name, but we know that it was Lope who wrote it because a rough draft was found among his letters.[10] In this dedication Lope again expresses his annoyance at seeing his plays being printed and claims that he did not write them for that reason, but with a 'diferente intento' [different purpose], that is, exclusively so that they would be performed on stage:

> Para satisfacer al autor de este libro del poco gusto que tiene de que se impriman las cosas que él escribió con tan diferente intento, no hallé medio más eficaz que dirigirle a V. Ex., a quien tanto ama, debe y desea servir.[11]

> [I could not find a more effective way to satisfy the author of this book for the little pleasure he finds in seeing in print what he wrote for such a different purpose, than to dedicate it to Your Excellency, whom he loves, to whom he is in debt and whom he desires to serve so much.]

These complaints had no effect whatsoever and *Partes V* and *VI*, both of which were published in 1615, were prepared by other editors eager to make money from Lope's name and work.[12] However, in 1616 Lope actively tried to put an end to the practice of others publishing his plays without his consent. That year the merchant Francisco de Ávila, who had compiled *Parte VI*, bought over twenty plays by Lope from different actors with the intention of preparing two new *partes* (which eventually became *Partes VII* and *VIII*). When Lope found out, he sued Ávila in order to try to bring to a halt the publication of those plays. In his legal action Lope claimed that the publication of his plays undermined his rights and his intention as a creator, because they were not works that had been written to be published, but to be performed:

> Dixo que él no vendió las dichas comedias a los autores para que se imprimiesen, sino tan solamente para que se representasen en los teatros: porque no es justo que se impriman algunas cosas de las contenidas en las dichas comedias.[13]

> [He said that he did not sell the aforementioned plays to the directors so that they could be published, but only so that they would be performed in theatres, because it is not right that some of things included in those plays should be published.]

---

[10] Victor Dixon, 'La intervención de Lope en la publicación de sus comedias', *Anuario Lope de Vega*, 2 (1996): 45–63.

[11] All quotations from the different *partes de comedias* are taken from *TESO: Teatro Español del Siglo de Oro*, CD-ROM database (Madrid: Chadwyck-Healey España, 1998).

[12] Jaime Moll, 'Los editores de Lope de Vega', *Edad de Oro*, 14 (1995): 213–22. The volume known as the *Parte V* of Lope was entitled *Flor de las comedias de diferentes autores. Quinta parte* [*Flower of Plays by Different Authors. Fifth Part*] and, although it presents itself as the follow-up to *Parte IV*, only one of the twelve plays it includes is actually by Lope. The fact that the publisher related this volume to the existing *Partes de comedias* by referring to it as the *Quinta parte* [Fifth Part] shows how Lope's name and fame was used by editors in order to attract potential readers.

[13] Ángel González Palencia, 'Pleito entre Lope de Vega y un editor de sus comedias', *Boletín de la Biblioteca Menéndez y Pelayo*, 3 (1921): 17–26 (pp. 25–26).

Notwithstanding Lope's plea, after the usual proceedings, the court determined that Francisco de Ávila had legitimately bought the plays and was therefore legally entitled to do with them as he pleased, and that Lope had surrendered his rights over his texts when he had sold them to the acting companies.

This event marks a turning point in Lope's relationship with the *Partes de comedias*. After losing the lawsuit he decided to take over the publication of his own dramatic work. By then there were other similar collections of plays. The printer Aurelio Mey, for example, had published two collective volumes of plays by several Valencian playwrights in 1608 and 1616, and Miguel de Cervantes had decided to publish his *Ocho comedias y ocho entremeses nuevos, nunca representados* [*Eight New Plays and Entremeses, Never Before Performed*] in 1615. Playwrights were resorting to print as a means of disseminating their plays and appealing to a public that increasingly wanted to read theatre, and Lope could not ignore this. In 1617 he collected copies of twelve of his plays from his actor friends and prepared *Parte IX*, the first in the series openly endorsed by him. In the prologue to the reader Lope repeated the idea that his plays were not conceived to be printed but to be performed, and justified his decision to publish them by claiming that in this way he could at least prevent others from publishing bad copies of his plays and ruining his reputation as a poet:

> me he resuelto a imprimirlas por mis originales, que aunque es verdad que no las escribí con este ánimo ni para que de los oídos del teatro se trasladaran a la censura de los aposentos, ya lo tengo por mejor que ver la crueldad con que despedazan mi opinión algunos intereses.

> [I have decided to print (these plays) following my original manuscripts, for even though it is true that I did not write them with this intention nor for them to be transferred from the ears of the theatre to the censorship of private chambers, I consider it better than to see the cruelty with which my reputation is torn to pieces by the self-interest of certain persons.]

Lope presented his decision to publish his plays as a lesser evil, a consequence of harmful practices begun by others; he stated that he was publishing his plays because external circumstances had forced him to protect his own creations and not because it was his initial will to do so. Confronted with the decision to prepare the editions himself or letting others do so, he decided that 'el menor daño es imprimirlas' [the lesser harm is publishing them], as Lope later stated in the prologue to *Parte XVII*, published in 1621. Lope justified his rejection of the printing of his plays on the grounds that the plays that were being printed presented textual corruptions, that some of the plays published under his name were not his and that the circumstances which surround the process of writing for the commercial theatre made plays unsuitable for private reading, because the playwright could not invest a lot of time in the elaboration of each text: they were not the result of many days of study — like epic poems — and were therefore unworthy of distribution through the printed word and of being scrutinized by readers. In other words, Lope argued that printed books were not the appropriate means for plays to circulate because the text alone was unable to reproduce theatricality — that is, the elements that are inherent to the staging of a play (mainly, the actors' performance) — and, therefore, did not reflect accurately the full intentions of the playwright. Under these circumstances, the text and its author are helpless with regard to criticism, because what is offered to the reader does not represent the totality of the play as conceived by the playwright.[14] These complaints, which Lope expressed in other texts, such as the *Epístola a Gaspar de Barrionuevo* [*Epistle to Gaspar de Barrionuevo*] included in the 1604 edition of the *Rimas*, reveal how a modern concept of authorship and its implications concerning textual property was taking shape in Lope's mind: he not only claimed legal rights over his own work, but also yearned to exert effective control over how his plays reached readers in terms of their textual integrity and the extent to which they accorded with his initial intentions as a literary creator.

However, soon after Lope decided to take over the task of printing his plays he started to appreciate the possibilities offered by the printed word. The best proof of this is that between 1617 and 1625 Lope published a total of twelve *partes* (*Partes IX–XX*), and was forced to halt only because of the prohibition on printed plays and novels in the kingdom of Castile from the latter date,[15] much to Lope's dismay, expressed in a letter to the poet Antonio Hurtado de Mendoza in 1628: 'Las *Comedias* de Alarcón han salido impresas: sólo para mí no hay licencia' [Alarcón's *Plays* have been printed; only I do not receive permission to publish].[16] Besides the fact that once Lope embraced the publication of his plays he did so enthusiastically, a discourse in favour of the printed page as a legitimate means for plays to reach their audience can also be traced in several of the prologues which accompany the *partes* he prepared. In the prologue 'El Teatro a los lectores' [The Theatre to the Readers], included in *Parte XI* (published in 1618), Lope promised to keep publishing his plays so that everybody could read 'en su casa o recogimiento con su familia lo que no todos pueden ver' [in their home or together with their family what not everyone can see]. Soon, however, Lope not only thought that printed plays had the ability to offer readers the same aesthetic pleasure that spectators enjoyed in the playhouses, but even considered the printed dramatic text superior to the performance itself. As Lope stated in the prologue to

---

[14] Roger Chartier, *Entre poder y placer: cultura escrita y literatura en la Edad Moderna* (Madrid: Cátedra, 2000); idem, 'La pluma, el taller y la voz: entre crítica textual e historia cultural', in *Imprenta y crítica textual en el Siglo de Oro*, ed. Pablo Andrés & Sonia Garza (Valladolid: Universidad de Valladolid & Centro para la Edición de los Clásicos Españoles, 2000), pp. 243–57.

[15] Jaime Moll, 'Diez años sin licencias para imprimir comedias y novelas en los reinos de Castilla: 1625–1634', *Boletín de la Real Academia Española*, 54 (1974): 97–103.

[16] *Epistolario de Lope de Vega Carpio*, ed. Agustín G. de Amezúa, 4 vols (Madrid: Aldus, 1935–43), IV, p. 131. During the time this prohibition was in effect re-editions of existing *partes* and new editions of plays attributed to Lope were made without the playwright's consent in the kingdom of Aragon and — as pirate editions — in Andalucía. A fraudulent *Parte XXIV*, for example, was published in Zaragoza in 1633 (the one considered authentic was published in Madrid in 1641). Lope himself had to resort to a printing press in Barcelona when he published his tragedy *El castigo sin venganza* in 1634 as a *suelta* (plays that were printed separately) in order to avoid the ban effective in the kingdom of Castile.

Parte XII (also published in 1618), printed plays were free from the series of 'accidentes' [vicissitudes] associated with performance, which prevented theatre-goers from fully enjoying the play and the poetry in it, an idea that Lope repeated in prologues to other *partes*. These 'accidentes' corresponded to spectators who did not appreciate the poetic virtues of the dramatic verses and disrupted performances with their shouts and noises, and to actors whose bad performances ruined well-written plays.[17] As Lope addresses the reader in the prologue:

> en tu aposento donde las has de leer nadie consentirás que te haga ruido ni que te diga mal de lo que tu sabrás conocer, libre de los accidentes del señor que viene tarde, del representante que se yerra y de la mujer desagradable por fea o mal vestida, o por los años que ha frecuentado mis tablas, pues el poeta no la escribió con los que ella tiene, sino con los que tuvo en su imaginación, que fueron catorce o quince.

> [in your room, where you are going to read the plays, you will not allow anybody to make noise or criticize what you will appreciate, free as you will be of the accidents of the gentleman who arrives late, of the actor who makes mistakes or the woman who is unpleasant due to her ugliness or poor dress, or because of all the years she has been on stage, for the poet did not write the role for a woman her age, but for the one he had in his imagination, who was fourteen or fifteen years old.]

According to Lope, readers (and not spectators) thus become the privileged recipients of plays, with whom the playwright can establish a relationship of complicity: the poet gains control over the text he is offering and can present it to his readers knowing that there will be none of the external interferences that can take place at the playhouses. The desire of the writer to exercise as much control as possible over his work in order to control circumstances which could influence the reception of the text is yet another example of how an incipient author-function — as Michel Foucault understood it[18] — was consolidated in Lope's *partes de comedias* between 1614 and 1625. Lope did not abandon this notion that printed plays offered him more control over his creation, as we can see in *La Dorotea*, an 'acción en prosa' [action in prose] published in 1632 and conceived to be read (in order to avoid the prohibition of printing plays), in whose prologue we find yet again a strong statement in favor of the possibilities offered by the printed page: 'el papel es más libre teatro que aquel donde tiene licencia el vulgo de graduar, la amistad de aplaudir y la envidia de morder' [paper is a freer stage than the one where the masses have permission to appraise, the familiarity to applaud and the envy to bite].[19]

---

[17] Maria Grazia Profeti, 'Comedias representadas/textos literarios: los problemas ecdóticos', in *Teatro, historia y sociedad*, ed. Carmen Hernández Valcárcel (Murcia: Universidad de Murcia & Universidad Autónoma de Ciudad Juárez, 1996), pp. 207–16.

[18] Michel Foucault, 'Qu'est-ce qu'un auteur?', in *Dits et écrits, 1954–1988*, 4 vols (Paris: Gallimard, 1994), I, pp. 789–821.

[19] Lope de Vega, *La Dorotea*, ed. José Manuel Blecua (Madrid: Cátedra, 1996). Although this prologue is signed by Francisco López de Aguilar, a good friend of Lope, we know that it was really penned by the playwright himself.

With the passing of the years Lope de Vega not only embraced print as a legitimate and beneficial way to promote his plays and reach his public, but also used the possibilities offered by the printed page as a way to promote himself as a writer within literary and political contexts.[20] Starting with *Parte XIII* (published in 1620), Lope decided to replace the opening dedication of each volume with twelve separate dedications, one for each play included in a *parte*.[21] On the one hand, this allowed him to reach far more potential patrons with each of his *partes*, for many of these dedications were directed to members of the nobility. We find the best example of this search for patronage in the play that opens *Parte XVI*, published in 1621: the mythological drama *El premio de la hermosura*, originally performed at the royal palace by members of the court and the royal family, which includes a dedication to Gaspar de Guzmán, the Count of Olivares and favourite of the recently crowned King Philip IV. At a time when Lope was trying to gain access to court circles dominated by Olivares in order to obtain the patronage of the new sovereign, the dedication of a play, especially the one that opened the *parte*, was a skilful strategy for Lope to promote himself and obtain the attention of the King's powerful favourite. At the same time, prologues and dedications to his printed plays served Lope's continuous and complex self-fashioning, as he used these preliminary texts to appear to his readers as a learned writer, frequently quoting classical sources to support his own ideas, as an innocent victim of envy and gossip, or as a neostoic who displays his contempt for worldly banalities, to mention just a few of the multifarious ways in which he represented himself in the *partes*. Lope also used these dedications and prologues to reinforce his position on the literary Parnassus and promote his own ideas about literature.[22] He did so, for example, by attacking his enemies in the literary field, such as the poets who followed Luis de Góngora's poetic style or the new playwrights who advocated plays based more on spectacular effects than on poetry and rhetoric, or by vindicating the literary value of his plays (and therefore of himself as a playwright) by enhancing the esteem comedy deserved compared to other prestigious genres. In this sense, Lope defended the social function of his plays, which were presented as useful entertainment even for gentlemen dedicated to serious matters, for they can improve public morals by reprimanding harmful behaviour, especially through historical plays. As Lope stated in the prologue to *Parte XIV* (1620): 'dellos [los poetas] y de mí [el teatro] se sacan tantos ejemplos con que venimos a ser de tan gran importancia a la República sin apurar las historias, los tiempos, los reyes y los sucesos' [from poets and theatre so many examples are obtained that we come to be of great importance to the republic, without exhausting stories, ages, kings and events]. When the ban on publishing plays and

---

[20] Teresa Ferrer Valls, '"Sustento, en fin, lo que escribí": Lope de Vega y el conflicto de la creación', in *Pigmalión o el amor por lo creado*, ed. Facundo Tomás & Isabel Justo (Rubí, Barcelona: Anthropos & Universidad Politécnica de Valencia, 2005), pp. 99–112.

[21] Thomas E. Case, *Las dedicatorias de Partes XIII–XX de Lope de Vega* (Chapel Hill, NC: University of North Carolina & Madrid: Castalia, 1975).

[22] Maria Grazia Profeti, 'Strategie redazionali ed editoriali di Lope de Vega', in her *Nell'officina di Lope* (Florencia: Alinea, 1998), pp. 11–44.

novels in Castile was lifted in 1634, Lope hastily continued publishing the series of his *partes de comedias*, although the two volumes he prepared (*Partes XXI* and *XXII*) only reached the booksellers after the playwright's death. Three more *partes* of plays by Lope (*Partes XXIII–XXV*) were published between 1638 and 1647, after which the series continued during the following decades as a miscellaneous collection of plays by various playwrights (including Lope) and consequently re-titled *Partes de diferentes autores* [*Parts by Different Authors*].[23]

In summary, Lope de Vega's *partes de comedias* dominated the market for printed plays during the first quarter of the seventeenth century and led the way for similar publishing enterprises by other playwrights, from Tirso de Molina to Juan Pérez de Montalbán, Ruiz de Alarcón and Calderón de la Barca. While Lope initially rejected the idea that his dramatic work should circulate among readers in printed form, he eventually embraced the editorial project of the *partes de comedias* and actively participated in the publication of his own plays. At the same time, Lope used his *partes de comedias* as cultural artefacts to promote himself in the competitive worlds of royal patronage and literary dominance. After his death new playwrights filled his place on the stage, but the existing twenty-five volumes of plays contributed decisively to his fame and to the preservation of a large portion of his dramatic work. From our own perspective as twenty-first-century spectators and readers of plays, when Lope had his plays face 'la censura de los aposentos' [the censorship of private chambers] and enter the realm of reading he was leading them along new paths towards modernity.

CHRONOLOGY OF FIRST EDITIONS OF LOPE DE VEGA'S
PARTES DE COMEDIAS

I	1604	*VIII*	1617	*XV*	1621	*XXII*	1635
II	1609	*IX*	1617	*XVI*	1621	*XXIII*	1638
III	1612	*X*	1618	*XVII*	1621	*XXIV*	1641
IV	1614	*XI*	1618	*XVIII*	1623	*XXV*	1647
V	1615	*XII*	1619	*XIX*	1624		
VI	1615	*XIII*	1620	*XX*	1625		
VII	1617	*XIV*	1620	*XXI*	1635		

[23] Jaime Moll, 'De la continuación de las partes de comedias de Lope de Vega a las partes colectivas', in *Homenaje a Alonso Zamora Vicente*, ed. Pedro Peira et al., 5 vols in 6 (Madrid: Castalia, 1988–96), III.2: *Literatura española de los siglos XVI–XVII* (1992), pp. 199–211.

Part 2: Poetry

4

Imagining Lope's Lyric Poetry
in the 'Soneto primero' of the *Rimas*

TYLER FISHER

A noteworthy feature of much Golden Age Spanish literature is its expressions of authorial self-consciousness. Writers of the period display a sharpened awareness of composition techniques and textual dissemination, of circulation patterns and readership — an awareness often incorporated into their texts through plots, tropes and other devices. Among such devices, metaphorical representations of texts and textual production offer particularly sophisticated expressions of how authors understood their craft, their product and their audience.

In the prologue to his *Novelas ejemplares* [*Exemplary Novels*], for example, Cervantes famously likens the collection to a 'mesa de trucos', a type of Italian billiard table then in vogue for public recreation.[1] The playful figure, as Cervantes develops it, embodies a recognition of the simultaneously subjective and communal nature of reading at a time when popular reading habits still included reading aloud to an audience of friends, family members or fellow-labourers.

A self-reflective figure could also illustrate its author's method. A generation after Cervantes, the courtier Juan de Andosilla finds the image of *centones* or patchwork garments to be useful for representing the design and nature of his piecemeal reworkings of Garcilaso de la Vega's poetry.[2] By this sort of figurative application, the term *centón* came to designate a specific sub-genre: a pastiche or literary amalgam composed entirely of fragments from earlier works in such a way that the fragments take on meanings different from those of the original sources.

And even when using a metaphorical commonplace, Sor Juana Inés de la Cruz imaginatively elaborates a text-as-progeny topos to suit her unique purposes. Her dedicatory sonnet to the Countess of Paredes in her *Inundación Castálida* [*Inundation of the Muses*] (1689) depicts her poems as children born to an

---

[1] Miguel de Cervantes Saavedra, *Novelas ejemplares*, ed. Jorge García López (Barcelona: Crítica, 2001), p. 18.

[2] Juan de Andosilla Larramendi, *Christo Nuestro Señor en la Cruz, hallado en los versos del príncipe de nuestros poetas, Garcilasso de la Vega, sacados de diferentes partes, y unidos con ley de centones* (Madrid: Viuda de Luis Sánchez, 1628); repr. in facsimile as *Centones de Garcilaso y otras poesías sueltas*, ed. Pedro Manuel Cátedra & Víctor Infantes (Barcelona: Litosefa, 1981), fol. ¶3v.

'esclava madre' [enslaved mother] who, by law, must surrender possession of her offspring to her mistress.[3] Sor Juana's metaphor at once conveys the poet's singular relationship to her patroness, suggests the intensely and intimately personal nature of the poems, and hints, we might imagine, at a sense of reluctant obligation in relinquishing them to her readership.

Billiard tables, patchwork clothes, indentured children: all three figures illuminate contemporary concepts of the creative impulse, the writing process and the authors' self-conceived role in relation to their texts and readers. Such figures are by no means unique to Early Modern Spain — in addition to examples from Classical literature, one could cite the fourteenth-century *Libro de Buen Amor* [*Book of Good Love*] for its description of itself as a musical instrument or 'pella' [ball] passed from hand to hand (coplas 70 and 1629)[4] — yet several factors combined to make Spanish literature of the period especially rich in metaphors for text and textual production. Contemporary debates and treatises on rhetoric and literary theory revived questions about the nature of texts, authorship and transmission. On a more practical level, the growth of the printed book trade, an increase in pirated editions, the establishment of a fixed, professional theatre and the emergence of *poeta* or author as a viable, professional vocation served to hone a cultural focus on issues of literary communication. Golden Age literature underwent nothing less than a self-conscious reevaluation of its own means and ends.

Among the Golden Age poets who participated in this reevaluation and left an artistic record of it by employing the sort of metaphors this essay has surveyed thus far, Lope de Vega exceeded them all in his sustained and explicit fascination with the creative process, the textual product, its reception and the various ways in which these could be represented. His lyrical works in particular offer a wealth of such representations. These enable us to examine Lope's perspectives on poetry from fresh angles as we consider the functions and implications of his metaphors in context. Characteristically for his era, Lope's representations of the literary endeavour exemplify both continuity with and divergence from Classical sources. Like Sor Juana, he modifies Classical and contemporary commonplaces to suit the poem or series of poems in which they appear and to articulate his arguments. The resulting figures are at once preceptive, expressing Lope's ideals for poetic composition and the properties of the resulting text, and self-consciously descriptive, reflecting his involved familiarity with all aspects of textual production and dissemination.

The most thoroughly developed metaphor for texts and textual production within Lope's lyrical *oeuvre* is the filial or text-as-progeny topos. This figure takes on particular prominence as the dominant image in the first sonnet of his *Rimas humanas* of 1602–9, and it reappears throughout ensuing works. The

---

[3] Sor Juana Inés de la Cruz, *Sonetos*, ed. Luis Íñigo-Madrigal (Madrid: Biblioteca Nueva, 2001), p. 27.

[4] Juan Ruiz, Arcipreste de Hita, *Libro de Buen Amor*, ed. Joan Corominas (Madrid: Gredos, 1973).

'Soneto primero' [Sonnet I] is at once an *ars poetica* for Lope's verse in general and a programmatic prologue for the *Rimas* collection in particular.

Antonio Carreño presents the text from the 1609 edition as follows:

> Versos de amor, conceptos esparcidos,
> engendrados del alma en mis cuidados,
> partos de mis sentidos abrasados,
> con más dolor que libertad nacidos;
>   expósitos al mundo en que perdidos,
> tan rotos anduvistes y trocados,
> que sólo donde fuistes engendrados,
> fuérades por la sangre conocidos;
>   pues que le hurtáis el laberinto a Creta,
> a Dédalo los altos pensamientos,
> la furia al mar, las llamas al abismo,
>   si aquel áspid hermoso no os aceta
> dejad la tierra, entretened los vientos;
> descansaréis en vuestro centro mismo.[5]

[Verses of love, scattered conceits, / fathered by my soul upon my cares, / offspring of my burning senses, / born with more pain than liberty; / abandoned to the world, where, lost, / you wandered so ragged and changed, / that only where you were begotten / would you be recognized by your blood; / since you steal the labyrinth from Crete, / from Daedalus your lofty thoughts, / your anger from the sea, your flames from the abyss, / if that fair asp does not accept you, / leave the earth, entertain the winds; / [there] you will rest in your own centre.][6]

Already the dedicatory *sextina* (a poem of six six-line stanzas) to Juan de Arguijo, which Lope included in the second (1604) and subsequent editions of the *Rimas*, anticipates the imagery of the 'Soneto primero': '¿A quién daré mis Rimas / y amorosos cuidados [...]?' [To whom will I give my Rhymes / and amorous cares?] the *sextina* begins, introducing the conflation of creative product and amorous emotion which Lope will take up again in the opening sonnet. 'A vos' [To you], to Arguijo the patron, the second stanza answers, and the anaphoric answer appears on four alternating lines beginning with line 7. With Arguijo as recipient and 'centro' [centre or target] for the *rimas* (line 10), 'más que sus versos letras tendrán vidas' [they will have more lives than their lines have letters] (line 18; p. 105); but the dedicatory *sextina* does not develop the idea of animate poetry further. Instead, the remaining stanzas feature a conventional description of the pastoral poet and a series of allusions to Apollo, Orpheus and the muses in praise of Arguijo as a patron of the arts.

---

[5] Lope de Vega, *Rimas humanas y otros versos*, ed. Antonio Carreño (Barcelona: Crítica, 1998), p. 117. Unless otherwise noted, all quotations are from this edition.

[6] Here I follow Arthur Terry's translation in his *Seventeenth-Century Spanish Poetry* (Cambridge: Cambridge University Press, 1993), p. 99, except for his translation of 'vientos' in line 13 as 'clouds', which I find inexplicable.

The inaugural sonnet, by contrast, elaborates in greater detail the idea of animate poetry with the figure of itinerant progeny. Its quatrains introduce, as Mary Gaylord Randel has observed, a personification of 'the historical scattering in manuscript versions, and probably in oral form as well, of Lope's verses prior to their collected publication in the *Rimas*'.[7] The quatrains offer a picture of the life of a poetic text as it circulated in Golden Age Spain, where traditions of manuscript and oral transmission of texts remained strong even long after printing was established. As manuscripts circulated, it was not uncommon for readers of the time to annotate, appropriate, amend, gloss or otherwise alter a text before communicating it (or a dubious copy) to successive readers. If the original author of a poem ever did come across circulated copies of his work, he would indeed have been likely to find the texts significantly modified, 'rotos [...] y trocados' [ragged [...] and changed] (line 6), and perhaps even difficult to recognize.

The series of four participles used in lines 5–6 to describe the transit of the *versos* ('expósitos', 'perdidos', 'rotos' and 'trocados') provides a fuller picture of Lope's understanding of textual circulation. There is also, I will argue, among the four a deliberate order, which corresponds to other meaningful patterns within the sonnet. First, 'expósitos' [abandoned] signals the sending forth of the *versos*, their dispatch to a condition of abandonment in a wider space than the interior 'alma' [soul] and 'sentidos' [senses] of the first tercet. Owing to its nominative possibilities, the participle also carries the sense of 'orphan' or 'foundling'. Sebastián de Covarrubias defines *expósito* in 1611 as

> El niño que ha sido echado de sus padres o de otras personas en los campos o en las puertas de los templos, desamparándolos [*sic*] a su ventura; y de ordinario son hijos de personas que padecerían sus honras o sus vidas si se supiesse cuyos son.[8]

> [The child who has been abandoned by his parents or by others in the countryside or at the doors of churches, leaving him to his fate; often they are children of people who would lose their honour or their lives if it were known whose they were.]

Covarrubias's definition, characteristically incorporating information about the word's broader cultural context, suggests a basis for the question of paternal recognition in lines 7–8. In light of this, 'expósitos' may reflect Lope's custom of circulating most of his poetry anonymously or pseudonymously prior to the publication of the *Rimas*.[9] Moreover, the idea of abandonment or orphanhood

[7] Mary Gaylord Randel, 'Proper Language and Language as Property: The Personal Poetics of Lope's *Rimas*', *MLN*, 101.2 (1986): 220–46 (p. 227).

[8] Sebastián de Covarrubias Orozco, *Tesoro de la lengua castellana o española* (1611), ed. Martín de Riquer (Barcelona: Horta, 1943; repr. Barcelona: Alta Fulla, 1993), p. 576.

[9] Near the end of his life, Lope returns to the ideas of recognition of authorship and the text as *expósito* in his mock prologue to *Rimas humanas y divinas del licenciado Tomé de Burguillos*. Under the ruse of compiling and publishing the fictitious Burguillos's verse in the *licenciado*'s absence, Lope introduces the book 'como si fuera expósito' [as if it were a foundling], but notes that 'conocerá el señor lector cuál es el ingenio, humor y condición de su dueño' [the reader will recognize the cast of mind, temperament, and disposition of its master], *Rimas humanas y divinas del licenciado Tomé de Burguillos y La gatomaquia*, ed. Antonio Carreño (Salamanca: Almar,

further underscores the detachment and effacement of the authorial progenitor in the sonnet. Any focus on the first-person speaker, already in the background of the sonnet, increasingly gives way to the actions and characteristics of the *versos* themselves. After the word 'expósitos', significantly, there is no further use of first-person pronouns as in the initial quatrain.

Abandoned to the vicissitudes of public circulation, the *versos* are 'perdidos' [lost]. The adjective points to the speaker's loss of ownership and control over the text. (Lope employs the same participle on a later occasion in reference to a personal letter which, with a conventional show of reluctance, he relinquishes to his patron for publication.[10]) Beyond the author's control, the *versos* become the property of a wider readership, with the result that the lost *versos* are 'rotos' and 'trocados', broken and altered. Even in a literary culture subject to the standardizing forces of the printing press, the circulation of both manuscript and printed works in Golden Age Spain involved accidental and deliberate textual modifications. Indeed, Lope's prologue to the 1609 edition of the *Rimas* openly invites the reader — though arguably with a shade of facetious raillery — to emend its contents: 'Lee si entiendes, y enmienda si sabes. Mas ¿quién piensa que no sabes?' [Read if you understand, and emend if you know how. But who would suppose that you do not know how?] (p. 108). For Lope, the fact that his poems would be altered during publication and circulation is an inevitable part of the process and, he posits, one which authors should bear in mind. In a letter to Don Juan de Arguijo, which serves as a prose introduction to the 1602 *princeps* edition of the *Rimas*, Lope condemns writers or literary critics who are ignorant of the alterations which can be introduced between the writer's draft and the printer's typesetting, between voices subsequently transmitting his text orally, or between the author's original and other, unauthorized versions: 'No saben la diferencia que va del borrador al molde, de la voz del dueño a la del inorante, de leer entre amigos o comprar el libro' [They do not know the changes which come between the author's draft and the form ready for printing, between the voice of the master and that of the uninstructed, between reading among friends or buying the book for oneself], he charges (p. 584).

Lope's *versos*, in print or manuscript or oral form, are passed from hand to hand, mouth to mouth; they circulate 'rotos' and 'trocados', according to the sonnet's description. The *dedicatoria* (dedication) to the 1609 edition of the *Rimas* reveals that its format was designed to facilitate handy transport; it was printed in response to readers' demands for a version of the *Rimas* 'solas y manuales' [alone — i.e. not printed alongside his epic *La hermosura de Angélica*— and easily held in one's hands] (p. 104).[11] The fourth participle in the

---

2002), p. 124. In *Burguillos*, the figure serves as a playful mask of authorial identity, much like Cervantes's claims to be 'padrastro' [step-father] of *Don Quijote*.

[10] Lope de Vega, 'La respuesta' [The Answer], in his *Obras poéticas*, I, ed. José Manuel Blecua (Barcelona: Planeta, 1969), pp. 889–91 (p. 889).

[11] The prologue to Baltasar Gracián's *El comulgatorio* [*The Communion Rail*] includes a vivid description of how a 'manual' text might be used and transported in the seventeenth century. Gracián states that he intends the book to be 'tan manual, que le pueda llevar cualquiera o en el seno o en la manga' [so handy, that anyone can carry it, either in his bosom or in his sleeve],

descriptive series of lines 5–6 ('trocados') not only indicates textual alteration, but also the exchange of texts — the literal, physical cycles of poetic commerce. Covarrubias again provides a helpful record of what the word would have meant for his contemporaries. He defines the verb *trocar* thus: 'Es lo mesmo que bolver, y el que trueca buelve y rebuelve las cosas como en rueda' [It is the same as to turn, and he who *trueca* turns things round and round as on a wheel] (p. 979). The four participles, then, span the process of textual circulation, from the initial dispersal of the 'expósitos', through their ruinous transit and ultimately to their circuitous return. The series comes full circle, mirrors the wider cycle of the quatrain and prepares the reader for lines 7–8, which describe the recognition of the *versos* when they return to the 'alma' [soul] of the poet, where they were first 'engendrados' [fathered].

The metaphor of the poem-as-progeny is a commonplace of Golden Age letters, an almost obligatory feature in literary prologues of the age. It is, not surprisingly, rooted in the Classical tradition, where it receives an early and extensive treatment in Plato's *Symposium*.[12] I propose that the *Symposium* provides Lope's source, whether directly or indirectly, for the central imagery of the 'Soneto primero'.[13] The first two lines of Lope's sonnet correspond with the language used in the dialogue between Socrates and his teacher Diotima. In both, analogies conflate love and the act of poetic creation. Diotima defines love as a universal desire for beauty, physical or ideal — a desire which strives for procreation, carnal or conceptual. 'Souls', Diotima argues, 'which are pregnant — for there certainly are men who are more creative in their souls than in their bodies, creative of that which is proper for the soul to conceive and bring forth: [...] among such souls are all creative poets and all artists who are deserving of the name inventor'.[14] Moreover, the *Symposium* describes the 'heat which is called love' as 'agony' (pp. 26–27), terms which parallel Lope's 'sentidos abrasados' [burning senses] and 'dolor' [pain] associated with love and the parturition of *versos*.

If Lope's acquaintance with the *Symposium*'s explanation of heated, amorous poetic creation were mediated through a contemporary author, Juan Huarte de San

---

Baltasar Gracián y Morales, *El comulgatorio*, in *Obras completas*, ed. Arturo del Hoyo, 2nd edn (Madrid: Aguilar, 1960), pp. 1015–1105 (p. 1016). Both *El comulgatorio* and the 1609 *Rimas* were printed in a handy sexto-decimo format.

[12] The figure appears also, though less prominently, in Plato's *Phaedrus*. Lope himself acknowledges Classical sources for the metaphor in his introduction to the 1620 *Justa poética* marking the beatification of San Isidro, in *Obras escogidas de Lope Félix de Vega Carpio*, ed. Federico Carlos Sainz de Robles, 3 vols (Madrid: Aguilar, 1946–55), II (1946), pp. 1569–83 (p. 1575).

[13] Lope's active familiarity with Plato's dialogues is well attested. Not only does he evince a mastery of Platonic ideas by incorporating them into a variety of texts, he demonstrates his direct knowledge of Plato's 'fábulas y imágenes matemáticas' [fables and mathematical images] in a letter to Don Francisco López de Aguilar, in which he quotes from a Latin translation of the *Symposium* ('Epístola nona: a Don Francisco López de Aguilar', in *Obras poéticas*, I, ed. José Manuel Blecua (Barcelona: Planeta, 1969), pp. 1311–18, p. 1312).

[14] Plato, Excerpts from the *Symposium*, *Phaedrus* and *Ion*, in *Classical and Medieval Literary Criticism: Translations and Interpretations*, ed. Alex Preminger et al. (New York: Ungar, 1974), pp. 25–48 (p. 28).

Juan's *Examen de ingenios para las ciencias* [*Study of Temperamental Aptitudes for Various Professions*] presents a likely source. Huarte de San Juan argues that poetry 'pide tres grados de calor; y esta calidad, tan intensa, [...] echa a perder totalmente al entendimiento' [requires three degrees of heat; and this heat, so intense, [...] spoils intellectual reasoning].[15] On this basis, Huarte de San Juan equates the sultry humoral makeup of poets and lovers. Luis Alfonso de Carvallo's *Cisne de Apolo* [*Apollo's Swan*], published in the same year as the first edition of Lope's *Rimas* (1602), echoes the *Examen*'s pseudo-scientific description of the fiery, sanguine poet-lover:

> en el verano se compone mejor que en invierno, por ser tiempo caliente y seco; y los mancebos enamorados por esta razón dan en poetas, que con la intensa afición del amoroso fuego vienen al grado de calor que para serlo es necesario. Y con la cólera viene también a escalentarse el celebro, de tal suerte que sólo con esto, sin otra ayuda de la naturaleza, se pueden hacer versos.[16]

> [in summer, one composes better than in winter, because the weather is hot and dry; and lovesick youths for this reason turn poets, for with the intense affection of amorous fire they attain the degree of heat necessary to be such. And the brain also warms with the choler, so that by this alone, without any other assistance from nature, one can compose verse.]

The picture of the ardent poet producing verse from his 'sentidos abrasados' [burning senses] was in vogue, as these examples attest. As a basis for Lope's image, Huarte de San Juan's and Carvallo's physiological explanations of 'qué complexión ha de tener el hombre para que tenga la imaginativa' [what bodily temperament man requires in order to have the imaginative faculty] (Carvallo, p. 98) lack only the *Symposium*'s explicit image of childbirth.

The sonnet's correspondence with the language of Plato's *Symposium* and with the figurative logic of sixteenth-century humoral theories lends a neat, causal, progressive consonance to the series of phrases in the quatrains. Such order provides little support for Carreño's reading of the two phrases of the first line as somehow representing two dissimilar or contrasting entities, 'dos nociones en juego, aparentemente contrapuestas: la expresión vivencial (los "versos de amor") y el discurso lírico que la configura: los "conceptos esparcidos"' [two notions in play, apparently counterposed: the expression of experience (the 'verses of love') and the lyrical discourse which configures it: the 'scattered conceits'].[17] Rather, the phrase 'conceptos esparcidos', like the subsequent phrase 'partos de mis sentidos abrasados', is appositional to the sonnet's initial substantive, an explanatory equivalent more in keeping with Lope's characteristic style of enumerating synonyms, adjectival constructions or epithets at the beginning of a

---

[15] Juan Huarte de San Juan, *Examen de ingenios para las ciencias*, ed. Guillermo Serés (Madrid: Cátedra, 2005), p. 407.

[16] Luis Alfonso de Carvallo, *Cisne de Apolo*, ed. Alberto Porqueras Mayo (Kassel: Reichenberger, 1997), p. 98.

[17] *Rimas humanas y otros versos*, ed. Antonio Carreño, notes, p. 943.

sonnet. The 'two notions' that really come into play here are Lope's frequently reworked ideas about *arte y naturaleza* (art and nature), which he subtly sets forth in the closing tercets.

Before turning our attention to the tercets, however, one further observation on the sonnet's first line should serve to elaborate an underdeveloped comment from recent criticism. Patricia Grieve and Felipe Pedraza Jiménez have both highlighted the resonance between Lope's phrase 'conceptos esparcidos' and the 'rime sparse' [scattered verse] of the inaugural sonnet in Petrarch's *Canzoniere* [*Song Book*].[18] Viewing the shared adjectival cognate as a case of direct borrowing, these critics note that Lope's first line immediately introduces a balance between literary imitation and autobiographical inspiration. Such a reading suits the emphasis most criticism of the *Rimas* has adopted, but it is not entirely convincing. First, it is not clear that Lope is in fact borrowing from Petrarch. The word *esparcidos* and its related forms were commonly employed in literature of the age to describe the dispersion of published texts. Granted, the word shared between the first line of one introductory sonnet and that of another collection is striking, but if Lope is indeed taking his cue from the *Canzoniere*, then the differences between the two sonnets are more telling. Such differences in themselves, of course, do not rule out the possibility that Lope is reworking Petrarch's sonnet, but the relationship between the two sonnets beyond the shared cognate is of greater interest. Whereas Petrarch's opening line addresses his audience, Lope addresses the personified *versos*. Instead of Petrarch's focus on his own youthful errancy ('mio primo giovenile errore', line 3), the *versos* themselves are the vagrant youths in the 'Soneto primero'; the 'mio vaneggiar' [my wandering] of Petrarch's line 12 becomes the cyclical wanderings of Lope's *versos*.[19] Lope's suppression of himself as author is a pointed departure from Petrarch's sonnet. Again we see Lope privileging poetic creation rather than personal experience. It is precisely the sonnet's central metaphor, the personification of the *versos* as battered, wayward offspring, that enables the sonnet to focus on art itself rather than on the author's life. This focus narrows in the tercets, in which, after having been described as subjects in the quatrains, the *versos* assume greater agency.

Most criticism devoted to Lope's opening sonnet has concentrated on the quatrains, with only scant analysis of the tercets, which carry forward the sonnet's argument and bring it to its climax. In keeping with traditional sonnet form, the increasingly enigmatic tercets of the 'Soneto primero' mark a divergence from the quatrains in tone and construction, yet they do not depart entirely from the

---

[18] Francesco Petrarca, *Canzoniere*, ed. Marco Santagata (Milan: Mondadori, 1996), p. 5. See Patricia E. Grieve, 'Point and Counterpoint in Lope de Vega's *Rimas* and *Rimas sacras*', *Hispanic Review*, 60.4 (1992): 413–34 (p. 417); Felipe B. Pedraza Jiménez, ed., Lope de Vega, *Rimas*, 2 vols (Ciudad Real: Universidad de Castilla-La Mancha, 1993–94), I, p. 184.

[19] Although the more common meaning of *vaneggiare* is 'to be delirious' or 'to rave', the *Vocabulario della lingua italiana*, ed. Rita Levi-Montalcini (Rome: Instituto della Enciclopedia Italiana, 1994) includes an acceptation more likely to have informed a possible reworking by Lope, and cites Tasso's *Gerusalemme liberata* [*Jerusalem Delivered*] to support the meaning 'to wander through space': 'Vaneggiare: [...] Vagare nel vuoto: *Ne le spelonche sue Zefiro tace, E'n tutto è fermo il vaneggiar de l'aure* (Tasso)' (*s.v.*).

argument and imagery established there. In rapid succession, the tercets present a series of objects, more or less abstract, which the personified *versos* are said to *hurtar* — that is, to appropriate, excel or match in a certain quality. A survey of Lope's other uses of the verb *hurtar* admits at least two distinct readings of the verb as used in the 'Soneto primero'. In its more literal sense, *hurtar* can mean 'to steal, to appropriate'. This is the acceptation Covarrubias records and which Lope frequently employs in a more or less negative sense to depict plagiarism or literary borrowing from peer, predecessor or muse. Randel interprets the *hurtar* of the 'Soneto primero' as a reference to 'the profession of poetic larceny', the standard 'aesthetic precept of the imitation of models' (p. 228). But this reading does not take into account the generally depreciatory sense with which Lope uses the verb in relation to literature, and it ignores the verb's second meaning. *Hurtar* also figures in the standard lexicon of hyperbolic Golden Age encomium, employed to compare two objects by descriptive correlation and often implying that the *hurtador* surpasses or possesses to a greater degree the quality said to have been *hurtado*. Such usage can be found in Spanish verse of the Petrarchan tradition in which an object of praise is said to *hurtar* or compete with an abstract entity or natural element. This latter meaning of the verb seems more likely for the *hurtar* of the 'Soneto primero'. The *versos* surpass or take on the characteristics of the four objects of the first tercet: they embody and transcend the enigmatic artifice of the labyrinth, the temerity of Daedalus's exalted thoughts, and the volatile passions of the sea and fiery abyss.

The cyclical series of objects thus appropriated or excelled follows a discernible elemental, spatial and narrative sequence built upon the myth of Daedalus and Icarus. Daedalus, according to the Greek myth, designed an ingenious labyrinth for the king of Crete. Later imprisoned within his own creation, he and his son Icarus escaped the island by flying away on wings fashioned from wax and gull feathers. But Icarus ignored his father's warnings against flying too close to the sun; the wax of his wings melted, and the boy plunged to his death in the sea.

Allusions to Daedalus and Icarus became a well-worn topos of Golden Age literature and were often connected to metaphorical descriptions of the act of composition. The myth was easily adaptable to various situations, well suited for moralizing and compatible with the conventional elements of the Petrarchan lexicon, such as imprisonment, rapturous transport, sun and torments. These possibilities made it a favourite for sixteenth- and seventeenth-century authors, who frequently exploited the myth in dedications, prologues and preliminary notes, generally accompanied by a pun on *pluma* ['quill' as both feather and pen].

In Lope's 'Soneto primero', the adaptation of this stock allusion transcends predictability by its artful subtlety and its fitness within the overall argument of the sonnet. The allusion follows upon the quatrains as if by suggestion, making further use of the figures of the creative father and his uncontrollable, lost autonomous offspring introduced in the opening lines. The narrative development of the Daedalus myth provides one of several ordering sequences in lines 9 to 11. In a series of rapid transitions, the sonnet's imagery departs from the Cretan labyrinth (line 9), rises to 'los altos pensamientos' [the lofty thoughts] (line 10), then plunges to the 'mar' [sea] and deeper still to the fiery abyss (line 11). These lines chart Daedalus's escape from an insular, subterranean imprisonment; his lofty flight; the fall of Icarus to the sea; and a descent to hellish depths — perhaps following as the consequent destination for the doomed, disobedient child. Concurrently, the series develops along an ordered unity of the four Classical elements: the earth (here associated implicitly with the labyrinth and the island of Crete), air, water, fire. In spatial terms, the series traces a cycle, an ascent and descent, outlining an itinerary for the peripatetic *versos* (who are the real agents in this sonnet, after all) and mirroring the departure-and-return cycle of the quatrains.[20]

But the 'abismo' of line 11 is not a final resting place. As contemporary readers steeped in Aristotelian physics would have expected, the lighter-than-air, unstable flames of line 11 must rise, as the *versos* themselves are enjoined to do in line 13. Thus, the cycle continues, open-ended. The wandering *versos* on the winds will come to rest in their self-same centre (line 14), another reference to Aristotle's account of gravitational forces, by which any entity left to itself was expected to tend towards its natural centre; in Lope's own words, 'todas las cosas que se mueuen, en llegando a su propio lugar, se quieten y descansen' [everything that moves, upon arriving at its proper place, must become calm and lie at rest].[21] Again, Lope recognizes the vagaries and volatile character of textual circulation. The sonnet ends at a point of paradoxical rest-in-flux, with the cyclical transit unfinished and the *versos* centred in the ethereal, mutable element.[22]

Critics have identified the 'áspid hermoso' [fair asp] of line 12 as the speaker's lady, the object of his unrequited desires.[23] Certainly, the image is one by which Lope represents the disdainful, unyielding beloved in other poems, such as Sonnet 132 of the same collection, which compares the impossibility of charming an 'áspid' with the futility of placing one's 'esperanza en mujer' [hope in woman] (lines 2, 14; p. 293). The 'áspid' also recalls the Classical topos of the snake

---

[20] Previous critics have likewise noted that the series of objects in the first tercet corresponds to the four elements of Classical physics, but have failed to point out the cyclical, spatial order of the four as Lope presents them: earth to air to water to fire — and a return from earth to air again in line 13. The cycle is a crucial thematic component of the 'Soneto primero', as we have seen in the quatrains' depiction of textual circulation.

[21] *Epistolario de Lope de Vega Carpio*, ed. Agustín G. de Amezúa, 4 vols (Madrid: Aldus, 1935–43), IV, p. 88.

[22] 'Los vientos' [the winds] of line 13 should be understood in relation to Lope's other uses of the word. While the image could and did carry suggestions of widespread fame in Golden Age literature, Lope repeatedly evokes the winds to underscore the ephemeral fragility of an author's product. In his commentary on 'Soliloquio IV' [*Fourth Soliloquy*], he refers to his verse as 'estas hojas débiles que el viento arrebata' [these fragile leaves which the wind snatches away] (cited in *Rimas humanas y otros versos*, ed. Carreño, p. 625), and, by metonymy, the speaker of 'Huerto deshecho' claims to have committed his writings to the wind, to have cast 'al viento plumas' [pens to the wind] (line 216, p. 744). The wind is a recurring feature of Lope's representations of textual dissemination.

[23] Terry, *Seventeenth-Century Spanish Poetry*, p. 100.

lurking in the grass — 'latet anguis in herba' in Virgil's third eclogue (line 93).[24] In Virgil's eclogue, the serpent serves as a reminder that all is not perfect in the pastoral landscape. The asp of the 'Soneto primero' similarly strikes a sobering note after the exuberance of the preceding lines. It evokes the latent hazards of the literary endeavour, the potential disappointments of reception — at once looking back to the description of the damaged *versos* in lines 5–8 and anticipating the insecurity of the wind in the final lines.

Whatever we take 'áspid' to signify in Lope's sonnet, the figure of the serpent follows by association from the image in the preceding line, 'las llamas' [the flames] of the 'abismo' [abyss], with their suggestions of the apocalyptic abyss and its serpent, the 'draco' [dragon] and 'serpens antiquus' [old serpent] of Revelation 12.9, the flames of hell and the serpent of Eden. If we read the final tercet as a portrayal of textual circulation, as a continuation of the argument taken up in the quatrains, the import of the equivocal closing lines becomes clearer. The *versos*, directed to an unreceptive individual in accordance with traditions of the Petrarchan sonnet, are subsequently remitted to a wider public, to a broader range of dissemination. Whatever occasion or individual may have incited the poetry, autobiographical or otherwise, the *versos* now belong to a more universal readership and will rest in their 'centro mismo' [own centre], to be accepted or rejected on their own merits.

There is yet another basis for the cyclical sequence of images in the tercets. In addition to being a picture of textual reception and circulation, the imagery suggests a representation of the very act of poetic composition. The tercets' spatial cycle corresponds neatly to Miguel Sánchez de Lima's description of contemplative composition in *El arte poética en romance castellano* [*Poetic Art in the Castilian Language*] of 1580. The passage is worth quoting at length:

> Mientras el Poeta esta componiendo, eleva el sentido en las cosas celestiales, y en la contemplacion de su criador, unas vezes sube al cielo contemplando aquella immensa y eterna gloria [...]. De alli baxa al infierno, siente las penas de los dañados [...]: otras vezes visita el Purgatorio, donde se para a mirar las penas que padecen aquellas ánimas de los fieles [...]. En estas y otras semejantes contemplaciones gasta su tiempo el verdadero y buen Poeta.[25]

> [When the Poet is composing, he elevates his perception to celestial things, and to the contemplation of his creator; at times, he rises to the heavens, contemplating that immense and eternal glory [...]. From there, he descends to hell, perceives the afflictions of the damned [...]: at other times, he visits Purgatory, where he pauses to

---

[24] *Virgil in Two Volumes*, ed. and trans. H. Rushton Fairclough, Loeb Classical Library, revised edn (Cambridge, MA: Harvard University Press; London: Heinemann, 1965), p. 26.

[25] Miguel Sánchez de Lima, *El arte poética en romance castellano* (1580), ed. Rafael de Balbín Lucas (Madrid: Consejo Superior de Investigaciones Científicas, Instituto 'Nicolás Antonio', 1944), pp. 43–44.

gaze upon the chastisements suffered by the souls of the faithful [...]. In these and other similar contemplations the true and good Poet spends his time.][26]

How, then, might the 'centro' of the sonnet's final line relate to such depictions of poetic imagination and contemplation? Baltasar Gracián provides a possible link in his treatise on *Agudeza y arte de ingenio* [*Wit and the Art of Ingenuity*] of 1648. He applies something like Sánchez de Lima's cyclical, spatial description of poetic contemplation more specifically to the writer's act of mentally forming a *concepto* (here, a poetic likeness or metaphor) and portrays this act as a process of selecting from appropriate *correspondencias* (correspondences) that surround a given subject, like spokes radiating from the hub of a wheel: 'Es el sujeto sobre quien se discurre y pondera [...] uno como centro de quien reparte el discurso, líneas de ponderación y sutileza a las entidades que lo rodean; esto es, a los adjuntos que lo coronan [...]. Los va careando de uno en uno con el sujeto' [The subject upon which one meditates and ponders is [...] like a centre from which contemplation distributes lines of consideration and subtle artifice to the entities which encompass it; that is, to the annexed elements which crown it [...]. He proceeds by comparing them one by one with the subject].[27] A successful, apt selection will produce expressive *agudeza* (wit). In other words, one might imagine the subject or tenor of a metaphor located at the centre of Gracián's conceptual wheel, with a variety of potential vehicles arrayed about it with varying degrees of correspondence.

Following Gracián's terminology, the 'sujeto principal' [principal subject], 'centro', or tenor of the primary metaphor in the 'Soneto primero' is the *versos* or *conceptos* themselves. The vehicle is the itinerant progeny. By Aristotelian physics, the *centro* is the principal state or elemental essence of the *versos*. By Gracián's theory, the *centro* is the conceptual key to the sonnet. The closing words of the sonnet, in light of Gracián's model, restate the self-reflective nature of the piece. Significantly, as I have previously intimated, this is a *centro* associated with 'los vientos' [the winds]. The ethereal texts are enjoined to return to their natural element, recalling Lope's associations of winds and words, winds and transience, fragmentation, scattering — which brings us back to the 'conceptos esparcidos' of the first line and suggests an overall cycle governing the sonnet's imagery. Even though an individual recipient, the 'áspid', might reject the *versos*, there is at least some hint of restful satisfaction that the texts will ultimately reach a wider, if indeterminate, audience.

The systematic order of the tercets and the allusion to Daedalus, the archetype of calculating artistry in Greek mythology, completes Lope's picture of poetic composition as a dual, balanced process of emotional inspiration tempered by

[26] Lope's and Sánchez de Lima's depictions are by no means isolated instances of this cyclical, spatial representation. We find the same idea in Shakespeare's *A Midsummer Night's Dream*: 'The poet's eye, in a fine frenzy rolling, / Doth glance from heaven to earth, from earth to heaven; / And as imagination bodies forth / The forms of things unknown, the poet's pen / Turns them to shapes [...]' (ed. Harold F. Brooks, The Arden Shakespeare, London: Methuen, 1979, 5.1.12–17).

[27] Baltasar Gracián y Morales, *Agudeza y arte de ingenio*, ed. Eduardo Ovejero y Maury (Madrid: La Rafa, 1929), 'Discurso IV', p. 14.

artistic precepts, just as natural, elemental cycles are governed by physical laws. The tercets qualify the dominant image of the quatrains, which might otherwise present an incomplete picture of seemingly spontaneous poetic generation arising from circumstances and feelings. Lope would later criticize the tendencies he perceived among the younger generations of poets for precisely this sort of unpolished, emotional outpouring in composition, and for their infatuation with poetry produced 'de la abundancia del corazón, efecto cierto de las asociaciones repentinas' [from the abundance of the heart, the inevitable result of impulsive associations].[28] As the apostrophe to the *versos* continues in the tercets, the sonnet reminds the reader that good poetic composition, despite appearances, is not merely a matter of succumbing to a *furor poeticus*. Rather, it is a balance between emotion and construct, between fiery passions and ordered precision.

Scattered children, battered ships[29] and tattered flotsam[30] — all are figures by which Lope portrays the literary endeavour in his *Rimas*. One could read these reiterated depictions of the fragile or damaged text as a positive statement, as Lope's avowal of his veteran status as an experienced poet. The sea-worn and battle-scarred *versos* of Sonnet 149, like those of the 'Soneto primero', may be scattered and broken, but they are also consequently time-tested, worldly-wise and worldly-weathered, having ultimately withstood the onslaughts of criticism and caprices of public taste. Read positively, the figure of the damaged text is not only an affirmation of the seasoned poet, but is necessarily a testimony to the fact that his works are being actively read in circulation. Like the poet who has overcome adversity and merits the prized epithet *Fénix* (Phoenix) — a title incessantly applied to Lope by his admirers and awarded by Lope in turn to his favourites — the figure of the mangled and recycled text suggests endurance and perpetuity, though, significantly, it is a perpetuity subject to conversions and alterations. On the other hand, Lope's figures of textual fragility also represent the sensibilities of *desengaño* ['disabusal'] applied to the act of textual production and circulation — a recognition of textual impermanence and the inconstancy of audiences, an author's more or less acquiescent acknowledgement of forces beyond his control. One can understand these metaphors as intentional manifestations of Lope's awareness of the perils of publication. He is conscious of what might be called a Law of Textual Entropy: literary production is not a tidy process; texts tend towards disorder.

The distinctive nature of Lope's recurring insistence on imagery of evanescence, fragility and dynamic ruin appears even more patent when contrasted with conventional contemporary figures, many of which exalt the architectural formidability and durability of poetic texts. Whereas Lope depicts brittle boats and errant foundlings, the 1608 'Discurso en loor de la poesía' [Discourse in Praise of Poetry] by an anonymous Peruvian poetess extols poets who construct paragons of artifice: 'fabrican [...] romances y sonetos / (como los de Anfión un tiempo a Tebas), / muros a África a fuerza de concetos' [they

---

[28] Lope de Vega, *Cartas*, ed. Nicolás Marín (Madrid: Castalia, 1985), p. 157.
[29] Sonnet 150 (p. 315).
[30] Sonnet 149 (p. 314).

fabricate [...] ballads and sonnets / (like those of Amphion for Thebes), / walls round Africa by the power of their conceits].[31] Félix de Lucio Espinosa y Malo likewise lauds the merits of writing in general in his *Epístolas varias* [*Various Epistles*] of 1675: 'las letras son como estatuas, y simulacros seguros que la mantienen [la voz] [...] puede su Autor pasarlas donde quiere' [the letters of the alphabet are like statues, and sure simulacra which preserve the voice [...] their Author can transmit them where he wishes];[32] and even Pedro Calderón de la Barca subscribes on at least one occasion to the claims that printed publication would make an author immortal. The printing press, Calderón affirms, grants 'duraciones que el tiempo no consuma, / por quien su autor segundo ser recibe' [durability which time does not consume, by which the author gains a second existence].[33] Such images and assertions run counter to Lope's portrayal of malleable, ephemeral texts. Far from being graven, fixed simulacra of the author's voice, the autonomous offspring of the 'Soneto primero' can evolve and stray and signify more than the author's intention at the time of composition: 'Essos versos os dirán más de mí que lo que yo sabía cuando los hize' [These verses will tell you more about me than I knew when I made them], Lope asserts through one of his characters *La Dorotea*.[34]

Images of construction and enduring artifice, in addition to being too rigid for the qualities Lope imagines for his texts, violate his ideal of the collaborative roles of *arte* and *naturaleza* in composition. Figures of walls and statues grant too much prominence to the artificial components of the literary endeavour — an aspect of such imagery which would lead Lope to adopt it for his arsenal when attacking the excesses of *culteranismo*. In a letter to the Duke of Sessa regarding Góngora's style, he condemns the 'edificio' [edifice] of second-rate *gongorista* imitators and their 'estupendas máquinas' [stupendous constructs] as the product of a 'fábrica portentosa' [astounding new manner of building].[35] As his polemic with Góngora grew more heated, Lope accused his rival of erecting a Tower of Babel, a 'torre de gigantes'.[36] The pejorative image is not only a critique of Góngora's difficult language but also of what Lope viewed as Góngora's overly artificial style.

Unlike those of Espinosa y Malo, moreover, Lope's metaphors predicate no such confidence in the author's ability to direct circulation wilfully. Lope's authorial figures do not retain control over the text beyond composition. He can

[31] Ventura García Calderón, ed., *Discurso en loor de la poesía*, in *El apogeo de la literatura colonial: las poetisas anónimas, el Lunarejo, Caviedes* (Paris: Desclée, de Brouwer, 1938), pp. 13–40 (lines 601–3, p. 33). According to legend, Amphion and his twin brother Zethus erected the walls and seven gates of Thebes. Amphion sang and played the lyre so charmingly that stones tore themselves from the earth and followed after Zethus in procession.

[32] Cited in Aurora Egido, *La voz de las letras en el Siglo de Oro* (Madrid: Abada, 2003), p. 53.

[33] Pedro Calderón de la Barca, 'Soneto al Maestro Joseph de Casanova', in José de Casanova, *Primera parte del arte de escrivir todas las formas de letras: escrito y tallado por el Maestro Joseph de Casanova* (Madrid: Diego Díaz de la Carrera, 1650), fol. ¶₂ᵛ, lines 10–11.

[34] Lope de Vega, *La Dorotea*, ed. Edwin S. Morby (Berkeley, CA: University of California Press; Valencia: Castalia, 1958; 2nd edn, revised, 1968), p. 370.

[35] Lope de Vega, *Obras poéticas*, I, ed. José Manuel Blecua, pp. 878–80.

[36] Lope de Vega, *Cartas*, ed. Nicolás Marín, p. 157.

indulge in fanciful speculation about what it would be like to accompany his printed texts in circulation, to provide the same 'viva voz y alma que el día que se leyeron' [living voice and soul as the day they were read] in a poetic tournament;[37] or he may allow a character in *La Dorotea* to contemplate what the presence of Lope's *alter ego* Burguillos would mean for the interpretation of one of his poems: 'Si aquí le tuviéramos, él nos sacara de muchas dudas en la tremenda esfinge deste soneto' [If we had him here, he would resolve many of our doubts about this tremendous sphynx of a sonnet] (p. 350). But Lope ultimately recognizes that texts in circulation are 'perdidos' [lost], Icarean playthings of the wind.

In Lope's metaphorical system, not only do the authorial figures relinquish control over textual dissemination, but the figures of the author themselves are unobtrusive, removed or eclipsed, rendered latent or passive. I have noted how the implied presence of the paternal, authorial speaker in the 'Soneto primero' increasingly gives way to a focus on the agency and characteristics of the filial texts themselves. The distance which the filial figure permits between author and product is crucial to Lope's metaphors for texts and textual production. It allows him to discard the images of simulacra, to exploit the images of dynamic agents, and to call into question the assumption of the author as principal meaning-maker. His suppressed or diminished authorial figure is far from being the centre of his imagined work, as the 'Soneto primero' makes explicit. The vagrant *versos* are said to rest in their self-same centre, a paradoxical rest in flux which leaves open the possibility of further change and disfigurement for the texts, rather than imposed limits, closure, and concretized meanings.

Lope's direct involvement with the printing of his works placed him in a unique position among the leading poets of the age who, in keeping with convention, tended to leave the printing of their poetry to friends, disciples and posthumous editors. His lifelong familiarity with printed publication — as well as with manuscript circulation, his youthful entanglements with manuscript libel, audiences' reactions in the theatres, the whims of patrons — endowed him with a seasoned, self-conscious perspective. His awareness encompasses what he accuses other poets of not sufficiently knowing: 'the changes which come between the author's draft and the form ready for printing, between the voice of the master and that of the uninstructed, between reading among friends or buying the book for oneself' (p. 584, previously cited). Lope draws on this awareness in order to imagine the full variety of audiences and modes of transmission his works encounter, the ultimately fragile nature of the text, and the range of receptions brought to bear on the transit of the texts throughout their repeated circulations.

---

[37] Lope de Vega, *Justa poética*, ed. Sainz de Robles, p. 1575.

5

'Quien en virtud emplea su ingenio ...':
Lope de Vega's Religious Poetry

ARANTZA MAYO

> Lector, no hay sílaba aquí
> que de oro puro no sea,
> que a quien en virtud emplea
> su ingenio sucede así.
>
> [Reader, there is no syllable here
> made of other than pure gold;
> It happens thus to those who put
> their wit to the service of virtue.][1]

Lope de Vega's religious poetry remains the least-known section of his work. While the *Rimas sacras* (1614) have attracted a significant degree of attention over recent years, this collection forms a comparatively small part of his copious religious lyrical production, estimated at around six-hundred-thousand lines, a substantial part of it still awaiting modern editions and studies that take account of its role and relevance within the broad landscape of Golden Age sacred poetry.[2]

Lope wrote on religious subjects throughout his career: his earliest documented collection is his *Los cinco misterios dolorosos de la Pasión y muerte de Nuestro Señor Jesucristo con su sagrada resurrección* (1582?),[3] followed almost two

---

[1] 'Lope de Vega al lector' [Lope de Vega to the Reader] in the preliminaries to Fernando de Camargo y Salgado's *El santo milagroso* [*The Miraculous Saint*]; Lope de Vega, *Poesía*, ed. Antonio Carreño, 6 vols (Madrid: Fundación José Antonio de Castro, 2002–5), VI, pp. 601–2. All translations are literal.

[2] Novo and Pedraza Jiménez have produced the most significant recent studies on the *Rimas sacras*: Yolanda Novo, *Las 'Rimas sacras' de Lope de Vega: disposición y sentido* (Santiago de Compostela: Universidade de Santiago de Compostela, 1990); Felipe B. Pedraza Jiménez, *El universo poético de Lope de Vega* (Madrid: Laberinto, 2003). The *Rimas sacras* themselves have just appeared in a much-needed critical edition by Antonio Carreño and Antonio Sánchez Jiménez ([Pamplona]: Universidad de Navarra; Madrid: Iberoamericana; Frankfurt am Main: Vervuert, 2006). The calculation of Lope's religious output is offered by José Rubinos, *Lope de Vega como poeta religioso* (Habana: Cultural, 1935), p. 9.

[3] For the dating of *Los cinco misterios* see the edition by César Hernández Alonso (Madrid: Instituto de Estudios Madrileños, 1987), pp. 2–5, and Alberto Blecua, 'De Granada a Lope: sobre

decades later by his hagiography of the patron saint of Madrid, *Isidro* (1599). A particularly fruitful period commenced around 1612, and in the space of four years Lope published his *Cuatro soliloquios* (1612), the partly versified *Pastores de Belén* (1612), his *Contemplativos discursos* and *Segunda parte del desengaño del hombre* (1613), the *Rimas sacras* (1614), the *Conceptos divinos al santísimo sacramento y a la Virgen Nuestra Señora* (1615) and the *Alabanzas al glorioso san José* (1616). This flurry of spiritual works was followed by the *Revelaciones de algunas cosas dignas de ser notadas de la Pasión de Cristo* published in 1621. *La Virgen de la Almudena* first appeared 'suelta' [individually] in 1623 but was reissued with the *Triunfos divinos, con otras rimas sacras* in 1625. The *Soliloquios amorosos de un alma a Dios* came out in 1626, followed by his *Corona trágica* in 1627 and the *Sentimientos a los agravios de Cristo, Nuestro Bien, por la nación hebrea* which was probably printed in 1632.[4] In addition, Lope wrote a number of individual short compositions for events such as *justas poéticas* (poetry competitions), including those celebrated in honour of St Teresa (1614) and St Isidro (1620, 1622).

With excessive frequency the majority of these works have been read as illustrations of spiritual turbulence of which there is no categorical evidence. In particular, a supposed spiritual crisis in the early 1610s, allegedly signalled by the author's self-reported ascetic practices (he famously informed the Duke of Sessa that 'me pego lindos zurriagazos todas las noches' [I give myself fine floggings every night]) and his joining of several secular religious associations, is said to have crystallized with the loss of his son Carlos Félix (1612) and his second wife Juana de Guardo (1613), moving him to take orders in 1614.[5] As a result of these events, the sacred works written in this period have been seen by many as accounts of public repentance. A different line of interpretation, more focused on the literary qualities of the poems than on the personal sincerity they may portray, considers his spiritual writings as a literary strategy: the creation of yet another elaborate mask probably designed to improve his own moral image and achieve a remunerated position in the court. In either case, the links between literature and biography play a significant role in informing the readings, something ultimately encouraged by the author's own tendency purposefully to blur his private and public lives. Particularly illustrative is his attribution of the *Soliloquios amorosos de un alma a Dios* (1626) to a French Carthusian named as Gabriel Padecopeo. Not only is the supposed author's name an anagram of Lope de Vega Carpio but four of its poems had already been published in his *Cuatro soliloquios* in 1612.

una fuente de *Los cinco misterios dolorosos*', *Anuario Lope de Vega*, 1 (1995): 9–17 (pp. 9 and 17).

[4] *Poesía*, ed. Carreño, VI, p. xxx.

[5] *Epistolario de Lope de Vega Carpio*, ed. Agustín G. de Amezúa, 4 vols (Madrid: Aldus, 1935–43), III, p. 58. Lope joined the secular Congregración de Esclavos del Santísimo Sacramento (Society of Slaves of the Most Holy Sacrament) in 1609, the Congregación del Oratorio de la calle del Olivar (Society of the Oratory of Olivar Street) in 1610, and the Congregación de la Orden Tercera de san Francisco (The Franciscan Third Order) in 1611. These secular associations had a social as well as a spiritual purpose and held regular meetings for prayer, mass and the celebration of particular devotions.

The barely ambiguous preliminaries by Montalbán and Valdivielso contribute to the outlining of the mask which is further elaborated upon in the biography of the Frenchman with which Lope introduces his supposed translation and where he recreates, rather glamorously, details of his own life. If all these details did not make the attribution transparent enough, Lope felt it necessary to 'confess' his authorship in his bio-bibliographical 'Égloga a Claudio'.[6]

The focus that both the issue of sincerity and the consideration of Lope's literary masks have attracted stands in contrast with the sidelining of the study of the devotional features of the texts themselves. Regardless of what literary devices Lope utilizes to create a persuasive repentant persona or, more questionably, whether his aim was to publicize a personal spiritual journey, he had to do it in a manner that was convincing from a devotional viewpoint to a readership highly conversant with a broad range of religious literary works. The purpose of this essay is thus to draw attention, if only at a very superficial level, to the devotional aspects of Lope's significant contribution to Spanish Golden Age religious poetry by highlighting the main features of their central devotional axis which are so frequently ignored. As will become clear in the course of the present work, this is not in any way to detract from the intrinsic value and interest of Lope's sacred production as literature, to subscribe to a vision of an original readership so devout and naive that it would not or could not consider the personal, political and social dimensions implicit in many elements and themes of these works, or to suggest that such an audience would indeed be indifferent to their literary merit.

It is useful to start by differentiating between two kinds of religious poetry both within Lope's output and in the broader context of the late-sixteenth and the first half of the seventeenth centuries. One type of verse is that which, apart from its lyrical qualities, has a clear devotional purpose and is thus meant to be read piously, as it contains 'conceptos divinos y espirituales que incitan al alma a la contemplación de las cosas celestiales' [divine and spiritual conceits which urge the soul to the contemplation of heavenly things].[7] This type, in its multiple variations, encompasses most Golden Age production, from *romances a lo divino* (religious ballads based on secular poetic models), such as the variously adapted 'Romance de Gaiferos' [Ballad of Gayferos], of which Valdivielso, López de Úbeda, Pedro de Padilla and Lope himself made versions, to more erudite and exegetical poeticizations of doctrinal matters such as Valdivielso's *Exposición parafrástica del Psalterio y de los cánticos del Breviario* [*Paraphrastic Exposition of the Psalter and of the Songs of the Divine Office*] (1623).[8] The second kind also deals with religious subjects but is more commemorative and

---

[6] 'Disfracé con anagrama / los soliloquios de mi ardiente llama' [I disguised with an anagram the soliloquies of my burning flame] (286–87); the poem was published without title or cover in 1632; *Poesía*, ed. Carreño, VI, pp. 25 and xviii.

[7] Fray Ambrosio de Vallejo in his 'aprobación' [approval] to the *Rimas sacras*, ed. Carreño & Sánchez Jiménez, p. 109.

[8] Further details of these particular *contrafacta* can be found in José de Valdivielso, *Romancero spiritual* [*Spiritual Ballads*], ed. J. M. Aguirre, Clásicos Castellanos, 228 (Madrid: Espasa-Calpe, 1984), pp. 132–33, and Lope de Vega, *Rimas sacras*, ed. Carreño & Sánchez Jiménez, p. 518.

political in nature than strictly devotional; in this class belong most works produced for *justas* (poetry competitions) in honour of a particular saint or festivity, such as the beatification of Saint Teresa or the passage of the Holy Sacrament to the Iglesia Mayor in Lerma, for which Lope produced some pieces.[9] This type also includes those poems aimed at forging or furthering links with a patron by upholding Catholic doctrine, as our author does in his *Corona trágica* with his liberal praise of Pope Urban VIII and the Hapsburg monarchs.

Most of Lope's religious verse falls into the first broad category and, as well as being interesting and valuable for the range of literary qualities it displays in terms of its imagery, musicality and linguistic plasticity, it offers its readership spiritually profitable diversion. In this respect, the role played by this type of poetry is not too distant from that which had once been fulfilled by medieval Books of Hours and continued to be fulfilled by the extremely popular spiritual treatises. As Luis de Granada's *Libro de la oración y meditación* [*Book of Prayer and Meditation*] exemplifies, these treatises were devoted to encouraging 'la meditación y consideración de las cosas divinas, y de los misterios principales de nuestra fe' [the meditation and consideration of divine things and the principal mysteries of our faith].[10] Unlike these guides, however, the vast range of religious subjects expounded by Lope, from the more popular aspects of devotion (such as the adoration of the shepherds in his *Pastores de Belén*) to complex doctrinal or theological points (the doctrine of transubstantiation in the *Triunfos divinos*) are mediated by crucial aesthetic and artistic concerns. Lope's poems hence offer their readership an experience which is akin to that of reading secular literature while drawing their attention to the works' spiritual dimension. These texts form a literary space which conjugates aspects of other kinds of sacred writing, from the socially enjoyed *comedias de asunto religioso* (plays with a religious theme) and *autos* (allegorical plays with a religious theme) — a public form of religious and didactic entertainment — to treatises and guides of devotion — focused on the individual practice of spiritual exercises — and which in its multiple variations can be closer to one or the other genre.

One of the works in which Lope most palpably combines devotion and spiritual guidance with the sort of entertainment that could be derived from a secular lyric or dramatic piece is his *Isidro* (1599), an epic hagiography devoted to the life of the patron saint of Madrid.[11] Although Lope would go on to write three different

---

[9] *Relación que en las fiestas de la beatificación de nuestra madre santa Teresa se celebraron en estos dos conventos nuestros de Madrid, san Hermenegildo y san Juan* (1614) and *Fiestas en la traslación del Santísimo Sacramento a la Iglesia Mayor de Lerma* (Valencia: José Gasch, 1612), in *Poesía*, ed. Carreño, VI, pp. 389–400 and 211–72.

[10] Granada, in the prologue to his *Libro de la oración y meditación*, in *Obras completas de Fray Luis de Granada: obras castellanas*, ed. Cristóbal Cuevas, 2 vols (Madrid: Turner & Fundación José Antonio de Castro, 1994–97), II, p. 6. In his 'The Problem of the "Best-Seller" in Spanish Golden-Age Literature', *Bulletin of Hispanic Studies*, 57.3 (1980): 189–98, Keith Whinnom notes that the book went through well over one-hundred editions between 1554 and 1679, becoming the indisputable 'best-seller' of the period (p. 194).

[11] Isidro was canonized by Pope Gregory XV on 12 March 1622, although he had been considered Madrid's patron since 1212.

comedias (plays) about the holy peasant and contributed to the *justas* (poetry competitions) in honour of his beatification and sanctification, Isidro is his first, most intimate and proselytizing work on the subject.[12] Formally, it combines elements from the *romancero* (ballads), both secular and sacred, and the *comedia* (drama) with a narrative style reminiscent of medieval and early modern hagiographies, an attractive combination for his readership.[13] In particular, the poem echoes well-known *Flos sanctorum* collections, such as Voragine's thirteenth-century *Legenda aurea* and the more contemporary version by Alonso de Villegas published in four volumes between 1578 and 1589.[14] Lope affirms that the poeticization of the saint's life increases its spiritual didacticism and appeal, arguing in his prologue that his use of 'versos castellanos' [Castilian metre] and 'humildes quintillas' [humble five-line stanzas] 'aumentarán la devoción en muchos, que por ser en verso parece que mueven con mayor eficacia' [will increase devotion in many individuals, because they seem to be more effectively moving by being in verse], thus suggesting that his is a particularly fruitful way of spreading Isidro's story.[15] While it is impossible to prove Pedraza Jiménez's affirmation that 'dinero, reconocimiento y la fama personal' [money, public recognition and personal fame] were Lope's motivations for writing the *Isidro*, his observation underlines how poetry of this kind had a wide appeal and could count on being well received.[16]

Isidro is 'un labrador español, / castellano y de Madrid' [a Spanish peasant, Castilian and from Madrid] (II, 704–5) whom Lope involves in a series of situations of the sort that he presents in his own religious *comedias* and that were common in *autos*: the poem includes an allegorical fight with Envy (II, 362–1000) and an almost mystical dream journey to the Holy Land (IV, 896–1000) as well as a liberal dose of miracles and trials; in canto VII alone Isidro's wife, María de la Cabeza, crosses the Jarama river walking over her own shawl to prove her chastity (681–90) and the saint makes a fountain spring to life (976–1000). Lope offers many careful and detailed depictions in delicate lyrical terms which are reminiscent of his secular *romances* (ballads). In particular he relishes the descriptions of Isidro and his bride on their wedding day. María de la Cabeza resembles an image of her own role model, the Virgin Mary, crowned in her precious purity (II, 181–85) while the 'labrador' [peasant] is a genuine 'castellano'

---

[12] For a study of the plays *La niñez de san Isidro* and *La juventud de san Isidro*, see Elaine M. Canning, *Lope de Vega's 'Comedias de tema religioso': Re-creations and Re-presentations* (Woodbridge: Tamesis, 2004), pp. 44–84.

[13] Américo Castro & Hugo A. Rennert, *Vida de Lope de Vega (1562–1635)*, 2nd edn (Madrid: Anaya, 1968; repr. 1969), p. 133, as well as Antonio Carreño, in Lope de Vega, *Poesía*, I, p. xxv, note stylistic similarities with *comedias*, *autos sacramentales*, religious and secular lyric and historical ballads.

[14] Santiago de la Vorágine (Jacobus de Voragine), *La leyenda dorada*, ed. José Manuel Macías, 2 vols (Madrid: Alianza, 1982). Villegas also wrote an independent *Vida de Isidro Labrador* [Life of Isidro the Labourer] (1592). A key source was the genealogical documents provided to him directly by Fray Domingo de Mendoza and which Lope acknowledges (*Isidro*, in *Poesía*, ed. Carreño, I, p. 205).

[15] *Isidro*, in *Poesía*, I, p. 207.

[16] Pedraza Jiménez, *El universo poético*, p. 77.

[Castilian] who rejects pernicious foreign influences both in religious beliefs and fashions and wears

> De paño abierto el gregüesco,
> no como agora tudesco,
> con tan nuevas invenciones,
> mas con pliegues y cordones
> más acomodado y fresco. (II, 136–40)

[His breeches were made out of broadcloth and not in the now fashionable German style full of new inventions; instead, they had folds and laces which made them more comfortable and fresh.]

He is a Spanish Everyman, a life-like and accessible example of sainthood on which every reader can attempt to model his or her own existence, however humble:

> No supo filosofía,
> física, ni teología
> como Isidro, luz del suelo,
> pero supo hallar el cielo
> llevando la fe por guía. (I, 286–90)

[He did not know philosophy, physics or theology like Isidore [of Seville], light of the earth; but, taking faith as his guide, he knew how to find heaven.]

In the first canto the author places great emphasis on how Isidro is an imitator of Isidore of Seville, regardless of his lack of 'ciencia' [science] and of magnificent clothes (I, 316–440), and although the 'villano' [peasant] is by no means a wealthy man or a scholar, he still achieves holiness because of his steadfast faith and willingness to shape his own actions according to existing models of sanctity, an imitation which is ultimately channelled towards Christ's own example. Their saintliness is realized not least because both men obey the Lord's precepts which are straightforwardly expounded in a moralizing manner throughout the text and which readers should follow if they are to emulate their local hero:

> no mentir era preceto [...]
> que aborrece Dios los labios
> de quien miente. (I, 486–89)

[not lying was a precept [...] because God abhors the lips of those who lie.]

The book's didactic aspects are similarly evident in the constant references to numerous biblical and church figures and episodes which help to illustrate events in Isidro's life but also point the reader to a multitude of complementary role models:

> Un Matatías prudente,
> un David, un Eleazar
> pudiera el viejo imitar,
> y él un Isaac obediente
> en la leña y el altar. (I, 641–45)

[The old man [Isidro's father] could resemble the prudent Mattathias, David and Eleazar, while Isidro brought to mind an obedient Isaac lying on the wood and the altar.]

The main sources for this stanza are listed beside it (1 Mach. 2 and 3 Reg. 21), as Lope is careful to annotate the margins with the foundations of many of his comparisons, images, precepts and concepts so that the more-educated reader who desires to consider any particular points in more depth or learn more about a specific figure may more easily do so. At the same time such annotations add more than a touch of erudite refinement and authority to an otherwise popular hagiography. The Vulgate is its main referent but a large number of authors, from St Augustine to Thomas Aquinas, as well as many writers from antiquity, are also cited. In addition, the poem is accompanied by a comprehensive appendix with the names of books and authors which Lope indicates will serve 'para la exornación de esta historia' [for the embellishment of this story], pointing to how a religious work such as *Isidro*, which is more closely related in formal terms to the *romancero* or the *comedia* than to a prose treatise, can serve both as edifying and pious reading as well as a solid basis for more sophisticated spiritual reflections, and is thus able to reach a large and diverse readership.[17]

Isidro's character as an entertaining hagiography which may have been approached with varying degrees of devotional engagement by Golden Age readers contrasts with that of other works which actively demand a more substantial spiritual and intellectual involvement from their audience. Many of these texts aim at the identification of the reader with the poetic speaker and insofar as they attempt to steer the spiritual reactions of their audience in a given direction — sorrow, joy, repentance, gratitude, etc. — they bear remarkable similarity with devotional guides, thus being at the other extreme of the literary space occupied by religious poetry, as formulated above. In these compositions, as the poetic speaker contemplates a particular spiritual image, event or concept, often in the first person, he leads his reader through a series of apposite thoughts and responses while allowing sufficient opportunity through the use of multi-layered conceits and biblical or similar allusions for the individual to consider independently related points that may emerge as a result.

Although there is no evidence to suggest that any specific collection of poems by Lope was ever intended to serve as a full guide to meditation, key aspects of Ignatius Loyola's *Spiritual Exercises* and the European meditative tradition they

---

[17] *Isidro*, in *Poesía*, ed. Carreño, I, p. 539.

summarize in such precise terms are manifest in the author's sacred lyric.[18] In particular, a reading of any of his Christocentric poems, especially those focused on the themes of repentance and spiritual intimacy with the Divinity, provides palpable confirmation that Lope was indeed familiar with Ignatius's manual and used its framework as a guide. Central to Ignatius's programme is the complementary engagement of the soul's three powers — memory, understanding and will — with a full exercise involving the successive action of each of these powers. Every power is dependent on the appropriate realization of its immediate antecedent, although memory, being the first, can be triggered by external elements, such as visual representations of the matter or episode to be contemplated. A small minority of Lope's poems recreate a full exercise, moving from an initial description or composition of place, through the spiritual consideration of the visualized event to the final emergence of one or more affections of the will. In the case of a sonnet entitled 'Fuerza de lágrimas' [The Power of Tears] this is achieved with extraordinary verbal economy.

> Con ánimo de hablarle en confianza,
> de su piedad entré en el templo un día,
> donde Cristo en la Cruz resplandecía
> con el perdón que quien le mira alcanza.
>   Y aunque la fe, el amor y la esperanza
> a la lengua pusieron osadía,
> acordeme que fue por culpa mía,
> y quisiera de mí tomar venganza.
>   Ya me volvía sin decirle nada
> y, como vi la llaga del costado,
> parose el alma en lágrimas bañada.
>   Hablé, lloré, y entré por aquel lado,
> porque no tiene Dios puerta cerrada
> al corazón contrito y humillado.[19]

---

[18] The subject has been considered to a varying extent in Antonio Sánchez Jiménez, 'Composición de lugar en las *Rimas sacras* (1614) de Lope de Vega: la influencia ignaciana', *Anuario Lope de Vega*, 10 (2004): 115–28; Pedraza Jiménez, *El universo poético*; Novo, *Las 'Rimas sacras' de Lope de Vega*; M. Audrey Aaron, *Cristo en la poesía lírica de Lope de Vega* (Madrid: Cultura Hispánica, 1967); Eberhard Müller-Bochat, 'Técnicas literarias y métodos de meditación en la poesía sagrada del Siglo de Oro', in *Actas del Tercer Congreso Internacional de Hispanistas*, ed. Carlos H. Magis (Mexico City: Colegio de México, 1970), pp. 611–17; and Arantza Mayo, *La lírica sacra de Lope de Vega y José de Valdivielso* ([Pamplona]: Universidad de Navarra; Madrid: Iberoamericana; Frankfurt am Main: Vervuert, 2007). Pedraza Jiménez has argued against the *Rimas sacras* being a full equivalent of the *Exercises*, but points out that some influence is a possibility. Sánchez Jiménez has illustrated various links with Ignatius's work in 'Composición de lugar en las *Rimas sacras* (1614) de Lope de Vega', while Mayo has examined the influence of the *Exercises* as a whole across a wide range of Lope's religious poetry. For the influence of Ignatius on Luis de Granada, see his *Guía de pecadores* [*The Sinners' Guide*], ed. José María Balcells (Barcelona: Planeta, 1986), p. xvi.

[19] *Triunfos divinos con otras rimas sacras*, in *Poesía*, ed. Carreño, V, p. 133.

[One day, with the intention of speaking to him frankly, I entered the merciful temple where Christ on the cross shone with the forgiveness achieved by those who look upon him.

Although faith, love and hope made my tongue audacious, I remembered that it was my fault and wished to take revenge upon myself.

I was about to turn away without speaking to him when, as I saw the wound in his side, my soul, bathed in tears, stopped.

I spoke, I wept, and I entered through that side, because God does not have a closed door for the contrite and humbled heart.]

In the quatrains the speaker describes going into a church in order to speak to the crucified Christ that presides over it ('con ánimo de hablarle en confianza' [with the intention of speaking to him frankly]). The first contact between sinner and Divinity is visual and the speaker is overcome by the Lord's immediate forgiveness ('el perdón que quien le mira alcanza' [the forgiveness achieved by those who look upon him]) which the crucified figure exudes. Although some affections ('la fe, el amor y la esperanza' [faith, love and hope]) flow before understanding has fully played its role, the middle power forces the sinner to realize that Christ's Passion 'fue por culpa mía' [was my fault], whereby shame (as illustrated by his tears, 'el alma en lágrimas bañada' [my soul, bathed in tears]), a more appropriate emotion than the 'osadía' [audacity] that had at first emboldened him, surges through him and the speaker decides to abandon his original purpose of addressing the Divinity ('ya me volvía sin decirle nada' [I was about to turn away without speaking to him]). However, in the first tercet he considers Christ's dead figure more carefully, pausing upon the meaningful wound in his side ('vi la llaga en el costado' [I saw the wound in his side]). It is then that true understanding of the paschal sacrifice ensues and the rest of the meditation is set out in remarkably compressed terms: 'hablé, lloré, y entré por aquel lado' [I spoke, I wept and I entered through that side]. The speaker has thus engaged in a colloquy, has achieved true repentance and has subsequently taken determined action to renounce his sins and abide by Christ's law by crossing the open 'puerta' [door] of his body. The final affections of the speaker's will ('corazón contrito y humillado' [contrite and humbled heart]) serve as further confirmation that he has concluded a fruitful meditation on which the reader may, again through imitation, model his own.

Poems like 'Fuerza de lágrimas' are nonetheless rare, and more often compositions take the form of an aid to memory, presenting a particular scene in rich detail so that the reader may be able to develop it according to the ability and depth of his own understanding and from where particular affections may subsequently flow. In addition to their clear association with meditative practices, the function of these texts is closely connected to that of Post-Tridentine visual representations conceived to arouse devotion in their viewers, from altarpieces and processional images to paintings and engravings.[20] Lope excels in his highly

---

[20] The Council of Trent in its twenty-fifth session (1563) formally encouraged the use of images to arouse devotion; Norman P. Tanner, ed., *Decrees of the Ecumenical Councils*, 2 vols (London: Sheed and Ward, 1990), II, p. 775.

textured descriptions of all episodes of the Passion, but he is also concerned with other events in Christ's life.[21] The sonnet 'A la visitación' [To the Visitation of the Virgin] — which portrays the expectant Mary's visit to her pregnant cousin Elizabeth and the joy experienced by the unborn John the Baptist — or the romance [ballad] 'Al nacimiento' [To the Birth] —in which Lope depicts in delicate bucolic terms the scene of the annunciation to the shepherds and their subsequent adoration of the holy child— are two of many possible examples of lyrically illustrated biblical events which are recommended by Ignatius for spiritual consideration.[22]

In yet another different kind of meditative text also close to the *Exercises*, Lope concentrates almost solely on affections, setting an example for the reader in how to channel emotions in a spiritually fertile manner through a colloquy with the Divinity. This is particularly obvious in his *Cuatro soliloquios*, 'obra importantísima para cualquier pecador que quisiere apartarse de sus vicios y comenzar vida nueva' [a most important work for any sinner who wants to move away from his vices and start a new life], whose full title eloquently describes the sort of spiritual exercise which the poems expound: *Llanto y lágrimas que hizo arrodillado delante de un crucifijo pidiendo a Dios perdón de sus pecados* [*Lament and Tears Shed by the Author While Kneeling Before a Crucifix Asking God Forgiveness for His Sins*].[23] Both tears and the request for forgiveness are central to Ignatius's programme, but also to these poems, where calls for mercy and outward expressions of sorrow are a constant.[24] In the 'Segundo soliloquio' [Second Soliloquy] the speaker exclaims: 'llorar quiero el desvarío / del tiempo que estuve ausente' [I want to lament the folly of the time I was absent], and is certain that tears will wash away his past sinful words: 'para limpiar la boca / quieren dar agua los ojos' [the eyes want to give water to clean the mouth]; yet full repentance is not easy to achieve and requires personal effort as well as the Divinity's help, a point made by Ignatius, who frequently reiterates the need to strive to grieve, be sad and weep. Lope's speaker underlines his efforts in his first soliloquy:

> Pero ya que me provoco
> en veros con tal dolor
> harto os he dicho, Señor,
> dejadme llorar un poco.[25]

[Given that it rouses me to see you in such pain I have often asked you Lord to let me cry a little]

---

[21] For a number of readings of paschal poems see Mayo, *La lírica sacra*, in particular chapters 2 and 3.

[22] *Rimas sacras*, pp. 240–41 and 535–38 respectively. For Ignatius's recommendations see sections [263] and [265] in any edition of his *Exercises*.

[23] *Cuatro soliloquios*, in *Poesía*, ed. Carreño, VI, p. 353.

[24] Some instances in which the exercitant is advised to request tears and sorrow in the *Exercises* can be found in sections [48], [55], [69] and [78].

[25] *Cuatro soliloquios*, in *Poesía*, ed. Carreño, VI, pp. 355–60, and *Spiritual Exercises* [195].

These different types of poems share a meditative and devotional core in common
with contemporary spiritual guides and, in particular, with the influential *Spiritual
Exercises*.

A different kind of composition which stands quite apart from the devotional
texts so far considered is concerned with the overt political aspects of religion.
Such is the case of the elaborate five-part epic *Corona trágica*, which focuses and
builds on beliefs and stereotypes about the Reformed church and its members
which were widely held in Golden Age Spain. Although far from being a popular
piece likely to attract a substantial audience, the poem is presented as a useful tool
to strengthen the Roman faith of its readers, as it provides 'ejemplo célebre y
estupendo a los verdaderos fieles católicos' [famous and wonderful example for
the true Catholic faithful] against the threat of infectious heretical beliefs.[26] The
book is designed to please and patently preaches to the converted, not least its
dedicatee, Pope Urban VIII, who is liberally praised in the text, predictably as an
example of virtue ('sacro Urbano' [holy Urban]) but less so as a literary model
('divino Orfeo' [divine Orpheus]).[27] *Corona trágica* is a poeticized chronicle of
the life of Mary, Queen of Scots, tightly packed with biblical and historical
references, whose main concern is to illustrate the cruelty and greed of heretical
Anglicans and, by contrast, the moral superiority and steadfastness of virtuous
Catholics. The conflict is epitomized by two contrasting figures, Elizabeth of
England and Mary of Scotland, and narrated from a biased historical perspective
which is the obvious product of militant Post-Tridentine Roman Catholicism.
Lope introduces his subjects as two equals in power, one of whom chose the
perilous route of heresy:

> Una reina os presento, una constante,
> invencible mujer, mujer y fuerte,
> cuyo pecho, católico diamante,
> con otro de crueldad labró la Muerte.[28]

[I give you a constant, invincible woman, a strong woman, whose heart, a Catholic
diamond, was carved by Death with another, cruel diamond.]

Mary, despite her colourful biography, is presented as an example of Christian
constancy and fortitude. Her execution, ordered by Elizabeth and described as
martyrdom, makes her 'invencible' [invincible], almost along the lines of Spain's
own Armada which set sail soon after her death, and confirms her moral
righteousness in the face of what seems to be an immediate defeat but, in Catholic
terms, becomes the ultimate victory. Lope borrows the commonplace but complex

---

[26] 'Aprobación' by Juan de Jáuregui, in *Corona trágica*, *Poesía*, ed. Carreño, V, p. 221.

[27] *Corona trágica*, in *Poesía*, ed. Carreño, V, p. 228. The Pope had composed a poem on the
subject in his youth. Lope's eulogy was duly rewarded by the award of the title of Doctor of
Theology as well as that of 'Caballero del Hábito de San Juan' [Knight of the Order of Saint
John].

[28] *Corona trágica* (I, 65–68), in *Poesía*, ed. Carreño, V, p. 229.

image of the diamond to describe both characters: diamonds possess rare beauty and strength and queens, by definition, are unique within their own countries and their roles demand exemplary virtue. Diamonds can only be scratched or cut by other diamonds and in this case, Elizabeth misuses her own power to inflict fatal damage on Mary's precious, Catholic heart. The English queen, despite having taken an usurped throne, has the potential to be a shining example of virtue by retreating into the Catholic fold but uses her own strength for destruction: a tacit warning for Christians to fulfil one's responsibilities with integrity, in a manner which implicitly echoes both the parable of the talents (Matthew 25:14–30) and that of the minas or pounds (Luke 19:12–27). These aspects may have been considered by some readers but in effect carry little devotional weight.

Although the poem can be slow in narrative terms and seem too subjected to the constraints of pouring open and lavish admiration on its Catholic characters to modern tastes, Lope's poetic ability is in evidence throughout the text in the vivid descriptions and subtly wrought concepts. Some of the English characters are described in a grotesquely damning manner, which is nonetheless eruditely referenced:

> Sangrienta Jezabel, nueva Atalía
> quedó de tronco tal, reinó en Bretaña
> dura esfinge Isabel, cuya porfía
> en sangre el mar de Calidonia baña;
> incestuoso parto de la arpía
> que el Hércules católico de España,
> pudiéndola matar, perdonó presa,
> para manchar la sacrosanta mesa.[29]

[A bloody Jezebel, a new Athaliah who came from such a trunk, Elizabeth, a severe sphinx, reigned over Britain and her obstinacy bathed the Caledonian sea in blood; she was the incestuous issue of the harpy that the Catholic Hercules of Spain, having the opportunity to kill her, forgave and imprisoned, for her to stain the sacred and holy table.]

Through a combination of biblical and mythological references Elizabeth is thus the bloodthirsty and death-bringing daughter of the tyrannical and idolatrous Anne Boleyn and a particularly vicious example of a monstrous, devilish and cruel creature who is contrasted with the heroic and semi-divine figure of the benevolent Spanish king.[30] The majority of the book's readership is unlikely to have drawn much spiritual stimulus from these details or the narrative as a whole. Mary, unlike Isidro, is a foreign and ultimately inaccessible model and although at a religious level the text may serve as warning of sorts to fend off the temptation

---

[29] *Corona trágica* (I, 129–36), in *Poesía*, ed. Carreño, V, p. 231.

[30] Jezebel was an Israelite queen who persuaded her husband Ahab to abandon his God in favour of Baal and ordered the persecution and execution of a number of prophets. Her daughter Athaliah followed her example by turning her husband Jeroham, king of Judah, away from the biblical God. Their stories are recounted in 1 and 2 Kings.

to give any consideration to anything or anyone non-Catholic, its devotional or true guiding content is negligible and stands in stark contrast with the thrust of its political statements.[31] Lope combines the development of the three powers of the soul in various ways throughout his works, sometimes incorporating all of them in the course of a single poem, but more often focusing on the action of a single power and thus preparing the ground for further individual spiritual considerations by the reader.

The small number of works briefly considered in this chapter exemplify in broad terms the main different types of religious poetry produced by Lope. With the exception of *Corona*, spiritual and devotional elements are an essential part of the texts' literary fabric, richly underpinning their formal and narrative structure as well as their imagery. These compositions were appreciated by their contemporary audience not just because of their genuine literary interest, or even because they were 'de Lope' [by Lope] and may have contributed something to his public persona, but because, in addition, they enabled their readers to engage intellectually as well as spiritually at a variety of levels with religious subjects of personal and social relevance. To borrow Fray Diego de Campos's words, the body of Lope's religious lyric 'es una obra de mucho ingenio, trabajo, y agudeza, y muy provechosa para divertir a los inclinados a poesías [...] porque leyendo este libro gozarán de admirables doctrinas, sazonadas a su paladar con el gusto de los versos' [it is a subtle, elaborate and witty work, very profitable for the entertainment of those inclined to poetry [...] because by reading this book they will enjoy admirable doctrines seasoned to their taste with the condiment of verse].[32]

---

[31] Lope's prologue is particularly enlightening in this respect; it also includes many contradictions that undermine his own work as a chronicler (*Corona trágica*, in *Poesía*, ed. Carreño, V, pp. 224–25.

[32] Fray Diego de Campo's *censura* [judgment] to José de Valdivielso, *Exposición parafrástica del Psalterio y de los cánticos del Breviario* (Madrid: Viuda de Alonso Martín, 1623), fol. ¶3ᵛ.

6

Outside In: The Subject(s) at Play in
Las rimas humanas y divinas de Tomé de Burguillos

ISABEL TORRES

I

The speaking subject of Lope de Vega's lyric poetry, the *yo lírico* (poetic 'I'), is uniquely plural.[1] Conceived on the borders of intimacy and imitation,[2] the poetic voice of Lope's early *Rimas humanas* (1602) has a mercurial fluidity which, while responding in part to the ontological uncertainty that is a general characteristic of the baroque aesthetic,[3] exposes a specific crisis of self-representation that pervades Lope's lyric trajectory.[4] Within an artistic environment that interrogates poetic creation as both a synchronic and diachronic process, and where lived experience (*erlebnis*) and art (*poesis*) are inextricably connected,[5] the subject

---

[1] Antonio Carreño has emphasised the fluid nature of Lope's *yo lírico* in his many articles on the poet. See, for instance, '"Amor regalado"/"amor ofendido": las ficciones del yo lírico en las *Rimas* (1609) de Lope de Vega', in *Hispanic Studies in Honour of Geoffrey Ribbans*, ed. Ann L. Mackenzie & Dorothy S. Severin, *Bulletin of Hispanic Studies* Special Homage Volume (Liverpool: Liverpool University Press, 1992), pp. 73–82; 'Los mitos del yo lírico: *Rimas* (1609) de Lope de Vega', *Edad de Oro*, 14 (1995): 55–72; '"Que érades vos lo más sutil del mundo": de *Burguillos* (Lope) y Quevedo', *Calíope*, 8.2 (2002): 25–50 (an expanded version of his earlier 'Los engaños de la escritura: las *Rimas de Tomé de Burguillos* de Lope de Vega', in *Lope de Vega y los orígines del teatro español: Actas del I Congreso Internacional sobre Lope de Vega*, ed. Manuel Criado de Val, Madrid: EDI-6, 1981, pp. 547–63).

[2] Mary Gaylord Randel has argued that a major difficulty in dealing with Lope's lyric poetry is his deliberate engagement with the practice of literary *imitatio*, so that what on the surface is manipulated to seem like intimacy based authority is, in fact, authority based on a creative strategy of imitation. See her 'Proper Language and Language as Property: The Personal Poetics of Lope's *Rimas*', *MLN*, 101.2 (1986): 220–46. See also Arthur Terry, who argues that 'biographical criticism has often done Lope a disservice [...] emphasising the man at the expense of the conscious artist', 'Lope de Vega: Re-Writing a Life', in his *Seventeenth-Century Spanish Poetry: The Power of Artifice* (Cambridge: Cambridge University Press, 1993), pp. 94–121 (p. 95).

[3] See Christine Buci-Glucksmann, *La Folie du voir: une esthétique du virtuel* (Paris: Galilée, 2002), p. 118.

[4] See Isabel Torres, 'Interloping Lope: Transformation and Tomé de Burguillos', *Bulletin of Spanish Studies* (forthcoming), which explores manifestations of transformation in Lope's lyric poetry.

[5] A particularly influential study in this context is Alan S. Trueblood, *Experience and Artistic Expression in Lope de Vega: The Making of 'La Dorotea'* (Cambridge, MA: Harvard University

emerges as a dynamic work in progress. And the subject voice is essentially dialectical, fashioned in tense recognition of authorities that exist outside the self, whether these are literary (predecessors, rivals, even implied readers), generic (the conventional resisting beloved of Petrarchan verse), or indeed socio-political (reflected in themes of disillusionment [*desengaño*] that are historically contingent, or in 'occasional poems' that are tied explicitly to an extraliterary context). Moreover, the emphasis placed on the threat of self-erasure (conveyed as the dark side of artistic creation), and on the ambiguous status of identity forged in language that is on loan to the speaker, suggests that there is more at stake when reading Lope's poetry than the issue of the 'imitative confession'; an even more 'troubling oxymoron' to negotiate.[6] The anxieties underlying the construction of a plural subject carry implications for lyric self-fashioning in the Baroque that are not only aesthetic, but epistemic. The selves that are assembled throughout Lope's verse (whether wearing pastoral, Moorish, Petrarchan, sacred, or even parodic masks) are self-consciously indeterminate, and are received at a multiply determined site of signification; that is, the unsettling interface of private and public.

The *yo lírico* moves along contradictory, interdependent axes, where private self meets public image, where intimate desire negotiates aesthetic or socio-cultural conventions and where creative control is compromised by an awareness of collective consumption. Occasionally these issues coalesce and the speaker's attempts to shape the subject in the text result in the objectification of the subject by the text.[7] This is exemplified in the Petrarchan-inspired poetics of the early *Rimas* where the subject of the poem confronts the problematic configuration of an identity that has no stable core, that is, in fact, the reflection of alterity. In the sonnet 'Era la alegre víspera del día' [It was the joyful eve of the day], the poetic persona recalls his capitulation to love upon first sight of Lucinda (generally identified as the fictional representation of Micaela de Luján, with whom Lope enjoyed a ten-year relationship). The final lines read:

> cuando amor me enseñó la vez primera
> de Lucinda en su sol los ojos bellos,
> y me abrasó como si rayo fuera.
>   Dulce prisión y dulce arder por ellos;
> sin duda que su fuego fue mi esfera,
> que con verme morir descanso en ellos. (lines 9–14)[8]

Press, 1974). See also Randel, who refers to a 'circular critical mode' ('Proper Language', p. 224) that operates when the reader translates Lope's art back into life.

[6] See Paul Julian Smith, *Writing in the Margin: Spanish Literature of the Golden Age* (Oxford: Clarendon, 1988), p. 76. The idea is reiterated by Randel, 'Proper Language', p. 224. Carreño engages critically with the concept in 'Amor regalado', pp. 78–79.

[7] This is particularly pertinent to the prologue sonnet of the *Rimas* (1602). See Torres, 'Interloping Lope', and chapter 5 of this volume.

[8] The poem is no. 34 in Lope de Vega, *Poesía selecta*, ed. Antonio Carreño, 4th edn (Madrid: Cátedra, 2003).

[When love showed me for the first time Lucinda's beautiful eyes [blazing] in her sun [i.e. face], and burned me like a shaft of sunlight. Sweet the imprisonment and sweet my burning desire for them [i.e. her eyes]; their fire was surely my sphere, for seeing myself die in them I find repose.]

The sonnet dialogues deceptively with memory, so that the surface recollection of an intimate first encounter is dependent upon a functioning collective memory for depth of meaning.[9] The poem reveals itself as a misleading medium of reflection, as autonomous art is confirmed in imitative practice. Within this specular context, writing fails entirely to concretise the self, and even the objectification of the subject in the searing gaze of the beloved is a *trompe l'oeil*. The subject speaks from a conventionally fragile narcissistic position, but this illusion of authority is further undermined as the poem projects only a resemblance of self. Paradoxically, the 'other' to whom the poetic subject surrenders autonomy is the self that is reflected in the eye of the beloved and returned in the gaze of the text. The symbolic and literal interconnectedness of the subjective gaze, memory and loss of self ('ver*me mor*ir' [seeing myself die]) leaves the critical issue of self-dissolution in art open and unresolved.

II

Lope de Vega's final lyric collection, the *Rimas humanas y divinas de Tomé de Burguillos*, was published in 1634, though many of the poems had been written and circulated earlier. While it represents a culmination of Lope's previous lyric poetry, drawing attention even in its title to the two collections of secular and sacred poetry published earlier (the *Rimas sacras* had appeared in 1614), the *Burguillos* poems continue to explore the problematic issues of textual authorship and ownership without seeking closure or resolution. On the contrary, with the creation of the false author/speaking subject Burguillos, Lope manipulates the fiction of a fixed self (whose lowly profession, social status, aesthetic views, and even physical appearance are predetermined for the reader),[10] in order to open out meaning in defiance of heterogeneity. The very shape of the collection celebrates diversity: 168 secular sonnets against the 11 sacred, in addition to a burlesque epic, the *Gatomaquia*, which utilises an overarching framework of absurd identification

[9] Following Joseph G. Fucilla, *Estudios sobre el petrarquismo en España* (Madrid: OGRAMA, 1960), p. 236, Carreño (in Lope, *Poesía selecta*) gives Petrarch's sonnet 3, 'Era il giorno ch'al sol si scoloraro', as the inspiration for Lope's sonnet. The play on words in verse 14 recalls the final line of Garcilaso de la Vega's Sonnet X, which reads: 'verme morir entre memorias tristes' [you [i.e. sweet tokens] desired to watch me die among sad memories].

[10] On the question of the historical authenticity of Tomé de Burguillos as presented in the dedication to the Duke of Sessa and in the 'Advertimiento al señor lector', see Carreño, 'Los engaños', pp. 549–50, and Juan Manuel Rozas, 'Burguillos como heterónimo de Lope', *Edad de Oro*, 4 (1985): 139–63 (pp. 144–45). Cecilia Pisos explores the pre-existing life of Tomé and the anti-*culto* dimension of the Burguillos poems with reference to Tomé's intervention in the *Justa poética* of 1620; see 'Burguillos y Góngora frente a frente', *Filología*, 26.1–2 (1993): 167–81.

(cat as human) to counter ideal epic pretensions, both aesthetic and ideological, with deflationary discourse and a marvellously ludic distorsion of verisimilitude. And it is this uniquely complex ludism that unifies the anthology. At the heart of the fiction/reality dialectic that the Burguillos/Lope relationship foregrounds for the reader is a playful process of subjectification which ensures that meaning never coincides with a single consciousness, or with a single poetic voice. This play (of words, of subjects) is the thing that paradoxically liberates a more authentic self, which promotes a flawed authoritative centre in order to demonstrate the resilience of authority in representation.

As I have argued elsewhere, the false Burguillos subject is much more dynamic than an alter-ego, pseudonym, or mask.[11] And it lacks, as Rozas acknowledges, the psychological distance to assume completely the role of heteronym.[12] There is a controlling aspect to Lope's role that García Santo-Tomás captures in his depiction of Burguillos as a ventriloquist's dummy,[13] but unless qualified, such an image relegates the reader to an overly passive position which denies parody the dynamic that makes it tick. Without the sense of a secret conspiratorial smile passing between writer and reader, the characteristic strategies of parody (inversions and distortions of referents, the infringement of literary and social decorum, the redeployment of literary conventions and forms in a new context) amount only to a massive communicative misfire.[14] The success of the parodic-burlesque text[15] depends on the reader recognising, and finding humour in, the discrepancy between absurd material representations and idealised authoritative discourses. Effective communication is often achieved in the transference of

---

[11] Torres, 'Interloping Lope'.

[12] See 'Burguillos como heterónimo', pp. 142–43. Rozas's comments are expanded in the Introduction to the most recent edition of the anthology. Engaging with Pessoa's concept of the heteronym to map out the co-ordinates of the role, he concludes that Burguillos is a conflicted heteronym with a problematic autobiographical dimension; see Lope de Vega, *Rimas humanas y divinas del licenciado Tomé de Burguillos*, ed. Juan Manuel Rozas & Jesús Cañas Murillo (Madrid: Castalia, 2004), pp. 34–35. All references to the *Burguillos* poems are taken from this edition.

[13] See 'Lope, ventrílocuo de Lope: capital social, capital cultural y estrategia literaria en las *Rimas de Tomé de Burguillos* (1634)', *Bulletin of Hispanic Studies* (Glasgow), 77.4 (2000): 287–303, an article which reads the poems as emanating from the disenchanted voice of a marginalised poet reviewing his life and his work.

[14] Rose's discussion of parody emphasises the transmutation of textual remnants in a new context, what she refers to as 'the comic refunctioning of preformed linguistic or artistic material'; see Margaret A. Rose, *Parody: Ancient, Modern, and Post-Modern* (Cambridge: Cambridge University Press, 1993), p. 52. See also Linda Hutcheon, *A Theory of Parody: The Teachings of Twentieth-Century Art Forms* (New York & London: Methuen, 1985), who demonstrates that, in allowing for the transfer and reorganisation of the past in the present text, parody paradoxically ensures the continued existence of the conventions being parodied (pp. 4–10).

[15] I use the compound term in recognition of the symbiotic relationship which exists between burlesque and parody, notwithstanding the fact that burlesque suggests an attitude of mockery and ridicule not necessarily pertinent in parody. For a succinct review of the attempts that have been made to classify burlesque in relation to cross-over genres such as parody, see Kimberly Contag, *Mockery in Spanish Golden Age Literature: Analysis of Burlesque Representation* (Lanham, MD & London: University Press of America, 1996), pp. 29–36, and also Rose, *Parody*, chapter 2, 'Distinguishing Parody from Related Forms'.

absurdity from the materialistic counter-text to the idealistic targets being mocked. In this parodic context, the Burguillos subject is a critical intervening figure between writer and reader, a catalyst that opens up a space for critique, but also for renewal.

Parody's preference for the material over the ideal is taken to literal extremes in the *Burguillos* poems. The illusion of the subject is constructed in materiality. In contrast to the elusive 'yo' of the early *Rimas*, who escapes us in the to-ing and fro-ing of art and biography, or the Gongorist subject's slippage into syntactical acrobatics that support aggressively open signifiers, Burguillos is grounded in the trivia of mundane life, both his own and the reader's.[16] Whereas in the *Soledades* [*Solitudes*], Góngora creates a protagonist/speaker who is entirely emptied of identity (without name, place, or single perspective), who is a defiant representation of the ambiguous relationship between the early modern subject and his environment, Lope de Vega insists on the who, what, where and when of his counterfeit subject, thus extending ambiguity into ambivalence. While ambiguous identity allows for the potential cancelling out of one authority by another (the anxiety which always underpins emulative poetics), a deliberately constructed ambivalent subject permits oppositional identities to co-exist and for authority to waver between them, and even, on occasions, to embrace both. Thus, depending on the poem in question, the reader identifies the 'yo' of the text as Tomé, or as Tomé masking Lope, or as Lope masking Tomé, or as the voice of Lope de Vega himself (whether constructed or real).

The poems and prose texts that introduce the 1634 collection correspond to conventional introductory formulae, that is, approbations, a dedication, a prologue to the reader and poetic eulogies. In the literary works published in the period these paratexts (authored by, addressed to, and referencing, real people) have an inevitable liminal quality, quite literally located on the threshold between life and art. The preliminary material that introduces the *Burguillos* poems, however, operates wholly within the parodic framework of the collection, giving the authorising border an enhanced plasticity and preparing the reader for the playfully subversive performance of subjectivity that will follow. Thus Valdivieso's approbation, which confirms the authorship of Tomé de Burguillos, is followed by that of Francisco de Quevedo, who authorises Tomé in the fragile linguistic space of the work's title, but legitimises the text by comparing its style to that of Frey Lope Félix de Vega Carpio. Lope's own dedication to the Duke of Sessa forges a 'yo' that speaks in the name of Tomé, followed by a preface to the reader which challenges assumptions that Burguillos is not actually real. The reader, who may be sceptical of fragile or circumstantial linguistic evidence (the brief biography, character sketch and physical description) is directed for corroboration to a portrait of Burguillos, which is not in itself authentic, but a copy of a canvas

---

[16] In a recent reading of the *Burguillos* anthology Adrián Pérez-Boluda explores how the poet creates a poetics of erotic *costumbrismo* through sensualising elements of prosaic reality; see 'Costumbrismo erótico y parodia antipetrarquista en el *Tomé de Burguillos* de Lope de Vega', *Calíope*, 12 (2006): 57–75.

painted by the artist Francisco Ribalta.[17] The self-portrait is, of course, of Lope,
laurel-wreathed and subverting the rejection of emblematic ideality that
characterises the materialistic Burguillos, who prefers olives as fruit over laurel as
symbol, and is wreathed always in thyme ('que más quiere aceitunas que laureles /
y siempre se corona de tomillos' [who prefers olives to bay leaves and is always
wreathed in thyme]). These verses close out a sonnet, ostensibly written by El
Conde Claros and addressed to Tomé, in which three subjects are at play in a
variegated voice. In a fusion of empirical person and poetic persona, Lope de
Vega becomes Claros, a manoeuvre that allows him to confirm his anti-*culto*
poetics, to absent (and present) Góngora from a subjective canonical tradition, and
to introduce his latest self-incarnation, a burlesquing Burguillos, as a worthy
successor to Garcilaso de la Vega and to Camoes. So before the reader enters
Tomé/Lope's alternative world, ambivalent subjectivity has been established and
polyvalence conveyed as its natural correlative.

The first of four programmatic sonnets reveals the three guiding principles of
the collection (a critique of Gongorist 'new poetry'; literary recreation; and a
preoccupation with time that was integral to the disillusioned literature of the
period),[18] but gives clear priority to the redeployment of courtly love/Petrarchan
topoi in a new burlesque disposition:

> oíd de un caos la materia prima,
> no culta como cifras de receta,
> que en lengua pura, fácil, limpia y neta,
> yo invento, Amor escribe, el tiempo lima. (lines 5–8)

[Listen to the raw material of chaos [i.e. poetry derived from the suffering of
unrequited love], not contrived [lit. 'not learned', with an aural pun suggesting 'not
hidden'] like prescription codes, for in language that is pure and simple, clean and
clear, I invent, Love writes, time polishes [away].]

The diminutive *ars poetica* of line 7 resonates with the terms of the *claros*/*cultos*
literary polemic and inserts Lope de Vega right into the centre of Tomé's opening
poem, a symbolic underlining of what might be considered the objective of the
entire anthology — an elderly Lope's attempts to reclaim the centre of Spanish
poetics.[19] But the process of poetic creation, as it is conveyed here, is rooted in an

---

[17] Aurora Egido, citing Pierre Civil, draws our attention to the evolving, controlled self-
portraits of Lope from the publication of the *Arcadia* in 1598; see 'Escritura y poesía: Lope al pie
de la letra', *Edad de Oro*, 14 (1995): 121–49 (p. 136). See also Antonio Sánchez Jiménez, *Lope
pintado por sí mismo: mito e imagen del autor en la poesía de Lope de Vega Carpio* (Woodbridge:
Tamesis, 2006) which offers the first substantial analysis of an evolving self-fashioning in Lope's
work, taking visual representation into account throughout (the Burguillos 'portrait' is discussed in
chapter 5).

[18] As noted by García Santo-Tomás, 'Lope, ventrílocuo de Lope', pp. 289–90.

[19] See also Sonnet 147, addressed to a Gongorist poet 'Libio', especially lines 5–8, where
Lope's presence is metaphorical but still central: 'Si vos, imperceptible, si remoto, / yo, blando,
fácil, elegante y puro; / tan claro escribo como vos escuro; / la vega es llana y intrincado el soto'
[Your style is [lit. you are] incomprehensible, distant, mine is [lit. I am] soft, easy, elegant and

ambivalent subject whose control over poetic invention is further compromised by the ambiguous role played by time (operating as a force for improvement, but also of erosion), and by an all too familiar subject matter (love).[20] It is true, as Rozas and others have suggested, that the prevalent view of the *Burguillos* poems as an 'anti-*canzoniere*' to the washerwoman Juana is fallacious (in that only 34 of the 168 compositions treat the amorous theme),[21] but it is equally true that Lope had a hand in guiding the fallacy. Aside from the fact that there are four programmatic sonnets instead of the usual one, and that all four turn on Burguillos' triple submission to love, to Juana and to love poetry, Lope had already proclaimed Juana as the subject of the anthology in the prologue (albeit misleadingly). In fact, he undermines Juana's identity as material subject by suggesting that her vulgar reality may be artificially constructed, that 'Juana' is a deceptive sign, a common label denoting a much loftier lady, a burlesque deflation of conventional poetic disguises. 'Juana', therefore, is Tomé's shepherdess, but extracted from the privileged site of the fertile *locus amoenus* and relocated to the banks of the dried-up Manzanares. She is no more real than, and as real as, Lope de Vega's Filis, Amarilis, Belisa, Camila Lucinda and Marfisa. One of the great and deliberate ironies of the anthology is that the ironic distance that enables the deconstructive voice of parody is not very distant after all. The poetic tradition parodied in the Juana poems not only includes Lope as former practitioner, but informs the practice that produces the parody.

III

The second sonnet of the collection encourages us to contemplate this poetic methodology in action: to confront the deceptive feigning that is involved in the transformation of life into art, a strategy the speaker simultaneously rejects and reinforces:

pure; my writing is as clear as yours is obscure; mine a flat meadow, and yours a tangled grove]. There is a clear pun on the author's name in 'vega', while opinion is divided over whether 'soto' is a veiled reference to the writer Pedro Soto de Rojas — a Gongorist poet but also a friend of Lope's (Lope wrote the eulogy which precedes Soto's 1623 anthology, *Desengaño de amor en rimas*).

[20] Daniel L. Heiple refers to these verses to support his argument that Lope's originality lies in great part in his view of poetry as an act of creation — invention over imitation; see 'Lope's Arte poética', in *Renaissance and Golden Age Essays in Honor of D. W. McPheeters*, ed. Bruno M. Damiani (Potomac, MD: Scripta Humanistica, 1986), pp. 106–19 (p. 118).

[21] See Rozas, 'Burguillos como heterónimo', pp. 145–46. Critical responses to Lope's poetry in general have been somewhat scant and with a tendency towards partial emphases, in comparison to the reception enjoyed by his drama. Responses to the *Burguillos* poems have been even fewer, if not further between. There are two main approaches: the text as parodic anti-text with an emphasis on 'desengaño amoroso y literario' (Carreño, in Lope, *Poesía selecta*, p. 381, and also Trueblood, *Experience*, p. 162); an historico-biographical approach which reads the poems in the context of the issues informing Lope's *ciclo de senectute* (e.g. Rozas & Cañas Murillo, in Lope, *Rimas*, pp. 20–21, and Felipe B. Pedraza Jiménez, 'El desengaño barroco en las *Rimas de Tomé de Burguillos*', *Anuario de Filología*, 4 (1978): 391–418).

Celebró de Amarilis la hermosura
Virgilio en su Bucólica divina,
Propercio de su Cintia, y de Corina
Ovidio en oro, en rosa, en nieve pura;
    Catulo de su Lesbia la escultura
a la inmortalidad pórfido inclina;
Petrarca, por el mundo peregrina,
constituyó de Laura la figura;
    yo, pues Amor me manda que presuma
de la humilde prisión de tus cabellos,
poeta montañés, con ruda pluma,
    Juana, celebraré tus ojos bellos:
que vale más de tu jabón la espuma
que todas ellas y que todos ellos.

[Virgil celebrated the beauty of Amarilis in his Eclogues divine [both work and lady]; Propertius celebrated Cynthia, and Ovid Corinna, in gold, in rose, and pure white snow; Catullus celebrated Lesbia's sculpture, thereby immortalising marble; Petrarch fashioned Laura's face, famous throughout the world; Now since I, a Cantabrian poet, with a primitive pen, am told by Love to boast that I am humbly bound by your hair [lit. 'boast of the humble prison of your hair'], Juana, I will celebrate your beautiful eyes; for the foam from your soap is worth more than all of them —women and writers.]

The poem pushes several intertextual buttons in a carefully crafted sequential sonnet that is more a celebration of subjective creativity based on reality than an attempt to forge idealistic associations. Meaning is derived in great part from the poem's relationship to the prior texts, literary predecessors and female subjects listed in the quatrains, but rather than casting doubt on the poem's autonomy, or uniqueness, deviance from conventional models serves to legitimise the speaker's emulative stance. A sense of continuity and rupture informs the emergence of the speaker in the tercets, where the self is textured in tense recognition of its reliance on the conventional rhetoric of amorous poetry, but also on an innovative impulse that can breathe new life into old images. Thus the poem acknowledges the inadequacy of the stereotypes it cannot do without, reiterating the speaker's subservience to a higher authority, employing conventional symbols of female power and beauty — hair and eyes — and dedicating the subject voice to a celebratory poetics. But whereas conventional motifs remain unchallenged in the following dedicatory sonnet, no. 3 (ice and fire, salamander, siren, moth and flame), the final tercet of Sonnet 2 confidently punctures Petrarchan pretensions. The meta-artistic finale has multiple antagonists: Juana, the speaker, the poetry, against a whole poetic legacy, Classical and vernacular. Ultimately the latter is deflated through its objectification in a poetics of experience, in which originality of concept and style is seen to owe something to origins that are non-literary, to the modest beginnings of the subject voice and the mundane activity of the subject matter. And there is an alternative splendour in this grounding. For the foam that in other aesthetic contexts might denote the emergence of water nymphs, the birth of Venus, or the fluid border of land and sea,[22] is not so much re-shaped in Tomé's poem as re-directed. In this transformed and transforming context a whole world of connotations converge and survive, but are submerged in Juana's suds.

The redeployment of conventional archetypes is also a feature of Sonnet 7, 'Bien puedo yo pintar una hermosura' [I am more than capable of depicting beauty], a poem which revels in its ambivalent subjects. The speaker is a dominant presence from the outset, and on this occasion has a single antagonist in the emulative arena, none other than Lope de Vega himself. Thus lyric self-creation in the present involves a confrontation with plural poetic selves of the past (lyric and pastoral), and depends on the agency of an informed and dynamic reader to realise manipulated life/art connections (the most obvious being the representation of Elena Osorio as Helen of Troy, or Filis). The poem authorises transgression on all levels, temporal, spatial and cognitive, ultimately proclaiming subjective creativity to know no bounds. The writer's freedom to rewrite reality can even transform Juana: 'basta que para mí tan linda seas' [It's enough that I find you so beautiful]. Whether or not Juana's beauty has the power to transform the world around her is the starting point of Sonnet 148. The poem opens in similar vein to no. 10, 'Describe un monte sin qué ni para qué' [He describes a mountain for no good reason], which engages in extreme terms with the reader's expectations of an erotic *locus amoenus*. Both poems open out hyperbolically into familiar idyllic territory, only to flummox the reader in a contrived anti-climax. Just as the speaker of no. 10 acknowledges that nothing ever happened to him (or, indeed, could happen to him) in a landscape too artificial to be true, the flowers and nightingales of no. 148 acquire a more authentic role, a linguistic alternative to stale rhetoric in the perspective of the speaking subject:

> Aunque decir que entonces florecieron,
> y por ella cantaron ruiseñores,
> será mentira, porque no lo hicieron.
>   Pero es verdad que, en viendo sus colores,
> a mí me pareció que se rieron
> selvas, aves, cristal, campos y flores. (9–14)

[Although I'd be lying if I said that fields flowered and nightingales sang for her, because they didn't. But truth be told, it seemed to me that the sight of her colours made woods, birds, silver streams, fields and flowers laugh.]

The triumph of the ending, however, is also its undoing. Identity constructed in and through the language of another will only ever acquire a partial, and subjective, truth.

The intentionality of language that emerges from a non-neutral frame of reference has ramifications for lyric self-creation that are both positive and

---

[22] Carreño provides a more detailed discussion of the symbolic associations of 'espuma' [foam], but reads the ending of the poem in terms of a deconstruction of antecedents; see 'Los engaños de la escritura', p. 555.

negative. On the one hand, language has the power to transform *ad infinitum* (so in Sonnet 115 Burguillos can imagine himself 'Paulo Emilio', or 'Burguitomico', simply by naming himself differently), but it also functions as a subjective interpretation of reality, rather than as a mimetic match. Thus Burguillos's self-transforming vision of Sonnet 115 is driven by a desire for self-validation through the assumption of alterity (in this case, identification with Classical authorities, or with foreignness); and a sparrow can become a goldfinch as a reward for intimacy with Juana (no. 101), only to be reinstated as a vile sparrow when that intimacy is abused (no. 102). Interpretation too is an intentional activity. In Sonnet 86, for instance, Juana's resistance to Tomé's attempts to constitute her in borrowed words is determined as much by her rejection of the speaker as by her rejection of the speech. The tercets read:

> Si digo que es la hermosa Policena
> dice que miento, porque no es troyana,
> ni griega si la igualo con Elena.
>   Eres hircana tigre, hermosa Juana;
> mas, ¡ay!, que aun para tigre no era buena,
> pues, siendo de Madrid, no fuera hircana. (9–14)

[If I refer to her as beautiful Polyxena, she says that I lie, because she is not Trojan, nor Greek if I compare her to Helen. You are a Hyrcanian tiger, beautiful Juana; but no, she wasn't good enough even to be a tiger, for being from Madrid she could never be Hyrcanian.]

Juana's opposition is presented as a desire for subjectively valid criteria and exposes the artificiality of a Petrarchan 'one size fits all' analogical formula. Although her voice is ventriloquised in the subject speaker's complaints, hers is the more effective assertion of self. The male speaking subject projects only a shadow of Lope's former Petrarchan self, and lacks linguistic mastery in the face of Juana's deliberately literal misreading of signs. In sonnets such as this one language is revealed as a variable commodity, and the gap between experience and articulation has implications for (and beyond) the self. Metalinguistic devices foreground the slippage between word and thing, and underline the flawed sense of self that is constructed on that slippery surface. Of course, underlying the entire collection is the perfectly imperfect example of the representational nature of self-invention, the ambivalent subject(s) that is/are Tomé/Lope.

Just as metalanguage and metadrama are interdependent, mutually reinforcing strategies of Lope's theatre, the *yo lírico* of the *Burguillos* poems performs the self in a highly theatricalised poetic environment.[23] The performative force of

---

[23] Demoor has remarked upon the theatricality involved in self-fashioning in language, linking it to Judith Butler's concept of performativity; see Marysa Demoor, ed., *Marketing the Author: Authorial Personae, Narrative Selves and Self-Fashioning, 1880–1930* (Basingstoke: Palgrave Macmillan, 2004), p. 14. Although the function of theatricality has yet to be fully explored in the *Burguillos* poems, its presence has been noted. See, among others, Trueblood, *Experience,* p. 15, and Rozas, 'Burguillos como heterónimo de Lope', p. 140, where he concludes that the use of the

these poems is often located not in the subject's reiteration of established linguistic contexts, but in its sudden deviance from them. This is particularly true of self-referential sonnets such as no. 9, 'Érase el mes de más hermosos días' [It was the month when days are at their most beautiful], which returns to the topos of 'Era la alegre víspera del día' [It was the joyful eve of the day] to rewrite the speaker's first encounter with the beloved. What is presented in the quatrains as the recollection of a biographical experience is turned on its head in line 9: 'No salió malo este versillo octavo' [This eighth wee line didn't turn out so badly]. The poem now presents itself as an event, the act of poetic creation. And as the reader is drawn in, and made aware of the reflective, modifying process that underlies art, the poem becomes a theatricalised site of experimentation where speaker, text and reader interact. Mascia notes that the speaker 'takes a step back after completing the task to admire it', and refers us back to Pedraza Jiménez's analysis of the relationship between poet and finished product.[24] But the chronology that is deceptive. The speaker steps in, as well as back, very much *in medias res*. His interruption in line 9 functions like an anti-text, breaking the illusion of the poem and splitting both the subject voice and the frame of the sonnet. The ending actually conveys the middle of a writing process and the reader is offered a double resolution — the one that is read and the one that is anticipated. The tercets of this sonnet make literal the traditional notion of lyric as 'utterance overheard';[25] in this case the reader overhears the speaker, who pretends to talk to himself.

On occasions the stage of the sonnet, and the gaze of the reader, are stretched by the inclusion of other speakers, or other characters, real or imagined. The subject speaker's relationship to them is often determined by an attitude of antipathy based on envy. Indeed, the spectre of envy shrouds the collection, despite the distancing effect of Burguillos' ironic perspective and the parodic prism through which the material is passed. Conventionally justified as the dark underbelly of authentic passion (see, for instance, nos 12, 144 and 151), envy also operates in an enhanced role as a powerful psychological catalyst that motivates attacks on degenerate nobility, misguided patronage and inept followers of Góngora.[26] What all these poetic manifestations have in common is a fractured subject who confronts in the experience of another, or others, the artistic accolades or erotic intimacy that might make self-realisation possible. This is very clearly illustrated in Sonnet 20, 'Envidia a un sastre que tomaba la medida de un

heteronym, like the play within the play, should be considered within the context of Baroque perspectivism.

[24] See Mark J. Mascia, 'To Live Vicariously Through Literature: Lope de Vega and his Alter-Ego in the Sonnets of the *Rimas humanas y divinas del licenciado Tomé de Burguillos*', *Romance Studies*, 19.1 (2001): 1–15 (p. 6).

[25] See Northrop Frye, *Anatomy of Criticism: Four Essays* (Princeton, NJ: Princeton University Press, 1957; repr. New York: Atheneum, 1965), p. 246.

[26] Rozas and Cañas Murillo make a strong case for reading many of the *Burguillos* sonnets, as well as aspects of the *Gatomaquia*, in the context of Lope's rivalry with the younger, Gongorist writer José Pellicer de Tovar, who obtained the post of *cronista real* (Royal Chronicler) in 1629. Lope lost out for the third time, having sought the position in 1611 and 1620. See *Rimas humanas y divinas*, ed. Rozas & Cañas Murillo, pp. 40–50.

vestido a una dama' [He envies a tailor measuring a lady for a dress], which dramatises anxieties of identity (artistic and amorous) within a highly charged erotic context:[27]

> Más eres sol que sastre (¡extraño caso!),
> Jaime, pues sólo el sol dicen que ha sido
> quien a la aurora le cortó vestido
> con randas de oro, en turquesado raso.
>   Tú le mides el pecho, aunque de paso,
> y yo en mis versos mis desdichas mido
> cortando galas en papel perdido,
> a manera de sastre del Parnaso.
>   Este soneto, Jaime, cosa es clara,
> que si dijese aquí lastre o arrastre
> el consonante dice en lo que para.
>   Mas si envidiar un sastre no es desastre,
> cuando te acerques a su hermosa cara,
> sé tú el poeta y déjame ser sastre.

[You are more a sun than a tailor, Jaime (a strange affair!), for they say that only the sun has cut out the dawn's clothes, in dark blue satin, with a lace trimming in gold. You measure her breast, although just in passing, and I measure out my sorrow in verse, cutting out my 'Sunday best' in waste paper [lit. cutting finery in wasted paper], like a tailor from Parnassus. One thing is clear about this sonnet, Jaime, suppose I were to say in line nine 'sailor' or 'gaolor' [lit. 'burden' and 'dragging,' but sound has priority over meaning here], the ending would come from the rhyme. But if envying a tailor doesn't spell failure, when you draw near to her beautiful face, you be the poet and let me take your place.]

Mascia offers a convincing reading of the sonnet, emphasising the specifically linguistic elements that give the text its metapoetic character, but sees little connection between the poem itself and its title.[28] This stance rather undercuts his appreciation of the ludic quality of the poem, since the linguistic game at play revolves around the subjective force exerted upon the term 'sastre' [tailor] by the lyric subject who operates under the influence of an erotic 'envidia' [envy].[29] The voyeuristic dimension of the poem is three-dimensionally transgressive: the

---

[27] The idea of the self as a controlling presence, but partially constructed, is a feature also of the *manso* sonnets of the early secular *Rimas*. Interpretation of the triangular relationship of *pastor/dueño* (speaker), *manso* (woman) and *mayoral extraño* (rival in love), conveyed in sexually suggestive language, is complicated by an intervening real-life triangle: Lope, Elena Osorio and Francisco Perrenot de Granvela. See Trueblood, *Experience*, pp. 104–14; Randel, 'Proper Language', pp. 234–37.

[28] See 'To Live Vicariously Through Language', pp. 7–8.

[29] See also in this context Sonnet 97, in which the speaker would change places with a flea who has the good fortune to bite Leonor's breasts. R. O. Jones situates Lope's poem at the intersection of two poetic traditions, French (salacious flea poems) and Italian (daring butterfly poems); see 'Renaissance Butterfly, Mannerist Flea: Tradition and Change in Renaissance Poetry', *MLN*, 80.2 (1965): 166–84.

reader's perception is guided by the subjective perspective of the speaker, whose desiring gaze transforms the mundane actions of the third-party male into a transgression of socially acceptable male/female relations.[30] The *yo lírico* is defined by the fact that it is and it is not 'sastre'. Tailor-made metaphors, however bizarre, are unproblematic. So within the illusion of the poem 'sastre' is 'sol' [sun], the prosaic measuring of the lady acquires the sensual enhancement of a mythological daybreak, and rhyming patterns almost write themselves into art. But within the concrete setting of the text the speaker cannot effect the most important transformation: to change places with the other and have access to the object of his desire. Thus words, however dynamically indeterminate, fail to bridge the gap between observation and action, art and life.

To some extent, Lope's theatricalised sonnets anticipate the modernist model of the dramatic monologue, but obviously without its depersonalised objective. For instead of masking subjectivity, the ambivalence at the heart of the *Burguillos* poems actually exposes the subject to a scrutiny that plays with personal poetics. In a series of dialogue poems (including one addressed to Francisco de Quevedo, no. 156), which emphasise speech as action and seem to operate within and beyond our understanding of the dramatic monologue, the reader is required to reconstruct a context in which the speaker emerges as a character, and to interpret the attitudes of the speaker as dramatised in the text.[31] But rather than promoting the notion of a free subjectivity,[32] sonnets such as 136, 'Discúlpase con Lope de Vega de su estilo' [He apologises to Lope de Vega for his style], actually connect and confuse alter ego and ego:[33]

> Lope, yo quiero hablar con vos de veras,
> y escribiros en verso numeroso,
> que me dicen que estáis de mí quejoso,
> porque doy en seguir musas rateras.

---

[30] For a more detailed reading of the erotic environment of the poem, see Pérez-Boluda, 'Costumbrismo erótico', pp. 68–69.

[31] The strategy of the dramatic monologue within contemporary Spanish poetry is analysed by Luís Martín-Estudillo, 'El sujeto (a)lírico en la poesía española contemporánea y su trasfondo barroco', *Hispanic Review*, 73.3 (2005): 351–70 (esp. pp. 363–66).

[32] For a succinct and lucid exploration of the modern lyric that includes a generic model which promotes depersonalised subjectivity, see Jonathan Culler, 'The Modern Lyric: Generic Continuity and Critical Practice', in *The Comparative Perspective on Literature: Approaches to Theory and Practice*, ed. Clayton Koelb & Susan Noakes (Ithaca & London: Cornell University Press, 1988), pp. 284–99.

[33] See also Sonnet 28, 'Cortando la pluma, hablan los dos' [Cutting the pen, both speak], where the dialogue form is explicitly exploited to draw together the principal themes of the collection (literary and social criticism) within an ambivalent arena of baroque multiperspectivism. Aurora Egido traces the trajectory of Lope's dialogue with his own work and situates the reiterations of 'pluma' within this, noting that the dialogue intensifies in the *Burguillos* poems and culminates in Sonnet 28. She follows Rozas in associating the ironic tone of the poem with Lope's disappointment at losing out to Pellicer in his bid for the post of *cronista real*; see Egido, 'Escritura y poesía', esp. pp. 142–49, and Rozas, 'Burguillos como heterónimo', p. 153.

> Agora invocaré las verdaderas,
> aunque os sea (que sois escrupuloso)
> con tanta metafísica enfadoso,
> y tantas categóricas quimeras.
>   Comienzo pues: 'Oh tú que en la risueña
> Aurora imprimes la celeste llama,
> que la soberbia de Faetón despeña!'
>   Mas, perdonadme, Lope, que me llama
> desgreñada una Musa de estameña,
> celosa del tabí de vuestra fama.

[Lope, I want to have a serious word with you, and write to you in elevated verse, for I hear that you are annoyed with me because I've succumbed to a lowly, common muse. Now I will invoke the true muse, although (being so meticulous), you may find all the metaphysics and uncompromising fantasy a bit tedious. So I begin: 'Oh you whose heavenly light [lit. 'flame'] is imprinted on the blissful dawn, whom proud Phaeton casts down …! But forgive me, Lope, for I am called away by a dishevelled Muse in serge, jealous of your 'taffeta-wearing' fame.]

On the surface the poem deals with the speaker's (Tomé's) desire for poetic authentification from a disapproving poetic authority (Lope de Vega).[34] But its dialogical quality has little depth. The poem's function is narcissistic, operating as a mirror in which the divided subject (Tomé/Lope) can contemplate and idolise the poetic self. This self will be made complete through a compromised act of poetic creation, that is, by Tomé's appropriation of an alternative (more genuine) muse in order to produce a new text in imitation of, and addressed to, Lope de Vega. The sonnet/mirror thus becomes a locus of deception, ruptured in the first tercet by Tomé's incompetent grappling with inherited topoi. Tomé's sonnet within the sonnet, or rather, partially constructed quatrain within the tercet, breaks the frame and, as in Sonnet 9, makes the sonnet form itself the subject of the poem. The text plays beautifully with a concept of creative process, but on this occasion one that is doomed to failure. It is significant that Tomé's improvised, appropriated voice cannot convince even its creator. Tomé seeks reconciliation with his own muse (presented as authorial submission in the ludic tradition of the poetological dramas of Classical elegy)[35] and with Lope, now in his favourite role as established poet. In the final analysis, Tomé's failure to imitate is converted into a display of poetic invention, securely fastened to the 'fama' of Lope de Vega. The concept of 'envidia' undergoes a positive transferral of value, now functioning as a barometer of Lope de Vega's renown.

---

[34] See also the companion sonnet, no. 137, also addressed to Lope. The sonnet ends with an ironic defence of burlesque poetry which is based on literary exemplum, illiterate reception and 'propio gusto' — an 'in' joke that directs self-validation against the self.

[35] See, for instance, Ovid's playful encounter with Cupid in the prologue poem of the first book of *Amores*, or the same deity's dominance over Propertius in the *Elegies*, 1, 1, 3–4.

IV

In the final sonnet of the secular poems, subject splitting becomes a question of mind over matter. The *yo lírico* who addresses the 'sacras luces del cielo' [sacred lights of heaven] (no. 161), that is, the stars, emerges unambiguously from the psyche of Lope de Vega, while Tomé is masked in metonym as an alternative, stylistic aberration, the 'otra lira' [other lyre] that is simultaneously self-centred and self-mocking but, ironically, not self-effacing. The sonnet synthesises the unsettling preoccupations of Lope's late work, [36] especially the lack of 'mecenazgo' [patronage], but the final tercet rises above the ramifications of 'envidia', concretising the poet's personal space, and liberating a resilient voice outside the reach of implied detractors. The lyric speaker's defiant self-assertion is expressed in the realistic terms of an idealised intellectual comfort zone: poetry, art and nature:

> Mas tengo un bien en tantos disfavores,
> que no es posible que la envidia mire:
> dos libros, tres pinturas, cuatro flores. (12–14)

[But one thing consoles me having lost your [the stars'] favour, that envy cannot touch two books, three paintings, four flowers.]

It is not so much that the Burguillos mask slips in this poem, but rather that its reconfiguration as theme paradoxically reinforces its burlesque purpose.

On other occasions, the subject play is provocatively presented in the very title of the poem. For instance, no. 124 informs the reader: 'parece que habla de veras' [he appears to speak 'for real']. This multilayered sonnet fuses the fluid identifications of Classical mythology and the conventional analogical infrastructure of amorous lyric to blur the boundaries between appearance and reality, art and life.[37] The familiar linguistic and symbolic discourse of the Trojan war, and the ill-fated love affair between Dido and Aeneas, is elucidated to reflect a fictional emotional situation whose experiential template is Lope's affair with Elena Osorio. The title of this poem asks the reader to accept an unstable Burguillos speaker for a text that flaunts outrageously its Lope credentials.[38]

But there are magnificent moments too when subject ambivalence is abandoned entirely, when the game is off, and the lyric voice of the sonnet transcends the anthology's parodic frame. A perfect example is Sonnet 78, entitled: 'Que al amor verdadero no le olvidan el tiempo ni la muerte. Escribe en seso' [Neither time nor

---

[36] On this sonnet as epilogue see Juan Manual Rozas, '"Sacras luzes del cielo": el soneto 161 de Burguillos, un epifonema de sus *Rimas humanas y divinas* y de la obra poética de Lope', ed. Jesús Cañas Murillo, *Anuario de Lope de Vega*, 6 (2000): 229–34.

[37] See also Sonnets 13 and 22, on the myths of Paris and Apollo/Daphne respectively, in which a similar strategy is employed. For a study of the lyric subject's recreation in mythological personae throughout the *Burguillos* poems, see Carreño, 'Los mitos del yo lírico'.

[38] For the presence of the Troy motif in the *Rimas humanas* (1602), see Trueblood, *Experience*, pp. 92–104.

death forget true love. He writes in sound mind]. The signifying universe of this poem spins on qualifications. The beloved is dead, but lives on in the speaker. The speaker is alive, but totally disoriented by images of lost love. The present is resolved, but inhabited by the vivid presence of the past. Memory is intimate, and powerfully confessional,[39] but also plays a crucial role in the creative process that extends beyond the private, opening up pre- and inter-textual channels that connect writer, reader, text and prior texts. Thus 'polvo' [dust] is a sign constantly in motion, signifying the definitive absence of the beloved (1); and the speaker's open-ended process of self-dissolution (9–11); but also recalling the eternalising poetics of Propertius (*Elegies*, 1, 19; 2. 13[b]) and the monumental grandeur of Quevedo's 'polvo enamorado' [enamoured dust]. The speaker's plea for silence serves only to bring the scattered conceits of Lope's early love poetry to the surface of a text that, once again, centres on the subject's capacity for poetic self-renewal. Burguillos, speaking 'en seso', or not, is always Lope *Fénix*.

It is fitting that the last ambivalent word on Lope's final lyric anthology should go to the unambiguous poet. Sonnet 78 reads:

> Resuelta en polvo ya, mas siempre hermosa,
> sin dejarme vivir, vive serena
> aquella luz, que fue mi gloria y pena,
> y me hace guerra, cuando en paz reposa.
>   Tan vivo está el jazmín, la pura rosa,
> que, blandamente ardiendo en azucena,
> me abrasa el alma de memorias llena:
> ceniza de su fénix amorosa.
>   ¡Oh memoria cruel de mis enojos!
> ¿qué honor te puede dar mi sentimiento,
> en polvo convertidos sus despojos?
>   Permíteme callar sólo un momento:
> que ya no tienen lágrimas mis ojos,
> ni concetos de amor mi pensamiento.

[Dust now, but ever lovely, that light that takes my life lives on serene, [and what] was once my pleasure and my pain wages war on me, but rests in peace. The jasmine, the pure rose, softly glowing in lily-white skin, is so alive to me that it sears my memory-laden soul: ash of a loving phoenix. Oh cruel memory of angry passion! What possible honour is there for you when the very remains of feeling have turned to dust? Let me be silent for just a moment: my eyes have no more tears, nor my mind conceits of love.]

---

[39] Rozas and Cañas Murillo date the poem between April 1632 (the death of Marta de Nevares) and August 1634.

Part 3: Drama

7

The *Arte nuevo de hacer comedias*:
Lope's Dramatic Statement

JONATHAN THACKER

> Not only what we say and how we say it
> is of importance, but also the
> circumstances under which we say it
> (Quintilian).

Lope de Vega's *Arte nuevo de hacer comedias en este tiempo*, first published in the fifth edition of his *Rimas* of 1609, was most likely given as a speech to a literary society called the Madrid Academy some months before it emerged in print. The 389-line text, almost entirely in Spanish[1] and taking the form of hendecasyllabic *versos sueltos* [blank verse], provides a reliable, if often tongue-in-cheek, condensation of his ideas about drama and playwriting at a period when his theatre had matured and he was at the height of his popularity. The *Arte nuevo* is clearly the first essential port of call for anyone interested in Lope's dramatic theory and practice. Indeed, because it was Lope, as his contemporaries and followers were well aware, who was the main driving force behind what came to be known as the *comedia nueva* [new theatre], its study is necessary to understand his whole era's dramatic output. Many would go further, considering the work to constitute 'el primer manifiesto del teatro moderno' [the first manifesto of modern theatre],[2] with the implication that Lope's speech, however poorly known outside Spain, is an important milestone in early modern European theatre.[3]

Elements of the *comedia nueva* can be discerned, in retrospect, in the late-sixteenth-century plays of writers such as the Sevillian, Juan de la Cueva, as well as Francisco Tárrega, Gaspar de Aguilar, Cristóbal de Virués and Andrés Rey de

---

[1] Lines 377–86 are in Latin, possibly not written by Lope, and possibly added before publication.

[2] The quotation comes from the introduction to Enrique García Santo-Tomás's edition (Madrid: Cátedra, 2006), p. 14. All quotations from the work are taken from this edition. Also thoroughly recommended is the edition of the *Rimas* by Felipe B. Pedraza Jiménez (Ciudad Real: Universidad de Castilla-La Mancha, 1993–94), where the *Arte nuevo* can be found in vol. II, pp. 355–93.

[3] The first translation of the *Arte nuevo* into English listed by García Santo-Tomás dates from 1914 (p. 106 and p. 125).

Artieda, all four working in a Valencia in cultural ferment at a time when Lope was himself unformed as a dramatist. However, it was the *madrileño* who knitted them together most effectively for the new, paying audiences of the Spanish playhouses.[4] It was Lope, unsurprisingly, as the undisputed popular champion of these *corrales*, a 'felicísimo ingenio destos reinos' [brilliant Spanish genius], who was invited to explain his principles, and to account for the new approach to theatre in the formal setting of an Academy gathering.[5]

The *Arte nuevo* must be read and understood, at least in part, then, as a speech, a performance, a rhetorical act, directed to a potentially hostile academic audience — or at least one with conservative elements.[6] There is a tension within it between the rhetorical *captatio benevolentiae* and a naked self-confidence. Structurally, and rhetorically, it can be roughly divided into three: up until line 127 Lope panders to the *doctos* (the educated audience) showing a concern with the past, with aspects of the history of drama and dramatic theory from Aristotle to sixteenth-century Spain; lines 128 to 361, which constitute the main body of his *arte*; and the concluding 28 lines, which are best described as an epilogue. In the shift from the first to the second section the writer feigns a recognition that his audience might be becoming bored with familiar literary history, and plays at remembering that his brief was 'que un arte de comedias os escriba / que al estilo del vulgo se reciba' [to write for you an art of creating plays / that satisfies the taste of the general public] (ll. 9–10). Thereafter, in the central section, he becomes less defensive and more assertive, outlining in broad brushstrokes many aspects of his own practice. The epilogue sees a return to the semi-apologetic Lope before there is a reiteration of his overarching self-justification. Scholars often think of the *Arte nuevo* as a manifesto (as we have already seen it described), but it is not properly such, or at least not entirely such. Neither is it bold or insistent enough to be a defence of poetry, although it is understandably often pigeon-holed as one. It is, rather, a practical man-of-the-theatre's guide to (and apologia for) what has been shown to work in the Spanish *corral*, in front of a mixed audience, at the turn of the seventeenth century.[7]

---

[4] Many of the Valencian dramatists' works are included in *Poetas dramáticos valencianos*, edited by Juliá Martínez, 2 vols (Madrid: Real Academia Española, 1929). For studies of the development of early Golden Age theatre, see García Santo-Tomás's edition of the *Arte nuevo*, esp. pp. 21–26 and footnotes.

[5] The epithet is from Cervantes's *Don Quijote*, I, 48, and the translation is from John Rutherford's English version of the novel (London: Penguin, 2000).

[6] In his introductory comments to the poem (II, pp. 37–67) Pedraza Jiménez explodes the critical myth that Lope might have been addressing a wholly antagonistic audience in the Academia. Alongside the classicists would have been some who were sceptical but ready to listen, and others still for whom the new theatre was 'un asunto de orgullo nacional del que participaron todos los grupos sociales' [a matter for national pride involving all social groups], II, p. 47.

[7] Even the term 'apología' is a problematic one, given that, as García Santo-Tomás convincingly argues, the hierarchical relationship between Lope and the Academy is the reverse of what one might expect (p. 54). Lope, as he rather pointedly reminds his audience in line 13, is a successful dramatist, not a dry theorist. He will educate them. In part then his dramatic statement is 'un acto de exhibicionismo' [an act of exhibitionism] (García Santo-Tomás, p. 61).

Before taking a closer look at the poem itself, three further general points are worth making. First, the work is not called (at least in its first edition) *El arte nuevo*. The absence of the definite article from the title is important because it suggests that the writer's intention was not to be prescriptive. Like Aristotle's *Poetics*, the *Arte nuevo* is primarily a description of theatrical practice: thus, where imperatives are employed, their function is to offer advice to the would-be *comedia*-writer. Indeed, its lack of punctiliousness is a defining feature of the work, perhaps explaining why it should have been interpreted by scholars in such different ways, both as a largely neo-classical text, and an often revolutionary one.[8] Lope is not a blinkered law-giver — it is just that his way of writing plays has been shown to be successful at the box-office. Second, the inclusion of 'en este tiempo' in the title suggests that the new art is a snap-shot of Lope's practice at the end of the sixteenth and the start of the seventeenth century. Although the *comedia nueva* is sometimes seen as formulaic — and some of its features, such as the three-act format, did remain very settled — there were distinct phases, fashions and developments even in the lifetime of Lope himself. The dramatist was proud of his achievements and, later in his career, he railed against, for example, the abuse of the *tramoya* [stage effect] by other dramatists, but he would not necessarily have expected his Spanish drama to remain static and unchanging, to have appealed indefinitely. Third, the *Arte nuevo* is not and should not be the only source of information about Lope's dramaturgy. His views on drama might be painstakingly pieced together — as have been Cervantes's views on the novel, for instance — from his practice and from comments scattered here and there in his works: in plays and their dedications, as well as from letters and the prologues to the *partes* in which many of his dramatic works were first published.[9] However, the *Arte nuevo*, like many a self-conscious reflection providing insights into the mind of a successful artist, is destined to retain its place of honour amongst Lope's theoretical writings. In the guide to it that follows an attempt will be made to consider, taking the implications of its form and context into account, the central question raised by our modern-day reading of the poem: how can Lope's dramatic theory be characterized?

The occasionally apologetic feel of the *Arte nuevo* comes, as we have mentioned, from Lope's defensive explanation to his educated audience of why Spanish theatre has departed from the rules and norms established by classical

---

[8] For an excellent overview of scholars' (mis)understanding of the poem, see Pedraza Jiménez, II, pp. 37–46.

[9] Luis C. Pérez and Federico Sánchez Escribano collect materials from a number of sources in their *Afirmaciones de Lope de Vega sobre preceptiva dramática* (Madrid: CSIC, 1961). Interestingly, they end their analysis of Lope's dramatic precepts, as he expresses them in various places, with the admission that 'nos ha sido imposible llegar a una conclusión inequívoca' [we have not managed to arrive at an unequivocal conclusion] (p. 209). The *Arte nuevo* can be judged alongside other early Spanish expressions of dramatic theory by Torres Naharro, Juan de la Cueva, Cervantes, Tirso de Molina, Cascales and others in *Preceptiva dramática española del Renacimiento y Barroco*, ed. Federico Sánchez Escribano & Alberto Porqueras Mayo, 2nd edn (Madrid: Gredos, 1972).

playwrights.[10] With the criticism of the *preceptistas* (those who would champion a poetics based on the old dramatic rules) in mind, Lope is anxious to reveal that he had read and thought about the classical authorities, in fact before he was ten years old (ll. 17–21), and had even written neo-classical plays at one time (ll. 33–34). He characterizes the works of classical authors, represented by the Roman comedians Terence and Plautus, as 'la verdad' (l. 44), but a truth or an ideal of authenticity that must be removed from his study, as he puts it, so that he can write in the only way that the undiscerning mass audiences of his day have come to accept. This process he calls 'hablarle en necio' [to pander to their ignorance] (l. 48). The battle was lost, he intimates, before he even came on the scene (ll. 22–27).

Much of Lope's knowledge of his classical forebears, such as Terence, Aristotle and Horace, stems, as Victor Dixon recalls in his chapter in this volume, from the fourth-century work by Donatus (on the first of these authorities) and Robortello's 1555 Latin commentary on the *Poetics*. His potted history of theatre and its primary definition, 'imitar las acciones de los hombres' [to imitate the actions of men] (l. 52) are taken, sometimes more or less translated, from the Italian's work. The playwright's purpose here seems to be to contrast the relative clarity in the definitions of the different genres of drama in olden times with the confused state of affairs that he has inherited. Thus whilst once upon a time 'por argumento la tragedia tiene / la historia, y la comedia el fingimiento' [the plot of tragedy comes from history and that of comedy from the imagination] (ll. 111–12), and its Ciceronian purpose was clear — to be a mirror to customs, an image of truth to set alongside history, it has become 'confuso' [mixed up] (l. 146). Again Lope apologizes (l. 151) for describing how to produce this monstrous mixture, or chimera (l. 150), and again he attributes his willingness to do so to his all-powerful paymasters, the *corral* audiences, so sadly following the dictates of 'gusto' [pleasure] rather than what is orderly, right and proper.

As he begins properly (in l. 157) to enumerate and explore briefly some of the ingredients and norms of his *comedia nueva*, Lope's characteristic slipperiness and related propensity to look both ways at the same time is evident. The line in question begins 'elíjase el sujeto' [choose the subject matter] as if he were about to begin a list of subjects suitable for dramatic treatment, or admit his own eclectic habits: the (Classically dubious) raiding of chronicles, ballads, hagiographies, sacred works, classical and contemporary Italian and Spanish literature, folk tales and so on for source materials. However, he distracts his audience with a consideration of the presence of monarchs in drama — important in itself, but just one aspect of the issue of what a playwright might justifiably

---

[10] Both Juan de la Cueva in his *Ejemplar poético* [Poetics] (1606) and Tirso de Molina in his *Cigarrales de Toledo* [Country Houses of Toledo] (1621), and even arguably Cervantes, in his play, *El rufián dichoso* [The Fortunate Ruffian] (1615), provide unapologetic, more overtly self-assured defences of the abandonment of some classical norms than Lope does in the *Arte nuevo*. Their contributions, which are not subject to the same rhetorical niceties as Lope's speech, are all included in the volume edited by Sánchez Escribano and Porqueras Mayo. Pedraza Jiménez helpfully details the main responses, positive and negative, to the *Arte nuevo* in the years following its publication in his introduction, II, pp. 38–39.

depict on the contemporary (broadly comic) stage. He approves of their presence, apologetically, and then produces two examples which wrong-foot the audience.[11] If we thought Lope was about to deal with plot-types, the inveterate digresser proceeds to 'illuminate' his point with an acknowledgement of Philip II's dislike of seeing kings on stage, and, more relevantly, he recalls Plautus's *Amphitruo* in which Jupiter disguises himself as the eponymous king in order to seduce his wife, Alcumena. With this characteristic legerdemain, Lope not only avoids opening up for debate the question of what are acceptable source materials for drama, he also undermines one of his earlier classical authorities by pointing out the celebrated Roman playwright's own departure from good practice. The boundaries of classical poetics to which he has paid lip-service are, Lope hints, not necessarily the impervious structures they seem. The attack is a subtle undermining of the academic certainties, not a frontal assault, and is possibly designed to surprise, to cause reflection and invite self-criticism.

If he has begun with a distraction, Lope continues in his famous lines on tragicomedy (ll. 174–80) with a child-like twisting of an argument that would leave his listeners scratching their heads. Having established that the mixture of Terence with Seneca, thus the comic with the tragic, produces a monster like the Minotaur, fruit of the *unnatural* union of Pasiphae with a bull, he avers that the resultant 'variedad deleita mucho' [variety gives great pleasure] (l. 178) because of its very resemblance to *nature*, in itself beautiful for its variety. The 'naturaleza/belleza' rhyming couplet (a flourish periodically used in the *Arte nuevo* to signal the end of a sub-section) has a finality that brooks no argument. These seven lines might be said to represent in microcosm the speech as a whole: in front of our very eyes Lope holds two positions, looks both ways, by sophistically turning a negative 'mixture' into a positive 'variety'. He accepts the theoretical inferiority of his unruly drama but both undermines that position through hints at its weakness (ancient drama was not always so orderly anyway; and why separate the two Aristotelian genres when life is not so compartmentalized?), and is assertive about the quality of the drama he writes.[12]

Lope moves swiftly on. In the matter of the so-called unity of action he reveals himself to be a follower of Aristotle, arguing that a play should maintain its focus on its central 'acción' [plot/story-line] (l. 182) without introducing extraneous episodes or detachable scenes. Lope probably has in mind here the gold-beater turned successful professional actor, Lope de Rueda (mentioned in l. 64), who had toured mid-sixteenth-century Spain with his troupe, making a lasting impression upon the young Miguel de Cervantes amongst others. Rueda's plays contained *pasos* [comic scenes] that were published (and could be performed) separately. In his own (inevitably experimental) early drama, for example in the four-act *Los*

---

[11] Lope habitually created monarchs for the *corrales*: so much so that he effectively reflected the many published treatises on kingship and statecraft for a popular audience. See the excellent *Playing the King: Lope de Vega and the Limits of Conformity*, by Melveena McKendrick (Woodbridge: Tamesis, 2000).

[12] In one clear sense, as I argue in my chapter on his comedies, the majority of Lope's dramatic works can be described as tragicomedies.

hechos de Garcilaso de la Vega y el moro Tarfe and the comedy *Las ferias de Madrid*, Lope had sometimes been happy to create colourful or comic individual scenes without worrying about whether they contributed to the development of the whole. Later, as the mature creator of a play such as *Fuente Ovejuna*, he would engineer a sub-plot or a comic scene to provide a supplement or a counterpoint to the main action. However revolutionary Lope's theatre has subsequently been seen to be, in the matter of unity of action he was conservative: Cervantes's radical theatrical experiments with plot development impressed neither Lope nor the *autores de comedias* [actor-managers] who had the purchasing power and knew what their audiences liked.

The *Arte nuevo* deals with the two other well-known neo-classical unities — of time and place — in its next section (ll. 188–210), another that ends with the full consonantal rhyme of the once opposing demands of 'gusto' [pleasure] and what is 'justo' [right]. These supposedly competing demands here become unified with an air of finality through the dramatic force of Lope's poetry and performance. Again the justification for changes of place (l. 198) and leaps in time (l. 195) within a drama comes from the impatience of the Spanish audience, who, Lope hyperbolically claims, are not satisfied unless they have seen on the stage in a couple of hours everything from Genesis to the Final Judgement (ll. 207–9). Here Robortello's Aristotle is contradicted, with a hint at a fleeting apology (190–92), but there is nothing to be done: especially when writing historical plays (l. 194) the dramatist will exceed the span of a single day in his re-imagining of events. He should try to condense the story into as short a time as dramatically feasible, allowing time to pass (years if necessary) in the two spaces between acts which, as it happens, are filled in the *corral* by other entertainments, notably the farcical *entremés* [interlude]. Typical in this respect is his late tragedy, *El castigo sin venganza*, in which time is allowed between acts two and three for the duque de Ferrara to fight in and return from the Papal wars, and for his wife and illegitimate son to develop their ill-starred love affair. It was eventually Tirso who pointed, in his *Cigarrales de Toledo* [Country Houses of Toledo], to the paradoxical nature of a unity (of time) that would tend to bring with it, willy nilly, a breach in the play's verisimilitude (by forcing important events improbably close together). Lope, as we have seen, is less intent upon flat contradiction of the Classical aesthetic.

Much of the remainder of the *Arte nuevo* concerns more practical advice to the would-be dramatist. The classical authorities are never far below the surface, however, with mentions of their names and interpreters far outweighing the odd reference to Spanish contemporaries such as Virués (l. 215) or the enigmatic Miguel Sánchez (l. 321). We shall continue to follow the order of the original poem in outlining and examining Lope's remaining advice, although the poet himself often seems to be following his own whims in structuring this central section of his *arte*. He does return to the question of the 'sujeto elegido' [chosen subject matter] (l. 211), first mentioned in l. 157, to give an apparent insight into his writing practice. Once he has his play's main story he sketches the plot in prose, attempting to limit the action of each act to the course of a single day (cf. ll.

195–97).[13] The mention of 'acto' [act] (l. 212) characteristically leads to a digression.[14] He recalls how it was the Valencian, Virués, who first moved from four-act plays, of the sort common in the 1570s and 1580s, to three acts, and how as an eleven- or twelve-year-old he had followed the old practice.[15] Implicitly, through the image of the baby crawling on all fours as representative of the infant genre, he expresses his approval of the change, one that lasted well beyond the seventeenth century. Lope's subsequent point about the importance of dividing the material to be dramatized into two parts (l. 231) is not an attempt to follow through the logic of this simile by suggesting two-act dramas, so much as a return to Robortello. He had, wisely in Lope's view, urged that the main story which is to be followed in the action be set out early in the piece, but that the resolution be delayed until the last moment to encourage, in Lope's words, the audience not to turn their backs on what they have been watching for three hours, and leave. On similar lines, the dramatist urges that the stage rarely be left empty, as the lack of activity provides a further excuse for restlessness (ll. 240–45). In his practice, Lope became expert at providing cover for possible on-stage lacunae, in particular through use of the set-piece sonnet to summarize a situation, as well as through the counter-point of the *gracioso*'s comedy.

So much for the bald structure of the play to be written. In line 246 Lope allows his would-be dramatist to begin composing verses. The language of the drama should, most importantly, suit the speaker, and be 'casto' [here, natural] and should only become more elaborate, overtly sophisticated, when the situation justifies it, when a character has a rhetorical end in mind. There is no contradiction here in the fact that Lope's drama is written in polymetric verse: he is referring to the words and style employed by the speaker. That the characters speak, unrealistically, in verse, is a given, as it is in Shakespeare. He goes on to discourage the use of the quotation of biblical and classical sources, such as are common in prose works, in a speech written for the stage, and to provide indicative examples of some of the words which should be avoided if one is properly to mimic the way people speak. One of these, 'hipogrifo' [hippogriff] (l. 268) was employed, certainly not innocently, by Calderón as the first word of the first play of the first part of his collected works, his famous *La vida es sueño* [Life is a Dream].[16] The playwright continues with some examples of how the

---

[13] Although autograph manuscripts of over forty of Lope's plays (not all complete) are extant, a lack of evidence makes it uncertain to what extent he used these prose sketches when planning a play. However, see Pedraza Jiménez's note on these lines in his edition of the *Rimas*, II, p. 374 and Fausta Antonucci, *Métrica y estructura dramática en el teatro de Lope de Vega* (Kassel: Reichenberger, 2007), p. 17, n. 36.

[14] On Lope's tendency to digress, see Tubau's contribution to this volume.

[15] As with several of Lope's claims about the history of the development of the theatre, there is some justification for what he writes here. Virués had self-consciously reduced the number of acts in his drama, but earlier three-act plays had been written.

[16] The hippogriff was a mythical-style beast, invented by Ariosto in his *Orlando Furioso*, in sixteenth-century Italy. Lope's objection to it seems to be that comprehension of the term depends on a reading knowledge of the Italian writer. Footnotes explaining what the hippogriff is have become otiose thanks to the *Harry Potter* books.

language should suit the speaker (ll. 269–79). His description of the lover's language is of interest as it sheds some light on the acting process and relationship between the actor and audience: 'con mudarse a sí, mude al oyente' [by becoming moved himself, he moves the audience-member] (l. 276). The transformation of the lover through the poetry that he or she speaks seems to suggest that — at least on some occasions — Lope favoured a naturalistic style of performance in which the empathetic response of the public was the goal. Lope deals here with the 'dama' [female character] too, played by an actress in the *corral*, and his lines again show how he appeals to two audiences simultaneously (in a passage reminiscent of his discussion of the combination of tragedy and comedy). On the one hand the playwright must show respect to women, through the female characters he creates, on the other the hugely popular 'disfraz varonil' [male disguise] (l. 283) should be permitted for the simple reason that the audiences enjoy the transvestism. Indeed, the cross-dressed *dama* was a staple of his and his contemporaries' comic drama. Again the 'calculadamente ambiguo' [calculatedly ambiguous] nature of the poem is laid bare.[17] This is another occasion on which Lope feels under pressure to defend the good character of his drama but, in the face of evidence of what the *corral* audiences pay to see, he has to conclude with an assertion and move on.

The question of verisimilitude, which has in fact been underpinning much of Lope's theory up to this point, is finally raised directly in lines 284–85. In disqualifying impossible events from the stage, Lope merely wants to ensure that the audience is not alienated, and shows a similar Aristotelian concern to that of Cervantes in his fiction. It is worth noting, perhaps, that plays with a strong supernatural element, with demonic or angelic characters on stage or voices off, or with miracles dramatized, were not considered to break the bounds of verisimilitude.

The focus shifts again in line 298 back to the structure, or the more practical matter of the organization of the plot. Lope's advice is to set up 'el caso' [the subject matter] in the first act, complicate it in the second, keeping the audience guessing about how the drama will be resolved, and even providing a twist so that the obvious outcome is ignored in favour of something surprising. In practice, the generic norms of the various sub-genres in which Lope wrote militate against a lot of surprises: plays usually end conventionally but the playwright is still able, like any good dramatic writer, to find ways of casting doubt over an expected conclusion, to make the audience anxious about the outcome, and even to defy expectations at times. The teasing ending of *El perro del hortelano* is a supreme example of his skill in this respect.

Much of the remaining advice offered by Lope is very loosely organized: he deals in quick succession with verse forms (ll. 305–12), the importance of rhetoric (ll. 313–18), 'engañar con la verdad' [deceiving with the truth] (l. 319) and related tricks of the trade (ll. 319–26), some favourite dramatic content (ll. 327–37), the length of the play (ll. 338–40) and satire (ll. 341–46), before reinforcing the

---

[17]   See Pedraza Jiménez, II, p. 47, and his analysis of this section in II, pp. 61–62.

impression of haste by admitting that he is running out of time (l. 349). His last short section before the epilogue, again heavily dependent on his principal source, Robortello, advises the Academy audience members where they can read further about classical stage decoration and costume (ll. 350–61). The purpose seems to be once again (as ll. 359–61 on the arbitrary nature of costume on the *corral* stage suggest) to illustrate ironically how different the world of the *comedia nueva* is from that of the more ceremonial, formal ancient drama.

Some of these final thoughts should detain us. Much has been written about Lope's advice on the use of verse forms, often with the intention of indicating that he did not follow his own precepts in this regard, for example that *redondillas* [a traditional octosyllabic form made up of quatrains rhyming ABBA] be used for love scenes (l. 312).[18] Whilst Lope's employment of different verse forms in the drama did change over time, his advice here is in fact broadly consistent with his own practice, especially when one takes into account that he has no intention of setting rules in stone and the fact that, in this particular case, his category of *redondillas* would also have included the very common *quintilla* [a similar form in five-line stanzas].[19]

Lope notes, with characteristic perspicacity, that his audiences enjoy the effects of a broad range of kinds of irony. Instances where a character either knowingly speaks the truth but is not believed or, without realizing it, anticipates a later action or alludes to a reality of which they are at the time unaware, are common in the *comedia*. A good example of the former is the case of Floriano, in *Los locos de Valencia*, who admits to a murder without gaining any reaction from those around him who are investigating it; and of the second type, one might think of the duque de Ferrara, in *El castigo sin venganza*, who encourages his son, Federico, to act in his stead while he is away. He does not, however, expect him to sleep in his bed with Casandra, his step-mother.[20] Of the types of subject matter that go down well with audiences, Lope singles out 'casos de la honra' [honour cases] (l. 327) and 'acciones virtuosas' [stories of virtue] (l. 329), and indeed, his output confirms his affection for both. Frequent amongst the latter type are his religious (often saints) plays. The former do not consist solely or even mainly of the type of wife-murder play so often associated with Calderón de la Barca: honour is an ingredient in countless plays, comic and more serious, and was clearly a code of behaviour with which audiences readily identified.

Lope's epilogue provides, as one would expect, a recapitulation. He repeats his own confession of guilt in the matter of breaking the rules, an offence, he further

---

[18] For further detail on the six types of verse forms Lope mentions and others he does not, see the Appendix to my *Companion to Golden Age Theatre* (Woodbridge: Tamesis, 2007), pp. 179–85. See also the excellent recent volume of studies edited by Antonucci, *Métrica y estructura dramática en el teatro de Lope de Vega*.

[19] See Pedraza Jiménez, II, p. 64. The fact that Lope's verse forms did change over time formed the basis of Morley and Bruerton's very successful method of dating his dramas: see their *The Chronology of Lope de Vega's 'Comedias': With a Discussion of Doubtful Attributions, the Whole Based on a Study of His Strophic Versification* (New York: The Modern Language Association of America, 1940).

[20] See Friedman's chapter in this volume for an in-depth analysis of the irony of this tragedy.

admits, he has exacerbated by daring to give advice to others who would do the same (ll. 362–65). But, he asks again, what else can he do? He has now offended repeatedly, as 477 of the 483 plays he has written (the number is presumably an exaggerated estimate despite its apparent precision) have violated the classical *arte*. The numbers prove the demand: these works 'deleita[n] el gusto' [delight the taste] (l. 376) of a public not, for once (in another subtle shift), referred to as the *vulgo*. There follow ten lines in Latin in general praise, after Cicero, of the theatre, and somewhat reminiscent of the duque de Ferrara's famous speech in act 1 of *El castigo sin venganza*. And with a final flourish Lope suggests that his whole command performance has been pointless (perhaps because in the end one cannot contain great art, or confine great artists, with simple rules) and asks his audience to relax and learn from the *comedia*, not worry about whether it happens to conform.

The fact that Lope delivers his speech 'con la sonrisa en los labios' [with a smile on his lips] does not mean that he fails to take his own theatre seriously.[21] When he began to show an active interest in the publication of his plays in *partes,* the dramatist took the opportunity to write prologues to them and dedications to individual works. In these short pieces, written with a reading audience in mind, a slightly different Lope emerges — one who is proud of his drama, not just of its appeal as entertainment to the *vulgo* but of its content and his own skill. He is often scornful of those who would criticize him for ignoring the rules, even characterizing them as mad to be so obsessed. It is probably fair to say, then, that his *Arte nuevo*, if it could ever be stripped of its necessary rhetoric, of the context in which it was delivered, would emerge as a bold statement of the need for theatre to evolve in order to continue to reflect the society for which it is written, the society at which it is aimed. However, as a poem delivered to an Academy, the speech cannot be unfettered from these considerations of its initial reception, and one is left to admire what has never been better described than as a 'juego de manos: el mago pone en el sombrero el conejo del teatro antiguo y saca la paloma de la comedia española sin que el oyente sepa exactamente cómo le han dado el cambiazo' [an act of legerdemain: the magician puts the rabbit of ancient theatre into the hat and pulls out the dove of the Spanish *comedia* without the audience member knowing exactly how the transformation has been made].[22] If Lope de Vega reveals anything for certain, it is that even when he discusses the theatre, he is a man of the theatre.

---

[21] The words are from Montesinos's study, quoted in Pedraza Jiménez, II, p. 42.
[22] See Pedraza Jiménez, II, p. 51.

8

Three Canonical Plays

ALEXANDER SAMSON AND JONATHAN THACKER

Lope de Vega's reputation today as a dramatist rests on a meagre proportion of his dramatic output. He suffers, as his successor Calderón de la Barca does, from the fact that only a small percentage of the plays he created are available in modern, scholarly editions and even fewer are regularly performed in theatres. One of the aims of this *Companion* is to reveal some of what lies beyond the theatrical canon, as the chapters that follow will demonstrate, but it would be perverse to ignore the recognised major works such as *El perro del hortelano*, *La dama boba*, *El caballero de Olmedo*, *Peribáñez y el comendador de Ocaña*, *Fuenteovejuna*, and *El castigo sin venganza* and the reasons they are considered great.[1] The first two in this list, both comic in nature, are examined in chapter 11, where they are placed in the context of Lope's other comedies; the last of them, a Spanish-style tragedy, has, as it deserves, a chapter of its own (chapter 15).

The remaining three plays are all serious in nature: *El caballero de Olmedo* (c. 1620), which will be dealt with last, is a fascinating mix of comic recourses with a tragic trajectory; the other two are so-called 'peasant honour' plays and are quite closely related. The works in question, *Peribáñez y el comendador de Ocaña* (c. 1605–8) and *Fuenteovejuna* (c. 1612–14), are perhaps the most widely studied, performed and translated of Lope's entire *oeuvre* today.[2] The extent to which this popularity distorts their place in his output reflects the story of the changing appropriations of these works in performance since their original appearance. Both dramas have come to occupy an important place in literary history not least as a result of their ideological complexity, a function of their commercialism and their creator's mastery of the resources of dramatic entertainment, as well as their

---

[1] These are the Lope plays most frequently edited in Spain as well as the ones most often published in English translation, for example in Jill Booty's and Gwynne Edwards's collections, *Lope de Vega: Five Plays* (*Peribáñez, Justice without Revenge, The Knight from Olmedo, Fuenteovejuna, The Dog in the Manger*), trans. Jill Booty, with an introduction by R. D. F. Pring-Mill (New York: Hill and Wang, 1961), and Lope de Vega, *Three Major Plays* (*Fuente Ovejuna, The Knight from Olmedo, Punishment without Revenge*), trans. Gwynne Edwards (Oxford: Oxford University Press, 1999). On the Lope canon and the reasons behind its formation, see Enrique García Santo-Tomás, *La creación del Fénix: recepción crítica y formación canónica del teatro de Lope de Vega* (Madrid: Gredos, 2000).

[2] Related 'peasant' plays, which have also proven popular, are *El villano en su rincón* (1611–15) and *El mejor alcalde, el rey* (1620–23).

availability to act as ciphers in a number of cultural and political contexts from Lorca's Spain to Pinochet's Chile.[3] The plots of both *Fuenteovejuna* and *Peribáñez* surround the irruption into idyllic rural communities of sexually rapacious and tyrannous authority figures. These men are, in both cases, *comendadores*. The term means 'knights-commander', or noblemen with habits from one of the three military orders. The *comendadores* enjoy jurisdiction over towns, a privilege which comes with various rights attached, such as the collection of rents and incomes from the local populace. There was a vogue for drama involving these figures, today often classified within a subgenre, the *comedia de comendadores*, which includes a play discussed later in this volume, *Los comendadores de Córdoba*.[4]

The plot of *Fuenteovejuna* was based on real events that had taken place in 1476. Lope's historical source, probably Francisco de Rades y Andrada's *Chrónica de las tres Órdenes y Caballerías de Santiago, Calatrava y Alcántara* (1572), described the violent murder by his vassals of Fernán Gómez de Guzmán, Comendador Mayor de Calatrava, following accusations of rape and robbery. A major factor in his historical murder appears to have been the presence of a standing army, stationed there under him in the service of the Portuguese king, and whose constant affronts and injuries to the local populace provoked them to revolt. The village of Fuenteovejuna had originally been under the jurisdiction of the city of Córdoba. However, in 1448 it had been occupied by a force under the seignorial mayor, Diego de Orellana, of the nearby towns of Gahete and Hinojosa. He was a nephew of the local feudal overlord, Gutierre de Sotomayor, a nobleman whose support for John II during the constant factional struggles of his reign had been rewarded with the grant of these places in 1444–45, along with another village, Puebla Alcocer, that belonged to Toledo. The claim that Fuenteovejuna belonged to these other towns was rebutted by the king in a letter to the town: 'Mucho soy marauillado el dicho maestre en tomar e ocupar la dicha villa de Fuenteovejuna [...] yo no fiz merçed a él ni a otra persona' [I am much amazed at the said master taking possession and occupying the said town of Fuenteovejuna [...] I have not made any grant to him or any other person].[5] There may be a hint of this family's dubious *modus operandi* in relation to these seized lands in the murder in 1464 of Gutierre's son and heir, Alonso de Sotomayor, by a disgruntled vassal, ten years before the defenestration of Fernán Gómez. John II ordered the restitution of the lands in his will, but his successor, Henry IV, then gifted the Cordoban towns to Pedro Girón, Master of the Military Order of Calatrava and

---

[3] See Paul E. Larson, '*Fuente Ovejuna*: History, Historiography, and Literary History', *Bulletin of the Comediantes*, 53.2 (2001): 267–90, and Christopher B. Weimer, 'he Politics of Adaptation: *Fuenteovejuna* in Pinochet's Chile', in *Echoes and Inscriptions: Comparative Approaches to Early Modern Spanish Literatures*, ed. Barbara A. Simerka & Christopher B. Weimer (Lewisburg, PA: Bucknell University Press, 2000), pp. 234–49.

[4] On this subgenre see the introductory essay to *Peribáñez y el comendador de Ocaña*, ed. Juan María Marín (Madrid: Cátedra, 1986), pp. 29–38. The latter example is discussed by Geraint Evans in chapter 14 below.

[5] Reproduced in Manuel Villegas Ruiz, *Fuenteovejuna: el drama y la historia* (Baena: Adisur, 1990), p. 86.

brother of his favourite, Juan Pacheco, Marqués de Villena. The town subsequently passed into the possession of Girón's heir, Rodrigo Téllez Girón. A grant by the king of a petition from Córdoba for the return of Fuenteovejuna in 1464 was never fulfilled as a result of the domination of the Royal Council throughout this period by a faction consisting of the father-in-law of Gutierre's son, Alvaro de Zúñiga, and the brothers Juan Pacheco and Pedro Girón. The town was occupied by force by the Fernán Gómez de Guzmán of the play again in 1468. Guzmán was lieutenant as Comendador Mayor of Calatrava to the Order's Maestre, Rodrigo Girón. A recent book about the litigation that lasted for more than a century surrounding the original grant of Gahete and Hinojosa to Gutierre de Sotomayor, which came to be known as the Belalcázar case, deals tangentially with the changes of ownership of the town, factional politics, royal administration of justice and its problems. It concludes with a reading of this play in relation to the arguments of the Jesuit political theorist Juan de Mariana against arbitrary government (often misunderstood as a defence of tyrannicide). The play and the Belalcázar case inflect the development of a debate about royal authority and the administration of justice in the crucial period between the civil wars, the faction-riven fifteenth century and the achievements of the Habsburg monarchy in the succeeding two.[6]

Lope's play foregrounds the civil-war context, mapping the conflict between town and *comendador* onto the struggle between on the one side the king of Portugal and Henry IV's heir, Juana la Beltraneja, and on the other the king's sister Isabella, whose bid for the throne was supported by Ferdinand of Aragon. It opens with Guzmán's attempts to persuade Rodrigo Girón to come out in support of la Beltraneja and attack Ciudad Real. While to an extent this may immediately have cast these figures as villains, given the reputation of Ferdinand and Isabella, the Catholic Monarchs' response to the murder and horror at the village's vigilante justice in some senses depoliticises the subplot of internecine strife and transforms it into a mere echo or reflection of the central plot.

The infamous nature of this story can be gauged from the fact that it became both a well-known aphorism and saying by the late sixteenth century as well as featuring in emblem books, designed to encourage meditation. A version of the story was incorporated into the first Spanish dictionary, Sebastián de Covarrubias y Orozco's *Tesoro de la lengua castellana* (1611): 'de do quedó el proverbio, cuando el delito es notorio y en particular no hallan quién lo haya hecho, siendo muchos los delincuentes, decir: Fuente Ovejuna lo hizo' [whence the proverb arose, when the crime is notorious and in particular they do not find those responsible, because many criminals are involved: Fuente Ovejuna did it].[7] The version in the emblem manual by the same author was even more fiercely condemnatory of the murder, describing it as a 'caso atroz' [appalling case], 'sin

---

[6] J. B. Owens, *'By My Absolute Royal Authority': Justice and the Castilian Commonwealth at the Beginning of the First Global Age* (Rochester, NY: University of Rochester Press, 2005), pp. 225–31.

[7] Sebastián de Covarrubias Orozco, *Tesoro de la lengua castellana o española* (1611), ed. Felipe C. R. Maldonado (Madrid: Castalia, 1995), p. 563.

Dios, ni Rey, sin ley' [without God, king or law], and 'hecho bárbaro, inhumano' [a barbarous, inhuman act].[8] This contrasts strongly with the tendency in modern critical readings and perform   the play to use the central conflict as an example of heroic resistance   ny of a noble, an interpretation implicit in Lope's play, although the   licates this approach with its ambivalent framing of a number of key   of the story. The great nineteenth-century critic Marcelino Menéndez   claimed that *Fuenteovejuna* was the 'obra más democrática en el teatr   o' [the most democratic work in Spanish theatre] and the tendency t   text in radical if not revolutionary terms underlies its popularity in R   a Tsarist production in 1876 to a series of performances of a version   ne monarchs from 1919 onwards.[9] Federico García Lorca staged a vers   e play in the town itself in 1935 with La Barraca, the travelling thea   ny, dressing the villain as a village *cacique*, and thus reading the play's   ubtext through the lens of Spanish colonial exploitation in the Americas.[10] There is no doubt that both this play and *Peribáñez* are highly political, although perhaps not in ways that those productions with a tendency to read the works in terms of the proletarian struggle might suggest.[11]

Lope's version personalises the conflict, excising whatever role the Cordoban authorities or wider political struggles may have played in fomenting resistance to the *comendador*, in favour of exploring a series of philosophical and political issues more pertinent to his own day, from notions of tyranny and justifiable disobedience, kings as God's representatives on earth, the role and authority of the noble caste, to the idealisation of rural communities in contrast to urban and courtly life. The debate about the nature of constituted authority and whether disobedience of such authorities could ever be justified had run through Europe in the sixteenth century and been given particular poignancy by the Reformation, beginning with William Tyndale's *The Obedience of a Christian Man* (1528), famously the book given by Anne Boleyn to Henry VIII that had begun the process of his conversion to the Reformed faith. The theme of 'alabanza de aldea y menosprecio de corte' [praise of the country and contempt for the court] was heightened by the stream of *arbitristas*' treatises on rural decline and the importance of Castile's agricultural heartlands to the power and security of Spain

---

[8] Sebastián de Covarrubias Orozco, *Emblemas morales* (Madrid: Luis Sánchez, 1610), fol. 297v, emblem 97.

[9] See Jack Weiner, 'Lope de Vega's *Fuenteovejuna* under the Tsars, Commisars and the 2nd Spanish Republic (1931–39)', *Annali Istituto Universitario Orientale, Sezione Romanza*, 24.1 (1982): 167–223, and Teresa Kirschner, 'Sobrevivencia de una comedia: historia de la difusión de *Fuenteovejuna*', *Revista Canadiense de Estudios Hispánicos*, 1.3 (1977): 255–71. The comment on the democratic credentials of the *comedia* by Menéndez y Pelayo is cited in Antonio Sánchez Romeralo, ed., *Lope de Vega: el teatro II* (Madrid: Taurus, 1989), capítulo IV, (a): *Fuenteovejuna*, p. 17.

[10] For a summary of the play's performance history see J. B. Hall, *Lope de Vega: Fuenteovejuna*, Critical Guides to Spanish Texts, 42 (London: Grant & Cutler, in association with Tamesis, 1985), and Suzanne Byrd, 'The Twentieth Century *Fuenteovejuna* of Federico García Lorca', *García Lorca Review*, 5 (1977): 34–39.

[11] William R. Blue, 'The Politics of Lope's *Fuenteovejuna*', *Hispanic Review*, 59.3 (1991): 339–41.

and her empire. Scholars have commented on the text's apparent allusions to Thomas Aquinas' notion of the common good, the Neoplatonism implicit in the hero Frondoso and heroine Laurencia's discussion of the nature of love and the denunciation of the deceptive courtly use of language in the city.[12] Lope provides arresting visual metaphors to explore these debates, exploiting to the full the dramatic possibilities of his material. For example, Fernán Gómez's beating of the aged mayor Esteban with his own staff of office visually embodies his abuse of justice and disregard for the reciprocal nature of feudal obligations, civil law, as well as the sacrament of matrimony that he has openly contemned by asking the old man to hand over his daughter. The world of arbitrary self-assertion is called into question by Frondoso's defence of Laurencia, leading Fernán Gómez to lament a disregard for social order that betokens for him the dissolution of all hierarchies and distinctions:

> ¡Que a un capitán cuya espada
> tiemblan Córdoba y Granada,
> un labrador, un moçuelo
> ponga una ballesta al pecho!
> El mundo se acaba, Flores.

[that a peasant, a mere lad, can aim a crossbow at the chest of a captain whose sword makes Cordoba and Granada tremble! The world is coming to an end, Flores] (lines 1044–48).[13]

Even the clownish Mengo, despite his argument that love is always self-love earlier in the play: 'nadie tiene amor / más que a su misma persona' [no one loves anything but their own self] (lines 401–2), heroically defends Jacinta from the *comendador*'s men, who eventually carry her off to service the army's sexual needs.

Another context essential for an understanding of this play is the humanist debate about the notion of virtue as the true nobility. The issue of the right to honour of the villagers is central. The *comendador* asks one of the aldermen contemptuously: '¿Vosotros honor tenéis?' [You, possess honour?] (line 987). While it could be argued that the play as a whole defends a contractual notion of legitimate authority based on a social compact and a constitutionalist view of governance, the vertical stratification of society and an absolute hierarchy demand a response that will be exemplary from the Catholic Monarchs even though the victim is a rebel and traitor against them. Early modern notions of justice were more concerned with reparation and the restoration of social order than with

[12] See for example Robert L. Fiore, '*Fuenteovejuna*: Philosophical Views on the State and Revolution', in *Hispanic Essays in Honor of Frank P. Casa*, ed. A. Robert Lauer & Henry W. Sullivan (New York: Peter Lang, 1997), pp. 103–11, and Donald Gilbert-Santamaria, *Writers on the Market: Consuming Literature in Early Seventeenth-Century Spain* (Lewisburg, PA: Bucknell University Press, 2005), '3: Violence, Agency and the Audience in *Fuenteovejuna*', pp. 63–82.
[13] Lope de Vega, *Fuente Ovejuna*, ed. Juan María Marín (Madrid: Cátedra, 1995). All references are to this edition.

specific victims. This was why punishment often took so spectacular, public, even theatrical a form. When Ferdinand hears of the case, his initial response is to order a 'castigo exemplar' [exemplary punishment], for this 'triste sucesso' [sad event] and 'grande atrevimiento' [great insolence] (lines 2025, 2016, 2024). This contrasts strongly with the villagers' constant invocations of the monarchs as when, in the very next scene, musicians sing '¡Muchos años vivan / Isabel y Fernando, / y mueran los tiranos!' [May Ferdinand and Isabella live many years and let tyrants die!] (lines 2028–30). Despite their loyalty, there follows the infamous torture scene during which women and children are subjected to interrogation on the rack in order to find out who is responsible for the *comendador*'s murder.

Indeed, violence is a constant theme in the play, with the civil war paralleling the town's popular insurrection. The obsessive self-assertion of the *comendador* has been apparent from the first scene with his angry response to a perceived lack of respect shown towards him by Rodrigo, Maestre of Calatrava, Fernán Gómez's (albeit young) master. This status anxiety about 'honor'/'honra' is displaced in this context in a speech drawing the youth's attention to the illustrious ancestry he needs to live up to. The relationship between masculinity and violence traced symbolically throughout the semantic structures of the text is given most explicit expression in Laurencia's speech, following her escape from the *comendador*'s house, in which the manhood of the male villagers is placed in brackets as a result of their supine acceptance of the *comendador*'s sexual violence. The heroine's vivid language is telling:

> Ovejas sois […]
> bárbaros sois, no españoles.
> ¡Gallinas! […]
> ¿Para qué os ceñís estoques?
> ¡Vive Dios, que he de trazar
> que solas mujeres cobren
> la honra destos tiranos,
> la sangre destos traidores!
> ¡Y que os han de tirar piedras,
> hilanderas, maricones,
> amujerados, cobardes!
> ¡Y que mañana os adornen
> nuestras tocas y basquiñas,
> solimanes y colores!

[You are sheep [...] you are barbarians, not Spaniards. Chickens! [...] Why do you bother to wear a sword? By God, I will make sure that us women alone regain our lost honour from these tyrants, through the blood of these traitors. And they'll pelt you with stones, spinning effeminate pansy cowards! Tomorrow you can wear our blouses and headscarves, make-up and blusher!] (lines 1758, 1769–70, 1773–83).

The gender inversion so powerfully presented in her speech finds a counterpart in the company of female soldiers she leads, the hunted 'gama' [doe] (line 781) is transformed into 'Cides' and 'Rodamontes' (line 1847). Imagery of hunting, the nobleman's preparation and training for war, was a commonplace in relation to the discourse of love. The manner of Fernán Gómez's death, defenestration and impaling on the women's pikes and swords is a symbolic reversal of his, the rapist's, penetration of the female body.

One of the most interesting questions raised by the play, in fact, is whether Laurencia has actually been raped. Lope's studied ambivalence on this point must be seen as highly significant. Her powerful speech suggests but does not state that she has been dishonoured:

> ¡Qué desatinos enormes,
> qué palabras, qué amenazas,
> y qué delitos atrozes,
> por rendir mi castidad
> a sus apetitos torpes!
> Mis cabellos, ¿no lo dizen?

[What enormous follies, what words and threats, what appalling crimes to make my chastity yield to his sordid desires! Does my hair not show it?] (lines 1745–50).

At the end of the play, in his plea to the Catholic Monarchs, Frondoso states: 'a no saberse guardar / ella, que en virtud florece, / ya manifiesto parece / lo que pudiera passar' [if she, flowering in virtue, did not know how to defend herself, it seems obvious what might have happened] (lines 2410–13). Other women in the play clearly have been, as Laurencia puts it euphemistically, 'descalabradas' [damaged / had their (maiden)heads bashed in] (line 195). A couple of names are even offered: Sebastiana, the wife of Pedro Redondo, and Martín del Pozo's wife barely two days after her wedding (lines 799–804). These apparently willing vassals qualify the *comendador*'s villainy and offer some grounds for the Catholic Monarchs' hesitancy to display clemency. The death of Fernán Gómez is a national and local purging; the reluctant pardon granted by the Catholic Monarchs sanctions the murder and elides the death of a political traitor and local tyrant. The actions of the peasants are ratified without being condoned.

Peribáñez y el comendador de Ocaña sets up a similar conflict between a rich countryman, his bride Casilda and a sexually rapacious *comendador*. Their wedding is interrupted by the unhorsing of the nobleman by a runaway bull, symbolising the loss of control and inability to master bestial passions that will lead to the play's tragic outcome. On awakening with Casilda tending to him he falls for her angelic beauty. The *comendador* ironically plays a part in his own downfall, by knighting Peribáñez and so conferring on him the honour whose loss the peasant will invoke in his justification for murder. Before stabbing the *comendador*, he asserts that despite being a 'pobre labrador' [a poor farmer], 'la honra es encomienda / de mayor autoridad' [honour is an endowment of greater authority] (III, lines 759 and 763–64). The issue of honour and status is again at the heart of this conflict.[14] In a further irony, shortly after Peribáñez is knighted, the two companies of soldiers, *hidalgos* and peasants from Ocaña, deliberately compete with each other as they march off to Toledo, in order to show greater 'brío' [spirit], the peasants sneering at 'estos judíos' [these Jews] (III, lines 375 and 382), a reference to the traditional association of the *hidalgo* class with blood tainted by Jewish or Moorish ancestry. One of the *comendador*'s servants describes Peribáñez as 'aunque villano, muy honrado' [although a peasant, very honorable] (I, line 830),[15] while Casilda's rejection of the nobleman's advances, a refrain that encapsulates the play in some senses, turns on her preference for 'Peribáñez / con su capa la pardilla, / que al Comendador de Ocaña / con la suya guarnecida' [Peribáñez with his dun cloak of rough cloth to the Comendador's embroidered velvet one] (II, lines 545–48). This perhaps politically conservative view of social distinctions and pride in low birth contradicts to some extent Casilda's own wish to make distinctions between herself and others on the basis of dress and status.

As they are about to travel to Toledo to see the Assumption day processions, Costanza, Inés and Casilda discuss what they are going to wear. Costanza alludes to silver braid, while Casilda mentions her outfit of 'terciopelo / sobre encarnada escarlata' [velvet over a fine scarlet wool], suitable for a married woman: Inés volunteers one of Casilda's skirts to Costanza because the colour of the one she has lent her does not go with her complexion, 'la de grana blanca es buena, / o la verde' [the fine white one is nice or the green one] (I, lines 670, 672–73, 687–88). When Peribáñez returns from Toledo and the painter's workshop, Casilda asks him what he has brought her:

> una chinelas abiertas,
> que abrochan cintas de nácar.
> Traigo más: seis tocas rizas,
> y, para prender las sayas,
> dos cintas de vara y media
> con sus herretes de plata.

[some open-toed shoes that do up with mother-of-pearl straps. I have also got six ruched headscarves and in order to adorn outer garments, a yard and a half of two ribbons with silver tags] (II, lines 959–64).

The interrogation of the honour code on the one hand is counterbalanced by this attention elsewhere in the play to the social and economic aspirations of the non-noble classes. Peribáñez's status is indicated by his election to the leadership of the religious brotherhood, whose icon of San Roque he accompanies to Toledo to be repaired and repainted. The subsequent scene in the painter's workshop makes

[14] See José María Ruano de la Haza, 'Teoría y praxis del personaje teatral áureo: Pedro Crespo, Peribáñez y Rosaura', in *El escritor y la escena, V: estudios sobre teatro español y novohispano de los Siglos de Oro*, ed. Ysla Campbell (Ciudad Juárez: Universidad Autónoma de Ciudad Juárez, 1997), pp. 19–35.

[15] All quotations are from the Juan María Marín edition cited in note 4.

remarkable use of the device of the stage portrait (of Casilda, commissioned by the *comendador*) for the play's anagnorisis.[16]

The issue of status is muddied and confused throughout the play. Oddly, although the *comendador* in their final meeting as Peribáñez leads the squadron of *labradores* off to war, confers *hidalgo* status on him 'haréos caballero' [I will make you a knight], 'le quieren her hidalgo' [they want to make him a gentleman] (III, lines 154 and 162), at no point in his speech to the king does he mention this apparently critical fact, instead simply presenting himself as 'de villana casta, / limpio de sangre, y jamás / de hebrea o mora manchada' [of peasant stock but pure lineage, unstained by Jews or Moors] (III, lines 948–50). He does, however, allude tellingly to his having been the mayor of the town for six years. On entering Enrique IV's presence and announcing who he is, the king's immediate reaction is to order his guards to kill him on the spot: 'Matalde, guardas, matalde' [Kill him, guards, kill him] (III, line 937). The original elevation of his status is ironically reconfirmed by the king's grant of the right for Peribáñez 'de traer armas / defensivas y ofensivas' [to bear arms, defensive and offensive] (III, lines 1036–37). Casilda is rewarded with four of the queen's dresses, an ironic complication of her protestation of contentment with her husband's 'dun coarse-cloth cloak'. Costume and dress play a central role in the play and the stage direction for this scene clearly states that Peribáñez enters 'todo de labrador, con capa larga' [dressed entirely as a peasant with a long cloak (as opposed to the fashionable short cloak or *ropilla*)] (III, line 925). The interplay between visual and verbal aspects of status and self-presentation is one of the most complex and interesting elements of this play's interrogation of issues surrounding class, status and honour.

As with *Fuenteovejuna*, the closure of the play contains potentially disturbing elements for a modern audience; the disproportionate revenge of the protagonist, its brutality in encompassing the death not just of the would-be rapist himself, but also his abettors in the house — Inés, Casilda's cousin, and Luxán, a servant of don Fadrique posing as an agricultural labourer. As Casilda comments coldly: 'No hay sangre donde hay honor' [there is no blood where honour is concerned] (III, line 810), but perhaps there is too much blood. This play is less about the licitness of social revolt than *Fuenteovejuna* and more concerned with the honour code, its role in society and the working out of its exigencies for specific individuals. In the case of the couple, although they are rewarded by the king, there is a certain hollowness to their vindication, as Peribáñez looks forward to resuming his life as a multiple murderer albeit with his honour intact.[17] The problem of the ending was apparent in the adaptation at the Young Vic, London (in 2003, in Tanya Ronder's

---

[16] For a discussion of the role and use of the portrait, see the chapter by Frederick de Armas in this volume. See also Lygia Rodríguez Vianna Peres, 'El retrato en la expresión barroca del teatro del Siglo de Oro: emblemática y teatralidad', in *Memoria de la palabra: Actas del VI Congreso de la Asociación Internacional Siglo de Oro*, ed. María Luisa Lobato & Francisco Domínguez Matito, 2 vols (Madrid: Iberoamericana; Frankfurt am Main: Vervuert, 2004), II, pp. 1507–22.

[17] See Susan Fischer, 'Staging Lope's *Peribáñez*: The Problem of an Ending', *Bulletin of Spanish Studies*, 82.2 (2005): 157–79.

prose translation directed by Rufus Norris), which transposed the action to the present day and polarised the representation of peasant and noble characters, playing down Casilda's approbatory response to the bloodbath at its climax. Its success as a production demonstrates how successful and engaging the play proves for audiences today; the critic Michael Billington wrote that 'at the end of an enthralling evening, one wonders why our experience of classic Spanish drama remains so sporadic'.[18]

Both peasant plays explore anxieties about status and monarchical control. They also contain elements of social criticism, picking up on *arbitristas'* complaints about corruption at court and the abandonment of the countryside by the traditional nobility in favour of the city. The series of plays about rich farmers supplanting corrupt noble authorities, ratified ultimately by the monarch, reflected social changes in the countryside towards the end of the sixteenth century, an increasingly impoverished *hidalgo* class and the rise of the wealthy landowning farmer. The topic was, however, double-edged, since the literary figure of the grasping and corrupt town mayor was as commonplace as that of the dignified low-born *cristiano viejo* [Old Christian], honourable and esteemed by his local community. The vacuum left by an impoverished *hidalgo* class and increasingly urban nobility was not entirely adequately filled by the honourable peasant. Such plays reflect on social order, individual worth and dignity, virtue, and the conflicts generated by reputation, desire, the arbitrary exercise of authority, on what it means to possess honour. The problems that arise when personal merit and quality do not tally with the expectations of social role are not unique to this period but explored in these works of art with a cogency and lucidity that make them endlessly fascinating.

El caballero de Olmedo, although its protagonist is a nobleman, also reveals Lope de Vega's alertness to the changing face of society in the early modern period. The drama, which has long fascinated scholars, is based partly on another play of the same name of about 1606, and, some have claimed, a sixteenth-century song, *El caballero*, which tells the story of the murder of a certain Juan de Vivero in 1521 between Medina del Campo and Olmedo. It is set in the early fifteenth century during the reign of John II of Castile.[19] Don Alonso, from Olmedo, has fallen in love with doña Inés, a woman from the rival town of Medina, who is being unsuccessfully courted by Don Rodrigo. So love-sick is Alonso that he pays a go-between, a Celestina-like figure, Fabia, to intercede on his behalf. The atmosphere of the play with Fabia's machinations (appeals to the devil, despoiling of dead bodies), Inés's lie to her father that she wants to become a nun, to avoid marriage to Rodrigo, and Alonso's and Tello's premonitions of doom (the dream of a goldfinch being caught by a hawk, a vision of his own shadow), leads the audience to the conclusion that the play will end unhappily. And yet, the plot with its love complications, stratagems and disguises is in some ways typical of a love

---

[18] Michael Billington, review of *Peribáñez*, *Guardian*, 9 May 2003.

[19] For a far-reaching discussion of the importance of history in the play see Lappin's fine new edition of it, aimed in particular at English readers, Lope de Vega, *El Caballero de Olmedo*, ed. Anthony John Lappin (Manchester: Manchester University Press, 2006), pp. 20–25.

comedy. (In other plays, such as Tirso de Molina's *Marta la piadosa*, a false vow of chastity to avoid an unwanted marriage is a comic ingredient.) In the third act, as he returns to Olmedo to see his parents, as he does every night, Alonso hears a snatch of song, 'Que de noche le mataron' [At night they killed him] (line 2374)[20] about his own death. A voice, at first mysterious, strikes fear into Alonso with the words:

> Sombras le avisaron
> que no saliese,
> y le aconsejaron
> que no se fuese
> el caballero,
> la gala de Medina,
> la flor de Olmedo.

[Shadows advised him not to leave and advised him not to go, the knight, the jewel of Medina, the flower of Olmedo] (lines 2386–92).

Sure enough, en route, Alonso is shot by his enemy, Rodrigo's men. When the king discovers the truth of the murder in an ironic ending, in which Inés's father offers her Alonso in marriage, he prepares to have Rodrigo and his friend Fernando executed. To add to the poignant sense of waste and what might have been, we learn that the king was about to promote the gifted Alonso.

The twentieth-century concern about whether *El caballero de Olmedo* can justifiably be labelled a tragedy, whilst understandable, has distracted some attention from the fascinating questions the work raises. It is unusual for Lope to deny well-matched lovers their happy ending in marriage in his drama. In other broadly tragic works such as *El duque de Viseo* or *El castigo sin venganza*, there is less teasing of the audience with the hint of a comic trajectory. How can this ambivalence be explained? One answer is that Lope takes more literally than ever his thought from the *Arte nuevo* that there is a beauty in the variety of nature and he reflects this on stage. The irony of the ending strikes a chord with audience members who well know that in real life the best laid plans and the most ardent desires can be cruelly dashed by fate or Providence. If there is a dominant lesson in the play it is that Don Alonso must be regarded, however misty-eyed his contemporaries might feel about it, as an anachronistic hero. The exquisite lover and self-sufficient knight who wears his nobility on his sleeve and trusts to the prowess of his sword arm, dies shot from a distance by an arquebus, powerless to defend himself. Jack Sage's insight seems apposite here:

If there is a flaw in Alonso's character, it is less likely to be connected with his behaviour as a lover than with his obsessive concern for heroics. Lope looks back at our fifteenth-century knight from the perspective of the seventeenth century, and the

---

[20] All quotations are taken from Lope de Vega, *El caballero de Olmedo*, ed. Francisco Rico (Madrid: Cátedra, 1999).

main subject of censure for seventeenth-century dramatists was the hero not the lover.[21]

Nevertheless, from the opening scene of the play the nobility of Alonso's love for Inés is undermined by the glee with which he greets the bawd, Fabia. His excessive words when the *gracioso*, Tello, leads her to him, '¡Oh peregrino dotor / y para enfermos de amor / Hipócrates celestial!' [O extraordinary doctor, celestial Hippocrates of the love-sick] (lines 44–46) are meant to be uncomfortably reminiscent of Calisto's to Celestina in Rojas's tragicomedy. Even the adjective 'celestial' is a hint of the textual genealogy. Like his literary forbear, Calisto — and, one may add, like the mad Don Quijote — Don Alonso seems to be naïvely incapable of operating effectively within his society, of seeing the implications of his actions upon normal flesh-and-blood people. It is perhaps no surprise that his figure was turned into a buffoon by the playwright Francisco de Monteser in his burlesque version of the story which may or may not have been inspired by Lope's play.[22]

The world of chivalry seems to be a thing of the past. However admirable a role model Alonso may be seen to be, Lope suggests that the complexity of the world makes a mockery of his values. A new kind of attitude and a new awareness will be required to survive. Although justice is served (albeit by a monarch 'famed for being unjust', according to Lappin, p. 24) when Rodrigo is punished for his jealousy it is too late for the knight to reap the rewards of marriage. He might have had those by acting in a different fashion. For once the escapism of Golden Age comic resolutions is undermined by Lope in a more pessimistic frame of mind.

Although elsewhere in this volume (see chapter 11) it is argued that Lope de Vega's dramatic vision is often predominantly comic — and indeed comedy in the shape of the *gracioso* is never far from the surface even in serious plays — it is a mistake to see him as an entertainer who gives only occasional thought to the didactic side of the Horatian dictum. In the three canonical plays discussed in this chapter, we see that Lope is acutely aware of tensions in the society in which he himself, lest it be forgotten, is trying unsuccessfully to rise. The nobleman, pillar of the social edifice, is seen to be fallible both when he fails to live up to the demands of his role and when he plays his part too well. Lope de Vega shows dramatically and undogmatically what other thinkers, notably Quevedo and Gracián, as well as a host of treatise writers, were keen to illustrate in their moral and philosophical works. The lasting appeal, mainly to readers, of these canonical dramas surely owes something to their creator's exceptional ability to reflect and reflect upon the still-relevant dynamics of the early modern world.

---

[21] See Jack Sage, *Lope de Vega: El caballero de Olmedo*, Critical Guides to Spanish Texts, 6 (London: Grant and Cutler, 1974), p. 65.

[22] The text of Monteser's spoof can be most easily found in *Comedias burlescas del Siglo de Oro*, ed. Ignacio Arellano et al. (Madrid: Espasa-Calpe, 1999), pp. 113–88.

9

Lope de Vega, the Chronicle-Legend Plays and Collective Memory

GERALDINE COATES

The plays categorized by Marcelino Menéndez Pelayo as 'Crónicas y leyendas dramáticas de España' [Dramatic Chronicles and Legends of Spain] collocate history and myth, chronicity and tradition, historical narrative and national drama. They are indebted to oral and literary forms which were the creative currency of the Middle Ages: chronicle, epic, and ballad. Spain has a lengthy and colourful ballad tradition which sets it apart from its European neighbours.[1] Spanish ballads, collectively known as the *Romancero*, are preserved as poetic texts from manuscripts set down in the fifteenth and sixteenth centuries and later printed texts, but, in essence, they are a traditional oral literary form belonging, in their earliest examples, to the zenith of Spain's Middle Ages. The ballad tradition cannot be discussed in isolation from that of the medieval Spanish epic, which represents a distinct but profoundly influential category of oral literature.[2] Epic is

---

[1] The main reasons for this, according to Smith, are the unity of form of the Spanish ballad, the sheer number of ballads produced and the good quality of the manuscripts and printed texts which preserved them (*Spanish Ballads*, ed. Colin Smith, 2nd edn [London: Bristol Classical Press, 1996]; repr. 2002, pp. ix–x). He also suggests that 'the ballad had early and strong beginnings in Spain because it was used to keep so much of the national past alive and to give voice to collective aspirations' (p. xi).

[2] Much critical discussion has taken place relating to the interconnection of ballad and epic and their respective origins. This is not the place to recount this in detail, but to advise the reader of the broad basis of the argument. The traditionalist view, propagated by the nineteenth-century Romantics, was that lyrics, epics and ballads were composed by the the the folk. Milá y Fontanals, in *De la poesía heroico-popular castellana* (1874), ed. Martín de Riquer & Joaquín Molas, (Barcelona: Consejo Superior de Investigaciones Científicas, 1959), proposed an individual author as the creative force behind each *romance*, a theory developed by his disciple, Menéndez y Pelayo. Menéndez Pidal developed a neo-traditionalist theory which suggested that the Spanish epic is essentially anonymous, was composed at the time of the events it describes, and developed continuously from the Visigothic age, undergoing a series of reworkings. He suggested that the habit of reciting the epics waned in the fourteenth and fifteenth centuries and certain parts of the epics were then reborn as ballads, recounting the most popular and dramatic moments. However, we know that some ballads derive directly from chronicles which had already incorporated heroic tales. Moreover, some ballads are simply adaptations and reworkings rather than true epic fragments. For his theories, see Ramón Menéndez Pidal, *Reliquias de la poesía épica española: acompañadas de Epopeya y romancero*, *I*, Reliquias de la Épica Hispánica, 1, 2nd edn (Madrid:

heroic narrative in verse, which might be the product of oral or written composition, and destined for popular or learned audiences. Through the recounting of exemplary deeds of heroes, the medieval Iberian epic tradition sought to entertain and inspire, as well as to inform and to unify the people. Spain's chronicle tradition is also interwoven with those of epic and ballad through an intricate history of mutual influence.[3] Spain's chronicles are not, by and large, dry historical artefacts, but literary works which often novelize history or represent it with a particular spin for the edification and unification of the people.

These vibrant forms of medieval literature inspired Early Modern dramatists, who were quick to recognize the theatrical potential of local and national history. In 1575, Jerónimo Bermúdez dramatized the story of Inés de Castro in *Nise lastimosa* [*Nise Piteous*] and *Nise laureada* [*Nise Triumphant*],[4] whilst in 1579 Juan de la Cueva staged a version of the epic legend of the siege of Zamora entitled *Comedia de la muerte del rey don Sancho* [*'Comedia' of the Death of King Sancho*] followed, in the same year, by two more plays based on Iberian epic material: *Tragedia de los siete infantes de Lara* [*Tragedy of the Seven Princes of Lara*] and *Comedia de la libertad de España por Bernardo del Carpio* [*'Comedia' of the Liberation of Spain by Bernardo del Carpio*].[5] Lope was likewise motivated by history; his first chronicle-legend play, *El casamiento en la muerte* (c. 1595–97), was based on the tale of Bernardo del Carpio. Due to his sensitivity towards

Gredos, 1980), and *La épica medieval española: desde sus orígenes hasta su disolución en el romancero*, ed. Diego Catalán & María del Mar de Bustos, Obras de Ramón Menéndez Pidal, 13 (Madrid: Espasa-Calpe, 1992). Bédier later developed a theory of the monastic origins of the epic, in Joseph Bédier, *Les légendes épiques: recherches sur la formation des chansons de geste* (Paris: Champion, 1908). More recently, Roger Wright developed an alternative theory of ballad precedence in 'How Old is the Ballad Genre?', *La Corónica*, 14 (1985–86): 251–57. His opinion is that ballads may be much older than previously thought. Some ballads, such as the Infantes de Lara and the Cid, may have preceded the respective epic texts and may have influenced the poets who composed these very epics. We are probably best advised to heed A. D. Deyermond's assertion that 'no single theory can explain the whole of epic poetry, or even the whole of Spanish epic' (*A Literary History of Spain: The Middle Ages* [London: Ernest Benn, 1971], p. 48).

[3] Spain's earliest chronicles are associated with the beginnings of the reconquest, promoted by the success of the Kings of Asturias in dealing with the Muslim attacks. See Kenneth Baxter Wolf, ed. and trans., *Conquerors and Chroniclers of Early Medieval Spain*, Translated Texts for Historians, 9, 2nd edn (Liverpool: Liverpool University Press, 1999), esp. pp. xv–xvii. The historiographical tradition in Spain underwent significant evolution in both its accuracy and approach (see, for example, D. G. Pattison, *From Legend to Chronicle: The Development of Epic Material in Alphonsine Historiography*, Medium Aevum Monographs, 13 [Oxford: Society for the Study of Mediaeval Languages and Literature, 1983]).

[4] For Bermúdez's plays see Alfredo Hermenegildo, ed., *El tirano en escena: tragedias del siglo XVI*, Clásicos de Biblioteca Nueva, 39 (Madrid: Biblioteca Nueva, 2002).

[5] Juan de la Cueva, *Comedia de la muerte del rey don Sancho y reto de Çamora, por don Diego Ordóñez*, in Cueva, *Comedias y tragedias*, ed. Francisco A. de Icaza, 2 vols (Madrid: Sociedad de Bibliófilos Españoles, 1917), I, pp. 11–53; *Los siete infantes de Lara*, in *El infamador, Los siete infantes de Lara y El ejemplar poético*, ed. Francisco A. de Icaza, Clásicos Castellanos, 60 (Madrid: Espasa Calpe, 1941), pp. 60–115; *Bernardo del Carpio*, ed. Anthony Watson, Exeter Hispanic Texts, 8 (Exeter: University of Exeter, 1974).

his sources, and his creative use of them, Lope became the best-known dramatist of Spain's history.

Lope's artistic engagement with chronicle and ballad sources informs the production of his historical plays. In the preface to *La campana de Aragón* he addresses the staging of history, praising the capacity of the theatre to bring what is literal and lifeless into the full dimensions of human experience. Moreover, the dramatization of history offers the possibility of containing all that is precarious about human life securely within the collective memory, and of preserving its most exemplary parts as immortal memories:

> La fuerza de las historias representada es tanto mayor que leida, cuanta diferencia se advierte de la verdad á la pintura y del original al retrato; porque en un cuadro están las figuras mudas y en una sola acción las personas; y en la comedia hablando y discurriendo, y en diversos afectos por instantes, cuales son los sucesos, guerras, paces, consejos, diferentes estados de fortuna, mudanzas, prosperidades, declinaciones de reinos y períodos de imperios y monarquías grandes [...] nadie podrá negar que las famosas hazañas ó sentencias, referidas al vivo con sus personas, no sean de grande efeto para renovar la fama desde los teatros á las memorias de las gentes.[6]

> [The impact of history on the stage is so much greater than when it is read, like the difference one perceives between reality and painting and between model and portrait; for in a picture the figures are mute and the characters adopt a single pose, and in the theatre they talk and move around, with changing emotions at different times, according to events, wars, times of peace, councils, different states of fortune, movements, times of prosperity, the downfall of kingdoms and periods of empire and great sovereignty. [...] With this in mind, nobody could deny that famous deeds and maxims, related live on the stage with characters, are of great use in revitalizing fame, taking it from the theatres to the memories of the people.]

Lope develops a theme found in Juan de Mariana's *Historia general* [*General History*] of 1601: the ability of history to create a memory which outlives time itself:

> La historia en particular suele triunfar del tiempo, que acaba todas las demás memorias y grandezas. De los edificios soberbios, de las estatuas y trofeos de Ciro, De Alejandro, de César, de sus riquezas y poder, ¿qué ha quedado? [...] Las historias solas se conservan.[7]

> [History in particular is the master of time, which does away with all other memories and accomplishments. Of those stately buildings, the statues and trophies

---

[6] Lope de Vega, *La campana de Aragón*, in *Obras escogidas de Lope Félix de Vega Carpio*, ed. Federico Carlos Sainz de Robles, 3 vols (Madrid: Aguilar, 1946–55), III (1955), pp. 835–72 (p. 835).
[7] Juan de Mariana, *Historia de España*, in *Obras del padre Juan de Mariana*, [ed. Francisco Pí y Margall], Biblioteca de Autores Españoles, 30–31, 2 vols (Madrid: Rivadeneyra, 1854), I, p. lii.

of Cyrus, Alexander, Caesar, of their riches and power, what remains? [...] Only histories endure.]

Lope's medieval sources sought, in their original setting, to inspire collective memory. The whole content of the social tradition in an oral culture, writes the anthropologist Jack Goody, is held in memory.[8] What is of social relevance is stored and passed on, while the rest is usually forgotten. Epic and ballad are often identified as the storehouses of collective memories. Whilst practically, and traditionally, memory plays a part in the actual performance of these works, thematically it underpins the entire epic, ballad, and indeed chronicle tradition, which trades in a language of commemoration and distinction. The present chapter will consider how Lope's reformatting of history for the stage seeks to foster collective memory in his own day, and how he employs his sources to this effect.[9]

Criticism of Lope's historical plays has conflated the Aristotelian distinction between poetry as an expression of the universal and history the particular.[10] A. A. Parker's view that 'dramatists are poets not historians' and that a historical theme was 'a medium for expressing a universal truth, nor for painting an historical picture'[11] is complemented by later readings.[12] Stephen Gilman speaks of Lope's gift for 'intuitive re-creation of poetry',[13] echoed by DeLys Ostlund,[14] while other critics have identified history as connecting an old order and a new.[15] Further

---

[8] Jack Goody, ed., *Literacy in Traditional Societies* (Cambridge: Cambridge University Press, 1968), p. 30.

[9] As a preliminary consideration, Roas refers to Lope's method of composing historical plays as comprising a perfect combination of details extracted from the chronicles, legendary material, and elements of his own invention; David Roas, 'Lope y la manipulación de la historia: realidad, leyenda, e invención en la *Comedia de Bamba*', *Anuario Lope de Vega*, 1 (1995): 189–208 (p. 190).

[10] Aristotle, *Poetics*, trans. S. H. Butcher (Mineola, NY: Dover Publications, 1997), Section 1, Part IX.

[11] A. A. Parker, *The Approach to the Spanish Drama of the Golden Age*, Diamante, 6 (London: The Hispanic & Luso-Brazilian Councils, 1957), p. 23.

[12] See Peter Burke, *The Renaissance Sense of the Past* (London: Edward Arnold, 1969), p. 143; Northrop Frye, *Anatomy of Criticism: Four Essays* (Princeton, NJ: Princeton University Press, 1957; repr. New York: Atheneum, 1965), p. 84; Joaquín Roses-Lozano, 'Algunas consideraciones sobre la leyenda de Bernardo del Carpio en el teatro de Lope de Vega', *Inti: Revista de Literatura Hispánica*, no. 28 (1988): 89–105 (p. 100).

[13] Stephen Gilman, 'Lope: dramaturgo de la historia', in *Lope de Vega y los orígenes del teatro español: Actas del I Congreso Internacional sobre Lope de Vega*, ed. Manuel Criado de Val (Madrid: EDI-6, 1981), pp. 19–26 (p. 26); '*Las almenas de Toro*: Poetry and History', in *Essays on Hispanic Literature in Honor of Edmund L. King*, ed. Sylvia Molloy & Luis Fernández Cifuentes (London: Tamesis, 1983), pp. 79–90 (p. 80).

[14] DeLys Ostlund, *The Re-Creation of History in the Fernando and Isabel Plays of Lope de Vega*, Ibérica, 18 (New York: Peter Lang, 1997), p. 7.

[15] Herbert Lindenberger, *Historical Drama: The Relation of Literature and Reality* (Chicago & London: University of Chicago Press, 1975), p. 5; Fernando Lázaro Carreter, *Lope de Vega: introducción a su vida y obra* (Salamanca: Anaya, 1966), pp. 70–71; Alan K. G. Paterson, 'Stages of History and History on Stage: On Lope de Vega and Historical Drama', in *Spanish Theatre:*

strands of criticism draw upon history as a pattern, a cycle or a process in Lope's work.[16] Lope tends toward the universal by recasting medieval history within a framework of growth and decline, a theme corresponding to the strong belief in historical cycles in his day.[17] Indeed, one of Lope's principal sources of written history, Florián de Ocampo's *Crónica general* [*General Chronicle*] of 1541, was a historical narrative based around the notion of fall and recovery which pursued the 'halo-conferring quality of mythical history'.[18] Its aim was less about the facts of history and more about the production of a shared, heroic memory:

> todo el universo entenderán el valor que siempre ha havido en los Hespañoles, como en que será exemplo a los presentes y venideros para seguir e imitar en los hechos heroycos a sus passados y desviarse de lo contrario.[19]

> the whole universe will appreciate the worth that the Spanish have always had, so that this will be an example to the present and future generations to imitate the heroic deeds of the past and to avoid what is wrong.

Lope's treatment of growth, loss, and continuity has clear appeal to the collective memory and can be effectively explored in the chronicle-legend plays set during the reconquest. Analyzing a selection of these plays, I shall illustrate that Lope's interpretation of the theme of cyclical history is a fluid one, and that his creative shaping of a collective memory lies in the translation of the fairly rigid pattern of historical change into a matter of imagination and association, myth and symbol.[20] The narrative of loss and regeneration that underpins the reconquest is evoked directly in *El último godo* (published 1647), where Spain's national foundation myth, that of King Roderick's seduction of the daughter of Count Julian and the subsequent unleashing of Muslim troops to invade the Iberian Peninsula in 711, is played out as a conflict of desires and a series of dislocations between appearance

---

Studies in Honour of Victor F. Dixon, ed. Kenneth Adams, Ciaran Cosgrove & James Whiston (London: Tamesis, 2001), pp. 147–56 (pp. 155–56).

[16] See Lindenberger, *Historical Drama*, p. 8; Renato I. Rosaldo, Jr, 'Lope as a Poet of History: History and Ritual in *El testimonio vengado*', in *Perspectivas de la comedia: colección de ensayos sobre el teatro de Lope, G. de Castro, Calderón y otros*, ed. Alva V. Ebersole, Colección Siglo de Oro, 6 (Valencia: Estudios de Hispanófila, 1978), pp. 9–32 (pp. 31–32); Carol Bingham Kirby, 'Observaciones preliminares sobre el teatro histórico de Lope de Vega', in *Lope de Vega y los orígenes del teatro español: Actas del I Congreso Internacional sobre Lope de Vega*, ed. Manuel Criado de Val (Madrid: EDI-6, 1981), pp. 329–37 (p. 330); Paterson, 'Stages of History', p. 154.

[17] Burke, *The Renaissance Sense of the Past*, p. 87.

[18] Robert B. Tate, 'Mythology in Spanish Historiography of the Middle Ages and the Renaissance', *Hispanic Review*, 22.1 (1954): 1–18 (p. 16). On the use of the Ocampo chronicle by Juan de la Cueva and Lope de Vega, see Geraldine Coates, 'The 1541 *Crónica general* and the Historical Theatre of Juan de la Cueva and Lope de Vega: An Epic Debt', *Bulletin of the Comediantes*, 60 (2008) (forthcoming).

[19] *Cortes de los antiguos reinos de León y de Castilla*, 5 vols (Madrid: Real Academia de la Historia, 1861–1903), v, p. 701.

[20] On Lope's imaginative faculty, see John Dagenais, 'The Imaginative Faculty and Artistic Creation in Lope', in *Lope de Vega y los orígenes del teatro español: Actas del I Congreso Internacional sobre Lope de Vega*, ed. Manuel Criado de Val (Madrid: EDI-6, 1981), pp. 321–26.

and reality.[21] The play begins with the election of Roderick as King of the Goths and his encounter with Zara, daughter of the King of Argel, who is to be baptized and marry the King. Roderick soon falls in love with the cursed daughter of Julian, Florinda, who is sent to accompany Zara and who has since her earliest days had premonitions of her role in the downfall of Spain. A letter reveals to Julian that a ring given to Florinda by her father has been broken by the royal rapier, which he interprets as a sign that his daughter has been deflowered and he must execute his revenge on the King. Julian brings the Moorish forces upon the Peninsula and the King is toppled, while Florinda commits suicide by jumping from a tower. The third and final act sees Pelayo successfully set about the reconquest of the land.

The tone of the play is sententious, even admonitory, whilst structurally it is predicated on tense contrasts which show Lope making full artistic use of the cyclical myth of loss and regeneration: power and submission, rise and fall, light and dark, inclusivity and exclusion, pleasure and torment, loyalty and betrayal. A compelling breach between what is preordained and what is liable to change shows the influence of chronicle and ballad versions of the legend; an aura of prophecy and predestination meets uncomfortably with the single-minded ambitions of the newly crowned Roderick, who wilfully interprets the fall of his crown and sceptre as a sign of imperial expansion rather than the omen of his demise. With the introduction of Florinda this aura gains force. Not only is she born to bring ills to Spain (641) but she seals the fate of the scapegoat King:

> ya sentenciado a morir
> en quien se ha de resumir
> las desventuras de todos. (643)

> [already sentenced to death
> he who shall stand for
> the misfortunes of all men.]

The narrative of demise is written into the play through finer means too. Artful use of language, especially in expressing disillusionment, suggests that the play stages a point of conversion and change: 'pensando hallar riqueza / halló tormento y castigo' [expecting to find riches / he found torment and punishement] (633); 'lo que es en paz traición / es en guerra estratagema' [what in peace is treachery / is in war strategy] (644); 'una hija hermosa, a veces / es destrucción de una casa' [a beautiful daughter, at times / is the destruction of a house] (641). This is most powerfully expressed in King Roderick's fall from royal power, charged with tragic anagnorisis:

---

[21] All quotations from the play are followed by page numbers, referring to Lope de Vega, *El último godo*, in *Obras escogidas de Lope Félix de Vega Carpio*, ed. Federico Carlos Sainz de Robles, 3 vols (Madrid: Aguilar, 1946–55), III (1955), pp. 629–59.

Ayer era rey de España
hoy, por mi desdicha extraña,
no tengo un palmo de tierra.
Del cielo ha sido el castigo;
sin remedio y sin amigo. (649)

[Yesterday I was King of Spain
today, through my strange misfortune
I possess not an inch of land.
The punishment has come from heaven;
without remedy nor companion.]

Lope's echoing of the *romancero* in this demonstrative paradigm of fortune's backsliding confirms his attempt to invest the theme of downfall with distinctly popular dimensions. The fall of Spain is condensed in the synecdochic passing of one human life, the literal closing of the King's eyes, whilst life itself is spurned by Roderick as a continual process of loss: 'donde es perder el vivir' [where to live itself is to lose] (650). What shades of humanity are lost in Roderick's demise are nevertheless recovered in the onset of reconquest by Pelayo. His bodily effort substitutes for the physical loss of Roderick, 'sudando sangre por los poros, / por restaurar este rincón de España' [sweating blood through his pores / to restore this corner of Spain] (656), yet he is also depicted as the lifeblood of myth, rising phoenix-like from the ashes of Roderick's demise (658). With impeccable juxtaposition of death and new life, Lope thus reconstructs the foundational model of fall and recovery espoused by medieval chroniclers. However, he introduces shrewd changes. Whereas the chronicles dwell on the watery grave of King Roderick by the River Guadalete and his mysterious epitaph at Viseo, Lope shifts focus toward the archetypal traitors Bishop Orpaz and Count Julian by assigning them an ominous end: Julian proclaims '¡Judas fui en vida, seré en muerte Judas!' [I was Judas in life, I will be Judas in death!] (654), whilst Orpaz's grave is inscribed with 'mal muere quien mal vive' [He who lives badly dies badly] (657). Here the sequence of contrasts and dislocations that represent growth and decline in the national context encounter a conclusive logic of private justice. This finality contrasts starkly with the mythical lives of Roderick and Pelayo, which are clearly intended to persist in the collective memory.

Growth and decline are at the heart of *El conde Fernán González* (1606–12). In this play, Lope adheres closely to the chronicle narratives and to the thirteenth-century *Poema de Fernán González*, developing their insistence upon territorial expansion and their almost lyrical preoccupation with time and memory, while exploiting a charming geographical contrast between court and country.[22] The play represents Fernán's career as the hero of Castilian independence, beginning with a prediction from a hermit that he will defeat the great Muslim leader Almanzor. Fernán must also battle through tense relations with the Kings of

[22] All quotations from the play are followed by line numbers, referring to Lope de Vega, *El conde Fernán González: tragicomedia*, ed. Raymond Marcus, Chefs-d'Oeuvre des Lettres Hispaniques, 4 (Paris: Centre de Recherches de l'Institut d'Études Hispaniques, 1963).

Iberia, which see him twice imprisoned and twice escape with the help of his wife, Sancha. The independence of Castile comes about in the end not through direct warfare as much as strategy; the King of León is left in a position where he is unable to pay an inflated debt for a hawk and horse Fernán sold him and is forced to give Castile its independence as remuneration.

In both epic and play, Fernán's interest in the perpetuation of his own memory, which occurs at the cusp of his fighting career, unites a tale of territorial recovery with the narrative of his heroic deeds. From the outset, Fernán seeks *fama* by proposing the construction of a place of worship to commemorate his divinely sponsored mission to emancipate Castile (87–88). Animating his men before battle, moreover, he urges them that a good name is won through arms, not inactivity, indicating that the personal pursuit of chivalresque honour is a key part of the culture of *fama*.[23] However, this culture also answers to the ecclesiastical complexion of the poem and its concerns with preparation for the life beyond. The pursuit of honour more acutely focuses the issue of memory on the interchange of the hero's individuality and his role in continuing the illustrious Gothic tradition. Although it is an important premise in the *Poema*, Lope expands this interface of past and present, using the hero as a means of thematizing man's relationship with the past. In the hero's person he evokes the great Pelayo and is explicitly named as 'restaurador segundo' [second restorer] (375), follower of Pelayo's lead (2339–40). However his attributes also suggest primacy:

> es el hombre más fuerte, más gallardo,
> más bravo, más famoso,
> que en España nació, ni está en memoria
> de hombres. (1775–78)

> [He is the strongest, most brave,
> most spirited, most great man
> ever to be born in Spain, or to dwell
> in the memories of men.]

While seeking to be remembered, Fernán thus crosses over into the realm of memory. As soon as he absents himself from the Christian cohorts they make a stone statue in his place, as an aid to the memory of his bravery and a symbol of loyalty. Moreover, towards the end of the play, when Fernán is in prison, one of the guards makes allusion to telling fireside tales about the Count:

> Las frías noches del invierno heladas
> se pudieran pasar contando historias
> del Conde, en todo el mundo celebradas. (2813–15)

> [Cold, frosty winter nights

---

[23] See María Rosa Lida de Malkiel, *La idea de la fama en la Edad Media castellana* (Mexico City: Fondo de Cultura Económica, 1952), p. 200.

> could be spent telling stories
> of the Count, applauded across the world.]

The evocation of the ballad tradition, most prominently the traditional ballad 'Buen conde Fernán González' [Good Count Fernán González], and the semi-erudite 'Juramento llevan hecho' [They Have Sworn an Oath] and 'Preso está Fernán González' [Fernán González is a Prisoner],[24] highlights the perpetuation of popular heroic tradition. While the hero strives to assert his future renown, therefore, he emerges as a character already encased in a heroic tradition, much of him composed of the past. The recollection of specific events in medieval history and in Fernán's life is therefore not the intention of the play. Lope encourages the audience instead to consider the past as a common ground and as a means of looking forward, thereby consolidating group identity through shared memory.

The dynamics of past and present, growth and decline, which underpin *El conde Fernán González* are complemented by a vision of change which picks up on one of the central themes of the medieval legend, the fluctuating bonds of loyalty. This is fundamental to the creation of a climate of instability. Internal strife between Fernán and the Kings of Spain is predicated on their deceitful politics, epitomized by Sancho Abarca's incursions into Castile during Fernán's absence, and Teresa of León's ruse, which culminates in a spell in prison when he is tricked into presenting himself at formal marriage *vistas*, a prelude to his union with Sancha of Navarre, and seized forthwith. Royal alliance with the Moors also stands in contrast to the territorial loyalty of the rustics; when Fernán González is ambushed at the *vistas* the country people regret having lost one of their own (1645–47). Furthermore, the play highlights the manipulative influence of courtiers in the royal circle, those whose loyalties wax and wane, 'amigos a lunas / con menguantes y crecientes' [fly-by-night friends / with waning and waxing phases] (2261–21, 2255–56). It is not until Sancha's pleading appearance before him that Sancho, the most just of the monarchs represented in the play, recovers an aura of rectitude and authority after choosing to believe his courtiers and not his protesting vassal. Quite apart from the bonds of loyalty, the play's vista of change is informed by a delicate tension between man's agency and the perceived vicissitudes of time and fortune. The Count refers to life's inherent capacity for change (890), a certitude he employs to advocate seizing the day. Nuño, meanwhile, voices the inevitability of decline: 'las cosas grandes dan mayor caída' [the greatest objects produce the biggest fall] (892), in terms which restate the reconquest myth of a fall from Visigothic greatness. In underlining the precipitate nature of time and the necessity of change, whilst maintaining constant recourse to the significance of the past, Lope thus establishes a framework for the immortalization of heroic memory which has intrinsic appeal for his own day.

---

[24] Jerome Aaron Moore, *The 'Romancero' in the Chronicle-Legend Plays of Lope de Vega* (Philadelphia, PA: University of Pennsylvania Press, 1940), pp. 84–87.

The fall and recovery motif locked into the collective memory is used with compelling flexibility in *Las almenas de Toro* (1618–19).[25] This epic narrative is based on the contentious endeavours of King Sancho II, eldest son of Ferdinand I, to retain the unity of his father's divided kingdoms, comprising a lengthy campaign to wrest the city of Toro from the hands of his sister, Elvira. A traitor, Bellido Dolfos, features in the play in keeping with the medieval sources of the legend. Whereas in chronicle accounts the traitor kills the King directly on the banks of the Duero with his own spear, in the play account he ensures that Sancho enters the city of Toro triumphant first and sends Elvira into exile. He then kills the King in this fashion later when he sets his sights on Zamora, a detail that is reported by another character, taking place outside the action of the play.

The tale traditionally lent itself to poetic interpretation, and Lope, whilst appropriating historical details from the version in the Ocampo chronicle, and clearly imitating its linguistic style, rhetorical patterns and medieval diction, appears to have seen innovative potential in this legend.[26] The narrative of the play remoulds the archetypal myth of growth and decline into an elastic world of myth, symbol and memory. The title of the play correctly suggests the importance of space, as well as its symbolic potential, within it, which is the first of the ways in which Lope augments the epic account for the purposes of collective memory. The 'almenas de Toro' [battlements of Toro] immediately evoke enclosure and resistance, territorial conservation and loss. More pertinently, they evoke the fifteenth- or sixteenth-century ballad of the same name, converting this play world into a symbolic space of popular meaning. This technique is sustained within the play itself:

> hasta en la cama se duerme
> el niño con las canciones
> que se han hecho a las almenas
> de Toro, y aún están llenas
> de tu historia mil naciones. (786)

> [even in bed the child
> falls asleeps to the songs
> that have been sung about the battlements
> of Toro, and a thousand nations
> are still full of your history.]

The predominant battlements of Toro, as the boundaries of collective memory, are a symbol of inclusivity. By promoting the fact that this space is already located in the Spanish collective memory, Lope foregrounds the success of the very process

---

[25] Quotations from the play are followed by page numbers, referring to Lope de Vega, *Las almenas de Toro*, in *Obras escogidas de Lope Félix de Vega Carpio*, ed. Federico Carlos Sainz de Robles, 3 vols (Madrid: Aguilar, 1946–55), III (1955), pp. 771–805.

[26] On Lope's deviation from his sources in this play and his poetic justification for doing so, see Thomas E. Case, 'Lope's *Las almenas de Toro*: An Example of the Poetic Interpretation of History', *Romance Notes*, 11 (1969): 333–38 (pp. 335–38), and Coates (forthcoming).

he is trying to re-inspire. Collective memory is already a subject of his play, as well as interwoven in its internal logic.

Lope's treatment of rise and fall within the play involves a richly allusive discourse of memory. This is achieved predominantly through the translation of the myth of rise and fall into a symbolic configuration of history and identity. This symbolism converges on Elvira, a character given a prominence not found in medieval chronicles, which concentrate instead upon the obstinacy and guile of her sister Urraca. Elvira is the axis around which growth and decline wheels in the play and of an intrinsically symbolic cast, representing both individual and land, past and present. A focus for contrast, her character is founded upon a basic opposition between corruption and purity. In this respect Sancho is her foil; one of the most arresting contrasts is the juxtaposition of his weapons with images from the natural world, of snow and light, which evoke Elvira's purity (774). As well as her associations with the natural world, Elvira, as defiant heroine, is inextricably linked with the city of Toro. Strong emphasis is placed upon borders in the assertion of her heroic stance; much of the action takes place around the city walls where Elvira's defence and Sancho's attack meet, and preservation and progress lock swords. Her emphatic speech at the end of the first act highlights her proud station:

> haránle un mar de sangre [...]
> y entonces verán, rodando
> del muro sus cuerpos troncos,
> qué doncella se pasea
> por las almenas de Toro. (783)

> [they will make it a sea of blood [...]
> and then they will see, as their
> lifeless bodies surround the wall
> what kind of lady walks
> the battlements of Toro.]

Lope upholds her heroism through physical stature; as she looms from the walls of Toro we gain a lasting impression of her silhouetted as both woman and symbol of strength. Even when she is toppled through deceit she is raised again through her assocation with the heavens (790, 796). Elvira also stands for the contest between old and new loyalties. After her disappearance, support for the new ruler Alfonso is viewed as the product of ambitious self-promotion (804), whilst Nuño suggests a return to the lessons of the past, asking if it were not better to imitate the good vassals of Count Fernán González (803). The connection with this epic hero confirms that Elvira is associated with collective benefit: a reconfigured, yet no less epic, guardian of independence and territory. Moreover, it ties collective memory into the fabric of the play by reiterating the exemplarity of the past. Lope thus constructs his heroine around a tension with particular application for his own time, as 'two currents of reform competed for attention —

one pressing for the return to ancient ways, the other for innovating change'.[27] Sancho's policy of unfettered ambition, which leads to personal and territorial decline, is counteracted in the play by the vision of a past age of moderation and order. Even that perspective, however, is divided by Elvira, the representative of stalwart ways but a model of initiative both in the play and beyond. In this splitting of past and future, stasis and progress, fall and rise, Lope replaces a qualitative insight into the deeds of history with a vision of historical change that converts the markers of time, space and identity into dynamics of social remembrance.

Lope wrote two plays treating the legend of Bernardo del Carpio, a nationalistic pseudo-history in response to French vaunting of the hero Roland which inspired medieval chroniclers.[28] The legend, set in ninth-century León, traditionally includes two parallel narratives: the fate of Spain against advances from the French and the constant threat of the Moors, and the fate of the Count Sancho Díaz, Bernardo's father, who has secretly, and controversially, married the sister of the King of Asturias-León and is thrown into prison in Luna. Bernardo is kept in ignorance of these events and brought up as the King's ward. When the secret of his father's condition is made known to him, he campaigns fiercely for his father's freedom, variously supporting and opposing his king. His military prowess proves so great that the King promises on numerous occasions to free his father as a reward but then reneges on his word as soon as peace was restored. In a nationalistic slant to the legend, Bernardo opposes the King's desire to hand over his kingdom to the French Emperor, Charlemagne, and fights ardently to secure freedom from the French threat. In the chronicle versions the King is forced to agree to San Díaz's release, but by then it is too late as the prisoner is already dead. Undeterred, the King and his men try to restore some semblance of life to the Count and present him regardless to Bernardo, who kisses the cold, dead hand of his true father.

El casamiento en la muerte and *Las mocedades de Bernardo del Carpio* (1599–1608) retain the essential political context of the medieval legend, Moorish presence in Iberia and resolute defence of the land in the name of Gothic continuity, but diverge in their treatment of this material, not least in their endings. That *El casamiento en la muerte* was the first of Lope's historical plays, produced early in the reign of Philip III, is borne out by the emphasis it places upon asserting the greatness of Spain. This is undertaken through direct use of the myth of reconquest and accompanied by a bombastic rhetoric of Spain's greatness

---

[27] J. H. Elliott, *Spain and its World, 1500–1700: Selected Essays* (New Haven, CT & London: Yale University Press, 1989), p. 257.

[28] The Bernardo legend is contained, for example, in the *Historia silense* of 1115; see Santos, Francisco Coco, ed., *Historia silense*, Textos Latinos de la Edad Media Española, Sección Primera: Crónicas, 2 (Madrid: Sucesores de Rivadeneyra, 1921). It is expanded in the *Chronicon mundi* (1236) by Lucas de Tuy; see Emma Falque, *Lucae Tudensis Chronicon mundi*, Corpus Christianorum: Continuatio Mediaevalis, 74 (Turnhout: Brepols, 2003); and in *De rebus Hispaniae* (1243) by Rodrigo Ximénez de Rada; see Ximénez de Rada, *Historia de rebus Hispanie, sive, Historia Gothica*, ed. Juan Fernández Valverde, Corpus Christianorum: Continuatio Medievalis, 72 (Turnholti: Brepols, 1987).

as 'cabeza del mundo' [head of the world] (66).[29] Yet there are cautionary undertones, reminders of failure which might serve an incipient insecurity about the reign of Philip III. Bernardo refers at one stage to King Roderick's loss of Spain and the danger of its recurrence:

> Que España, que Dios no quiera,
> por un Rey que fue lascivo
> se perdió la vez primera,
> y agora por un Rey casto
> es posible que se pierda. (53)

> [That Spain, against God's wishes,
> because of a lascivious king
> was ruined for the the first time,
> and because of a chaste king
> it is possible that it will ruined now.]

King Alonso's character is constructed in the play through careful use of elements of the Roderick legend described above. One scene describes how Spain's victory in battle is found depicted in a cave at Roncesvalles (72), which is reminiscent of Roderick's fabled insistence upon entry to the forbidden house in Toledo and his unlocking of the chest to find the image of Spain's defeat painted on a white cloth.[30] Clearly Lope employs the Roderick myth to excite a memory of Spain's greatness but also to suggest that the exemplary is still to be sought after in his own time, perhaps desirably in its ruler. Indeed, Lope's epic poem *La hermosura de Angélica* (1602) also includes the intrusion of Roderick, this time in a sealed tower in Toledo. Emilie Bergmann notes that this allusion to Rodrigo's reckless disregard for tradition 'sounds a clear warning to the new king'.[31] Moreover, both the Bernardo and Roderick legends, predicated on exponential betrayals, inform the play's marked climate of deceit; the criticism of Ganelon as 'un vasallo de dañado pecho' [a vassal of corrupted breast] (69) might stand more broadly for man's damaged integrity, his shaken faith in king and fellow men. The expectation and discovery of deception are frequently voiced in the play, from the political assertion that 'siempre te engañan traidores' [traitors always trick you]

---

[29] Quotations from *El casamiento en la muerte* and *Las mocedades de Bernardo del Carpio* are followed by page numbers, referring to *Obras de Lope de Vega*, XVII: *Crónicas y leyendas dramáticas de España*, ed. Marcelino Menéndez Pelayo, Biblioteca de Autores Españoles, 196 (Madrid: Atlas, 1966), pp. 2–48 (*Las mocedades*) and 49–93 (*El casamiento*).

[30] On Roderick's entry into the forbidden house see, for example, the chronicle of the Egyptian Ibn Abd-el-Hakem (pp. 18–22), *Estoria de los godos* (pp. 87–88), *Estoria de España* (p. 307), and *Crónica General de España de 1344* (pp. 94–97). The 'casa de Hércules' is also referred to in various *romances*: 'En Toledo está Rodrigo', 'En Toledo está Rodrigo, el rei malaventurado', 'Don Rodrigo rey de España', 'Don Rodrigo, rey de España por la su corona honrar', 'La entrada en la casa de Hércules', 'El palacio de Hércules'. For discussion of the legend, see Ruiz de la Puerta, 1977.

[31] Emilie Bergmann, 'The Painting's Observer in the Epic Canvas: *La hermosura de Angélica*', *Comparative Literature*, 38.3 (1986): 270–88 (p. 275).

(62) to concerns about the inconstancy and broken word of the King (66, 85), to the fraudulent insubstantiality of the monarch offering Bernardo his dead father. *Las mocedades de Bernardo del Carpio*, the later play, although more subtle in its treatment of growth and decline, echoes this collapse of sociopolitical bonds. Enmity between the peninsular kingdoms is exacerbated by the retraction of interpersonal loyalty and growth of antagonism. Even love is analogous with loss, woman with weakness and political instability (7). This crisis of loyalty finds arresting form in the physical contrast between Sancho Díaz's loss of vision and the King's grasping omnipotence: 'está en su mano el poder de poner y quitar leyes' [the power to implement and abolish laws is in his hands] (14).

As a parallel to the military action, both plays narrate the imprisonment of Bernardo's father. The divergent ending of the plays with regard to the fate of San Díaz is telling. In the earlier of the two, *El casamiento en la muerte*, Bernardo is permitted to see his father but finds him already dead and in a scene of lyrical *desengaño* (disillusionment) voices his dashed hopes, comparing himself with one who buys false gold from a thief (92). Despairing of remaining a bastard, Bernardo unites his dead father with his mother in marriage. This apparently morbid ending thematizes continuity and legitimacy, completing a consistent emphasis upon loss and death in the play which supports the notion of growth and regeneration for Spain. Bolstering this revival, in the second act optimistic reference is made to fortune, 'que se muda siempre de males a bienes' [which always changes from bad to good] (71). This seems to be confirmed by the demise of the French. Dudón tells Roland of the downfall of Charlemagne, repeating the Emperor's recourse to the *ubi sunt*:

> ¿que es de tu esfuerzo pasado?
> ¿qué es de tus Doce famosos,
> que dieron al mundo espanto? (78)

> [what has become of your former strength?
> what has become of your twelve famous men
> who spread fear throughout the world?]

Roland dies alluding to 'las lenguas de la fama' [the tongues of fame] (78), thus continuing the theme of memory. Moreover, the narration of Don Beltrán's death is presented as a ballad: 'Por la matanza va el viejo / por la matanza, adelante' [For the kill goes the old man, for the kill, pressing forward] (82), with obvious appeal to collective memory.[32] The expiry of French greatness in the play creates a language of remembrance which ultimately frames the life of Bernardo and serves to promote the myth of Spanish rejuvenation.

In *Las mocedades de Bernardo del Carpio* Bernardo's father remains alive, but this makes the play no less critical of the King. When braving what is supposed to

---

[32] A less literal translation, as provided by Wright, might be 'Over the battlefield / goes the old man'; Roger Wright, ed. and trans., *Spanish Ballads with English Verse Translations* (Warminster: Aris & Phillips, 1987), p. 54.

be the enchanted castle of Luna, which once more evokes the palace in Toledo and the 'casa de Hércules', Bernardo encounters his incarcerated father and the King promises to free Sancho and allow him to marry. This twist in a well-known epic tale of heroism tinged with grief and disappointment most likely serves a political end, presenting the King as a more humane individual. However, the subtext is far from complimentary. The reunion of father and son is conflated with issues of disloyalty and secrecy, not to mention the narrative of royal irresponsibility rekindled by the enchanted castle. The circumstances of Sancho's imprisonment are couched in betrayal; given away by Rubio and tricked by the King, he is kept from public knowledge in a cell, to the point that Bernardo is astonished by the degree of covertness: 'Tanto encubrir, ¿qué será? […] este caso en tantos días / no pudo estar encubierto' [So much secrecy, what is to be made of it? [...] this predicament could not have remained secret for so long] (40). In fact this leads into the manifest question of memory, as Sancho asks:

> ¿Es posible que mi historia
> está de vos ignorada,
> pues en Castilla y León
> hasta los niños lo cantan? (44)

> [Is it possible that my story
> is unknown to you,
> when in Castile and León
> even children sing of it?]

Bernardo's father has become a symbol of intrinsic corruption at the heart of the polity. At the end of the play, with his own release and with this allusion to the story seeping into the public domain and playing on the lips of the most innocent, corruption breaks out fully. The Count's fame thus serves to direct the theme of memory towards the threat of destructive internal politics. It is a narrative of freedom, union and progress at one level, but, more latently, the play engages with contemporary political backslidings. Thus Lope's two Bernardo plays present superficial similarities but differ in their employment of the theme of growth and loss. *El casamiento en la muerte* adheres more strictly to the organizing myth of loss and reconquest in its assertion of Spanish greatness and inquietude over its ruler, whilst *Las mocedades de Bernardo del Carpio*, through subtle but constant affirmations of corruption, indicates that some years into Philip III's reign internal cracks in the system may be deepening.

Drawing some conclusions, the plays discussed here engage with the dynamic of growth and loss which lies at the heart of the reconquest myth, but Lope breaks down and enlivens this theme, projecting it onto the stage with figurative appeal. It has been said that 'change is inherent in the drama, since it is that aspect of human experience which the genre exists to imitate',[33] but Lope's understanding of the way change is implanted in collective experience suggests that memory also funds his theatre. The internal composition of Lope's chronicle and ballad sources is doubtlessly mnemonic, and key to their continuing popularity in Golden Age Spain. Recognizing the lines of popular ballads must have been intensely emotive for the play's audience,[34] and remembering would place the individual within a broader framework of belonging. Lope exploits these factors in his theatre, but creates a deeper, subtler layer of memory in his emotive and protean treatment of Spain's past.

El último godo manifestly presents the theme of historical change in its adherence to the narrative of the fall of Spain. However, it represents a series of internal literary conflicts and contrasts which invest the processes of political change and continuity with a metaphorical quality that breathes life and interest into the medieval myth. In *El conde Fernán González*, meanwhile, an inherent sensitivity towards change is mapped out in the insistence upon time as a relative concept, an inner measurement which is overcome by the hero's insistence upon a life beyond, and by his straddling of novelty and tradition. *Las almenas de Toro* presents growth and loss in terms which exploit the symbolic potential of space and the device of literary contrast. Seizing with acute sensitivity upon the suggestiveness of the epic and ballad versions, Lope's poetics spark the collective memory. Finally, of the two Bernardo plays, *El casamiento en la muerte* combines the historical framework of the reconquest and the political vista of growth and loss with an aura of myth, inspired by the legend of King Roderick and the fall of Spain. The unusual ending represents a point of divergence from chronicle and ballad sources, so that death and its aftermath become a theme which Lope converts into a discourse of continuity and regeneration. *Las mocedades de Bernardo del Carpio* retains an epic dynamism befitting its subject matter and is ambitious in its political reach, yet succeeds in refining and nuancing a vision of insidious corruption.

In his chronicle-legend plays, therefore, Lope demonstrates that collective memory answers to a different language from that of historical report. It cannot solely be kindled in the recapitulation of lessons and events, but in altering and extending the very discourse of history. Knowledge of the past is a form of growth: 'no saber lo que antes de nosotros había pasado, era ser siempre niños' [not knowing what has taken place before our time consigns us to be forever children],[35] but the ability of Lope's theatre to re-shape history and fashion collective memory represents social and artistic progress at an altogether different level.

---

[33] Leroy R. Shaw, *The Playwright and Historical Change: Dramatic Strategies in Brecht, Hauptmann, Kaiser and Wedekind* (Madison, WI & London: University of Wisconsin Press, 1970), p. 3.

[34] Ramón Menéndez Pidal, *L'Épopée castillane à travers la littérature espagnole*, trans. Henri Mérimée (Paris: Armand Colin, 1910), pp. 205–6.

[35] *La campana de Aragón*, p. 835.

10

Sacred Souls and Sinners:
Abstinence and Adaptation in Lope's Religious Drama

ELAINE CANNING

El teatro religioso de Lope no ha sido objeto de atento estudio, aunque lo merecía.[1]

[Lope's religious plays have not generated sufficient critical analysis, although deserving of it.[2]]

Lo religioso, the religious component of Lope's twenty-nine *comedias de tema religioso*, has repeatedly attracted and distracted Golden-Age scholars. However, since the challenge to traditional investigations into the theological aspects of these plays by insightful recent studies on their more complex features, Lope's religious drama has been gaining status in *comedia* circles as a corpus of works deserving of increased critical attention. While his hagiographical and biblical texts are naturally set within a religious framework, it is through the intricate fusion of *lo sagrado* and *lo profano*, the sacred and profane, that plot development, action, thematic concerns and audience expectations are determined and explored. Furthermore, the conventional characters found in many of Lope's most celebrated secular *comedias*, including lovers, jealous rivals, *graciosos* (comic servants) and role-players, are also common types in his religious plays. The aim of this essay is to foreground the complexity at work within Lope's religious drama by focusing on three key representative texts. *San Nicolás de Tolentino*, *El robo de Dina* and *Lo fingido verdadero* exemplify the challenge to textual, character, theatrical and religious boundaries found in Lope's entire corpus of religious plays. As will become evident in due course, the relationship between *santo* (saint) and *gracioso*, the exploitation of metatheatrical devices and the process of the re-creation of source texts for the *corral* are crucial to an understanding of the significance of Lope's religious drama as a whole. These issues are teased out through two principal themes, namely abstinence and

---

[1] Lope de Vega, *Barlaán y Josafat*, ed. José F. Montesinos (Madrid: Centro de Estudios Históricos, 1935), pp. 189–90.

[2] Translations of quotations are my own.

adaptation. While Lope's saints often opt for an abstemious lifestyle, they conflict with gluttonous servants who not only relish good food and wine but are also frequently tempted by females in their presence. Sexual appetite may not be a common preoccupation for the more saintly, but that is not to say that human love plays no part in their lives. In *La juventud de San Isidro* (1622), for example, Isidro experiences the pain of separation from his beloved spouse in order to dedicate himself to God, while Clara, the principal protagonist of *La buena guarda* (1610), exchanges divine love for human love when she abandons her position as *abadesa* (abbess) in order to escape with her lover, Félix. The fluidity of role highlighted by Clara manifests itself in many of Lope's religious *comedias* where characters adapt both voluntarily and unwittingly to a variety of parts. This process of adaptability and adaptation not only triggers a range of audience responses but also complements the literal adaptation of material for the stage. By reworking selected hagiographical and biblical sources, Lope problematizes contemporary issues and continues to toy with audience expectations. The following analyses of the themes of abstinence and adaptation in *San Nicolás*, *El robo* and *Lo fingido* shed light on several of the key issues highlighted above. What is more, they encourage a reading of Lope's religious works from the dual perspective of *lo sagrado* and *lo profano* in order to comprehend the intricacies which lie at the heart of these dramatic texts.

Abstinence and Appetite in *San Nicolás de Tolentino*

San Nicolás de Tolentino (1613–15) (prob.1614)[3] is a dramatization of the life of St Nicholas of Tolentino (1245–1305), a devout Augustinian monk and Patron of the Holy Souls. He was renowned for his daily preaching and visits to the poor, as well as his healing qualities. An ascetic in the extreme, he rejected worldly pleasures in order to dedicate himself to his religious vocation. Yet *San Nicolás de Tolentino* is not just a play about abstinence, charity and miracles. With the inclusion of Ruperto, the *gracioso*, a character 'íntegramente creado por Lope'[4] [entirely of Lope's invention], it also addresses the themes of temptation, gluttony, indulgence and human weakness. Moreover, through the responses of Nicolás and Ruperto to food, the play interrogates the traditional categorization of saint as flawless sacred soul and *gracioso* as sinner.

Rejection of food and the promotion of abstinence and prayer are constant concerns for Nicolás throughout the play. According to the *labrador*/peasant of

---

[3] The dates of composition of the three plays analyzed here are taken from S. Griswold Morley and Courtney Bruerton, *Cronología de las comedias de Lope de Vega* (Madrid: Editorial Gredos, 1968).
[4] Delfín Leocadio Garasa, *Santos en escena* (Buenos Aires: Cuadernos del Sur, 1960), p. 48.

Act II, Nicolás even fasted three days per week as a child (II, 252).[5] In addition, before both he himself and Ruperto become Augustinian friars, Nicolás encourages fasting rather than excess during the period of *fiestas* (I, 243); his advice is 'celebrallas santamente' (I, 241) [celebrate them in a holy fashion]. Following their entry into the monastery, Nicolás' austere lifestyle becomes much more pronounced due to the stark contrast with Ruperto's ongoing complaints about his hunger pangs. In fact, when a Jewish doctor diagnoses lack of sustenance as the cause of Nicolás' subsequent illness and orders a quail to be prepared for him, the saint experiences incredible 'tormento', or anguish at the thought of having to break his vow not to eat meat (II, 261). Ruperto, on the other hand, is tormented by the very absence of food. Spiritual health, that is, nourishment by faith, is advocated by Nicolás. According to his philosophy, 'el alma es vida del cuerpo; / la vida del alma es Dios;' (II, 258) [the soul is the life of the body; / the life of the soul is God]. Furthermore, in his lecture to Ruperto on the benefits of abstinence, he makes reference to St Chrysostom's claim that fasting is the food of the soul (II, 259). However, the restoration of Nicolás' physical health thanks to the curative properties of the Bread of Heaven administered by the Virgin upholds the Christian concept of Christ as the Bread of Life. Nicolás maintains that the bread he has received is 'medicina de la Reina del Cielo' (II, 263) [medicine of the Queen of Heaven] and that the Virgin, like the 'Médico eterno', the eternal Doctor, cures with bread (II, 262). Indeed, Nicolás' own *panecitos*, little bread rolls, are divinely ordained and their restorative qualities are confirmed by angelic voices who claim that they will bring 'saludes' (III, 272) [health]. In addition to the provision of the blessed *panecitos*, Nicolás strives to satisfy the hunger of the needy by other means. His personal rejection of food and belief in spiritual nourishment does not make him lose sight of the necessity of food for the survival of others. The production of food and water at the hands of the saint takes place thanks to divine intervention, something which Nicolás never loses sight of. After feeding a hungry crowd, he informs them: 'Vuelvan mañana al convento, / que Dios para todos da' (II, 254) [Come back to the monastery tomorrow, / for God provides for all]. Similarly, when he miraculously produces a spring in the role of 'agustino Moisés' (Augustinian Moses), he attributes the miracle to God – '… Dios es autor, Dios solo ha sido' (III, 268) [God is responsible, it was God by himself]. While it is evident that Nicolás' charitable deeds are aided by the divine, they are also protected by celestial mediation, even when some degree of deception is involved. In an attempt to dupe the Prior to get food to the hungry, Nicolás claims that he is carrying herbs, rather than bread. The bread is transformed into herbs when observed by the Prior, but miraculously returns to its former state when Nicolás reaches the crowd. Thus, Nicolás confirms Morrison's contention that the saint, according to Lope, '… is not without his contradictions … He advocates

---

[5] The edition of the play used for the purposes of this essay is contained in *Obras selectas*, estudio preliminar, biografía, bibliografía, notas y apéndices de Federico Carlos Sáinz de Robles, 2nd edn, 3 vols (México: Aguilar, 1991), III (Teatro 2), 239–74.

truthfulness, but he does not hesitate to color or withhold truth when it seems advantageous to do so.'[6] Given that Nicolás' harmless recourse to deceit is brought about because of his desire to administer help to others, as well as the fact that his actions are endorsed by the Heavens, his virtuous qualities remain untarnished. In contrast, Ruperto adopts the same title of friar as his master, but his relationship with food and his views on spiritual and physical health are quite different.

Leoni maintains that 'Lope offers his audiences *graciosos* who are more than just a shadow to be forgotten at the play's end.'[7] Due to his tripartite function within the play, Ruperto is arguably of greater dramatic significance than the principal protagonist. He serves not only to make the holy saint more accessible to the *corral* audience but also to highlight the dichotomies present in the figure of the *gracioso* himself. What is more, he provides much needed comedy in a work which would otherwise be a sober staging of Nicolás' disciplined existence. Ruperto is the embodiment of the religious and profane; as an Augustinian friar, he never loses his appetite and remains the gluttonous yet loyal servant of Nicolás. In fact, the very reason why he joins the Augustinians is because his master incites him to follow him. He acknowledges that love of his master can generate the unexpected and he openly admits that he exhibits a series of traits uncharacteristic of a religious individual, including arrogance, non-conformity and idleness (I, 249). Unsurprisingly, then, he faces derision from Celia, his love interest, when he reveals his new vocation. When he explains to her that God usually kills two birds with one stone (I, 250), little does he realize that lack of food will cause him to contemplate the proximity of death. Once in the monastery, he complains that he is dying of hunger – 'que de hambre estoy muriendo' (II, 257). His subsequent inability to remove food from his thoughts affects his behaviour, reactions, relationships and speech and is exploited fully for comedic effect. The *gracioso*'s discourse is particularly playful and reflects the clash between the religious and the secular which he epitomizes. He announces, for example, that the food prepared for the Provincial will contain 'carne de honestidad' (II, 256) [meat of honesty], thus clarifying that the purity associated with the ingredient makes it permissible. This *carne* is a far cry from the *carne*, or flesh of the female which can tempt a man and cause his downfall. Ruperto is fully aware of the temptation of *carne* prompted by the female body and as a result, he initially refuses to look up when Celia delivers a basket of food to him.[8] Such is Ruperto's love of food that he imagines a blood connection with a pot, referring to it as 'una hermana olla' (II, 257) [a sister pot]. In addition, the religious significance of *hermana*

---

[6] Robert R. Morrison, *Lope de Vega and the Comedia de Santos*, Ibérica, XXXIII (New York: Peter Lang, 2000), pp. 92–93.

[7] See Monica Leoni, *Outside, Inside, Aside. Dialoguing with the Gracioso in Spanish Golden Age Theatre* (New Orleans: University Press of the South, Inc., 2000), p. 55.

[8] The association of the female with temptation is also addressed in *El divino africano/The Divine African*. When a woman enters and asks Agustín to listen to her complaint, he states: 'No quiero alzar la cabeza' (I don't want to raise my head). See Lope de Vega Carpio, *El divino africano*, in *Obras selectas*, III (Teatro 2), 205–37 (III, 230).

means that Ruperto's description of his affiliation with the pot is fitting for his new holy environment. Similarly, several of Ruperto's enquiries about Celia's cooking are deliberately imbued with secular and religious connotations. Principal among these is whether Celia still makes her *obispillos* (II, 258), literally her 'little bishops'. According to Covarrubias, the *obispillo* signifies both 'boy bishop' and 'un cierto morcillón', a type of blood sausage.[9] Arguably, the *gracioso*'s interest in both the *obispillo* and 'puerco en sal' (II, 258) [salted pork] substantiates his position as a *cristiano viejo*, an old Christian.[10] As well as that, the reference to the Boy Bishop has notable connections with Nicolás himself. The Boy Bishop, who led the festivities of the choirboys on 28 December, Holy Innocents' Day, was usually chosen on 6 December, the Feast of St Nicholas of Myra (or Bari).[11] It is claimed that Nicholas of Tolentino was named after Nicholas of Bari due to the fact that he was conceived following his parents' pilgrimage to the holy man's tomb to pray for a son.[12] The subtle link established between the *gracioso*'s appetite and his master is symbolic of the complicated interweaving of paradoxical elements throughout the play.

Ruperto's obsession with food leads him to engage in inappropriate forms of behaviour. Such is his craving for a 'morcilla' [blood sausage] that he steals one from the kitchen at the same time that Nicolás takes bread to feed the hungry. Desperation leads to the duping of the Prior, but Ruperto's actions, unlike his master's, are not protected by the divine. In fact, his gluttony is punished when the blood sausage is transformed into a snake. For a second time, he behaves rashly when he hides the basket of food and wine brought by Celia, his angel (II, 258). Anxious to sample its contents, he fails to see that Celia is undeserving of the celestial classification that he has granted her and is more of a temptress, the personification of Eve who promises his downfall. Through the incorporation of the snake and Eve figure, key components of the Adam and Eve biblical narrative, the perils of temptation and gluttony are recalled. Ruperto, however, is saved from indulgence thanks to divine intervention and Nicolás. While the *morcilla* is removed by the supernatural, the basket is physically removed by Nicolás and given to a poor student. According to Nicolás, Adam and Eve 'comiendo pierden / la justicia y la inocencia' (III, 266) [lose justice and innocence through eating].

---

[9] See Sebastián de Covarrubias Orozco, *Tesoro de la lengua castellana o española* (Madrid: Turner, 1977), p. 833.

[10] In *La buena guarda*, Carrizo, like Ruperto, represents the embodiment of the religious and profane as he fulfils the roles of *sacristán* (sacristan) and *gracioso*. What is more, by lamenting the absence of ham, he highlights his link with the *cristiano viejo* even after he has abandoned his position as sacristan. For a more detailed discussion on this, see Elaine Canning, 'Identity and the Refashioning of Role in *La buena guarda*: The Cases of Carrizo and Félix, *BSS*, LXXXIV (2007), 859–69.

[11] See *New Catholic Encyclopedia*, prepared by an editorial staff at The Catholic University of America, Washington, District of Columbia, 17 vols (New York: McGraw-Hill, 1967), II, 741.

[12] In a commentary on Nicolás' origins and how he came to take Holy Orders, the *labrador* makes reference to the visit of Nicolás' parents to the tomb of St Nicholas of Bari (II, 252).

Ruperto, on the other hand, is rescued from a similar sinful act and is redeemed by his holy protectors.

When it comes to protecting his master and witnessing his miracles, the *gracioso* continues to inject humour into critical episodes. On learning that Nicolás is being attacked by the Devil and his cohorts in his cell, Ruperto appears 'armado graciosamente con una escoba en un palo largo y un tapadero de tinaja' (III, 271) [humourously armed with a long-handled broom and a clay pot lid]. His armoury, well suited to one so obsessed with the domestic sphere, provides visual compatibility with his role as comic servant. What is less traditionally associated with the *gracioso* is the courage that Ruperto displays in his encounter with the Devil. Protection of his master takes precedence over his fear of Hell's fire and he does not stop until he has ejected the enemy.[13] His loyalty to Nicolás is thus unquestionable and is highlighted further by his belief in the power of the saint's *panecitos*. When one is used to quell the flames of a fire at Ruperto's suggestion, the *gracioso* provides irrefutable proof that his master is indeed a worker of miracles. In contrast, his reactions to two of Nicolás' miracles appear to verge on the irreverent. When Nicolás brings a roasted quail back to life, Ruperto vows to eat it, despite having witnessed the miracle (II, 263). Subsequently, when the saint creates a spring to satisfy thirst during a period of drought, the *gracioso* comments that he would like some wine to be miraculously produced and ponders the extent of thanks he would give to God should this happen (III, 268). These light-hearted comments do not display a level of disrespect for the saint's accomplishments; after all, the *gracioso* has more than verified the esteem in which he holds his master. Rather, Ruperto's quips serve to make the supernatural more digestible, more palatable. Indeed, he clearly illustrates Dassbach's definition of the comic servant who accompanies the miracle worker:

> … el gracioso humaniza al santo y lo acerca al espectador, al mostrarle su aceptación de lo sobrenatural como algo natural y tan real como cualquier suceso ordinario.[14]

> [… the comic servant humanizes the saint and brings him closer to the spectator by demonstrating to him his acceptance of the supernatural as something as normal and real as any ordinary event.]

In other words, Ruperto not only testifies to the state of holiness of his master but likewise increases his accessibility to the *corral* audience.

Through the exploitation of the themes of appetite and abstinence, characterization becomes a complex feature of *San Nicolás de Tolentino*. On the one hand, Nicolás and Ruperto are categorized as what they essentially are – holy saint and gluttonous *gracioso*. However, the exposition of a more 'human' saint

---

[13] In Act I, Ruperto admits that reference to Hell's fire turns him to ice – 'Cuando en el infierno toco, / su fuego me vuelve hielo' (I, 247).

[14] Elma Dassbach, *La comedia hagiográfica del Siglo de Oro español*, Ibérica, XXII (New York: Peter Lang, 1997), p. 154.

and courageous *gracioso* is set against a backdrop of food-related episodes, imagery and discourse. Furthermore, the obsession and rejection of food not only reinforces important Christian doctrine such as the dangers of temptation and Christ as the Bread of Life, but more importantly it triggers a clash between the religious and secular, the spiritual and physical. Ruperto is the epitome of the fusion and confusion of *lo sagrado* and *lo profano*. He strives to adapt to his blessed milieu, but he cannot compete with the sacred soul of his master. His response to food highlights his fallibility.

Adaptation and Adaptability: *El robo de Dina* and *Lo fingido verdadero*

The practice of adapting texts and the roles assigned to characters is one which Lope embraces in his religious drama. By reworking his source material and manipulating metadramatic devices, especially role-playing within the role and the play within the play, he persistently challenges audience expectations. In *El robo de Dina* (1615–22), one of four plays which takes its subject matter from the Scriptures, he exposes and problematizes contemporary issues, while in *Lo fingido verdadero* (approx. 1608), the most metadramatic play of Lope's entire corpus, both religious and secular, he plays with notions of illusion and reality in order to produce varying levels of confusion.

El robo de Dina is based on Genesis 31.17–35.5 and presents a series of occurrences including the flight of Jacob from his father-in-law, Laban, Laban's pursuit of Jacob and ultimate reconciliation with him and Jacob's encounter with his twin brother, Esau. However, the main action of the play is taken from Genesis 34 and concerns the rape of Jacob's daughter Dinah (Dina in the play) by Shechem, son of Hamor the Hivite. Both the play and the relevant chapter of Genesis end with the deceitful massacre of Siquen/Shechem and his male subjects and the emergence of an angel who urges Jacob to take up residence in Bethel. What has been described by Alan E. Knight as the 'inherently dramatic nature' of the rape of Dinah is developed by Lope in a lengthy act II of what is only a two-act play.[15] The choice of title, *El robo de Dina* stresses the exploitation of the female body, the literal theft of Dinah's virginity by the active male and the establishment of the male (subject) v. female (object) dichotomy. It therefore encapsulates the principal themes of the play – lust/passion, dishonour and vengeance. Furthermore, the overbearing male presence conveyed by the title recalls the style of the source material – it is a 'male-centred' or 'male-oriented' text, where Dinah's views on the rape and her emotional responses to it are absent, as are her feelings about Shechem and marriage. Instead, Shechem's attraction to

---

[15] See Alan E. Knight, 'The Enacted Narrative: From Bible to Stage in Late Medieval France', *Fifteenth-Century Studies*, 15 (1989): 233–44 (p. 236). It has been suggested that *Los trabajos de Jacob/The Trials of Jacob* (1620–30) constitutes the missing third act of *El robo*. *Los trabajos de Jacob* is Lope's fourth and last biblical play and is based on Genesis 37–47 which recounts the story of Joseph and his brothers.

Dinah is pinpointed, as well as the fury of Jacob's sons when they discover that their sister has been raped. References to 'his heart', 'their grief' and 'his delight' abound in the biblical narrative. Conversely, Dina is given a voice in Lope's play; she expresses her reactions to Siquen's advances, the rape, her hatred of him and her desire for bloody vengeance. Indeed, as Yarbro-Bejarano points out, '… she prefers death to remaining, unavenged, the permanent signifier of her male relatives' dishonor' (p. 88).[16] In this respect, Dina comments to her father: 'tu honor y mi afrenta venga, / si no en Siquen, en mi sangre,' (II, 39) [avenge your honour and my affront, / if not in Siquen then in my blood].[17] Furthermore, the beauty of Dina is emphasized throughout the play, a feature which is not stressed in the biblical text. The original Dinah naturally wins favour with Shechem, but the attractiveness of Lope's female is developed right from Dina's encounter with her uncle Esaú in the first act, who describes her as a 'hermosa dama', a beautiful lady (I, 15). By the end of act I, Siquen has witnessed Dina's beauty first hand and has sacrificed his soul to her eyes, which have enslaved him. This hunter now replaces his sport with the pursuit of Dina, despite his former acknowledgment of his negative view of love. According to him, love can only bring a 'trágico fin' (I, 16) [tragic end], words which unquestionably foreshadow his own fateful ending. Siquen the hunter is eventually haunted by a *sombra*, the shadow of his death, despite Alfeo's insistence that it forms part of his fantasy and imagination (II, 47). Thus, the inevitability of his death is suggested and ultimately expected as dramatic tension builds from the early scenes of act I.

Character development in *El robo* is complemented by the problematic treatment of the theme of honour, the presentation of the theme of deception and the possibility of varying audience responses to the depiction of the Jews. With regard to the recuperation of honour, there are conflicting attitudes towards the theme of vengeance within the play. Jacob, for example, informs his sons: 'la venganza es bárbara en los sabios / cuando tienen remedio los agravios' (II, 44) [revenge is a barbarous act in wise men / when there is a solution to insults].[18] But Jacob's resolution to the problem – the marriage of Siquen and Dina – is not acceptable to his sons, nor to his dishonoured daughter Dina, who see murder as the only way forward. According to Yarbro-Bejarano, 'Murder is most likely if the wife has been used sexually by the rival, either with her consent … or through rape' (*Feminism*, p. 132). In Genesis, Jacob's stance on the issue of revenge is difficult to determine; we do not hear him support marriage as a solution, but we do hear him rebuke his sons for the slaughter of the Shechemites. In *El robo*, the difference of opinion between father and children concerning Siquen's

---

[16]   Yvonne Yarbro-Bejarano, *Feminism and the Honor Plays of Lope de Vega* (West Lafayette, Indiana: Purdue UP, 1994), p. 88.

[17]   Lope de Vega Carpio, *El robo de Dina*, in *Obras de Lope de Vega*, ed. Don Marcelino Menéndez y Pelayo, Biblioteca de Autores Españoles, 157–59, VI–VIII (Madrid: Atlas, 1963), VIII, 7–50.

[18]   See Canning, 'Identity and the Refashioning', pp. 862–63 for further information on warnings against revenge and the theme of honour from a Christian perspective in other Lopean plays.

punishment leads to outright deception of Jacob. In other words, responses to the honour code determine the level of deception generated within the play. Having decided to murder Siquen, Leví nonetheless informs his father: '... el acuerdo nuestro / es que con ella se case;' (II, 45) [... we are in agreement / that he should marry her]. The deception of the father is coupled with the deception of the Shechemites, but more brothers are implicated in *El robo* than in the source material. The presentation of the sons as calculating, cruel individuals who not only commit murder but deliberately negate their father's wishes may pave the way for a possible anti-Semitic reading of the dénouement.[19] On the other hand, the brothers seek vengeance in line with the dictates of the honour code, while Jacob's reputation, if not that of his sons, remains intact.

Finally, an analysis of the additions to *El robo* would not be complete without reference to the role of the *gracioso*. Bato, through his gullibility, fearfulness and pursuit of love injects humour and provides a stark contrast to the self-serving Siquen. Bato's unreciprocated love for Zelfa mirrors that of Siquen for Dina, but rather than take his beloved by force, Bato demonstrates self-sacrifice and perseverance despite his fear. One of the clearest examples of this, and without doubt the most comical scene in the play, concerns Bato's attempt to fetch some 'magic water' at Zelfa's request. Led to believe that he has to overcome a talking serpent in order to get the water, Bato literally faces his demons until he discovers that he has been tricked. The simplicity of Bato, who reappears in *Los trabajos de Jacob*, demonstrates a level of innocence which counterbalances the more sombre themes of lust, deception and murder which feature in both the play and the biblical narrative.

Ticknor asserts that in the time of Lope, audiences 'brought a willing faith' to representations of saints' plays.[20] Through modification of his source material, Lope converts the story of Dinah into a play that appeals to more than just the faith of his spectators. *El robo* explores and problematizes many of the themes which preoccupy Lope in his secular drama, including the role of the female and the *gracioso* and the implications of deception, dishonour and revenge. In other words, thanks to the re-creation of selected chapters from Genesis, Lope approximates *El robo* to his secular plays in terms of thematic trajectory.

The interplay between the religious and the profane, divine love and human love and illusion and reality determines the dramatic action of *Lo fingido verdadero*. A re-creation of the life of St Genesius, patron saint of actors,

[19] The Jews are upheld as a 'santo pueblo hebreo' in *La hermosa Ester*, a play in which Lope deliberately omits the murder of Haman and his sons by the Jews. For an in-depth analysis of this biblical play, see Canning, '*La hermosa Ester* and the Re-creation of the Biblical Esther', in *Lope de Vega's comedias de tema religoso: Re-creations and Re-presentations* (Woodbridge: Tamesis, 2004), pp. 9–43. In contrast, Alexander Samson notes Lope's 'ambiguous representation of the *hebreos*' in *El niño inocente de La Guardia*. See his 'Anti-Semitism, Class, and Lope de Vega's *El niño inocente de La Guardia*', *Hispanic Research Journal*, 3.2 (2002): 107–22 (p. 120).

[20] George Ticknor, *History of Spanish Literature*, 3 vols (London: John Murray, 1849), II, 210.

Lo fingido constitutes Lope's most skilful interrogation of the *theatrum mundi* topos, a motif explored by many seventeenth-century Spanish writers and artists. Weisinger states that:

> *Theatrum mundi* is … an extended metaphor; the world is symbolized as a theatre, and all its events, or plot, and all its inhabitants, or *dramatis personae*, are depicted as taking place and acting within its confines and within its particular terms as a medium of representation.[21]

The illusory nature of life explicit in *theatrum mundi* is encapsulated in the play's title, *Lo fingido verdadero*. What is more, it links directly to seventeenth-century Spain's theocentric view of the world as stage, a preparation for the true role to be embraced in the afterlife. With its focus in act III on the conversion and martyrdom of St Genesius, *Lo fingido* is categorized as a *comedia de santos*, a hagiographical play. However, as indicated by Dixon, its 'metateatralidad' [metatheatricality] is 'el atractivo primordial de la obra de Lope' [the most appealing feature of Lope's work].[22] In act I, a representation of the rise to power of the emperor Diocletian (Diocleciano), characters engage in positive and negative forms of role-playing within the role. Acts II and III are each dominated by a play within the play in which Ginés is the principal protagonist. While the subject matter of his first inset play is human love, divine love features in the second and in both cases, the boundaries between the inset play and main play, or illusion and 'reality', become blurred. An enquiry into the metatheatrical devices of role-playing within the role and the play within the play draws attention to the unpredictable nature of reality. Both inset plays serve to confound the *corral* audience, the inner audience and the actors themselves who role-play within their prescribed roles. What is more, the second play within the play reshapes Ginés' 'true' role, that is his role within the main play, by casting him into a part which he embraces fully but never sought. It is the second play within the play which concerns us here.[23]

In act III, Diocleciano requests a performance based on the portrayal of a baptized Christian. Ginés obliges, not knowing that he will become the Christian he is impersonating. His conversion frustrates the expectations not only of the inner audience (Diocleciano and his favourites) and the actors within the inset play, but also those of the outer, *corral* audience. Despite several spectators' familiarity with the hagiographical text, the play within the play is constructed in such a way that it is impossible to determine at what point the conversion actually

---

[21]   Herbert Weisinger, '*Theatrum Mundi*: Illusion as Reality', in *The Agony and the Triumph: Papers on the Use and Abuse of Myth* (East Lansing: Michigan State UP, 1964), 58–70 (p. 59).

[22]   See Victor Dixon, '"Ya tienes la comedia prevenida … La imagen de la vida": *Lo fingido verdadero*', *Cuadernos de teatro clásico*, 11 (1999): 53–71 (p. 55).

[23]   A comprehensive analysis of acts I–III in terms of their metatheatrical properties is not possible within the scope of this essay. For a detailed study of role-playing within the role and the play within the play in *Lo fingido*, see Canning, '*Lo fingido verdadero* as metaplay', in *Lope de Vega's comedias de tema religioso*, pp. 95–127.

occurs. Ambiguities abound from rehearsals to the dénouement when Ginés reveals to both audiences that he has received baptism. The fusion of illusion and reality commences when an offstage voice addresses Ginés during rehearsals. On his representation of the Christian, the voice asserts: 'no le imitarás en vano, / Ginés, que te has de salvar' (III, fol. 280r) [You will not play the part in vain, Genesius, for you will be saved].[24] Although he considers that the voice could have emanated from the Heavens, he concludes, mistakenly, that it belongs to Fabio, a member of his troupe. Subsequently, just before the inset play begins, he vows to follow Christ:

> ¡Cristo mío, pues sois Dios,
> vos me llevaréis a vos,
> que yo desde ahora os sigo!
>
> (III, fol. 280v)

> [My Christ, as you are God, you will direct me to you, for I will
> follow you from this point onwards!]

Yet it is unclear to the *corral* audience whether his remark forms part of the warm-up or whether Ginés has already accepted Christianity. Once the play gets under way, Ginés' improvisations and deviations from the script make it difficult to ascertain whether he is speaking as himself or as León, the character he is supposedly playing. What is more, the baptismal scene is particularly difficult to decipher; an angel addressing Ginés by his real name, rather than León, invites him to receive baptism. In order for Ginés' baptism to be 'real', it would have to be carried out by a celestial angel, rather than Fabio, the actor designated to play the part. However, the captain and inner audience make an association between the alleged celestial angel and Fabio, calling into question whether the baptism is part of the main or inset play. When Ginés finally asserts himself as a Christian, he does so by employing theatrical language, describing his transformation and its implications as a series of acts:

> Césares, yo soy cristiano,
> ya tengo el santo bautismo,
> esto represento yo,
> porque es mi autor Jesucristo;
> en la segunda jornada
> está vuestro enojo escrito,
> que en llegando la tercera
> representaré el martirio.
>
> (III, fol. 282v)

[24] Lope de Vega Carpio, *Lo fingido verdadero*, in *Decimasexta parte de las comedias* (Madrid: Viuda de Alonso Martín, 1621), fols 261r–84v. All quotations are taken from this edition.

[Caesars, I am a Christian, I have now received holy baptism. This is the part I am playing because my director is Jesus Christ. Your anger is written in the second act, and when the third act comes, I'll perform martyrdom.]

As he faces martyrdom, he looks forward to his part within the *comedia divina* scripted by God: 'mañana temprano espero / para la segunda parte' (III, fol. 284v) [early tomorrow I await the second part of this play]. Through the use of the play within the play, Lope questions the very essence of reality and identity at the same time that he reinforces his audience's theocentric world view. Double images, unexpected role-change and the merging of dramatic fiction and reality point to the intangibility of reality and the complicated process of self-discovery. What is evident, however, is the redeeming power of divine love which determines Ginés' true role.

As Lope's saints and sinners pursue passions and vocations, secular and religious worlds merge to complicate characterization and plot. The adaptation of source material and the employment of metadramatic devices add further levels of dramatic multiplicity. Ultimately, the analyses of *San Nicolás*, *El robo* and *Lo fingido* highlight that there is much more to Lope's *comedias de tema religioso* than simply 'lo religioso'.

11

Lope, the Comedian

JONATHAN THACKER

> Di, Lucindo, ¿a un padre noble
> los buenos hijos engañan?
>
> [Tell me, Lucindo, do good children
> deceive a noble father?]
> (*La discreta enamorada*)[1]

When Lope de Vega writes of having composed plays 'sin el arte' [without art] or 'contra el arte' [against art] (*Arte nuevo*, lines 16, 135) it is not, he claims, because he is ignorant of the classical precepts to which he refers, but because he cannot survive as a dramatist without the approval of his audience. The public's less educated majority (the 'vulgo'), he avers, has become accustomed to a monstrous variety within a play. Whilst such variety may be undesirable because it is disorderly in aesthetic terms, it can at least claim a certain beauty in its proximity to 'naturaleza' [nature] (line 179), since life itself is varied.[2] Lope's attitude to contemporary drama, as to many things, is calculatedly ambivalent: his academic audience — the *Arte nuevo* is written as a speech to Academy members — can sense both a staged frustration that one can no longer write pure comedy or pure tragedy, and a boldness in his assumed role of defender of this new hybrid, which the erudite will not deign to support.

But what exactly are the mixed plays which warrant the composition of a new art? In a basic sense the term 'tragicomedy' will do to describe them: they are, in Lope's words, 'lo trágico y lo cómico mezclado, / y Terencio con Séneca' [the tragic and the comic combined, Terence with Seneca] (lines 174–75). There is not a rigid separation of the high-born from lesser mortals, as a classical 'art' would require from tragedy and comedy; the stakes to be played for are not consistently either very great or fairly insignificant; the ending is no longer either calamitous or just happy; the movement of the play is neither uniformly from calm to turbulence nor in the opposite direction; the didactic norms of encouraging the

---

[1] Lope de Vega, *Arte nuevo de hacer comedias*; *La discreta enamorada*, Colección Austral, 842 (Madrid: Espasa-Calpe, 1948), p. 152.

[2] Lope de Vega, *Arte nuevo de hacer comedias*, ed. Enrique García Santo-Tomás (Madrid: Cátedra, 2006). See chapter 7 for a consideration of this important text.

rejection or embracing of a certain approach to life are muddied; the rigid distinction between the origins of the two genres in history or in fiction is dissolved; and high and low styles are mixed.[3] It is thus not incorrect to dub the bulk of Lope's dramatic output 'tragicomic', but the epithet, broadly understood, sheds little light on most works.

A bolder assertion would be the claim that Lope de Vega most naturally penned plays that are comic in nature, *comedias cómicas* as it seems sensible to call them.[4] The assertion is bold because of the sheer number of plays one needs to assess, because there has been a reluctance to define or decide what 'comic' actually means for Lope, and because so many works remain to be tested in the crucible of performance.[5] There is such a thing as a Lopean tragedy, a 'political' Lope emerged particularly in his usually historical 'kingship' plays, he wrote serious dramas with peasant protagonists, he was inspired by the lives of saints and the Old Testament to dramatize religious stories, and he frequently plundered ballads and epics (including the influential Ariosto) for broadly serious plots; but beyond these non-comic categories there lies this host of other works.[6] These plays tend not to follow the classical legacy of provoking audience laughter at the ridiculous, the clumsy or the ugly. Instead their comic mode is identifiable in the habitual, indeed predominant, recourse to wit of all kinds (often *agudeza* in dialogue, or *ingenio* in trickery) and its role in the unfolding and resolution of the drama. Such plays do often follow the classical norm of ending happily, in marriage(s), but both through their endings and as their plots are developed, they may engage thoughtfully, critically, in short, seriously, with the world they are ineluctably related to.

Part of the explanation for Lope's exploitation of the comic mode can be found in the fortunes of sixteenth-century Spanish drama: the successful, money-making

---

[3] These seven principal differences between classical tragedy and comedy are paraphrased from López Pinciano's *Philosophía antigua poética*, of 1596, the most important Spanish discussion of classical artistic theory of the period; see Alonso López Pinciano, *Obras completas*, I: *Philosophía antigua poética*, ed. José Rico Verdú (Madrid: Fundación José Antonio de Castro, 1998), pp. 382–83. As El Pinciano recognizes, these generic distinctions were not rigidly adhered to even in classical times.

[4] The adjective is necessary because of the triple meaning of *comedia* in Spanish; see my *A Companion to Golden Age Theatre* (Woodbridge: Tamesis, 2007), pp. 144–46.

[5] Scholars are sometimes surprised when plays they have studied emerge in unexpected guises when staged. This can further complicate what is already a complex matter of definition.

[6] This is perhaps especially true in the early period, up until 1598; see Juan Oleza, 'Del primer Lope al *Arte nuevo*', 'Estudio preliminar' to Lope de Vega, *Peribáñez y el comendador de Ocaña*, ed. Donald McGrady, Biblioteca Clásica, 53 (Barcelona: Crítica, 1997), pp. ix–lv (pp. xvi–xxi). For a consideration of the tragedies, see Gail Bradbury, 'Tragedy and Tragicomedy in the Theatre of Lope de Vega', *Bulletin of Hispanic Studies*, 58.2 (1981), pp. 103–11; on political Lope (including the peasant plays), see Melveena McKendrick, *Playing the King: Lope de Vega and the Limits of Conformity* (Woodbridge: Tamesis, 2000); on saint's plays, see Robert R. Morrison, *Lope de Vega and the 'Comedia de Santos'*, Ibérica, 33 (New York: Peter Lang, 2000), and Elaine M. Canning, *Lope de Vega's 'Comedias de tema religioso': Re-creations and Re-presentations* (Woodbridge: Tamesis, 2004); on Lope's use of the chronicles, see Coates's chapter in the present volume, and of the ballads, see Jerome Aaron Moore, *The 'Romancero' in the Chronicle-Legend Plays of Lope de Vega* (Philadelphia, PA: University of Pennsylvania Press, 1940).

theatre was popular comedy, whether in the form of the Italian *commedia dell'arte*, which he enjoyed watching in Madrid as a young man, or the entertaining plays of the itinerant troupes, such as that of Lope de Rueda, with their detachable comic scenes similar to the farcical *entremés*. For whatever reason, the brief flurry of classical-style tragedies, written by Virués, Cervantes and others as the first permanent playhouses opened in the Spain of the 1570s and 1580s, failed to catch the imagination of the play-going public.[7]

In his early period then, the two decades or so from when he started to write plays until the temporary closure of the theatres in 1598–99, Lope's drama is very varied, as he begins to find a distinctive voice by avoiding what the public has not taken to and trying to adapt and mimic forms and genres which have been box-office or publishing successes.[8] In a study of fourteen urban comedies written between about 1590 and 1606, Ignacio Arellano stresses in particular Lope's dependence on the often seedy and ignoble worlds of Boccaccio's *Decameron* and of the *Celestina*.[9] Not all of Lope's early plays are comic, of course, but many are, even though elements of their content, characterization, structure and language can seem alien to those who have read chiefly his mature comedies and those of his contemporaries and followers, especially Calderón de la Barca.[10] Indeed, *Las ferias de Madrid* of 1587–88, has appeared to be 'extraño y escandaloso' [odd and scandalous] to scholars, who have also hesitated in the face of the wife-murder play, *Los comendadores de Córdoba* (1596), which 'could without strain be played for laughs as a black farce'.[11] The former play, with its unusual resolution involving the murder of Patricio, husband of the *dama* (female lead),

---

[7] For further details and bibliography on sixteenth-century theatre, see my *Companion to Golden Age Theatre*, chapter 1.

[8] See, for analyses of this important formative period, Lavonne C. Poteet-Bussard, 'Algunas perspectivas sobre la primera época del teatro de Lope de Vega', in *Lope de Vega y los orígenes del teatro español: Actas del I Congreso Internacional sobre Lope de Vega*, ed. Manuel Criado de Val (Madrid: EDI-6, 1981), pp. 341–54; Frida Weber de Kurlat, 'Lope-Lope y Lope-preLope: formación del subcódigo de la comedia de Lope y su época', *Segismundo*, 12, nos 23–24 (1976): 111–31; and Juan Oleza, 'La propuesta teatral del primer Lope de Vega', *Cuadernos de Filología* (Valencia), 3.1–2: *La génesis de la teatralidad barroca* (1981): 153–223, and 'Del primer Lope al *Arte nuevo*'. For a specific example of Lope standing on the shoulders of Ariosto, see my 'Lope de Vega's Exemplary Early Comedy, *Los locos de Valencia*', *Bulletin of the Comediantes*, 52.1 (2000): 9–29, esp. pp. 23–25.

[9] Ignacio Arellano, 'El modelo temprano de la comedia urbana de Lope de Vega', in his *Convención y recepción: estudios sobre el teatro del Siglo de Oro* (Madrid: Gredos, 1999), pp. 76–106. Of *La viuda valenciana*, he writes: 'Toda la trama se desarrolla en el tono de cuento boccaccesco, desenvuelto y cómico, de un erotismo directo y sin paliativos' (p. 87).

[10] Oleza, 'Del primer Lope', reckons that there are some thirty comedies amongst the plays by Lope that can certainly be dated before 1599, as against about twenty *dramas*. He divides them into five types, comedias 'pastoriles, palatinas, novelescas, urbanas y picarescas' [pastoral, palace, novelesque, urban and picaresque] (p. xvi), but scholars are not always in agreement as to categorizations of individual plays.

[11] The first quotation is from Arellano, p. 88 and the second from Melveena McKendrick, 'Celebration or Subversion?: *Los comendadores de Córdoba* Reconsidered', *Bulletin of Hispanic Studies* 61.3 (1984): 352–60 (p. 359). *Los comendadores de Córdoba* is not usually taken to be a comedy, but McKendrick's claim is certainly justifiable. See also Evans's contribution to this volume.

Violante, by her father to allow her an unexpected 'happy' ending in marriage to her lover, Leandro, is just one of a number of experimental urban comedies of the period.[12] The manner in which dishonour is avoided in *Las ferias de Madrid* is indeed striking: the father, Belardo, explains in a soliloquy delivered over the body of his son-in-law, whom he has stabbed in the buttocks:

> El honor ha de vivir.
> Es mujer, y pudo errar,
> y yo padre, y perdonar,
> y éste mortal, y morir.[13]

> [Honour must survive.
> She is a woman, susceptible to error,
> I am a father, and can forgive,
> and this man is mortal, and can die.]

As it happens, Patricio is a despicable man, himself unfaithful to Violante, but his death could not have been played comically once the norms of the *comedia de capa y espada* (cloak and sword play) had become set in the early years of the seventeenth century.[14] *Las ferias* has a feel quite distinct from later comedies in other ways too: there is little unity of action — less than half of the stage business relates to the central story — for Lope is primarily interested in setting up the 'ambiente erótico-festivo de las ferias' [erotic-festive atmosphere of the fairs/fêting] which he does by populating the stage with certain city types who play tricks on others, dress up, and try their hands at seducing *madrileñas*.[15] The cast is consequently large and the characters are a mixture of picaresque and bourgeois types; the scene is set mainly in the street, not within the house; and the register of the language is low with frequent bawdiness and sexual double-entendres.

By the time of *Los locos de Valencia* (1590–95), a play set in Europe's first asylum for the mentally ill and written only a few years after *Las ferias*, Lope has still not settled on all his staple comic ingredients, but there is now a clear focus on a central action, however unlikely its elaboration. As in *Belardo el furioso* (1586–95), a pastoral comedy with a strong autobiographical element, and many

---

[12] In his introduction *to El acero de Madrid* (Madrid: Castalia, 2000), Stefano Arata mentions *La bella malmaridada* (1596), *El mesón de la corte* (1588–95), *La francesilla* (1596), *El Grao de Valencia* (1589?) and *Viuda, casada y doncella* (1597) alongside *Las ferias de Madrid* (p. 23).

[13] Lope de Vega, *Las ferias de Madrid*, ed. Donald McGrady (Newark, DE: Juan de la Cuesta, 2006), lines 3167–70.

[14] The *capa y espada* play, a type of urban comedy set in contemporary times and involving the love affairs of the minor nobility or bourgeoisie, became the dominant comic form in the *corrales* after about 1600. The other major sub-genre was the *comedia palatina* (palace comedy). See my *Companion to Golden Age Theatre*, p. 150, and Felipe B. Pedraza Jiménez, *Lope de Vega* (Barcelona: Teide, 1990), p. 127, for further definition of these related forms.

[15] The quotation is from David Roas, ed., *Las ferias de Madrid*, in *Comedias de Lope de Vega: Parte II*, dir. Alberto Blecua & Guillermo Serés, 3 vols (Lleida: Milenio & Universitat Autònoma de Barcelona, 1998), III, pp. 1823–1967 (p. 1827).

other early works, the playwright remains keen to advertise the kinship of his output to established literary forms (here Ariosto), but there is strong evidence too of a fuller, more developed and more independent comic vision. The Valencian hospital provides Lope with a chance to contrast the behaviour of apparently sane individuals with those who are actually mad or feigning madness, to dramatize a theme treated by Erasmus and others. Again it is a 'Belardo' (one of the authorial spokesmen in Lope's drama), an inmate, who, as well as reminding the audience of the Horatian commonplace that drama should delight and instruct,[16] provides a lesson on which the audience would do well to ponder:

> Porque en este tiempo
> no me daréis un hombre tan perfecto
> que no haya hecho alguna gran locura,
> y vos podéis juzgar por vuestro pecho
> lo que conozco yo por vuestra frente. (lines 2568–72)

> [Because these days
> you can't show me a man so perfect
> that he hasn't committed some great act of madness,
> and you can determine from your heart
> what I can tell from your face.]

Belardo well knows that there is a difference, remorselessly and resourcefully exploited by Lope in his comedies, between the composed and conformist face presented to the world and the anarchic inner world of desire and semi-hidden urges. This nether world is revealed in comedy through madness, jokes and the escape from intolerable pressures created by suppressed feelings. The playwright develops a comic voice that will rarely be mordant: he is too sympathetic to these human foibles to produce social satire in the same vein as a Francisco de Quevedo. For Lope, the attraction of comedy is in part the access it gives to a world in which fantasies can be lived out, in which the kinds of wish fulfilment and self-expression that social pressures habitually deny, are momentarily possible. The rational sometimes needs to be escaped, and in the upside-down world dramatized, the seething brains of the lunatic, the lover and the poet (Belardo is a mad poet) can be apprehended a realm no less significant for being beyond cool reason.

It is no surprise then, given the marginalization of women's desires within early modern Spanish society, to find Lope de Vega increasingly placing a female figure at the heart of his comic plays. The title of *Las ferias de Madrid* may betray an interest in the capital, and the anonymity it provides, at a time when a certain sexual licence is possible; *Los locos de Valencia* may suggest an equal concern with male and female development in love, although within a wider fascination with what constitutes madness; later titles, however — *La viuda valenciana*

---

[16] Lope de Vega, *Los locos de Valencia*, ed. Hélène Tropé, Clásicos Castalia, 277 (Madrid: Castalia, 2003), lines 2502–7.

(1595–1603), *La bella malmaridada* (1596), *Viuda, casada y doncella* (1597), *Los melindres de Belisa* (1604–8), *La discreta enamorada* (1606), *La dama boba* (1613), *El perro del hortelano* (1613–15), *La vengadora de las mujeres* (1613–20), *La moza de cántaro* (pre-1627), *Las bizarrías de Belisa* (1634), to name a few — reveal an increasing tendency to recognize the importance of the woman as the hub around which the action spins. This action is now as likely to take place inside the house/palace as in the street, the garden, the church and the city square. The central female figure is intriguing in herself, enticingly transgressive, but also *representative* of the freedom to act that the forces of patriarchy and social conservatism would curtail.

Viuda, casada y doncella, one of the last works from the early period, can usefully represent Lopean comedy as it evolves further towards its mature form. Here there is unity of action, although the play has myriad sources,[17] and in spite of the evident holes in the plot and its lack of verisimilitude, most of the other elements of Lope's mature urban comedy are present. The faithful lovers, Clavela and Feliciano, triumph over the hurdles of a nagging maid, Leonora, a litigious lover, Liberio, who is favoured by Clavela's father, Albano, and the latter's hostile opposition to their union, and manage to secure a marriage. The father (or brother) and spurned lover(s), acting against the desires of the central pair(s) of lovers and in thrall to money or honour, are almost invariably central to Lope's comic plots henceforth. In the case of *Viuda, casada y doncella* the marriage is interrupted before being consummated, allowing Lope to maintain an undercurrent of erotic double-entendres throughout, since Clavela remains *casada* (a married woman) but *doncella* (a virgin), a state her would-be conquerors are desperate to change. When Feliciano is feared drowned, Albano bullies his daughter into taking Liberio as a second husband, only to find that Feliciano turns up as an unwelcome wedding guest, having somehow returned from captivity in North Africa and become fortuitously rich. It falls to Feliciano finally to sleep with his wife and Liberio suffers the same fate that his rival once did, gnashing his teeth in his sexual frustration: '¿No hubo dónde cayese, / no hubo una calentura / que un hora le detuviese?' [Could he not have had a fall, could he not have had a fever that would have delayed him by an hour?] (lines 2949–51).

The other very significant comic ingredient that begins to develop in the 1590s, and is a feature of *Viuda, casada y doncella*, is the figure of the *gracioso* (comic servant). Celio, in this case, acts as a comic foil to his master, displaying many of the usual anti-heroic characteristics of his type — gluttony, cowardice, lust, a mercenary streak, misogyny, religious intolerance — but also a ready wit and endearing faithfulness to Feliciano. In this case Celio marries nobly, thus taking a more prominent role than is usual for his character-type in the comedy's dénouement. The *gracioso*, who has a number of forbears in Classical, as well as Italian and Spanish popular drama, will not subsequently part from his master in

---

[17] See the introduction to the edition by Ronna S. Feit and Donald McGrady (Newark, DE: Juan de la Cuesta, 2006), pp. 7–22.

Lopean comedy, whether the play is set in palace or city.[18] Indeed his role's importance is magnified in plays such as *El perro del hortelano* and *La discreta enamorada*, where he is responsible for reading signs or inventing strategies which help the *galán* (male lead) to succeed in his amorous quest.

After a short gap Lope began to write for the stage again when the *corrales* (playhouses) reopened in 1599, and so began a period that is marked by a preponderance of *dramas*, especially historical plays, rather than comedies. This change to more serious subject matter may have come about at least in part as the result of moral criticisms made by opponents of the theatre and against which the theatre had to defend itself.[19] The types of comedy Lope would now write settled more recognizably into the main categories of *palatinas* and *urbanas* (or *de capa y espada*). Whilst the playwright was still wont to search for plot ideas in the Italian *novella*, and whilst his comic vision continued to develop, as we shall see, the plays themselves became a little more formulaic. However, it would be a mistake to see this last development as negative: in the series of plays which see beautiful, clever women overcome (sometimes self-inflicted) obstacles on the path to their desired marriage, Lope produces some of his most memorable characters and his most coruscating drama. He is at the height of his comic powers.

La discreta enamorada (1606), inspired by one of Boccaccio's stories, advertises its comic credentials in the opening scene in which an aunt, Belisa, is outfoxed by her protégée, Fenisa.[20] The play, which alternates outdoor settings largely inaccessible to Fenisa with her home in which she can control events with ease, charts the *dama*'s successful winning of Lucindo, the *galán* for whom she has fallen. Its novelty lies in the fact that Fenisa cleverly makes use of predictable male behaviour to achieve her ends, making her presence in the male world out of

---

[18] One early example of a *gracioso* in a *comedia palatina* is Tristán in *El mármol de Felisardo* (1594–98). On this comic type in Lope's plays see the studies by Jesús Gómez, *La figura del donaire o el gracioso en las comedias de Lope de Vega* (Sevilla: Alfar, 2006), and José F. Montesinos, 'Algunas observaciones sobre la figura del donaire en el teatro de Lope de Vega' (1925), in his *Estudios sobre Lope de Vega* (Salamanca: Anaya, 1967), pp. 21–64. The *gracioso*, once developed, arguably allowed Lope to concentrate much of the low humour which is such a feature of his early comedies into a single figure.

[19] So suggests Poteet-Bussard in 'Algunas perspectivas', p. 344, and Oleza discusses the same issue in 'Del primer Lope', pp. xxviii–xxix. In 1598 and again in 1599 the city of Madrid, keen for the *corrales* to reopen, petitioned the king. The reasoning behind the requests shows how important the morality of the theatre had become, and how susceptible comedies were to criticism: see Emilio Cotarelo y Mori, ed., *Bibliografía de las controversias sobre la licitud del teatro en España* (Madrid: Revista de Archivos, Bibliotecas y Museos, 1904), pp. 421–25. Nevertheless, if Teresa Ferrer is correct in believing that *La viuda valenciana* was written in 1599 or 1600 (Lope de Vega, *La viuda valenciana*, ed. Teresa Ferrer Valls (Madrid: Castalia, 2001), pp. 9, 17–18), some doubt would be cast on this theory of self-censorship. This fine comedy features a young widow, Leonarda, who satisfies her sexual desires but is not keen to marry — a topic certain to antagonize the moralists.

[20] *El acero de Madrid* (1607–9) has a similar opening scene: see Arata's edition of the play. (Whilst most dates for plays mentioned in this chapter are taken from S. Griswold Morley & Courtney Bruerton, *The Chronology of Lope de Vega's 'Comedias'* (New York: The Modern Language Association of America, 1940), those for *El acero de Madrid* and *La discreta enamorada* are given by Arata, pp. 17–20.)

doors unnecessary. By instructing Lucindo's father, the captain, whom she agrees to marry against her will, to tell his son to stop courting her so brazenly, she makes him understand (thanks in part to his servant, the quick-witted Hernando) that she wants him to do so. Fenisa's plans almost come unstuck due to the intervention of Lucindo's former lover, but the setback, typical of Lope's unfolding plots, is temporary and her merry dance ends in laughter as she tricks the captain into her aunt's bed and takes Lucindo for herself. The comic treatment of such generational strife has a long pedigree and what Lope does (and what of course his contemporaries and successors, including Calderón, do repeatedly) is search for novelty within the established form. The originality can come from the setting, unusual stratagems or twists in the plot, changes in characterization or the balance of the family members/pairs of lovers included, and other surprise elements. In the beautifully structured *La discreta enamorada*, the *gracioso*'s forced courting of the older Belisa, his female cross-dressing and the irony of the captain acting inadvertently as his fiancée's go-between, are examples of the play's comic novelty.

In his early fifties, Lope produced two of his most complex and far-reaching comedies: *La dama boba* and *El perro del hortelano*. The former is essentially a *capa y espada* play set in Madrid, and the latter, a palace play set in Naples, is perhaps the best known of Lope's works thanks in part to Pilar Miró's film version of 1995.[21] The usual ingredients of these comic sub-genres are in place, but evident too is an increased sense of seriousness, of the sort that some commentators demand of great comedy.[22] As well as enjoying the unravelling of a comic plot, the audience is left feeling a little uncomfortable, with questions left dangling in spite of the generic resolution of the action. In *La dama boba*, the comic novelty which keeps the audience in thrall lies in the splitting of the protagonist: here two sisters, the bluestocking, Nise, and the ignorant Finea, are the pair of unruly marriageable daughters to whose courtships we are party. Their father, Otavio, unusually for the *barba* (old man type), is a reasonable man who simply wants to see his daughters happily married, and just behaving more normally: 'pues la virtud es bien que el medio siga: / que Finea supiera más que sabe, / y Nise menos' [since virtue involves following a happy medium: I wish Finea knew more than she does, and Nise less].[23] The personal development of the sisters, one educated by her love for Laurencio, the other able to accept Liseo's devotion and descend from her haughty pedestal, is comically desirable, but it only masks the kinds of base motivations at play — greed, pride, envy — in the confused society Lope depicts.

El perro del hortelano ends with another kind of deception which barely hides the chaos reigning beneath the surface. A socially unacceptable marriage between

---

[21] *La dama boba* has been made into a film more recently; see Wheeler's contribution to the present volume.

[22] For an up-to-date summary and assessment of approaches to comedy in the academy, see chapter 2 of Andrew Stott, *Comedy* (New York and London: Routledge, 2005), pp. 17–39.

[23] Lope de Vega, *La dama boba*, ed. Diego Marín, 9th edn (Madrid: Cátedra, 1985), lines 237–39.

the love-struck countess Diana and her lowly secretary Teodoro has been engineered by the resourcefulness of the *gracioso*, Tristán, who persuades a doddery old count, Ludovico, that the secretary is his long-lost son. As an audience we are asked to keep quiet about the subterfuge which permits the union, a sure sign that the ending is fragile: 'que a nadie digáis se os ruega / el secreto de Teodoro' [Please don't tell anyone Teodoro's secret].[24] The action of the play manages to maintain a skilful balance between the traditional comic vicissitudes and often farcical action of an on-off courtship, and a tenderness and lyricism that ensures the audience cares about the outcome for the characters, in particular Diana's servant Marcela, whom Teodoro abandons (more than once) when he sees where his fortune might land him. Again human nature is laid bare. What is particularly interesting about these more mature comedies is that Lope is clearly engaged intelligently with the way his society functions: he reflects in the mirror of his comic drama some truths which he has recognized about how the powers — political, religious, economic — that shape society function. Lope himself was a secretary who failed to rise above his social station in spite of his accomplishments, but Teodoro's success within the comic world is an acknowledgement that the kind of honour or status in society that is guaranteed by birth rather than achievements is a sham. He is perfectly capable of playing the aristocrat; indeed his confession to Diana of Tristán's mischief-making renders him morally superior to the countess's noble suitors who are attempting to have him murdered. Teodoro's faked genealogy may also be Lope's sly comment on the convenient marriages arranged between noble Spanish families fallen on hard times and the better-off *converso* (New Christian) stock many Spaniards thought inferior.[25]

The unseemly scramble for economically advantageous marriages in his mature urban comedy and the hypocrisy of the noble classes in the *comedia palatina* perhaps indicate that Lope has honed his comic vision. Whilst maintaining basic elements which please an audience and produce laughter and ridicule (the creation and development of farcical situations, disguise and misunderstanding, the *gracioso*, moments of wit and stock satire), he allows a darker view of humanity to emerge, and survive the generic closure.[26] Other later comedies would seem to confirm this shifting balance: both *La moza de cántaro* and *Amar sin saber a quién* (1620–22) involve on-stage murders, which, whilst not unknown in comedy, overshadow the happy resolution of the protagonists' comic trajectories. In the former play, the heroine, María, murders one of her suitors who has struck,

---

[24] Lope de Vega, *El perro del hortelano*, ed. Victor Dixon (London: Tamesis Texts, 1981), lines 3379–80.

[25] For important readings of these mature comedies within their generic contexts, see Donald R. Larson, '*La dama boba* and the Comic Sense of Life', *Romanische Forschungen*, 85.1 (1973): 41–62, and J. W. Sage, 'The Context of Comedy: Lope de Vega's *El perro del hortelano* and Related Plays', in *Studies in Spanish Literature of the Golden Age Presented to Edward M. Wilson*, ed. R. O. Jones (London: Tamesis, 1973), pp. 247–66.

[26] If we are correct to note such a movement in the relatively small number of comedies considered here then Lope foreshadows the trajectory of Calderón's comic drama, from light-hearted in the 1620s to dark and disturbing by the end of the following decade.

and so dishonoured, her father, and runs away from Ronda to Madrid disguising herself as a servant-girl. In the capital she has to resist further attentions from her *indiano* (rich man returned from the New World) master, as well as from her fellow servants. The road to marriage with Juan, the nobleman who recognizes her qualities and loves her faithfully, is a tough one: her status as *mujer esquiva* (shrewish woman) seems justifiable when most of the men she meets are violent and try to take sexual advantage of her. Usually Lope will tame his shrews, as with Nise in *La dama boba*, but in this case the fun — the laughter detectable at the end of *La discreta enamorada*, for example — disappears from the unravelling of the comic plot under the weight of human vice.[27]

In another fine mature comedy, *Amar sin saber a quién*, Lope produces a clever variation on the theme of the mystery lover. Yet, despite the similarity of the central idea, the play is quite different in feel to *La viuda valenciana*. Typically for a *comedia de capa y espada*, a stranger, Don Juan, arrives in a city (here Toledo) with business to transact. However, such an *ingénu* habitually becomes caught up in the action of the first scene, which then ties him to an obligation and ultimately a woman whom he will marry. In this case Don Juan is mistaken for the murderer of Don Pedro, and spends the first two acts of the play in prison. He meets Leonarda, another *mujer esquiva*, when her brother admits to her that he is the murderer, and she offers to help the unfortunate Juan, in prison in his stead. She takes him money and letters, becoming his anonymous female admirer. Juan is intrigued by and falls in love with the picture of Leonarda he paints in his imagination, but he is unable to act to pursue her because of the bonds physical, and later social, which tie him. Lope's comic point, it would seem, is to be found in these constant references to imprisonment: the demands of life lived in a group stymie personal expression and trap the individual until all freedom is gone. Even in the comedy's dénouement the dramatist insists, wittily, on Don Juan's continuing 'imprisonment', as his former rival in love, Don Luis, to whom he has a binding obligation, brings him back to Leonarda's house with the words:

> Y pues ya todos sabéis
> que es prisión el casamiento
> que sola la muerte rompe,
> contigo le dejo preso.[28]

> [And since you all know
> that marriage is an imprisonment
> ended by death alone,
> I leave him with you, a prisoner.]

The exuberance of earlier comedies is suppressed even in the happy ending, to be replaced by a wryness, a world-weariness even, as if Lope may have stopped believing in the youthful individual's ability to change his or her role in the world.

---

[27] Lope de Vega, *La moza de cántaro*, ed. José María Díez Borque (Madrid: Austral, 1990).

[28] Lope de Vega, *Amar sin saber a quién*, ed. Carmen Bravo-Villasante (Salamanca: Anaya, 1967), lines 3028–31).

Pedraza too recognizes a change in Lope's comedy in this late period, seeing a 'tendencia a reducir la importancia de la sicología y a acentuar el movimiento escénico' [a tendency to reduce the importance of psychology and to accentuate the stage business] (p. 138), which may be either an anticipation of, or a rapid adaptation to, Calderón's comic norms.

We claimed above that Lope was most naturally a comic dramatist and it may be worth returning briefly to how and why that might have been so. Unlike Calderón and some of his other contemporaries, Lope never received recognition at court, in spite of his fame and popularity and in spite of sometimes appearing to have attached himself to the right faction.[29] His background and unruly youth made him something of an outsider and his attitude to authority in its various guises shows him to have been an extrovert with a strong rebellious streak, however patriotic he felt. There are dangers, of course, in linking a writer's work too closely to biographical data or to what we perceive to be his disposition, but Lope can certainly be seen to have helped to create a forward-thinking drama which reflected the early-modern change in the role of the individual in society. Part of this change, this sense of possessing an ability to fashion oneself within the social group, is expressed in the freedom individual (comic) characters are given to mould the world that surrounds them.[30] In comedy there exists a licence to rebel, within the generic norms of course, and Lope makes use of the genre to allow his characters to express themselves, to explore 'las posibilidades de una vida diferente' [the possibilities of a different life].[31] If this wording appears to ascribe too modern an intention to Golden Age comedy, then perhaps, with Blue, we can accept that in comedy:

> Marriage for love [...] can be seen as a poetic, displaced metaphor for
> achievement by merit rather than by traditional ties [and comedies] can be
> read as re-presentations in a different register of the hopes and dreams of
> many people who flocked to Madrid seeking advancement and a better life.[32]

The heady appeal and power of comedy, if not always the individual laughs, surely stem from the bold stand it dramatizes against the forces of conservatism. This is the case whether one believes with the new historicists that 'the comic as a medium for the message of dissent' is in the end permitted and contained by the ruling culture for its own ends, or, more positively, that the marginal, the comic

---

[29] See Ferrer's introduction to *La viuda valenciana*, in which she chronicles Lope's involvement with the wedding of Philip III in Valencia in 1599, p. 14.

[30] The wording of the document which advises the king on the closure of the *corrales* in 1598 clearly reveals how great a threat to the status quo the theatre was thought to be in this period: see Cotarelo, pp. 392–97.

[31] Bruce W. Wardropper, 'La comedia española del Siglo de Oro', addendum to Elder Olson, *Teoría de la comedia* (Barcelona: Ariel, 1978), p. 234.

[32] William R. Blue, *Spanish Comedy and Historical Contexts in the 1620s* (University Park, PA: Pennsylvania State University Press, 1996), pp. 85–86. Blue's insight refers to comedies by different authors from the 1620s, but it can easily apply to Lope in earlier decades.

can be 'genuinely creative and disruptive', revealing 'the contradictions and unacknowledged dependencies' within the hierarchy.[33]

In Lope de Vega's own statements on dramatic theory, within and beyond the *Arte nuevo*, the dramatist does not put forward a theory of comedy, nor does he think consciously of the comic in terms of power structures, transgression and marginal dissent. However, his sympathy or natural affinity for comedy is certainly expressed in his attraction to and elaboration of plots which involve wit, exaggerated characterization, deception, disguise, madmen and fools, uncertainty, liminal moments, cunning and intelligence, the world turned upside down. He goes behind the scenes of Reason. The winners in his plays (and not just those we can comfortably describe as *comedias cómicas*) are often the characters who perform unpredictably, who overturn expectations, who dare to uncover the hypocritical or self-serving motivations of their enemies with genuine emotion or the unadorned truth.[34] A triumph based on such a performance conventionally earns forgiveness and recognition from the opposition, just as the *gracioso* is habitually pardoned for his failings because he is quick-witted and funny: 'Que por este buen humor / le has de perdonar' [You must forgive him on account of his good humour].[35]

[33] The quotations are taken from Stott, *Comedy*, pp. 35, 36 and 37.

[34] See my 'Lope de Vega, *El cuerdo loco*, and "la más discreta figura de la comedia"', *Bulletin of Hispanic Studies*, 81.4 (2004): 463–78, for an example of a serious play resolved with a comic stratagem.

[35] The example, quoted in Luis C. Pérez & Federico Sánchez Escribano, *Afirmaciones de Lope de Vega sobre preceptiva dramática* (Madrid: Consejo Superior de Investigaciones Científicas, 1961), p. 53, is taken from Lope's *Arauco domado*.

12

Lope de Vega's Speaking Pictures:
Tantalizing Titians and Forbidden Michelangelos
in *La quinta de Florencia*

FREDERICK A. DE ARMAS

Italian Renaissance art is exhibited throughout Lope de Vega's plays, creating a museum of words where Michelangelo, Raphael, Titian, Federico Zuccaro, Jacopo Bassano and many others enhance the works with their designs, and design new meanings with their art. Simonides of Ceos refers to poetry as speaking pictures — and Lope unleashes verses that recreate art through allusions to art and through ekphrasis.[1] While Lope's references to Michelangelo are few and often puzzling, allusions and ekphrases of Titian's canvases abound in his texts.[2] In spite of the wealth of material, almost nothing has been written on the subject except for a few essays that have turned to discrete problems in the relationship between Titian and Lope, including questions of empire, mythology, melancholy, Orientalism, and the portrayal of women.[3]

---

[1] *Ekphrasis* is a narrative description of a visual work of art. It derives from the Greek *ek* meaning 'out' and *phrasis* or 'speak'. For examples of ekphrasis see Frederick A. de Armas, ed., *Ekphrasis in the Age of Cervantes* (Lewisburg, PA: Bucknell University Press, 2005).

[2] In *La Dorotea*, the eponymous heroine is described as a sculpture by Michelangelo, be it a Venus or a Lucretia; and in a burlesque sonnet, 'Lo que hiciera Paris si viera a Juana' [What Paris would do if she saw Juana], Lope describes a Venus that resembles a statue by Michelangelo, but at the same time pokes fun at it. See Frederick A. de Armas, 'Lope de Vega and Michelangelo', *Hispania*, 65 (1982): 172–79.

[3] See Elaine Bunn, 'Negotiating Empire and Desire in Lope de Vega's *Carlos V en Francia*', *Hispanic Review*, 72.1 (2004): 29–42, on empire; Timothy Ambrose, 'Lope de Vega and Titian: The Goddess as Emblem of Sacred and Profane Love', in *Writing for the Eyes in the Spanish Golden Age*, ed. Frederick A. de Armas (Lewisburg, PA: Bucknell University Press, 2004), pp. 167–84, on mythology; Debra Collins Ames, 'Love Melancholy in *La quinta de Florencia*', *Bulletin of the Comediantes*, 44.1 (1992): 45–58, on melancholy and art; Frederick A. de Armas, 'The Allure of the Oriental Other: Titian's *Rossa Sultana* and Lope de Vega's *La Santa Liga*', in *Brave New Words: Studies in Spanish Golden Age Literature*, ed. Edward H. Friedman & Catherine Larson (New Orleans: University Press of the South, 1996), pp. 191–208, on Orientalism; and María Asunción Gómez, 'Mirando de cerca "mujer, comedia y pintura" en las obras dramáticas de Lope de Vega y Calderón de la Barca', *Bulletin of the Comediantes*, 49 (1997): 273–93, on the portrayal of women. In addition, Javier Portús, *Pintura y pensamiento en la España de Lope de Vega* (Hondarribia: Nerea, 1999) contains a wealth of information and

This essay seeks to provide an introduction to the uses of ekphrasis in Lope's plays by singling out one of his works and studying its pictorial aspects in detail. In *La quinta de Florencia*, an ekphrastic passage that seems to refer to a painting by Titian is attributed to Michelangelo.[4] But before turning to this puzzle, another question must be resolved which impinges upon it: why does Lope de Vega resort to ekphraseis in his plays, a classical device that is virtually absent from Italian Renaissance theatre and even from French neo-classical drama? And, what are his models in this rhetorical move?

At the inception of *La quinta de Florencia*, we find that César, the Duke's secretary, has constructed a pleasure villa outside Florence, surrounded by fountains and gardens. The wealth of its interior is described in terms of works of art:

> Puse famosas pinturas
> de aquel artífice en ellas,
> que en el pincel y en el nombre
> es un ángel en la tierra.
> Allí mil ninfas desnudas
> daban con sus carnes bellas
> imaginaciones locas
> entre soledades necias. (lines 289–96)[5]

> [I placed famous paintings
> of that artisan within,
> who by brush and by name
> is an angel on earth.
> There, thousands of naked nymphs
> triggered with their beautiful flesh
> wild imaginings
> among foolish solitudes.]

The description of César's collection would not only recall collections of art in Italy and Spain, but would also foreground the erotic quality of these 'museums'. Art works of mythological subject matter, and particularly nudes, were seldom painted in Spain since erotic figures contrasted strongly with paintings of religious subjects favored by the Church. Wealthy collectors in Spain avidly sought to

---

thoughtful commentary, but, given its scope, it cannot deal with developing the complexity of some of the textual problems that are posed.

[4] In studies I published more than two decades ago, 'Italian Canvases in Lope de Vega's *Comedias*: The Case of *Venus and Adonis*', *Crítica Hispánica*, 2 (1980): 135–42, and 'Lope de Vega and Michelangelo' (1982), I argued that the attribution of the ekphrasis to Michelangelo could help interpret the play. I am now going beyond those interpretations and arguing that we must consider both Michelangelo and Titian in order to understand the ekphrasis of *Venus and Adonis*.

[5] Quotations from the play are taken from Lope de Vega, *La quinta de Florencia*, ed. Debra Collins Ames, Teatro del Siglo de Oro: Ediciones Críticas, 65 ([Valparaiso, IN]: Valparaiso University; Kassel: Reichenberger, 1995).

purchase or copy canvases by Italian masters on mythological subjects. Jonathan Brown asserts that: 'the possession of fine pictures became a badge of identity for the social elite'.[6] Consequently the ekphrastic presence of Italian canvases within the play would increase the 'value' of the representation and would entice those 'in the know' to discourse upon art and upon its meanings within and without the *comedia*. Lope enhances the sparse elements of scenery in the public theatres with this vision of erotic and aristocratic opulence that calls upon the sense of sight and thus brings forth from recollection artistic images in the connoisseur. Indeed, by displaying his own knowledge of art, Lope de Vega is fashioning himself as an aristocratic poet, one who can converse with the most fastidious of courtiers.[7]

But, how did Lope come up with such an enticing and felicitous use of ekphrasis, one that will be central to the development of the play's action? In his *Arte nuevo de hacer comedias* Lope proclaims that he is the initiator of a new type of theatre. He argues that in order to succeed in this endeavour he must lock away the works of Plautus and Terence.[8] This denial on his part simply serves to hide a kind of anxiety of influence, particularly when it comes to ekphrasis. Lope, I will argue, models and develops many of his uses of ekphrasis from Terence — and this device will be picked up by his successors, Tirso de Molina and Calderón de la Barca. While Spain imported from Italy complex stage devices and movable scenery, ekphrasis has little precedent in the Italian works that impelled the development of Spanish theatre.[9] Lope and his successors then are indebted to a Roman author who was particularly well known, since his texts were often used in

---

[6] Jonathan Brown, *Kings and Connoisseurs: Collecting Art in Seventeenth-Century Europe* (Princeton, NJ: Princeton University Press, 1995), p. 244.

[7] Antonio Sánchez Jiménez discusses Greenblatt's self-fashioning as an 'autofiguración' by the poet who constructs his own identity and fame. But while Greenblatt asserts that self-fashioning occurs in opposition to a threatening Other, Sánchez Jiménez asserts that 'Lope no necesita oponerse explícitamente a nada para crear una imagen determinada de sí mismo, sino que más bien le basta asociarse a una tradición ya formada' [Lope does not need explicitly to oppose himself to something in order to create a specific self-image; it is sufficient to associate himself with an already formed tradition]; *Lope pintado por sí mismo: mito e imagen del autor en la poesía de Lope de Vega Carpio* (Woodbridge: Tamesis, 2006), p. 10. The same occurs here, as he fashions himself as an aristocratic poet.

[8] 'Y cuando he de escribir una comedia, / encierro los preceptos con seis llaves, / saco a Terencio y Plauto de mi estudio [...]' [and when I have to write a comedy I lock in the precepts with six keys, I banish Terence and Plautus from my study], Lope de Vega, *Arte nuevo de hacer comedias*, ed. Enrique García Santo-Tomás (Madrid: Cátedra, 2006), lines 40–42. See Irving Rothberg, 'Algo más sobre Plauto, Terencio y Lope', in *Lope de Vega y los orígenes del teatro español: Actas del I Congreso Internacional sobre Lope de Vega*, ed. Manuel Criado de Val (Madrid: EDI-6, 1981), pp. 61–65, on the importance of Terence in Lope. For O'Connor there is a significant difference between Lope and Terence, since in the latter: 'The active female parts in his plays are more likely to be assigned to loose young women and to mature matrons [...] For women are, in fact, ancillary to Terence's theatrical *fabulae*', Thomas Austin O'Connor, *Love in the 'Corral': Conjugal Spirituality and Anti-Theatrical Polemic in Early Modern Spain*, Ibérica, 31 (New York: Peter Lang, 2000), p. 230.

[9] Terence's *Eunuch* played in Ferrara in 1499 and was so popular it was shown twice more at the instigation of Isabella d'Este; see Cathy Santore, 'Danae: The Renaissance Courtesan's Alter Ego', *Zeitschrift fur Kunstgeschichte*, 54.3 (1991): 412–27 (p. 499). It is thus surprising that Italian comedies generally do not use ekphrasis.

schools from antiquity through the Middle Ages and into the Renaissance — there are more than six-hundred preserved manuscripts of his works.[10]

In Terence's *Eunuch*, Chaerea after his encounter with the young and beautiful slave Pamphila explains what occurred: 'She sits in her room, in the middle of all this bustle inspecting / a picture on the wall. A famous subject: Jupiter launching / a shower of gold into Danaë's lap. I began to inspect it / myself. It repaid attention. Encouraging: here was a god / Long ago, who'd played almost the same game [...] / I might be only human, but couldn't I do the same?' (III.3, lines 584–88, 591).[11] A painting has transformed the lover's intentions; it has impelled him to rape Pamphila as she sleeps. Through his main character, Terence shows the impact of erotic art, how it can arouse the observer, Chaerea, and set him into action. Chaerea's emotions also impact upon the play's spectators, who become voyeurs in a scene that has a strong visual impact. Art, then, seems as dangerous as Plato would have it be. It creates forbidden intimacies and arouses emotions that Plato would have tamed through reason. But Terence is unrepentant. His arguments would be radically different from those of Plato or Counter-Reformation moralists. While a god can force a mortal in antique mythology, a citizen can enjoy a slave in antique culture. In his *History of Sexuality*, Michel Foucault explains how even in dreams the sexual actor must play the role of social actor. Thus, a favorable dream would show, for example, a citizen sexually penetrating a slave.[12] This would not only be acceptable practice, but a good omen, since: 'the word *soma*, which designates the body, also refers to riches and possessions; whence the possible equivalence between the "possession" of a body and the possession of wealth' (III, p. 27). Chaerea's action, albeit not a dream, turns out to be a good omen. At the play's denouement, Pamphila is revealed as the long-lost daughter of a citizen of Athens, and thus Chaerea can court her and enjoy her body and her family's wealth. The myth of Danaë, showered by wealth, has served to bring wealth to both the main characters in the play.

Augustine often cited the passage from Terence 'to demonstrate the evil effects of lascivious pictures'.[13] During the Spanish Golden Age, Juan de Pineda and Juan de Mariana, for example, provide us with a long moralizing discussion of Terence's *Danaë*. They maintain that Golden Age works which exhibit such 'paintings' can have a deleterious effect on the morality of the audience. These

---

[10] During the Renaissance, Petrarch wrote his biography, Boccaccio annotated one of his manuscripts, Ariosto (now lost) and Machiavelli translated the *Andria*, which was produced in Florence in 1476.

[11] Quotations are from Terence, *The Comedies*, trans. Palmer Bovie, Constance Carrier & Douglass Parker, ed. Palmer Bovie (Baltimore, MD & London: The Johns Hopkins University Press, 1992).

[12] Michel Foucault, *The History of Sexuality*, trans. Robert Hurley, 3 vols (New York: Random House, 1986), III, pp. 32–33.

[13] 'Hence the young profligate in Terence [...] accepts this as authoritative precedent for his own licentiousness, and boasts that he is an imitator of God', St Augustine, *The City of God*, trans. Marcus Dods, intr. Thomas Merton (New York: The Modern Library, 1950), p. 46; see Carlo Ginzburg, *Clues, Myths, and the Historical Method*, trans. John & Anne C. Tedeschi (Baltimore, MD: The Johns Hopkins University Press, 1989), p. 77.

treatises dutifully refer the reader to Augustine.[14] It may not be a coincidence that the much debated and forbidden *Danaë* was the subject of Titian's first mythological 'poesie' given to the young Philip II, even before he became king. Acquired in 1554, it was in the Alcázar in Madrid when Rubens saw it and imitated it in 1603–4.[15] Titian painted this scene at least twice; the second was commissioned by Alessandro Farnese so that he could view the nude image of his mistress under the cover of mythology.[16]

[14] Chapter XIII of Mariana's work includes this passage: 'Ultimamente, con la torpeza de las cosas y de las palabras despertaban á malos deseos y maldades, y con delictos fingidos encendian á los verdaderos por los ojos y orejas, la cual es una peste gravísima, haciendo entrar la torpeza con tanto mayor fuerza, que en pecar al ejemplo de los dioses, á los cuales muchas veces se atribuian las torpezas, si no merecian loa, á lo menos eran dignos de perdon, pues con sola la mirada de una imágen deshonesta, vemos que los hombres se encienden y mueven á semejantes delictos desta manera [...]' [Lately, lascivious and awkward things and words have awakened many to evil wishes and wickedness, and with imagined crimes led to real sins of eyes and ears — which is a grave plague, letting lust enter more forcefully through. In attributing their sin to the example of the pagan gods, if they did not deserve to be praised, at least they were worthy of being forgiven, since by just looking at an improper image, we see that men excite themselves and are moved to similar crimes in this manner], Juan de Mariana, *Tratado contra los juegos públicos*, in *Obras del padre Juan de Mariana*, [ed. Francisco Pí y Margall], Biblioteca de Autores Españoles, 30–31, 2 vols (Madrid: Rivadeneyra, 1854), II, p. 434. At this point, Mariana describes the scene in Terence. Then, he concludes: 'Ciertamente como con enseñanza del cielo, como dice san Agustin, lib. i de las Confesiones, cap. 16, donde trae este lugar de Terencio, lo cual es necesario que acontezca con mayor vehemencia cuando estas cosas y semejantes en las comedias se representan' [Certainly as if taught by the heavens, as Saint Agustin argues in the first book of his *Confessions*, chapter 16, where he discusses the place of Terence, these things happen with more vehemence when these and similar things are represented in plays] (ibid.). Juan de Pineda goes even further, claiming that Princes should take care of the paintings they allow: 'y no nos queda sino cualificar tan gran pecado de pintores desalmados, y el descuido de los príncipes que no castigan cosa tan prejudicial en el reino' [and nothing is left but to credit such terrible sins to malevolent painters, and the negligence of the princes who do not punish things so hurtful in the kingdom], Juan de Pineda, *Diálogos familiares de la agricultura cristiana*, ed. Juan Meseguer Fernández, 5 vols, Biblioteca de Autores Españoles, 161–63, 169–70 (Madrid: Atlas, 1963–64), IV, p. 66.
[15] 'Fue conseguida por Felipe II en 1554. En 1623 probablemente ya estaba en el Alcázar de Madrid [...] Cabe suponer que Rubens la viera en el Alcázar en 1603–4' [Philip II acquired it in 1554. In 1623 it was most likely to be in the Alcázar of Madrid [...] It can be assumed that Rubens had seen it in the Alcázar in 1603–4], Simon A. Vosters, *Rubens y España: estudio artístico-literario sobre la estética del Barroco* (Madrid: Cátedra, 1990), p. 39.
[16] As both Carlo Ginzburg and Pierre Civil have noted, this image was considered the epitome of the erotic. Piere Civil asserts: 'Muy famoso en la época, el tema de Dánae y Júpiter se consideraba como la representación erótica por antonomasia. San Agustín había utilizado para condenar las pinturas lascivas el ejemplo de un personaje de una comedia de Terencio excitado a la vista de tal cuadro' [Popular in the period, the subject of Danaë and Jupiter was considered to be the erotic representation par excellence. Saint Agustin had used the example of a character from a play by Terence who was aroused at the sight of such painting in order to condemn lascivious works of art], Pierre Civil, 'Erotismo y pintura mitológica en la España del Siglo de Oro', *Edad de Oro*, 9 (1990): 39–49 (p. 46). Ginzburg also comes to the same conclusion: 'Thanks to the condemnation by Augustine, the scene of love between Jove and Danae, as we have seen, came to be considered in the sixteenth century the very prototype of the image created to excite the beholder sexually' (Ginzburg, *Clues, Myths, and the Historical Method*, p. 81). In spite or because of its forbidden aura, the image was copied many times during the early modern period; see Hans

Well aware of the moral tradition forbidding the use of erotic ekphrasis in the manner of Terence, Lope picks it up and makes it the centerpiece of *La quinta de Florencia*. The evocation of nude nymphs (so typical of Titian) is but the beginning of Lope's uses of art. César in his opulent *otium* dozes off in his villa surrounded by erotic designs. His slumber recalls and reverses that of Pamphila in Terence. It also brings to mind Foucault's *soma*, where the dream refers to wealth and the body:

> Miraba a Venus y Adonis
> una tarde en una siesta,
> el con el bozo dorado,
> y ella con doradas trenzas [...]
> Cupidillo, que jugaba
> con un carcaje de flechas,
> – yo pienso que aunque pintado
> es discreción que se tema –
> diome deseo de amar
> una mujer como aquélla. (lines 297–300; 305–10)

> [He looked at Venus and Adonis
> one afternoon during his sleep,
> he with his golden beard,
> and she with her golden locks [...]
> Little Cupid, who played
> with a quiver,
> (I believe that even though painted
> it is wise to fear him)
> it triggered within me the wish to love
> a women like her.]

The opulence of the dream-like vision is underlined by the emphasis on golden objects. Jupiter's golden shower in Terence's play has been replaced by yet another luminous scene — let us recall the emphasis on golden light and its reflections in Titian's *Venus and Adonis*. Furthermore, the viewer's response to the ekphrasis clearly derives from Terence. Like Chaerea, Lope's César wants to possess such a woman. Looking for his Venus both in Florence's aristocratic circles and even in the countryside, he discovers her by a fountain:

> Llegué a una fuente nativa,
> que entre dos pintadas peñas
> formaba aquel manso arroyo [...] (lines 341–43)

> [I arrived at a local fountain,
> Which between two painted rocks
> Formed that gentle stream]

Tietze, 'An Early Version of Titian's *Danaë*: An Analysis of Titian Replicas', *Arte Veneta*, 8 (1954): 199–208.

Although, as Debra Ames has noted: 'Tales so abound in popular medieval lyric of women who meet their lovers at nearby springs or wash their hair and clothes there as prelude to an amorous encounter',[17] the two painted ('pintadas') hills may alert us to a possible pictorial allusion or allusive ekphrasis. In Titian's *Sacred and Profane Love* we view two women sitting by a fountain with a body of water in the background, presumably stemming from the spring. There are indeed two painted hills in the background. While in Lope's play we have a simple peasant woman, who seems to have nothing to do with Titian's figures, her presence in this particular setting can be of great importance. Both César and Laura must decide what will be the outcome of Cupid's darts (and we see him in the painting, turning the waters). As he does, we recall that Laura is also in the process of cleaning. Is Venus, in Ficinian terms, to be a terrestrial or celestial image — or worst still, will César reject the Platonic Venuses in favor of the bestial goddess who is spurned by Ficino? The fact that Laura has 'los blancos brazos desnudos' [naked white arms] (line 357) may be an indication that she stands as guide to the celestial realms, very much like the nude Venus in Titian's painting. But, what will be César's reaction?

The answer is not long in coming, and it takes us back to Terence. Once again, it appears as if there is an unbreachable class difference. Laura is a peasant woman, a washer woman, the daughter of a miller. César's friend, Octavio, asks in disbelief: '¿Que lava y es molinera?' [She washes and is a miller?] (line 400). But César persists in claiming that she is a 'bello retrato / de aquella Venus' [beautiful portrait / of that Venus] (lines 405–6). To foreground the impossibility of such a union in a hierarchical society, Octavio conceives of bestiality as less offensive:

> Que más quisiera que una cierva,
> un galápago, una araña
> te enamoró con sus piernas,
> que no una mujer tan vil. (lines 369–73)

> [I would rather that a doe,
> a turtle, a spider
> wooed you with her legs,
> than such a vile women]

While in Terence Pamphila is thought to be a slave, here Laura is also derided for her social position. And, as in Terence, it is thought that no harm can come to the man in using force on someone of baser rank.

One major difference between Terence's and Lope's play has to do with the art works depicted. Why does Lope move away from Danaë and turn to Venus? At first this does not seem to make sense since it is a move from a scene of power and rape (which would suit César's desires) to a scene of mutuality of desire. I have come to believe that in this shift Lope is introducing a puzzle for his learned audience, one that calls upon the connoisseur, and thus includes Lope in an aristocratic conversation. From the early 1550s to 1562 Titian sent to Philip II a series of mythological paintings of strong erotic content. Philip eventually commanded Titian to refrain from sending him any more erotic art. While the first painting was the *Danaë*, the second was *Venus and Adonis*.[18] Thus, Lope, with a wink to the informed audience, is replacing one painting with its companion piece. In order to contrast the frontal view of Danaë, Titian shows Venus's back as she holds on to Adonis, who is off to the hunt. While Danaë is passively receiving the golden gift, Venus is actively preventing her lover's departure.[19] This is important for the play, since Laura is no Danaë. She is shown to have agency and will-power, dismissing César in spite of his power. It may be argued that Danaë would have been a better subject, since César is constantly attempting to gain Laura by showering upon her gifts and wealth. But Laura successfully refuses her earthly Jupiter, thus denying the Danaë model. On the other hand, she is truly a 'Venus labradora' [peasant Venus], a Ficinian Venus, who in her guise and manner guides César to higher realms of love and desire.

Although César's description touches upon a number of elements in Titian's painting, what we have is a transformative ekphrasis, one that changes some of the elements in the original work of art to better suit its new placement.[20] Lope captures the golden luminescence of Titian's painting, but misplaces some of the objects from the canvas. Adonis's javelin is no longer on the ground, but in his hand, as he prepares for the chase. It is true that the dogs are panting 'sacando al aire las lenguas' [sticking their tongues out] (line 303) and that Cupid is present in the scene. But while in Titian the god of love slumbers under the shade of a tree, in Lope's play he is playing with his arrows. The change is crucial, for, while in the myth erotic enjoyment gives way to the hunt, in Lope the arrows of desire and aversion are still to play their role. César has not yet met his *labradora* nor has Laura gazed upon the courtier.

In order to slyly make the case for Titian, César, in the play, mentions in the third act that art works in his villa are not just by Michelangelo, but also by Titian.[21] Another element that reinforces the notion that *La quinta de Florencia*

---

[18] The mythological works sent to Philip include: *Danaë* and *Venus and Adonis* (Prado), *Perseus and Andromeda* (Wallace Collection, London), *The Rape of Europa* (Gardner Museum, Boston), *Diana and Actaeon* and *Diana and Calisto* (Ellesmere Collection, on loan to the National Gallery of Scotland), and *The Death of Actaeon* (National Gallery, London).

[19] In this, Titian departs from Ovid's *Metamorphoses*, as Pedrocco has noted: 'In Ovid's text Adonis leaves during Venus's absence. Titian, instead, condenses the myth into a single image and modifies the theme by introducing the goddess, who desperately tries to retain her lover', Filippo Pedrocco, *Titian* (New York: Rizzoli, 2000), p. 228.

[20] For a typology of ekphrasis see Frederick A. de Armas, *Quixotic Frescoes: Cervantes and Italian Renaissance Art* (Toronto & London: University of Toronto Press, 2006), pp. 9–13.

[21] César states: 'De Michael Angel son aquellos cuadros, / y del Ticiano aquella Filomena, / que forzada se queja de Tereo' [Those paintings are by Michelangelo./ and by Titian is that Philomena, who being forced, complains of Tereus] (lines 2727–29). Although popular in Renaissance writings, the myth of Philomela as found in Ovid's *Metamorphoses* was not particularly popular in Renaissance art. One exception is the fresco by Sebastiano del Piombo

contains an ekphrasis of Titian's *Venus and Adonis* is one that is external to the work. Although Lope often alludes to Titian in his works, I have only been able to find one ekphrasis of Danaë.[22] Terence's and Titian's image can be found in *El Perseo*.[23] On the other hand, Lope de Vega shows a predilection for alluding to and/or describing *Venus and Adonis*.[24] In *La viuda valenciana*, a play composed contemporaneously with *La quinta de Florencia*, Titian's painting is unequivocally evoked.[25] Here, one of Leonarda's suitors, Valerio, disguises himself as a merchant of prints and exhibits a number of mythological scenes to his beloved, hoping that she will react with desire. Thus, once again art is used for its effect on the passions. Indeed, the first print presented by Valerio is 'El *Adonis del Tiziano* / que tuvo divina mano / y peregrino pincel' [The *Adonis* of Titian / who had a marvellous hand / and a distinctive brush] (lines 890–92).[26]

But, if Lope is referring to Titian, why attribute the painting to Michelangelo? During the Renaissance many argued for masking, or copying without it being noticed — only someone truly knowledgeable would perceive the subtle transformation of one work into another.[27] And masked copying could at times become an *aemulatio*, the desire to improve upon the original, emerging from a strong artistic rivalry, as Rona Goffen argues.[28] The discovery of the antique

---

found in the Sala di Galatea at the Villa Farnesina in Rome. Sebastiano's style was thought to imitate Michelangelo's. Thus, we have yet another reversal — a painting ascribed to Titian should be viewed as a work by an imitator of Michelangelo.

[22] This is not to say that there are no allusions to Danaë in Lope's works. In *La bella aurora*, ancient amorous deceits are invoked: Jupiter's rape of Europa and of Danaë. Also in *El amor enamorado* these two transformations of Jupiter are equated to treachery to be performed in the night.

[23] In his edition of Lope de Vega's *La fábula de Perseo, o La bella Andrómeda* (Kassel: Reichenberger, 1985), p. 15, Michael D. McGaha has noted Lope's borrowing from Titian.

[24] I have posited that there is an ekphrastic reference to Titian's painting in the *Égloga Amarilis* (1633), although Teresa Ferrer Vals in her edition of *La viuda valenciana* (Madrid: Castalia, 2001), p. 168, n. 129, believes Lope is referring to another painting. In *La Angélica*, canto XVIII and in *La prueba de los amigos*, the painting is attributed to Raphael. However, the latter actually points to Titian. See Frederick A. de Armas, 'Pinturas de Lucrecia en el *Quijote*: Tiziano, Rafael y Lope de Vega', *Anuario de Estudios Cervantinos*, 1 (2004): 109–20.

[25] In her introduction to the play, Teresa Ferrer Vals explains that Lope returned from Valencia to Madrid in July or August of 1599. She posits that 'quizá fuese durante los últimos meses del año 1599 o muy de comienzos de 1600, cuando la redactó' [perhaps it was written during the last months of the year 1599 or the beginning of 1600] (p. 26). The play could have had its debut in Valencia in the theatre of La Olivera, with the company of Gaspar de Porres at this time.

[26] The second print derives from Raphael, the third is by the engraver Cornelius Cort (Titian's friend and collaborator), while the fourth is by Federico Zuccaro. For a discussion of Titian's painting and its function in *La viuda valenciana*, see Frederick A. de Armas, 'Lope de Vega and Titian', *Comparative Literature*, 30 (1978): 338–52; 'Italian Canvases in Lope de Vega's *Comedias*'; and 'De Tiziano a Rafael: pinturas y libros en *La viuda valenciana* de Lope de Vega,' in *Actas del XIV Congreso de la Asociación Internacional de Hispanistas*, ed. Isaías Lerner, Robert Nival & Alejandro Alonso, 4 vols (Newark, DE: Juan de la Cuesta, 2004), II, pp. 165–72.

[27] Fredrika H. Jacobs, 'Aretino and Michelangelo, Dolce and Titian: Femmina, Masculo, Grazia', *The Art Bulletin*, 82 (2000): 51–67 (p. 58).

[28] Rona Goffen, *Renaissance Rivals: Michelangelo, Leonardo, Raphael, Titian* (New Haven, CT & London: Yale University Press, 2002).

statue of the *Sleeping Hermaphrodite* led to Michelangelo's *Leda and the Swan*. Both Titian's *Danaë* and his *Venus and Adonis* were modelled after Michelangelo's painting.[29] In the first, imitation is quite straightforward — the pose of Danaë recalls that of Leda. There is a masking of imitation, however, in the second work. While Michelangelo's women have a strongly masculine quality to them, Titian attempts the reverse in his *Venus and Adonis* by including feminine qualities in Adonis.

This opposition is also found in Lope's play. As a *mujer esquiva* (disdainful woman) Laura may be perceived in this period as having both masculine and feminine qualities, and her veiled reference to Michelangelo's Leda may define her as such. Of course, if this is the case, the allusion also foreshadows her eventual submission to César, since the *esquiva* is forever humbled in misogynous plays, and Jupiter is forever fulfilling his lusts.[30] But, if there are masculine qualities in Laura, are there feminine ones in César? Can the popular playwright afford to engage in such a characterization at a time when the notion of masculinity was in crisis?[31] Certainly César is the Duke's secretary and as such enjoys a close friendship, a space of secrecy and intimacy that may at times seem beyond the ordinary. This feminization is also found in César's own villa, where he lives alone, surrounded by beautiful art objects. In Castiglione's *The Courtier*, we are presented with a new era where the perfect courtier is expected to appreciate art, play musical instruments, and even paint. But Castiglione's text also reveals the anxieties over feminization in pursuing the arts. One of the speakers in the Italian work complains: 'I think that music, like so many other vanities, is most certainly very suited to women, and perhaps also to some of those who have the appearance of men, but not to real men who should not indulge in pleasures which render their minds effeminate'.[32] In Lope's work, we are presented with a courtier who has an almost excessive passion for art and may thus be labelled by some as effeminate.

---

[29] The unearthing of the statue of the *Sleeping Hermaphrodite* is for Mary Pardo the basis for Michelangelo's *Leda and the Swan*, and even Titian's *Venus and Adonis*. Frederick Hartt has pointed to the similarities between Michelangelo's (lost) painting and Titian's *Danaë*; see his *History of Italian Renaissance Art: Painting, Sculpture, Architecture*, 4th edn, rev. by David G. Wilkins (New York: Harry N. Abrams, 1994), p. 595.

[30] A similar allusion, as noted, is found in *La viuda valenciana* (line 231), which may once again bring together these two rivals, Michelangelo and Titian.

[31] According to Cartagena-Calderón: 'El siglo XVII vio en España una creciente preocupación por la masculinidad. La opinión cada vez más extendida era que el imperio se había ido irremediablemente a la ruina por haberse presuntamente desvirilizado' [In the seventeenth century, Spain saw a growing concern for masculinity. The growing opinion was that the empire had irremediably gone to ruin because it had presumably feminized], José Cartagena-Calderón, '"Él es tan rara persona": sobre cortesanos, lindos, sodomitas y otras masculinidades nefandas en la España de la temprana Edad Moderna', in *Lesbianism and Homosexuality in Early Modern Spain: Literature and Theater in Context*, ed. María José Delgado & Alain Saint-Saëns (New Orleans, LA: University Press of the South, 2000), pp. 139–75, p. 139.

[32] Baldassare Castiglione, *The Book of the Courtier*, trans. George Bull (Harmondsworth & Baltimore, MD: Penguin, 1967), p. 94.

Contemplating the *Venus and Adonis*, César wishes to remove the face of Adonis from the canvas and add his own:

> Otras veces, en su rostro
> retratar el mío quisiera,
> porque pintura a pintura
> gozara lo que pudiera. (lines 328–32)

> [Other times, in his countenance
> I would like to paint mine,
> because painting upon painting
> I would enjoy all that I could]

There is then a kind of mimetic or triangular desire aroused by the painting.[33] Both César and the painted Adonis are rivals for Venus's favours. But, by imagining that his face is now upon the painting and that he takes on a youthful male body, César is both expressing his desire for Venus and desiring the body of Adonis. According to Lodovico Dolce, Titian succeeded in having in Adonis 'handsome beauty which would have its share of femininity, yet not be remote from virility'.[34] So, César is both desiring a male body and transforming his own body into a more feminized one.

Pointing to homoeroticism and feminization Lope is evoking the rivalry between Titian and Michelangelo as well as the conflictive art and desire of these two painters. In doing so, he is not only dialoguing with the art connoisseur, but he is inscribing in his plays important issues of style and gender. Titian was known in the Renaissance for his *colorito* (colour), a quality thought to belong to the feminine, and thus he is able to use colour to flesh out his erotic feminine nudes. Michelangelo, on the other hand, was known for his design, a masculine quality.[35] But, this was a subversive masculinity for the times, since it was one that desired male bodies. By bringing both artists together, Lope seeks to show that his play has the appropriate rhetorical flowers or feminine adornments — ekphrasis, as well as an impeccable (masculine) design. He even brings both elements together, since the play is framed by ekphrasis, one in the first and a second in the third act, thus reinforcing the play's design with the pictorial adornments.[36] And the play also points to the changing construction of the

---

[33] Gómez, 'Mirando de cerca', p. 280.

[34] Mark W. Rosskill, *Dolce's Aretino and Venetian Art Theory of the Cinquecento* (New York: New York University Press for the College Art Association of America, 1968), p. 213. Dolce adds that in art, women 'would embody an indefinable quality of manhood, and in a man something of beautiful womanhood — an amalgam which is hard to achieve and agreeable and was (if we are to believe Pliny) supremely prized by Apelles' (ibid.).

[35] For the opposition between the feminine colours of Titian and the masculine designs of Michelangelo, see Philip Sohm's important article 'Gendered Style in Italian Art Criticism from Michelangelo to Malvasia', *Renaissance Quarterly*, 48.4 (1995): 759–808.

[36] The main ekphrasis is that of *Venus and Adonis* which impels César to desire Venus and provides agency to Laura, the Venus of the play. In act three, the ekphrasis is of *Philomela and Tereus*, picturing César's lustful violence.

masculine and feminine as a courtly society moves away from chivalric poses to new kinds of poses.[37]

Finally, the erotics of the play are also linked to the politics of the work, since Duke Alessandro, in spite of his supposed generosity, persecuted Michelangelo in Florence (although none of this appears in Lope's play). Only a command from the Pope saved the artist.[38] Lope's poetry is mute as to the implications of a forbidden Michelangelo.[39] However, his speaking pictures tantalize the viewer to approach erotic bodies and contemplate forbidden desires. This pictoric presence recalls the Habsburg Court, with its tensions between opulence and restraint. Through art, Lope perfects his art using colour and design to reflect and reflect upon the anxieties of gender. In doing so, he fashions himself as both a new Michelangelo and a new Titian. His *arte nuevo* is thus monstrous, alluring, genre- and gender-bending, resembling the figures of the Hermaphrodite which served as models for Italian art.

---

[37] In 1528, with the publication of *The Courtier*, the anxiety derived from the changing roles of men and women was inscribed in a best-selling book: 'Castiglione reconoce claramente el riesgo que para el cortesano constituye la adopción de una masculinidad que ya de por sí se encuentra, con su protocolo de refinamiento y cortesía, al borde de la feminidad' [Castiglione clearly recognizes the risks that consist in a courtier adopting a masculinity that at that moment finds itself at the border of femininity, with its protocol of refinement and courtesy] (Cartagena-Calderón, pp. 152–53).

[38] 'An order was issued to seek out Michelangelo and kill him. He, fortunately, was hidden away in the house of a friend. In November, letters from Clement urged that Michelangelo be treated in a friendly way; and before the year was out he was back at work in the Medici Chapel', Howard Hibbard, *Michelangelo* (New York: Harper & Row, 1974), p. 223.

[39] As Melveena McKendrick rightly argues, there is a 'sort of critical restraint, of self-censorship, that operates in Lope's theater', *Playing the King: Lope de Vega and the Limits of Conformity* (Woodbridge: Tamesis, 2000), p. 105. But Lope used a 'decir sin decir,' a 'range of enabling stratagems of commentary and interrogation' (p. 108).

13

Performing Sanctity:
Lope's Use of Teresian Iconography in *Santa Teresa de Jesús*

BARBARA MUJICA

The hagiographical play *Santa Teresa de Jesús* offers us the opportunity to observe how Lope and others helped shaped the image of a woman who, in the early seventeenth century, was fast becoming a kind of super-star. Lope wrote three plays based on St Teresa, none of which has survived as a pristine autograph. Nevertheless, even the adulterated versions help to show how the visual language of sanctity associated with St Teresa that was emerging in the early seventeenth century found expression on the Lopean stage.

The three plays on Saint Teresa attributed to Lope are *La Madre Teresa de Jesús* [*Mother Teresa of Jesus*], now lost, *La bienaventurada Madre Santa Teresa de Jesús* and *Vida y muerte de Santa Teresa de Jesús*. A play entitled *Comedia famosa de la bienaventurada Madre Santa Teresa de Jesús, monja descalza de Nuestra Señora del Carmen* appears in volume V of the 1890 RAE *Obras de Lope de Vega,* although Lope's authorship has been challenged.[1] Marcelino Menéndez Pelayo believed the play that appears in the RAE collection to be by Lope because of its style and possibly because it was mentioned in the 1618 *El peregrino en su patria,* although he admitted it could be a *refundición* by Vélez de Guevara of one the Phoenix's earlier works (p. L). Morley and Bruerton cast doubt on Lope's authorship of *Vida y muerte* based on its versification.[2] The Italian Hispanist Elisa Aragone Terni concluded that all of the existing manuscripts of Lope's St Teresa plays had been so badly dismembered and recomposed over the years that they defied individualization (pp. 9–12).

Upon examining MS 16579 of the Biblioteca Nacional, entitled *La Madre Teresa de Jesús, fundadora del Carmen*, Marco Presotto notes: 'Si trata de una

---

[1] Lope de Vega (attr.), *Santa Teresa de Jesús, monja descalza de Nuestra Señora del Carmen,* in *Obras de Lope de Vega,* V: *Comedias de vidas de santos y leyendas piadosas; Comedias pastoriles,* ed. Marcelino Menéndez Pelayo (Madrid: Real Academia Española, 1890), pp. 467–503. Quotations from the play are taken from this edition, and are followed by the act and line number(s). For an examination of Lope's plays on Saint Teresa and the difficulties in reconstructing them, see Elisa Aragone Terni's Introduction to her edition of *Vida y muerte de Santa Teresa de Jesús* (Messina & Florence: Casa editrice D'Anna, 1970).

[2] Morley, S. Griswold & Courtney Bruerton, *Cronología de las comedias de Lope de Vega* (Madrid: Gredos, 1968), p. 449.

raccolta non ordinate dei vari frammenti delle due commedie lopiane dello stesso tema' [In question is a disordered collection of assorted fragments of two *comedias* by Lope on the same theme].[3] These include segments of the first and third acts of *La bienaventurada Madre Santa Teresa de Jesús* and an autograph fragment of the second act of *Vida y muerte*. In 1970 Terni published as *Vida y muerte de Santa Teresa* a reconstruction of extant manuscripts from the Biblioteca Nacional and other libraries, not all of which are in Lope's hand.[4] In spite of the monumental work done by Terni, numerous questions still remain about these *comedias*. It is clear, though, that Lope did write plays about St Teresa and that he contributed to the printed versions that we have (which show considerable overlap), even if he is not the sole author.

My purpose here is not to authenticate editions of Lope's St Teresa plays — an impossible task — but to illustrate how Lope and perhaps his imitators used Teresian iconography theatrically in order to help construct a national icon. Although both *comedias* make use of familiar images of Teresa, in this article I will focus on the BAE edition, because its pared-down portrayal of the saint's story corresponds so closely to the depictions of her career in prints and paintings of the period.[5] Through the use of allegorical figures representing temptations, *Vida y muerte* develops Teresa psychologically as she struggles to reach a state of perfect detachment. In contrast, *Santa Teresa de Jesús* presents a somewhat more straightforward image of the saint.

There is no evidence in the play that Lope[6] (or Vélez) actually read Teresa's own writing. Teresa wrote her *Vida* [*Life*] at the behest of spiritual directors anxious for her to prove her orthodoxy at a time when, as a woman, an ecstatic, and a reformer of *converso* background, she was suspect. Besieged by the Inquisition as well as adversaries within her own Order, Teresa had to step gingerly, establishing her spiritual authority by constantly recalling her mystical experiences. At the same time she had to avoid the appearance of self-importance, considered reprehensible in a woman. Thus, she often presented herself as a miserable sinner who only by God's mercy enjoyed spiritual favours. However, when Lope wrote *Santa Teresa de Jesús* , probably for Teresa's canonization in 1622 or possibly for her beatification in 1614, he was not interested in depicting his subject's insecurities. His task was to celebrate her as a Spanish saint at a time when in Rome the Church hierarchy was anxious to express its gratitude to Spain for defending the faith against Protestantism, and at home, national morale was low. Like all hagiographic literature, the play was not meant to create a realistic portrait of the subject, but to inspire awe and devotion.

---

[3] Marco Presotto, *Le commedie autografe di Lope de Vega: catalogo e studio* (Kassel: Reichenberger, 2000), p. 370.

[4] For an overview of the manuscript research on the Teresa plays attributed to Lope, see Presotto, pp. 370–72.

[5] A comparison of the two plays and their use of Teresian iconography is projected for a later time.

[6] For the sake of simplicity, in this article I will refer to Lope as the author, rather than employ the cumbersome 'Lope and his co-authors and imitators'. I am, however, fully aware that Lope may not have been the sole author.

A Problematic Saint

During her lifetime, Teresa had been a divisive figure, and the controversy surrounding her was not over by the time she was proposed for canonization. Teresa was a 'spiritual', a member of a reform movement that sought to promote a personal, intimate relationship with God through mental prayer. Rather than empty rites or vocal prayers recited perfunctorily, Teresa stressed *recogimiento* (interiority) and contemplation as means of attaining spiritual knowledge. During Teresa's lifetime mental prayer and claims to mysticism met with harsh resistance, in particular from Dominican theologians suspicious of ecstatics. These detractors, who held that doctrinal instruction should be reserved for university trained *letrados,* found Teresa's writings transgressive. Their view was that 'for the general population, spirituality should be limited to the practice of vocal prayer, traditional ceremonies, listening to sermons about the pursuit of the Christian virtues, and obeying one's confessors'.[7] Since women were barred from universities, where theology was taught, their spiritual experience was usually affective rather than intellectual. Teresa's validation of female spirituality — that is, non-academic spirituality — through her writing and foundations alarmed conservative theologians. Critics of Teresa, such as the papal nuncio Felipe Sega, who called her 'a restless, gadabout, disobedient, and contumacious woman',[8] and the Inquisitor Alonso de la Fuente, who tried to have her books banned on the grounds that they were inspired by the devil, were incensed that a woman should be recognized as a spiritual teacher.[9] When canonization procedures for Teresa were initiated early in the seventeenth century, some theologians were still arguing that her mystical doctrine was diabolical in origin and that her writings should be outlawed.

From 1523 until 1588 no saint had been canonized, partly in response to Protestant depictions of Catholics as superstitious and idolatrous and partly due to uncertainty on the part of some Catholic reformers about the intercessory power of saints. By the end of the sixteenth century, however, clerics concerned about the incursions made by Protestants into previously Catholic areas sought new canonizations as a means of galvanizing the faithful. Holy persons such as Teresa, Isidro Labrador, and Ignatius of Loyola were likely candidates because they had a popular following. They also had value to the institutional church, 'which needed strong Tridentine models for the laity, role models who respected the church hierarchy, adhered to the sacramental system, and, in short, epitomized what it

---

[7] Elena Carrera, *Teresa of Avila's Autobiography: Authority, Power and the Self in Mid-Sixteenth-Century Spain* (London: Modern Humanities Research Association & Maney, 2005), p. 79.

[8] Quoted in *The Complete Works of Saint Teresa of Jesus*, trans. E. Allison Peers, 3 vols (London: Sheed and Ward, 1946; repr. 1953, 1963, 1975, 1978), III, p. 150. This oft-quoted condemnation appears in nearly every modern biography of Teresa.

[9] Alison Weber, *Teresa of Avila and the Rhetoric of Femininity* (Princeton, NJ: Princeton University Press, 1990), p. 160.

meant to be a "good Roman Catholic"'.[10] However, the active, mobile life that Teresa had led and the kind of spirituality she had practised made her a difficult candidate for canonization. It was necessary to reconstruct her, to transform her into a model of feminine virtue characterized by humility and obedience. Teresa's popular following would not have been enough to ensure her canonization, explains Peter Burke.[11] Other factors had to come into play. Her candidacy succeeded, argues Ahlgren, due to the persistent pressure on the Pope from the Spanish king and nobility, the convincing depiction of Teresa as a role model for women, and the Church's endorsement of mysticism as an element of Counter Reformation identity.[12] Pierre Delooz contends that all saints are reconstructions; their lives are remodelled in conformity with a collective image of sanctity, not of the period in which they lived, but of the period that elevated them as models of holiness.[13] Peter Burke notes that saints are cultural indicators: 'Like other heroes, they reflect the values of the culture which sees them in a heroic light' (p. 45). Unsurprisingly, Lope depicts those aspects of Teresa's life that concur with Counter Reformation notions of female sanctity.

Images of Teresa

By the time Lope wrote *Santa Teresa de Jesús* , Teresa's books were widely available. Fray Luis de León published Teresa's major works, except for *Fundaciones,* in 1588, only six years after her death, and the books were quickly disseminated throughout Europe. These books show us Teresa as she wished to portray herself: assertive yet humble, audacious yet orthodox, self-confident yet self-denigrating. Several scholars, most notably Alison Weber, have argued that the rhetoric of self-deprecation that characterizes Teresa's writing is a strategy for veiling her claims to spiritual authority behind a façade of modesty. If Teresa at times depicts herself as a flighty woman, she counterbalances this image by insisting on her spiritual wisdom, derived directly from God and bestowed on her through visions and locutions. In *Fundaciones* she transforms herself into a heroic figure, a kind of spiritual *pícara* who scraps with all kinds of authority figures, including confessors, provincials, lawyers, and property owners, in order to carry forward the Reform — thereby establishing her as a shrewd political manoeuverer as well as a holy woman. The need to be both assertive and humble creates an exquisite tension in Teresa's writing and also accounts for her stylistic messiness.

---

[10] Gillian T. W. Ahlgren, *Teresa of Ávila and the Politics of Sanctity* (Ithaca, NY & London: Cornell University Press, 1996), p. 146.

[11] See Peter Burke, 'How to be a Counter-Reformation Saint', in *Religion and Society in Early Modern Europe, 1500–1800*, ed. Kaspar von Greyerz (London: German Historical Institute & George Allen and Unwin, 1984), pp. 45–55 (pp. 46–48).

[12] Gillian T. W. Ahlgren, 'Negotiating Sanctity: Holy Women in Sixteenth-Century Spain', *Church History*, 64.3 (1995): 373–88 (p. 380).

[13] See Pierre Delooz, 'Towards a Sociological Study of Canonized Sainthood in the Catholic Church', in *Saints and their Cults: Studies in Religious Sociology, Folklore and History*, ed. Stephen Wilson (Cambridge & New York: Cambridge University Press, 1983), pp. 189–216.

Her books are full of caveats, backtracking, and expressions of incertitude that enable her to maintain a posture of diffidence.

However, Lope would not have had to have read any of Teresa's books in order to write his play. By the end of the sixteenth century, several biographies were available, among them Diego de Yepes's *Vida, virtudes y milagros de la Bienaventurada Virgen Teresa de Jesús* [*The Life, Virtues and Miracles of the Blessed Virgin Teresa of Jesus*] (1587), Francisco de Ribera's *La vida de la madre Teresa de Jesús, fundadora de las Descalzas y Descalzos* [*The Life of Mother Teresa of Jesus, Founder of the Discalced Female and Male Orders*] (1590), and Jerónimo Gracián's *Declaración en que se trata de la perfecta vida y virtudes heroicas de la Santa Madre Teresa de Jesús* [*Declaration Which Treats of the Perfect Life and Heroic Virtues of the Holy Mother Teresa of Jesus*] (1611).[14] As the titles suggest, the purpose of these books was to celebrate Teresa's works and miracles, not to offer a realistic portrait of the reformist nun. More influential still were the iconographic drawings and paintings depicting highlights of Teresa's life. These created a vivid, graphic image of Teresa's supernatural powers in the public's mind. The triumph of print culture meant that such images could reach a wide audience. By the sixteenth century, female saints increasingly came to dominate the Catholic imagination. Frances E. Dolan asserts that: 'For post-Reformation Catholics, the saint's life became a feminized genre'.[15] In Protestant England, saints' lives circulated in manuscript and print, and were propagated through engraved images. These lives, which served to unite and inspire Catholics, contributed to Protestant propaganda, which characterized Catholicism as a feminized religion, one in which women were worshipped and prayed to, a carnivalesque, topsy-turvy faith.

Much of the Teresian iconography of the seventeenth century was inspired by the twenty-five engravings of the *Vida B. Virginis a Iesu*, created in Antwerp, in 1613, by Adriaen Collaert and Cornelis Galle.[16] The latter was a member of the circle of Christopher Plantin, a shrewd businessman who ran the largest printing firm in Western Europe and managed to maintain Catholic affiliations while at the same time serving Calvinists.[17] These engravings illustrate the principal events in Teresa's life as described in her writings, highlighting the supernatural and miraculous. The Collaert and Galle prints depict Teresa's three-day paroxysm, Teresa casting out demons, Teresa in the company of the Virgin, St Peter and Paul, Teresa reviving her dead nephew, Teresa being encouraged to found convents by

---

[14] Fray Luis's concise *De la muerte, vida, virtudes y milagros de la Santa Madre Teresa de Jesús* may predate these biographies, but this work was not published until 1883, in the *Revista Agustianana*, vol. 5. A modern edition appears in Luis de León, *Obras completas castellanas I.Ed. Félix García, O.S.A.* (Madrid: Biblioteca de Autores Cristianos, 1991), pp. 921–41. Another appeared the same year edited by María Jesús Mancho and Juan Miguel Prieto (Salamanca: Universidad, 1991).

[15] Frances E. Dolan, *Whores of Babylon: Catholicism, Gender, and Seventeenth-Century Print Culture* (Ithaca, NY & London: Cornell University Press, 1999), p. 176.

[16] I wish to thank Dr Christopher Wilson for sharing the Collaert and Galle images with me.

[17] Elizabeth L. Eisenstein, *The Printing Revolution in Early Modern Europe* (Cambridge: Cambridge University Press, 1983), p. 178.

the Virgin and St Joseph, Teresa being crowned by God after founding the first Discalced Carmelite convent, Teresa levitating, and Teresa being led out of the darkness in Salamanca by a pair of angels. These images penetrate Teresa's visions, depicting the miracle with the same realism as the living person, thereby making the viewer witness to the supernatural event. Like much medieval and early modern art, they blur the line between the worldly and otherworldly. The prints spread immediately throughout Catholic areas, and would inspire Teresian iconographers well into the eighteenth century. In 1614, the year of Teresa's beatification, Francisco Villamena depicted Teresa writing by inspiration of the Holy Spirit, a theme also adopted by Hieronymus Wierix, Josefa de Óbidos, and many others.[18]

The scene from Teresa's writing most often depicted is the Transverberation, in which an angel in bodily form plunges a large golden dart with an iron, fire-tinged tip into her heart. Teresa describes the experience in her *Vida:* 'Este [dardo] me parecía meter por el corazón algunas veces, y que me llegaba a las entrañas. Al sacarle, me parecía las llevaba consigo, y me dejaba toda abrasada en amor grande de Dios' [It seemed to me that this angel plunged the dart several times into my heart and that it reached deep within me. When he drew it out, I thought he was carrying off with him the deepest part of me; and he left me all on fire with great love of God] (XXIX, 13).[19] Among those who depicted the Transverberation were Collaert and Galle (1613), Peter Paul Rubens (1614), Anton Wierix (before 1624), and Josefa de Óbidos (1672). A banner depicting the Transverberation adorned the interior of Saint Peter's Basilica in Rome on the day of Teresa's canonization. The most famous representation of the Transverberation is probably the statue created by Gianlorenzo Bernini (1647–52), now in Santa Maria de la Vittoria in Rome. As Christopher Wilson has shown in his study of Teresian iconography in the New World, images of the Transverberation proliferated in the Spanish colonies, as Carmelites sought a unifying icon to give cohesiveness to their order.[20]

Reconstructing Teresa for the Stage

Santa Teresa de Jesús draws on this burgeoning corpus of Teresian iconography. The play depicts Teresa's life from her first conversion in adolescence to her

---

[18] Luís de Moura Sobral, *Pintura e poesia na época barrocca: a homenagem da Academia dos Singulares a Bento Coelho da Silveira* (Lisboa: Estampa, 1994), pp. 50–54. A painting on this subject attributed to Velázquez also exists.

[19] *The Collected Works of St. Teresa of Avila*, trans. Kieran Kavanaugh, O.C.D. & Otilio Rodríguez, O.C.D., 3 vols (Washington, DC: Institute of Carmelite Studies, 1976–85), I. All English translations from Teresa's *Vida* are from this edition. Spanish quotes are from *Libro de su vida*, ed. Dámaso Chicharro (Madrid: Cátedra, 1993).

[20] Christopher Wilson, 'Saint Teresa of Ávila's Martyrdom: Images of Her Transverberation in Mexican Colonial Painting', *Anales del Instituto de Investigaciones Estéticas* 74–75 (1999): 211–33.

death. The first act represents the worldly Teresa and her decision to serve God; the second, her visions and foundations; the third, her miracles and death. Lope's purpose is not really to tell Teresa's story, the highlights of which would have been familiar to his audience, but to celebrate her virtues and miracles.

As a master playwright, Lope knew that no matter how appealing his subject, he must entice his spectators. The first act portrays Teresa in the secular world. Here Lope uses all the tried and true devices of a *comedia de enredos* and exploits the traditional themes of honour and love. In her *Vida,* Teresa mentions in passing a relationship with a young man: 'era el trato con quien por vía de casamiento me parecía poder acabar en bien' [the friendship with one of my cousins was in view of a possible marriage] (II, 9).[21] To quell the gossip, her father, Don Alonso, places her in the convent of Nuestra Señora de la Gracia (not in La Encarnación, where she starts her career in Lope's play). There she will spend nearly twenty years before launching the reform. Teresa writes that at the time, she had no desire to become a nun, but that she finally concluded that: 'los trabajos y pena de ser monja no podía ser mayor que la del purgatorio' [the trials and hardships of being a nun could not be greater than those of purgatory] (III, 6). However, if Lope knew about her initial aversion to conventual life, he chose to ignore it, transforming Teresa into an avid postulant. He replaces this unidentified cousin with two characters, Don Diego and Don Ramiro, rivals for Teresa's hand.

Attempting to advance their cause at a party at Teresa's house, the two men engage in the usual passing of secret missives, fits of jealousy, confrontations and show-downs. Don Alonso, behaving like an archetypal honour hero, becomes livid upon learning that men are courting his daughter: 'Quien tiene hijas que casar / de vidrio tiene el honor' [Whoever has marriageable daughters, / his honour is made of glass] (I, 338–39). Lope not only creates a dramatic situation he knows will appeal to audiences, but places Teresa in the stock role of *dama* — a tactic that serves dual purposes. First, it enables him to exploit for maximum dramatic effect Teresa's radical — indeed, miraculous — transformation from society belle to holy woman when she opts to leave behind the colourful life of parties and suitors to enter the convent. Second, it allows the audience to identify Teresa with a national 'type'. Since Teresa's canonization was in part a celebration of Spain's role in the defence of the faith, her Spanish identity is an issue. In addition to the *dama, galanes,* and *hombre de honor,* Lope introduces another stock character, a *graciosa* named Petronila, whose cheeky remarks serve to contrast with Teresa's high-mindedness.

Lope enhances the attractiveness of the first act for audiences by incorporating music and dance into the party scene. Teresa dances with her brother, while Teresa's sister, Juana (who in real life was thirteen years junior), dances with her future husband, Don Juan del Valle. In her *Vida* Teresa does indeed describe her adolescence as a flurry of social activities, a time when she craved the world's

---

[21] Kavanaugh and Rodríguez do not identify the man, and their translation of the passage is quite loose. However, it is clear from the Spanish that Teresa was involved with a man and believed that any dishonour arising from this liaison could be remedied by marriage.

vanities, including perfumes and pretty clothes. Lope manages to depict her as a self-confident, socially adept young girl, while at the same time maintaining her aura of virtue by having her dance only with a family member.

Although Lope leads the audience to realize that Teresa is always guided by God, he maintains the integrity of the first act by excluding allegorical or supernatural characters. In this act, Teresa is still 'of this world'. Here, Lope substitutes humor for awe. Teresa flees the party for the Convent of La Encarnación in order to figure out which of the two suitors she should accept. As she reflects, she overhears the Sacristan conversing with Don Diego's servant, Leonido. However, she perceives only the Sacristan's words, which she interprets as a divine message:

LEONIDO:	Amigo, luego saldré.
TERESA:	Dios, ¿con cuál marido iré?
SACRISTÁN:	Con Cristo se puede ir.
TERESA:	Con Cristo una voz me dijo;
	el cielo debe de hablar. (I, 813–17)[22]

[LEONIDO:	All right, friend, I'm off.
TERESA:	Oh, God, which husband should I choose?
SACRISTÁN:	Go with Christ.
TERESA:	A voice told me to go with Christ;
	heaven must be speaking to me.]

This humorous interval marks Teresa's transition from the secular to the sacred. When Don Alonso arrives to take her home, she has already decided to devote her life to God. Although the *graciosa* Petronila will infuse the entire play with humour, it is only in the first act that Teresa contributes to the hilarity, since the second two acts depict her in another dimension, already a saint in intimate contact with God.

The depiction of the worldly Teresa in the first act is fundamental to the construction of her image of sanctity. Building on Judith Butler's notions of gender as 'performed', Christopher Gascón argues that sanctity could also be 'performed' through the representation of certain stylized acts, manners and stances that were associated with holiness.[23] These were sometimes different for men and women. Men were routinely depicted doing battle with evil, while women were depicted defending their virginity. Early modern notions of female sanctity reflected societal values, and the significance even such stalwart defenders of marriage as Fray Luis de León placed on virginity determined that audiences would see celibacy as fundamental to holiness.[24] Gascón explains:

---

[22] I have added my own line numbers. The BAE edition is not numbered.

[23] Christopher D. Gascón, *The Woman Saint in Spanish Golden Age Drama* (Lewisburg, PA: Bucknell University Press, 2006), p. 15.

[24] '[...] el estado del matrimonio en grado y perfección es menor que el de los continentes o vírgenes' [in merit and perfection matrimony is inferior to celebacy or virginity], Luis de León,

'Through the holy woman's preservation of her virginity and strict asceticism, she enacts in ritual form the transformation of the poslapsarian Eve into the Virgin Mary' (ibid.). By rejecting marriage and embracing celibacy, Teresa performs a kind of ritual act[25] which signifies to the audience her initiation in the path of holiness.

It may seem curious that Teresa's first spiritual awakening takes place during a humourous scene in which she mistakes the Sacristan's voice for God's. However, a characteristic often associated with holiness in both the Old and New Testaments is the ability to read signs. Words and events whose significance eludes ordinary people are perceived to be imbued with meaning by the spiritually sensitive. Rather than diminish the sacredness of the moment in which Teresa turns toward God, the humour might have had the contrary effect. Distracted by laughter, spectators may have been suddenly jolted into the realization of God's mystical communication with Teresa through the Sacristan's words. The humour may well have heightened the audience's awareness of the mysterious and unexpected ways in which God imparts spiritual knowledge and of Teresa's receptiveness to God's will.

The contrast between the first act and the rest of the play is evident from the initial scene of the second *jornada,* which opens with an enactment of the Transverberation. Both the playwright and his audiences would have been familiar with the scene either from the Collaert and Galle engraving, shown below, or some other image. Rather than dramatize a saint's story through plot and character development, Lope presents the audience with a series of *tableaux vivants* inspired by Teresian iconography. As in the Collaert and Galle engravings, the boundary between this world and the other disappears. Visions and miracles are depicted with the same immediacy and realism as earthly situations. While the historical Teresa maintained a certain vagueness regarding these events, deferring to the judgment of her confessors regarding their authenticity and expressing herself through rhetorical devices that convey incertitude, Lope, like the iconographers, purges all ambiguity. Worldly and otherworldly characters are equally vivid and tangible.

The Angel, lance in hand, plunges its flaming tip into Teresa's heart: 'la punta de este dardo fuego tiene, / fuego de amor, que enciende y nunca abrasa' [this dart is tipped with fire / the fire of love, which ignites and never burns] (II, 954). Teresa reacts ecstatically: 'Herid, herid con golpes más continos; / dejadme el pecho, si gustáis, rasgado' [Wound me, wound me with continual thrusts; / if you want, leave my breast ripped apart] (II, 961). Gascón remarks that 'The *comedia de santos* [...] usually echoes in some way Christ's ritual transformation from human to divine', often through a rite of passage that 'affirms the subject's new sacred status' (p. 31). The female emerges from this rite of passage as 'a liminal figure between the human and the divine' (p. 37).

'La perfecta casada' in *Obras completas castellanas I*, ed. Félix García (Madrid: Biblioteca de Autores Cristianos, 1991) pp. 223–358, p. 244.

[25] Gascón examines the ritual aspects of *Vida y muerte* in *The Woman Saint,* pp. 64–79.

Transverberación de Santa Teresa

Often this process involves violence, such as an act of martyrdom, as the holy person becomes Christ-like through mimicking Christ's sacrifice. Christopher Wilson has shown that both in Europe and colonial America the Transverberation, the scene from Teresa's life that artists most often depicted, was seen as an image of martyrdom.[26]

Lope collapses into one event the Transverberation and Teresa's long-term girlhood illness, which plunged her into a coma, convincing everyone that she was dead and ready for burial, according to her description in her *Vida*, V. In Lope's play, Teresa slumps onto a bed and remains there during the first part of the second act. The *tableau vivant* depicting Teresa's inert body signals the spectators that Teresa — and they, as witnesses — are entering a new dimension. Teresa remains in this position during an exchange between the Abbess and other characters, which is followed by a debate between Ángel, Demonio and Justicia. In all, Teresa is prostrate for 197 verses. The length of the *tableau* alone would have intensified the impact of the visual image. Through this powerful depiction of death and rebirth, Lope reinforces the notion that Teresa, pierced and penetrated by God's love, returns to the world transformed.

Just as the Mass engages congregants through the use of familiar symbols and rites, this hagiography integrates the spectators by presenting them with familiar scenes to which they respond emotionally. Numerous performance theoreticians (Brook, Grotowski, Schechner, Bennett) have discussed the ways in which any theatrical event is ideologically encoded. Karen Gaylord explains that 'the spectator serves as a psychological participant and empathic collaborator in the maintenance and "truth" of the fictive world onstage, is "taken out of himself" and

---

[26] Christopher Wilson, 'Saint Teresa of Ávila's Martyrdom: Images of Her Transverberation in Mexican Colonial Painting', *Anales del Instituto de Investigaciones Estéticas*, 74–75 (1999): 211–33.

becomes for the time part of an ad hoc collective consciousness, ready to find meaning and significance in the events taking place on stage'.[27] Susan Bennett clarifies: 'The spectator comes to the theatre as a member of an already constituted interpretive community and also brings a horizon of expectations shaped by [...] pre-performance elements'.[28] These, in the case of Lope's audience, would include familiarity not only with Teresa's story, but with the visual signs associated with female sanctity, on display in churches and public areas as well as in private homes, in books and on prayer cards. Prevalent were images of the Virgin, meek, mild, and submissive. Sherry Velasco has shown the importance of *estampas,* or print engravings, which functioned as devotional objects for people of all socioeconomic backgrounds and served to inspire devotion to particular saints, thereby promoting the Crown's ideological and theological stance. Indeed, religious imagery appeared on furniture such as writing secretaries, plates, and even dinnerware.[29] Yet, Lope's tableaux are not what director Peter Brook calls 'everyday images', images that tie spectators to their quotidian lives, so familiar and boring that they are easily overlooked. Instead, these images, like the *estampas,* are meant to amaze and arouse, to free spectators to transcend the boundaries of the mundane and enter the realm of the miraculous.[30] In the image of the recumbent Teresa, the early modern Spanish spectator must have seen reflections of Mary, ever acquiescent to God's will.

Like Collaert and Galle, Lope creates a dramatic space in which the invisible becomes visible and the impossible is commonplace; that is, natural law yields to the supernatural. Thus, when Teresa's confessor Mariano prays for her recovery, the audience witnesses the results, as Justicia, Angel and Demonio wrestle for Teresa's life. Christian Baroque stresses the didactic mission of art; it is an artist's duty to concretize abstractions and, through the creation of allegorical characters, show spectators truths they cannot otherwise witness. In the second act of the play, Teresa does not work miracles. Rather, miracles are worked upon her. The first is her revival. When she regains consciousness, she describes the battle for her soul that the audience has just observed. Lope transforms the otherworld into a tangible organism so that the spectators can see and therefore believe. These scenes may have been inspired by engravings such as Collaert and Galle's 'Santa Teresa

---

[27] Karen Gaylord, 'Theatrical Performances: Structure and Process, Tradition and Revolt', in *Performers and Performances: The Sociology of Artistic Work,* ed. Jack B. Kamerman & Rosannne Martorella (South Hadley, MA: J. F. Bergin; New York: Praeger, 1982), pp. 135–50 (p. 136).

[28] Susan Bennett, *Theatre Audiences: A Theory of Production and Reception* (London: Routledge, 1990; 2nd edn, 1997), p. 139.

[29] See, for example, the lustered plate with an angel in prayer from the Musée du Louvre, and the painted plate depicting Saint Clare (identifiable by her Franciscan hood), flanked by Saint Peter (identifiable by his keys) and a generic martyr, in Catherine Hess, *Italian Ceramics, Catalogue of the J. Paul Getty Museum Collection* (Los Angeles: Getty Publications, 2002), pp. 117 and 170.

[30] Sherry M. Velasco, 'Visualizing Gender on the Page in Convent Literature', in Marta V. Vicente and Luis R. Corteguera (ed.), *Women, Texas and Authority in the Early Modern Spanish World* (Aldershot: Ashgate, 2003), p. 236.

sufriendo el paroxismo, que la tuvo cuatro días sin sentido, y en el cual se le revelaron grandes misterios' [Saint Teresa suffering the paroxysm that left her unconscious for four days, during which great mysteries were revealed to her] and 'Victoria de Santa Teresa sobre los espíritus del infierno' [Victory of Saint Teresa over the spirits of Hell].

Santa Teresa sufriendo el paroxismo

Victoria de Santa Teresa

The following *tableau* represents Teresa as *fundadora* (founder). Here Teresa's struggle to introduce a more primitive, authentic spirituality into monastic life and the opposition of ecclesiastical authorities — described in *Vida* and *Fundaciones*

— are problems easily resolved. Although in real life God may have, as Teresa believed, charged her with the initiation of the Carmelite Reform, He did not remove the bureaucratic complexities of applying for patents, financing the purchase of houses, or negotiating contracts. If Lope was even aware of all these impediments, by the seventeenth century they were relevant only for their contributions to the image of Teresa triumphant. The important point was that God himself had guided Teresa's footsteps, a notion reinforced by images such as the Collaert and Galle print showing God crowning Teresa after her first foundation.

Coni Iruǵts primo noue reformationis in vrbe Abulǎ monaſterio, in eodem mentdis oratiom viſtantes vacans, a IESV Chriſto ſponſo ſuo, ob varios in eius obſervio paſſos labores, corona fulgentiſſima crónitur.

Coronación de Santa Teresa

In Lope's play, St Peter, St Paul, and the Child Jesus intervene in person when Teresa's confessor tries to plant the seeds of doubt in her mind. In a vision described by Teresa in *Vida* and often depicted in art, the Virgin and St Joseph give Teresa a rosary. Here, Jesus himself gives her the rosary, thereby signalling his gratitude for her serving as God's tool. Immediately afterward, angels in work clothes complete the construction of her convent for friars. In *Fundaciones* and her Letters, Teresa complains constantly about money — the need to buy supplies, pay labourers and landlords, and furnish chapels. In Lope's play, when Juan del Valle offers her money (in real life he bought the house for the Carmel of San José), Teresa refuses because Christ's angels require no payment. Through scenes such as these Lope removes Teresa from the practical concerns of the everyday world and conveys iconographically the divine nature of her mission.

In her books, Teresa routinely depicts herself as an instrument of God's will, downplaying her own abilities and importance. However, her letters show that she exerted tremendous power and influence over the Order she founded, controlling even the minutiae of convent life, often from afar. As I have argued elsewhere, Teresa succeeded as *fundadora* because she was a brilliant administrator, fundraiser, financial manager, legislator, and politician.[31] However, during the course of the seventeenth century, these talents were considered not only irrelevant, but even embarrassing by Church and Carmelite authorities.[32] Uncomfortable with the image of a tough, independent female founder, they sought to recast Teresa according to conventional notions of Catholic womanhood, a project in which the arts played a major role, due to the importance the Council of Trent placed on them for the propagation of the faith. The performance of sanctity required images of holy women who, like Mary, acquiesced unquestioning to God's demands. Thus, rather than celebrate Teresa's agency in the Reform, Lope portrays her as a compliant daughter through whom God works wonders.

The third act of the play is devoted to Teresa's miracles. The post-Vatican II Church has focused rather on Teresa's spiritual wisdom, exalting her as a writer rather than as a miracle-worker. However, the seventeenth-century audience was avid for miracles. Lope not only represents the miracles Teresa mentions in her *Vida*, but also invents a few of his own. In her fine study of early modern hagiographic plays, Elma Dassbach points out that 'cuando se trata de mujeres santas, el aumento de poderes sobrenaturales es especialmente pronunciado' [in the case of women saints, the proliferation of supernatural powers is particularly pronounced], undoubtedly because prejudices against women made it necessary to reinforce their claim to sanctity.[33] As Act III opens, Teresa has founded twenty-seven convents (although in real life she founded only seventeen), and is on her way to Alba de Tormes, where she will die. When Teresa cuts her finger on a cord, Don Juan de Valle bandages it with his handkerchief, then rips the cloth in two and tucks half in his doublet, by his heart. When Don Diego hears of Valle's marriage to Juana, he becomes furious and shoots him, but the handkerchief miraculously blocks the bullet. Repentant, Don Diego takes vows, and it is he and not John of the Cross (who has not yet found his way into the popular imagination) or Antonio de Heredia who becomes Teresa's first male Discalced Carmelite.

Teresa's best-known miracle is probably the resuscitation of her dead nephew. In the Collaert and Galle engraving, Teresa recuperates the boy from a collapsing convent wall. In the *comedia,* Lope plays the scene for optimum dramatic effect. Doña Juana enters with the child in her arms, agonizing over how she will break the devastating news to her husband. When he arrives, Juana, disconsolate, struggles to withhold the truth. When at last the grieving father turns to Teresa for an explanation of what distresses his wife, the saint begs God to save the child, who opens his eyes and reprimands her for yanking him out of heaven.

---

[31] Barbara Mujica, *Lettered Women: The Correspondence of Teresa de Ávila* (Nashville, TN: Vanderbilt University Press, 2008), chapter 5.

[32] On other efforts to reconstruct Teresa's image in accordance with Catholic convention, see *Lettered Women,* chapter 6.

[33] Elma Dassbach, *La comedia hagiográfica del Siglo de Oro español: Lope de Vega, Tirso de Molina y Calderón de la Barca*, Ibérica, 22 (New York: Peter Lang, 1997), p. 73.

Santa Teresa resucita a un sobrino

The culmination of the play is Teresa's mystical marriage and union with Christ in death. Carrying a cross, Teresa kneels and prays, thereby realizing another *tableau vivant.* Teresa was commonly depicted crucifix in hand, above her a cozier with a banner reading IHS, which is sometimes repeated on her breast. Other images show her receiving Christ's hand in mystical marriage, surrounded by angels. In the Collaert and Galle engraving, Christ gives Teresa his left hand, while holding a crucifix in his right.

Alianza de Santa Teresa con el Verbo

Here *Amor Divino* (Divine Love) appears in the form of Christ carrying his crown of thorns. Recognizing him as true spouse, she takes his barbed headdress, which in her hands becomes laden with roses. This completes the icon — Teresa, whose incorrupt body famously emitted the aroma of roses, follows Christ to heaven. The rest of the characters comment on the exquisite perfume, except for Petrona, who lacks a sense of smell. Teresa's final miracle, which she works from heaven, is to restore the *graciosa*'s olfactory capabilities.

The practice of adapting popular iconography to the stage was not, or course, limited to hagiographic theatre. In his study of Velázquez's portraits of monarchs, Antonio Feros notes that Lope de Vega and other authors adapted to the stage the same images of power that painters used in their royal portraits. As in the case of saints, the purpose of these images was not to offer an accurate portrait of the king, but to represent him as 'inaccessible, untouchable, irresistible, almost invisible and possessing a divine aura', thereby inspiring awe in his subjects.[34] Just as Lope turned to prevailing images of monarchy when depicting kings onstage, he and his imitators probably turned to prevailing images of sanctity when portraying Teresa.

The representation of Teresa's visions and miracles, often in scenes reminiscent of hagiographic art, appealed to both the spectators' comfort in the familiar as well as their appetite for the extraordinary and spectacular. However, as Elma Dassbach points out, it would be a mistake to see the depiction of miracles simply as a means of fulfilling the audience's desire for spectacle. These scenes met a spiritual need in a public accustomed to sanctity being represented coherently and tangibly in literature and art (p. 114). By comparing Teresa's self-portrait in her writings such as *Vida* and *Fundaciones* to Lope's depiction of her in *Santa Teresa de Jesús* , we can see how far her image had evolved in just forty years. We can also see how Lope may have drawn on existing art forms to enhance the Teresian myth.

---

[34] Antonio Feros Carrasco, '"Sacred and Terrifying Gazes"', in *The Cambridge Companion to Velázquez*, ed. Suzanne L. Stratton-Pruitt (Cambridge: Cambridge University Press, 2002), pp. 68–86, p. 74.

14

Masculinities and Honour in *Los comendadores de Córdoba*

GERAINT EVANS

Men and women falling in love; men fighting over women or fighting for their nation; men preoccupied with their reputation: these staple plot elements of the *comedia* developed by Lope involve gendered characters in situations where issues of gender drive the action. While many of their predicaments may be recognisable as relevant to human beings of either sex, much of the *comedia*'s appeal and fascination derives from the tension between the subject and the perceived norms of masculine and feminine behaviour of their culture. The instability and constructed quality of gender is further foregrounded when the occasional woman dresses and successfully passes as a man, or when a male's sense of himself as a man threatens to unravel before us. Marriage, the conventional goal of many plays, involves the male protagonist, not as an asexual, ungendered representative of the human norm, but as a heterosexually orientated half of a hegemonic relationship based on gendered hierarchy. Segregation of the audience by sex would only have increased the partisan response to the actions on stage,[1] and as Lope's *Arte nuevo* reveals a playwright acutely aware of his audience, it is unsurprising that his writing responds to the dynamics of the *corral* (playhouse).

Los comendadores de Córdoba (1596)[2] has been seen by several critics as important for understanding Lope's subsequent representations of masculine honour.[3] The male protagonist is the Veinticuatro de Córdoba (a *regidor* or

---

[1] For an idea of how male and female spectators behaved, see Juan de Zabaleta, *El día de fiesta por la mañana y por la tarde* (1654, 1660), ed. Cristóbal Cuevas García (Madrid: Castalia, 1983), pp. 312, 318.

[2] Lope de Vega, *Los comendadores de Córdoba,* in *Obras de Lope de Vega*, XXIV: *Crónicas y leyendas dramáticas de España*, ed. Marcelino Menéndez Pelayo, Biblioteca de Autores Españoles, 215 (Madrid: Atlas, 1968), pp. 1–60. All references are to this edition, by act and page number(s). The translations given here are mine. For the dating of this and other plays mentioned, see S. Griswold Morley & Courtney Bruerton, *Cronología de las comedias de Lope de Vega* (Madrid: Gredos, 1968).

[3] Donald R. Larson, *The Honor Plays of Lope de Vega* (Cambridge, MA & London: Harvard University Press, 1977), pp. 38–39; Melveena McKendrick, 'Celebration or Subversion?: *Los comendadores de Córdoba* Reconsidered', *Bulletin of Hispanic Studies,* 61.3 (1984): 352–60 (p. 359); Alix Zuckerman-Ingber, *El bien más alto: A Reconsideration of Lope de Vega's Honor Plays* (Gainesville, FL: University Presses of Florida, 1984), p. 44.

alderman), whose wife Beatriz and niece Ana we find ogling men from a window and then flirting with Jorge and Fernando, two *comendadores* (knights-commander) of a military order. As reward for active service against the Moors, King Fernando presents a diamond ring to the Veinticuatro, who passes this ring to his wife as a symbol of their marital union, but she in turn gives the ring to her admirer Jorge as a token of her lust. When the king notices his gift on the finger of the rival, he indignantly questions the Veinticuatro, provoking feelings of jealousy, shame and insecurity in the latter. Setting a trap for his wife, he catches her and Jorge about to consummate their passion, and exacts a vengeance which is almost unparalleled in world theatre, killing his wife, niece, both male lovers, several servants and the household pets. He surrenders, expecting punishment, but is pardoned by the king, who seemingly rewards him with another wife.

The events have a historical basis: in 1448, Fernando Alonso did indeed kill his wife, two maidservants and two knights commander, escaping punishment by taking advantage of a pardon issued in 1444 by Juan II to murderers who were prepared to spend a year in the town of Antequera, which at that time was a Christian stronghold close to the border of the Islamic kingdom of Granada. In the following 150 years, several literary accounts appeared, including Juan Rufo's *romance* (ballad) of 1596, which was Lope's main source.[4] Rufo had shifted the date forward from 1448 to the capture of Granada in 1492 and the effective ending of the Muslim occupation of the Peninsula. Lope, with his appreciation of dramatic potential, retains the anachronism.

To appreciate the multiple meanings for an early modern audience, we must look at how Lope dramatises his raw material: examining linguistic tone, characterisation and the context of individual actions, particularly the ending. In the second half of the twentieth century such sensitive readings led to the honour-vengeance plays of Calderón, and Lope's later period, being reinterpreted as critiques of the concern for reputation and of the victimisation of women. However, as Melveena McKendrick showed in 1984, *Los comendadores* could still be seen as an uncritical representation of wife-murder. She quotes Duncan Moir, who in 1970 contrasted Lope with the newly accepted view of Calderón: 'parecen ser, en efecto, muy distintas, si no diametralmente opuestas, la moralidad de *Los comendadores de Córdoba*, *La locura por la honra* y *La victoria de la honra*, de Lope, y la de las tres tragedias calderonianas [*El médico de su honra*, *A secreto agravio, secreta venganza* and *El pintor de su deshonra*]' [Indeed, the morality of Lope's *The Knights-Commander of Córdoba*, *Madness through Honour* and *The Victory of Honour* seems very different from, if not diametrically opposed to, that of the three Calderonian tragedies].[5] In 1977, Donald Larson argued that the play presented the Veinticuatro in a positive light: 'the model of Spanish manhood', a hero who acts to save his social reputation in a

---

[4] Juan Rufo, *Las seiscientas apotegmas y otras obras en verso*, ed. Alberto Blecua, Clásicos Castellanos, 170 (Madrid: Espasa-Calpe, 1972).

[5] Edward M. Wilson & Duncan Moir, *A Literary History of Spain: The Golden Age: Drama, 1492–1700* (London: Ernest Benn, 1971), p. 63; see McKendrick, 'Celebration or Subversion?', p. 353.

way comparable to that of the Cid (pp. 64, 53). McKendrick argues that 'rather than a confident celebration of traditional values, *Los comendadores* is an uneasy play which teeters on the edge of the ridiculous',[6] and Alix Zuckerman-Ingber also details how humour is a tool employed in a critique of honour conventions (p. 30). The ability to laugh at masculine weakness and failure is later placed within a literary and historical context by Alison Sinclair, who discusses the representation of the cuckold and the man of honour.[7]

Gender in early modern Spain is linked to the ubiquitous concept of honour, which, as the anthropologist J. G. Peristiany explains, is an intrinsic part of social development:

> All societies have rules of conduct, indeed the terms 'society' and 'social regulations' are coterminous. All societies sanction their rules of conduct, rewarding those who conform and punishing those who disobey. Honour and shame are social evaluations and thus participate of the nature of social sanctions.[8]

Honour is also about the prestige and value of an individual:

> Honour is the value of a person in his own eyes, but also in the eyes of his society. It is his estimation of his own worth, his claim to pride, but it is also the acknowledgement of that claim, his excellence recognized by society, his *right* to pride.[9]

Perceived value can be based on civic or spiritual virtue, but, especially when the opinion of society is instrumental, it may be based on rank, race, or socially acceptable behaviour. In the Middle Ages a distinction had been forged between two terms: *honor*, based on innate qualities expected of the aristocracy, and *honra*, based on the verb *honrar* and involving praise gained by actions, but by the seventeenth century Sebastián de Covarrubias claims that the two terms are similar, and in the *comedia*, differences are elided.[10]

Various types of honour are represented in the play, and all are shown to be precarious. The importance of vertical hierarchy, specifically of rank or blood, to a sense of self is seen as characters proudly talk of lineage and royal connections. The Veinticuatro is acutely aware of his status and, exaggerating his inferiority to the king, calls himself a 'tosco aldeano' [coarse rustic] (I, p. 9b). There are suggestions he might be of Jewish blood (I, p. 6a; III, p. 48a), while his

---

[6] 'Celebration or Subversion?', p. 354.

[7] Alison Sinclair, *The Deceived Husband: A Kleinian Approach to the Literature of Infidelity* (Oxford: Clarendon; New York: Oxford University Press, 1993), pp. 133–41.

[8] J. G. Peristiany, ed., *Honour and Shame: The Values of Mediterranean Society* (London: Weidenfeld and Nicholson, 1965), p. 9.

[9] Julian Pitt-Rivers, 'Honour and Social Status', in *Honour and Shame*, ed. Peristiany, pp. 21–77 (p. 21).

[10] As, for example, in *Los comendadores*, III, pp. 47b–48a. See Julio Caro Baroja, 'Honour and Shame: A Historical Account of Several Conflicts', in *Honour and Shame*, ed. Peristiany, pp. 79–137 (p. 84); Sebastián de Covarrubias Orozco, *Tesoro de la lengua castellana o española* (Madrid: Turner, 1977), s.v. 'honor'.

sycophancy and reluctance to leave the royal presence comically show his desire for the reflected glory of royalty. Zuckerman notes that Galindo, a mere servant, can feel superior to the mulatto slave Rodrigo, who in turn attempts to belittle Galindo as a Jewish *converso*. She argues that the obsession with race is too sensitive to be discussed openly by nobles but can be 'hidden away among the servants and camouflaged as comic relief'.[11]

The final violence, enacted in the cause of lost honour, is preceded and contextualised by a much-quoted definition of honour as social construction. The Veinticuatro, his sense of identity now threatened by awareness of his wife's infidelity, rhetorically asks what honour is, provoking us to consider the question, before providing an explanation in which the verb use, especially the past participle, makes it clear how honour derives from others:

> VEINTICUATRO: ¿Sabes qué es honra?
> RODRIGO: Sé que es una cosa
> que no la tiene el hombre.
> VEINTICUATRO: Bien has dicho:
> honra es aquella que consiste en otro;
> ningún hombre es honrado por sí mismo,
> que del otro recibe la honra un hombre.
> Ser virtuoso hombre y tener méritos
> no es ser honrado; pero dar las causas
> para que los que tratan les den honra. (III, pp. 47b–48a)

> [VEINTICUATRO: Do you know what honour is?
> RODRIGO: I know it is something
> which a man does not possess.
> VEINTICUATRO: Well said,
> for honour exists in others.
> No man is honoured by himself
> but from another receives honour.
> Being a man of virtue and merit
> does not make you honoured. You must give cause
> for those who know you to honour you.]

He rejects two possibilities of masculine honour. First, his understanding leaves no room for virtue, thus tapping into early modern debates. Many writers, especially clerics, building on Classical and Christian thinkers, emphasised that true honour lay in virtue,[12] either seen in terms of civic values or how individuals

---

[11] Zuckerman-Ingber, *El bien más alto*, p. 42. McKendrick develops the arguments of Albert Sicroff and Américo Castro, that anxiety over *limpieza de sangre* (purity of blood), and the possible stain of *converso* blood, fuel the literary convention of the stain of sexual dishonour, so that the former is transferred onto the latter; see 'Honour/Vengeance in the Spanish "Comedia": A Case of Mimetic Transference?', *Modern Language Review*, 79.2 (1984): 313–35.

[12] See Pitt-Rivers, 'Honour and Social Status', p. 24; Caro Baroja, 'Honour and Shame', pp. 83, 122. The tension between honour as inner virtue and honour as social reputation is an important aspect of *Lazarillo de Tormes*.

are seen by their own conscience and by God, rather than by other humans. Moralists felt compelled to stress this only because of the opposing tendency in society to see honour not in terms of morality but in terms of social reputation. As the anthropologist Michael Herzfeld concluded in a modern study of masculinities, 'there is less focus on "being a good man" than on "being good at being a man"'.[13]

Social honour thus exists not in the individual but in others' perception, and it is not the quality of actions themselves which count, but whether they are effective in causing others to treat you with honour. Further, the emphasis on perception means that a man who has experienced a potentially dishonourable situation does not lose social honour unless others know. Hence, in *El castigo sin venganza*[14] the Duke attempts to plot a secret revenge, in order to protect his sense of self:

> Pero de tal suerte sea
> que no se infame mi nombre; [...]
> Y no es bien que hombre nacido
> sepa que yo estoy sin honra,
> siendo enterrar la deshonra
> como no haberla tenido. (lines 2748–49, 2752–55)

> [But let it be in such a way
> that my name is not defamed. [...]
> Let no man alive
> know that I am without honour,
> burying my dishonour
> being as if it had never existed.]

This concern for reputation, and irrelevance of the truth, gives great power to the spoken word, especially from those who influence opinion:

> VEINTICUATRO: Las palabras de los reyes
> son balas de pieza gruesa,
> que matan con sólo el aire,
> puesto que el cuerpo no ofendan. (III, p. 60a)

> [The words of a king
> are cannonballs
> which kill with only the air
> even though they harm not the body.]

Words are thus more harmful than sticks and stones, which is why the *comendadores* refuse to mount the spirited horses of Córdoba (I, p. 4a): they are afraid of falling, not because of the physical pain but because of the ridicule it

---

[13] See David D. Gilmore, *Manhood in the Making: Cultural Concepts of Masculinity* (New Haven & London: Yale University Press, 1990), p. 30.
[14] See the essay by Edward Friedman on this play, chapter 15 in this volume.

would bring. More than that, words can kill reputation: immediately after the king has reprimanded him for the loss of the ring, the Veinticuatro refers to his 'honor difunto' [dead honour] (II, p. 39b). The poetic device of personification, treating an abstract object or concept as if it were alive, here has a basis in reality: in social groups where acceptance is based on reputation, the exclusion resulting from unacceptable behaviour can make loss of honour seem like social death.[15] As Rodrigo, whose words spur him to action, says, honour is a 'ley del mundo' [law of the world] (III, p. 50a), a social rule which is unwritten, and for that reason stronger, because infringement brings not official punishment but social insecurity or even exclusion.[16]

The trajectory of the protagonist's honour is elegantly expressed by the ring. On the relatively bare stage of the *corral*, the limited range of props could take on great symbolic value. The ring which the king gives the Veinticuatro, for long periods visible on the hands of four actors, is a symbol of honour which is both visually and verbally integrated into the dramatic action. To the Veinticuatro it was reward and recognition of his valour in war: 'un diamante en un anillo, / de mis servicios empresa' [a diamond set in a ring / impresa of my services] (III, p. 59b). An impresa was originally a visual design on a knight's shield to record and inspire valour and, as Covurrubias records, the practice of a king honouring his knights with a ring goes back beyond ancient Rome to the Old Testament.[17] In a Europe when war was more common than peace, and many men, including literary figures such as Lope, fought for their nation,[18] military valour was a conspicuous aspect of masculinity, and, as Matthew Stroud points out, by keeping Rufo's false chronology, Lope brings the grandeur of the Conquest of Granada to bear on the Veinticuatro's actions.[19] Like a modern day state honour, the ring is thus a reward for his deeds as a man and soldier, which shows the vertical dynamics of honour, for the male subject receives a sense of identity from the

---

[15] Caro Baroja, 'Honour and Shame', p. 85. In the thirteenth-century book of moral and social codes, *Las siete partidas*, a man defamed was described as dead to the world, to the extent that death might be better for him than life: Alfonso X, the Wise, *Las siete partidas del sabio rey don Alonso el Nono: nuevamente glosadas por el licenciado Gregorio López* (1555), facsimile edn, 3 vols (Madrid: Boletín Oficial del Estado, 1974), Segunda Partida, título 13, ley 4.

[16] Jeremy Robbins explains the anxiety caused by the nebulous and unstable quality of gender laws in 'Male Dynamics in Calderón's *A secreto agravio, secreta venganza*', *Hispanófila*, 117 (1996): 11–24 (pp. 17–19).

[17] Sebastián de Covarrubias, *Tesoro*, 'anillo': 'los anillos se dieron en señal de honra' [rings were given as a sign of honour]. Rings are presented by kings in Esther 3.10; 8.2. For *empresa*, see Covarrubias, 'emprender'.

[18] Garcilaso de la Vega (a descendant of the character in this play) died fighting for Spain in France in 1536, Cervantes bore arms for the Christian Holy League against the Turks at Lepanto in 1571, Calderón fought in the Castilian force which suppressed the Catalan Rebellion of 1640, while Lope himself sailed with the ill-fated Armada of 1588.

[19] Matthew D. Stroud, '*Los comendadores de Córdoba*: realidad, manierismo y el barroco', in *Lope de Vega y los orígenes del teatro español*, ed. Manuel Criado de Val (Madrid: EDI-6, 1981), pp. 425–30 (p. 427).

arbiter of reputation, the king, situated at the apex of the system.[20] The ring is thus a visual symbol of his acceptance as a man.

Identity is commonly constructed against a perceived other: black against white, civilisation against barbarism, Spanish against Muslim, while adult masculinities are principally constructed against two social groups: boys and women.[21] Gayle Rubin describes how gender identity is formed by the repression of 'natural similarities [...] in men, of whatever is the local variation of "feminine" traits; in women, of the local definition of "masculine" traits',[22] while anthropological studies show the importance of rites of passage for constructing masculinities which leave behind boyhood, and exclude the feminine.[23] Regarding the rejection of boyhood, Jorge and Fernando are proud that war has made men of them: '¡Cuánto se ha holgado de vernos / tan robustos y soldados! / que nos dejó niños tiernos' [How pleased he was to see us / such robust soldiers / having left us tender boys] (I, p. 3b). Regarding the rejection of femininity, Ana and Beatriz, discussing what makes a man attractive to women, repeat the adjective 'robusto' to express their view of acceptable masculinity:

> ANA: En fin, ¿robusto ha de ser?
> BEATRIZ: Y lo contrario te asombre;
>   que no es bien que tenga el hombre
>   semejanza de mujer. (I, p. 11a)

> [ANA: And so, a man must be robust?
> BEATRIZ: The opposite would shock you;
>   for it is not right that a man
>   should have the aspect of a woman.]

These two 'others' combine when the comendadores express their reluctance to risk humiliation should they ride through Córdoba, specifically because it is a city where 'cualquier niño o mujer' [any child or woman] (I, p. 4a) is an expert equestrian.

One of the most important rites of passage by which a male leaves behind boyhood and becomes accepted as a man within society has been marriage, which creates ties and responsibilities to establish him within a community, while also

---

[20] For a historical discussion of this phenomenon, see Caro Baroja, 'Honour and Shame', pp. 84, 98.

[21] A third group is homosexuals; for a study of a gay *gracioso*, see Peter E. Thompson, *The Triumphant Juan Rana: A Gay Actor in the Spanish Golden Age* (Toronto, University of Toronto Press, 2006).

[22] Gayle Rubin, 'The Traffic in Women: Notes on the "Political Economy" of Sex', in *Toward an Anthropology of Women*, ed. Rayna R. Reiter (New York: Monthly Review Press, 1975), pp. 157–210 (pp. 179–80).

[23] Gilmore, *Manhood in the Making*, pp. 26–29. A good example from the *comedia* is Guillén de Castro's play *La fuerza de la costumbre* [*The Force of Custom*], which dramatises the parallel but unequal construction of masculinities and feminities by rites of passage which exclude the opposite; see Jonathan Thacker, *Role-Play and the World as Stage in the 'Comedia'* (Liverpool: Liverpool University Press, 2002), pp. 19–34.

complying with the demand for heterosexuality. Yet while marriage helps to
construct masculinity, it also threatens it. The Veinticuatro's odd claim that
married men have a greater obligation to fight for their country (I, p. 9a) suggests
a fear that marriage can soften men, who are made for arms rather than the
domestic world of pleasure. Despite his theoretical praise of marriage, throughout
the play the Veinticuatro shows a desire to be in the company of men, and a
strange reluctance to return home, lingering in the presence of the king, who has
to insist on sending him back (I, pp. 9b, 10a).

Discussing the benefits of married life, the rhetorical rejection of
counterarguments simply reminds us of their existence, and while his words praise
the wedded state, the double interrogative merely begs questions.

> ¡Oh, cuánto gusto recibo!
> ¿Quién pone en casarse mengua?
> ¿Quién era aquel ignorante
> que habló mal del casamiento? (I, p. 19a)

> [Oh, what pleasure I receive!
> Who could disapprove of marriage?
> Who was so ignorant
> as to speak ill of matrimony?]

As Sinclair points out, while the marriage rite marks a passage into full
masculinity, it also leaves the husband vulnerable to infidelity (p. 119). In this
play Lope makes great use of dramatic irony, with the audience knowing more of
events than the speaker. The praise of marriage above suggests that any doubter
should experience the benefits of marriage for himself: 'verá lo que es ser casado'
[he will see what it is to be married] (I, p. 19a). But this is exactly what we have
seen, for Lope places this speech after we have witnessed his wife ogling men
from a window and flirting outrageously in their presence, so while the husband
does not explicitly state the arguments against marriage, we already know and
understand them. When he finally realises the extent of his wife's infidelity, he
considers the theatricality of life and the roles humans are expected to play, with
words which express this paradox of marriage: 'la honra, autor de mis bodas, /
me vino a dar el verdugo' [Honour, the creator of my marriage, has cast me as the
executioner] (III, p. 56a). To obtain honour as a man, he married, but marriage has
destroyed his honour and life.

However, the stigma of marital infidelity has traditionally been imbalanced, for
while both partners may feel the pain of rejection, the husband may feel the
additional social shame of the cuckold. The problem arises from the importance
patriarchy has tended to lay upon controlling the sexuality of females, with the
virginity of the unmarried woman watched over by father or brothers, and the wife
expected to be faithful. Hence the Veinticuatro's security in his belief that Beatriz
is modestly confined to the domestic sphere: 'Yo aseguro que está ya / puesta
entre cuatro paredes' [I assure you she is now / enclosed within four walls] (II,

p. 38b). Part of the Veinticuatro's perceived dishonour is thus that he has failed to control the sexuality of both his wife and the niece who lives within his household.[24] On the other hand, men, both unmarried and married, have been allowed greater sexual freedom by society. This double standard is seen in Lope's *El castigo sin venganza*, where the extra-marital activities of the Duke are sinful but do not threaten social honour, while those of his wife Casandra do. The dishonour of the woman is transmitted to the husband who has failed to control her, and is now branded a cuckold. The double standard entails social stigma only from female infidelity, so the terms cuckold and its Spanish equivalent 'cornudo' ('he who wears the horns') were traditionally applied only to men, with no female equivalent. As Sinclair points out, 'patriarchy and society do not permit masculine language to be used for purposes it would rather ignore', and both legal and creative literature have tended to dwell on infidelity by the female rather than the male (pp. 34, 19).

The second social function which Covarrubias ascribed to the ring was to express the union of husband and wife, but here Lope develops its use as a visible symbol of masculine honour invested in woman:

> VEINTICUATRO: Beatriz, entre este dedo y el pequeño
> y grande, luego al corazón aplico
> este diamante, aqueste anillo rico,
> más que por sí, por el valor del dueño. [...]
> Guardadle bien, que os doy en esta prenda
> valor, crédito, anillo, plata y oro,
> lealtad, fe, honor, hacienda, sangre y vida. (II, p. 23b)

> [Beatriz, between the large and small finger.
> to the heart I give
> this diamond, this precious ring,
> precious not for itself, but for the worth of its owner.
> Guard it well, as in this gift
> I give you worth, credit, ring, silver and gold,
> loyalty, faith, honour, wealth, blood and life.]

The ring's worth derives not from intrinsic value but from the social worth of its owner, his credit, now invested in Beatriz. The ring traces the honour dynamics of the play: from the king to the husband, to his wife, to her lover Jorge, on whose hand it is seen by the king, who reprimands the Veinticuatro, who in solitude four times recalls the king's words of censure, emphasising how the symbol and the concept are conflated in his mind.

> 'Si a tu mujer se la diste,
> que tu mujer te la dé'.
> ¿Dice la honra o la piedra? [...]

---

[24] In Rufo's *romance*, Ana is a secretary: Lope's change increases the familial responsibility.

que más por la posta fue
honra que en mujer consiste. (II, p. 39b)

['If you gave it to your wife,
let your wife give it back.'
Does he mean my honour or the ring? [...]
Honour that resides in woman
has taken flight.]

It is the reprimand from the king which initiates his path towards the recovery of honour through violence. The second act closes with the husband throwing and retrieving his hat, which, because of its capacity to hide his imaginary horns, he calls a 'cartel', or libellous poster (II, 39b–40a), [25] publicising his state of cuckoldry.

Now his honour is in jeopardy, the Veinticuatro finally questions traditional values and the honour system, while regretting his earlier words on marriage:

¿Cuál fue el villano que la honra santa,
que es de los hombres el mayor tesoro,
que debiera engastarse entre diamantes,
la puso en vasos de sutiles vidrios,
que con cualquiera golpe que dan, quiebran?
La honra se derrama como el agua.
¿Qué dije bien del casamiento? (III, p. 49a)

[Holy honour,
man's greatest treasure
which should be set among diamonds;
who was the villein who
placed it in vessels of fragile glass
which break at the slightest touch,
spilling honour like water?
What praise did I heap on marriage?]

Seeing honour as holy, he again blurs the moralists' distinction between virtue and honour, his reference to glass echoing the popular saying, 'La mujer y el vidrio siempre están en peligro' [women and glass are always in danger], [26] while his description of dishonour as spilt water comes only seconds before the *comendadores*, who cause his dishonour, drop a cup of water (II, p. 49b).

The double standard's emphasis on female sexuality is problematic because it tends to accept no middle ground between modesty and licentiousness, encouraging a binary thought pattern which sees a woman as either chaste or unchaste, good or evil, perfect or imperfect, gold or lead, heaven or hell (III, p. 49a;

---

[25] 'Cartel suele llamarse el libelo infamatorio, que se fija secretamente en los cantones', Covarrubias, s.v. 'carta'.

[26] Gonzalo Correas, *Vocabulario de refranes y frases proverbiales* (1627), ed. Louis Combet (Bordeaux: Féret, 1967), p. 204b.

I, p. 19a). The husband either has honour or has none, with dishonour experienced as the 'abismo' [hell] (p. 58a) and his restoration of identity seen as a return to the heavens (III, p. 60a). Similarly, dishonour is often expressed as a stain, which however small, sullies the whole.[27] It was a cliché of early modern literature that the stain can be washed clean, not with water, but with blood, as the bloodshed of revenge re-asserts the self-identity of the offended party over those who have offended him. The Veinticuatro and Rodrigo embody masculine identity in the sword that redresses an affront:

VEINTICUATRO:	¡Ea, desnuda la espada,
	no te mueva compasión!
RODRIGO:	Entra, que si entra manchada
	de afrenta y mala opinión,
	saldrá con sangre lavada. (III, p. 56a)

[VEINTICUATRO:	Now, unsheathe the sword,
	And be not swayed by compassion!
RODRIGO:	Enter, for the sword that enters stained
	by affronts and bad opinion
	will exit washed clean by blood.]

The killing not only of the wife but the rival reminds us that honour and masculinity concern a relationship between men. The pains of jealousy derive not only from his lost love, but also from injury to masculine self-esteem, because the new male lover is seen as a rival, a usurper, who, by taking the first man's place, pushes the latter downward in the perceived hierarchy of masculinity, compounding the social inferiority already noted. Honour here is social rather than moral, so the cause of dishonour is seen not in terms of sin but rather as an affront to self-esteem, which leaves no possibility of forgiveness, and the only remedy is to re-assert the self over those who caused the affront, a remedy expressed repeatedly in terms of recovering or settling a debt ('cobrar'): by the Veinticuatro, who talks with veiled menace to his wife (III, pp. 44a, 45a), and explicitly by Rodrigo, acting as the voice of masculine imperative:

RODRIGO:	Señor, que agora es tiempo
	de cobrar el honor que te han quitado.
VEINTICUATRO:	¿Que, en efeto, perdí mi honor, Rodrigo?
RODRIGO:	Señor, no le ha perdido quien le cobra. (III, p. 47b)

[RODRIGO:	Sir, now is the time
	to recover the honour they have taken
VEINTICUATRO:	So it is true, I have lost my honour, Rodrigo?
RODRIGO:	Sir, he who recovers it has not lost it.]

---

[27] As Mary Douglas points out, pure dirt exists only in the mind, not in the object observed; *Purity and Danger: An Analysis of the Concepts of Pollution and Taboo* (London: Routledge, 1984; 1st edn 1966), p. 2.

At the end, having killed his wife and her lover, he no longer feels like living, but before he can die he seeks judgment from the king, the arbiter of masculine honour, who reproached him for the loss of the ring. As in the historical source, the king gives him another wife, which may be seen on the surface as a reward, and the king's approval seems to restore his spirits: 'Cuanto he pedido me das: / has confirmado mi honor' [You give me all I ask for / and confirm my honour] (III, p. 60b). The voice of the dead woman and the woman offered as her replacement in the marriage contract are silent amid the voices of men.

Thus far we have analysed how the play dramatically explores the machinations of the masculine mind whose sense of identity is under threat, but we have not considered how audiences might have responded. In Lope's novella, *La prudente venganza*, a husband escapes justice after taking revenge on his unfaithful wife, killing her, the lover and two servants, yet at several points the narrator steps forward to suggest interpretations:

> Y he sido de parecer siempre que no se lava bien la mancha de la honra del agraviado con la sangre del que le ofendió, porque lo que fue no puede dejar de ser [...] satisfaciendo los deseos de la venganza, pero no las calidades de la honra, que para ser perfecta no ha de ser ofendida.[28]

> [I have always believed that the stain of honour is not washed clean by the blood of the offender, for what once was does not cease to be [...] This merely satisfies the desire for revenge, not honour, which is only perfect if it has not been offended.]

Drama usually lacks such direct narration to guide our responses, but many aspects of *Los comendadores* do suggest irony, and thus a range of interpretations which may diverge from those of the protagonists. The Veinticuatro reminds the audience of a third symbolic meaning of the ring, deriving from Classical myth, of Prometheus bound to a rock by chain and ring, his liver eternally eaten by an eagle:[29]

> Si el anillo antiguamente
> era de prisión señal,
> ésa tendré eternamente;
> que de águila tan real
> ser presa es honra excelente. (I, p. 9b)

> [If rings were in antiquity,
> a sign of imprisonment,
> I will wear this one eternally,
> for to be captive of such a royal eagle,
> is an honour most excellent.]

---

[28] Lope de Vega, *La prudente venganza*, in *Novelas a Marcia Leonarda*, ed. Francisco Rico (Madrid: Alianza, 1968), pp. 107–42 (p. 141).

[29] See Covarrubias, 'anillo'.

The king later repeats the image of prison back to him (II, p. 38b). By accepting the ring, he enters willingly into the eternal cycle of honour transactions: of affront and revenge, which, being based on prestige rather than virtue, precludes the possibility of forgiveness, and thus has no end. Similarly, as Jaime Fernández points out, he again enters into an arranged marriage to a younger woman whom he has not met, so renewing the prospect of marriage without love, and the cycle of masculine honour and retribution may continue.[30] The Veinticuatro is also likened to the phoenix (III, p. 51b), which dies to be reborn, but what is renewed here is not only honour, as Larson argues (pp. 51–52), but the cycle of honour as worldly revenge and retribution.

Audience reaction is also guided by tone, and while earlier critics treated the play as tragedy, the most important re-readings of the play have come from McKendrick and Zuckerman, who show how the excess of honour posturing spills over into the burlesque, with the tone set early by the ridiculous refusal of Jorge and Fernando to ride through Córdoba, for '*caballeros* who are frightened of *caballos* and prefer to walk are a contradiction in terms'.[31]

In 1596, Lope was still developing the dramatic use of the *gracioso*, a type used here to introduce the theme of masculine rivalry. The first sword brandished and the first discussion of infidelity involve the *graciosos,* as does the first talk of revenge killing: 'Hágote voto solene / que pueden doblar por él' [I give you a solemn vow, that they can toll the bells for him] (I, p. 15a). In early modern literature, parallels between masters and servants often serve to stress differences in character, but here they suggest similarities, and, as McKendrick notes, when the master engages in behaviour already seen in the *graciosos*, he is brought down to their ignoble level.[32] Rather than a hero, he is to be laughed at.

The Veinticuatro is an exaggerated version of masculinity who, oversensitive to his reputation as a man, cares too much about what the king thinks, and perceives his affinity with Orlando, the hero of Ariosto's *Orlando furioso* (III, p. 55b), who in a jealous rage uproots trees and kills peasants and animals.[33] At the end, the Veinticuatro loses all sense of proportion, killing not only the lovers, the servants, but dogs, cats, the monkey and a parrot as well, thus taking to ridiculous extremes his rage and the need to silence witnesses to dishonour. Whereas Rufo's protagonist stabs his wife once, Lope's stabs her six times, perhaps making a joke at the expense of a man who has been unable to penetrate his wife himself.

---

[30] Jaime Fernández, '*Los comendadores de Córdoba:* ¿un caso de honor recobrado?', *Bulletin of the Comediantes,* 38.1 (1986): 55–62 (p. 58). A similar renewal of the cycle ends *El médico de su honra* [*The Physician of His Honour*], attributed to Lope, which was reworked with the same title by Calderón.

[31] McKendrick, 'Celebration or Subversion?', p. 355.

[32] McKendrick, 'Celebration or Subversion?', p. 356.

[33] Links with Ariosto are demonstrated by Frederick de Armas, who shows the contrast with Orlando as well as Hercules. Whereas Hercules kills lions, the Veinticuatro kills unarmed servants and animals; Frederick A. de Armas, 'La estructura mítica de *Los comendadores de Córdoba*', in *Actas del X Congreso de la Asociación Internacional de Hispanistas*, ed. Antonio Vilanova, 4 vols (Barcelona, PPU, 1992), I, pp. 763–72. We might argue that the contrast presents him as non-heroic and ridiculous.

Zuckerman argues that when the king compares him to the ancient Cordobans Seneca and Lucan (III, p. 60b), the more thoughtful of the audience would have seen the irony, as he has displayed the opposite of the self-control represented by these Stoics (p. 28).

Above all, the *gracioso* introduces humour to the scene in which the husband supposedly recovers his honour. The audience must have laughed at the sight of Galindo and Esperanza, rolled in mats, waddling onstage, then giving us a running commentary of the carnage. Galindo wishes he could escape by turning into a flying ant (III, p. 57a), and when the monkey is killed, immediately calls himself a 'mona', which, as well as 'monkey', means 'drunkard', which *graciosos* invariably were (III, p. 57b).[34] Zuckerman stresses the burlesque of the Veinticuatro's '¿esteras para el verano?' [mats for summer?] (III, p. 58b), his pun on the 'negro' who is now a 'blanco' [target] (III, p. 57a),[35] and surely the audience would have laughed when the Veinticuatro later announces the death of the parrot (III, p. 60b). Lope's *El cuerdo en su casa*, an unequivocal comedy, looks back on this scene, suggesting Lope himself saw it as humorous: 'No perdonó / a un papagayo que hablaba / porque no se lo decía / y a una mona, porque hacía / señas de hablar, y callaba' [He spared not / the talking parrot / because it did not tell him / and a monkey who knew signs / but kept mum].[36]

Humour serves to undercut the pomposity and rigidity of masculine honour, yet a further function of humour is explained by Sinclair, who applies the object relations theories of the psychoanalyst Melanie Klein. Sinclair suggests that literature can enable our psychological growth by representing examples of psychic trauma, allowing us to work through responses to them. She traces literary representations of marital infidelity and identifies three main types. First the cuckold, such as January in Chaucer's *Merchant's Tale* or *Miller's Tale*, where narrator and audience seem able to laugh at the foibles of male foolishness, and to be given the chance to contemplate their own weakness and mortality; secondly, the man of honour, who cannot tolerate the stain on his sense of self; and thirdly, the nineteenth-century novel of adultery, where readers are encouraged to understand and empathise with both the deceived male and the female who has been driven to seek affection elsewhere. *Los comendadores* would seem a burlesque on the second type, which, like the first, invites us to laugh at the extremes of male behaviour. The unwelcome is thus not just tolerated, but seen as part of the totality of experience.[37]

In *La prudente venganza*, Lope presents the fleeting possibility of a man able to tolerate a blemish on his honour:

---

[34] Covarrubias, 'mona'. The monkey and parrot are additions of Lope.

[35] Zuckerman-Ingber, *El bien más alto*, p. 30.

[36] *El cuerdo en su casa*, in *Comedias escogidas de frey Lope Félix de Vega Carpio*, III, ed. Juan Eugenio Hartzenbusch, Biblioteca de Autores Españoles, 41 (Madrid: Rivadeneyra, 1873), pp. 443–64, (p. 462a).

[37] Alison Sinclair, *The Deceived Husband*, p. 53.

Ya sabía Laura todo el suceso y, como veía tan alegre a Marcelo, parecíale algunas veces que era de aquellos hombres que, con benigna paciencia, toleran los defectos de las mujeres propias.[38]

[Laura now knew everything, and seeing Marcelo so happy, at times she thought he must be one of those men who with benign patience can tolerate defects in their own wives.]

In the event, the chain of dishonour and vengeance is carried through to its logical and bloody conclusion by a cuckolded husband turned murderer, but the possibility of alternatives has been raised.

As humour may encourage distancing and contemplation, so too does metatheatrical imagery,[39] which has two effects: first it suggests that honour itself is a performance, one which requires the individual to conform to a social role, and secondly, it foregrounds the fictionality of the representation. First the Veinticuatro connects honour with theatre and role-play:

> ¡Ay, honra, veisme aquí ya
> en vuestro teatro puesto,
> como todo hombre lo está. (III, p. 55b)

> [Ah, honour, here you see me
> standing in your theatre
> like all men.]

Honour itself is called an 'autor' [theatre producer] (III, p. 56a), and the Veinticuatro glimpses that he is a 'figura' [stage character] playing the role of 'verdugo' [executioner] (III, p. 56a), conforming to what is expected of his gender, performing for an audience of his fellow characters, who will judge him accordingly, as do the king and Rodrigo, for it is the reprimand of the king and later the urging of Rodrigo (III, 47b) that push him towards action. Secondly, theatre is not real life but a fiction: the events of 1448 notwithstanding, real life wife-murders were no more common than now and did not go unpunished:[40] the Veinticuatro himself expects to be executed (III, p. 60b). Revenge and honour in the theatre could be seen as conventions of literature rather than of the real world, but conventions that many spectators welcomed. As Lope in his *Arte nuevo* admitted, 'los casos de la honra son mejores, / porque mueven con fuerza a toda gente' [affairs of honour are the best / because they move deeply one and all] (lines 326–27). But whereas Larson argues that the play shows a ritual of masculine assertion which draws the audience in to participate vicariously, re-affirming their belief in traditional values such as the honour/vengeance code

---

[38] *Novelas a Marcia Leonarda*, p. 139.

[39] For an investigation of metatheatre and role-play in the *comedia*, see Thacker, *Role-Play and the World as Stage in the 'Comedia'*.

[40] McKendrick, 'Honour/Vengeance', pp. 313–16

(pp. 60–61), Zuckerman argues that the humour also lets us draw back to contemplate these rituals (p. 36). Lope even gives us an example of vicarious revenge, as the jealous Rodrigo, who cannot see beyond the dramatic convention, compensates for his own cuckoldry through goading his master into action and participating in the slaughter.

Los comendadores, written when Lope was still exploring the possibilities of the *comedia nueva*, is regarded by Larson as a prototype for the Spanish honour play (p. 39). McKendrick and Zuckerman also see it as significant, but in its subversion of conventions, both social and theatrical. McKendrick went on to analyse the humour in two other 'wife-murder' plays by Lope which take further his burlesque treatment of honour conventions: *La victoria de la honra* (Morley & Bruerton: 1609–15), in which the comic plot allows actions which would be unacceptable to the audience in a serious play, and *La locura por la honra* (Morley & Bruerton: 1610–12), which contains parodies of literary representations of masculine honour, including *Orlando furioso* and the medieval *romance* 'Blanca sois, señora mía' [You are white, my lady].[41] While the critical disagreement outlined above arises partly from the difficulties in reading texts (from the past) and the desire to make hidden meanings visible, it must always bear in mind the horizon of expectations of the seventeenth century rather than those of the twenty-first, and it is clear that Lope wrote both for those spectators who attended the theatre in the hope that conventions, both social and theatrical, would be re-inforced, and for those who were able to interpret signs and meanings which call into question convention, and open up an imaginative space to explore the psychology of jealousy, loss, and masculine esteem.

---

[41] Melveena McKendrick, 'Lope de Vega's *La victoria de la honra* and *La locura por la honra*: Towards a Reassessment of his Treatment of Conjugal Honour', *Bulletin of Hispanic Studies*, 64.1 (1987): 1–14.

15

El castigo sin venganza and the Ironies of Rhetoric

EDWARD H. FRIEDMAN

Literary categories and labels are useful in a paradoxical way, and more so in the aftermath of poststructuralism. Frames allow for typologies and for groupings of texts, yet if similitude is a point of departure, difference — differentiation, distinction, divergence, deviation — ultimately will inform the critical or analytical act. Take the case of the (for many) 'first modern novel', *Don Quijote*, which is easy to classify and even more likely to resist, or to defy, classification. It serves as an example of realism, as contrasted with the idealistic fictions of sentimental, chivalric, and pastoral romance, but it has more in common with modernist and postmodernist responses to eighteenth- and nineteenth-century narrative realism than with the objectives and conventions of the authors cataloged as realists. Not only is realism relative, dependent on a significant 'other' to shape its identity, but it also is compromised from the start, separated from the signified in the mediating space of words that attempt to capture things. In *Don Quijote*, Cervantes breaks from idealism in an ironic way. His realism is inflected by an antithetical force, that of metafiction, which takes the narrative in an opposing direction that substitutes self-reflexivity for mimesis. It is not realism or metafiction but the dialectics of realism and metafiction that defines the rhythm, movement, and tone of *Don Quijote*.[1] In the *Arte nuevo de hacer comedias* and in his dramatic works themselves, Lope de Vega balances comedy and tragedy in a variety of forms. In those plays that veer toward comedy, the threat to honour and the potential for catastrophe yield to the upside-down perspective of saturnalian inversion; happy endings (often punctuated by multiple marriages) result from breaking rules in ways that would not be sanctioned in 'real' society. In the more serious plays, the dénouement frequently illustrates tragedy averted and acknowledgment of the guiding principles of society. *El castigo sin venganza* (1631),[2] one of Lope's later works, is particularly interesting in

---

[1] This is a thesis of my study *Cervantes in the Middle: Realism and Reality in the Spanish Novel from 'Lazarillo de Tormes' to 'Niebla'* (Newark, DE: Juan de la Cuesta, 2006).

[2] I have used the editions of *El castigo sin venganza* by C. A. Jones (Oxford: Pergamon Press, 1966), José María Díez Borque (Madrid: Espasa Calpe, 1987), and Antonio Carreño (Madrid: Cátedra, 1998).

generic terms, given that the playwright categorizes the text as a tragedy.[3] By Lope's own criteria, that denomination must be qualified.

Derived from the Phaedra myth and from literary and historical variations on the theme, *El castigo sin venganza* centres on the Duke of Ferrara, a profligate who, under pressure from his constituents, arranges to marry the noblewoman Casandra.[4] The Duke had recognized and looked after in a most generous fashion his illegitimate son, the count Federico, whom he hoped to make his heir. He sends the reluctant Federico to Mantua to accompany the bride-to-be to her new home. On the road, Federico saves Casandra after a coach accident, and their attraction is mutual and strong. When the Duke ignores his young wife, he affords the opportunity for her to become more attached to Federico, who, in turn, is struggling to moderate his passion. The Duke receives an order to serve the Pope in Rome, and he entrusts Casandra's care to Federico. Motivated by love and by the desire for revenge, Casandra offers herself to her stepson, who cannot refuse her, although both know that they will suffer for their recklessness. On his return, after four months away, the Duke declares that he is a reformed man. He pledges that his dissolute behaviour is a thing of the past and that henceforth he will treat his wife with due courtesy. The Duke's niece Aurora, deeply enamored of Federico, has witnessed the intrigue, and she secretly alerts her uncle to what has transpired in his absence. To punish them for their sin — rather than to take vengeance on them, as he justifies his action — the Duke devises a plot whereby Federico unwittingly will murder Casandra and then be killed for that crime.

Following the model of classical tragedy, Lope allows fate to control the emotions and the destinies of the three principal characters, who all are victims of circumstance. Persuaded by popular opinion, the Duke marries against his inclinations and against his will. Casandra, who expects devotion and consideration on the part of her husband, is abandoned physically and emotionally. Federico neither wishes to escort Casandra nor to stay with her in the court. He would prefer to accompany his father, but is forbidden to do so. Federico and Casandra cannot avoid each other, and they elect not to resist their yearnings,

---

[3] For an analysis of Lope's view of tragedy over time, see José María Díez Borque, 'Lope de Vega trágico: juventud-madurez', *Ínsula*, no. 658 (2001): 18–22. See also Edwin S. Morby, 'Some Observations on *Tragedia* and *Tragicomedia* in Lope', *Hispanic Review*, 11.3 (1943): 185–209; Gwynne Edwards, 'Lope and Calderón: The Tragic Pattern of *El castigo sin venganza*', *Bulletin of the Comediantes*, 33.2 (1981): 107–20; Bruce W. Wardropper, 'Civilización y barbarie en *El castigo sin venganza*', in *'El castigo sin venganza' y el teatro de Lope de Vega*, ed. Ricardo Doménech (Madrid: Cátedra & Teatro Español, 1987), pp. 191–205; and Antonio Carreño, '"... La sangre / muere en las venas heladas": *El castigo sin venganza*, de Lope de Vega', in *Hispanic Essays in Honor of Frank P. Casa*, ed. A. Robert Lauer & Henry W. Sullivan, Ibérica, 20 (New York: Peter Lang, 1997), pp. 84–102.

[4] See the introductions to the Jones and Díez Borque editions for commentary on sources. See also C. B. Morris, 'Lope de Vega's *El castigo sin venganza* and Poetic Tradition', *Bulletin of Hispanic Studies*, 40.2 (1963): 69–78; Duncan Moir, 'The Classical Tradition in Spanish Dramatic Theory and Practice in the Seventeenth Century', in *Classical Drama and Its Influence: Essays Presented to H. D. F. Kitto*, ed. M. J. Anderson (New York: Barnes & Noble, 1965), pp. 191–228; and Manuel Alvar, 'Reelaboración y creación en *El castigo sin venganza*', *Revista de Filología Española*, 66.1–2 (1986): 1–38.

despite their awareness of the consequences of transgression. The Duke routinely has abused women, and he neglects his wife. He claims that the experience in Rome has inspired him to turn over a new leaf, and he is ready to be the ideal husband and father, but his professed transformation comes too late. Angered by the treachery committed against him, bound by the laws of honour, and pained by the need to hurt those closest to him, he must bring about justice. The case illustrates what Alexander A. Parker calls 'diffused responsibility', in which several parties share accountability for the tragic outcome.[5] An air of doom or fatalism envelops the dramatic events, as if there were no escape from death and destruction. The story, whatever its specific source or sources, seems familiar. The characters are enacting predetermined roles in which a tragic impulse — a tragic push — is felt at all times. One might say that passion predominates over reason, but that would imply a choice that fate seems to deny to the protagonists, each of whom understands the correct course of conduct but becomes powerless before fate. Lope juxtaposes the inevitability of tragedy with poor judgment and improper behaviour, but the first overshadows the second. That is, he stresses the inexorable over the manageable, the tragic inscription over self-discipline. *El castigo sin venganza* is not an allegory of the theological battle of determinism versus free will, but instead a projection of determinism onto a formula for tragicomedy.

A paraphrase of the plot of *El castigo sin venganza* might suggest the spirit of pure tragedy, an unmediated rush toward the fulfilment of a foreshadowed disaster, with dramatis personae as pawns of fortune. Once Casandra and Federico have cast prudence aside — spurred as they are by the Duke's negligence — their fate is sealed. Once the Duke's honour has been blemished, and his dishonour known to others, he has no alternative but to eradicate the stain. The unity of action is based on the progression from crime to punishment. At the conclusion, the Duke has regained his honour. Aurora will marry the Marquis Gonzaga, who will take her with him to Mantua, out of the Duke's purview. Order ostensibly having been restored, the Duke will be alone to contemplate his complicity in the annihilation of his family. He has lived a life of debauchery, betrayed his wife, and led his son into a trap. His metamorphosis is a matter of words, not deeds, and the damage already has been done. The Duke rationalizes the execution of the offenders; he accentuates his participation in the proceedings by elaborating on the scheme that he has invented to rid himself of dishonour. His explanation may strike the spectator as more incriminatory than convincing. There is an ideological foundation for his rationale, but this is a play about emotions, about impulsiveness, and about the physical nature of human beings. The ending is ironic, to a large extent because philosophy and theology enter the picture, somewhat belatedly. The situation builds on ardor, obsession, and a taste for danger, essentially on the absence of reason, and the conceptualization of the problem and its solution may come as a bit of a surprise. This hardly represents the beginning

---

[5] A. A. Parker, 'Towards a Definition of Calderonian Tragedy', *Bulletin of Hispanic Studies*, 39.4 (1962): 222–37, esp. p. 228.

of irony in the play. On the contrary, it is the culmination of a pattern of irony that functions from the opening to the final scene.[6]

In this tragedy, the influence of Lope's tragicomedy is apparent, as is the lesson in metafiction — and the interface of realism and metafiction — of *Don Quijote*. Lope crosscuts from the gravity of the primary plot to metaliterary, or metadramatic, interventions. A suspension of disbelief vies with a consciousness of the world as stage, and the poetic discourse is self-consciously ironic, drawing attention to technique over sentiment. The play commences with the Duke in disguise, deceiving women in the darkness of night and abetted by his servants Ricardo and Febo. Ricardo remarks that night itself is a cape that conceals the heavens, and the exchange shifts to the highly figurative language of the new poetry. Metacommentary on art and on the practice of deception — that of the Duke and of women who cuckold their husbands — supersedes, to a degree, the initial action of the play, to create a dispassionate, cynical, and burlesque tone. The Duke seeks an assignation with Cintia, a lady of the evening recommended by Ricardo, but she (as an agent of exposition) contends that the party in question cannot be the Duke, for he has resolved to curtail his decadence, and to emend his reputation, by marrying Casandra. She further argues that such audacity would be improper on the part of Federico, but that it would be inexcusable on the part of the Duke. The Duke continues the exposition, in a speech in which he laments having to give up his freedom and having to deprive Federico of his inheritance, but he vows to forsake the licence of his past. In the same speech, he refers to the negative impact of eavesdropping on the private conversations of others, and this anticipates his hiding to hear Federico and Casandra toward the end of the third act. As the Duke and his servants approach the house of a theatre manager, where a well-known actress is rehearsing her lines, Lope takes advantage of the occasion to address elements of drama. The Duke describes the theatre as a mirror to life and emphasizes the mode of tragicomedy, which blends the sombre with the risible. The dialogue falls within the domain of tragicomedy, yet it occurs in a play that Lope has identified as a tragedy.

The next scene features Federico and his servant Batín, the key provider of comic relief. The melancholy Federico expresses his resentment at his father's decision and his distaste for the charge of attending to Casandra, whom he regards, never having met her, as 'poisonous'. The two men discuss the notion of

---

[6] On the topic of irony, see David M. Gitlitz, 'Ironía e imágenes en *El castigo sin venganza*', *Revista de Estudios Hispánicos*, 14.1 (1980): 19–41; and Currie K. Thompson, 'Unstable Irony in Lope de Vega's *El castigo sin venganza*', *Studies in Philology*, 78.3 (1981): 224–40. On the language of the play, see Janet Horowitz Murray, 'Lope through the Looking-Glass: Metaphor and Meaning in *El castigo sin venganza*', *Bulletin of Hispanic Studies*, 56.1 (1979): 17–29; Melveena McKendrick, 'Language and Silence in *El castigo sin venganza*', *Bulletin of the Comediantes* 35.1 (1983): 79–95; Margit Frenk, 'Claves metafóricas en *El castigo sin venganza*', *Filología*, 20.2 (1985): 147–55; Roberto González Echevarría, *Celestina's Brood: Continuities of the Baroque in Spanish and Latin American Literatures* (Durham, NC & London: Duke University Press, 1993), pp. 66–80; Frederick A. de Armas, 'The Silences of Myth: (Con)fusing Eróstrato/Erasístrato in Lope's *El castigo sin venganza*', in *Hispanic Essays in Honor of Frank P. Casa*, ed. A. Robert Lauer & Henry W. Sullivan, Ibérica, 20 (New York: Peter Lang, 1997), pp. 65–75.

changing one's habits. Both Batín's *exemplum* and Federico's rejoinder contain the image of the lion (or lioness), and Batín introduces the theme of vengeance. He reminds his master that he has had a series of 'stepmothers' and that now he will only have to suffer one, and a high-born one at that. Heeding a woman's cry for help — complemented by Batín's aside that he should only be as attentive to his future stepmother — Federico rescues none other than Casandra, and their bonding is immediate and profound. Casandra alludes to Fortune, which in her mind has brought them together. Lope then inserts a comic counterpoint, in which Batín enters with Casandra's maid Lucrecia in his arms. The ensuing dialogue between Casandra and Federico takes the concept of maternity — she as his soon-to-be mother, he as having instantly been reborn — to clearly ironic levels. The signifiers indicate motherhood, but the undercurrent hints of love at first sight. The couple talk about a harmonious relationship and perfect coexistence, but the audience will comprehend that drama stems from conflict. Federico reiterates his position when the Marquis Gonzaga appears, and this intensifies the irony. Lucrecia perceives that her mistress would rather be with Federico than with his father, and Casandra returns to the subject of Fortune. Batín similarly presumes that his master would be more inclined to have Casandra as a wife than as a mother, and Federico urges that they make haste, in order not to arouse suspicion.

In a dialogue with Aurora, the Duke reproaches those who have coerced him into marriage. He regrets the unintentional hurt that he has caused Federico. Aurora answers that the fault is not his, that Fortune bears the blame. When she articulates her love for Federico, the Duke enthusiastically agrees to support her matrimonial plans, confident as he is that his son's feelings are as strong as those of his niece. Batín enters with news of the imminent arrival of Casandra and Federico. He announces that the two have got along beautifully, that each has enchanted the other, and that they could be taken as 'true' mother and son. The Duke welcomes Casandra as one who, as his wife, will bring increased honour to his family. Casandra maintains that the greatest gift that Fortune has bestowed upon her is to give her Aurora as a friend, and Aurora promises to serve Casandra in any way that she can. With his father and cousin as witnesses, Federico swears his allegiance to Casandra through service, loyalty, and 'true obedience', and the Duke praises his discretion. The Marquis pays his respects to Aurora and attributes their meeting to his good luck. When Federico and Batín remain alone on stage, the count bemoans the strength of his imagination and begs God to shield him from the thoughts and dreams that cloud his vision.[7] He prays that his fantasies stay in his mind. Batín guesses the cause of his turmoil. Federico concedes that he envies his father for possessing what is, for him, unattainable. Love may be impossible, but jealousy is not, and, in the closing speech of Act I, Federico predicts that he will die of a love that is forbidden to him. Lope develops a poetic system laden with irony. He is by no means subtle in the linking of language to circumstance. Characters are feeling one thing and saying another,

---

[7] On the motif of imagination, see Susan L. Fischer, 'Lope's *El castigo sin venganza* and the Imagination', *Kentucky Romance Quarterly*, 28.1 (1981): 23–36.

and the particular configuration of irony is an obvious recourse that enhances the drama and the poetry, if not necessarily the tragic import, of the play.

Act II opens a month later, with Casandra's protest, to Lucrecia, concerning her despondency. She insists that a noble lineage does not guarantee happiness. She rails against her mistreatment by the Duke, who has not been with her since their wedding night, and she proclaims that she will not endure indignities of this type. She mentions Federico's melancholic state and deems the two of them to be the prey of an unkind destiny. She warns that the Duke someday will pay for his disdain. The Duke brings up the possibility of Federico marrying Aurora. The dialogue is especially ironic, because Federico cannot admit the truth and the Duke has to counter bogus arguments. Away from his father, Federico cries that he is drowning in sorrow so intense that he continually stands between living and dying. Batín breaks the momentum by comparing him to a hermaphrodite. Federico concludes his plaint by noting that his agony is so intense that he has no room for reason, only for feeling. He can barely speak, for the divide between his soul and his tongue is wider than that between heaven and earth. One cannot fail to notice, however, that the count, like his fellow characters, is anything but tongue-tied. When Casandra ascribes Federico's anguish to jealousy over the Marquis's pursuit of Aurora, Aurora feels certain that her cousin's mind is elsewhere. In a crucial dialogue between Casandra and Federico, she registers her dissatisfaction over her husband's insensitivity; she calls the Duke a tyrant and his palace a prison. A sobbing Federico cannot escape his own plight, his desperation, his obsession with death. Discomfited by his tears, the only excuse for which is lost honour, Casandra admonishes him to act like a man and — whether believing this or not — impugns Aurora for causing his heartache. Federico, in a circuitous fashion, sets the record straight; he is in love with a woman who is beyond his reach. Casandra presses him to confess his love to the lady, whoever she may be, for love revealed is less dangerous than that which is kept buried.

A critical moment in the play is Casandra's soliloquy in the middle of the second act. She reintroduces and underscores four major themes: the imagination, propriety, revenge, and honour. She realizes that, despite the fact that appearances can be misleading, she is probably the object of Federico's love. Nonetheless, she hesitates to renounce the sacrament of marriage. It would please her to avenge her husband's infidelity, but she can visualize his sword stained by her blood. Federico has many outstanding qualities, yet she should not let herself fall into mortal error. Up to now, she has erred only through dishonourable thoughts, which she has not made public. Although preserving her good name is of the utmost importance, she cannot refrain from reflecting on love and vengeance. Casandra again tells Aurora that Federico is jealous of the Marquis. Aurora disagrees, but she will feign affection to stir a response in Federico. She gives the Marquis a ribbon in front of Federico; she submits, in an aside, that this 'amorous revenge' does a disservice to her love. Federico has no reaction to this staged scene, and Batín deduces why his master seems unperturbed. In the meantime, the Duke has been notified of his charge from the Pope. Federico wants to go with him, but his father demands that he stay at home to protect his property and, presumably, Casandra. In another soliloquy, Casandra once more ponders the boundaries of love and revenge. She feels that retribution is warranted, but that love should never manifest itself through treachery. Federico is very much in the middle of her ruminations, as are, if less discernibly, issues of honour and personal integrity. As Federico approaches, she places determination above everything; her fears have vanished. He is in the depths of melancholy, torn by the clash of love and duty but irrevocably devoted to Casandra. In a gloss on the traditional phrase 'sin mí, sin vos y sin Dios' [without myself, you, and God], Federico rues his loss of self (through absorption in grief), his love object (who belongs to another), and God (for whom he substitutes an adored woman). Cognizant of his heresy yet unable to contain his love, he is forlorn and helpless. Federico and Casandra cannot separate love from guilt or fatalism. Their parting words at the end of the act are filled with references to death.

Act III opens with Aurora's account to the Marquis of the offences of Casandra and Federico in the Duke's absence. She has spied on them out of jealousy and resentment, and she cites their exploits as shameless, befitting only heathens. The affront is too apparent to go undetected or unpunished. The Marquis holds that there is every chance that blood will be spilled on the Duke's triumphant return; this 'Achilles of Ferrara' will have to fight to redeem his fame and honour. He advises Aurora to marry him and depart with him for Mantua. Batín shares the news that the Duke has arrived and that he is on his way to the palace, eager to greet his son and wife. Preparing for the confrontation, Federico yet again feigns jealousy of the Marquis, and Aurora condemns the hypocrisy of his strange and inconsistent melancholy. Batín, who has heard Aurora's protest and does not quite trust his master's reputed ignorance of what is going on, engages in a comic excursus on forgetfulness. Turning down his servant's offer of aid, Federico can only convey that he does not know the root of his dilemma. He has but minutes to confer with Casandra before the Duke invades their clandestine space. They cannot elude the imagery of death, just as they will not be able to elude death itself. Federico affirms in an aside that he can feel death looming. In search of a diversionary tactic, he will try to persuade his father that he is in love with his cousin and ready to marry her. Casandra adamantly opposes the idea. She threatens to expose their sins publicly if he follows through with the plan. She would rather lose her life than have him marry Aurora.

The reunion is played out in contradictory modes. Virtue and vice have been interchanged. The Duke is overjoyed to be home, elated by his victory and his reception by the Pope, heartened by the report that Federico has governed well while he was away, anxious to see his family and to herald his conversion. Federico and Casandra must deal with their guilt. Batín and Ricardo debate the Duke's reformation, Ricardo highlighting the new humility and an attitude that borders on the saintly, and Batín asserting that leopards rarely change their spots. When the Duke questions Batín about Federico's administration of the household, the servant gives him answers replete with double entendres: the count has been as successful on the domestic front as the Duke at war; never has a stepmother had a better relation with a stepson, doubtlessly due to her righteousness. The

Duke's high spirits are dampened when he reads the correspondence that awaits him. One letter, which bears the unmistakable imprint of Aurora, communicates the treason that jeopardizes his honour and proposes that he keep Federico and Casandra under surveillance. He deliberates on the cause of his disgrace, and he wonders if the heavens are avenging his past vices, although he endeavours to excuse his misdeeds by comparing them favourably with those of the biblical King David, whose offences were more egregious and whose punishment was less severe. He cannot fathom why the two would want to destroy his honour. He prays that if he kills Federico, the heavens will give his son new life so that he could be punished again for duplicity of this magnitude. Before he tests his adversaries, he differentiates between punishment and vengeance. He has the right to retaliate in such a manner as to reckon with the offense without publicizing his dishonor; the private act is poetic justice (or justice in an absolute sense), whereas revenge implies not only a personal decision but a public display, which would go against the broader concept of justice and the conventions of honour. Hence, a cardinal rule of the honour code: the publicizing of dishonour can only further tarnish an individual's or a family's honour. In the baroque reversal of appearance and reality, the former enjoys the privileged position.

When Federico enters to request Aurora's hand in marriage, the Duke becomes the purveyor of ironic strategies. He says that he is positively disposed to sanction the nuptials, but that this is a family affair and that he should ask his mother's permission. Federico balks at the task, and he hints that his relation with Casandra has not been as ideal as it might seem, since she cannot forget that he is the son of another woman. The Duke replies that he would have wished that she had shown even stronger love to Federico than to himself. His instinct tells him that Federico is lying, but he will watch the two in order be assured of their complicity. Speaking with Casandra, who lavishly praises Federico and says that he is the living image of his father, the Duke cunningly taunts her by noting that if they are so similar, it is possible that she has mistaken the son for the father. He adds insult to injury by mentioning Federico's bid to marry Aurora, who is present. Aurora resolutely declines, for lack of love, and Casandra backs her up. Hidden behind the tapestries, the Duke hears the all-encompassing conversation between the two lovers. Convinced that the Duke will do everything to defend his honour, Federico advocates ending the relationship, and Casandra calls him a coward. That is enough for the Duke, who plots his 'punishment'. He will have Federico execute a traitor (in reality, Casandra, who has been bound and covered), and consequently have his son executed for the crime. The Duke raises his voice to curse honour as the enemy of mankind and woman — always weaker than man, always susceptible to corruption — as the receptacle of honour. The misogynistic detail regarding the weakness of women intimates that the Duke credits Casandra with a larger portion of culpability. The Duke grants Aurora permission to marry the Marquis, and she will permit Batín to go with them to Mantua, thereby removing from the realm three witnesses to the wrongdoing. The Duke sets his ploy into motion, and his discourse gives a spiritual, or theological, cast to the death sentence. He argues that God is behind him, to grant him the precise mechanism for effecting justice without revenge.[8] Batín concludes the play by designating it as a lesson, from Italy, for the Spanish public.

El castigo sin venganza incorporates the deep structure of classical tragedy, in which characters are relegated to performance of a dramaturgy that they cannot control. Oedipus's search for Laius's killer demonstrates an ironic undoing of his power; a master plot defeats him. The new king is the detective and his own prey, and the audience relishes and shudders at the search. Tragedy is about disillusionment; it is a deconstruction of the myth that human existence involves choice. A rudimentary but viable analogy would be to cast tragic characters as puppets, with the power of the strings belonging to an independent, and far more potent, energy. An operative verb in this context might be *drive*, for the players are driven by what seem to be their own feelings and needs, but they are subject to an authority that one could depict as 'from above'. By having the Duke allude to God and divine retribution, and to the agency of Federico and Casandra, Lope removes the play from its classical grounding. The Duke holds his son and wife responsible for their actions, for their decisions, and he appreciates, though conditionally, his own defects. (His allusion to King David brilliantly captures his egotism and his way of thinking, and it places the play in the Judeo-Christian realm, as well. The fact that his analogy is not completely valid makes a rhetorical statement in itself.) Before the action proper begins, characters discuss poetry and theatre, notably the subgenre of tragicomedy that Lope foregrounds in the *Arte nuevo*. That model does not disappear when he places *El castigo sin venganza* under the rubric of tragedy. The discussion of the so-called 'new poetry' of the period places the writer of dramatic poetry in the centre. Language becomes an instrument of irony while exposing the art — the artfulness — behind the creation and conspicuously obstructing the path toward a pure tragic realism. In short, ingenuity serves art better than it serves tragedy. If Oedipus's metadrama is absorbed into a higher drama, the Duke's plot operates in both its immediate social setting and, at least according to his rationalization, in the celestial order, neither of which represents the universe of ancient tragedy.

It could be said that in *El castigo sin venganza* Lope mediates Lope. Self-referentiality, metatheatre, theology, and, most pointedly, tragicomedy compete with the tragic vision, with the tragic intertext. The Duke intercedes at each juncture within the dramatic spectrum. Until the end, he is vice personified, and he pushes Federico into the arms of Casandra. His moral evolution occurs offstage, and the audience must take his word for a change in outlook — be it sincere or not — that comes too late to alter the ending. There is no catharsis here, and likely no cause for empathy. The Duke does not decry the system in which he must operate; on the contrary, he rushes to punish the guilty parties, and he can do so with impunity, without compromising his social position or admitting his

---

[8] See Antonio Carreño, 'La "sin venganza" como violencia: *El castigo sin venganza* de Lope de Vega', *Hispanic Review*, 59.4 (1991): 379–400. See also Donald R. Larson, *The Honor Plays of Lope de Vega* (Cambridge, MA & London: Harvard University Press, 1977), esp. pp. 131–58; and Antonia Petro, 'El chivo expiatorio sustitutorio: *El castigo sin venganza*', *Bulletin of the Comediantes*, 55.1 (2003): 23–46.

complicity. Federico is a man with a conscience, being pulled at in two directions. He loves his father, but that love is tinged with resentment. He loves Casandra, but the shadow of rectitude hovers over him. He aims at a cover-up; she will not consent to it. Casandra has the pride and arrogance of the aristocracy. She is a strong-willed woman who refuses to abide by the Duke's neglect. For her, Federico is simultaneously a love object and an instrument of vengeance. If he is plagued by guilt, she is angry, embittered, and entitled to go after the love that her husband denies her. She is the least cautious of the main characters and, arguably, the blindest to her fate. Federico is trapped by indecisiveness, the Duke by social protocol, and Casandra by an inflexible temperament; in this respect, she is the closest to the classic archetype.[9]

The three characters, along with Aurora and Batín, have impressive, and distinctive, verbal talents. They are wordsmiths, and, for them, language is not merely a means to an end but an end in itself. They deploy conceits and an array of linguistic manoeuverings under the most adverse conditions. Ironic discourse jointly supplements and runs the risk of overpowering the plot line and the tragic dimensions of the play. So, too, does Lope's dependence on the norms of the honour code, as portrayed in the cultural artifacts of early modern Spain. While tragic inevitability is not absent in *El castigo sin venganza*, Lope does not slip seamlessly out of the frame of his 'new art' as he renders — ironically, in the final analysis — the face-off between tragedy and tragicomedy.

Critics have often contrasted Lope, as a creator of dramatic action, with Calderón, as a creator of poetic language. The dichotomy tends to slight not only the beauty of Lope's poetry but also the relevance of the linguistic base of his plays. *El caballero de Olmedo*, for example, takes the courtly love motif of dying for love to the extreme. The play's dénouement is predetermined by a *seguidilla* on the death of the protagonist, Don Alonso. Using the go-between Fabia as a healer of amorous illnesses, Lope exaggerates the metaphorical discourse, only to actualize the metaphor by having a jealous rival and his accomplices kill the title character. The play, with its comic intrigue in Acts I and II, may be deficient as a tragedy, at least by classical standards, but the unity of action (the road, literal and figurative, to the hero's death) is replicated in the movement from vocalizing about death to ceasing to exist. The language of *El caballero de Olmedo* centres, as well, on the interplay of vision and blindness; Don Alonso does not heed the signs that warn him of imminent danger, as he relishes the sweet suffering of a

---

[9] On characterization, see, among numerous others, T. E. May, 'Lope de Vega's *El castigo sin venganza*: The Idolatry of the Duke of Ferrara', *Bulletin of Hispanic Studies*, 37.3 (1960): 154–82; Peter W. Evans, 'Character and Context in *El castigo sin venganza*', *Modern Language Review*, 74.2 (1979): 321–34; Matthew D. Stroud, 'Rivalry and Violence in *El castigo sin venganza*', in *The Golden Age Comedia: Text, Theory, and Performance*, ed. Charles Ganelin & Howard Mancing (West Lafayette, IN: Purdue University Press, 1994), pp. 37–47; Theresa Ann Sears, 'Like Father, Like Son: The Paternal Perverse in Lope's *El castigo sin venganza*', *Bulletin of Hispanic Studies* (Liverpool), 73.2 (1996): 129–42; and Robert ter Horst, '"Error pintado": The Oedipal Emblematics of Lope de Vega's *El castigo sin venganza*', in *'Never-Ending Adventure': Studies in Medieval and Early Modern Spanish Literature in Honor of Peter N. Dunn*, ed. Edward H. Friedman & Harlan Sturm (Newark, DE: Juan de la Cuesta, 2002), pp. 279–308.

love that will lead to his downfall.[10] In Lope's best-known play, *Fuenteovejuna*, much revolves around a single word — the name of the village itself — as a symbol of unity and collective defence. Lope borders on subversion by having the inhabitants of Fuenteovejuna take the law into their own hands. The playwright ingeniously has the villagers praise the Catholic Monarchs when they attack the Comendador as a tyrant worthy of assassination; they know the rule, but this is, for them, a justifiable exception. Lope brings into the dialogue, early in the first act (lines 275 ff.), a fascinating but rather indecorous conversation among selected villagers on the themes of language (the use of euphemisms, among other topics), harmony, the customs of love, and self-love. The philosophizing peasants would seem to go against Lope's call for linguistic decorum in the *Arte nuevo*,[11] but they fit nicely into a frame of subtle subversion, and they point to the ways in which a carefully chosen rhetoric can support, and even surpass, the dramatic action.

The self-referential and metatheatrical aspects of *El castigo sin venganza* allow Lope to comment on the compositional process while seeking to involve his audience in a tragic predicament. His recourse to honour both updates precedent and alienates the plot from the classical model, and the play dramatizes the confrontation between the 'ancients' and the 'moderns', advocates of the glories of the past and proponents of change. Within this scheme, irony becomes a means of reconciliation, a common denominator, a link to antiquity but noticeably updated, and as a form of punctuation. The rhetoric of irony in the play joins together words that unknowingly foreshadow the conclusion and words whose deceptive qualities escape the receiver of the message, but, importantly, not speaker or the audience. Verbal dexterity is crucial to the ending, to the Duke's rationale. What has gone before the Duke's distinction between punishment and revenge has suggested that one must be vigilant in detecting and interpreting rhetorical artifacts, which may be designed just as easily to shield, camouflage, or reconfigure than to validate the truth. It is probably not coincidental that Lope decided to ask the reader to trust the word of the Duke at the end of the play. The Duke's new self is never realized on stage; rather, he avows his change and proceeds to contemplate his strategies for 'punishment'. The play cautions one to 'read' with a degree of scepticism, that is, to be aware and wary of the power of words. The Duke gives his word that he is ready for the responsibilities of matrimony, and he repeats that oath in the marriage ceremony itself. He then breaks his word, and an analysis of the ending must take into account his veracity and his motives. On several levels, then, Lope admonishes his audience to listen well, to enjoy an intricately crafted poetic object, and to judge a verbal construct as a potential analogue and antithesis of deeds. As he rewrites tragedy, he rewrites irony, but with reverence in each case.

---

[10] My edition of *El caballero de Olmedo* (Newark, DE: Juan de la Cuesta, 2004) includes an introduction and bibliography (pp. 11–51). See esp. pp. 21–32.

[11] See the edition of Enrique García Santo-Tomás (Madrid: Catédra, 2006), lines 269–79, p. 146; and Francisco Ruiz Ramón's edition of *Fuenteovejuna*, Clásicos Almar, 23 (Salamanca: Colegio de España, 1991).

Part 4: Prose

16

Life's Pilgrim: *El peregrino en su patria*

ALEXANDER SAMSON

El peregrino en su patria was published in early 1604 in Seville,[1] the city where Lope's mistress at that time, the actress Micaela Luján, was living with five of their eventual seven illegitimate children born before their breakup in 1608. The name of the novel's protagonist, Pánfilo de Luján, pays homage to her. A sonnet to the pilgrim in the preliminaries is attributed to her (although it was probably ghost-written for her by Lope, given that she was illiterate) through her pseudonym, Camila Lucinda, the dedicatee of an extended, classically inspired eclogue in the text, 'Serrana hermosa' [Beautiful mountain girl], a paean to their passion. At around the same time that Lope's novel appeared, Micaela presented a petition demanding the stewardship of the estate of her late husband Diego Díaz, who had died in Peru the previous year having left for the New World, abandoning his wife, in 1596. Lope acted as her guarantor in relation to the estate, worth possibly as much as 700 ducats. The first witness to her claim was, intriguingly, Mateo Alemán, the author of the picaresque novel *Guzmán de Alfarache* (1599, 1604) and a resident of the same parish as the two lovers.[2] *El peregrino* was republished a further seven times between this Seville edition of Clemente Hidalgo and the last Madrid edition of 1618, an indication of its popularity, at least contemporaneously.

Although prose is probably the least critically regarded genre of Lope's output today, in terms of the dissemination of his work in the early seventeenth century this novel was the first extended piece by him to be translated into both English and French. Vital D'Audigier's French translation *Les diverses fortunes de Panfile et Nise* appeared in 1614, while the English translation *The pilgrime of Casteele*, likely to have been the work of William Dutton, a lawyer matriculated at Exeter

---

[1] Lope's friend Tomás Gracián Dantisco signed the *aprobación* or official approval for publication in Valladolid on 25 November 1603, referring to his friend as 'peregrino y fénix'.

[2] On Micaela and the circumstances of the text's publication see Francisco Rodríguez Marín, 'Lope de Vega y Camila Lucinda', *Boletín de la Real Academia Española* 1.1 (1914): 249–90 (pp. 271–74, esp. p. 271); Juan Bautista Avalle-Arce's introduction to his edition of *El peregrino en su patria* (Madrid: Clásicos Castalia, 1973), pp. 13–16; and Américo Castro & Hugo A. Rennert, *Vida de Lope de Vega (1562–1635)*, 2nd edn (Madrid: Anaya, 1968; repr. 1969), pp. 100–9.

College, Oxford in 1611 or 1612,[3] came out in 1621. The English version retained
fragments of the original Spanish; for example, the tags in Everardo's prison cell
are left untranslated: 'the word was from Ouid, and saith thus: O quanta pena es
viuir, vida enojosa y forcada / Y quando la muerte agrada; ser impossible, morir'
[oh how painful it is to live an irksome and unchosen life / and when death is
pleasing, for it to be impossible to die].[4] As in the earlier French edition of 1614,
Dutton omitted all four of the interpolated *autos sacramentales* and most of the
poetry, simplifying and focusing the story on Pánfilo and Nise by getting rid of
digressions and numerous 'extraneous' episodes. The first verses not omitted by
the English translator were the songs sung by Nise to Leandro and his reply,
which were curiously left by him in the original Castilian. This points to the likely
projected use of the translation as phrase book, cultural and language-learning tool.
A second variant reissue appeared in London in 1623 in the context of the Prince
of Wales's surprise visit to Madrid to woo the Spanish Infanta, with a dedication
that underlined Lope's status as 'in his owne Countrey one of the choysest Spirits,
which hath beene bred there in many yeares'.[5] Lope's story inspired John
Fletcher's play *The Pilgrim*, whether through contact with the original or in this
translation. The title in the French and changes to both translations reveal the
specific ways in which the text was read abroad to emphasise the classically
inspired love story and downplay precisely those features highlighted by Lope
elsewhere as original about his own prose, its copiousness, erudition, and generic
and stylistic variety:

> ya de cosas altas, ya de humildes, ya de episodios y paréntesis, ya de historias, ya de
> fábulas, ya de reprensiones y ejemplos, ya de versos y lugares de autores, pienso
> valerme, para que ni sea tan grave el estilo que canse a los que no saben, ni tan
> desnudo de algún arte que le remitan al polvo los que entienden.[6]

> [I plan to make use of things whether elevated or humble, episodes and parentheses,
> histories, fables, cautionary tales and moral examples, verses and the well-known
> sayings of famous authorities, in order that its style is not so serious as to tire out the
> unlearned, nor so bereft of any stylishness that the lettered consign it to oblivion.]

The interest of Lope's novel in literary history has come to focus almost
exclusively on the lists of his *comedias* which accompanied it, because of their

---

[3] See the entry on this translation in P. E. Russell & D. M. Rogers, ed., *A Catalogue of
Hispanic Manuscripts and Books before 1700 from the Bodleian Library and Oxford College
Libraries, Exhibited at the Taylor Institution, 6–11 September* (Oxford: Dolphin Book Co. for
Primer Congreso Internacional de Hispanistas, 1962), no. 82, p. 26; also the discussion of it in
Dale B. J. Randall, *The Golden Tapestry: A Critical Survey of Non-Chivalric Spanish Fiction in
English Translation (1543–1657)* (Durham, NC: Duke University Press, 1963), pp. 102–12.
[4] Lope de Vega, *The Pilgrime of Casteele* (London: Edward Allde for John Norton, 1621),
p. 20 [BL C.57.e.23.].
[5] Lope de Vega, *The Pilgrime of Casteele*, 2nd edn (London: Edward Allde for John Norton
and Thomas Dewe, 1623), sig. A2r.
[6] Lope de Vega, *Novelas a Marcia Leonarda*, ed. Julia Barella (Madrid: Biblioteca Nueva,
2003), pp. 132–33.

function as indispensable tools in the attribution and dating of his plays. There is no convincing explanation, however, for the falling away in the reception of this text, undoubtedly popular in its day, other than Lope being known subsequently predominantly as a playwright. *El peregrino* does not compare unfavourably with work by other prose writers of the epoch and should be a worthy and worthwhile member of the canon of early modern Spanish prose fiction.

The context of the work was the phase of Lope's career, during the ban on theatrical production that lasted from 1598 until 1599, when he had turned his hand to other media and activities away from the theatre. He probably entered the service of Don Pedro Fernández de Castro, shortly after the latter began to title himself Marqués de Sarria (his father Fernando Ruiz de Castro, VI Conde de Lemos, was about to take up his Viceregency of Naples), some time towards the end of 1598. Lope was initially his first *gentilhombre* and then secretary.[7] *Arcadia*, a pastoral novel, as well as his poem about the pirate Sir Francis Drake, *La Dragontea*, both appeared in 1598, followed the next year by his popular devotional religious poem *Isidro* and the encomiastic *Fiestas de Denia*, a festival text commemorating the celebrations that followed the marriage of Philip III and Margaret of Austria in Valencia in 1599 on the ancestral estates of the royal favourite, the Marquis of Denia (later Duke of Lerma), father-in-law and uncle of Lope's then patron. The king had been forced to remain in the east by the ravages of plague in Castile, so Lope was no doubt drafted in to bolster the awesome display of courtly power mounted by the Sandoval y Rojas family, either by his patron or directly by Lerma himself, as he exerted his stranglehold on the government of Spain in the early stages of the new regime, through its representations and the instigation of a new culture of visibility and display.[8] These events were interlaced with the plot of *El peregrino*: Pánfilo and his friend Everardo arrive in Valencia a few days after 'el Rey Católico se hubiese casado en ella con la preciosa perla Margarita' [the Catholic king married that precious pearl Margaret], to watch the second interpolated *auto*, *Las bodas entre el alma y el amor divino*, which had in reality originally been performed in a public square there as part of the wedding celebrations.[9] In the text the pilgrim catches the performance ahistorically a year after it was actually performed. A description of Lope in a contemporary news pamphlet in the context of his participation in the 1599 festivities underlines the extraordinary favour he enjoyed and how close he was to the centres of power:

---

[7] Eduardo Pardo de Guevara y Valdés, *Don Pedro Fernández de Castro, VII conde de Lemos (1576–1622): estudio histórico* (Santiago de Compostela: Xunta de Galicia, 1997), p. 257.

[8] See Lope de Vega, *Fiestas de Denia*, ed. M. G. Profeti, with historical notes by B. J. García García, Secoli d'Oro, 41 (Florence: Alinea, 2004), and Guevara y Valdés, *Don Pedro Fernández de Castro*, p. 62.

[9] Patrick Williams, *The Great Favourite: The Duke of Lerma and the Court and Government of Philip III of Spain, 1598–1621* (Manchester: Manchester University Press, 2006), p. 60 and notes. On this see also Felipe B. Pedraza Jiménez, '*Las bodas entre el alma y el amor divino*: texto, espectáculo y propaganda ideológica', in *La fiesta de Corpus Christi*, ed. Gerardo Fernández Juárez & Fernando Martínez Gil, Estudios, 84 (Cuenca: Universidad Castilla-La Mancha, 2002), pp. 235–51.

Pues passando adelante con estas fiestas de carnestoliendas, digo que el húltimo día dellas, que fué martes, a las dos horas después de mediodía, salieron de la ciudad por el sobredicho portal del Real huna hermossa y gallarda quadrilla de caualleros disfrasados de máscaras muy bien apuestos con sus cavallos, siendo el principal el Marqués de Sarria [...] yvan delanteras dos máscaras ridículas quel huno dellas fué conoscida ser el poheta Lope de Vega, el qual venía vestido de botarga, ábito italiano, que hera todo de colorado, con calsas y ropilla seguidas y ropa larga de levantar, de chamelote negro, con una gorra de terciopello llano en la cabesa, y éste yva a cavallo con huna mula vaya ensillada a la gineta y petral de cascaveles y por el vestido que traya y arsones de la silla llevava colgando diferentes animales de carne para comer, representando el tiempo del carnal.[10]

[On the last day of the Lenten carnival, which was Tuesday, at 2 o'clock, a beautiful and elegant party of gentlemen left the city through the Real gate, wearing masks, with well-trapped horses, the principal rider being the Marquis of Sarria [...] one of the two at the front of the party in ridiculous masks was known to be the poet Lope de Vega, who was dressed in a loose fitting all-in-one red Italian outfit like Botarga, with jerkin and breeches overlaid and long gown of black camlet, with a flat velvet cap on his head, and he was riding a cream mule saddled with short stirrups and a breast strap with bells and on his costume and hanging from the saddle tree cuts of meat from different animals, representing Shrovetide.]

The festival text he penned for Lerma was as much about the construction of a courtly persona for himself, about projecting an image of the erudite poet in the service of a noble elite, dignified and elevated by his gift, as it was a token of his gratitude to his patron, the Marquis of Sarria, and the royal favourite, and a record of what actually transpired. This image is incarnated in the description here of the rich fabrics of his Italian-style clothing, velvet and camlet (silk with camel-hair), and forming part of an 'elegant party of gentlemen', although the outfit also alluded to the origins of his fame in entertainment and comedy: the 'botarga' was associated with the *commedia dell'arte*. The frontispiece of *El peregrino* encoded many aspects of this same process of self-fashioning. Lope identified himself as the humble pilgrim appearing on the right through the sonnet, allegedly by Micaela, as well as through the topical allusions to public events in which he had participated. His friend and censor Tomás Gracián Dantisco referred to him as 'peregrino y fénix' [pilgrim and phoenix], and there was yet another reworking of identifiable autobiographical material, his affair with Elena Osorio in the 1580s,[11] which had ended unhappily with his exile from Madrid for ten years and whose mark haunted him right up until his 1632, septuagenarian *La Dorotea*.[12] At the bottom was a coat of arms consisting of nineteen towers belonging to the mythic

---

[10] Eduardo Juliá Martínez, 'Lope de Vega en Valencia en 1599', *Boletín de la Real Academia Española*, 3 (1916): 541–59 (p. 542). See also Matías de Novoa, *Memorias de Matías de Novoa, ayuda de cámara de Felipe IV*, 4 vols (Madrid: Imprenta de Miguel Ginesta, 1878–86), I, p. 176.

[11] The story of Tirso and Aurelia and the sonnet composed by Everardo before the ruins of Sagunto, playing on the obvious echo between Helen of Troy and Elena.

[12] See on this chapter 18 by Xavier Tubau in this volume.

Bernardo del Carpio, to which Lope had laid claim for, it seems, no reason other than the coincidence of their surnames, and which had driven Góngora to ridicule his rival's pretensions of nobility in a sonnet telling him to stop making towers out of bacon, an allusion to his second wife, Juana de Guardo, who was the daughter of a wealthy meat merchant: 'No fabrique más torres sobre arena, / si no es que ya, segunda vez casado, / nos quiere hacer torres los torreznos' [Don't build any more towers on the sand, / if it is not that now, married for a second time, / you want to build towers out of rashers of bacon].[13] This was the second time the coat of arms had been used by Lope in print and he took this opportunity to rebuff Góngora's slighting and scathing criticism by placing a medusa stabbing a heart on the left, a figure of Envy, with the words 'Velis nolis Invidia' below, completed by his blason, meaning something like 'whether you like it or not, Envy, I am Lope'.[14] Some exemplars of the first edition also contain a woodcut portrait of Lope[15] with three additional Latin tags, referring again to envy, fame and the difficulty of finding anything of a particular kind perfect in all respects. Even while this highly self-conscious act of image-making insisted on the figure of Lope as pious and humble Christian pilgrim, it simultaneously underlined his uniqueness and laid claim to a questionable nobility, vociferously defended along with his fame and status as a poet — 'al honesto trajabo sigue la fama' [fame follows honest hard work][16] — from attacks by other writers, rebuffed for their envy of his talent: 'no conozco en España tres que escriban versos' [I know of no more than three in Spain able to write verse] (p. 56), and referring ultimate judgment to eternity.

Lope's story drew inspiration from the fashionable Byzantine Greek romances of Heliodorus and Aquiles Tatius (the *Aethiopian History* and *Leucippe and Clitophon* respectively), prototypes for Cervantes's *Persiles y Sigismunda* (1617); classical stories about lovers who overcome a multitude of adversities and eventually emerge from a labyrinth of encounters and episodes to be united.[17] In his 1613 play *La dama boba* the clever Nise refers to Heliodorus as a 'griego poeta divino' [divine Greek poet], despite being a writer of prose, going on to define poetic prose, in what could be a description of Lope's own *El peregrino*, as 'hermosa / varia, culta, licenciosa, / y escura aun a raros ingenios. / Tiene mil exornaciones / y retóricas figuras' [beautiful, / varied, cultivated, licentious, / and obscure even for rare intellects. / It has a thousand adornments / and rhetorical figures].[18] The Lopean novel shared three key features with its antique models, love, adventure and religion, but differed in its heterogenous incorporation of

---

[13] Luis de Góngora, *Obras completas*, ed. Juan & Isabel Millé y Giménez, 6th edn (Madrid: Aguilar, 1967), p. 534.

[14] See Juan Eugenio Hartzenbusch, 'Cervantes y Lope de Vega en 1605: citas y aplicaciones relativas de estos dos esclarecidos ingenios', *Revista Española*, 1 (mayo de 1862): 169–86, and the discussion by Avalle-Arce in his edition of *El peregrino*, pp. 18–21.

[15] See figure A23 and chapter by David McGrath in this volume.

[16] *El peregrino en su patria*, ed. Avalle-Arce, p. 57. All quotations are taken from this edition.

[17] His title was taken from an Italian source, Jacopo Caviceo's *Il peregrino* (1508); see Dale Randall, *The Golden Tapestry*, p. 104.

[18] Lope de Vega, *La dama boba*, ed. Diego Marín (Madrid: Cátedra, 2005), p. 75, lines 281 and 298–302.

chivalric, sentimental, pastoral and picaresque elements. There is an intensification of degradation; the vicissitudes suffered by the protagonist, his imprisonment on numerous occasions, capture and Algerian slavery, where Nise finds him 'desnudo y flaco' [naked and emaciated] (p. 359), condemnation to wander as a vagrant, 'ya tan mal tratado, los pies corriendo sangre, quemado el rostro y los cabellos revueltos' [now so mistreated, blood dripping from his feet, his face sunburnt and matted hair] (p. 441), are framed by catechistic drama and a wealth of moral and religious *exempla*, in other words are contained within a Christian cosmology ruled over by Tridentine Catholicism rather than fate and chance. His tribulations are meant to be interpreted as quasi-religious experiences. There is also a clear debt to the *comedia* in the shifting, playful confusion of identities; the crossdressed Nise becomes Don Felis for Pánfilo's sister Finea, her lover and Nise's brother Celio stabs his own sister unwittingly, mistaking her for a rival, while Pánfilo ends up assuming a false identity for a second time in the service of Nise's family as Mauricio, secretary of Lisardo, Nise's brother, while he persuades Leandro, a Catalan admirer of Nise, to assume his identity. Both are banged up until the real Pánfilo can be identified. Also, rather than eroticism, in keeping with its Catholic reformed agenda, *El peregrino* represents a test of constancy and example of virtue, an inversion of romance or an anti-picaresque, resorting instead to variety of incident and the production of *admiratio* or amazement in the reader through the marvellous to keep its audience entertained.

Despite the apparent didactic and orthodox content of this tale, set significantly in the 'Año Santo' [Holy Year] 1600, the papal Jubilee year dedicated to the promotion of good works amongst the faithful, shortly after they escape from Toledo the protagonist, Pánfilo, attempts to rape Nise (pp. 354 and 356). While Nise 'con tanta castidad la vemos seguir su comenzado propósito' [with such chastity we see her stick to her original intent] (p. 423), Pánfilo remains 'al fin hombre, muchas veces se hubiera rendido a su apetito, si ella no gobernara con su modestia el freno de aquella furia' [in the end a man, who would have given in on countless occasions to his baser appetites if her modesty had not been able to govern that unruliness] (p. 338). Such ingenuous touches temper the novel's moral and didactic Counter Reformation agenda. The representation of the lovers is, furthermore, highly mediated in a literary sense. The scene in which Pánfilo discovers his feelings for Nise by means of a portrait and then a mirror echoed scenes from Jean Renart's *Lai de l'ombre*, Margarita of Navarre's *Heptaméron*, Martorell's *Tirant lo blanc*, the *Arcadia* by Sannazaro, Garcilaso's *Second Eclogue* and Gil Vicente's *Tragicomedia de Amadís*.[19] The prominent religious elements remain structural devices rather than being integrated into the narrative structure of the text as allegory, as they were in Jerónimo de Contreras's *Selva de aventuras* [*Forest of Adventures*] (1565); the invocations of the Virgin and visits to her three principal shrines (Montserrat, Guadalupe, and del Pilar) are simply vehicles to display the author's rich erudition in legends, hagiography and

---

[19] On these literary echoes see Bienvenido Morros Mestres, 'El arte de la seducción en *El peregrino en su patria*', *Anuario Lope de Vega*, 6 (2000): 147–62.

Mariology.[20] Criticism that religion simply adds to the novel's *copia* or copiousness is supported by the failure to exploit its oxymoronic title, a pilgrim in his own land, which while alluding to a rich medieval culture surrounding the figure and institution of pilgrimage,[21] the *peregrinatio vitae*, is constantly twinned with its secular counterpart, the *peregrinatio amoris*. As one critic has written: 'estar enamorado es la condición esencial del peregrino cristiano' [being in love is the fundamental state of the Christian pilgrim].[22] The notion of pilgrimage here has more to do with exile and adventure as the best teachers of experience, wisdom and virtue, an idea picked up on by later thinkers from Salas Barbadillo to Gracián as peculiar to the Spanish in the context of their vast imperial dominions. The attempt to embody the values of the Catholic Reformation fails in its excessive self-consciousness and inability to incorporate spiritual values within characterisation and plot development, which remain ultimately a novelisation of a *comedia de capa y espada* (cloak and sword play).[23] According to Lope in the *Novelas a Marcia Leonarda* he was able to fulfil his obligation to write 'habiendo hallado tantas invenciones para mil comedias' [having come up with so many ideas for a thousand plays], and in the preliminaries to *La desdicha por la honra* [*Misfortune through Honour*], even more specifically, he reveals: 'yo he pensado que tienen las novelas los mismos preceptos que las comedias' [I have always thought that novels have the same basic foundations as drama], specifying that this means giving 'gusto al pueblo, aunque se ahorque el arte' [pleasure to people, even though tradition be damned].[24]

The preface to *El peregrino* was highly atypical, eschewing any pretence of *humilitas* in favour of a robust defence of his dramaturgy, a self-adulatory affirmation of his talent and erudition. The list of his *comedias* provided the *aficionado* with proof of his prodigious creativity as well as a checklist designed to 'advertir a los que leen mis escritos con afición' [to warn those who earnestly read my writings], and there are readers in Italy, France and the Indies, he went on to add, in a world of circulated manuscript copies derived from performance originals and the first publications of pirate copies of his work. The plays are listed neither chronologially, alphabetically nor thematically but according to the *autores* [actor-managers] to whom they had been sold. Subsequent references to particular actors (in any given moment associated with particular companies) appearing in specific named *comedias* has allowed us to refine the datings of Morley and Bruerton.[25] He litters the introduction to the list of *comedias* with

---

[20] On the complex relationship between *El peregrino* and Greek or Byzantine romance see '*El peregrino en su patria* de Lope de Vega desde la poética del romance griego', in *Lope en 1604*, ed. Xavier Tubau (Lleida: Milenio & Universitat Autònoma de Barcelona, 2004), pp. 95–122.

[21] The word *peregrino* in Spanish has a range of meanings from strange, unusual, rarely seen to temporary, passing, worldly and mutable, alteration and vicissitude.

[22] Avalle-Arce, Introduction to *El peregrino*, p. 31.

[23] Antonio Vilanova, 'El peregrino andante en el *Persiles* de Cervantes' (1949), in his *Erasmo y Cervantes*, Palabra Crítica, 8 (Barcelona: Lumen, 1989), pp. 326–409 (p. 370).

[24] Lope de Vega, *Novelas a Marcia Leonarda*, ed. Barella, pp. 75 and 133.

[25] See Thornton Wilder, 'New Aids Toward Dating the Early Plays of Lope de Vega' (1952), in his *American Characteristics and Other Essays*, ed. Donald Gallup (Lincoln, NE: Authors

classical citations, many in Latin, from Seneca, Aristotle, Plato, Cicero and Plutarch. The focus and defence of his talent as a writer of poetry culminates with the claim he has written 5,160 pages of poetry, which swelled along with the the list of *comedias* from the 230 in 1604 to 462 by 1618 and to 23,100 pages of verse.[26] In an indirect and prophetic response to criticism of him he suggests: 'Si algo agrada, comúnmente alaban el natural del dueño, niegan el arte' [if they find something pleasing, often they praise the author's gift, but deny his art] (p. 56). This idea of Lope as an 'untutored genius', a brilliant writer of drama but not especially profound, has dogged his reputation into the twenty-first century. The display of genuine erudition in this introduction,[27] his ironic reflection on the denial of his 'arte', undermines suggestions of artlessness. In his *Arte nuevo de hacer comedias en este tiempo* (1609) he might reject the 'arte' [practice or rules] of classical precept in favour of a populist poetics, based on what works in the theatre, seeking to follow the 'arte que inventaron / los que el vulgar aplauso pretendieron / porque, como las paga el vulgo, es justo / hablarle en necio para darle gusto' [the method created / by those who sought the applause of commoners, / since it is they who pay for these plays, it is only fair / to please them with foolish talk].[28] The four catechistic religious dramas incorporated in each of the first four books (*La Maya* is the only *auto sacramental*, dealing directly with the Eucharist) taken together with his promise to publish ten *comedias* in the sequel to *El peregrino*, it has been argued, demonstrate that for him the concept of autonomous printed editions of plays destined for private readers as potentially lucrative literary objects had still not crystallised in Lope's thought.[29] In this sense, *El peregrino* was a means for him to put four devotional offerings before a public banned from the theatre in Madrid between November 1597 and April 1599, gathering dust since that period, that showed off his royal connections, theological erudition, piety and doctrinal orthodoxy, even while they testified to and defended his calling as playwright. The construction of his persona as an artist in the introduction rested primarily on his gifts as a writer of poetry, learning and social connections. Nevertheless, while the interpolated plays may demonstrate his lack of awareness of the value of the medium of print in relation to drama *per se*,[30] the practice of including dramatic compositions in prose works

---

Guild Backinprint, 2000), pp. 257–66; S. Griswold Morley & Courtney Bruerton, *Cronología de las comedias de Lope de Vega* (Madrid: Gredos, 1968).

[26] Lope de Vega, *El peregrino en su patria*, ed. Avalle-Arce, pp. 56 and 64.

[27] See also the chapter by Victor Dixon in this volume on Lope's considerable Latin and less Greek.

[28] Lope de Vega, *Arte nuevo de hacer comedias*, ed. Enrique García Santo-Tomás (Madrid: Cátedra, 2006), pp. 132–33, lines 29–30, 45–48.

[29] On the introduction see Luigi Giuliani, 'El prólogo, el catálogo y sus lectores: una perspectiva de las listas de *El peregrino en su patria*', in *Lope en 1604*, ed. Xavier Tubau (Lleida: Milenio & Universitat Autònoma de Barcelona, 2004), pp. 123–36.

[30] As can be seen from elsewhere in this volume, especially chapter by García Reidy, Lope initially viewed printing his drama with suspicion, given that it could only fully live in performance. His perspective on this issue clearly changed, as is apparent both from his increasing involvement in the publication of his own dramatic oeuvre as well as the explanatory and self-justificatory prefaces and paratextual material that accompanied it.

was not unprecedented; other contemporaries known better as prose writers, like Alonso Jerónimo de Salas Barbadillo, who fulsomely praised *El peregrino*, did the same, including the *comedia El gallardo Escarramán* [*Gallant Escarramán*] in his *El sutil cordobés Pedro de Urdemalas* [*The Subtle Cordoban Pedro de Urdemalas*] (Madrid, 1620), while Alonso del Castillo Solórzano included *Los encantos de Bretaña* [*The Enchantments of Brittany*], *La fantasma de Valencia* [*The Phantom of Valencia*], and *El marqués del Cigarral* [*The Marquis of Cigarral*] in his *Las fiestas del jardín* [*The Festivities in the Garden*] (Valencia, 1634).[31] Their ultimate model may have been again Jerónimo Contreras's *Selva de aventuras* (1565). In both the nearly contemporary translations by D'Audigier and Dutton, however, the *autos* were omitted altogether. In spite of this, the plays have a structuring role in relation to the story, underlining the ways in which the amorous trials of the pilgrim can be paralleled with religious themes.

The issue of whether his prose was the subset of his literary output least regarded by Lope himself is more complex. In the prologue to the first of his so-called *Novelas a Marcia Leonarda* he admitted: 'una novela ha sido novedad para mí, que aunque es verdad que en el *Arcadia* y *Peregrino* hay alguna parte deste género y estilo' [a novella is a novelty for me, despite it being true that there are aspects of this genre and style to be found in the *Arcadia* and *Peregrino*], nevertheless he suffered from the 'temor de no acertar' [worry about not getting it right].[32] His apparent hesitancy in putting pen to paper to produce a set of prose works for his lover Marta de Nevares, however, smacks of mock humility in the light of his subsequent assertion of his own originality: 'sé que no la ha oído ni es traducida' [I know that it has not been heard before, nor is it translated] and the defence of an anti-populist poetics of prose (in contrast to what might be expected from his pronouncements on the theatre), encapsulated by the assertion that 'habían de escribirlos hombres científicos o por lo menos grandes cortesanos, gente que halla en los desengaños notables sentencias y aforismos. Yo, que nunca pensé que el novelar entrara en mi pensamiento [...]' [they ought to be written by wise men or at least great courtiers, people who uncover in tribulation striking philosophical examples and aphorisms. I, who never thought that writing novels would enter into my very thought] (p. 75), and clearly then exemplified in his own work by his frequent asides and discussion of *autores* (authorities) on a range of topics from music to gunpowder, love and music to portraiture. Juan Ignacio Ferreras has suggested that *El peregrino* showed Lope to be 'más experimentador de la novela que novelista auténtico' [more an experimenter with novelistic form than a true novelist].[33] The Fénix's poetics of prose fiction, set out in the long excursus at the beginning of book IV about poetry and history, shows that he was

---

[31] Lope de Vega, *El peregrino en su patria*, ed. Avalle-Arce, p. 24.

[32] Lope de Vega, *Novelas a Marcia Leonarda*, ed. Barella, p. 73. See also on the Novelas Rafael Sánchez Martínez, 'El requiebro en las Novelas a Marcia Leonarda', in Memoria de la palabra: Actas del VI Congreso de la Asociación Internacional Siglo de Oro, Burgos-La Rioja, 15–19 de julio 2002, ed. María Luisa Lobato & Francisco Domínguez Matito, 2 vols (Madrid: Iberoamericana; Frankfurt am Main: Vervuert, 2004), II, pp. 1609–18.

[33] Juan Ignacio Ferreras, *La novela en el siglo XVII* (Madrid: Taurus, 1988), pp. 40–41.

both serious and artful as a novelist. The injunction to include journeys and travel, variety of incident, and the dependence of true *admiratio* on verisimilitude are all explored through a wealth of contemporary theory from Pinciano to Cervantes, Castelvetro to Tasso, and detailed comparisons are drawn between Lope's pronouncements about his practice and that of Mateo Alemán or Tirso de Molina.[34] The narrative strategies of the 'poeta histórico' [historical poet] in this text sought to move the reader not merely through verisimilitude, something that left space for the Christian legitimate marvellous (i.e. miracles, ghosts, supernatural occurrences), but with the truth (given its contemporary and familiar geography, real historical characters, local details and colour and so forth) in order to render its audience more receptive to its doctrinal and didactic content. These techniques, however, presented a fresh difficulty: how to move and transmit wonder in a context too familiar to its audience, other than by piling up discovery and incident, the greatest weakness of this text, especially in its breathless conclusion. The story is mediated by an unstable narrator who moves from the third-person omniscience of the chronicler to a first-person eyewitness, from past to present tenses, and eventually implicates the reader with the use of the first-person plural, as well as seeking to get the reader to identify with the narrator by dramatising his own reception of the story.[35] At the opening of Book v, the narrative voice shifts from the past: 'podíamos alabar a nuestros peregrinos' [we could praise our pilgrims], to the metafictional, studied imprecision of the present: 'No sé si en este mismo estado se halla Finea; pero como a mí no me toca el disculparla, sino la prosecución de la narración propuesta' [I don't know if Finea is in this same state, but since it is not up to me to make excuses for her but rather to continue the proposed story], and finally back to the past and third person narration: 'Declinaba el sol de la mitad del día' [the midday day was going down] (p. 423). The lack of organic unity in the text, with its episodic structure, mixing of genres (prose, poetry, and drama), its unseemly haste in drawing all the threads of the plot together as it reaches a conclusion, rather than climax or culmination, has led one critic to describe it as 'una novela mosaico' [a mosaic novel].[36]

Book 1 begins *in medias res* with the pilgrim washed up on a beach near Barcelona. He is rescued by some fisherman, before being held up at gun point by members of an armed gang led by Doricleo, a Catalan gentleman who has become a renegade and robber in despair at the loss of his beloved Florinda to a rival, Filandro, after the latter kidnapped and raped her disguised as a Turkish pirate before being arrested but then pardoned on agreeing to marry his victim. The pilgrim's companion (Nise) has been held by their captain Doricleo. On trying to liberate her he is shot in the arm by him and taken off into the mountains to be

[34] On this section of the text, see Guillermo Séres, 'La poética historia de *El peregrino en su patria*', *Anuario Lope de Vega*, 7 (2001): 89–104.

[35] Javier González Rovira, 'Estrategias narrativas en *El peregrino en su patria*', in *Lope en 1604*, ed. Xavier Tubau (Lleida: Milenio & Universitat Autònoma de Barcelona, 2004), pp. 137–49.

[36] Rafael Osuna, '*El peregrino en su patria*, en el ángulo oscuro de Lope', *Revista de Occidente*, n.s., nos. 113–14 (August–September 1972): 326–31 (p. 330).

hanged. After being released by his captors, he travels to Barcelona where, recognised by one of the fisherman and wrongly associated with the thieving bandits, he is thrown in prison, where he is befriended by the gentleman Everardo, locked up for the murder of Telémaco, husband of the beautiful, although 'no tan casta como la romana' [not as chaste as the Roman one] (p. 98), Lucrecia, with whom his best friend Mireno has become hopelessly infatuated. Despite their falling out over his friend's amorous pursuit of her he protects the fleeing Mireno from Telémaco by hiding the ladder he has used to scale the walls of a tower, adjacent to the gardens, the backdrop for their erotic adventures. Forced to admit his affair, Everardo again attempts to dissuade his friend; however, Erfila, Mireno's discarded and jealous ex, seduces Telémaco in revenge and reveals his wife's adultery. Returning suddenly the cuckolded husband murders his wife and her lover and is then killed himself in turn by the waiting Everardo. This tale of misfortune is unravelled using the series of emblems displayed in his cell, which encode the series of *sententiae* or moral lessons the reader is meant to draw from it along the way. As always with Lope in this text, their application and applicability, however, is far from obvious.

Released following Doricleo's pardon, the pilgrim witnesses the performance of the first *auto*, the *Viaje del alma*, before making his way at the outset of Book 2 to Montserrat, where, as he ascends, he is joined by a German and a Flemish pilgrim, who discuss contemporary religious conflicts, including the suffering of English Catholics, 'holocaustos (que así llamo yo a Inglaterra, pues cada día ofrece en sí tantas vidas de mártires al cielo)' [holocausts (that is what I call what is happening in England, since every day sees so many lives of yet more martyrs being despatched to heaven)] (p. 149), as well as sharing devotional tales such as that of an icon painter whose brilliance in depicting the ugliness of the devil incenses Satan, prompting him to take revenge on him by making him fall in love with the wife of a soldier and then ensuring the whole village catch them as they elope. The two are imprisoned and due to be beheaded, but before their execution, they are miraculously released after the painter intercedes with the Virgin, whom he has depicted so beautifully. The woman returns to her husband's bed, her hair miraculously regrown, and persuades him it has all been a dream. He seeks confirmation from the villagers, who, finding the cells empty, are convinced of the same. The pilgrims encounter a series of hermits, who instruct them with profitable *exempla* and cautionary tales of a religious complexion. Urbano, for example, offers them a litany of biblical quotations and commonplaces about the penitential value of tears, drawn from the Psalms, Ezekiel and Luke and the church fathers Bernard, Gregory and Jerome, stories such as those of Judith and David and Bathsheba, ending his discourse with a *romance* (ballad) 'Bien podéis, ojos, llorar' [Well might you shed tears] and the story of a penitent blasphemer saved by his tears despite a 'mal enseñada familia' [ill-taught family] and his father 'creyendo que había de ser muy hombre' [believing he would be a real man] for mouthing such oaths (p. 168). At the mountain's peak the hermit Tirso tells the story of his love affair with Aurelia, who after five years rejects him for Feliciano, whose discarded lover Menandra in turn betrays the pair to him. In revenge, the jilted partners become lovers, provoking Aurelia to be jealous of Tirso and win him back. They flee to Italy and, caught in a storm, make religious vows. Juan Bautista Avalle-Arce (p. 4, notes 11 and 12) argues that this tale is another reworking of Lope's experience with Elena Osorio and proposes the following identifications: Tirso (in this story) = Fernando (in *La Dorotea*) = Lope, Aurelia = Dorotea = Elena Osorio, Feliciano = don Bela = Granvelle,[37] Menandra = Marfisa. The different ending and the common nature of love triangles of this kind both in life and art make such a reading, I believe, questionable. The other pilgrims flee with the daughter of an innkeeper and jewellery, leaving him to resist attempts to arrest him and flee towards Valencia, where he encouters his jailbreaking friend Everardo. After passing Sagunto, they reach the city and watch the performance of the *Las bodas entre el alma y el amor divino*, days after Philip III and Margaret of Austria's wedding.

On visiting the famous asylum in Valencia, the *hospital de los locos*,[38] one of the city's principal tourist attractions, at the outset of book 3 he recognises his lost companion crossdressed as a man and the lovers Pánfilo and Nise are momentarily reunited before she is carried off for calling him husband and he is violently ejected trying to prevent the warders from caging her. In the street he regains consciousness in the arms of Celio, Nise's brother, who recounts, without realising to whom, how a suitor for his sister's hand, Pánfilo, had pretended to leave for Flanders but returned secretly to work in their house, feigning a profound melancholy. To cheer him up, Nise sings a romance composed by him in order to reveal his feelings discreetly for her. Nise's father revives the abandoned marriage plans with Pánfilo unbeknown to them and informs his daughter that she is soon to marry. The two, not realising that he is the prospective husband, abscond. Celio, sent after them to avenge his family honour, visits Pánfilo's mother, where he falls in love with his sister Finea, whom he then elopes with to France, from where, after killing a French nobleman out of jealousy, he is forced to flee back to Spain without her. After Celio's departure in search of Finea, Pánfilo rescues Jacinto from a street fight and persuades him to get him into the hospital. Celio entertains himself in Zaragoza with a performance of *La Maya* and examines a gallery of portraits of Philip II and III, Greek and Roman worthies, with lists of *auctoritates* on their lives and works.

A discussion of prose fiction opens book 4, before the main narrative thread is resumed with Pánfilo and Nise paraded before an Italian count Emilio Anguilara, who decides to take her with him while he is returned to the asylum. Shipwrecked again, Nise, still crossdressed, makes her way to Marseilles, where she encounters Finea; pretending to have known her brother as a captive in Constantinople, she recounts how Nise and her brother, after leaving Toledo, had headed to Seville, where they were recognised and forced to flee to Lisbon, with her disguising herself as a man for the first time. A soldier, a friend of Nise's older brother

---

[37] It is conjectured that the lover who supplanted Lope was José Francisco Perrenot de Granvela or possibly his brother Juan Tomás, nephew of the bishop of Arras and great minister of Charles V and Philip II.

[38] The setting, of course, of an earlier play by Lope, *Los locos de Valencia* (early 1590s).

Lisardo, who is serving under Archduke Albert of Austria, regent of the Netherlands, is warned of their arrival and seeks out Pánfilo. The two escape with a Portuguese captain and head to Ceuta in North Africa, where he is captured in a skirmish and carried as a captive to Fez. Nise learns Arabic and, taking the name Azán Rubín, follows him dressed as a moor with the merchant Alí Iajer, whose nephew she pretends to be. She persuades him to buy Pánfilo from his master Salí Morato, escaping back to Ceuta with the merchant's daughter Lela Axá and Fátima in tow, from where they are sent to Lisbon and then travel on to Rome, where the *moricas* are baptised. They decide to put off their wedding until they can return to their parents and Toledo; travelling around Italy and France, they disembark from Nice and are shipwrecked, bringing the tale back to where it began. Picking up in the present again, Pánfilo is liberated from the hospital by Jacinto and, returning to Barcelona, is imprisoned again for the violence committed resisting arrest on Montserrat. Nise and Finea reach Perpignan, where they attend the performance of *El hijo pródigo*.

Arriving back in Barcelona just as Pánfilo is brought out to be executed, the two women witness him being saved by Jacinto on the order of the Duke for being mad. As he is taken back to Valencia, the women are arrested under the suspicion that the disguised Nise, or Felis, as she is known by Finea, has forced 'his' female companion to become 'his' adulterous mistress. Celio returns to Barcelona, rejects Finea and awaits her supposed lover on his release, whom he stabs, not realising that it is his own sister. Pánfilo returns and reveals the whole story to Celio before searching for Nise. Jacinto is injured after challenging his friend when his sister Tiberia, angry at the rejection of her advances, accuses him of her rape in a letter to her brother. As Pánfilo puts distance beween himself and Barcelona yet again he comes across a mortally injured gentleman, Godofre, whom he carries to a nearby monastery, where he expires in his arms just as a search party looking for him passes by. Suspecting he is responsible, the victim's brother Tirso carries him off and imprisons him in the tower of his family home, after the real traitor, Godofre's best friend Tansilo, tries to shoot him, from where he is rescued by the charity of the youngest sister Flérida, before fleeing to Zaragoza. From there he sets out and, staying overnight in a haunted lodge, lives through what the bible-seller George Borrow described as 'the best ghost story in the world', a terrifying parade of ghosts, torches lit and then snuffed out, animals and demons who threaten, undress, throw water over and ridicule the unsuspecting traveller, before stealing the jewels given to him by Finea and letters from Nise, which provokes him to confront them despite his fear, chasing them outside before they disappear into a waterwheel.[39] In the morning he sets out for Guadalupe, in which monastery he is overtaken by the bearer of a letter from Flérida recounting how Godofre's

[39] Cited by Francisco Javier Díez de Revenga Torres, 'La imaginación en Lope de Vega: los espacios de *El peregrino en su patria*', in *Loca ficta: los espacios de la maravilla en la Edad Media y el Siglo de Oro*, ed. Ignacio Arellano ([Pamplona]: Universidad de Navarra; Madrid: Iberoamericana; Frankfurt-am-Main: Vervuert, 2003), pp. 189–202 (p. 190). There is an edition of this story published separately as *Las aventuras de Pánfilo: cuento de espantos* (Madrid: Jímenez Fraud, 1920) with drawings by R. Romero Calvet.

lover had revealed the guilt of Tansilo, who killed his friend out of jealousy over her. Wandering through the open country, the pilgrim encounters the rustic Fabio, who gets him work as a cowherd for Nise's father, who has an estate in that part of Toledo. A servant of the host who has taken in the injured Nise, Leandro, falls in love with her, but she flees on learning that Celio has been released from prison, fearing he will make another attempt on her life. Finea is taken under the protection of Lisardo, Celio's older brother, on his way back from Flanders and ends up in Toledo in the house of her lover. Lisardo takes Pánfilo unwittingly into his service, at first as a stable hand but then as chamberlain and secretary, in which capacity he is reunited with his sister Finea, with whom Lisardo has fallen in love. Lisardo hears of Leandro's arrival in Toledo in search of the fugitive Nise and, assuming he is Pánfilo, entrusts the real Pánfilo with his murder. Lisardo and his father surprise Pánfilo and his doppelganger Leandro, and both are arrested until it can be determined which is the real one. Meanwhile, Nise and Jacinto encounter each other and travel to Madrid, where they are joined by Pánfilo's mother and youngest sister Elisa before moving on to Toledo. Celio meanwhile encounters Tiberia on the way there too and in his parents' house all the protagonists are finally reunited. Finea marries Celio, Pánfilo Nise, Lisardo Tiberia and Leandro Elisa, weddings celebrated with the performance of ten plays, and other fiestas about which the reader is referred to a promised second part.

The symmetry of dishonour in the main plot subverts any anticipation of the bloody revenge that typified *comedia* plots, 'casos de la honra'[40] [tales of honour], and points to an evanescent creativity, working at the margins, oppositionally, and against societal norms, rather than an insider shoring up the social *status quo* and championing orthodoxy. Pánfilo, lover of everything, universal lover and figure of the author, like Lope, defeats readerly expectation with his mutual forgiveness of Celio. Unexpected and at times progressive stories, characterised by their excess, full of humanist and unorthodox elements, anticipate the extraordinary, impassioned plea against honour killings and bloody revenge against either men or women in the *Novelas a Marcia Leonarda*: 'he sido de parecer siempre que no se lava bien la mancha de la honra del agraviado con la sangre del que le ofendió, porque lo que fue no puede dejar de ser y es desatino creer que se quita porque se mate al ofensor' [I have always believed that the stain of dishonour is not washed away from the injured party with the blood of the offender, because what was can not cease to be and it is madness to believe that it is removed through the death of those responsible] (p. 237). This notion echoes through the numerous stories within this text that involve sexual revenge through infidelity, symmetrical bed-hopping to even the scores between erring and jilted lovers. The variety of scenarios and outcomes depicted, from the painter and soldier's wife, who are forgiven, to the culminating story on his ascent of Montserrat of Tirso and Aurelio, which could end bloodily but in fact ends in a convent, represent the ambivalent and contradictory responses to be found in Lope's work to the dictates of honour. The very excess and contradictory nature of his novel answers the fundamental

---

[40] Lope de Vega, *Arte nuevo*, p. 149, l. 327.

question raised as to whether it still works, given the very different way we read, in far less directed and pragmatic, end-orientated ways. Although the moral architecture of the novel may not quite add up to a defence of Counter-Reformation orthodoxy, its fragmentary nature and plurality lend themselves to a postmodern resurgence in the fortunes of the pilgrim. Lope's own relationship to the very erudition he advocated is ironic. After the discussion of love at the end of book 1, quoting Plotinus, Plato and so on, the pilgrim was well aware of 'la vana filosofía de esta fábula' [the vain philosophy found in this myth] (p. 143). While classical commonplaces and aphorisms were meant to guide and rule contemporary mores and behaviour, their power disappears in the face of grief and other raw human emotions, in the same way that his moralising is eclipsed by the excess of his amorous adventures. Whether unique or temporary, it is ultimately perhaps this work that embodies best of all Lope's own 'desdichas peregrinas' [ever-changing misfortunes],[41] professional, personal and artistic.

---

[41] From his dedication to the Marqués de Priego.

17

Novelas a Marcia Leonarda

ALI RIZAVI

The so-called *Novelas a Marcia Leonarda* published in two separate miscellanies of long poems, verse epistles and four *novelas*, *La Filomena* (1621) and *La Circe* (1624), have commanded relatively few — and disparate — responses from critics. This fact arises from the presentation of the textual matter to the reader and traces of self-fashioning in the form of autobiography. One such act of self-representation is Lope's claim that the *Novelas a Marcia Leonarda* were written at the request of 'la señora Marcia Leonarda', whom critics have identified as Lope's lover Marta de Nevares; the mediated character of the narration carries significant implications for the role of femininity in the fictional content of the stories, discussed below.

The first *novela*, *Las fortunas de Diana*, is the only prose piece published in *La Filomena*, and relates the wanderings and trials of Diana, who falls in love with a young man socially inferior to her and bears his child. The second, *La desdicha por la honra*, is a *novela morisca* (Moorish romance) in the manner of *El Abencerraje y la Hermosa Jarifa* [*Abencerraje and the Fair Jarifa*]. It relates the love of a brave *morisco*, protected by the Viceroy of Naples, for a Sicilian Christian, his discovery that he is descended from the noble Moors (the Abencerrajes), and his escape from Italy to Constantinople in order to accomplish great feats to facilitate his ultimately unsuccessful return to his homeland, Spain. The third, *La prudente venganza*, echoes the theme and tight structure of a *drama de honor*, such as Lope's late masterpiece, *El castigo sin venganza* (1631). The fourth and final one, *Guzmán el Bravo*, is an abridged prose eulogy, the heroic account of a man of Herculean fortitude and strength, Don Felis, behind which stands the figure of Don Gaspar de Guzmán, the then favourite of Philip IV.

Critical commentary has tended to focus on three features of the texts. Earlier critics generally concentrated on the theatricality of these novellas; Georges Cirot and Walter Pabst analyzed them as *comedias* (plays) in prose, since Lope appears to conflate the two genres in *La desdicha por la honra*, stating: 'tienen las novelas los mismos preceptos que las comedias, cuyo fin es haber dado su autor contento y gusto al pueblo' [novellas obey the same rules as the *comedia*, whose purpose is for the author to give contentment and pleasure to the people].[1] A more recent

---

[1] All references are from the following edition: Lope de Vega, *Novelas a Marcia Leonarda*,

point of view, voiced by Marina Brownlee, argues that these stories constitute a response to Cervantes and an attempt to subvert the Cervantine vision of the *novela*.[2] Lastly, Juan Diego Vila and Fernando Capello have examined the role of the female narratee in enabling the writer to reach a female audience.[3]

However, taking *Guzmán el Bravo* as a case study, I would like to focus on several neglected aspects of these *novelas*. First I argue that they are a clear attempt to attract the patronage of the apparatus surrounding the new monarch, Philip IV; the significance of the high quality of the two volumes, discussed below, strongly suggests this motivation. Secondly, I suggest that the long poems should be read together with the *novelas*. More specifically, in these *novelas*, Lope experiments with the writing of encomia in different registers: *La Circe*, in a formal meter, the *octava real*, and *Guzmán el Bravo*, in prose and in low register, appropriate for a genre which Lope considered 'humilde'. In his detailed survey of the genre in Spain, *La nouvelle en Espagne*, Jean-Michel Laspéras argues that the layout of the two miscellanies *La Filomena* (1621) and *La Circe* (1624), alternating *novelas* with poetry of various kinds, seems deliberate in design, seeking to test the notion of the three discrete styles of writing: sublime, medium and low.[4] Indeed, *La Circe* and *Guzmán* form a diptych, displaying, in different styles, related subject-matters, the central figures of which are Ulysses and Hercules: Ulysses the continent man and prudent ruler, and Hercules, a figure with which the iconography of Hapsburg Spain was closely associated. In a departure from the contrast which Lope draws between fable (creative fiction or myth) and history (narration of true facts) in other works of narrative prose, he appears to suppress such a distinction in *Guzmán el Bravo*, for the benefit of his distinguished subject-matter.[5] Thirdly, I show how Lope, by introducing female

---

ed. Antonio Carreño (Madrid: Cátedra, 2002). See Georges Cirot, 'Valeur littéraire des nouvelles de Lope de Vega', *Bulletin Hispanique*, 28.4 (1926): 321–55; Walter Pabst, *Novellentheorie und Novellendichtung: zur Geschichte ihrer Antinomie in den romanischen Literaturen*, 2nd edn (Heidelberg: Carl Winter, 1967), p. 183.

[2] Marina Scordilis Brownlee, *The Poetics of Literary Theory: Lope de Vega's 'Novelas a Marcia Leonarda' and their Cervantine Context* (Madrid: José Porrúa Turanzas, 1981).

[3] Juan Diego Vila, 'Lectura e imaginario de la femineidad en *Las Novelas a Marcia Leonarda*', in *Silva: studia philologica in honorem Isaías Lerner*, ed. Isabel Lozano-Renieblas & Juan Carlos Mercado (Madrid: Castalia, 2001), pp. 697–708; Fernando Capello, 'La Femme inspiratrice et réceptrice de la nouvelle au XVIIe siècle', in *Images de la femme en Espagne au XVIe et XVIIe siècles: des traditions aux renouvellements et à l'émergence d'images nouvelles*, dir. Augustin Redondo (Paris: Publications de la Sorbonne, Presses de la Sorbonne Nouvelle, 1994), pp. 365–79.

[4] Jean-Michel Laspéras, *La Nouvelle en Espagne au Siècle d'Or* (Montpellier: Castillet, 1987), p. 178.

[5] 'A ninguno parezca nuestro peregrino fabuloso [...] que desdichas de un peregrino no solo son verosímiles, pero forzosamente verdaderas' [Let no one think that our pilgrim is mythical [...], for the misfortunes of a pilgrim are not only realistic, but necessarily true], *El peregrino en su patria*, in *Prosa*, I: *Arcadia; El peregrino en su patria*, ed. Donald McGrady, Obras Completas de Lope de Vega, 33 (Madrid: Fundación José Antonio de Castro, 1997), p. 660; 'Si algún defeto hubiere en el arte [...] sea la disculpa la verdad: que más quiso el poeta seguirla que estrecharse a las impertinentes leyes de la fábula' [If there is any artistic defect [...], let truth be the excuse: for the poet preferred to follow truth than to adhere to the impertinent laws of fiction], 'Al teatro', in *La Dorotea*, ed. Edwin S. Morby (Madrid: Castalia, 1980), p. 61.

character types drawn from the margins of society, goes far beyond using female figures and other non-Spanish figures as mere receptors for his narrative, as Juan Diego Vila and Fernando Capello have argued; indeed, these seemingly passive figures are the catalysts for the heroic feat of Don Felis.

First since these four *novelas* were insertions into *La Filomena* and *La Circe*, the title *Novelas a Marcia Leonarda* is itself an editorial fiction. It does not appear on the elaborate frontispiece of either miscellany; nor indeed do the titles of any of the four stories, which are respectively: *La Filomena con otras diversas rimas, prosas y versos* and *La Circe con otras rimas y prosas*. Significantly, each work has an important dedicatee. *La Filomena* was dedicated to Doña Leonor Pimentel. The Pimentel family had been influential under Philip III and Leonor's spouse, the Count of Benavente, was *mayordomo mayor* (High Steward and head of household) to the recently crowned Philip IV's Queen; Leonor herself was lady-in-waiting to the Infanta María. The Benaventes thus held sway at the Queen's court. Furthermore, the mother of the Count-Duke of Olivares, Don Gaspar de Guzmán y Pimentel, dedicatee and addressee of *La Circe*, also belonged to the Pimentel family. The joint addressee is Doña María de Guzmán, Olivares's daughter. Lope's clear purpose is to seek patronage from the Pimentel family, as well as the Count-Duke of Olivares:

> Vos honor de las letras; vos, Mecenas, [...]
> en tanto que la sangre de mis venas
> los elementos de mi vida acaban,
> seréis mi Sol [...][6]

> [You, who are the honour of the arts; you, their Maecenas,
> Until the blood flowing in my veins ends my life-matter,
> You shall be my Sun.]

Events prompted Lope to seek such favour. As Ruth Lee Kennedy pointed out, the death of Philip III coincided with a dramatic shift in artistic patronage. Indeed, Lope had been declined the position of royal chronicler in 1620; and in 1621, Vélez de Guevara wrote *Más pesa el rey que la sangre* [King before Kin], a play which not only glorified the loyalty of Don Alonso Pérez de Guzmán (i.e. Guzmán el Bueno, founder of the Medonia Sidonia dynasty, to whom Lope alludes in his *novela*) to the Spanish crown, but also stressed how indebted Philip's kingdom was to that branch of the Guzmán family.[7] Material evidence suggests that both works, particularly *La Circe*, were intended as precious gifts for

---

[6] Lope de Vega, *Prosa*, IV: *La Filomena; La Circe*, ed. Antonio Carreño, Biblioteca Castro, Obras Completas de Lope de Vega, 39 (Madrid: Fundación José Antonio de Castro, 2004), III, p. 154, lines 1, 5–8. All quotations are from this edition.

[7] Ruth Lee Kennedy, *Studies in Tirso, I: The Dramatist and his Competitors, 1620–26* (Chapel Hill, NC: University of North Carolina Press, 1974), pp. 65–213; 'Attacks on Lope and His Theatre in 1617–1621', in *Hispanic Studies in Honor of Nicholson B. Adams*, ed. John Esten Keller & Karl-Ludwig Selig (Chapel Hill, NC: University of North Carolina Press, 1966), pp. 57–76.

members of the Madrid court whose star was then in the ascendant. *La Filomena* was published in two editions, a quarto by Alonso Martín at Madrid and another in octavo by Sebastián Cormellas, at Barcelona. It seems that *La Circe* was only ever published in a beautiful quarto by Alonso Martín of Madrid.[8] Unlike many other of his works in prose and poetry, the *novelas* or the poems do not seem to have been republished in Lope's lifetime, supporting the suggestion of non-literary motives for the genesis of these volumes.[9]

The potential for myth and mythologizing is fully exploited to fulfil this purpose, as the preliminary sonnet of *La Circe*, 'A Circe' [To Circe], demonstrates:

> Rinde tu ciencia, y con temor retira
> de los Guzmanes rayos los febeos,
> hija del sol, humilla tus trofeos,
> su luz respeta, su grandeza admira.

> [Yield up your science, withdraw in awe
> from the Guzmán family the rays of Phoebus,
> Daughter of the sun, tame your victories.
> Respect its light, bewonder its greatness.]

In this context, the Guzmán family, equated with the Sun-God, Apollo, leader of the Muses, will outshine the temptress, Circe, a point reiterated in the Prologue: 'Están las musas tan obligadas al favor que el excelentísmo señor conde de Olivares les hace, premiando los ingenios que las profesan que, como a restaurador suyo, le deben todas justas alabanzas y dignos ofrecimientos' [The Muses are so obliged to His Excellency the Count of Olivares for the favour which he grants them by rewarding the minds which practice them. As their renewer, they owe him all fitting praises and worthy offerings]. The evocation of the Guzmán family and Apollo in the same stanza, together with the use of planetary imagery, enhances Olivares's identification with that god's role as healer and patron of the arts.

It is perhaps fitting that this paean, pregnant with political overtones, should then proceed to assimilate the figure of Ulysses, the archetypal steadfast man and

---

[8] Antonio Palau y Dulcet, *Manual del librero hispanoamericano*, 28 vols, 2nd edn (Barcelona: Palau Dulcet; Oxford: The Dolphin Book Company, 1948–1977), vol. 25 (1973), pp. 521–22. It is noteworthy that the first edition of the *Novelas ejemplares* (1613) was published in two editions, in-quarto and in-octavo, and this seems to have been common practice amongst popular writers of the day. See, for example, the entries for María de Zayas: vol. 28, pp. 375–77; Pérez de Montalbán: vol. 13, p. 90. Only the hyper-prolific Castillo Sólorzano seems not to conform to the rule: vol. 3, pp. 289–91.

[9] After Lope's death the *novelas* were published once in an anonymous-sounding 1649 collection, *Novelas amorosas de los mejores ingenios de España* (Zaragoza: Viuda de Pedro Verges, 1648), BL 1074.d.27. For the publishing history of some of Lope's prose and poetry, see Palau y Dulcet, vol. 25: entries for *La Arcadia* (pp. 504–5) *El peregrino en su patria* (p. 510) and *La Dorotea* (pp. 525–26); and poetry, *Rimas sacras* (pp. 516–17) *Rimas humanas y divinas* (pp. 527–28).

ruler, into Olivares. However, Lope's Ulysses is a moralized version of the figure from Antiquity: he refrains from sexual contact with Circe, in marked contrast to the account in Homer, *Odyssey*, X (133–574) or Ovid, *Metamorphoses*, XIV (223–440):

> Entró luego en la quadra en que dormía,
> Que no la resistieron las criadas,
> Que aunque era novedad no era osadía. (III, p. 53)

> [He entered thereafter in her bed-chamber,
> Which her maids did not resist,
> Though he had never done it before, it was not temerity.]

This tends to conform to Lope's view of the use of mythology in literary creation: as censor of Baltasar de Vitoria's *Teatro de los dioses de la gentilidad* [*Theatre of the Pagan Gods*] (1619), an important encyclopaedia of mythology, he observes in the Imprimatur that the work constituted 'antes bien una lección importantísima a la inteligencia de muchos libros, cuya moralidad envolvió la antigua Filosofía en tantas fábulas, para exornación [...]' [foremost a most important lesson in our understanding of many books, the moral of which ancient Philosophy wrapped in so many fables, as an adornment].[10] Lope follows quite closely the essence of Vitoria's glosses on Circe concerning the metamorphosis of men into beasts, which is presented as a 'teología mitológica' [mythologized theology] (fol. 638, I), and in the warnings to avoid bodily subservience to woman or the animal self.

The allegorized Olivares, Ulysses, protects the ship of state against perils that deceive the senses and reason, making Circe, the enchantress queen whose potions caused men to lose their reason, a fitting antagonist. Ulysses, however, possesses the self-discipline to vanquish attractive — but eventually destructive — impulses:

> No tiempla a todos rígida y severa
> la virtud de Catón, que están templados
> en las leyes communes. Y estos tales
> convierte Circe en fieras y animales. (I, p. 102, lines 3–7)

> [The virtue of Cato, unbending and severe,
> does not govern all, who abide
> in laws for ordinary men. And such men
> Circe turns into beasts and animals.]

In *Guzmán el Bravo*, the third *novela* in the *editio princeps* of *La Circe*, the mythological figure detectable in Don Felis is Hercules, a figure intimately linked to the iconography of the Spanish Habsburg state. Indeed, the Habsburgs claimed descent from Hercules, who had cleaved a passageway from the Atlantic to the Mediterranean, the two waterways which anchored the prosperity of Spain.

---

[10] Fray Baltasar de Vitoria, *El teatro de los dioses de la gentilidad* (Madrid: Imprenta Real, 1676), unpaginated.

Charles V's motto, 'Plus ultra' [Beyond] is derived from the Pindaric metaphor 'Ad Herculis columnas' [To the columns of Hercules] and the phrase 'Non plus ultra' [Not beyond], which also became associated with Hercules in the later sixteenth century; simultaneously, it evokes the Ulyssean dream of sailing beyond the Pillars of Hercules.[11]

> El Hercules Tebano, que fue contemporáneo del invencible Sansón, es sin duda el que no vino a España; [...] dicen que fue pusilánime, cobarde y flojo; [...] que se echó en la hoguera a quemar y que el barquero Neso le forzó a Deyanira a vista de ojos. Todo eso lo tengo por fabuloso, pues ninguna de estas cosas se puede presumir de hombre de tanta estofa.[12]

> [The Theban Hercules, who was a contemporary of the invincible Samson, is doubtless the one who did not come to Spain; [...] it is said that he was pusillanimous, cowardly and weak; [...] that he hurled himself on the pyre to immolate himself and that the boatman, Nessus, raped Deianira before his eyes. I consider all this to be untrue, since none of these things is conceivable for a man of such great calibre.]

Vitoria thus removes any imperfection or cowardice from a character which he closely relates to Spain and to the shaping of the Spanish identity, and no Deianira impedes the destiny of the Spanish Hercules, identified with the Count-Duke of Olivares in *Guzmán el Bravo*. A simile yokes together Spain with Felis and Hercules: when Felis defeats one of his Moorish opponents in battle, he is 'como Hércules al hijo de la Tierra' [like Hercules with the son of the Earth] (p. 327). Like Ulysses, he is portrayed as protector and succourer of his nation.

On another level, Don Felis's epithet 'el Bravo' invites comparison with Guzmán el Bueno, the distant forebear of Olivares, who had protected the city of Tarifa in Andalusia from the Moors in 1296, as a reward for which Guzmán received a dukedom. For, although Lope provides an accurate description of Olivares's family background, he is complicit in furthering the aggrandizement project of the 'junior' branch from which the Count-Duke, his father, Count Enrique, and his grandfather, Pedro, hailed: a strategically placed semi-colon attaches the 'junior' branch to the more famous Medina Sidonia line:

> Ha habido insignes y valerosos hombres, como fueron don Pedro Ruiz de Guzmán, año de mil y ciento; don Alonso Pérez de Guzmán, principio de la casa de Medina Sidonia, a quien su sepulcro llama 'bienaventurado', y con otros muchos, dignos de eterna memoria; don Pedro de Guzmán, hijo del duque don Juan, primero conde Olivares, que en servicio del emperador Carlos hizo valerosas hazañas. (p. 290)

---

[11] Earl Rosenthal, '*Plus Ultra, Non plus Ultra*, and the Columnar Device of Emperor Charles V', *Journal of the Warburg and Courtauld Institutes*, 34 (1971): 204–28. For the importance of Hercules in pictorial representation under Philip IV, see José Álvarez Lopera, 'La reconstrución del Salón de Reinos: estado y replanteamiento de la cuestión', in *El palacio del Rey Planeta: Felipe IV y el Buen Retiro*, ed. Andrés Úbeda de los Cobos (Madrid: Museo Nacional del Prado, 2005), pp. 91–167.

[12] Vitoria, *El teatro de los dioses de la gentilidad*, fol. 67.

[There have been many great and valorous men, as Don Pedro Ruiz de Guzmán, in the year eleven hundred; Don Alonso Pérez de Guzmán, founder of the house of Medina Sidonia, whose tomb calls him 'the blessed,' and many others, worthy of eternal memory; Don Pedro de Guzmán, son of Duke Don Juan, the first Count Olivares, who accomplished valorous feats in the service of the Emperor Charles.]

In fact, Don Gaspar's grandfather, Pedro de Guzmán, had even contested — unsuccessfully — in the courts the title of Duke of Medina Sidonia, which carried great status (and revenue).[13]

Although the fictional content of *Guzmán el Bravo* is informed, as is that of *Las fortunas de Diana* or *La desdicha por la honra*, by wanderings, imprisonment, concealment of identity and the inevitable recognition scenes, it is the manipulation of fiction and history to create myth which defines its literary interest and makes it diverge from the aesthetic of the other *novelas*. Praise of the Guzmán family at the opening and conclusion of the *novela* situates them at the heart of the myth-making enterprise, and lends powerful determinacy to the narration, befitting its addressee. Yet this is done in a manner reminiscent of popular legend, rather than the formal encomium in *La Circe*. At the start of *Guzmán el Bravo* the narrator informs his reader or listener:

En una de las ciudades de España [...] estudió desde sus tiernos años don Felis, de la casa ilustrísima de Guzmán [...] ellos son grandes de tiempo immemorial [...]
(p. 289)

[From his earliest years, Don Felis, of the most illustrious house of Guzmán, studied in one of the cities of Spain. [...] They have been great since time immemorial.]

Likewise, the fable-like orality at the end of the narrator's discourse suggests that Fame will disperse herself as people come into contact with Lope's text:

Fuese a vivir en sus lugares [...], donde yo le conocí, si bien en sus mayores años, pero con el mismo brío porque el defeto de la naturaleza del cuerpo no ofende el valor del ánimo. Este, señora Marcia, es el suceso de Guzmán el Bravo.

[He returned to live on his lands [...], where I met him; although he was advanced in years, he possessed the same brio, for the feebleness of the body does not detract from the courage of the spirit. This, señora Marcia, is the story of Guzmán the Brave.]

Lope combines his idealizing and edificatory understanding of myth with (remote and recent) historical events important for Spain. Simultaneously, myth-making acquires two faces — public and private — in order to appeal to the reading or

---

[13] J. H. Elliott, *The Count-Duke of Olivares: The Statesman in an Age of Decline* (New Haven, CT & London: Yale University Press, 1986), pp. 7–45.

listening public by softening the distinction between public and private spheres. For example, Don Felis protects Spain at Lepanto, a significant victory for Philip II and Spain:

> Hizo con una espada y rodela tan notables cosas don Felis que allí se le confirmó el nombre de Bravo; y rindiendo una galera sacó vientidós heridas de flechas y cuchilladas, que a quien le vía ponía espanto, porque en [...] las cuchilladas [parecía] toro [...] (p. 301)

> [Don Felis achieved with his sword and the shield such great things that he was granted the epithet of Brave; and he vanquished a galley, suffering twenty-two arrow wounds and knife wounds, so much so that whoever saw him was frightened, because, with his knife wounds, he seemed to be a bull.]

Conversely, seemingly banal details, such as Felis's popularity at university, maintain human interest by leaving traces of biography: this echoes the Count-Duke's election as rector in November 1603 of his alma mater, the University of Salamanca.[14]

Just as the *novela* form is used to create legend in a register different from that of *La Circe*, the narrative also negotiates a passage through the conventionality which a mythologizing representation of Olivares (and, by extension, Olivares's association with the Habsburg monarchy) imposes upon it. For instance, when Felis is involved with an *hidalgo* in a duel which 'hizo temblar la tierra' [made the earth tremble] (p. 336), a conventional outcome is presented: he is temporarily exiled from the city where the duel is fought, although the king subsequently pardons him. Significantly, Felis's feats are accomplished outside Spain, at Lepanto, in Flanders and North Africa: this distant show of strength ensures that, in fiction at least, Spain remains a sphere in which loyal servants do not outshine potentially jealous masters.

However, interference from the margins of the fictional space — in the form of women, Jews, Moors, unexpected happenings in exotic settings, especially in Don Felis's North African captivity — exercises crucial influence in blurring the contours of that conventionality, acting centrifugally on the effect which the text exercises upon its reader. For example, on the one hand, figures of authority in Felis's North African captivity, though Jewish and Moorish, are depicted in a favourable light. Felis loyally serves his Jewish master, David, and thereafter Salárraez, the Moorish ruler of Tunis: in turn, they behave decently towards him. Strikingly, Felis is likened to Hercules defeating Antaeus, a Libyan Titan, whilst he is defending Salárraez, and his feats for Salárraez mirror those which he accomplishes for the Habsburg monarchy; even the state apparatus which Felis defends for Salárraez is explained in terms which remind the reader of Spain's Moorish past: 'Salárraez, su rey o alcaide, puesto por el Gran Turco, que esta manera de reyes, como los virreyes entre nosotros, usaron los moros en España [...] y así había reyes en Alcalá, en Jaén [...] y en otras partes de las Españas [...]'

---

[14] Elliott, *The Count-Duke of Olivares*, p. 18.

[Salárraez, his king or his *alcaide*, installed by the Turkish Sultan. This type of king is akin to viceroys in our country, which the Moors used in Spain; thus there were kings in Alcalá, Jaén [...] and other parts of Spain] (p. 320). On the other hand, the depiction of other Moors and Jews is rather ambiguous: David's daughter, Susana, who attempts to seduce Mendoza, Felis's squire, is described as rather less chaste than the Susanna of the Old Testament, who had spurned the advances of the Elders; when Mendoza tearfully admits the embarrassing situation to Felis, Felis alludes to the story of Joseph and Potiphar, whose wife falsely accused Joseph of seducing her when he had repulsed her advances: 'mira que esta mujer es hebrea y se acordará de la historia de Josef, si quieres imitarle [...]' [Look this woman is a Jew and she will remember the story of Joseph, if you wish to emulate him] (p. 316). Likewise, the Moors seem cowardly when Felis, repelling Moors who attempt to take advantage of David's frailty, is insulted as a 'perro cristiano' [Christian dog] (p. 319). Yet Salárraez is depicted as honourable, since he keeps his promise to Felis.

This ambiguity is reinforced in two important North African recognition scenes: when Salárraez questions Don Felis about his true identity, he informs him that he belongs to the Guzmán family of Spain, which elicits even greater respect from the Moorish ruler. However, when Mendoza's true identity is revealed as Felicia, a woman of modest birth and even more modest virtue who had once unsuccessfully wooed Don Felis, his reaction is less disdainful than before but no less determined: 'No te espantes, Felicia, que no te haya conocido, que aunque te visitaba no te vía; tan aprisa miro yo los rostros de las mujeres de mis amigos' [Felicia, don't be frightened that I didn't recognize you; although I was close to you, I didn't see you; so fleetingly do I look at the faces of my friends' wives] (p. 317). As in *Las fortunas de Diana*, assuming a new identity enables a level of social intercourse between characters which would otherwise be impossible: effectively, once Mendoza/Felicia's true identity is rediscovered, the relationship assumes a paternal dimension. Don Felis assumes responsibility for Mendoza/Felicia's future, rescuing her from the embarrassment of having to reveal herself to Susana by setting off a false fire alarm, and, upon their return to Spain, ensures her future by marrying her to a *hidalgo* and providing her with a generous dowry.

Notwithstanding the seeming passiveness, at first sight, of the various incarnations of the female figure in *Guzmán el Bravo*, Felicia/Mendoza, Isbella (the lady Don Felis woos upon his return to Spain), as well as the allegorical figure of Spain also act upon Felis. Vilas's argument that the female is a receiver or 'consumed' figure is true insofar as she hears or listens to the story. However, for fictional purposes, the female figure is also the catalyst for Felis's feats, and serves as example or counterexample for the reader. A light-hearted example is Don Felis's serenading Isbella, a 'gentilísima dama' [a most gentle lady] and sister of a 'valiente caballero' [valiant gentleman] (p. 332): nevertheless, she does not marry without her brother's approval. Such use of the female figure is further reflected in the messages of the *romances* (ballads) Felis sings for Isbella, and the one Felicia/Mendoza sings for Susana. 'Filis', the woman evoked in both *romances*, changes shape to fit the purpose of the song; for Susana, the meretricious Filis 'envid[a] de falso' [casts dishonest looks] (p. 312). This reflects Susana's behaviour, as the song of Mendoza and Don Felis makes patent in its concluding line: 'No quiero tanto pesar por tan pequeño placer' [I don't want such great cares for such little pleasure] (p. 314). By contrast, the *romance* for Isbella contains echoes of eclogue and elegy: Filis is metamorphosed into the woman whom the lover misses during his forced absence. An apostrophic lament implores the allegorical figure of Spain to report Felis's suffering to his beloved; of course, the love she witnesses is chaste and decorous:

> ¡Ay mar de España!,
> si pisa tus riberas
> aquella labradora […]
> le digas: "Bella Filis,
> esto llaman tormenta
> ausentes de su patria,
> que por el mar navegan,
> pero las que padece
> quien ama y quien desea
> el puerto de tus brazos,
> en más rigor le anegan. (p. 333)

> [Ah, seas of Spain!
> If that peasant girl
> sets foot on your shores, [...]
> tell her: 'Lovely Filis
> this is what those who ply the seas,
> away from their countries, call a storm;
> but those suffered by
> one who loves you and yearns
> for the safe harbour of your arms
> submerge him in greater trials.]

In the same way that using two distinct registers enables Lope to transcend the normally formal language of encomium, his use of *romance* lends a protean character to the language of courtship, which is normally stylised and formal in structure, as Christina Lee rightly points out in her study of the rhetoric of courtship in these *novelas*.[15] Indeed, as Antonio Carreño explains, song and recital performances of *romances* were not only popular amongst people of all classes in Golden Age Spain but also served to edify the public and celebrate its highest values.[16] They are used by Lope to similar effect in this *novela*.

The hybrid nature of these *novelas* pulls the reader's perceptions in opposite directions by making him or her question whether these are 'mere experiment[s]',

---

[15] Christina H. Lee, 'The Rhetoric of Courtship in Lope de Vega's *Novelas a Marcia Leonarda*', *Bulletin of Spanish Studies*, 80.1 (2003): 13–31.

[16] Antonio Carreño, *El romancero lírico de Lope de Vega* (Madrid: Gredos, 1979), pp. 13–54.

to use Walter Pabst's dismissive expression;[17] whether they constitute fiction with an allegorical purpose, as the long poems do in large measure; and to what extent the boundaries of established practice are blurred, both in terms of subject-matter and genre. I have shown how Lope blurs the distinction between fable and history and between the high and the low styles by creating formal eulogy in both.

Furthermore, as an example to illustrate the links between the *novelas* and the poems, I have tried to suggest above that *Guzmán el Bravo* can be read as a gift in exchange for which royal protection is sought, as well as a commentary on fortitude and love towards woman and one's country; and, equally, *La Circe*, as an allegory of good conduct for someone leading the ship of state.

However, I would suggest that the interconnectedness of the subject-matter of the long poems and *novelas* also lies in their exemplarity as a dialectic on love (a quality which Lope, either playfully or churlishly, denies Cervantes's *Novelas ejemplares*).[18] For instance, one can read *Las fortunas de Diana* and *La Andrómeda* together as narrations on heroism and perfect love; *La prudente venganza* and *La Filomena*, as a study on frustrated desire and revenge; and *La desdicha por la honra,* which does not have a 'mirror' poem, as a meditation of perfect love thwarted by circumstances and otherness, a theme also present, as we have seen, in *Guzmán el Bravo*.

Earlier critics focused on the theatricality of these *novelas*. I would suggest that the significance of poetry has been somewhat underemphasized. In the form of ballads, poetry is a vehicle for conveying significant messages in the stories. Lope's endeavour to extend the boundaries of poetic expression in prose is exemplified in the use of rhetorical devices, for instance, simile and digression. In his witty comment concerning the use of hackneyed Petrarchan similes: 'fue hermosa como el sol' [she was as beautiful as the sun], which, according to Lope, obscure the conveying of poetic meaning in literary creation. Similarly, Lope's extensive deployment of digressive glosses in the *novelas* acquires a dimension rather different from the hitherto-emphasized admonitory or ironic,[19] when examined in the light of his comments about poetic imitation in the prologue to his *comedia El cuerdo loco* (1602): 'La alteza de las locuciones, términos y lugares felizmente escritos, las sentencias, el ornamento, propiedad y hermosura esquisita que se encuentran en los mejores poetas' [The loftiness of the turns of phrase, expressions and the loci felicitously wrought, the adornment, decorum and exquisite beauty which is found in the greatest poets].[20] The yoking of decorum and sententiousness with aesthetic considerations of clarity is evident in *Guzmán*

---

[17] Pabst, *Novellentheorie und Novellendichtung*, p. 153.

[18] 'Confieso que son libros [Cervantes's *Novelas ejemplares*] de grande entretenimiento, y que podrían ser ejemplares, como algunas de las *Historias Trágicas* del Bandello' [I acknowledge that they are very entertaining books, and that some might have well have been exemplary in the manner of the *Istorie tragiche* of Matteo Bandello] (pp. 105–6).

[19] Gonzalo Sobejano, 'La digresión en la prosa narrativa de Lope de Vega y en su poesía epistolar', in *Estudios ofrecidos a Emilio Alarcos Llorach*, 5 vols (Oviedo: Universidad de Oviedo, 1976–83), II (1978), pp. 469–94.

[20] Lope de Vega, *El cuerdo loco*, ed. José F. Montesinos (Madrid: Centro de Estudios Históricos, 1922), p. 6.

el Bravo, and particularly in *La prudente venganza*, deliberately composed in a style of pared-down elegance to increase the tension of its sinister unfolding and to convey its stark message.[21] In a critique in *La Filomena* of the poetic style associated with Góngora and his followers, entitled 'Respuesta de la nueva Poesía' [Reply to the New Poetry], Lope adumbrates similar concerns about poetic style and the function of the clarity of language in transmitting poetic lessons.

Lastly, I believe that Lope's soliciting patronage from powerful women (Leonor de Pimentel and María de Guzmán) in *La Filomena* and *La Circe* and the not inconsiderable presence of fictional female characters in the *novelas*, coupled with the increasing realization in recent research that the female Maecenas was not a figure absent from Early Modern Spain, provide grounds for reassessing the role of femininity in these works.[22] I would go as far as to argue that Lope's experimentation in high and low styles, so accomplished in his mythologizing eulogies found in *Guzmán el Bravo* and *La Circe*, is likewise detectable in his relationship with his female addressees, formal in the poems, familiar and playful in the *novelas*.

It is by examining these intricate threads which Lope weaves into these *novelas* — especially from his poetry and the principles of his dramatic practice, rather than incidental similarities between one *novela* and a play or clusters of plays — that one could gain a deeper understanding of a text which strives to expand the possibilities of writing in a genre in which conventions and practice were still in the incipient stages of their development in the early seventeenth century.

---

[21] 'Ésta fue la prudente venganza, si alguna puede tener este nombre, no escrita, como he dicho, para ejemplo de los agraviados, sino para escarmiento de los que agravian' [This was the prudent vengeance, if any [such act] can bear that name, which was not written, as I have said, as an example for those who are affronted but as a lesson to those who cause affront] (p. 284).

[22] Concerning the Mendoza family, see Helen Nader, ed., *Power and Gender in Renaissance Spain: Eight Women of the Mendoza Family, 1450–1650*, (Urbana, IL: University of Illinois Press, 2004).

La Dorotea: A Tragicomedy in Prose

XAVIER TUBAU

The presence of his personal life in Lope de Vega's literary output, noticed by his contemporaries and studied exhaustively by scholars in modern times, acquires a particular intensity in the case of his youthful love for Elena Osorio. The couple's relationship probably began around 1583 and ended abruptly in early 1588 when Lope was exiled to Valencia as a result of the satires he penned against Elena and her family. The motive for the attacks is to be discovered in the appearance of a rich, new suitor, Francisco Perrenot de Granvela, who was of a higher social standing than Lope and was favoured by Elena and her family, to his detriment.[1] The conversion of these episodes into literature began immediately, taking the form of *morisco* and pastoral ballads which were very widely circulated at the time and collected in later years in a number of anthologies; they were subsequently inspirational in the creation of individual scenes and even the entire plots of plays (for example, *Belardo el furioso*), as well as the composition of short stories (*La prudente venganza*), passages of epic works (such as canto XIX of *La hermosura de Angélica*) and lyric poems (such as the *mayoral* [farm steward] cycle of sonnets).[2] The conception of a project such as *La Dorotea* (1632), a lengthy prose dialogue written when Lope was approaching 70 and presented as the 'history' of these events, clearly indicates the exceptional place that this experience had in the writer's memory.[3]

---

[1] The statements made during the course of Lope's trial for libel can be read in A. Tomillo & C. Pérez Pastor, *Proceso de Lope de Vega por libelos contra unos cómicos* (Madrid: Fortanet, 1901).

[2] See Edwin S. Morby, 'Persistence and Change in the Formation of *La Dorotea*', *Hispanic Review*, 18.2 (1950): 108–25 and 195–217; and Alan S. Trueblood, *Experience and Artistic Expression in Lope de Vega: The Making of 'La Dorotea'* (Cambridge, MA: Harvard University Press, 1974), pp. 48–201.

[3] Although Lope avers that *La Dorotea* is a work composed at the time of the events it narrates, scholars are in broad agreement that it was written from scratch at the start of the 1630s; see Edwin S. Morby, 'Introducción' to *La Dorotea*, 2nd edn, revised (Berkeley, CA: University of California Press; Madrid: Castalia, 1968), pp. 20–23 (all quotations are taken from this edition, with orthography modernized unless it alters the phonetic peculiarities of the original). The passage most often quoted on the subject is from the *Égloga a Claudio* [*Eclogue to Claudio*], written at the start of 1632: 'Póstuma de mis musas *Dorotea*, / y por dicha de mí la más querida, / última de mi vida / pública luz desea' [The latest fruit of my Muses *Dorotea*, and perhaps my best

A short summary of the plot will reveal the importance of its autobiographical component to the work. Dorotea and the young poet Don Fernando have been lovers for five years. Gerarda, an old go-between who is a friend of Dorotea's mother, Teodora, persuades her to break off this liaison and look kindly upon the suit of Don Bela, a rich *indiano* (returnee from the New World), who has fallen for the young woman. Dorotea at first refuses but in the end explains to Don Fernando that she has no choice in the matter. He feels betrayed, and after an argument with her, makes up his mind to flee in desperation to Seville, taking his servant Julio, and not without first having managed to obtain jewels from Marfisa, a former lover, with the story that he has to leave town as a result of a murder he has committed. Dorotea attempts suicide by swallowing a diamond ring, but fails to end her life, and after recovering, eventually accepts Don Bela. Three months after leaving, Fernando returns to Madrid, still in love with Dorotea, and learns what has happened. By chance one night he comes across Don Bela, underneath a window of Dorotea's house, and in a fight he wounds him with his sword. A few days later Fernando and Dorotea, her face hidden and accompanied by Gerarda's daughter Felipa, meet in the Prado; he recounts to her the story of his life, and when Dorotea reveals her identity, the lovers are reconciled. An elated Fernando returns home, only to find Marfisa, aware of his deceit, berating him for his conduct. He then admits to his servant, Julio, that the reconciliation with Dorotea was in fact the end of his love affair, and that he has decided to return to Marfisa. However, before finally abandoning her, he remains with Dorotea for a further two months. The latter discovers this new deception, and in a fit of pique, burns her lover's portrait and all his letters to her. The accidental deaths of Gerarda and Don Bela then lead to the work's tragic conclusion.

La Dorotea was interpreted by nineteenth-century scholarship, interested chiefly in the biographical elements of the work, as an accurate autobiographical account of the love affair between Lope and Elena Osorio. Criticism since then, however, has paid more attention to the artistic elaboration of the text and has warned that the treatment particular episodes receive and the characterization of individuals (unlike what happens in a play such as *Belardo el furioso*) are not so much dependent upon a hypothetical desire to relate the events of the past faithfully as on the exigencies of the plot itself, intimately linked to the conventions of contemporary theatre, and to the objectives pursued by Lope through the work. These cannot be separated from certain very specific personal and editorial circumstances. Thus, whilst the basic plotlines might correspond with the history of a youthful love affair and the characterization in some cases seems to coincide with the real-life existence of its historical protagonists, the substance of *La Dorotea* cannot be explained from a biographical perspective, but rather from the perspective of the writer's own literary output.[4] Although it is

---

loved, last of my life, desires the light of day], in *Rimas humanas y otros versos*, ed. Antonio Carreño (Barcelona: Crítica, 1998), pp. 712–13.

[4] See José F. Montesinos, 'Lope, figura del donaire' (1935), in his *Estudios sobre Lope de Vega* (Salamanca: Anaya, 1967), pp. 65–79 (pp. 65–67), and the 'Advertencia' to *La Dorotea*,

clear, then, for example, that Elena Osorio is Dorotea, it is also true that for his female protagonist's characterization Lope made use of features taken from other women, such as Marta de Nevares; likewise, whilst it is not impossible that the character and behaviour of Francisco Perrenot square with those of Don Bela, it is equally obvious that his depiction as a neo-Platonic lover owes something to the same sort of literary projections Lope indulged in as part of his relationship with Marta de Nevares.[5]

The scenes, characters and situations which are created in *La Dorotea* cannot be examined, as we have claimed, in isolation from the drama of the period.[6] The work offers up the characteristic elements of a *comedia de capa y espada* [cloak and sword play], with an urban backdrop (Madrid) against which the lovers' dialogues are spoken (by Dorotea, Don Fernando and Don Bela), as well as those of their servants (Celia, Julio and Laurencio respectively). There is the lovers' courtship at the lady's grille, the night-time encounter and duel between gentlemen in love with the same lady, and the down-to-earth version of the lovers' feelings expressed through the mouths of their servants, to mention three examples.[7] On the other hand, Lope makes use, in *La Dorotea*, of formal features and episodes belonging to tragedy: the division into five acts and the presence of the chorus at the end of these acts is one case in point, and the prophetic dream of Don Fernando (I, 4, pp. 81–83), the arrival of the messenger with bad tidings (V, 11, p. 455) and the importance given to the theme of vengeance (with the exemplary ending) are others.[8] This mixture of elements common to both comedy and tragedy is characteristic of contemporary theatre and would not have

---

ed. Morby, 2nd edn (1968), p. 40. See also Francisco Márquez Villanueva, 'Literatura, lengua y moral en *La Dorotea*', in his *Lope: vida y valores* (Río Piedras: Universidad de Puerto Rico, 1988), pp. 143–267.

[5] With other characters, such as Gerarda, whose primary model is the go-between Celestina of Fernando de Rojas's tragicomedy, Lope seems to have exploited many of the characteristics of the actress Jerónima de Burgos (another former lover of his). On the subject of the influence of *La Celestina* in *La Dorotea*, technical as well as character-related, see María Rosa Lida de Malkiel, *La originalidad artística de 'La Celestina'* (Buenos Aires: Eudeba, 1962), and Bienvenido Morros Mestres, 'El género en *La Dorotea* y la imitación de *La Celestina*', in *'La Dorotea': Lope de Vega*, ed. Monique Güell (Paris: Ellipses, 2001), pp. 93–111.

[6] José F. Montesinos indicated that in order to study this work 'habrá que recurrir siempre a la comedia como contraste' [one must always return to the *comedia* with which to contrast it], in 'Las poesías líricas de Lope de Vega' (1925–26), in his *Estudios sobre Lope de Vega* (Salamanca: Anaya, 1967), pp. 129–213 (p. 201). See also Alda Croce, *La 'Dorotea' di Lope de Vega: studio critico seguito dalla traduzione delle parti principali dell'opera* (Bari: Laterza, 1940), pp. 132–41; and Trueblood, *Experience*, pp. 324–50.

[7] However, the relationship of master and servant is not consistently at one with the model to be found so regularly in the writer's plays; on this issue, see Montesinos, 'Lope, figura del donaire', pp. 67–68.

[8] On the tragic elements of the work, see Laura Alcoba, 'Présence du tragique dans *La Dorotea*', in *'La Dorotea': Lope de Vega*, ed. Monique Güell (Paris: Ellipses, 2001), pp. 5–12; and José Montero Reguera, '*La Dorotea* como tragedia', in *Silva: studia philologica in honorem Isaías Lerner*, ed. Isabel Lozano-Renieblas & Juan Carlos Mercado (Madrid: Castalia, 2001), pp. 479–85. On vengeance, see Jean-Pierre Étienvre, 'Castigo y venganza en *La Dorotea*', *Anuario Lope de Vega*, 8 (2002): 19–34.

surprised a reader of the work — we should not assume, therefore, that there exists an ironic intention on the part of the writer. The association of tragedy with noble characters and comedy with the low-born, central to classical theory, had disappeared from the commercial theatre by the end of the sixteenth century. The choice of five acts, and above all the inclusion of the chorus (in imitation of Seneca's tragedies), are undoubtedly the work's most original aspects as far as a challenge to dramatic theory is concerned.

The summary of the plot of *La Dorotea* makes evident the parallels that exist between the work and certain scenes and characters in Lope's own theatre. It does not, however, allow one to notice a basic feature of the work: *La Dorotea* is, as Edwin S. Morby indicates, 'menos acción que comentario de acciones' [less action than commentary on actions]. Lope's prose had always tended towards the digressive, a feature of which he was well aware:[9] it was usual as he wrote for one notion to call to mind another, by analogy, and for that one to suggest a third, until the point at which the original idea with which he had started his writing became lost in the course of successive thematic breaks in the discourse. However, in *La Dorotea* this tendency is taken to the extreme. In a scene in the first act, in which Gerarda continues to try to persuade Teodora that Don Bela is a better catch for Dorotea than Don Fernando, a reference to the *décimas* [ten-line stanzas] that Fernando writes prompts the memory of their inventor, Vicente Espinel, and in turn another invention is mentioned — the five-string guitar — which opens the way for reflections on the neglect some instruments and certain dances have fallen into, to be replaced these days by others which are more showy and lascivious. Thus, mention of the detail of a poetic genre employed by Fernando ends up becoming a lament for the fleeting nature of things.

The movement of the characters, in spite of what the plot summary might seem to suggest, is minimal. In fact, some of the episodes are not even presented directly, but narrated after the event by their protagonists: for example, the three months that Don Fernando's visit to Seville and Cadiz lasts (IV, 1), or the deaths of Don Bela and Gerarda (V, 11). And a simple listing of the occasions on which the work's protagonists speak face to face during the course of the five acts offers a clue to explaining this 'falta de movimiento' [lack of movement]: the two main characters, Dorotea and Don Fernando, speak only twice (I, 5; IV, 1); Don Fernando and Marfisa also speak on two occasions (I, 6; IV, 8); likewise Marfisa and Dorotea (II, 3; IV, 1); Dorotea and Don Bela once (II, 5); and the two gentlemen in love with Dorotea, Don Fernando and Don Bela, barely once, in a very short scene (III, 9).[10]

---

[9] The quotation is from Morby's 'Introducción', p. 11. Lope explains himself via don Fernando in the following way: 'Pero volviendo de esta digresión a la historia (que ninguna deja de tener sus episodios, ni se ofende la buena retórica como no sean largos), sabed, César, que Marfisa [...]' [But returning from this digression to the story (for no story is without its episodes which, provided they are not long, do not offend against the laws of rhetoric), let me tell you, César, that Marfisa ...] (V, 3, p. 412).

[10] See Morby, 'Introducción' to his edition, pp. 18–19 (the quotation is his). On the problem of time in the work, see Alban Forcione, 'Lope's Broken Clock: Baroque Time in the *Dorotea*', *Hispanic Review*, 37.4 (1969): 459–90.

Reflection on characters' actions and feelings is as important here as the actions themselves, to the extent that many scenes of the work develop from simple conversations about issues which are not necessarily associated with the central plot line. The clearest case of this happening occurs in the two scenes (IV, 2 and 3), featuring secondary characters — the astrologer César, Ludovico and Julio, Fernando's servant — which are dedicated to a commentary on a Gongorine sonnet ('Pululando de culto, Claudio amigo' [Brimming over with enthusiasm for *culto* poetry, friend Claudio]). Through these characters Lope mocks the poetic language of Góngora and his commentators. As usual, the writer appears to defend the author of the *Soledades* [*Solitudes*] and limit his criticisms to his imitators, but the explicit rejection of metaphors employed by Góngora in his most important poems (for example 'cítara de pluma' [feathered zither]) confirms once again the negative assessment Lope made of certain of the Corboban poet's more extreme elements. Lope also satirizes the indiscriminate use of books of quotations by Góngora's commentators, who adduced, 'venga o no venga a propósito' [whether apposite or not], all the 'lugares comunes' [commonplaces] that they could find in Stobaeus's *Florilegium*, Nanus Mirabellius's *Poliantea* or the *Calepino*, edited by Conrad Gesner (IV, 2, p. 319). This general critique of the commentators' methodology, coming at the start of the 1630s, was certainly tied in with an attack on José Pellicer, whose commentary on Góngora's most important works had been published in 1630.[11]

The critique of the use of commonplaces, however, emerges in the context of a work in which the characters employ them repeatedly in their arguments or in order to explain an opinion, so adding to the slow pace of the action, upon which we have already remarked. Characters provide commentaries on topics such as love, hatred, jealousy, gold, wine, water, rivers and suicide, and they tend to make use of quotations from authors ancient and modern, from any and every discipline, of apothegms, mythological references or emblems to illustrate their point of view on the matter in question.[12] I shall give just one example: one of Fernando's statements about Dorotea ('yo la quiero y la aborrezco' [I love her and I hate her] (III, 1) brings up a classical anecdote, from Aristotle 'en el libro primero *De la*

---

[11] On the polemic between Lope and Pellicer, see Juan Manuel Rozas, 'Lope contra Pellicer (historia de una guerra literaria)', in his *Estudios sobre Lope de Vega* (Madrid: Cátedra, 1990), pp. 133–68. On this passage of *La Dorotea*, see Begoña López Bueno, 'Las tribulaciones "literarias" del Lope anciano: una lectura de *La Dorotea*, IV, ii y iii', *Anuario Lope de Vega*, 11 (2005): 145–63.

[12] See the excellent notes by Edwin S. Morby to his edition of *La Dorotea*; and the following works by Alan S. Trueblood, 'Plato's *Symposium* and Ficino's Commentary in Lope de Vega's *Dorotea*', *Modern Language Notes*, 73.7 (1958): 506–14; and 'The *Officina* of Ravisius Textor in Lope de Vega's *Dorotea*', *Hispanic Review*, 26.2 (1958): 135–41. On the emblems mentioned in the work, see Christian Bouzy, 'L'Emblématique des lieux communs dans *La Dorotea*: Lope de Vega dans l'entre-deux', in *Lectures d'une oeuvre: 'La Dorotea' de Lope de Vega*, ed. Nadine Ly (Paris: Éditions du Temps, 2001), pp. 65–123. On the influence of these cultured traditions on the formation of the characters' discourse of love, see Lía Schwartz Lerner, 'Tradition and Authority in Lope de Vega's *La Dorotea*', in *Cultural Authority in Golden Age Spain*, ed. Marina S. Brownlee & Hans Ulrich Gumbrecht (Baltimore, MD: The Johns Hopkins University Press, 1995), pp. 3–27.

generación de los animales' [in book 1 of the *Generation of Animals*], about a woman 'que tuvo amores con un etíope' [who made love to an Ethiopian]; immediately thereafter, a reply by Fernando ('es digna de ser amada' [she is worthy of love]) becomes the point of departure for the discussion of two further Aristotelian quotations, the first one on the concept of the 'good' with regard to friendship ('en las *Éticas*' [in the *Ethics*]), the second on the happiness of lovers in their moments of greatest sadness ('en el libro primero de los *Retóricos*' [in book 1 of the *Rhetoric*]). This dialogue between the individual experiences of the characters and classical and contemporary learning, whilst seeming strange to the modern reader who might feel that 'la expresión sincera de los sentimientos y las reminiscencias eruditas' [sincere expression of feelings and erudite allusions] are incompatible, was perfectly normal at a time when these sort of references were thought indispensable for any written composition.[13] The naturalness of the pairing, in a literary text, of immediate experience with bookish allusions is explained both by the exercises in composition practised in grammar and rhetoric classes, which stimulated just such opportune employment of these materials, and by publications of the period which made such a method of composition easier by their provision of very full indices.

Another distinctive element of *La Dorotea* is the considerable number of lyric compositions sung and recited during the course of the work. On the one hand there are the five choruses that close the acts, an attempt to adapt classical verse forms to Spanish, through which, as well as linking the work to the genre of classical tragedy, Lope presents a summary of the main issue dealt with in each act (from the initial 'Love' to 'Vengeance' and the 'Message' or lesson derived from each case). On the other hand, a series of poems are sung and recited by the main characters and these have been included so that the reader 'descanse' [can relax] 'de la continuación de la prosa, y porque no le falte a *La Dorotea* la variedad, con el deseo de que salga hermosa' [from the continuation of the prose, and so that *La Dorotea* does not lack variety, and in order for the work to turn out beautiful] ('Al teatro' [To the audience], p. 51). Amongst these compositions, scholars have singled out, for its high quality, the ballad that begins 'A mis soledades voy / de mis soledades vengo' [Into my solitude I go, from my solitude I come] (I, 4, pp. 87–91) and the series of piscatory idylls (written in the *romancillo* [six-syllable ballad] form) dedicated to the death of Marta de Nevares (poetically known as Amarilis) in 1632.[14] Most of these ballads, *endechas* [four-line verses of six or seven syllables with even lines assonating], sonnets and *villancicos* [traditional songs] were composed in the years, months and even weeks running up to the writing of *La Dorotea*, and only in the cases of two

---

[13] The quotation is from Lida de Malkiel, *La originalidad*, p. 331.
[14] See Leo Spitzer, '"A mis soledades voy ..."', *Revista de Filología Española*, 23 (1936): 397–400; Edwin S. Morby, 'A Footnote on Lope de Vega's *barquillas*', *Romance Philology*, 6 (1952–53): 289–93; Guillermo Serés, '"A mis soledades voy ...": fuentes remotas y motivos principales', *Anuario Lope de Vega*, 4 (1998): 327–37; and Nadine Ly, 'Mémoire théorique et mémoire de l'âme: la matière de poésie et la poésie dans *La Dorotea* de Lope de Vega', in *Lectures d'une oeuvre: 'La Dorotea' de Lope de Vega*, ed. Nadine Ly (Paris: Éditions du Temps, 2001), pp. 137–224 (pp. 179–224).

sonnets can we be certain that they were written deliberately for the place they occupy in the work.[15]

The recurrence of the well-known episode of Lope's youthful love, the presence of elements belonging to his theatrical works, the mixture of comic and tragic elements, and its obviously digressive and lyrical nature, are some of the most important aspects of the work as far as its content is concerned. However, Lope scholars have for many years wondered what might have made the writer embark upon a literary project with these characteristics. It is true that *La Dorotea* is taken to have the same objectives as the body of work published throughout the 1620s: literary success measured by re-editions of texts; prestige amongst the aristocrats interested in culture and cultured men of the period; benefits in the form of positions appointed by the Crown.[16] Yet there is another factor which better explains the choice of *La Dorotea*'s format. As Lope scholars of the last few decades have noted, the legal climate in which the world of publishing operated could cause, for example, the delay in publication of a finished work or indeed even redirect the literary creativity of an author towards genres he had not assayed before. Thus the delay in the publication of Lope's *Jerusalén conquistada* (whose *licencia* [licence required from the civil authorities], requested in the summer of 1605, was not granted until August 1608) was due to the drastic reduction in the number of *licencias* granted to works of fiction between April 1605 and the beginning of 1608. Similarly, the composition of narrative poetic texts such as *La Dragontea*, the *Isidro* or the *Fiestas de Denia*, can be explained chiefly by the interruption to theatrical activity in the *corrales* imposed under Philip II, and which ran (with a few exceptions) from May 1598 to April 1600.[17] The decision to write a work such as *La Dorotea* with its particular generic characteristics cannot be explained either if one fails to take into account the prohibition on the granting of *licencias* to plays and short stories within the kingdoms of Castile, which was in operation from May 1625 until 1634.[18] Some writers, such as Juan Pérez de Montalbán, got around the ban by including plays and novellas in a miscellany (*Para todos* [*For Everyone*], 1632). Others managed to have a *licencia* granted by writing a play in prose, as was the case in 1631 with the Spanish translation of Jorge Ferreira de Vasconcelos's *Eufrosina* (originally published in Portuguese in 1555). The case of *Eufrosina* (also divided into five

---

[15] The first describes Dorotea's burial of Fernando's portrait (IV, 1); the second is the sonnet to which we have already alluded, in which Gongorine poetry is mocked (IV, 2).

[16] The work can be classified, in this regard, within the 'de senectute' cycle studied by Juan Manuel Rozas, 'Lope de Vega y Felipe IV en el "ciclo *de senectute*"', in his *Estudios sobre Lope de Vega* (Madrid: Cátedra, 1990), pp. 73–131 (p. 109); see also Francisco Javier Ávila, '*La Dorotea*: arte y estrategia de senectud, entre la serenidad y la desesperación', *Edad de Oro*, 14 (1995): 9–27.

[17] On the first case, see Jaime Moll, 'Los editores de Lope de Vega', *Edad de Oro*, 14 (1995): 213–22 (p. 217); and on the second, Felipe B. Pedraza Jiménez, 'Introducción' to Lope de Vega, *Rimas*, 2 vols (Ciudad Real: Universidad de Castilla-La Mancha, 1993–94), I, pp. 9–119 (p. 12).

[18] See Jaime Moll, 'Diez años sin licencias para imprimir comedias y novelas en los reinos de Castilla: 1625–1634', *Boletín de la Real Academia Española*, 54 (1974): 97–103; and '¿Por qué escribió Lope *La Dorotea*?', *1616: Anuario de la Sociedad Española de Literatura General y Comparada*, 2 (1979): 7–11.

acts with scenes) must have been important in the original conception and composition of *La Dorotea*:[19] the partial reproduction of Francisco de Quevedo's prologue to Vasconcelos's play in the preliminaries to *La Dorotea* suggests that Lope wanted both texts to be read in the same generic context. His work is neither a play in verse of the usual sort (like those that made up the collections of plays in his *Partes*, whose publication, incidentally, was also interrupted in 1625), nor a prose narrative in the style of the contemporary novellas.[20] It is not by chance, then, that the term *comedia* does not appear in the title of the work — where the word *acción*, from neo-Latin theatre, is chosen — and nor is it used with specific reference to *La Dorotea* in the preliminaries — where it is called *fábula*, that is, 'theatrical work'.[21] Nor is it a surprise that the objectives of the work should be in tune with the moral concerns of the Junta de Reformación [the body set up to reform public morals], which had given rise to the prohibition, in claiming to advise readers 'que andan con el apetito y no con la razón, qué fin tiene la vanidad de sus deleites y la vilísima ocupación de sus engaños' [who act according to appetite rather than reason, of the consequences of the vanity of their pleasures and their despicable concern with their misguided actions] ('Al teatro', p. 52).[22]

The important prologue addressed 'Al teatro' [To the audience] sees Lope combine several theoretical concepts in order to characterize his work generically. Although the term 'comedia' is not employed, the whole prologue presupposes that *La Dorotea* is a play ('esta fábula' [this theatrical work]): from the title of the prologue itself ('Al teatro') or Fame's final words ('Senado, esta es *La Dorotea* [...]' [Audience, this is *La Dorotea* ...] (V, 12, p. 457), to the way that the work is envisaged in terms identical to the 'comedias de hombres ignorantes' [plays by men who know nothing], printed, under his name, by 'libreros de Sevilla, Cádiz y otros lugares del Andalucía' [booksellers from Seville, Cadiz and other towns in Andalusia]. Telling too are the writers and texts put forward in order to refer to the purpose of the work and the issues it contains (Aristophanes, Plautus, Terence, *La Celestina*, *Eufrosina*). The use of prose instead of verse is justified on two grounds, one theoretical, the other practical: first Lope recalls the truism that poetry can be written in verse or in prose, an assertion that can be read within the frame of Aristotelian literary theory (*Poetics*, I, 1447b), but whose formulation

---

[19] See Karl Vossler, '*Euphrosina*', *Corona*, 8 (1938): 514–33. This translation had three *aprobaciones* [endorsements] (all of them signed by friends of Lope), the first of which was issued on 17 September 1629. The *privilegio* [author's 'privilege'] is signed on 16 December 1630 and the *tasa* [the book's price] on 11 August 1631. Lope must have got wind of this edition well before its publication in the summer of 1631.

[20] Only from this vantage point can we can make sense of Lope's allusion to the novelty implied by the introduction of poems into the work: 'aunque esto pocas veces se vea en las [letras] griegas, latinas y toscanas' [even if this is rarely seen in Greek, Latin or Italian letters] ('Al teatro', p. 51). All of Lope's prose works, from the pastoral to the Byzantine novel, include poems, following the conventions of these narrative genres.

[21] Anne Cayuela alerts us to the caution shown by authors with regard to the use of terms such as *novela* and *comedia* in this period, in 'La prosa de ficción entre 1625 y 1634: balance de diez años sin licencias para imprimir novelas en los reinos de Castilla', *Mélanges de la Casa de Velázquez*, 29.2 (1993): 51–76.

[22] On this didactic purpose to the work, see Trueblood, *Experience*, 529–631.

here owes a direct debt to a passage belonging to medieval literary theory (taken from Savonarola's *Apologeticus*).[23] Secondly, he indicates that the choice of prose was better suited to the work's content, 'porque siendo tan cierta imitación de la verdad, le pareció que no lo sería hablando las personas en verso como las demás [comedias] que ha escrito' [because as it is (meant to be) so true an imitation of life, it seemed to him that it would not be were characters to speak in verse as they do in the other (plays) he has written]. The truth of the events imitated in his play (for a play is 'imitación de la vida, espejo de la costumbre e imagen de la verdad' [an imitation of life, mirror of customs and image of truth], according to the maxim attributed by Donatus to Cicero) requires a more natural style, free from the artifice of versification. In the choice of prose for this work the aforementioned prohibition on the publication of plays (in verse, it was understood) probably weighed more heavily than an apparent desire for literary veracity, given that for Lope and his contemporaries using verse did not necessarily imply any distancing from the real world. (*Arcadia* and *El peregrino en su patria* move further from reality than *La dama boba* or *Fuente Ovejuna*, for example.) Yet this statement is important because it introduces the problem of poetic fiction and truth, a concern of the central section of this prologue, and one to which some of the characters within the work even refer metaliterarily (see III, 4, p. 236, and V, 3, p. 405). If the reader were to notice any defect in the 'arte' of the work, that is, in its general artistic composition, the excuse is that what is narrated is 'verdad' [the truth], because 'el poeta más quiso seguirla que estrecharse a las impertinentes leyes de la fábula ["obra teatral"]' [the dramatist was keener to follow the truth than to be bound by the inappropriate rules of the theatrical work], that is, by the way in which contemporary works for the theatre developed almost mechanically. 'El asunto fue historia' [The subject matter was history], writes Lope, and his play is a polished 'imitación' [imitation] of those facts from the past, which does not mean that the 'argumento' [story line] is not adorned with 'donaires y colores retóricos' [wit and rhetorical colour], 'erudición' [erudition], deceptions and truths suited to the context, and generally speaking, 'tantas partes de filosofía natural y moral' [so many components of natural and moral philosophy] ('Al teatro', p. 53).

The distinction between historical facts (history) and fictitious facts (fiction) as the basis for a dramatic story line is central to the writer's theoretical thinking.[24]

---

[23] On the use of this passage from *Apologeticus* and Lope's interpretation of its contents, see Xavier Tubau, *Una polémica literaria: Lope de Vega y Diego de Colmenares* ([Pamplona]: Universidad de Navarra; Madrid: Iberoamericana; Frankfurt am Main: Vervuert, 2007), pp. 139–144. Scholars have suggested several approaches to *La Dorotea* from the perspective of Aristotle's *Poetics*; see Trueblood, *Experience*, 201–6; and Nadine Ly, '*La Dorotea*: la question du genre', *Les Langues Néo-Latines*, 95, no. 319 (2001): 41–68, and 'Mémoire théorique et mémoire de l'âme: la matière de poésie et la poésie dans *La Dorotea* de Lope de Vega', in *Lectures d'une œuvre* (pp. 137–79).

[24] The dedications to his plays provide repeated testimony to this opposition, which Lope, like many of his contemporaries, does not view as problematic; see Juan Oleza, 'Del primer Lope al *Arte nuevo*', 'Estudio preliminar' to Lope de Vega, *Peribáñez y el comendador de Ocaña*, ed. Donald McGrady (Barcelona: Crítica, 1997), pp. ix–lv (pp. xxxviii–xliv).

From this approach, Lope only needed to take a further step and call to mind the association of history with tragedy and fiction with comedy (following Donatus's commentaries on Terence, mentioned in the *Arte nuevo*, lines 111–12) in order to find a generic denomination which suited his work: tragicomedy. For a work which, in addition to the elements common to the cloak and sword play, combined historical truth with those 'nuncios y coros' [messengers and choruses] which he viewed as paradigmatic of tragedy (in the prologue to *El castigo sin venganza* of 1631), as well as taking *La Celestina* as a model, no doubt demanded such a denomination. Lope in the end chose 'acción en prosa', and the reason he did so is most probably to be sought in the prohibition on the issuing of *licencias* for plays.[25]

---

[25] This chapter, originally written as '*La Dorotea*: una tragicomedia en prosa' was translated by Jonathan Thacker.

Part 5: The Afterlife

19

Lope as Icon

DAVID MCGRATH

Lope de Vega has always been a byword for excellence in Spanish letters, so it is remarkable that portraits of him have until recently received little critical attention. We have to go back to 1935 to find the only monograph on the subject, by Enrique Lafuente Ferrari, the then Keeper of Prints at the Prado,[1] whose *Los retratos de Lope de Vega* is a model of economic thoroughness that still reads remarkably well today, and provides a comprehensive selection of images. Indeed, until the emergence of the Lope portrait pages on the excellent *Biblioteca Virtual Cervantes* website[2] (which draws heavily on Lafuente for its images) it has been the sole source of access to portraits in sufficient numbers for purposes of comparison and collation. Although new information has come to light from Pérez Sánchez[3] and Jordán de Urríes[4] in terms of the location and dating of one important portrait mentioned by Lafuente, it is safe to assume that it will remain the benchmark for identifying the various strands of Lope portraiture for many decades.

In fact, there has been a revival of interest generally in Lope's image on the part of art historians and literary critics. Most notable among these is Javier Portús,[5] whose *Pintura y pensamiento en la España de Lope de Vega* appeared in 1999 and describes the cult of portraiture in Golden Age Spain that gave rise to the vast number of contemporaneous images of this most celebrated of playwrights. His analysis of Lope's role in their deliberate cultivation and their typology has been complemented by the appearance of Antonio Sánchez Jiménez's *Lope pintado por sí mismo*,[6] which deals with Lope's equally assiduous self-inscription in his

---

[1] Enrique Lafuente Ferrari, *Los retratos de Lope de Vega* (Madrid: Imprenta Helénica, 1935).

[2] Biblioteca Virtual Cervantes, Lope de Vega (retratos), at website http://www.cervantes virtual.com/bib_autor/Lope/retratos.shtml, pp. 1–3.

[3] Alfonso E. Pérez Sánchez, *Pintura española de los siglos XVII y XVIII en la Fundación Lázaro Galdiano* (Madrid: Fundación Lázaro Galdiano & Fundación Pedro Barrié de la Maza, 2005).

[4] Javier Jordán de Urríes y de la Colina, 'El coleccionismo del ilustrado Bernardo Iriarte', *Goya*, nos 319–20 (July–October 2007): 259–80.

[5] Javier Portús Pérez, *Pintura y pensamiento en la España de Lope de Vega* (Hondarribia: Nerea, 1999).

[6] Antonio Sánchez Jiménez, *Lope pintado por sí mismo: mito e imagen del autor en la poesía de Lope de Vega Carpio* (Woodbridge: Tamesis, 2006).

writings, but also bristles with discussion of the merits (or otherwise) of his portraits.

The present chapter seeks to build on this renewed interest to make a selection of his portraits once again available between the covers of a book, the illustrations being accompanied by a brief commentary sufficient for the purposes of general orientation. The text provides an opportunity to develop some of Lafuente's observations about the way some images of Lope have proliferated and prospered in the public imagination, while others — often of superior artistic quality — have not. Central to this is the question of how far Lope's popular image represents a conceptual vision of how he ought to look, as against substantial evidence of how he actually did look. In other words, I wish to look at the icon versus the man, and the impact of the manipulation of Lope's image during his own lifetime as artists adjusted their depiction of him. This naturally affected their later counterparts' image of him in monuments, frontispieces of published works, literary manuals and so on.[7]

The latter part of this article is devoted to a discussion of a portrait of Lope mentioned in the inventory of the will of his close friend and associate, the court painter Juan van der Hamen. The present location of this painting is unknown, but I want to consider it in the light of another portrait of the *Fénix* attributed to Juan Carreño de Miranda, which is housed in the Lilly Library, Indiana, and seems to have been overlooked.[8]

I

Before embarking upon a discussion of Lope's physical appearance, it would be as well to be reminded of the way the seventeenth-century artist, subject and viewer saw pictorial likeness. In his essay on the portrait and reality,[9] Finaldi reminds us that Covarrubias in 1611 and Francisco Pacheco in 1645 defined the art of portraiture as the faithful reproduction of the sitter's features in order that they might be transmitted to posterity (p. 150), but such aspirations were to be heavily circumscribed by the circumstances surrounding the actual execution of any such commission. Portús has identified the considerations which outstrip the importance of mere physical verisimilitude in Early Modern Spanish portraiture:

---

[7] For the minutiae of attribution, dating, provenance and location of images, I refer the reader to Lafuente, Portús, Sánchez Jiménez, Pérez Sánchez and Jordán de Urríes. There are also incidental references to Lope portraiture in studies by David Martin Kowal, *Ribalta y los ribaltescos: la evolución del estilo barroco en Valencia* (Valencia: Diputación Provincial de Valencia, 1985) and Juan Manuel González Martel, *Casa Museo Lope de Vega: guía y catálogo* (Madrid: Real Academia Española & Comunidad de Madrid, 1993) which are well worth examination.

[8] In this excursion into art history, I have been particularly indebted to Nigel Glendinning, Juliet Wilson Bareau, Marta Cacho Casal, Jeremy Roe and Zahira Véliz Bomford for their experience and guidance. Any assertions made and errors committed are of course my own.

[9] Gabriele Finaldi, 'Retrato y realidad: Ribalta, Zurbarán, Ribera', in *El retrato español: del Greco a Picasso*, ed. Javier Portús Pérez (Madrid: Museo Nacional del Prado, 2004), pp. 150–69.

Una de las características que definen el retrato español de la Edad Moderna es que con él frecuentemente se buscaba más que la plasmación de los rasgos psicológicos que individualizaban y distinguían al modelo, su caracterización como integrante de un determinado grupo social mediante la multiplicación de elementos (trajes, cortinajes, muebles, etc.) que son ante todo símbolos de estatus.[10]

[One of the defining characteristics of the Spanish portrait in the Modern Era is that it went beyond the quest to depict the psychological traits that distinguished a particular individual, seeking rather to indicate his position as a member of a given social group via a proliferation of elements (costume, draperies, furnishings, etc.) which are principally symbols of status.][11]

Portús's assertion that it is the depiction of psychological realism and the signification of status, rather than likeness, that are the criteria of representational fidelity is reinforced by Finaldi's allusion to supposed evidence of physical verisimilitude which can be shown to be completely illusory. He cites the example of a celebrated series of portraits of friars by Zurbarán from around 1630:

Cuando se puso a realizar la serie de 'retratos' de célebres teólogos mercedarios [...] todos los cuales (con una excepción) habían fallecido ya antes de que comenzase a pintarlos, parece ser que utilizó a diversos modelos de mercedarios vivos que hicieron las veces de sus precursores. Fray Francisco Zumel, célebre filósofo y profesor, además de general de la orden, había muerto en 1604, pero Zurbarán, en lugar de pintar un retrato póstumo basándose en una imagen anterior o en una máscara mortuaria, decidió emplear la iconografía con la que tradicionalmente se representa a un doctor de la Iglesia, solemne, reflexivo y divinamente inspirado en sus escritos, combinarla con la atenta observación de un modelo vivo y, después, inscribir en el lienzo sencillamente el nombre de Zumel. De hecho el mismo modelo aparece representado también como otro teólogo difunto, fray Pedro Machado. (pp. 153–54)

[When he came to paint the series of 'portraits' of celebrated Mercedarian theologians [...] all of whom (with one exception) were dead before he began, he appears to have used a selection of living Mercedarian models who played the part of their forebears. Fray Francisco Zúmel, a celebrated philosopher and teacher and General of the order, had died in 1604, but rather than painting a posthumous portrait, based on a earlier image or a death mask, Zurbarán decided to employ the traditional imagery of a church doctor, solemn, reflective and divinely inspired in his writings, combine it with the close observation of a living model, and then simply inscribe the canvas with Zúmel's name. The same model in fact appears as another deceased theologian, Fray Pedro Machado.][12]

---

[10] Portús Pérez, *Pintura y pensamiento*, p. 166.

[11] Except where otherwise indicated, all translations are my own.

[12] Quotations from Finaldi's article are taken from the English version of the catalogue: 'Portrait and Reality: Ribalta, Zurbarán, Ribera', in *The Spanish Portrait: From El Greco to Picasso*, ed. Javier Portús Pérez (London: Scala, 2004), pp. 146–65. Here Zumel's name has gained an accent.

It appears, then, that physical resemblance could even be discarded altogether in certain circumstances, one being the desire to transmit a controlled image to posterity.

Finaldi also points to a much more nuanced example of dubious adherence to verisimilitude, the well-known case of the portrait by Ribera of the bearded woman *Maddalena Ventura* with child at breast. Portrait commissions by Ribera's sponsors in Naples normally fell to Stanzione 'y a otros artistas de origen flamenco más proclives a plasmar a sus modelos con rasgos atractivos' [and to other artists of Flemish extraction more inclined to produce attractive renditions of their sitters] (p. 154). The tendency of painters from the Low Countries towards a sympathetic representation is illustrated by Winkel's comment on Dutch female portraiture of the time:[13]

> Portrait painters took certain liberties when [...] depicting the subject's face. In studying seventeenth-century sources [...] we are struck first and foremost by a near-obsessive preoccupation with smooth, white skin. [...] In reality, few would have had smooth skin in those days, if only because everyone suffered a bout of smallpox at some point. Those who survived were frequently scarred for life with deep pockmarks, yet in portraiture all the faces are equally smooth, and pockmarked faces are nowhere to be found. A burlesque entitled *The Painter through Love* (1682) undoubtedly refers to prevailing practice, when the young lady whose portrait is being painted says: 'The original surely merits no great praise; / But the good master will easily erase / The blemishes encountered in the face'. (p. 72)

The *Maddalena Ventura* project seems to have been awarded to Ribera by the Spanish viceroy in order to guard against such cosmetic adjustments, and because it was hoped to achieve an absolutely faithful and unadorned record of this human phenomenon (or as the inscription on the picture has it: 'EN MAGN   NATURA MIRACVLVM'). This proto-documentary approach was even bolstered by a written record of the portrait's execution by way of authentication of the likeness. Despite such precautions, Finaldi casts doubt on the reliability of the outcome by comparing it to another well-known painting by Ribera: 'Si comparamos la cabeza del harapiento filósofo *Demócrito* [...] con la de Maddalena Ventura descubriremos no sólo curiosas similitudes de tratamiento y caracterización, sino indicios de que el proceso de elaboración de ambos cuadros, que implica una detallada observación del modelo, resulta muy similar' [a comparison between the head of the ragged philosopher *Democritus* [...] and that of Maddalena Ventura reveals not only intriguing similarities in handling and characterisation but suggests that the process of elaboration, which involves detailed observation of the sitter-model, is very similar in the two pictures] (p. 152). It could be, then, that the models for Ribera's *Maddalena* and *Democritus* were one and the same person.

---

[13] Marieke de Winkel, 'The Artist as Couturier: The Portrayal of Clothing in the Golden Age', in *Dutch Portraits: The Age of Rembrandt and Frans Hals* (The Hague: Royal Picture Gallery Mauritshuis; London: National Gallery; Zwolle: Waanders, 2007), pp. 65–73.

4

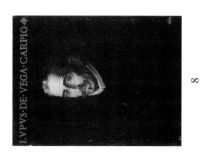

LVPVS·DE·VEGA·CARPIO

8

3

7

2

6

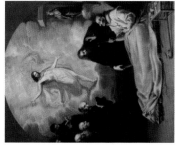

1

5

12

11

10

9

16

15

14

13

20

24

LOPE DE VEGA.

19

23

17

22

EL ARTISTA.

18

21

28

32

27

31

26

30

25

29

So a facial likeness as conceived in Early Modern Europe does not necessarily correspond to current notions. This is not to say that the series of images of Lope that we are about to consider never give an accurate idea of how he looked in real life, but that physical verisimilitude is only one of several factors to be taken into account.

II

Much in the way that Shakespeare's defining physical characteristics are his bald pate and perfunctory facial hair, the shorthand version of Lope de Vega's distinguishing features are his aquiline nose, penetrating gaze, primped moustache and strangely modern quiff. The Hispanic world is familiar with his emblematic face. To take Madrid as an example, one can see it not only painted on tiles or printed on ephemera at bars in Huertas and Santa Ana [1], but also atop the sober statue by Fuxà [2] outside the Biblioteca Nacional, or in the 1862 bust by Ponzano on the mural [3] in the hallway of his house (now the Casa Museo de Lope de Vega). The fact that such images are only an approximation of how he looked is, of course, central to the cultivation of a signifying object. Lope's picture has been developed beyond the mere representation of his appearance, and has taken on the status of an icon, so that the features of this man have come to equate to a kind of a national champion of the Arts.

This is Lope as presented posthumously: 'of a certain age', no longer young (though certainly not old), elegantly combining the wisdom of maturity with continued creative energy. But where does this consensus come from? There was after all a plethora of images of the poet in his own time, or, as his acolyte Pérez de Montalbán characteristically overstated it, 'no hay casa de hombre curioso que no tenga su retrato, o ya en papel, o ya en lámina, o ya en lienzo' [anyone with an enquiring mind will have a portrait of him, whether on paper, or in a print, or on canvas, in his house].[14] Not all of these images would have depicted Lope as a mature man, but often much more fresh-faced, and for centuries since his death these have hardly been reproduced at all — the same fate that has befallen other excellent images from his old age which showed him as he really must have looked, in one instance, with unsparing candour.

One can point in the first instance to the overriding influence of the death-mask as transformed by Herrera Barnuevo [4] into a plaster bust. Preserved from the gaunt sparseness of senile decay, Lafuente sternly denounced 'los falseamientos que el escultor se permitió [...] por ejemplo el presentar abiertos los ojos a capricho del que los modeló' [the falsifications which the sculptor indulged in [...] for example in presenting the eyes open, modelled at the whim of the artist] (p. 35). However, Portús has observed that the completion of a death-mask then represented 'algo para lo que sólo ciertas personas muertas en olor de santidad o pertenecientes a la Casa Real tenían el honor de prestar sus rostros' [something for

---

[14] Portús Pérez, *Pintura y pensamiento*, p. 161.

which only those persons who had died in an odour of sanctity, or who were members of the Royal household, had the privilege of lending their faces].[15] So the undertaking must in itself have been commemorative rather than clinical in nature. If the commission of the bust was yet another example of Lope's endearing vanity (even from beyond the grave), or made at the behest of zealous admirers, it seems more than likely that the sculptor would have brought some sympathetically creative element to his efforts, and reinvigorated the face and hairline of his subject.

The same impulse must have underpinned the well-known and rather similar painted portrait from 1630 now in the Lázaro Galdiano Museum in Madrid [5]. The collector and artist, Carderera, who owned the portrait at one stage, optimistically described it (from the dubious vantage point of the late nineteenth century) as 'casi coetáneo' [almost contemporaneous], but once again we see an unnaturally vigorous and full-faced subject with a fine growth of red hair, whose aspect reflects early middle age rather than a man of at least 68, and so the image must have been heavily retouched.

This hypothesis is supported by a comparison of the bust and the Lázaro Galdiano picture to a portrait of Lope from 1632 by Vicente Carducho. This painting shows an all too believably bald and emaciated figure, only three years from death, kneeling in reverence at the *Death of the Venerable Odón de Novara* [6]. Here Lope is visible as the central figure of the three on the lower left of the picture. In modest detail only, he takes his place among those in vigil at the deathbed of a pious colleague. Decidedly unheroic in aspect and overwhelmed by the subject's last agony, this likeness [7] is certainly a more satisfying and technically accomplished work of art than the two images discussed so far, but it has been overlooked by posterity as it seeks to conjure an appropriate image. Why is this? What are the factors that must have inhibited the diffusion of a more naturalistic Lope image?

Apart from the decline in aesthetic appeal that decrepitude naturally entails, and which might have dissuaded copyists from taking their inspiration from a somewhat depressing reality, there could be mundane reasons. The painting was originally completed for the monastery of El Paular in its remote location in the Sierra de Guadarrama, and was therefore not accessible to the general viewer. Furthermore, the identification of the kneeling figure as Lope is relatively recent, so perhaps those involved in the posthumous manufacture and distribution of images simply did not know that this affecting figure was Spain's most illustrious playwright.

Whatever the circumstances, those seeking inspiration during his lifetime and in decades immediately following his death have unsurprisingly preferred the reassurance of images of a more robust *Fénix*. One of the best-known examples of these is the portrait in the Hermitage Museum, St Petersburg — its influence on editions of his writings being presumably what Lafuente had in mind when, dismissing the traditional attribution to Tristán, he described it as having become

---

[15] Portús Pérez, *Pintura y pensamiento*, p. 170.

'el casi único retrato aceptado oficialmente del Fénix' [practically the only officially accepted portrait of the *Fénix*] (p. 65). This portrait shows him fuller-faced, although lined and grey, and in clerical collar (having been ordained in 1614) [8].

Another painting often reproduced [9] is presently in the keeping of the Casa-Museo and is by an unknown artist. Again in clerical garb, Lope is shown in three-quarter view with his hand pointing at various books including *La Dorotea*, published in 1632, thus providing the picture's *terminus a quo*. This shows a rather more vigorous Lope than is apparent in the Hermitage portrait and seems to have been executed in the same largely commemorative spirit as the Herrera Barnuevo bust and the Lázaro Galdiano portrait. Once again it seems unrealistically youthful in aspect for a man of 70.

The Lázaro Galdiano portrait had already featured the Cross of Malta which was to become a regular feature of the iconography of Lope for future generations. Probably conferred in 1627, its frequent presence in images of him is a telling indication of his relentless social aspiration, although, as Sánchez Jiménez points out, it was far less prestigious than Lope might have hoped (p. 40, note 48). The Cross motif is combined with that other indicator, the clerical sobriety so gloomily apparent in the Hermitage portrait, in another painting now at the Biblioteca Nacional. Here the insignia feature prominently on the cassock as well as the cloak [10]. Lafuente identifies this sombre image as the unalloyed source of various nineteenth-century versions of the playwright's features: by Rosell (prior to 1860) [11] and Maura in 1876 [12] and 1890 (pp. 65–68). This picture was first recorded in 1760 and is poorly executed compared to its precursors, which include an excellent copper engraving by the French artist resident in Spain Jean de Courbes, a frequent illustrator of Lope editions. As the frontispiece of *Laurel de Apolo* (1630), it shows a greying and middle-aged Lope, though still with dark eyebrows and moustache, around his fiftieth year. Once again the poet looks grey but vigorously hirsute, and rather younger than his 68 years [13]. (There is an indifferent copy of it in an eighteenth-century edition of *El peregrino en su patria* [14].)

In fact, images of the mature Lope that have remained in the public consciousness tend to portray him as middle-aged rather than old, and even veer towards ruddy good health. They enjoy a significant afterlife as illustrations to printed works of Lope and public monuments representing him. It is only in the Carducho picture that we get anything like a glimpse of the gaunt and diminished 70 year-old he is more likely to have been. Such images invest in his status as a man of the cloth, rather than that of the man of letters, a posture often enhanced by the presence of the Cross of Malta. They are inevitably circumscribed by the social aspiration which inspired their existence, and do not therefore necessarily reflect the likeness of the subject at the moment of their artistic creation (often difficult to determine in any case). As such, they resist attempts to create a chronological sequence for them by reference to physical characteristics such as hair colour or facial lines and skin tones.

III

The signifying elements just described in terms of his facial features and his attire were to become formulaic in subsequent centuries in the illustration of editions of Lope's works or in literary manuals. This is the era which saw the rise of the 'official' type of Lope portraiture (to borrow Lafuente's terminology). Images take on a series of developments which conflate or detach symbols as required, and which begin to reflect not just his status as a cleric but also his pre-eminence as a man of letters. This process seems to have been initiated by an anonymous portrait which has also been in the Lázaro Galdiano Museum since some time after 1935. Its origins are unknown, but it belonged to the collector Luis Navas at the start of the twentieth century before being briefly lost,[16] and has also been identified by Lafuente with a canvas in the collection of Juan de Iriarte from 1760, mentioned by La Barrera.[17] The portrait shows Lope around his sixtieth year, Lafuente observing that the facial characteristics are, once again, those of the death-mask bust (p. 78). Here, he is sitting at a table covered in books, papers and the paraphernalia of a writer [15], and is wearing a cassock and cape with the Cross of Malta hanging low on his chest, visible just above his right hand, which is pointing to a niche containing a statue of Apollo. Two volumes bearing titles, *Arcadia* (from 1598) and *Laurel de Apolo* (from 1630) can be discerned — the latter just below the statue. Pérez Sánchez comments:

> Aunque Lafuente Ferrari lo considera obra probablemente del siglo XVIII, un estudio más atento del cuadro obliga a considerarlo todavía dentro del XVII y de mano de algún artista madrileño no despreciable. Tela y materia son, indudablemente, de este siglo y la calidad de los objetos de la mesa —libros, gafas, tintero y tijeras— es muy notable, con técnica próxima a lo que hacían por los años de 1650–60 los bodegonistas madrileños del tipo de Burgos Mantilla. (p. 135)

> [Although Lafuente Ferrari considers it probably to be an eighteenth-century work, a closer study of the picture requires a dating still in the seventeenth, and by the hand of an artist from Madrid — one not without merit. The canvas and materials date unquestionably from that century, and the quality of the objects on the table — books, glasses, inkwell and scissors — is very high, and technically close to that achieved around the years 1650–60 by still-life artists of Madrid such as Burgos Mantilla.]

---

[16] Navas was a collector living in Madrid in the first three decades of the twentieth century, of whom little else is known.

[17] One of three brothers, Juan de Iriarte formed one of the most important collections of paintings in Spain in the eighteenth century. The Lope portrait was originally displayed in one of two *gabinetes* alongside portraits of artists and other writers. At his death in 1771, Iriarte's entire estate passed to his brother Bernardo, including this portrait. A sale in 1842 confirms it as having once belonged to Juan de Iriarte and mentions an attribution to Alonso Cano (Jordán de Urríes, 'El coleccionismo', pp. 262–64).

This version of his appearance is the source of many subsequent engravings and lithographs; for example, that of a bust by Carmona in Sedano's *Parnaso español* of 1770 [16][18] — a version that was copied by Morales for the review *El artista* in 1835 [17].

The composition with the pointing right hand is reproduced in reverse in an engraving by Selma, the image probably being one among several executed from his collection at the instigation of Bernardo and Domingo de Iriarte for the *Cuadernos iconográficos* [*Notebooks of Iconography*] series *Retratos de los españoles ilustres* [*Portraits of Illustrious Spaniards*] of 1791 [18].[19] Here the poet looks less advanced in years, and with darker hair, but the prominent cheekbones preserve the resemblance to the Herrera Barrionuevo bust.

Lafuente's comments on the context for the development of this series of images are illuminating:

Los estudios de iconografía no tenían precedentes en España, y así fue grande la dificultad de encontrar retratos auténticos, habiendo que recurrir, como observó Carderera en su *Catálogo de retratos* [...] 'a las diminutas estampas del *Parnaso español*, de Sedano, y a las de varias portadas de libros, grosamente estampadas en madera'. Allí salió este retrato de Lope de Vega, dibujado por Rafael Ximeno y grabado por Fernando Selma; era pues el primer retrato oficial de Lope, y ello explica el favor que ha gozado. La efigie de Selma se unió a las de Carmona y Tejada;[20] a estas dos versiones vino a añadirse, en el siglo XIX, la del pseudo Tristán de Rusia; estas tres han acaparado, puede decirse, hasta ahora, la pretensión de representar la efigie del poeta. (p. 81)

[Iconographic studies had no precursors in Spain, and so it was very difficult to find authentic portraits, and one had to resort, as Carderera observed in his *Catálogo de retratos* [...] 'to the miniature prints in the *Parnaso español* by Sedano, and to the crude woodcuts in various frontispieces of books'. This is the source of this portrait of Lope de Vega, drawn by Rafael Ximeno and engraved by Fernando Selma. As such, it was the first official portrait of Lope, and this explains the favour it has enjoyed. The Selma likeness was then joined by those from Carmona and Tejada, and in the nineteenth century, the supposed Tristán effort (now in Russia) came to be added to these two versions. It could be said that, up to now, these three have monopolised the claim to represent the poet's likeness.]

Lafuente thus identifies three essential strands of standard Lope portraiture. The one represented by the Selma image was itself to be exploited, for a refined view of the face only, in a lithograph by Rey in the mid-nineteenth century [19]. It is this version of the playwright's face, after a journey of 300 years, that is

[18] Jordán de Urríes notes that the Iriarte portrait 'sirvió a Carmona para su grabado en el *Parnaso español*' [was used by Carmona for his engraving in the *Spanish Parnassus*] and explains that it was reduced to a bust within an oval in order to fit the *Parnaso* format (p. 262).

[19] *Retratos de los españoles ilustres, con un epítome de sus vidas* (Madrid: Imprenta Real, 1791).

[20] Moreno de Tejada was an eighteenth-century engraver whose image of Lope is mentioned by Lafuente (p. 51) but not reproduced in his monograph.

immediately recognisable as the source for the painted tiles at the Taberna del León de Oro in Madrid.

This is the culmination of a self-referential process which has drawn upon a small group of portraits in order to produce the instantly recognisable cultural icon whose face is known even to those who may never have read or seen his plays. The plaster bust castigated by Lafuente for its 'falseamientos', the early strands of painted portraiture, and those images adorned with the Cross of Malta, together form the basis of Lope's most accessible image-type. During the centuries following his death, new emphasis was placed on his literary achievements while his physical aspect was subjected to constant re-interpretation by painters, engravers and lithographers. These have fixed in the popular imagination an icon of Lope in his mature years with more or less elderly looking variants, according to commission or whim. His status not only as a cleric, but as a man of letters, is now apparent, both within the iconography itself, or in his allocation of a place among other writers of the first rank (as in the *Cuadernos iconográficos* series). Today his image can be found on the front of bars alongside portraits of Quevedo, Cervantes *et al.*

IV

So what has become of contemporaneous portraits that somehow escaped inclusion in the narrow conspectus of images studied? We know of a portrait by the Valencian artist Francisco Ribalta, thought to have been painted between 1621 and 1625, but now lost. However, it may survive in the sense that an anonymous woodcut copied 'de un lienzo en que le trasladó al vivo el catalán Ribalta' [from a canvas done of him from life by the Catalan Ribalta] precedes the *Rimas humanas y divinas de Tomé de Burguillos* of 1634 [20].[21] It is crudely finished, but shows him full-faced, grey-haired and, according to Sánchez Jiménez, in burlesque mode, crowned with laurel or — absurdly — thyme (*tomillos*) (pp. 223–25).

Arguably inspired also by the Ribalta portrait is an image of Lope that outshines all those mentioned so far for its technical accomplishment and psychological acuity. This is a 1625 copper engraving by Pedro Perret from *Triunfos divinos* showing him in a cassock, with silver close-cropped hair [21]. Perhaps uniquely among all the images under discussion, the age of the subject seems to correlate with his chronological age and the known date of publication. The 63 year old Lope wears the air of proud resignation appropriate to the features of one who has already led an exhausting life, with even greater travails to come.

Even though this brilliant image has the mature, heroic resonance much sought-after by literary patriots, it has only in the twentieth century begun to receive the dissemination it merits. Lafuente attributes the lack of impact of the Perret image in the eighteenth and nineteenth centuries to sparse use of it in editions of the text which it was meant to accompany (pp. 68–69).

---

[21] Kowal, *Ribalta y los ribaltescos*, p. 256.

Its fate mirrors that of a similarly intriguing image, this time of the young Lope, one with which scholars are now familiar, though it disappeared almost entirely from view for 300 years. Francisco Pacheco in his *Libro de descripción de verdaderos retratos de ilustres y memorables varones* [*Book Describing the True Portraits of Illustrious and Famous Men*] of 1598[22] included an image of Lope in warm colours showing a fashionable young man with a carefully trimmed beard, foppish moustache and a ruff or *lechuguilla* calculated to reflect Lope's aspiration to the condition of nobility. Indeed, this image already shows that Lope thought status at least as important as likeness in his portrait. Although it lacks a caption [22], Lafuente has identified it definitively as being of Lope (pp. 32–33), and as the inspiration for several frontispiece engravings between 1598 and 1613: *Arcadia* (1598) [23], *Isidro* (1602) [24], *El peregrino en su patria* (1604) [25] and *Jerusalén conquistada* (1609) [26].

Unfortunately the woodcuts which derive from Pacheco's original are mediocre in quality, and three of them feature the notorious Carpio coat of arms, complete with its nineteen towers, an affectation which inevitably attracted the derision of contemporaries such as Góngora. Lope was of course to construe this mockery as a manifestation of the *envidia* intended to blight his phonemenal popular success — much of the impetus for his lifelong self-promotion being predicated upon resistance to his detractors. Nevertheless, the success of this series of images was relatively short-lived, to judge from the fact that 'Pacheco's Lope' has not been favoured by artists and editors in subsequent centuries, and only makes an isolated reappearance in 1804 in an image by Fonseca, in Pellicer's *Tratado histórico sobre el origen y progresos de la comedia y del histrionismo en España* [*Historical treatise on the origin and development of the theatre and acting in Spain*], which is clearly based on the *Isidro* image [28].

Commenting on the contrast between the more youthful and the more mature images, Portús nevertheless finds they have much in common:

[Lope] ha pasado de ser un joven elegante y un tanto arrogante a convertirse en clérigo maduro y algo escéptico. Sin embargo, existen varios y significativos puntos de contacto. Del escritor aparece invariablemente sólo su busto y no existen elementos que se refieran a su condición de hombre de letras. Lo que sí hay en casi todos los retratos son símbolos alusivos a su posición social —no siempre verdadera—, y así, mientras que los tres primeros están acompañados por un blasón que nos habla de sus pretensiones nobiliarias, en el que grabó Juan de Courbes se insiste de manera reiterativa en la posesión de la Cruz de Malta, que le concedió el Papa Urbano VIII y muestra colgada del pecho y cosida al hábito. Vemos, pues, que todas estas efigies tienen como común denominador el hecho de que eran ante todo testigos de la posición que el escritor ocupaba —o mejor dicho, que quería ocupar— en el orden social.[23]

---

[22] Francisco Pacheco, *Libro de descripción de verdaderos retratos de ilustres y memorables varones*, ed. Pedro M. Piñero Ramírez & Rogelio Reyes Cano (Seville: Diputación Provincial de Sevilla, 1985).

[23] Portús Pérez, *Pintura y pensamiento*, p. 166.

[Lope has gone from being an elegant and somewhat arrogant young man to a mature and rather sceptical cleric. Nevertheless, there exist several significant points in common. The image of the writer only ever takes the form of a bust and there are no elements referring to his status as a man of letters. What we do see however, in almost all of the portraits, are symbols alluding (not always accurately) to his social position. So, whereas the first three are accompanied by a coat of arms which reveals his pretensions to nobility, the one engraved by Jean de Courbes repeatedly insists on his possession of the Cross of Malta, conferred on him by Pope Urban VIII. This is shown hanging upon his chest and sewn upon his habit. We see, therefore, that all these depictions share the common denominator of being, primarily, evidence of the position that the writer occupied — or rather, wished to occupy — in the social order.]

It is difficult to be sure why the image of the youthful Lope remained unfamiliar until quite recently. It could be partly due to the fact that Pacheco's famous compendium of portraits, so often referred to nowadays, was broken up and consigned to oblivion until well into the nineteenth century. Even when it resurfaced, the frustrating lack of a caption for the image we now know to be Lope must have cast doubt on its identification, and may perhaps have dissuaded editors from using it. The insufficient quality of contemporaneous engravings that flowed from it could also have dissuaded artists of the time from taking inspiration from them. Perhaps Lope himself favoured a change of approach in his campaign for universal recognition, and approved the transition from foppish *caballero* to seasoned cleric — at least for public consumption — which characterised the development of his image for centuries afterwards.

V

Apart from the vagaries of accessibility, influence and popularity, many images of Lope have not come down to us simply because they have been lost. Kowal's resumé is useful here: apart from the portrait by Ribalta mentioned, he reports that Lope was first portrayed as an adolescent, and quotes Montalbán's description of him 'sentado en una silla, escribiendo en una mesa, rodeado de perros, monstruos, duendes, monos y otros animales, unos gesticulando, otros ladrando, y él escribiendo sin apercebirse de ellos' [sitting in a chair, writing at a table, surrounded by dogs, monsters, imps, monkeys and other animals, some gesticulating, others barking, and he writing without even noticing them]. The location of this portrait is unknown, the same fate that has befallen another effort, prior to 1602, by Pedro Guzmán el Cojo who, according to sonnet LXII of Lope's *Rimas*, depicted him crowned with laurel leaves. Another lost image dates from around 1624 in Madrid, from the hand of an otherwise unknown Florentine painter, Francesco Gianetti, who had been commissioned to paint Lope's portrait by the Neapolitan poet Giovanni Battista Marino (p. 256).

It may well be that some of these pictures will resurface at some stage, particularly when we have a good description of them, or when, as a product of archival work, existing images can be matched to Lope portraits. The search is, in fact, already underway for one of the most intriguing descriptions of missing Lope portraits. Jordan mentions an item listed in the post-mortem inventory of the collection of the Marqués de Leganés as 'un retrato de media bara en quadro, de medio cuerpo, Lope de Vega, de mano de Vanderhamen' [a portrait half a *vara* square, half length, Lope de Vega, by Vanderhamen].[24] Jordan links this picture to a portrait of Lope listed as number 58 in the post-mortem inventory of the artist himself (although all the pictures in this collection are assigned the same dimensions — three quarters of a *vara* high by half a *vara* wide). Jordan suggests that these two are 'the same or a similar portrait' (p. 166), and asks, in the light of this information, if it might have been the source of the Perret engraving:

> In the tercentenary of Lope's death, Enrique Lafuente Ferrari published a study of the known portraits of the great dramatist, which, although a bit dated today, has not been superseded in its conclusion that the most sensitive likeness of Lope is the engraving made in 1625 by the Antwerp engraver active in Spain, Pedro Perret. Neither Lafuente Ferrari nor anyone else in 1935 knew that Van der Hamen had portrayed Lope [...] It is not implausible that the engraving reflects Van der Hamen's lost portrait, but if it does not, it is almost certain that the artist's original must have been a painting at least as good as those others we can attribute to him. (pp. 166–67)

This may well be the case, and I would like to make a suggestion as to the portrait's possible location. There is a portrait that is at least equal in technical and psychological depth to the Perret engraving, and which has been in the Lilly Library, Indiana, for some years. The picture, apparently done in oil on canvas, measures 24 inches high by 20 inches wide,[25] and is attributed to Juan Carreño de Miranda (1614–85) with a dating of c. 1664 [29].[26]

What first strikes the viewer is its naturalism, together with the intense contrast of light and shadow. The dark unadorned background, a graduated series of deep browns, gives the face and figure immense physical presence, the black garb and

---

[24] William B. Jordan, *Juan van der Hamen y León and the Court of Madrid* (New Haven, CT & London: Yale University Press, 2005), p. 199.

[25] Attempts to align modern measurements with those of the seventeenth century are fraught with difficulty. This is typically because of vague and generalised estimates such as are apparent in the two inventories in question, where it is not stated either whether these include any frame. In *Un palacio para el rey: el Buen Retiro y la corte de Felipe IV* (Madrid: Taurus, 2003) Brown and Elliott define *vara* as 0.84 metres (p. 257), which comes out at 32.76 inches for purposes of the present discussion of the Lilly portrait. On the Brown/Elliott basis, three-quarters of a *vara* is 24.57 inches, half a *vara* is 16.38 inches, and third of a *vara* 10.92 inches. This would make the Lilly canvas measure just under three-quarters of a *vara* high, and slightly less than two-thirds of a *vara* wide.

[26] I wish here to express my grateful thanks to Professor Breon Mitchell and the staff of the Lilly Library at the University of Indiana for providing me with an excellent high-resolution digital image for examination. Further information on the portrait is limited: it was purchased by the bibliophile and benefactor J. K. Lilly from the Schneider-Gabriel Galleries, New York City, in September 1939 and exhibited at the Herron Gallery's *Portraits XVII to XIX Centuries from Indiana Collections* in 1945 (catalogue number 8). The portrait then came into the Lilly Library with J. K. Lilly's gift of books in 1954. Based on this data, inquiries by me into its provenance have to date proved fruitless.

cape allowing the spectacular falling ruff to illuminate the fresh youthful face of the subject, where the painter has achieved a remarkably luminous and smooth sense of the sitter's complexion. The eyes, pale and devoid of lashes, seem to derive from Dutch or Flemish pictorial conventions, and although the pose looks reminiscent of El Greco's *Caballero de la mano en el pecho* [*Gentleman with his hand on his breast*] of the previous century, here it is reversed, with the left hand placed over the breast.[27]

The identification of Lope as the subject certainly seems plausible: the hairline, moustache, beard, and facial proportions are in keeping with all the images so far discussed. Most crucially, they appear to duplicate exactly those of our most useful guide, the Perret engraving, whose modelling of the nose, lips and eyes is identical, as is the direction of the light source. In terms of the age of its subject, though, the Lilly portrait rather recalls the Pacheco drawing, with its upturned moustache and spirit of youthful vigour — a little tempered by the dark jacket and cape perhaps, but lifted by the exuberant ruff.

The Lilly dating, which has not been determined by scientific means, does of course fit with Carreño's career, and the idea that it might be a centenary commemorative portrait is an appealing one. Unfortunately, there is no record of the artist having undertaken such a project, and there is no signature on the front or information on the back of the canvas that might be of help (although it must be said that Carreño did not make a habit of signing his paintings). The major reservation in attributing it to him, however, is that its technique differs from that of his usual style, which is much more loose and free.

The smooth brushwork of the Lilly portrait, the way the light falls upon the face of the sitter, the pose, background and facial style, do on the other hand, recall several portraits done by Juan van der Hamen (1596–1631). The description of the portrait in the collection of the Marqués de Leganés as 'de medio cuerpo' [half length] would seem to fit. The drab backdrop was much favoured by him (and many other artists) for portraiture, but it is the creamy pallor of the subject's fair — almost Northern European — face that is most reminiscent of his other work. In some of his portraits, Van der Hamen seems to manipulate his light source so as to obliterate the lines of age. If one compares the youthful faces of the subjects of *Portrait of a Young Page* (1625–30, location now unknown) [30] and *Offering to Flora* (1627) [31] to that of one the artist's most important patrons, the more mature Jean de Croÿ, II Comte de Solre (1626) [32], one sees that the painter has managed to suffuse his sponsor's face with the same glow of early youth so visible in his juvenile sitters, without in any way obscuring the fact that he was at that time thirty-eight years of age (which is rather conveyed by his bulk and physical presence). It could of course be a coincidence, but Solre's face seems to

[27] The whole pose with the left hand across the breast (which is unusual) is an exact duplicate of that seen in Rembrandt's *Portrait of Johannes Wtenbogaert* from 1633 [27]. This image from the Rijksmuseum, Amsterdam, was drawn to my attention by my wife Yvonne. I am indebted to other members of my family also in the preparation of this chapter: to my brother Chris, who first informed me of the existence of the Lilly Library portrait; and to my son James for the bar front image of Lope [1].

be so similar to Lope's in the Lilly portrait that it looks as if they could have been painted by the same artist. Individual painting style can transmit this effect at times — even between subjects who do not, in reality, resemble each other. Thus we have faces that are unmistakably by Murillo, El Greco, Zurbarán and so on.

Obviously, caution needs to be exercised here. Although it is true that Van der Hamen was very much part of Lope's inner literary-artistic circle in the 1620s, Portús is no doubt correct in observing that the thirty-year age difference probably implies the absence of 'una amistad profunda entre ambos' [a deep friendship between the two] (p. 143). Portús nevertheless points out that in two sonnets Lope does comment appreciatively on the young artist's skill as a painter of flowers and of portraits, 'uno de los cuales tuvo precisamente como modelo al propio escritor' [one of which was actually of the writer himself] (p. 146).

With similar caution, one must bear in mind that although Van der Hamen has a Flemish name, it does not make him a Flemish painter. The son of a Flemish family that had emigrated in the late 1580s, he cut his artistic teeth, as Brown explains, studying Spanish and Flemish techniques alike for the still-lifes for which he is more particularly famous.[28] Jordan is also careful to dispel notions that the artist underwent 'an early formation in the "Flemish" manner followed by a gradual hispanicization', adding for good measure that he 'was at his core as deeply italianate an artist as most of his peers'. His suggestion is rather that Van der Hamen 'borrowed openly and enthusiastically from contemporary Flemish painting when it suited his clients' taste' (p. 24). In other words, he demonstrates that willingness to manipulate the likeness according to the sitters' wishes which was identified as a commonplace in Flemish portraits of the period at the beginning of this chapter. In any event, the capacity to render the glow of unblemished youth is plainly on display in the Lilly portrait.

The suggestion that the Lilly portrait may account for either or both of those mentioned in the Leganés and Van der Hamen post-mortem inventories can, of course, only be a tentative one. In questioning the attribution of the portrait, I am conscious that circumstantial evidence is just that, and far from conclusive.

The question of the falling ruff is also problematic. Although fashionable around the turn of the seventeenth century, it would have seemed anachronistic painted so much later by Van der Hamen during the years of his friendship with Lope. The tradition of depicting elderly subjects clad in the fashions of their younger days, as seen so often in Dutch painting, does not seem to apply here because Lope's face is so youthful. From this perspective, the Lilly portrait appears to be an attempt to capture a moment in the decade around 1600.

It would of course be useful to examine and date the portrait by scientific means. The quality of the portrait would certainly justify such technical work. If it can definitively be assigned to either Carreño (as a centenary commemorative piece?) or to Van der Hamen (as an affectionately retrospective tribute to an admired but rather vain friend?) then the effort will have been more than worth it. On the other hand, if it turns out to be a mocked-up version from eighteenth- or

---

[28] Jonathan Brown, *Painting in Spain 1500–1700* (New Haven, CT & London: Yale University Press, 1998), p. 114.

nineteenth-century hands, then it surpasses any of the contemporary rivals mentioned in this article, and can take its place among those images of the *Fénix* with which we began: a manufactured icon perhaps, but one of superior quality.

A Modern Day *Fénix*: Lope de Vega's Cinematic Revivals

DUNCAN WHEELER

Ever since Ramón Menéndez Pidal referred to a Lope play as a 'verdadero cinedrama' [genuinely cinematic drama],[1] commentators have persistently noted the cinematic quality of the *comedia*, with its rapid scene changes and prioritising of action over characterisation. Nonetheless, there is no real tradition, beyond the occasional one-off project, of filming Golden Age plays for the silver screen. Even if we resist the arguably unfair comparison with Shakespeare, the *comedia* lags behind other native Spanish literary works. As Peter W. Evans notes:

> There have been comparatively few adaptations of Golden-Age plays. Even in the 20s and in the 60s and in the early 70s when, for different historical reasons, the Spanish cinema was repeatedly turning to the country's literary heritage, film-makers were rarely inspired by the *comedia*.[2]

In the case of Lope de Vega, there have, to date, been the following cinematic adaptations: *Fuenteovejuna* (1947), *La moza de cántaro* (1953), *Fuenteovejuna* (1972), *La leyenda del alcalde de Zalamea* [*The Legend of the Mayor of Zalamea*] (1973), *El mejor alcalde, el rey* (1973), *El perro del hortelano* (1996) and, most recently, *La dama boba* (2006). With a total of seven screen appearances, there have been more films based on Lope's plays in Spain than of any other native seventeenth-century dramatist; nevertheless this popularity is only relative, and is placed in sharp relief when one considers that there have been ten adaptations of both *Don Quijote* and *Don Juan Tenorio*.[3] In this article, I will offer a brief history of the production and reception of these seven films, paying particular

---

[1] Ramón Menéndez Pidal, 'El Rey Rodrigo en la literatura', *Boletín de la Real Academia Española*, 11 (1924): 519–85 (p. 541).

[2] Peter W. Evans, *From Golden Age to Silver Screen: The Comedia on Film*, Papers in Spanish Theatre History, 5 (London: Department of Hispanic Studies, Queen Mary and Westfield College, 1997), p. 1.

[3] There have been various films of Calderón's works made abroad and there have been more screen adaptations of his plays than of Lope's in total. However, within Spain, Lope has a slight lead. For more details on all screen adaptations of the *comedia* see Ana Calvo Sastre, Lola Millás & Antonio Papell, *Literatura española: una historia de cine* (Madrid: Polifemo, 2005). This book, which provides an exhaustive catalogue of films based on Spanish literary works, has a chapter dedicated to film adaptations of Golden Age dramatic works (pp. 48–52).

attention to Antonio Román's *Fuenteovejuna,* Pilar Miró's *El perro del hortelano* and Manuel Iborra's *La dama boba.*[4]

Lope made his screen debut in 1935 with *La musa y el Fénix* [*The Muse and the Phoenix*], written by Eduardo G. Portillo and directed by the German filmmaker Constantin David. The film was a fictional recreation of the playwright's life and times rather than an adaptation of one of his works. It was another non-Spanish director, Jean Renoir, who then planned to make the first screen adaptation of a Lope play with *Fuenteovejuna* in the late 1930s, but the project ground to a halt when the Republicans began to lose the Civil War.

Fuenteovejuna is the fictional re-telling of a real-life historical event where the inhabitants of the eponymous town rose up against, and murdered, their overlord. In Lope's play, the revolt is a consequence of the abuses they suffer at the hands of the Comendador, Fernán Gómez; amongst other offences, he interrupts a wedding to kidnap the bride, Laurencia, and imprisons Frondoso, the groom. On the national level, Gómez's treachery and moral bankruptcy are indicated by his support for the opposition in a Civil War waged against the rightful heirs to the Spanish throne, Ferdinand and Isabella. Having killed the Comendador, the inhabitants of *Fuenteovejuna* want to be placed under the protectorate of the Catholic monarchs. Despite the political allegiance of the townspeople, this act of local insurgence cannot go unpunished and an investigation is undertaken at the personal behest of Ferdinand and Isabella. The town unanimously agrees to share responsibility for Gómez's murder, declares 'Fuenteovejuna lo hizo' [Fuenteovejuna did it], and remains united even in the face of torture. In an ambivalent ending, a lack of evidence forces the Catholic Monarchs to pardon, although not excuse, their actions.

From the advent of the Spanish Civil War, Golden Age literature, and the *comedia* in particular, performed an important role in the consolidation of Nationalist ideology.[5] Seventeenth-century literary works were often presented as the embodiment of a national spirit that had been corrupted and was therefore in need of forceful resuscitation. *Fuenteovejuna* very quickly became an emblematic work because it was felt to encapsulate precisely those values most in need of recuperation and, also, because it was seen to have been perverted through deviant productions in the Soviet Union and within Spain itself. Given its subject matter and iconic status, it is perhaps not surprising that *Fuenteovejuna* became the first *comedia* to be filmed in the dictatorship period. However, its contested legacy ensured a far from easy transition from page to screen. In 1942, Carlos Arévalo tried to direct a film version of the play and was even granted a shooting permit. Though the reasons as to why this film was never completed are unknown, Pepe Coira has suggested that it was probably due to the regime's known aversion to

---

[4] I would like to thank the Filmoteca in Madrid, especially Trinidad del Río, for their help in enabling me to view these adaptations.

[5] For a detailed analysis of the production and reception of the *comedia* in recent times, see Duncan Wheeler, 'The Performance History of Golden-Age Drama in Spain (1939–2006)', *Bulletin of the Comediantes*, 60.2 (2008) (forthcoming).

overly authoritarian plots at the end of the Second World War and their lack of trust in the director to deal with such sensitive material.[6]

Three years after the collapse of Arévalo's project, Antonio Román voiced an interest in filming a high-budget screen version of *Fuenteovejuna*. As far as the establishment of the time was concerned, Román was a far safer director; he had been a scriptwriter on the infamous *Raza* [*Race*] (1941), written by Franco as an idealistic retelling of his own life, and his most recent film had been the hugely patriotic, and successful, *Los últimos de Filipinas* [*The Last Ones in the Philippines*] (1945). His screenwriter, José María Pemán, was also a stalwart of the regime, and the film obtained its shooting permit in August 1946.

Román made every effort to ensure that the film was ideologically sound and this is reflected in his choice of three advisors: Major General Luis Bermúdez de Castro gave counsel on military matters; Father Antonio Figora on religious matters; and Cayetano Luca de Tena, director of the Teatro Español, on locations and sets. *Fuenteovejuna* was awarded the category of 'national interest' by the state administration,[7] although the state censor did object both to Laurencia's use of the term 'maricones' [queers] (it was replaced by 'maritones' [pansies]) and to the original ending where the townspeople and their monarchs march into Portugal in a bellicose manner (this was simply cut from the film).[8] This level of official support, the fact that the film had the largest set ever erected for a national production, Román's reputation, and a famous cast (in particular Amparo Rivelles, popularly known as Amparito, one of the most popular Spanish actresses of the 1940s), ensured prominent media coverage.

The film itself, though enjoyable, is hardly subtle; Román's biographer claims that it is the director's most overtly political film.[9] There are scenes, early in the film, not present in Lope's play-text, of a local priest criticising Fernán Gómez's behaviour; the *Comendador* does not appreciate this polite admonishment and rather melodramatically smashes the communion chalice. The Catholic Monarchs are idealised to a degree not even intimated by Lope; when Ferdinand doubts whether they can go to *Fuenteovejuna* because of the weather, Isabella stands firm, claiming: 'No hay justicia de tiempo seco y justicia de tiempo de agua. Más pronto corre el mal ejemplo que las nubes' [There is not justice for dry weather and justice for wet weather. Bad habits travel faster than clouds]. On hearing the inhabitants' stories, there is not the pragmatic acquiescence of the play-text but a maternal sigh of 'Pobre gente' [poor people] followed by shots of mass

---

[6] Pepe Coira, *Antonio Román: un cineasta de la posguerra* (Madrid: Editorial Complutense, 2004), p. 118.

[7] This category, introduced in 1944, optimised the chances of success for a film that was looked on favourably by the regime. A film awarded this category was booked into the best theatres and was premiered during the most favourable seasons, and exhibitors were obliged to continue showing the film as long as film attendance was, on a weekly basis, over fifty per cent of the theatre's capacity.

[8] The censorship files for films produced during this period are available for consultation at the Archivo General de la Comunidad in Alcalá de Henares. The box numbers for *Fuenteovejuna* are 36/03317 and 36/03299.

[9] Coira, *Antonio Román*, p. xiv.

celebration as the monarchs pass through *Fuenteovejuna*. The film also avoids the darker elements of the play, as the torture scenes and most of Laurencia's famous diatribe against the town's men are removed. Furthermore, Laurencia (Rivelles) is able to escape from the *Comendador*; she bites him and then jumps into the river below. This quintessentially Spanish actress functions here as a kind of metonym for the heroic value inherent in the work as a whole; self-abnegation through death is construed as more honourable than violation. Not surprisingly, Laurencia survives the perilous escape, thus providing an ideal pretext to show *Amparito* in revealingly wet attire whilst remaining within the realms of moral propriety.

Still from Antonio Román's *Fuenteovejuna* (1947)

The shooting of the film was plagued by bad weather and there were persistent rumours of financial difficulties. *Fuenteovejuna* was eventually premiered in a gala presentation in Burgos on 10 October 1947, and then opened in Madrid on 20 November at the Cine Coliseum. Although a few reviewers were disappointed, and quite justifiably so, by the heavily hyped set design, the film was very well received by critics. From the pages of *Primer Plano*, López Rubio spoke of the film as 'uno de los mayores éxitos del cine español' [one of the greatest successes of Spanish cinema] and 'este gran esfuerzo de nuestro cine' [this great effort of our cinema],[10] whilst Gómez Tello praised the work for projecting, with sincerity and panache, Lope's original vision: 'Un pueblo entrañable, vigorosa, con una

---

[10] López Rubio, José, '*Fuenteovejuna* ovacionada', *Primer Plano*, 23 November 1947: 4.

convincente frontera de su orgullo y su justicia y con un sentimiento de fidelidad que —¡ay!— era lo que se torcía en unas versiones teatrales mugrientas y tumultuosas de las que más vale no acordarse' [A close and resolute community that presents a convincing front of pride and justice with a sense of fidelity that, alas, was precisely that which was perverted in some repulsive and unruly theatrical versions that we would do better to forget].[11] Furthermore, the Diplomatic Office used multiple stills from the film in a 1949 document produced to encourage foreign investment in the Spanish Film Industry, alongside the proud boast that 'For this type of picture — which may be produced with whatever pomp may be desired — Spain is a fountain of dazzling inspiration'.[12] However, in spite of this, *Fuenteovejuna* was the first of Román's films not to be awarded a prize by the Sindicato Nacional Español and it was a commercial disappointment that caused financial ruin in the director's production company, Alhambra. Nonetheless, the film has remained part of the popular imagination and when Román died in 1989, most obituaries made specific references to *Fuenteovejuna*, despite the fact that he had directed over thirty works.

Lope's next foray onto the silver screen was in Florián Rey's *La moza de cántaro*.[13] Rey, director of the landmark film *La aldea maldita* [*The Cursed Village*] (1930), is arguably the most important Spanish director of the silent era. He worked as a filmmaker in Nazi Germany and then returned to Spain to try and help rebuild the Spanish film industry. However, by this stage he was already past his prime, and he specialised in *españoladas* that delighted in the kind of kitsch and sentimental images of Spain that Berlanga was to parody in *Bienvenido Mister Marshall* [*Welcome, Mr Marshall*] (1953). Rey's version of Lope's play fits firmly into this tradition and featured the very popular singer, Paquita Rico, whose strong vocal chords were not matched by her acting skills. The film had a relatively high budget for the time and, prior to its release in Spain, enjoyed success in Argentina and Italy. This financial investment in a national production alongside foreign success allowed the producers to argue successfully that the censor's original category of *interés B* ought to be elevated to *interés A,* and the film was also awarded the category of 'national interest'.[14]

Rico's celebrity status and appeal amongst lower-class audiences was seen to be crucial to the film's appeal. According to the trade magazine *Cine Asesor*: 'el anuncio de este film despertará expectación y su estreno se esperará con interés, máxime si se exhibe antes algún traylers que, al recoger las canciones de la

[11] Gómez Tello, José Luis, '*Fuenteovejuna*' (review), *Primer Plano*, 23 November 1947: 23.

[12] Diplomatic Information Office, *The Spanish Cinema* (Madrid: Diplomatic Information Office, 1949), p. 14.

[13] In 1951 the Falangist director José Antonio Nieves had attempted to direct a cinematic adaptation of *La estrella de Sevilla* (sometimes attributed to Lope). However, the project was prohibited by the Spanish censor; they objected to it on the basis of its supposed anti-monarchical sentiments. However, this was not the first time that Nieves had had problems with the censor. The prohibition was probably a consequence of their antipathy to the director, rather than a genuine objection to the play. See Román Gubern, *La censura: función política y ordenamiento jurídico bajo el franquismo (1936–1975)* (Barcelona: Ediciones Península, 1981), p. 131.

[14] Box no. 36/03460 in the Archivo General.

protagonista, aumentarán el deseo de verlo' [the announcement of this film will generate expectation and its release will be anticipated with interest, especially if trailers are screened in advance featuring songs by the protagonist, which will increase the public's desire to see it].[15] However, the commentator qualifies these remarks by observing that 'la película en sí no es una obra de arte' [the film, in itself, is not a work of art], and it is difficult to disagree with this assessment. The film lacks any dramatic coherence or depth and is structured so as to allow Rico to burst into song on the flimsiest pretext. Rey eschews the more complex and dark aspects of Lope's play-text, which tells the story of Doña María, who kills a man to defend her father's honour and then is forced to disguise herself as a peasant girl, Isabel, to escape recriminations. For example, the sexual aggression María suffers when disguised as a servant is shrouded in risible farce. Furthermore, the melodramatic aspects of the plot are exaggerated beyond any reasonable grounds of credulity. María/Isabel's beauty is such that the King, Felipe IV, falls in love with her. He visits Isabel at night and says that when a king is in love, he wants to be thought of not as a king but as a suitor. Isabel then reveals her true noble identity and Felipe says that her father was correct to have described her, earlier in the film, as 'la más bella flor de Andalucía' [Andalusia's most beautiful flower]. At this point, María/Isabel's suitor, Don Juan, crashes through the window intent on challenging the King. Once informed of Felipe's true identity, however, Juan goes down on one knee and says how he loves María. Felipe asks María if this love is reciprocated, and on hearing that it is, he graciously relinquishes his role as a suitor and judiciously acts as a king, saying that they will marry and that he will be the best man. This then provides the perfect opportunity for a celebratory and mawkish final wedding scene.

Not only was the film an artistic failure but it failed to live up to its commercial promise. According to the Filmoteca's (admittedly not always reliable) statistics, only one hundred and fifty-nine tickets were sold for this film with a total gross of twenty-five euros and seventy-four cents.[16] Even if this figure is not completely reliable, it is certain that the film's theatrical release in Madrid only lasted ten days. Given this disastrous showing, it is perhaps not surprising that Rey would soon leave filmmaking to open a bar in Benidorm, and that it would be nearly twenty years until Lope would return to the big screen.

In the early 1970s, Televisión Española produced two versions of *comedias* designed to increase awareness of Golden Age drama both in Spain and abroad: Juan Guerrero Zamora's *Fuenteovejuna* and Mario Camus's *La leyenda del alcalde de Zalamea*. Both were produced primarily for television but were also given theatrical releases. The two films can be seen as responses, or even corrections, to earlier screen adaptations. At this time, Román's *Fuenteovejuna* and José G. Maesso's version of Calderón's *El alcalde de Zalamea* (1953) were both the best-known and most propagandistic films based on the *comedia*.

---

[15] Anon., '*La moza de cántaro*' (review), *Cine Asesor*, no. 615 (1954): unpaginated.

[16] The Filmoteca's box-office statistics are available on-line at http://www.mcu.es and are quoted in euros.

Guerrero Zamora's updating of *Fuenteovejuna* performed respectably at the box-office but was markedly less successful in other respects. The film is too long, and, in sharp contrast to Román's film, not only refuses to eschew violence but clumsily foregrounds even the most latent hint of aggression in Lope's play-text. For example, there are extended torture scenes and we see the *Comendador* rape three women: María, Marcela and Manuela.[17] The censor objected to some of the more explicit content and ordered some serious cuts; Guerrero Zamora was sufficiently offended not to attend the film's premiere. The director explicitly stated that he had a political motive in making the film: '[...] propuse *Fuenteovejuna*. ¿Por qué? Implicaba una gran trascendencia social su contenido, que además no suelen tener las obras clásicas' [I suggested *Fuenteovejuna*. Why? Because its content is of great social significance and, furthermore, this is not typical of classic works].[18] This version focuses on the social and psychic effects of a community ruled by fear, but any political aim is undermined by aesthetic shortcomings that were characterised by many critics as 'mera falta de oficio cinematográfica' [a basic lack of cinematic competence].[19] Most reviews criticised the use of verse, but the fact that this would not be seen as problematic in Camus's film suggests that the problem was less in the verse itself that its application. In *Fuenteovejuna* it ruthlessly exposes the limitations of most of the cast, and technical ineptitude prevents the director from applying restraint to the risible theatrics on display.

Mario Camus has a reputation as being both a serious and a left-wing filmmaker. *La leyenda del alcalde de Zalamea* marked the first time that the potential complexities of a Golden Age text had been brought to life on the silver screen. Camus uses a combination of Lope and Calderón's versions of the story to forge a vision that focuses heavily on both the abuse of power and the actions of the military, thereby refusing to offer anodyne dramatic closure. This new approach to the *comedia* on screen is reflected in the choice of casting; whilst Maesso's film had starred Alfredo Mayo, 'el galán español por antonomasia, que igual servía para Pedro Crespo que para capitán de los Tercios' [the Spanish matinee idol par excellence, as well suited for the role of Pedro Crespo as he was for a military captain],[20] Camus cast Francisco Rabal and Fernando Fernán Gómez (the former known for his work with Buñuel, the latter in works that formed part of the Nuevo Cine Español [New Spanish Cinema] movement) as Crespo and Don Lope respectively. The film exceeded expectations and was a commercial and critical success; it also became the first TVE production ever to be broadcast on French and Italian state television. This came as much as a

---

[17] Thomas Austin O'Connor has written an excellent article on the changes that Guerrero Zamora has made to Lope's play text; see his 'Culpabilidad, expiación y reconciliación en la versión de *Fuenteovejuna* filmada por Juan Guerrero Zamora', in *Hispanic Essays in Honor of Frank P. Casa*, ed. A. Robert Lauer & Henry W. Sullivan, Ibérica, 20 (New York: Peter Lang, 1997), pp. 122–31.

[18] Mery Caravajal, 'Entrevista con Juan Guerrero Zamora', *Pueblo*, 20 November 1972: 35.

[19] Alfonso Sánchez, '*Fuenteovejuna*' (review), *Informaciones*, 30 November 1972: 31.

[20] M. A. Bastenier, '*El alcalde de Zalamea*: Calderón no era culpable', *El País*, 13 May 1983: 36.

surprise to Camus as to anyone: 'Lo hice para televisión y no pensé que pudiera tener el éxito que está teniendo' [I did it for television, and it never occurred to me that it would be so successful].[21]

In 1973, Rafael Gil directed a Spanish-Italian co-production of *El mejor alcalde, el rey* based on a script adapted by José López Rubio, a previous recipient of the Premio Nacional de Teatro [National Theatre Prize]. Lope's play contrasts the lives of noble peasants, Sancho and Elvira, and their honourable courtship with a lascivious and despotic overlord, Don Tello, who kidnaps Elvira before her wedding can take place; unlike *Fuenteovejuna*, where the villagers collectively take their revenge, retributive justice is here administered by the King in person. Gil is often thought of as the quintessential Francoist filmmaker; he received more national prizes from the regime than any other director, and at the time of his death in 1986 he was planning to make a film of the dictator's life. Nevertheless, these facts ought not to detract from his artistic achievements. He made over fifty films, his 1947 adaptation of *Don Quijote* is thought by many to be the best screen adaptation of Cervantes's novel, and his version of Lope's play is accomplished and well acted. The film was a modest commercial success and was well received by critics, who commended López Rubio's adaptation for the 'la actualización de los diálogos, de los que se ha eliminado el empaque literario' [the modernisation of the dialogue, from which all literary excess has been shed],[22] whilst also praising 'la corrección en la factura técnica de un veterano y equilibrado profesional que conoce muy bien su oficio' [the technical prowess of a veteran and well-grounded professional who knows his trade very well].[23]

In line with the trend of other Spanish literary adaptations of the early 70s, and in contrast to adaptations of the *comedia* from the 40s and 50s, *El mejor alcalde, el rey* foregrounds the sexual and violent aspects of the play. The film was classified, as were all the *comedia* adaptations of the period, as being suitable only for patrons over the age of eighteen, or over the age of fourteen if accompanied by an adult. This restrictive rating was at odds with the principles that underpinned these projects as attempts to increase awareness and knowledge of Spain's cultural patrimony; as one of the censors wrote in his report on *El mejor alcalde, el rey*, 'aunque hubiese sido mi deseo darla para 14 y menores' [though I would have liked to classify the film as suitable for 14 and under], this proved impossible, 'dado que está hecho de manera bastante tosca y la personalidad del Conde es tan barbara y cruel' [given that it is shot in a rather crude tone and the Count's character is so barbaric and cruel].[24]

Rey's film is visually reminiscent of Roman Polanski's controversial film adaptation of *Macbeth* (1971), which had recently enjoyed great success in Spain. Tello's castle is presented as a decadent den of iniquity, and his moral depravity is indicated through his grotesque and uncontrolled carnality. Early on, the film cuts

[21] Jesús María Santos, 'Entrevista con Mario Camus, director cinematográfico', *El Adelanto*, 3 August 1973: 12.

[22] Alfonso Sánchez, '*El mejor alcalde, el rey*' (review), *Informaciones*, 30 April 1974: 37.

[23] Florentino Soria, '*El mejor alcalde, el rey*' (review), *Arriba*, 6 May 1974: 22.

[24] Box no. 36/04445 in the Archivo General.

from an idyllic village scene to a banquet of Bacchanalian excess where Tello unceremoniously gorges on food and drink; later on, the camera lingers on the greasy and fleshy contours of his body as he washes. An incestuous subtext is introduced between Tello and his sister, Feliciana, who also shows a sexual interest in Sancho. Whilst Tello lusts after Elvira, he gives Feliciana permission to have sex with Sancho who is, at the time, being tortured. Following some explicit torture scenes, a sub-plot, not present in the play-text, is introduced where Feliciana comes to Sancho's rescue and rather fetishistically tends his wounds. She then goes to kiss him, but is sharply rebuked as Sancho strangles her. The scene where Elvira is violated is also depicted in graphic detail as, although the camera cuts away before the actual rape can take place, there is a long scene where we see Tello ripping off her clothes and then reporting to his sister that 'No me importa que llore. Estoy acostumbrado' [It doesn't bother me that she cried. I'm used to it].

After *El mejor alcalde, el rey*, it would be over twenty years before another director would direct a film based on one of Lope's plays. In fact, in the interim Spain did not produce a single film based on the *comedia* at all. This was most probably a consequence of the fact that, in the transition period, Golden Age drama was often thought of as a reactionary art-form that had enjoyed special treatment under Franco. There were three primary factors that helped resurrect the *Fénix* in *El perro del hortelano*.[25] First the success of the Compañía Nacional de Teatro Clásico (CNTC), formed in 1986, had raised awareness and interest in Spanish classical drama. Secondly, the success of Kenneth Branagh's *Much Ado about Nothing* (1993) and Jean-Paul Rappeneau's *Cyrano de Bergerac* (1990), especially amongst young people, had proven that there might be an audience for this kind of film adaptation. The third and, probably, decisive factor was the formidable and tenacious nature of the film's director, Pilar Miró.[26]

By the time she made *El perro del hortelano*, Miró had directed a series of classic works for the small screen, and had worked for the CNTC (as had screenwriter Rafael Pérez Sierra, costume designer Pedro Moreno, and lead actor Carmelo Gómez). Though lacking a substantial tradition in her homeland, Shakespeare adaptations provided Miró with inspiration and confidence. In an article in *El Mundo*, Miró reminisced on the formative impression left by Renato Castellani's *Romeo and Juliet* (1954), the first Shakespeare adaptation she had ever seen, and the importance of other adaptations by Orson Welles and Branagh.[27] Her appreciation of these productions created in her an acute case of 'Shakespeare envy'. She argued elsewhere that 'no valoramos lo que tenemos' [we do not value what we have] and that whilst 'nadie se extraña cuando se adapta

---

[25] This was not the first time that *El perro del hortelano* had been filmed. In 1977, the Soviet director Yan Frid directed a Russian-language version of the play, *Sobaka na sene*, for television.

[26] Alongside her impressive resumé of successful and often controversial films — *Gary Cooper, que estás en los cielos* [Gary Cooper who art in Heaven] (1980), *El crimen de Cuenca* [The Cuenca Crime] (1981) — the director had previously been Director-General of Film and had passed the controversial Miró Law, which focused state investment on a small number of 'quality' films in the early 1980s.

[27] Pilar Miró, 'Síntomas de envidia', *El Mundo*, supplement ('La Esfera'), 25 January 1997: 2.

a Shakespeare [...] todo el mundo se sorprendió cuando pensamos llevar al cine a Lope de Vega' [nobody bats an eyelid when Shakespeare is adapted but everyone was surprised when we thought of bringing Lope to Vega to the big screen], arguing that 'si esta película no se ha rodado antes es porque somos demasiados críticos con lo nuestro' [the reason that this film has not been shot before is that we are too critical of our own patrimony].[28] In light of this observation, it is rather ironic that there seems to be no record of Miró referring to previous film adaptations of the *comedia*, whilst Pérez Sierra tried actively to distance the film from what he termed 'aquellas versiones vulgarizadas de los dramas de Lope y Calderón' [those dumbed-down versions of Lope and Calderón's dramas].[29] This cultural amnesia was also reflected in the film's press coverage, which claimed, incorrectly, that this was the first *comedia* adaptation to be rendered in verse.[30]

Raising money for the film was an uphill struggle, but eventually, with ministerial support, contracts with television channels, distribution advances, and bank subsidies, the producer, Carlos Ramón, was able to raise the film's budget of 271 million pesetas and filming commenced in Portugal in June 1995. However, five weeks into the shoot, Ramón went bankrupt due primarily to his lack of experience as a producer and the financiers' scepticism over whether audiences would pay to go and see a *comedia* in verse. The Portuguese crew harboured fears that they would never be paid and decided to take the film's costumes as insurance. Following some anxious negotiating, the thought that a film facing bankruptcy would have an adverse effect on future productions in Portugal led three of the largest producers in Spanish cinema (Enrique Cerezo, PC; Lola Films; and Cartel) to invest in the project and shooting resumed in August 1995.

Even when completed, the film faced further problems when it was not chosen as part of the official selection in the 1996 San Sebastian Film Festival. However, *El perro del hortelano* was shown out of competition on a large screen where, according to Diego Galán, most critics did not even bother to attend, but nonetheless 'tuvo una gran acogida. El público siguió el verso con interés y coronó la proyección con una ovación cerrada' [it was very well received. The audience followed the verse with interest and, at the end, gave the film a standing ovation].[31] Present at the screening were the curators of the Argentine Mar de Plata Festival, who chose to screen the film, which ultimately won the highest prize, the Ombú de Oro. Only once the film had secured this foreign accolade did

---

[28] Manuel Montero, 'Miró: "Despreciamos nuestra cultura"', *El Periódico*, 26 November 1996: 58.

[29] Rafael Pérez Sierra, 'Versión cinematográfica de *El perro del hortelano*', in *Lope de Vega: comedia urbana y comedia palatina: Actas de las XVIII Jornadas de Teatro Clásico, Almagro, 11, 12 y 13 de julio de 1995*, ed. Felipe B. Pedraza Jiménez & Rafael González Cañal (Almagro: Universidad de Castilla la Mancha, 1996), pp. 107–14 (p. 108).

[30] Miró did nevertheless pay more attention to verse than any other director has. The three lead actors had an intensive training course with verse coach Alicia Hermida before shooting began. This level of rehearsal is very unusual; ten years later, Hermida would have only 15 days to train the actors in preparation for *La dama boba*; interview by Duncan Wheeler with Alicia Hermida (conducted in Madrid, 16 September 2007).

[31] Diego Galán, *Pilar Miró: nadie me enseñó a vivir*, (Barcelona: Plaza & Janés, 2006), p. 383.

it receive a release date at home. Due largely to Miró's status amongst Spain's cultural elite, the film's domestic release in November 1996 was a veritable media feast. José María Aznar held a lunch for the director and the actors, whilst Don Juan Carlos, a personal friend of Miró, attended the premiere.

Still from Pilar Miró's 1996 film

Now that it had finally been released, *El perro del hortelano* achieved the rare feat of charming critics and audiences alike. It was the ninth most successful film at the Spanish box-office in 1996 and the sixth most successful in 1997, ultimately grossing over three million euros. In addition, it won a series of high-profile awards, including seven Goyas. Reviewers heaped praise not only on the work itself but also on its cultural significance as a film that presented a Golden Age play to a mainstream audience, thereby establishing a precedent for future adaptations. Alberto Bermejo spoke in *El Mundo* of how 'No cabe duda de que *El perro del hortelano* sienta un precedente importante en el panorama del cine español' [There can be no doubt that *El perro del hortelano* establishes an important precedent within the context of Spanish cinema],[32] and Miguel García-Posada argued in *El País* that 'es el encuentro de los clásicos y del cine auténticamente moderno. Se abren, pues, unas expectativas nuevas, un horizonte que creíamos clausurado para siempre' [it is the coming together of the classics and genuinely modern cinema. It therefore opens new horizons of a kind that we

---

[32] Alberto Bermejo, 'Fiel, sobria y brillante', review of *El perro del hortelano*, *El Mundo*, 25 January 1997: 3.

thought would remain forever closed].[33] The review from *La Vanguardia* was even more effusive: 'se puede afirmar que a Pilar Miró le ha salido una película no sólo inhabitual para la historia del cine español, sino, sobre todo, gratificantemente gozosa para la vista, oído, y en suma, la salud física y mental del espectador' [one can safely say that Pilar Miró has produced a film that is not only unusual within the history of Spanish cinema but is, above all else, pleasing on the eye and ear is, in overall terms, conducive to the viewer's physical and mental well-being].[34] Whilst there is an element of hyperbole in such appraisals, the film is undeniably a triumph. It has excellent production values, is visually stunning and features outstanding performances from Emma Suárez, Carmelo Gómez and Ana Duarto.

Though the script remains relatively faithful to Lope's verse, Miró uses cinematic devices to deliver a romantic comedy that is far removed from the 'dark comedy' of the play text.[35] As I have argued elsewhere:

> costume functions alongside other semiotic systems (mise-en-scène, star presence, choice of scenes, music) to transfer attention away from the axes of class to gender divides. This transferral ensures that a narrative of desire, repression and evasion is assimilated into the world of romance, a place where quotidian impediments are kept at bay.[36]

Whilst, as Evans rightly observes, a film of this type, 'with its own codes, both cinematic and non-cinematic, may be regarded not as a violation but as a selective

---

[33] Miguel García-Posada, 'Un perro muy particular' (review of *El perro del hortalano*), *El País*, 6 February 1997: 32.

[34] Diego Muñón, '¿Quién sabe lo que quiere el público?', *La Vanguardia*, 26 November 1996: 23.

[35] Edward M. Wilson & Duncan Moir, *A Literary History of Spain: The Golden Age: Drama, 1492–1700* (London: Ernest Benn, 1971), p. 52.

[36] Duncan Wheeler, '*We Are Living in a Material World and I Am a Material Girl*: Diana, Countess of Belflor Materialised on the Page, Stage and Screen', *Bulletin of Hispanic Studies*, 84.3 (2007): 267–86 (p. 277). I have refrained from discussing the film's artistic merits in detail in this chapter because there are already various studies that offer detailed readings of the film. In addition to my own article, see Mark Allison, 'Pilar Miró's Last Two Films: History, Adaptation and Genre', in *Spanish Cinema: Calling the Shots*, ed. Rob Rix & Roberto Rodríguez-Saona (Leeds: Trinity and All Saints, 1999), pp. 33–45; María José Alonso Veloso, '*El perro del hortelano*, de Pilar Miró: una adaptación no tan fiel de la comedia de Lope de Vega', *Signa: Revista de la Asociación Española de Semiótica*, 10 (2001): 375–93; Elaine Canning, '"Not I, My Shadow": Pilar Miró's Adaptation of Lope de Vega's *The Dog in the Manger* (1996)', *Studies in European Cinema*, 2.2 (2005): 81–92; Esther Fernández & Cristina Martínez-Carazo, 'Mirar y desear: la construcción del personaje femenino en *El perro del hortelano* de Lope de Vega y de Pilar Miró', *Bulletin of Spanish Studies*, 83.3 (2006): 315–28; Enrique García Santo-Tomás, 'Diana, Lope, Pilar Miró: horizontes y resistencias de clausura en *El perro del hortelano*', in *'Otro Lope no ha de haber': atti del Convegno Internazionale su Lope de Vega, 10–13 febbraio 1999*, ed. M. G. Profeti, 3 vols (Florence: Alinea, 2000), II, pp. 51–61; Antonio Jaime, *Literatura y cine en España (1975–1995)*, Signo e Imagen, 61 (Madrid: Cátedra, 2000), pp. 210–31; María del Mar Mañas Martínez, 'Reflexiones sobre *El perro del hortelano* de Pilar Miró', *Dicenda: Cuadernos de Filología Hispánica*, 21 (2003): 139–56; Juan Antonio Pérez Millán, *Pilar Miró: directora de cine*, 2nd ed., expanded and updated (Madrid: Ediciones Calamares, 2007), pp. 247–70.

interpretation of the original' (p. 2), the result in this case is that this adaptation 'tendrá más de testamento cinematográfico de Pilar Miró que de comedia palatina de Lope de Vega' [will be remembered more as a Pilar Miró film than as a palace comedy by Lope de Vega].[37] Along with Miró's high profile in Spain, this change in emphasis has ensured that the film has been over-identified with the director at the expense of the playwright. This fact helps to explain why, given the film industry's obsession with box office returns and the desire to create products of a kind that have a proven track record, *El perro del hortelano* failed to establish a precedent; another decade would pass before Lope received a further cinematic makeover.[38]

At the time of writing, Manuel Iborra's *La dama boba* is the most recent addition to the select canon of films based on the *comedia*. It was theatre director Miguel Narros who first suggested that Iborra ought to film a version of Lope's play, as it dealt inventively and beautifully with the perennial subject of his work: love. In his screenplay, Iborra was determined to retain Lope's verse but to jettison what he considered to be the more erudite and pedantic aspects of the play-text in order to focus on the central love-story between Finea and Laurencio that would provide the basis for a film that he hoped would be 'suavemente teatral' [lightly theatrical].[39]

Although Miró's film had failed to establish a precedent, it still constitutes the benchmark against which all other adaptations will be judged; hence the publicity surrounding the film foregrounds the connection with *El perro del hortelano*, and most reviewers have compared the two works. Like Miró, Iborra also had a feeling of cultural belatedness and comments he made at the film's premiere at the Malaga Film Festival in March 2006 were almost verbatim copies of the kind of observations that she had made ten years earlier:

> Sería maravilloso que esta película sirviera para que todos los años pudiéramos hacer uno o dos filmes sobre Lope, Calderón o Zorrilla ... a todos nos gusta ver las películas de Shakespeare que hacen los ingleses, pero es que nosotros tenemos clásicos y textos maravillosos que se deberían hacer, y no estaría mal que se convirtiera en un hábito.[40]

> [It would be marvellous if this film served as an impetus for us to make one or two films every year based on the works of Lope, Calderón or Zorrilla... all of us enjoy seeing the Shakespeare adaptations that the English produce, but we also have classics and texts that ought to be filmed, and it would no bad thing if this were to become a habit.]

---

[37] Enrique García Santo-Tomás, *La creación del Fénix: recepción crítica y formación canónica del teatro de Lope de Vega* (Madrid: Gredos, 2000), p. 390.

[38] At the time of her death in 1997, Miró was planning to direct a film version of Lope's *El castigo sin venganza*, but it was not to be.

[39] Interview by Duncan Wheeler with Manuel Iborra (conducted in Madrid, 15 May 2007).

[40] José María Camacho, '*La dama boba*, el cine en verso', *ABC*, 24 March 2006: 34.

This desire was shared by Televisión Española, who provided fifty per cent of the budget as part of a proposed plan to provide funding to bring a Spanish classic to the silver screen once a year.[41] Iborra is a popular and well-respected film and television director and *La dama boba* features a powerhouse cast including Silvia Abascal, José Coronado and Verónica Forqué. Initially, the film's prospects seemed positive. It won a series of high-profile awards at the Malaga Film Festival,[42] received a healthy amount of media exposure and advertising, and was shown on some of the most high-profile screens in the country.

In artistic terms, Iborra's work is arguably the most successful film version of a *comedia* ever made. The standard of performance is good, with the actors working well as an ensemble cast and employing a very physical form of acting to bring the comic brio of Lope's verse to life. The setting and costumes create a series of appetising visual tableaux, and the film employs the camera judiciously to focus on the facial expressions of the different actors, thus allowing for the kind of intimacy that would be difficult to achieve in a large theatre. Iborra exploits the visual potential of the cinematic medium to cut many superfluous lines and, in my opinion, brings scenes to life in a far more inventive and vivacious manner than any previous adaptation has achieved.

Lope's play tells the story of two sisters, one a bluestocking (Nise) and the other an idiot (Finea), who discover, through love, the means through which to shed their respective excesses: pedantry and stupidity. If the film has a weakness, it is that it is rather one-dimensional in its focus on the comic aspects of the play. For example, the replacement of the father, Octavio, with a hysterical mother removes both intimacy and any real sense of paternal threat; similarly, in Lope's play-text, Laurencio is initially attracted to Finea for pecuniary reasons but the film skirts around these more cynical motivations. Modern-day cinema audiences are accustomed to a more hybrid approach to genre and straight comedy can come across as rather old-fashioned; this impression is bolstered by the casting of Coronado who, as Chris Perriam has noted, 'must be the epitome of the old-style leading man to a significant segment of the audience'.[43] This sense of cultural anachronism was a source of antagonism in most reviews, which generally ranged from the lukewarm to the cautiously positive. The critic from *El País* spoke of 'una ambientación muy cómoda, pero de andar por casa' [a very pedestrian and unchallenging mise-en-scène],[44] whilst Javi Vara complained in *Cinemanía* of how 'podría haberse hecho hace 20 años en el mal sentido de la hipótesis' [it is no compliment to say that this film could have been made 20 years ago].[45]

If *La dama boba* has not been an unqualified success with the critics, then it has proven even less popular with audiences. Whatever we take as our point of

---

[41] At the time of writing, it is not clear whether TVE will continue with this plan or not.

[42] Silvia Abascal won the prize for best actress; Lorenzo Caprile for best costume design; and Macarena Gómez and Roberto San Martín for best actors in a supporting role.

[43] Chris Perriam, *Stars and Masculinities in Spanish Cinema: From Banderas to Bardem* (Oxford: Oxford University Press, 2003), p. 201.

[44] Mirito Torreiro, 'A vueltas con el amor' (review of *La dama boba*), *El País*, 24 March 2006: 37.

[45] '*La dama boba*' (review), *Cinemanía*, April 2006: 119.

comparison (Shakespeare adaptations, the director's previous films, adaptations of Spanish literary works, comedies in general), the film has not been a commercial success. Prior to its release, Spain's best-selling film magazine, *Fotogramas*, spoke of 'El loable riesgo de Manuel Iborra en *La dama boba*: reivindicar a Lope de Vega en tiempos del SMS' [The admirable risk of Manuel Iborra: to revive Lope de Vega in the age of text-messaging];[46] in purely financial terms, it does not seem that this risk has initially paid off. However, to judge the film solely in these terms is reductive in that it fails to take into account other considerations, such as the success that it has enjoyed in special screenings organised for schoolchildren. Equally, the film may very well enjoy a healthy afterlife on DVD and/or television.

As we have seen, Lope's cinematic career has been sporadic at best; he has been the servant of many masters, who have sought to appropriate his works for a variety of agendas, and only very occasionally has this favour been returned with adaptations that genuinely attempt to render his plays as cinematically credible works suitable for modern-day audiences. There is still no tradition in Spain of filming versions of Golden Age plays, and it seems unlikely that this is an omission that will be remedied in the near future. The failure of a film of *La dama boba*'s calibre to capture the popular imagination does not inspire faith in the commercial viability of the *comedia*. Though the unpredictable, and often capricious, nature of Spanish film production makes it unwise to be too firm in our predictions, it nevertheless seems unlikely that a twenty-first-century *Fénix* will be coming to a cinema screen near you anytime soon.

---

[46] '*Fahrenheit 451*' (review), *Fotogramas*, April 2006: 45.

21

Lope in Translation: Opening the Closed Book

DAVID JOHNSTON

Just before the end of the First World War Barrett Clark turned his gaze from the conflagration in Europe to bemoan the fact that 'the drama of Spain, early and modern, has in English-speaking countries been sadly neglected'. Referring to Golden Age theatre in particular, he glumly acknowledged that Lope de Vega, Tirso and Calderón, whom he described as the 'greatest of dozens of dramatists of the time', were still a 'closed book' to British and American audiences.[1] Nearly ninety years later, Melveena McKendrick's survey of sixteenth- and seventeenth-century Spanish theatre ends in similar plaintive style:

> the dramatic genius of sixteenth and seventeenth-century Spain is virtually unrecognized outside the circle of Hispanic studies. In the mid-1980s, when two of Calderón's plays, *Life is a Dream* and *The Mayor of Zalamea*, were put on in London [...] British theatre critics hailed the discovery of a remarkable 'new' dramatist. More recently the National Theatre's production of Lope de Vega's *Fuenteovejuna* elicited a similar response. The fact is that not just two remarkable playwrights but a remarkable theatre to all intents and purposes still awaits rediscovery.[2]

On one level, this is of course an issue of reception. In spite of the creative responses of nineteenth-century translators like Fitzgerald, whose freewheeling versions of six Calderón plays retain much of their playable freshness today,[3] or of pioneering directors like Joan Littlewood, whose memorable mid-twentieth-century production of *Fuenteovejuna*, like that of García Lorca's La Barraca, grafted Lope's play into the living tissue of contemporary ideological conflict, a whiff of cultural marginalisation lingered for a long time around a great deal of Spanish writing. In 1965, in his *La difícil universalidad española*, Guillermo de Torre harked back to the thought of Baltasar Gracián in order to analyse the

---

[1] Quoted by John Gassner in his Preface to *Great Spanish Plays in English Translation*, ed. Ángel Flores (New York: Dover, 1991), p. 3.

[2] Melveena McKendrick, *Theatre in Spain: 1490–1700* (Cambridge: Cambridge University Press, 1989), p. 270.

[3] Pedro Calderón de la Barca, *Six Dramas of Calderon: Freely Translated by Edward Fitzgerald* (London: William Pickering, 1853).

apparent national self-obsession which pervaded much Spanish writing and which served to foster the belief that it was unwelcomingly introverted, narrowly local, an emaciated literature, like Rocinante, with all its prickly bones sticking out:

> Hallaremos quizá la explicación última en el espíritu autocrítico tan desenfrenado —estimulante como fermento interno, desconcertante para quienes lo ven desde fuera — que caracteriza todo lo español; en la acedía, la aspereza con que los españoles juzgan o más bien trituran, a veces, los valores propios, con una violencia, una crueldad de la que es difícil encontrar equivalente en otras literaturas.[4]

> [Perhaps the explanation ultimately lies in that intense spirit of self-criticism — stimulating as an internal fermenting agent, but off-putting to those seeing it from the outside — which characterizes everything Spanish; in the acidity, the harshness with which Spaniards judge, or rather tear to shreds, at times, their own values, with a violence and a cruelty for which it is difficult to find an equivalent in other literatures.]

Guillermo de Torre is undoubtedly right to preface this assertion with a note of caution. There are, after all, many examples of writers — Sean O'Casey, for example — whose blistering attacks on configurations of national identity or scenarios of national history have not prevented them from being read or performed, and widely translated. Socially committed writing for the stage in particular generally displays a number of common patterns of construction that promote audience complicity — this is surely one of the factors that allows for that sense of the 'revenant', the haunting, that critics like Marvin Carlson detect as a key factor of spectator engagement.[5] But rather than socially committed in the most obvious sense it probably would be more accurate to refer to the playwrights of the Spanish Golden Age as culturally engaged, preoccupied with the expression of those sensibilities that are secured by local experience and those that, equally, are dislocated within it. It is the constant return to these cultural engagements in the work of writers like Lope de Vega that has prompted the view — misguided perhaps, but influential certainly — that this is a 'national' theatre whose frame of reference can only be understood through the framework of local history. A closed book, by any other name.

The notorious Reichenberger/Bentley dispute which began in the late 1950s focused characteristically on qualities of the *comedia* which they termed, respectively, the 'unique' and the 'universal'.[6] In other words, these critics continue to perceive this as a problem of reception. Without putting it quite in these terms, what Reichenberger detects at the heart of Lope de Vega's work is a model of Spanish ethnicity that, in this particular critic's eagerness to articulate the basis of a national theatre, elides the multicultural and multilingual roots that

---

[4] Guillermo de Torre, *La difícil universalidad española* (Madrid: Gredos, 1965), p. 12.

[5] See Marvin Carlson, *The Haunted Stage: The Theatre as Memory Machine* (Ann Arbor, MI: University of Michigan Press, 2001).

[6] Arnold G. Reichenberger, 'The Uniqueness of the *Comedia*', *Hispanic Review*, 27.3 (1959): 303–16; Eric Bentley, 'The Universality of the *Comedia*', *Hispanic Review*, 38.2 (1970): 147–62.

Lope's work shares with other traditions, among them, of course, Latin theatre and commedia dell'arte. Such ethnicity is inevitably modelled historically and territorially, but it is rooted in language, in mother tongue. Castilian Spanish was being explicitly promoted as a 'natural' language throughout the sixteenth century, with all the connotations of national integrity, ethnic distinctiveness and uniqueness that such an enterprise entails. Figuratively speaking, Lope's work occupies, dominates and, indeed, in any number of plays, extends the language-nation space. Its reach and focus are resolutely national, and its ultimate audience — the one to which, at least, it addresses itself as a reflective medium — is that of the empowered. In this it enacts the tactics of power symptomatic of *translatio imperii*, drawing on the capacities of translation from other sources, classical and more contemporary, to transform both meanings and places, eliding difference in its endeavour to discern a Spanish hegemony.

The same charge could be levelled, however, and indeed with no less cause, at Shakespeare's theatre, as Bentley cogently replied. And, of course, Lope too had his own groundlings, to whom he gave compelling situations meshed into fast-moving pieces, where thought and action were communicated simultaneously through tightly controlled imagery and resonant paralinguistic signs. By emphasising Lope's language as a series of vivid dramatic actions rather than as a vector of the national situation, its history and its aspirations, Bentley sets out the case for Lope's apparent 'universality'. In contradistinction, Reichenberger's protectionist defence of Lope's closed-book status is predicated precisely upon the way in which his theatre engages with the specific locations and dislocations of its moment. These two stances have profound implications for how we might approach the process of translating Lope de Vega's plays, and for what sort of product we might wish to see as emerging from that process.

Perhaps the issue, therefore, is one of translation rather than simply of reception, of process rather more than product. It is certainly true that, while there may have been no discernible shortage of translations of individual plays or of willing translators over the years, this has not been reflected in the number of professional productions of Lope's work that have taken place (Jonathan Thacker counts only twenty-two professional Lope productions, the majority of them in small-scale arthouse theatres, in Britain from 1900 to the present day).[7] This disjunction seems, on the surface, to give some credence to Reichenberger's view that Lope's theatre is too reflective of the very specific traumas of this hothouse society at root, too concerned with supporting the ideology of nascent nationhood at superstructure. Certainly, throughout most of the twentieth century, Lope may have acceded to the status as a major figure of world theatre, but such recognition was merely notional. His work, with apparently little to say to us, was rarely produced on stage. The ninety largely barren years that separate the parallel complaints of Barrett Clark and McKendrick certainly suggest that

---

[7] Jonathan Thacker, 'History of Performance in English', in *The Spanish Golden Age in English: Perspectives on Performance*, ed. Catherine Boyle & David Johnston (London: Oberon, 2007), pp. 15–30.

Reichenberger's assertion of philological difference (mapped from national aspiration) was well founded.

With the singular exception of John Osborne, whose interest in Lope rapidly waned after his 1966 version of *La fianza satisfecha — A Bond Honoured*[8] — there was certainly no Fitzgerald among those translators, no single writer who was willing, as Fitzgerald had done with Calderón, to allow these plays to make some sort of demand on the current attention of spectators, either in the pitch of their language or the contestatory nature of their subject matter. So it is no coincidence that the Lope production that McKendrick specifically refers to, while it certainly marks a paradigm shift in translation method at least, is nonetheless, in marketing terms, a revival of sorts. *Fuenteovejuna*, this time in Adrian Mitchell's memorable version produced by the National Theatre in 1989, had traditionally been perceived, with all of the brash assurance of British theatre's ignorance of the *comedia*, as the one Lope play that transcends, consciously or unconsciously, the ideological agenda and limited sweep of its author. So had it not been for the pioneering work of London's Gate Theatre in the early 1990s, then under the artistic directorship of Stephen Daldry and subsequently (and crucially) of Laurence Boswell, it is unlikely that English-speaking audiences would have had much further access to Lope's work. Because, of course, as always in theatre, there is a financial factor that weighs heavily over every other consideration. The fact that the Gate paid its actors only expenses, a method deemed artistically liberating by some and ethically buccaneering by others, allowed these resource-intensive plays finally to find their way back to where they always belonged: on the stage. Perhaps inevitably therefore it was only when that most resource-rich of all theatre companies, the Royal Shakespeare Company, turned its attention to the *comedia*, over a decade later, that a new Spanish Golden Age season was born.

A comparison of Mitchell's translation and those of Jill Booty, whose *Lope de Vega: Five Plays*, published twenty years earlier, was a landmark in the barren terrain of Lope in English translation,[9] shows clearly how the writing practice of each translator reflects the core assumptions of Bentley and Reichenberger respectively. In spite of Booty's explicitly stated intention to assert Lope as a living force in theatre, her translations derive from philological rather than dramaturgical analysis, privileging what Walter Benjamin, in his seminal *The Task of the Translator*,[10] termed the 'accidental', allowing the text to be heavily textured with a level of detail that Booty considered as authenticating, and which contemporary audiences would inevitably experience as obfuscating. Mitchell, on the other hand, brings a poetic eye to the play, shaping the language for contemporary performance, ensuring that the play's original capacity to raise

---

[8] John Osbourne, *A Bond Honoured: A Play (from Lope de Vega)* (London: Faber & Faber, 1966).

[9] *Lope de Vega: Five Plays*, trans. Jill Booty, with an introduction by R. D. F. Pring-Mill (New York: Hill and Wang, 1961).

[10] Walter Benjamin, 'The Task of the Translator' (1923), in his *Illuminations*, ed. Hannah Arendt, trans. Harry Zohn (New York: Harcourt, Brace & World, 1968), pp. 69–82.

issues of power, morality and collective retribution was re-activated for a twentieth-century audience. This states the issue succinctly. If Lope was to function on the stage — if theatres were to risk substantial investment in inevitably expensive productions, the translations had to be stage-worthy — they had to work as plays and they had to have something to say to contemporary audiences.

More radically, of course, we might also say that translation as a cultural method reveals the profound fault lines in the essentialist values of uniqueness and universality alike. Bentley's defence of Lope's universality, based on a whole series of undeniable dramaturgical qualities, takes a sentient view that threatens to peddle Lope, across the range of his plays, as by and large the provider of a sort of theatrical froth, excellent in its own way, but, nonetheless, form divorced from substance. It is a view of universality that fashions its paradigm on the unthinking acceptance of the universality of Shakespeare — in the case of the English writer, the exportable value of his particular substance was rarely called into question. Gary Taylor addresses this paradox head on:

> We assume that Shakespeare's thirty-odd plays contain more of humanity than the five hundred plays of Lope de Vega we have not read [leading] I do not doubt, to our neglecting all those aspects of humanity which Shakespeare neglected, on the assumption that anything outside the circle of his art does not exist.[11]

It is an assumption that is 'in the sweep of human culture, just a trick of perspective: a local illusion'. Dennis Kennedy's influential *Foreign Shakespeare* provides a more compelling intercultural paradigm that replaces this essentialist and, of course, ideologically driven, sense of universality.[12] Where Shakespeare exists most vividly is in the multiple Shakespeares generated at the interstices of cultures, shaped and re-shaped by the performative possibilities and cultural resonances that vary from encounter to encounter. Is it time now to begin to imagine the multiple Lopes that may be generated through the contingency of intercultural contact?

To speak of the universal qualities of a writer is to imagine that translation is a simple matter of the cross-cultural duplication of essential and, for that reason, inviolable qualities and values. Echoes of that very different sort of imagination, this time rooted in philological concerns, surfaced in the surtitles polemic that arose in the midst of the RSC's preparations to take the plays of the Spanish Golden Age season to Madrid's Teatro Español, when the possibility of providing surtitles based on the original plays rather than on the new versions was discussed.[13] But reality duplicated is not real. It is, in the most literal sense,

[11] Gary Taylor, *Reinventing Shakespeare: A Cultural History, from the Restoration to the Present* (New York: Weidenfield & Nicholson, 1989), p. 386.

[12] Dennis Kennedy, *Foreign Shakespeare: Contemporary Performance* (Cambridge: Cambridge University Press, 1993).

[13] See David Johnston, 'Lope de Vega in English: The Historicised Imagination', in *The Comedia in English*, ed. Susan Paun de García & Donald Larson (Woodbridge: Tamesis, 2008).

meaningless. Reality is what has been transformed by meaning, by our interpretation of its contexts, signs and signifiers. Reality therefore, like the text, is constituted by discourse rather than by truth, configured by meanings that are generated and re-generated in every act of reception. Even the briefest survey of contemporary translation theory will demonstrate its tendency to worry over and to problematise any act of cultural exchange or transaction. After all, translation embodies the attempt to replicate in one language and grammar an act of discourse from a language and grammar that are 'other' to us, with all the connotations that postmodernism has granted that term. It is in this context that Sanford Budick and Wolfgang Iser influentially describe how the product of translation passes through a liminal space in which two cultures intermingle, before what tends to be known as the 'third space', the space inhabited by the translation as new text, is elaborated.[14] Translation, therefore, is centrally concerned with difference; crucially, its apprehension of — or its relationship to — the target text or culture is metaphorical rather than metonymic. For Lawrence Venuti, 'a translated text should be a site at which a different culture emerges, where a reader gets a glimpse of a cultural order and resistency'.[15] Venuti's notion of translation as a process, in which a target language is foreignised through contact with a source other, arguably underpins much of contemporary translation theory, that perceives each translation to be a hinge between specific moments, located within ever-shifting interstices and temporary intercultures. Thus:

> Translation is not only the intellectual, creative process by which a text written in a given language is transferred into another. Rather, like any human activity, it takes place in a specific social and historical context that informs and structures it [...] In the case of translation, the operation becomes doubly complicated since, by definition, two languages and thus two cultures and societies are involved.[16]

Richard Jacquemond might have added 'two systems of production and reception' to his binary list, but the fact remains that in its broadest sense translation implies cross-cultural negotiation between two contexts that are both very specific and very different. This recognition now allows us to destabilise Budick and Iser's notion of the third space, leading instead to the awareness that plays in translation, no less than in production, inhabit not a third terrain, but multiple terrains in which the crossing points are infinite.

What does this mean for Lope in translation? For scholars, surely it suggests that as Lope is performed more and more frequently across the English-speaking world (the prestige productions of the RSC have ensured that this particular

---

[14] See especially Sanford Budick & Wolfgang Iser, ed., *The Translatability of Cultures: Figurations of the Space Between* (Stanford, CA: Stanford University Press, 1996).

[15] Lawrence Venuti, *The Translator's Invisibility: A History of Translation* (London: Routledge, 1995), p. 305.

[16] Richard Jacquemond, 'Translation and Cultural Hegemony: The Case of French-Arabic Translation', in *Rethinking Translation: Discourse, Subjectivity, Ideology*, ed. Lawrence Venuti (London: Routledge, 1992), pp. 139–58 (p. 139).

wagon is beginning to roll[17]) and in other theatre cultures (mediated in this case, whether we like it or not, through the availability of English-language translations), there will have to be a recognition that the different Lopes that emerge in the mapping of global Lope performance are not accidental distortions of some notional essence. We must be clear: this is an attitude that persists. For was this not what the proponents of using the original Spanish as the basis for the RSC surtitles were effectively saying? Of course to-date Lope studies have naturally been centred on considerations of his original language and the environment, cultural, social and political, in which his work was produced (in the double sense of that word, as plays and as responsive artefacts). All of that is secured and will continue, but if we are to see Lope's work performed on the international stage, where it has a natural place, the understanding and formal assessment of his work must also now begin to fall to translators, critics, editors and commentators whose training and primary allegiance may well not be in Hispanic Studies. That may go without saying for some; others will consider it an issue of concern. The fact remains, however, that professional multilingual performances of Lope's work — university based productions are discountable in that they are often infused with a philological zeal that casts a museological pall over the performance — challenge us to look beyond Lope as a literary creator, and to delve into the manifold but temporary completions that each encounter and each production imply. In the last number of years, the importation of speech-act theory into a number of critical approaches to Lope's plays has given a nod in the direction of the plays' performative qualities. But this is still to ignore the fact that it is the property of theatre to offer performances of the same play, reinfleshments of the same character, and interpretations of the same lines, that may vary enormously from one set of production specifics to the next.

This chapter however, is not simply another exhortation to consider Lope's plays as scripts for performance. A number of critics already do that, and with notable acuity. What it does argue, however, is that the pre-origins of Lope's work are multicultural, its scope is multilayered, and its afterlife will inevitably be multilingual. From the perspective of translation, of course, any multilingual status cannot be contained within a perceived monolingual space or identity, or within a philological or nationalising project, without articulating a series of powerful cultural paradoxes. One such paradox is rooted in the frequently encountered view that translation automatically imposes loss. Echoing Frost's famous dictum that poetry is what is lost in the translation, proponents of this view tend to see Lope in translation as a Lope somehow *manqué*. Surely a Lope shorn of his language by the process of linguistic and cultural transfer cannot be anything other? Of course, any translator for professional performance will naturally have worried about this problem. Lope's stage language is highly organised and concise — where it is not, there is usually another dramatic purpose being served (stories, tall-tales and elaborated classical references tend to belie

---

[17] The RSC version of *The Dog in the Manger*, for example, received three major professional productions in the United States, one in Australia and one in the Czech Republic, between 2005 and 2008.

hidden agendas and unacknowledged motivations). The rich polymetric forms of Lope's stage language are very often seen as performing some essential quality that must be maintained in translation. But should all Lopes therefore be polymetric? For example, in the introduction to his published translation of *The Dog in the Manger*, Victor Dixon argues:

> Translators of Golden-Age Spanish plays face from the outset the difficult and debatable question of form. Some opt for prose; but to my mind, since the *comedia* is an essentially stylized genre, steeped in a diverse poetic tradition, and dependent for much of its impact on the evocative potential of verse, to do so is unthinkable. In the case of Lope de Vega, one of Spain's very greatest poets, it would be a betrayal; the *traduttore* would be truly a *traditore*.[18]

This sets very clearly delimited parameters around the extent to which Dixon is actually prepared to countenance a debate on form. But within those parameters he usefully sets out some of the possible solutions and difficulties that present themselves: blank verse (too grave?), pentameters (in Round's phrase, 'sub-Shakespearian pastiche'?), partially rhyming neo-Shakespearian pentameters (his eventual solution). Such a think-aloud protocol is entirely appropriate for the practising translator. But, as we have seen, there can be no justification for pre-setting paradigms for the translation of any author or text. If a translator wishes to write a verse translation, then that is a perfectly valid choice. But, as with any choice he or she needs to assess the pitfalls. And broadly speaking, assuming that the translator, à la Ranjit Bolt, is actually capable of manipulating stage verse, one needs to bear in mind that rhyme in English tends to be more clever that Spanish rhyme, which is very often achieved from the internal echoing of grammatical endings or common suffixes. Cleverness, as an end in itself, rapidly becomes self-satisfied, and there is the danger that the play may begin to sink under the weight of its own linguistic smugness. The fact that there are whole library shelves full of such translations, published notably by academic houses, did — and does — little to turn the pages of Lope's closed book. Stage poetry, as García Lorca argued, requires the body of the actor to make it real. The oral medium of performance and the literary analysis of verse, the gestural and the logocentric, may well run at odds to each other. Laurence Boswell, referring to his work with Spanish actors on a production of *El perro del hortelano*, describes the physicality of Lope's verse forms in terms that are no less relevant for the translator:

> I think one of the great mistakes that people make with verse is that they see it as existing beyond the body. Because it requires a certain mental effort to understand what's being said, people tend to see verse as the fruit of a mental process, distant from the physicality of the actors. The verse is a sensual thing, an erotic, physical,

---

[18] Lope de Vega, *The Dog in the Manger*, trans. and ed. Victor Dixon, Carleton Renaissance Plays in Translation, 21 (Ottawa: Dovehouse Editions Canada, 1990), p. 5.

emotional thing, that needs to be experienced in the body and understood as a psychosocial element.[19]

Returning to Frost's complaint, clearly there are many creative strategies that different translations can adopt in order to obviate or to compensate for any perceptible loss. One such strategy, one among many possible strategies, that I have used is the eight-beat line as the default metre for my Lopes in translation. The foreshortening of the pentameter assures the rhythm of the action, meaning that the play delivers itself, as Lope's plays should, with a theatrical energy that, in turn, energises the audience. RSC director Jonathan Munby notes how this device also communicates something of the play's theatrical otherness to an English-speaking audience:

> Working with actors from the RSC who were very skilled at verse speaking, they took to this like ducks to water, but were constantly aware that it felt very different. I think it was the missing two syllables from the iambic pentameter that they were used to, that gave the play [in this case *Madness in Valencia*] its extraordinary momentum [...] The iambic pentameter sounds very English [...] there is something impatient, impassioned, about the eight-beat verse line — its drive — which means that it has an otherness: it forces us as English practitioners to think in a slightly different way.[20]

The default line allows variants to be picked up by the attentive spectator. In *The Dog in the Manger*, for example, twelve-beat lines became immediately expressive of the ponderous pomposity of the Marqués Ricardo, while six-beat lines caught the urgent intensity of Teodoro's feverish imaginings of his longed-for flight and dreaded fall.[21] In that way at least, some of the melodramatic functionality of Lope's polymetric system is restored, as different metres underscore shifts in emotional key and narrative turning points. But in Munby's assessment of form, surely what is most notable is his sense that English practitioners are challenged by forms that are other to them into searching for and hopefully creating a style of performance that captures some of the difference that Lope de Vega marks on the English-speaking stage.

This is a small but telling example of the sort of paradoxes that open up when the work of a writer like Lope, the Phoenix of Spain, so closely associated with national aspirations, is extended through multilingual and multicultural spaces. Yet Lope himself, like virtually every other playwright to whom we now accord classic status, freely plundered sources and forms from a variety of cultures and times. Right from Chaucer and Dante through to the mid-seventeenth century,

---

[19] David Johnston, 'Interview with Laurence Boswell', in *The Spanish Golden Age in English: Perspectives on Performance*, ed. Catherine Boyle & David Johnston (London: Oberon, 2007), pp. 148–54 (p. 150).
[20] David McGrath, 'Interview with Jonathan Munby', in *The Spanish Golden Age in English*, pp. 133–40 (p. 134).
[21] See Lope de Vega, *The Dog in the Manger*, trans. David Johnston, Absolute Classics (London: Oberon, 2004).

translatio was also synonymous with invention: with the creation of new expressive forms, rooted in a broad range of discursive, rhetorical and interlingual traditions. Shakespeare, Lope, Calderón, later Molière and Goldoni, for example, all produce at one moment the 'latest' in a concatenation of multilingual accounts: recognisable European stories, but whose cultural eclecticism is subsequently press-ganged into the much more confined project of the construction of a national space inhabited by a national canon.

This takes us into the heart of the paradoxes of translation: sameness through difference, metonymy rooted in metaphor. But as a paradox, of course, it is not new:

> In medieval Latin, the word *translatio* was often taken to be synonymous with *expositio* (interpretation). If this equation is taken seriously it provides a justification for understanding vernacular translations not simply as attempts to transfer meaning unchanged from one language to another but as readings of source texts, part of whose purpose may indeed lie in their difference from those texts.[22]

As early as 1199 the great Sephardic philosopher Maimonides had written in a letter to Ben Tibbon, one of the translators associated with the first period of the School of Toledo:

> The translator must above all clarify the development of thought in the original, then write it, comment upon it, and explain it so that the same process of thought is clear and comprehensible in the new language. That is how Hunain ben Ishaq translated Galen and his son Ishaq translated Aristotle.[23]

The act of translation-as-interpretation revivifies the earlier text, relocating it in a way that re-energises not only the cultural and semantic charge of the 'original' text, but also refocuses its hermeneutic surplus. In other words, each act of interpretation creates an object that is different from the object it reflects. It takes it into a different place. The idea that the act of translation is also an act of transposition — an act of appropriation that Lope and Shakespeare at different times carried out almost unthinkingly as an accepted part of their practice — has nonetheless seemingly radical connotations for how we might think of translation today. To understand those radical connotations perhaps we have to return to the paradoxes of these extraordinary cultural projects. No matter how much Lope's overall theatrical project is seen as configuring some sort of national theatre, each text remains marked by the *difference*, the *otherness*, of the cultures it translates and relocates in its *grand récit* of a developing sense of Spanishness.

---

[22] Quoted by Stephen Kelly, 'Translating Cultures: Suggestions from the Middle English Prose *Brut*', in *Metaphrastes, or, Gained in Translation: Essays and Translations in Honour of Robert H. Jordan*, ed. Margaret Mullett, Belfast Byzantine Texts and Translations, 9 (Belfast: Belfast Byzantine Enterprises, 2004), pp. 91–102 (p. 98).

[23] My translation. Quoted in Miguel Ángel Vega, ed., *Textos clásicos de teoría de la traducción* (Madrid: Cátedra, 1994), p. 23.

There have been numerous studies of how Lope exploited his sources. Together these borrowings and importations bring much vividness and variety to his theatre. As we see happening increasingly with classical productions around the world (for instance, the Teatro Piccolo's productions which explored the echoes of Plautus in both *The Comedy of Errors* and Goldoni's *The Twins*), the intercultural practice of translation frequently amplifies the narrative echo of these borrowed sources in the new target text. *The Gentleman from Olmedo*, for example, presents itself, in one possible translation, as a product of the great European ballad tradition, its direct story line, its overhanging sense of doom, its insistent patterns of dialogue, all reminiscent to its new spectators of a tradition they already know. They may not rationalise it like this, but they may hopefully feel some of that familiarity — that haunting sense of déjà vu in the unknown that, in Carlson's analysis of reception, deepens — and authenticates — spectator experience on the haunted stage.

What is certainly true is that the translator need not consciously be concerned with importing cultural difference in the act of translation for that difference to survive in the translated text. As the words of Munby and Maimonides, quoted above, suggest, from radically different contexts, there is implicit in working with translated words a sort of journeying into otherness. This emphasis on hermeneutics, as a principle of theatre (in the case of the English director) and as a structuring principle of translation (as far as the Sephardic philosopher is concerned) brings the translator to focus on the role of interpretation, of hermeneutics, as a trigger for the ability of spectators here and now, of contemporary audiences, to re-activate the play's political, ethical, social strategies and aims. The logic of this focus demands in turn that the translator confronts the play's cognitive and affective dimensions, and filters them through his or her own contemporary experience. The issue of the play's reception becomes then not merely a question of the text's immediate or historical milieux but a dilemma of the confrontation between literary-historiographical practice and translation. This is the essence of the matter, and there are important issues to consider here from the perspective of the translator of historical plays.

Performance, of course, always takes place in the here and now of an audience. If Lope's theatre has been a closed book — and Thacker's statistical analysis provides forceful corroboration that it is — it is not because his mind and the way in which he captures a vision of life for the stage are irretreviably foreign from the perspective of the English-speaking translator. It is because we have not made an effort to bridge the schism between his past and our present, his there and our here. This constitutes the major fault-line between Lope's theatre and the English-language (or any other language) spectator. Translators, unlike literary historians, cannot afford to adopt a detached position by avoiding being critics of their own cultures. Critical positions such as Reichenberger's constitute a reluctance to admit the effects of culture — and history — upon their own critical procedures. The act of contextualising, for example, Lope de Vega's audience seems to require such critical writers to de-contextualise themselves; this act of de-contextualisation, in turn, legitimates the authors' detachment from the historical material they subsequently write about, bringing an apparent objectivity, that in reality is little more than rhetorical force, to their conclusions. Thus much literary historicism and reception history reinscribe the contradiction at the heart of how Western historiography imagines time. That contradiction consists of the schism between past and present. In presenting themselves as somehow aloof from (or invariably subject to) the historical mechanisms of their own cultures, these authors bifurcate between past and present and thereby dispel any sense their work might provide of the aliveness in the present of texts written in the past.

The 'aloof from' and the 'subject to' have profound implications for the shaping strategies for the writing of translations. On the surface, they can be seen as the writing tactics suggested by the extremes of domesticating and foreignising. But in practice they have as much to do with how the translator situates him or herself in relation to the cultural utility of the text in question. Central to this is the view that there is a disabling premise at the heart of Western historiographical discourse that prevents us from experiencing — experiencing in an active way, as somebody in the theatre can experience — the pastness of past things — in other words, their historicity. In *The Writing of History*, Michel de Certeau writes memorably:

> Historiography takes for granted the fact that it has become impossible to believe in the presence of the dead that has organised (or organises) the experience of entire civilizations [...] By taking for granted its distancing from tradition and the social body, in the last resort historiography is based upon a power that in effect distinguishes it from the past and from the whole of society.[24]

It is this extraordinary ability of translation both to safeguard the past and to project that past into the present moment of performance that allows us to view the sort of extension that the act of translation brings to a text as being necessarily temporary, inherently contingent. When, for example, in 2004, the Watermill Theatre wanted to re-stage my version of Lope's *The Gentleman from Olmedo*, which had featured in the original Gate Theatre season, I therefore felt compelled to re-write the translation in a way that was designed to promote the play's historical hybridity. The language, in terms of its formal arrangement and the positions it struck between the naturally occurring and the richly stylised and pleonastic, created a linguistic environment that was both other and accessible, as a number of critics noted. The opening speech of Alonso, the eponymous gentleman, is crucial in that it not only establishes the parameters of that linguistic environment — creating the trust that allows the spectator to become complicit with the truths of performance — but it also proposes the Neoplatonic correspondences that are implicit in the idea of requited love and which give this society its moral currency:

How could any man call this feeling love,

---

[24] Michel de Certeau (1988). *The Writing of History*, trans. Tom Conley (New York & Chichester, NY: Columbia University Press, 1988), p. 6.

when love hides its face, then takes flight?
We love and so are loved, reflecting
in perfect form and substance nature's law
that two souls join together so to live.
Our eyes met, our glances crossed and, so, fixed
a flame in my heart that still rages.
She looked directly at me: her eyes flickered,
her face changed ... and hope soared within.
For if those eyes saw me as mine saw her,
then I think she must love me, as I love her.
But if in that glance her eyes did not see,
no sooner am I reborn to life
than I shall die, unseen and alone.[25]

This one example must stand as a synecdoche for the linguistic fabric of the entire play. But it should serve to give an insight into one possible way of achieving the synchronic historicism in which each professionally performed Lope will be embedded. The translator can also engage in tactics of re-construction, restoring to individual instances the human understanding that allows connections to be made by contemporary audiences. This is a clear functioning of hermeneutics as a structuring element of translation, and it may take any number of formal interventions at macro- and micro-textual levels. There is no space in an essay of this nature to illustrate what form such interventions may take. Moreover, translational tactics will normally derive from textual strategy, and that in turn will be contingent upon the conjunction of performance specificities.

Much literary history, like any museological practice, has played a fundamental role in fabricating, maintaining and disseminating many of the essentialist and historicist fictions that congeal cultural movement and academic innovation. Of course, Lope's theatre world, characterised as it was by fluidity and immediacy of purpose, was notably concerned with the specificities of performance. As a writer he was preoccupied with the urgent need to produce a constant stream of new plays, and, as a self-regarding stamp of his professional status, declared himself as unconcerned with theatrical legacy. This primacy of production over posterity promotes a very different culture of creativity than that which currently prevails in most mainstream theatre environments, where other pressures, not least among them academic-critical, cause greater attention to be given to the publication in print. A predominantly oral approach treats the written text as simply a temporary means of transmission which, all too often, is disregarded once the performers assume ownership of the language. Once again, we are marauding into the well-worn issue of stage versus page, but translation no less than performance frees the play from what Michael Goldman sharply calls 'its mere textuality'.[26] This need, in the crucible of theatrical preparation, to prioritise the oral over the written explains the difficulties with which subsequent generations of editors grapple as

[25] Published by Caos Editorial (Madrid) on www.caoseditorial.com.
[26] Michael Goldman, *On Drama: Boundaries of Genre, Borders of Self* (Ann Arbor, MI: University of Michigan Press, 2000), p. 52.

they seek to reconcile and mediate between conflicting written sources. A stage-translator concerned to open Lope's closed book on the English-speaking stage will inevitably be sceptical about the possibility of understanding performance solely through the printed word. Bill Worthen pointedly asks:

> Is it possible to understand performance through the scripted form of dramatic texts? [...] Is the form of a printed book an adequate delivery system for plays? Is it a delivery system at all?[27]

There is a growing interest in Lope's theatre in Britain. Eighteen of the twenty-two professional productions recorded by Thacker have taken place since 1990. For that to continue, for Lope the writer to survive in multilingual afterlives, it is time to open the closed book and enrich its logocentric codes with the stage languages of the gestural and the paraverbal. Literary critics of Lope imagine one sort of writer. But translators and directors will inevitably carry that imagination into different arenas. And difference, and histories of difference inevitably haunt any attempt to render one language into another. The play undergoes interpretation anew each time it is performed with the framework of such difference, and in the process the original play constantly reveals its own mobility, its own inherent instability. As Derrida notes:

> The translation will truly be a moment in the growth of the original, which will complete itself in enlarging itself [...] And if the original calls for a complement, it is because at the origin it was not there without fault, full, complete, identical to itself.[28]

Each translation of Lope, each performance, just like any act of reading, brings its own completion to bear. And, in turn, each completion feeds into the sense of the many possibilities of his work. There is a long way to go before we can talk of opening up the many Lopes, as we now can of the multiple Shakespeares. But, at least, we are beginning to turn the pages.

---

[27] W. B. Worthen, *Print and the Poetics of Modern Drama* (Cambridge: Cambridge University Press, 2006), p. 213.

[28] Quoted in Kelly, 'Translating Cultures', p. 102.

TRANSLATIONS OF TITLES

We have offered in this list translations that are for the most part as literal as possible, although some works, especially plays, have several alternative titles in English.

Poetic works

Alabanzas al glorioso san José [*Eulogies to the Glorious St Joseph*]

Arte nuevo de hacer comedias en este tiempo [*The New Art of Writing Plays*]

Las bodas entre el alma y el amor divino [*The Marriage between the Soul and Divine Love*]

Los cinco misterios dolorosos de la Pasión y muerte de Nuestro Señor Jesucristo con su sagrada resurrección [*The Five Sorrowful Mysteries of the Passion and Death of Our Lord Jesus Christ with His Holy Resurrection*]

La Circe con otras rimas y prosas [*Circe with Other Lyric Poems and Prose Pieces*]

Conceptos divinos al santísimo sacramento y a la Virgen Nuestra Señora [*Divine Conceits on the Most Holy Sacrament and Our Lady the Virgin*]

Contemplativos discursos [*Contemplative Discourses*]

Corona trágica [*Tragic Crown*]

Cuatro soliloquios [*Four Soliloquies*]

Descripción de la Tapada [*Description of the Country Estate*]

La dragontea [*The Dragontea*]

Égloga a Claudio [*Eclogue to Claudio*]

Fiestas de Denia [*Festivals at Denia*]

La Filomena con otras diversas rimas, prosas y versos [*Philomena with Other Various Lyric Poems, Prose Pieces and Verses*]

La gatomaquia [*The Gatomachia*]

La hermosura de Angélica [*The Beauty of Angelica*]

Huerto deshecho [*Ruined Garden*]

Isidro [*Isidro*]

El jardín de Lope de Vega [*Lope's Garden*]

Jerusalén conquistada [*Jerusalem Conquered*]

Justa poética y alabanzas justas al bienaventurado San Isidro [*Poetic Tournament and Just Eulogies to the Most Favoured Saint Isidro*]

Laurel de Apolo [*The Laurel of Apollo*]

Pastores de Belén [*Shepherds of Bethlehem*]

Revelaciones de algunas cosas dignas de ser notadas de la Pasión de Cristo [*Revelations of Certain Things Worthy of Note in the Passion of Christ*]

Rimas [*Lyric Poems*]

Rimas humanas [*Secular Lyric Poems*]

Rimas humanas y divinas del licenciado Tomé de Burguillos [*Secular and Sacred Lyric Poems by the Licenciate Tomé de Burguillos*]

Rimas sacras [*Sacred Lyric Poems*]

Segunda parte del desengaño del hombre [*The Second Part of the Disillusionment of Man*]

Sentimientos a los agravios de Cristo, Nuestro Bien, por la nación hebrea [*Lamentations for the Wrongs Done to Christ Our Beloved by the Hebrew Nation*]

'Serrana hermosa' [Beautiful mountain girl]

Soliloquios amorosos de un alma a Dios [*Amorous Soliloquies of a Soul to God*]

El triunfo de la fe en los reinos del Japón [*The Triumph of the Faith in the Realm of Japan*]

Triunfos divinos con otras rimas sacras [*Divine Triumphs with Other Sacred Lyric Poems*]

La Virgen de la Almudena [*The Virgin of the Almudena*]

Dramatic works

El acero de Madrid [*The Steel-Water of Madrid*]

Las almenas de Toro [*The Battlements of Toro*]

Amar sin saber a quién [*To Love without Knowing Whom*]

El amor enamorado [*Love Enamoured*]

Arauco domado [*The Araucans Tamed*]

Barlaán y Josafat [*Barlaam and Josaphat*]

El bastardo Mudarra [*Mudarra, the Bastard Son*]

Belardo el furioso [*The Frenzy of Belardo*]

La bella Aurora [*The Fair Aurora*]

La bella malmaridada [*The Mismarried Beauty*]

La bienaventurada Madre Santa Teresa de Jesús [*The Blessed Mother St Teresa of Jesus*]

Las bizarrías de Belisa [*The Gallantries of Belisa*]

El Brasil restituido [*Brazil Reconquered*]

La buena guarda [*The Erring Nun*]

El caballero de Olmedo [*The Knight from Olmedo*]

La campana de Aragón [*The Bell of Aragon*]

El cardenal de Belén [*The Cardinal of Bethlehem*]

Carlos el perseguido [*Charles the Pursued*]

Carlos Quinto en Francia [*Charles V in France*]

El casamiento en la muerte [*Marriage in Death*]

El castigo sin venganza [*Punishment without Revenge*]

Los comendadores de Córdoba [*The Knights-Commander of Córdoba*]

El conde Fernán González [*Count Fernán González*]

El cuerdo en su casa [*The Sensible Man at Home*]

El cuerdo loco [*The Sane Madman*]

La dama boba [*The Dim-Witted Lady*]

La discreta enamorada [*The Clever Girl in Love*]

El divino africano [*The Divine African*]

El duque de Viseo [*The Duke of Viseo*]

Los embustes de Fabia [*Fabia's Tricks*]

El esclavo de Roma [*The Slave of Rome*]

Los esclavos libres [*The Free Slaves*]

La Estrella de Sevilla (attributed to Lope) [*The Star of Seville*]

La fábula de Perseo, o La bella Andrómeda [*The Fable of Perseus, or, The Fair Andromeda*]

Las ferias de Madrid [*The Fairs of Madrid*]

Lo fingido verdadero [*The Feigned Truth*]

La francesilla [*The French Girl*]

Fuente Ovejuna or *Fuenteovejuna* [*Fuenteovejuna*]

El galán de la Membrilla [*The Gallant from Membrilla*]

Las grandezas de Alejandro [*The Greatness of Alexander*]

El Grao de Valencia [*The Port of Valencia*]

Los hechos de Garcilaso de la Vega y el moro Tarfe [*The Exploits of Garcilaso de la Vega and the Moor Tarfe*]

La hermosa Ester [*Beautiful Esther*]

El hijo pródigo [*The Prodigal Son*]

El hombre de bien [*The Good Man*]

El honrado hermano [*The Honourable Brother*]

La imperial de Otón [*Otón's Vassal*]

Las justas de Tebas [*The Tournament at Thebes*]

La juventud de San Isidro [*The Youth of Saint Isidro*]

Los locos de Valencia [*Madness in Valencia*]

La Madre Teresa de Jesús [*Mother Teresa of Jesus*]

El maestro de danzar [*The Dancing Master*]

El mármol de Felisardo [*The Marble of Felisardo*]

La Maya [*The Mayan*]

El médico de su honra [*The Physician of His Honour*]

El mejor alcalde, el rey [*The Best Mayor, the King*]

Los melindres de Belisa [*The Caprices of Belisa*]

El mesón de la corte [*The Inn of the Court*]

Las mocedades de Bernardo del Carpio [*The Youthful Deeds of Bernardo del Carpio*]

La moza de cántaro [*The Girl with a Pitcher*]

La niñez de san Isidro [*St Isidro's Childhood*]

La obediencia laureada [*Obedience Rewarded*]

Las paces de los reyes y judía de Toledo [*The Kings' Peace and the Jewess from Toledo*]

Peribáñez y el comendador de Ocaña [*Peribáñez and the Commander of Ocaña*]

El perro del hortelano [*The Dog in the Manger*]

El premio de la hermosura [*Beauty's Prize*]

El príncipe despeñado [*The Prince Hurled from a Height*]

La prueba de los amigos [*The Test of Friendship*]

La quinta de Florencia [*The Country House in Florence*]

El rey sin reino [*The King without a Realm*]

El robo de Dina [*The Rape of Dinah*]

Roma abrasada [*Rome Burned*]

San Nicolás de Tolentino [*St Nicholas of Tolentino*]

La santa liga [*The Holy League*]

Santa Teresa de Jesús [*St Teresa of Jesus*]

El secretario de sí mismo [*His Own Secretary*]

El serafín humano [*The Human Seraph*]

Servir a señor discreto [*To Serve a Sensible Master*]

El último godo [*The Last of the Goths*]

La vengadora de las mujeres [*The Avenger of Her Sex*]

El verdadero amante [*The True Lover*]

Viaje del alma [*Journey of the Soul*]

Vida y muerte de Santa Teresa de Jesús [*The Life and Death of St Teresa of Jesus*]

El villano en su rincón [*The Peasant in his Corner*]

Virtud, pobreza y mujer [*Virtue, Poverty and Woman*]

Viuda, casada y doncella [*Widow, Wife and Maiden*]

La viuda valenciana [*The Valencian Widow*]

Prose works

Arcadia [*The Arcadia*]

La Dorotea [*Dorotea*]

Epistolario [*Letters*]

El peregrino en su patria [*The Pilgrim in His Homeland*]

Novelas a Marcia Leonarda [*Novels for Marcia Leonarda*]
    Las fortunas de Diana [*The Fortunes of Diana*]
    La desdicha por la honra [*Misfortune through Honour*]
    La prudente venganza [*The Prudent Revenge*]
    Guzmán el Bravo [*Guzmán the Brave*]

GUIDE TO FURTHER READING

(Full publication details of the works mentioned in this section can be found in the bibliography.)

A figure as significant and fascinating as Lope Félix de Vega Carpio has predictably attracted the attention of numerous admirers over the centuries, with centenaries of his birth and death in particular leading to voluminous re-assessments of his biography and the nature of his poetic genius. Nevertheless, one cannot help but be surprised at the number of obvious gaps in the scholarship and literature on his life and works. For the scholar the most egregious lack is of good critical editions of his oeuvre. Non-canonical plays often still have to be read in the nineteenth-century editions of Hartzenbusch and Menéndez y Pelayo, or the thirteen volumes of Cotarelo published between 1916 and 1930. However, the future in this respect looks brighter as the excellent and handsomely produced editions of the ProLope group at the Autónoma in Barcelona, which follow the order of the *Partes*, gradually remedy this problem. More popular editions, for example of plays such as *La viuda valenciana*, edited by Teresa Ferrer (Castalia) and the four *Novelas a Marcia Leonarda*, edited by Antonio Carreño, (Cátedra), are also helping to make Lope's works more readily available. And academic presses, such as Edition Reichenberger and Iberoamericana/Vervuert are also publishing high-quality editions, bibliographies and scholarly studies. The former has produced several editions over the past two decades of lesser-known Lope plays such as *La quinta de Florencia*, by Debra Collins Ames, as well as important bibliographical works by Marco Presotto and Maria Grazia Profeti, and the latter, Lope's epic poem, *La hermosura de Angélica* by Marcella Trambaioli, as well as the *Rimas sacras*, edited by Carreño and Sánchez Jiménez. Good, available scholarly editions of Lope's works will continue to underpin re-assessments of his prose, poetry, drama, and indeed his biography.

The best brief introduction to Lope de Vega's life and works in English is Victor Dixon's chapter in *The Cambridge History of Spanish Literature* (ed. David T. Gies). A fine longer study in Spanish with the same scope is Felipe B. Pedraza Jinénez's *Lope de Vega*. This is more up-to-date than Francis C. Hayes's *Lope de Vega*, in the Twayne's World Author Series, although the latter volume is still useful for English-speaking readers. Many encyclopaedia entries on Lope unfortunately repeat myths created by early biographers and as a consequence should be treated with caution.

Life

Although many notable figures have produced biographical studies of Lope de Vega – Lord Holland in the nineteenth century, Astrana Marín, la Barrera, Azorín, Entrambasaguas – there is a clear need for a new scholarly biography of the man. The publication by Krzysztof Sliwa of his two-volume *Cartas, documentos y escrituras del Dr Frey Lope Félix de Vega Carpio* in 2007 provides the bedrock for such a study, although Charles Davis's *27 documentos de Lope de Vega en el Archivo Histórico de Protocolos de Madrid* must now also be taken into account. The most reliable full biography is still H. A. Rennert's, with Américo Castro's additions, *Vida de Lope de Vega (1562–1635)*, whose second edition was published by Anaya in 1968, although the original appeared as long ago as 1919. Aspects of Lope's life are deftly dealt with by, amongst others, Elizabeth Wright in her fascinating *Pilgrimage to Patronage* which neatly combines historical and literary studies to produce a convincing portrait of Lope in his middle years, and Javier Portús Pérez in his study of painting and thought in Lope's Spain, *Pintura y pensamiento en la España de Lope de Vega*. Antonio Sánchez Jiménez's recent book, *Lope pintado por sí mismo: mito e imagen del autor en la poesía de Lope de Vega Carpio* emphasizes the point that several contributors to this *Companion* make, that Lope was adept through his poetry at self-fashioning, presenting different faces at different times and for different audiences.

Lope's first biographer, Juan Pérez de Montalbán's brief but hugely influential work, the *Fama póstuma a la vida y muerte del doctor frey Lope Félix de Vega Carpio y elogios panegíricos a la inmortalidad de su nombre*, whose title betrays the author's attitude to his subject, has recently been re-edited very usefully by Enrico di Pastena.

Poetry

As is the case with Lope's drama and prose, much of the most influential scholarship appears in introductions to editions and in journal articles rather than in monographs. Indeed, this is even more the case with the poetry. However, Pedraza Jiménez does provide a good, clear overview of the landmarks of Lope's verse in his *El universo poético de Lope de Vega*, a study that also provides further detailed bibliographical guidance to the reader. Other very stimulating studies are Juan Manuel Rozas's collected *Estudios sobre Lope de Vega*, Aurora Egido's 'Lope al pie de la letra', in *La voz de las letras en el Siglo de Oro*, and, written in English, Arthur Terry's chapter 'Lope de Vega: Re-Writing a Life', in *Seventeenth-Century Spanish Poetry: The Power of Artifice* as well as much of Alan S. Trueblood's *Experience and Artistic Expression in Lope de Vega: The Making of* La Dorotea. This last study is by no means limited to the prose drama mentioned in the title. Indeed chapter 3, for example, deals with Lope's prolific ballad-writing, an aspect not treated in this *Companion*.

Pedraza Jiménez proves to be an excellent guide again in his two-volume edition of the *Rimas*, which includes the *Arte nuevo* (see below). The *Rimas sacras* are introduced and edited by Carreño and Sánchez Jiménez in the edition mentioned above and Lope's religious poetry is dealt with in Mayo's recent monograph, *La lírica sacra de Lope de Vega y José de Valdivielso*. Although there is relatively little critical bibliography on the *Rimas humanas y divinas del licenciado Tomé de Burguillos*, the recent edition of the text by Rozas and Cañas Murillo provides an excellent overview of the key issues in its introduction. Antonio Carreño's *Poesía selecta* should also be consulted, especially in terms of constituting a trajectory for Lope's poetic voice.

A brief guide to Lope's epic poetry, another neglected area, can be found in the second chapter of Pedraza's *El universo poético de Lope de Vega* and Elizabeth Wright's above-mentioned monograph explores Lope's often complex reasons for composing and publishing his epics. The best modern edition of one of the poems is Trambaioli's of *La hermosura de Angélica*.

Drama

Overviews of Lope de Vega's drama are difficult to write because of the sheer scale and variety of his output. Chapters of McKendrick's *Theatre in Spain* and Thacker's *A Companion to Golden Age Theatre* attempt the task. There are a number of good monographs on sub-genres of Lope's theatre: Donald R. Larson's *The Honor Plays of Lope de Vega* is a very well-balanced study; kingship plays are best served by Melveena McKendrick's *Playing the King* which supersedes other studies of this grouping and argues that Lope is a much more political dramatist than previous generations have thought; Robert R. Morrison introduces the saint's plays in *Lope de Vega and the* comedia de santos, and Elaine Canning's study, *Lope de Vega's comedias de tema religoso: Re-creations and Re-presentations*, takes the study of this area on substantially. Other obvious areas, such as Lope's use of history, the development of his idea of comedy and performance studies are not so well served. The volume recently edited by Fausta Antonucci entitled *Métrica y estructura dramática en el teatro de Lope de Vega* promises to re-ignite interest in two less-fashionable areas of study.

Despite its date of publication, S. Griswold Morley and Courtney Bruerton's work on the chronology and authenticity of Lope's dramatic works, based on analyses of the playwright's use of verse forms, remains essential to scholars. Lope's thoughts on dramatic theory are collected usefully in Pérez and Sánchez Escribano's *Afirmaciones de Lope de Vega sobre preceptiva dramatic*, and the surest analysis of his *Arte nuevo* occurs in Pedraza Jiménez's edition of the *Rimas*. Enrique García Santo-Tomás's Cátedra edition of the poem is also reliable and more easily accessible.

Much of the most stimulating scholarship written on Lope's theatre occurs in collections of essays, book chapters, introductions to editions and translations of his works and specialist journals, such as the *Anuario Lope de Vega*. José F.

Montesinos's *Estudios sobre Lope* is replete with acute observations about aspects of Lope's drama, as is R. D. F. Pring-Mill's introduction to *Lope de Vega: Five Plays*, translated by Jill Booty. Juan Oleza's 'La propuesta teatral del primer Lope de Vega' in *La génesis de la teatralidad barroca*, is a basic guide to some of the norms and concerns of his early drama. Individual editions of Lope plays well worth consulting are: Francisco's Rico's of *El caballero de Olmedo*, Victor Dixon's of *El perro del hortelano* and the same scholar's bilingual edition of *Fuente Ovejuna*, Ruano and Varey's of *Peribáñez y el comendador de Ocaña*, Pedraza Jiménez's of *El castigo sin venganza*, Teresa Ferrer Valls's of *La viuda valenciana*, Hélène Tropé's of *Los locos de Valencia* and Stefano Arata's of *El acero de Madrid*. And there are Grant and Cutler Critical Guides to Spanish Texts by Jack Sage to *El caballero de Olmedo* and J. B. Hall to *Fuenteovejuna*.

Finally García Santo-Tomás has recently begun to trace the reception of Lope through the centuries with his fascinating and very welcome *La creación del 'Fénix': recepción crítica y formación canónica del teatro de Lope de Vega*.

Prose

The most helpful introductions to Lope's prose works are to be found in the very solid editions of many of them which have emerged in recent decades. Castalia have produced: the pastoral romance, *La Arcadia*, one of the most popular of Lope's works in the seventeenth century but now less frequently the object of scrutiny, in Edwin S. Morby's edition; *El peregrino en su patria*, edited by Juan Bautista Avalle-Arce; *La Dorotea*, also the work of Morby; and additionally a selection of *Cartas*, edited by Nicolás Marín. In Cátedra, José Manuel Blecua's edition of *La Dorotea* emerged in 1996 to rival Morby's and even more recently the *Novelas a Marcia Leonarda*, edited by Carreño, have emerged.

The outstanding critical work on Lope's prose is Trueblood's already cited *Experience and Artistic Expression in Lope de Vega: The Making of* La Dorotea. Two monographs shed light on the short stories Lope wrote, after Cervantes: Carmen R. Rabell's *Lope de Vega: el arte nuevo de hacer 'novelas'* and Marina Scordilis Brownlee's *The Poetics of Literary Theory: Lope de Vega's 'Novelas a Marcia Leonarda' and their Cervantine Context*.

Translations

Only a tiny proportion of Lope's oeuvre has been translated into English, almost all of it drama. This is perhaps partly because of the difficulties translation poses. Translators debate vigorously the rights and wrongs of translating polymetric verse as prose and the desirability of remaining absolutely loyal to the original or of adapting for a modern audience. The two best-known collections of plays are *Lope de Vega: Five Plays* (*Peribáñez, Justice without Revenge, The Knight from Olmedo, Fuenteovejuna, The Dog in the Manger*), done by Jill Booty, and *Three*

Major Plays (*Fuente Ovejuna/ The Knight from Olmedo/ Punishment without Revenge*), translated by Gwynne Edwards. For further published versions of plays, some commissioned for performance, see the second appendix to Thacker's *A Companion to Golden Age Theatre* or the web-site of the Association for Hispanic Classical Theatre.

Translations of some of Lope's lyric poems exist in various collections of Spanish or Golden Age verse, but there has been no systematic attempt to render the whole – a prodigious undertaking. There is, however, an impressive version of the prose work, *La Dorotea*, by Alan S. Trueblood and Edwin Honig, published after seven years of toil, in 1985.

BIBLIOGRAPHY

Names in brackets at the end of individual entries indicate the contributors who have cited this source.

Aaron, M. Audrey, *Cristo en la poesía lírica de Lope de Vega* (Madrid: Cultura Hispánica, 1967). (Mayo)

Abd al-Hakam, Ibn, *Ibn Abd-el-Hakem's History of the Conquest of Spain*, trans. John Harris Jones (Göttingen: Kaestner, 1858). (Coates)

Ahlgren, Gillian T. W., 'Negotiating Sanctity: Holy Women in Sixteenth-Century Spain', *Church History*, 64.3 (1995): 373–88. (Mujica)

———, *Teresa of Ávila and the Politics of Sanctity* (Ithaca, NY & London: Cornell University Press, 1996). (Mujica)

Alcoba, Laura, 'Présence du tragique dans *La Dorotea*', in *'La Dorotea': Lope de Vega*, ed. Monique Güell (Paris: Ellipses, 2001), pp. 5–12. (Tubau)

Alfonso X, the Wise, *Las siete partidas del sabio rey don Alonso el Nono: nuevamente glosadas por el licenciado Gregorio López* (1555), facsimile edn, 3 vols (Madrid: Boletín Oficial del Estado, 1974). (Evans)

Allison, Mark, 'Pilar Miró's Last Two Films: History, Adaptation and Genre', in *Spanish Cinema: Calling the Shots*, ed. Rob Rix & Roberto Rodríguez-Saona, Leeds Iberian Papers (Leeds: Trinity and All Saints, 1999), pp. 33–45. (Wheeler)

Alonso, Dámaso, *En torno a Lope: Marino, Cervantes, Benavente, Góngora, los Cardenios*, Biblioteca Románica Hispánica, 178 (Madrid: Gredos, 1972). (Dixon)

Alonso Veloso, María José, '*El perro del hortelano*, de Pilar Miró: una adaptación no tan fiel de la comedia de Lope de Vega', *Signa: Revista de la Asociación Española de Semiótica*, 10 (2001): 375–93. (Wheeler)

Alvar, Manuel, 'Reelaboración y creación en *El castigo sin venganza*', *Revista de Filología Española*, 66.1–2 (1986): 1–38. (Friedman)

Álvarez Lopera, José, 'La reconstrución del Salón de Reinos: estado y replanteamiento de la cuestión', in *El palacio del Rey Planeta: Felipe IV y el Buen Retiro*, ed. Andrés Úbeda de los Cobos (Madrid: Museo Nacional del Prado, 2005), pp. 91–167. (Rizavi)

Ambrose, Timothy, 'Lope de Vega and Titian: The Goddess as Emblem of Sacred and Profane Love', in *Writing for the Eyes in the Spanish Golden Age*, ed. Frederick A. de Armas (Lewisburg, PA: Bucknell University Press, 2004), pp. 167–84. (De Armas)

Ames, Debra Collins, 'Love Melancholy in *La quinta de Florencia*', *Bulletin of the Comediantes*, 44.1 (1992): 45–58. (De Armas)

Amezúa, Agustín G. de, ed., *Epistolario de Lope de Vega Carpio*, see Vega, Lope de.

Andosilla Larramendi, Juan de, *Christo Nuestro Señor en la Cruz, hallado en los versos del príncipe de nuestros poetas, Garcilasso de la Vega, sacados de diferentes partes, y unidos con ley de centones* (Madrid: Viuda de Luis Sánchez, 1628); repr. in facsimile as *Centones de Garcilaso y otras poesías sueltas*, ed. Pedro Manuel Cátedra & Víctor Infantes (Barcelona: Litosefa, 1981). (Fisher)

Anon., *Novelas amorosas de los mejores ingenios de España* (Zaragoza: Viuda de Pedro Verges, 1648). (Rizavi)

Anon., '*La moza de cántaro*' (review), *Cine Asesor*, no. 615 (1954): unpaginated. (Wheeler)

Anon., '*Fahrenheit 451*' (review), *Fotogramas*, April 2006: 45. (Wheeler)

Antonucci, Fausta, ed., *Métrica y estructura dramática en el teatro de Lope de Vega*, Teatro del Siglo de Oro: Estudios de Literatura, 103 (Kassel: Reichenberger, 2007). (Thacker, 7)

Arata, Stefano, 'Teatro y coleccionismo teatral a finales del siglo XVI (el conde de Gondomar y Lope de Vega)', *Anuario Lope de Vega*, 2 (1996): 7–23. (Reidy)

Arellano, Ignacio, *Historia del teatro español del siglo XVII* (Madrid: Cátedra, 1995). (Ruano)

———, 'El modelo temprano de la comedia urbana de Lope de Vega', in his *Convención y recepción: estudios sobre el teatro del Siglo de Oro*, Biblioteca Románica Hispánica, 413 (Madrid: Gredos, 1999), pp. 76–106. (Thacker, 11)

———, Juan M. Escudero & Abraham Madroñal, ed., Luis Quiñones de Benavente, *Entremeses completos*, I: *Jocoseria*, Biblioteca Áurea Hispánica, 14 ([Pamplona]: Universidad de Navarra; Madrid: Iberoamericana; Frankfurt am Main: Vervuert, 2001). (Ruano)

Aristotle, *Poetics*, trans. S. H. Butcher (Mineola, NY: Dover Publications, 1997). (Coates)

Armas, Frederick de, see De Armas, Frederick.

Armas, José de, *Cervantes y el duque de Sessa: nuevas observaciones sobre el Quijote de Avellaneda y su autor* (Habana: P. Fernández, 1909).

Astrana Marín, Luis, *Vida azarosa de Lope de Vega*, 2nd edn (Barcelona: Editorial Juventud, 1941).

Augustine, Saint, *The City of God*, trans. Marcus Dods, intr. Thomas Merton (New York: The Modern Library, 1950). (De Armas)

Ávila, Francisco Javier, '*La Dorotea*: arte y estrategia de senectud, entre la serenidad y la desesperación', *Edad de Oro*, 14 (1995): 9–27. (Tubau)

Azorín, *Obras completas*, 9 vols, ed. Ángel Cruz Rueda (Madrid: Aguilar, 1948–63). (Dixon)

Barrera, Cayetano Alberto de la, see La Barrera, Cayetano Alberto de.

Bastenier, M. A., 'El alcalde de Zalamea: Calderón no era culpable', El País, 13 May 1983: 36. (Wheeler)

Bataillon, Marcel, Varia lección de clásicos españoles, Biblioteca Románica Hispánica, 77 (Madrid: Gredos, 1964). (Rizavi)

Bédier, Joseph, Les légendes épiques: recherches sur la formation des chansons de geste (Paris: Champion, 1908). (Coates)

Benjamin, Walter, 'The Task of the Translator' (1923), in his Illuminations, ed. Hannah Arendt, trans. Harry Zohn (New York: Harcourt, Brace & World, 1968), pp. 69–82. (Johnston)

Bennett Susan, Theatre Audiences: A Theory of Production and Reception (London: Routledge, 1990; 2nd edn, 1997). (Mujica)

Bentley, Eric 'The Universality of the Comedia', Hispanic Review, 38.2 (1970): 147–62. (Johnston)

Bergmann, Emilie, 'The Painting's Observer in the Epic Canvas: La hermosura de Angélica', Comparative Literature, 38.3 (1986): 270–88. (Coates)

Bermejo, Alberto, 'Fiel, sobria y brillante', review of El perro del hortelano, El Mundo, 25 January 1997: 3. (Wheeler)

Biblia Sacra iuxta Vulgatam Clementinam, ed. Alberto Colunga & Laurentio Turrado, Biblioteca de Autores Cristianos (Madrid: Editorial Católica, 1965). (Fisher)

Biblioteca Virtual Cervantes, Lope de Vega (retratos), at website http://www.cervantesvirtual.com/bib_autor/Lope/retratos.shtml, pp. 1–3. (McGrath)

Billington, Michael, review of Peribáñez, Guardian, 9 May 2003. (Samson & Thacker, 8)

Blecua, Alberto, 'De Granada a Lope: sobre una fuente de Los cinco misterios dolorosos', Anuario Lope de Vega, 1 (1995): 9–17. (Mayo)

Blue, William R., 'The Politics of Lope's Fuenteovejuna', Hispanic Review, 59.3 (1991): 339–41. (Samson & Thacker, 8)

———, Spanish Comedy and Historical Contexts in the 1620s (University Park, PA: Pennsylvania State University Press, 1996). (Thacker, 11)

Bouzy, Christian, 'L'Emblématique des lieux communs dans La Dorotea: Lope de Vega dans l'entre-deux', in Lectures d'une oeuvre: 'La Dorotea' de Lope de Vega, ed. Nadine Ly (Paris: Éditions du Temps, 2001), pp. 65–123. (Tubau)

Bradbury, Gail, 'Lope's Plays of Bandello Origin', Forum for Modern Language Studies, 16 (1980): 53–65. (Dixon)

———, 'Tragedy and Tragicomedy in the Theatre of Lope de Vega', Bulletin of Hispanic Studies, 58.2 (1981): 103–11. (Thacker, 11)

Brook, Peter, The Empty Space (Penguin: Harmondsworth, 1968). (Mujica)

Brown, Jonathan, Kings and Connoisseurs: Collecting Art in Seventeenth-Century Europe (Princeton, NJ: Princeton University Press, 1995). (De Armas)

———, Painting in Spain, 1500–1700 (New Haven, CT & London: Yale University Press, 1998). (McGrath)

——— & J. H. Elliott, Un palacio para el rey: el Buen Retiro y la corte de Felipe IV, edn revisada y ampliada (Madrid: Taurus, 2003). (McGrath)

Brownlee, Marina Scordilis, *The Poetics of Literary Theory: Lope de Vega's 'Novelas a Marcia Leonarda' and their Cervantine Context* (Madrid: José Porrúa Turanzas, 1981). (Rizavi)

———, 'Lope's Conception of Literary Theory: The Example of the *Novelas*', *Kentucky Romance Quarterly*, 30.2 (1983): 149–57. (Rizavi)

Buci-Glucksmann, Christine, *La Folie du voir: une esthétique du virtuel* (Paris: Galilée, 2002). (Torres)

Budick, Sanford & Wolfgang Iser, ed., *The Translatability of Cultures: Figurations of the Space Between* (Stanford, CA: Stanford University Press, 1996). (Johnston)

Bunn, Elaine, 'Negotiating Empire and Desire in Lope de Vega's *Carlos V en Francia*', *Hispanic Review*, 72.1 (2004): 29–42. (De Armas)

Burke, Peter, *The Renaissance Sense of the Past* (London: Edward Arnold, 1969). (Coates)

———, 'How to be a Counter-Reformation Saint', in *Religion and Society in Early Modern Europe, 1500–1800*, ed. Kaspar von Greyerz (London: German Historical Institute & George Allen and Unwin, 1984), pp. 45–55. (Mujica)

Byrd, Suzanne, 'The Twentieth Century *Fuenteovejuna* of Federico García Lorca', *García Lorca Review*, 5 (1977): 34–39. (Samson & Thacker, 8)

Calderón de la Barca, Pedro, 'Soneto al Maestro Joseph de Casanova', in José de Casanova, *Primera parte del arte de escrivir todas las formas de letras*: *escrito y tallado por el Maestro Joseph de Casanova* (Madrid: Diego Díaz de la Carrera, 1650), fol. ¶2v. (Fisher)

———, *Six Dramas of Calderon: Freely Translated by Edward Fitzgerald* (London: William Pickering, 1853). (Johnston)

Calvo Sastre, Ana, Lola Millás & Antonio Papell, *Literatura española: una historia de cine* (Madrid: Polifemo, 2005). (Wheeler)

Camacho, José María, '*La dama boba*, el cine en verso', *ABC*, 24 March 2006: 34. (Wheeler)

Canet Vallés, J. L., 'Las comedias manuscritas anónimas o de posibles "autores de comedias" como fuente documental para la reconstrucción del hecho teatral en el período áureo', in *Teatros y vida teatral en el Siglo de Oro a través de las fuentes documentales*, ed. Luciano García Lorenzo & J. E. Varey, Colección Támesis, Serie A: Monografías, 145 (London: Tamesis, 1991), pp. 273–83. (Ruano)

Canning, Elaine M., *Lope de Vega's 'Comedias de tema religioso': Re-creations and Re-presentations*, Colección Tamesis, Serie A: Monografías, 204 (Woodbridge: Tamesis, 2004). (Canning) (Mayo) (Thacker, 11)

———, '"Not I, My Shadow": Pilar Miró's Adaptation of Lope de Vega's *The Dog in the Manger* (1996)', *Studies in European Cinema*, 2.2 (2005): 81–92. (Wheeler)

———, 'Identity and the Refashioning of Role in *La buena guarda*: The Cases of Carrizo and Félix', *Bulletin of Spanish Studies*, 84.7 (2007): 859–69. (Canning)

Canonica-de Rochemonteix, Elvezio, *El poliglotismo en el teatro de Lope de Vega*, Teatro del Siglo de Oro: Estudios de Literatura, 11 (Kassel: Reichenberger, 1991). (Dixon)

Capello, Fernando 'La Femme inspiratrice et réceptrice de la nouvelle au XVIIe siècle', in *Images de la femme en Espagne au XVIe et XVIIe siècles: des traditions aux renouvellements et à l'émergence d'images nouvelles: colloque international, Sorbonne et Collège de France, 28–30 septembre 1992*, dir. Augustin Redondo, Travaux du Centre de Recherche sur l'Espagne des XVIe et XVIIe siècles, 9 (Paris: Publications de la Sorbonne, Presses de la Sorbonne Nouvelle, 1994), pp. 365–79. (Rizavi)

Caravajal, Mery, 'Entrevista con Juan Guerrero Zamora', *Pueblo*, 20 November 1972: 35. (Wheeler)

Carducho, Vicente, *Diálogos de la pintura: su defensa, origen, esencia, definición, modos y diferencias*, ed. Francisco Calvo Serraller (Madrid: Turner, 1979). (Dixon)

Carlson, Marvin, *The Haunted Stage: The Theatre as Memory Machine* (Ann Arbor, MI: University of Michigan Press, 2001). (Johnston)

Caro Baroja, Julio, 'Honour and Shame: A Historical Account of Several Conflicts', in *Honour and Shame: The Values of Mediterranean Society*, ed. J. G. Peristiany (London: Weidenfeld & Nicolson, 1965), pp. 79–137. (Evans)

Carreño, Antonio, *El romancero lírico de Lope de Vega*, Biblioteca Románica Hispánica, 285 (Madrid: Gredos, 1979). (Rizavi)

———, 'Los engaños de la escritura: las *Rimas de Tomé de Burguillos* de Lope de Vega', in *Lope de Vega y los orígines del teatro español: Actas del I Congreso Internacional sobre Lope de Vega*, ed. Manuel Criado de Val (Madrid: EDI-6, 1981), pp. 547–63. (Torres)

———, 'La "sin venganza" como violencia: *El castigo sin venganza* de Lope de Vega', *Hispanic Review*, 59.4 (1991): 379–400. (Friedman)

———, '"Amor regalado"/"amor ofendido": las ficciones del yo lírico en las *Rimas* (1609) de Lope de Vega', in *Hispanic Studies in Honour of Geoffrey Ribbans*, ed. Ann L. Mackenzie & Dorothy S. Severin, *Bulletin of Hispanic Studies* Special Homage Volume (Liverpool: Liverpool University Press, 1992), pp. 73–82. (Torres)

———, 'Los mitos del yo lírico: *Rimas* (1609) de Lope de Vega', *Edad de Oro*, 14 (1995): 55–72. (Torres)

———, '"... La sangre / muere en las venas heladas": *El castigo sin venganza*, de Lope de Vega', in *Hispanic Essays in Honor of Frank P. Casa*, ed. A. Robert Lauer & Henry W. Sullivan, Ibérica, 20 (New York: Peter Lang, 1997), pp. 84–102. (Friedman)

———, '"Que érades vos lo más sutil del mundo": de *Burguillos* (Lope) y Quevedo', *Calíope*, 8.2 (2002): 25–50. (Torres)

———, '«De esta manera de escribir tan nueva»: Lope y Góngora', in *Lope en 1604*, ed. Xavier Tubau (Lleida: Milenio & Universitat Autònoma de Barcelona, 2004), pp. 43–59. (Samson & Thacker, Introduction)

Carrera, Elena, *Teresa of Avila's Autobiography: Authority, Power and the Self in Mid-Sixteenth-Century Spain*, Legenda (London: Modern Humanities Research Association & Maney, 2005). (Mujica)

Cartagena-Calderón, José, '"Él es tan rara persona": sobre cortesanos, lindos, sodomitas y otras masculinidades nefandas en la España de la temprana Edad Moderna', in *Lesbianism and Homosexuality in Early Modern Spain: Literature and Theater in Context*, ed. María José Delgado & Alain Saint-Saëns, Iberian Studies, 37 (New Orleans, LA: University Press of the South, 2000), pp. 139–75. (De Armas)

Carvallo, Luis Alfonso de, *Cisne de Apolo*, ed. Alberto Porqueras Mayo, Teatro del Siglo de Oro: Ediciones Críticas, 82 (Kassel: Reichenberger, 1997). (Fisher)

Case, Thomas E., 'Lope's *Las almenas de Toro*: An Example of the Poetic Interpretation of History', *Romance Notes*, 11 (1969): 333–38. (Coates)

———, *Las dedicatorias de Partes XIII–XX de Lope de Vega: estudio crítico con textos*, Estudios de Hispanófila, 32 (Chapel Hill, NC: University of North Carolina & Madrid: Castalia, 1975). (Dixon) (Reidy)

Castiglione, Baldassare, *The Book of the Courtier*, trans. George Bull, Penguin Classics, L192 (Harmondsworth & Baltimore, MD: Penguin, 1967). (De Armas)

Castillejo, David, *Las cuatrocientas comedias de Lope: catálogo crítico* (Madrid: Teatro Clásico Español, 1984). (Ruano)

Castro, Américo & Hugo A. Rennert, *Vida de Lope de Vega (1562–1635)*, 2nd edn (Madrid: Anaya, 1968; repr. 1969). See also Rennert. (Mayo) (Samson) (Samson & Thacker, Introduction)

Cayuela, Anne, 'La prosa de ficción entre 1625 y 1634: balance de diez años sin licencias para imprimir novelas en los reinos de Castilla', *Mélanges de la Casa de Velázquez*, 29.2 (1993): 51–76. (Tubau)

Certeau, Michel de, *The Writing of History*, trans. Tom Conley (New York & Chichester, NY: Columbia University Press, 1988). (Johnston)

Cervantes, Saavedra, Miguel de, *El ingenioso hidalgo Don Quijote de la Mancha*, ed. Luis Andrés Murillo, 2 vols, Clásicos Castalia, 77–78, 3rd edn (Madrid: Castalia, 1982). (Thacker, 7)

———, *Don Quijote de La Mancha*, ed. Francisco Rico, Biblioteca Clásica (Barcelona: Instituto Cervantes & Crítica, 1998). (Fisher)

———, *Entremeses*, ed. Nicholas Spadaccini, Letras Hispánicas, 162, 13th edn (Madrid: Cátedra, 1998). (Reidy) (Samson & Thacker, Introduction)

———, *Don Quixote*, trans. John Rutherford (London: Penguin, 2000). (Thacker, 7)

———, *Novelas ejemplares*, ed. Jorge García López, Biblioteca Clásica, 49 (Barcelona: Crítica, 2001). (Fisher)

Chartier, Roger, *Entre poder y placer: cultura escrita y literatura en la Edad Moderna* (Madrid: Cátedra, 2000). (Reidy)

———, 'La pluma, el taller y la voz: entre crítica textual e historia cultural', in *Imprenta y crítica textual en el Siglo de Oro*, ed. Pablo Andrés & Sonia

Garza, Clásicos Españoles, 22 (Valladolid: Universidad de Valladolid & Centro para la Edición de los Clásicos Españoles, 2000), pp. 243–57. (Reidy)

Checa, Fernando, *Tiziano y la monarquía hispánica: usos y funciones de la pintura veneciana en España (siglos XVI y XVII)* (Madrid: Nerea, 1994). (De Armas)

Cirot, Georges, 'Valeur littéraire des nouvelles de Lope de Vega', *Bulletin Hispanique*, 28.4 (1926): 321–55. (Rizavi)

Civil, Pierre, 'Erotismo y pintura mitológica en la España del Siglo de Oro', *Edad de Oro*, 9 (1990): 39–49. (De Armas)

Coates, Geraldine, 'The 1541 *Crónica general* and the Historical Theatre of Juan de la Cueva and Lope de Vega: An Epic Debt', *Bulletin of the Comediantes*, 60 (2008) (forthcoming). (Coates)

Coira, Pepe, *Antonio Román: un cineasta de la posguerra* (Madrid: Editorial Complutense, 2004). (Wheeler)

Collaert, Adriaen, Cornelis Galle, Roderico Lasso, and Albrecht, *Vita S. Virginis Teresiæ a Iesv ordinis carmelitarvm excalceatorvm piae restavratricis* (Antverpiæ: Apud Ionnem Galleum, 1630). See also Galle, Cornelio. (Mujica)

Compte, Deborah, 'The Sojourn in the Garden: The Pastoral Tradition in Lope de Vega's *Novelas a Marcia Leonarda*', *Hispania*, 76.4 (1993): 656–63. (Rizavi)

Contag, Kimberly, *Mockery in Spanish Golden Age Literature: Analysis of Burlesque Representation* (Lanham, MD & London: University Press of America, 1996). (Torres)

Corral, José del, *Las composiciones de aposento y las casas a la malicia* (Madrid: Instituto de Estudios Madrileños, 1982). (Ruano)

Correas, Gonzalo, *Vocabulario de refranes y frases proverbiales* (1627), ed. Louis Combet, Bibliothèque de l'École des Hautes Études Hispaniques, fasc. 34 (Bordeaux: Féret, 1967). (Evans)

Cortes de los antiguos reinos de León y de Castilla, 5 vols (Madrid: Real Academia de la Historia, 1861–1903). (Coates)

Coso Marín, Miguel Ángel, Mercedes Higuera Sánchez-Pardo & Juan Sanz Ballesteros, *El teatro Cervantes de Alcalá de Henares: 1602–1866. Estudio y documentos*, Fuentes para la Historia del Teatro en España, 18 (London: Tamesis, 1989). (Ruano)

Cotarelo y Mori, Emilio, ed., *Bibliografía de las controversias sobre la licitud del teatro en España* (Madrid: Revista de Archivos, Bibliotecas y Museos, 1904). (Thacker, 11)

———, *Ensayo sobre la vida y obras de D. Pedro Calderón de la Barca* (Madrid: Revista de Archivos, Bibliotecas y Museos, 1924). (Ruano)

Covarrubias Orozco, Sebastián de, *Emblemas morales* (Madrid: Luis Sánchez, 1610). (Samson & Thacker, 8)

———, *Tesoro de la lengua castellana o española* (1611), ed. Martín de Riquer (Barcelona: Horta, 1943; repr. Barcelona: Alta Fulla, 1993). (Fisher)

————, *Tesoro de la lengua castellana o española* (Madrid: Turner, 1977). (Canning) (Evans)

————, *Tesoro de la lengua castellana o española* (1611), ed. Felipe C. R. Maldonado, rev. Manuel Camarero, Nueva Biblioteca de Erudición y Crítica, 7, 2nd edn (Madrid: Castalia, 1995). (Samson & Thacker, 8)

Croce, Alda, *La 'Dorotea' di Lope de Vega: studio critico seguito dalla traduzione delle parti principali dell'opera*, Biblioteca di Cultura Moderna, 348 (Bari: Laterza, 1940). (Tubau)

Croyden, Margaret, *Conversations with Peter Brook, 1970–2000* (New York: Faber and Faber, 2003). (Mujica)

Cruz, Sor Juana Inés de la, *Sonetos*, ed. Luis Íñigo-Madrigal, Nuestros Poetas, 4 (Madrid: Biblioteca Nueva, 2001). (Fisher)

Cueva, Juan de la, *Comedia de la muerte del rey don Sancho y reto de Çamora, por don Diego Ordóñez*, in Cueva, *Comedias y tragedias*, ed. Francisco A. de Icaza, 2 vols (Madrid: Sociedad de Bibliófilos Españoles, 1917), I, pp. 11–53. (Coates)

————, *Los siete infantes de Lara*, in *El infamador, Los siete infantes de Lara y El ejemplar poético*, ed. Francisco A. de Icaza, Clásicos Castellanos, 60 (Madrid: Espasa Calpe, 1941), pp. 60–115. (Coates)

————, *Bernardo del Carpio*, ed. Anthony Watson, Exeter Hispanic Texts, 8 (Exeter: Univerity of Exeter, 1974). (Coates)

Culler, Jonathan, 'The Modern Lyric: Generic Continuity and Critical Practice', in *The Comparative Perspective on Literature: Approaches to Theory and Practice*, ed. Clayton Koelb & Susan Noakes (Ithaca & London: Cornell University Press, 1988), pp. 284–99. (Torres)

Dagenais, John, 'The Imaginative Faculty and Artistic Creation in Lope', in *Lope de Vega y los orígenes del teatro español: Actas del I Congreso Internacional sobre Lope de Vega*, ed. Manuel Criado de Val (Madrid: EDI-6, 1981), pp. 321–26. (Coates)

Dassbach, Elma, *La comedia hagiográfica del Siglo de Oro español: Lope de Vega, Tirso de Molina y Calderón de la Barca*, Ibérica, 22 (New York: Peter Lang, 1997). (Canning) (Mujica)

Davis, Charles, ed., *27 documentos de Lope de Vega en el Archivo Histórico de Protocolos de Madrid* (Madrid: Comunidad de Madrid, 2004). (Dixon) (Samson & Thacker, Introduction)

De Armas, Frederick A., 'Lope de Vega and Titian', *Comparative Literature*, 30.4 (1978): 338–52. (Dixon) (De Armas)

————, 'Italian Canvases in Lope de Vega's *Comedias*: The Case of *Venus and Adonis*', *Crítica Hispánica*, 2.2 (1980): 135–42. (De Armas)

————, 'Lope de Vega and Michelangelo', *Hispania*, 65.2 (1982): 172–79. (De Armas)

————, 'La estructura mítica de *Los comendadores de Córdoba*', in *Actas del X Congreso de la Asociación Internacional de Hispanistas: Barcelona, 21–26 de agosto de 1989*, ed. Antonio Vilanova, 4 vols (Barcelona, PPU, 1992), I, pp. 763–72. (Evans)

————, 'The Allure of the Oriental Other: Titian's *Rossa Sultana* and Lope de Vega's *La Santa Liga*', in *Brave New Words: Studies in Spanish Golden Age Literature*, ed. Edward H. Friedman & Catherine Larson, Iberian Studies, 12 (New Orleans: University Press of the South, 1996), pp. 191–208. (De Armas)

————, 'The Silences of Myth: (Con)fusing Eróstrato/Erasístrato in Lope's *El castigo sin venganza*', in *Hispanic Essays in Honor of Frank P. Casa*, ed. A. Robert Lauer & Henry W. Sullivan, Ibérica, 20 (New York: Peter Lang, 1997), pp. 65–75. (Friedman)

————, 'De Tiziano a Rafael: pinturas y libros en *La viuda valenciana* de Lope de Vega', in *Actas del XIV Congreso de la Asociación Internacional de Hispanistas: New York, 16–21 de julio de 2001*, ed. Isaías Lerner, Robert Nival & Alejandro Alonso, 4 vols (Newark, DE: Juan de la Cuesta, 2004), II, pp. 165–72. (De Armas)

————, 'Pinturas de Lucrecia en el *Quijote*: Tiziano, Rafael y Lope de Vega', *Anuario de Estudios Cervantinos*, 1 (2004): 109–20. (De Armas)

————, ed., *Ekphrasis in the Age of Cervantes* (Lewisburg, PA: Bucknell University Press, 2005). (De Armas)

————, *Quixotic Frescoes: Cervantes and Italian Renaissance Art* (Toronto & London: University of Toronto Press, 2006). (De Armas)

De Armas Wilson, Diana, '"Passing the Love of Women": The Intertextuality of *El curioso impertinente*', *Cervantes*, 7.2 (1987): 9–28. (De Armas)

Delooz, Pierre, 'Towards a Sociological Study of Canonized Sainthood in the Catholic Church', in *Saints and their Cults: Studies in Religious Sociology, Folklore and History*, ed. Stephen Wilson (Cambridge & New York: Cambridge University Press, 1983), pp. 189–216. (Mujica)

Demoor, Marysa, ed., *Marketing the Author: Authorial Personae, Narrative Selves and Self-Fashioning, 1880–1930* (Basingstoke: Palgrave Macmillan, 2004). (Torres)

Deyermond, A. D., *A Literary History of Spain: The Middle Ages* (London: Ernest Benn, 1971). (Coates)

Díez Borque, José María, '¿De qué vivía Lope de Vega? Actitud de un escritor en su vida y ante su obra', *Segismundo*, 8, nos 15–16 (1972): 65–90. (Reidy)

————, *Sociedad y teatro en la España de Lope de Vega* (Barcelona: Antoni Bosch, 1978). (Dixon)

————, 'Lope de Vega trágico: juventud-madurez', *Ínsula*, no. 658 (2001): 18–22. (Friedman)

Díez de Revenga Torres, Francisco Javier, 'La imaginación en Lope de Vega: los espacios de *El peregrino en su patria*', in *Loca ficta: los espacios de la maravilla en la Edad Media y el Siglo de Oro: actas del coloquio internacional, Pamplona, Universidad de Navarra, abril, 2002*, ed. Ignacio Arellano, Biblioteca Áurea Hispánica, 26 ([Pamplona]: Universidad de Navarra; Madrid: Iberoamericana; Frankfurt-am-Main: Vervuert, 2003), pp. 189–202. (Samson)

Diplomatic Information Office, *The Spanish Cinema* (Madrid: Diplomatic Information Office, 1949). (Wheeler)

Dixon, Victor, '"Beatus... nemo": *El villano en su rincón*, las "polianteas" y la literatura de emblemas', *Cuadernos de Filología* (Valencia), 3.1–2: *La génesis de la teatralidad barroca* (1981): 279–300. (Dixon)

———, 'La comedia de corral de Lope como género visual', *Edad de Oro*, 5 (1986): 35–58. (Dixon)

———, 'Lope de Vega no conocía el *Decamerón* de Boccaccio', in *El mundo del teatro español en su Siglo de Oro: ensayos dedicados a John E. Varey*, ed. J. M. Ruano de la Haza, Ottawa Hispanic Studies, 3 (Ottawa: Dovehouse Editions Canada, 1989), pp. 185–96. (Dixon)

———, 'The *Emblemas morales* of Sebastián de Covarrubias and the Plays of Lope de Vega', *Emblematica*, 6.1 (1992): 83–101. (Dixon)

———, 'Lope de Vega, Chile and a Propaganda Campaign', *Bulletin of Hispanic Studies*, 70.1 (1993): 79–95. (Dixon)

———, 'La intervención de Lope en la publicación de sus comedias', *Anuario Lope de Vega*, 2 (1996): 45–63. (Reidy) (Samson & Thacker, Introduction)

———, '"Ya tienes la comedia prevenida ... la imagen de la vida": *Lo fingido verdadero*', *Cuadernos de teatro clásico*, 11 (1999): 53–71. (Canning)

———, 'Lope Félix de Vega Carpio', in *The Cambridge History of Spanish Literature*, ed. David T. Gies (Cambridge: Cambridge University Press, 2004), pp. 251–64. (Samson & Thacker, Introduction)

———, 'La huella en Lope de la tradición clásica: ¿honda o superficial?', *Anuario Lope de Vega*, 11 (2005): 83–96. (Dixon)

——— & Isabel Torres, '*La madrastra enamorada*: ¿una tragedia de Séneca refundida por Lope de Vega?', *Revista Canadiense de Estudios Hispánicos*, 19.1 (1994): 39–60. (Dixon)

Dolan, Frances E., *Whores of Babylon: Catholicism, Gender, and Seventeenth-Century Print Culture* (Ithaca, NY & London: Cornell University Press, 1999). (Mujica)

Domínguez Ortiz, Antonio, *Las clases privilegiadas en la España del Antiguo Régimen*, Colección Fundamentos, 31 (Madrid: Ediciones Istmo, 1973). (Samson & Thacker, Introduction)

Douglas, Mary, *Purity and Danger: An Analysis of the Concepts of Pollution and Taboo* (London: Routledge, 1984; 1st edn 1966). (Evans)

Edwards, Gwynne, 'Lope and Calderón: The Tragic Pattern of *El castigo sin venganza*', *Bulletin of the Comediantes*, 33.2 (1981): 107–20. (Friedman)

Egido, Aurora, 'Lope de Vega, Ravisio Textor y la creación del mundo como obra de arte', in *Homenaje a Eugenio Asensio*, ed. Luisa López Grigera & Augustin Redondo (Madrid: Gredos, 1988), pp. 171–83; repr. in her *Fronteras de la poesía en el Barroco*, Filología, 20 (Barcelona: Crítica, 1990), pp. 198–215. (Dixon)

———, 'Escritura y poesía: Lope al pie de la letra', *Edad de Oro*, 14 (1995): 121–49. (Torres)

———, *La voz de las letras en el Siglo de Oro* (Madrid: Abada, 2003). (Fisher)

Eisenstein, Elizabeth L., *The Printing Revolution in Early Modern Europe* (Cambridge: Cambridge University Press, 1983). (Mujica)

Elliott, J. H., *The Count-Duke of Olivares: The Statesman in an Age of Decline* (New Haven, CT & London: Yale University Press, 1986). (Rizavi)

———, *Spain and its World, 1500–1700: Selected Essays* (New Haven, CT & London: Yale University Press, 1989). (Coates)

Entrambasaguas, Joaquín de, *Estudios sobre Lope de Vega*, 3 vols (Madrid: Consejo Superior de Investigaciones Científicas, 1946–58). (Dixon)

———, 'Un códice de Lope de Vega autógrafo y desconocido' *Revista de Literatura*, 38 (1970): 5–117. (Samson & Thacker, Introduction)

Étienvre, Jean-Pierre, 'Castigo y venganza en *La Dorotea*', *Anuario Lope de Vega*, 8 (2002): 19–34. (Tubau)

Evans, Peter W., 'Character and Context in *El castigo sin venganza*', *Modern Language Review*, 74.2 (1979): 321–34. (Friedman)

———, *From Golden Age to Silver Screen: The Comedia on Film*, Papers in Spanish Theatre History, 5 (London: Department of Hispanic Studies, Queen Mary and Westfield College, 1997). (Wheeler)

Falque, Emma, *Lucae Tudensis Chronicon mundi*, Corpus Christianorum: Continuatio Mediaevalis, 74 (Turnhout: Brepols, 2003). (Coates)

Fernández, Esther & Cristina Martínez-Carazo, 'Mirar y desear: la construcción del personaje femenino en *El perro del hortelano* de Lope de Vega y de Pilar Miró', *Bulletin of Spanish Studies*, 83.3 (2006): 315–28. (Wheeler)

Fernández, Jaime, '*Los comendadores de Córdoba*: ¿un caso de honor recobrado?', *Bulletin of the Comediantes*, 38.1 (1986): 55-62. (Evans)

Fernández Gómez, Carlos, *Vocabulario completo de Lope de Vega*, 3 vols (Madrid: Real Academia Española, 1971). (Dixon)

Feros, Antonio, '"Sacred and Terrifying Gazes"', in *The Cambridge Companion to Velázquez*, ed. Suzanne L. Stratton-Pruitt (Cambridge: Cambridge University Press, 2002), pp. 68–86. (Mujica)

Ferrer Valls, Teresa, '"Sustento, en fin, lo que escribí": Lope de Vega y el conflicto de la creación', in *Pigmalión o el amor por lo creado*, ed. Facundo Tomás & Isabel Justo (Rubí, Barcelona: Anthropos & Universidad Politécnica de Valencia, 2005), pp. 99–112. (Reidy)

Ferreras, Juan Ignacio, *La novela en el siglo XVII*, Historia Crítica de la Literatura Hispánica, 7 (Madrid: Taurus, 1988). (Samson)

Finaldi, Gabriele, 'Retrato y realidad: Ribalta, Zurbarán, Ribera', in *El retrato español: del Greco a Picasso*, ed. Javier Portús Pérez (Madrid: Museo Nacional del Prado, 2004), pp. 150–69. Translated as 'Portrait and Reality: Ribalta, Zurbarán, Ribera', in *The Spanish Portrait: From El Greco to Picasso*, ed. Javier Portús Pérez (London: Scala, 2004), pp. 146–65. (McGrath)

Fiore, Robert L., '*Fuenteovejuna*: Philosophical Views on the State and Revolution', in *Hispanic Essays in Honor of Frank P. Casa*, ed. A. Robert Lauer & Henry W. Sullivan, Ibérica, 20 (New York: Peter Lang, 1997), pp. 103–11. (Samson & Thacker, 8)

Fischer, Susan L., 'Lope's *El castigo sin venganza* and the Imagination', *Kentucky Romance Quarterly*, 28.1 (1981): 23–36. (Friedman)

———, 'Staging Lope's *Peribáñez*: The Problem of an Ending', *Bulletin of Spanish Studies*, 82.2 (2005): 157–79. (Samson & Thacker, 8)

Flores, Ángel, ed., *Great Spanish Plays in English Translation*, with a preface by John Gassner (New York: Dover, 1991). (Johnston)

Forcione, Alban, 'Lope's Broken Clock: Baroque Time in the *Dorotea*', *Hispanic Review*, 37.4 (1969): 459–90. (Tubau)

Foucault, Michel, *The History of Sexuality*, trans. Robert Hurley, 3 vols (New York: Random House, 1986). (De Armas)

———, 'Qu'est-ce qu'un auteur?', in *Dits et écrits, 1954–1988*, ed. Daniel Defert & François Ewald, with the collaboration of Jacques Lagrange, 4 vols (Paris: Gallimard, 1994), I, pp. 789–821. (Reidy)

Frenk, Margit, 'Claves metafóricas en *El castigo sin venganza*', *Filología*, 20.2 (1985): 147–55. (Friedman)

———, *Entre la voz y el silencio: la lectura en tiempos de Cervantes*, Biblioteca de Estudios Cervantinos, 4 (Alcalá de Henares: Centro de Estudios Cervantinos, 1997). (Rizavi)

Friedman, Edward H., *Cervantes in the Middle: Realism and Reality in the Spanish Novel from 'Lazarillo de Tormes' to 'Niebla'*, Juan de la Cuesta Hispanic Monographs, 26 (Newark, DE: Juan de la Cuesta, 2006). (Friedman)

Frye, Northrop, *Anatomy of Criticism: Four Essays* (Princeton, NJ: Princeton University Press, 1957; repr. New York: Atheneum, 1965). (Coates) (Torres)

Fucilla, Joseph G., *Estudios sobre el petrarquismo en España*, Anejos de la Revista de Filología Española, 72 (Madrid: OGRAMA, 1960). (Torres)

Fuentes III, see Varey, J. E. & N. D. Shergold. (Ruano)

Galán, Diego, *Pilar Miró: nadie me enseñó a vivir*, (Barcelona: Plaza & Janés, 2006). (Wheeler)

Galle, Cornelio and Adrián Collaert, *Estampas de la vida de la Santa Madre Teresa de Jesús. Grabadas por los famosos artistas Cornelio Galle y Adrián Collaert, impresas en Amberes en 1613, ahora reproducidas en facsímil y publicadas por Carlos Sanz, en ocasión de la conmemoración del IV centenario de la reforma de la Orden Carmelitana* (Madrid: Carlos Sanz, 1962). (Mujica)

Garasa, Delfín Leocadio, *Santos en escena* (Bahía Blanca: Instituto de Humanidades & Universidad Nacional del Sur, 1960). (Canning)

García-Bermejo Giner, Miguel M., 'Transmisión y recepción de la obra teatral en el siglo XVI', in *Historia del teatro español*, ed. Javier Huerta Calvo, 2 vols (Madrid: Gredos, 2003), I, pp. 527–48. (Reidy)

García Calderón, Ventura, ed., *Discurso en loor de la poesía*, in *El apogeo de la literatura colonial: las poetisas anónimas, el Lunarejo, Caviedes*, Biblioteca de Cultura Peruana, 5 (Paris: Desclée, de Brouwer, 1938), pp. 13–40. (Fisher)

García-Posada, Miguel, 'Un perro muy particular' (review of *El perro del hortalano*), *El País*, 6 February 1997: 32. (Wheeler)

García Santo-Tomás, Enrique, *La creación del Fénix: recepción crítica y formación canónica del teatro de Lope de Vega*, Biblioteca Románica Hispánica, 421 (Madrid: Gredos, 2000). (Wheeler) (Samson & Thacker, 8 and Introduction)

———, 'Diana, Lope, Pilar Miró: horizontes y resistencias de clausura en *El perro del hortelano*', in *'Otro Lope no ha de haber': atti del Convegno Internazionale su Lope de Vega, 10–13 febbraio 1999*, ed. M. G. Profeti, 3 vols (Florence: Alinea, 2000), II, pp. 51–61. (Wheeler)

———, 'Lope, ventrílocuo de Lope: capital social, capital cultural y estrategia literaria en las *Rimas de Tomé de Burguillos* (1634)', *Bulletin of Hispanic Studies* (Glasgow), 77.4 (2000): 287–303. (Torres) (Samson & Thacker, Introduction)

Gascón, Christopher D., *The Woman Saint in Spanish Golden Age Drama* (Lewisburg, PA: Bucknell University Press, 2006). (Mujica)

Gaylord, Karen, 'Theatrical Performances: Structure and Process, Tradition and Revolt', in *Performers and Performances: The Sociology of Artistic Work*, ed. Jack B. Kamerman & Rosannne Martorella (South Hadley, MA: J. F. Bergin; New York: Praeger, 1982), pp. 135–50. (Mujica)

Gaylord Randel, Mary, see Randel, Mary Gaylord.

Gea Ortigas, María Isabel, *El plano de Texeira* (Madrid: Ediciones La Librería, 1999). (Ruano)

Genealogía, see Shergold, N. D. & J. E. Varey. (Ruano)

Gil Enríquez, Andrés, *El ensayo*, in Hannah E. Bergman, ed., *Ramillete de entremeses y bailes: nuevamente recogido de los antiguos poetas de España, siglo XVII*, Clásicos Castalia, 21 (Madrid: Castalia, 1970), pp. 337–46. (Ruano)

Gilbert-Santamaria, Donald, *Writers on the Market: Consuming Literature in Early Seventeenth-Century Spain* (Lewisburg, PA: Bucknell University Press, 2005), '3 – Violence, Agency and the Audience in Fuenteovejuna', pp. 63–82. (Samson & Thacker, 8)

Gilman, Stephen, 'Lope: dramaturgo de la historia', in *Lope de Vega y los orígenes del teatro español: Actas del I Congreso Internacional sobre Lope de Vega*, ed. Manuel Criado de Val (Madrid: EDI-6, 1981), pp. 19–26. (Coates)

———, '*Las almenas de Toro*: Poetry and History', in *Essays on Hispanic Literature in Honor of Edmund L. King*, ed. Sylvia Molloy & Luis Fernández Cifuentes, Colección Tamesis, Serie A: Monografías, 98 (London: Tamesis, 1983), pp. 79–90. (Coates)

Gilmore, David D., *Manhood in the Making: Cultural Concepts of Masculinity* (New Haven & London: Yale University Press, 1990). (Evans)

Ginzburg, Carlo, *Clues, Myths, and the Historical Method*, trans. John & Anne C. Tedeschi (Baltimore, MD: The Johns Hopkins University Press, 1989). (De Armas)

Gitlitz, David M., 'Ironía e imágenes en *El castigo sin venganza*', *Revista de Estudios Hispánicos*, 14.1 (1980): 19–41. (Friedman)

———, 'Inquisition Confessions and Lazarillo de Tormes', *Hispanic Review* 68 (2000): 53–75. (Mujica)

Giuliani, Luigi, 'El prólogo, el catálogo y sus lectores: una perspectiva de las listas de *El peregrino en su patria*', in *Lope en 1604*, ed. Xavier Tubau (Lleida: Milenio & Universitat Autònoma de Barcelona, 2004), pp. 123–36. (Reidy) (Samson)

Goffen, Rona, *Renaissance Rivals: Michelangelo, Leonardo, Raphael, Titian* (New Haven, CT & London: Yale University Press, 2002). (De Armas)

Goldman, Michael, *On Drama: Boundaries of Genre, Borders of Self* (Ann Arbor, MI: University of Michigan Press, 2000). (Johnston)

Gómez, Jesús, *La figura del donaire o el gracioso en las comedias de Lope de Vega*, Alfar Universidad, 143 (Sevilla: Alfar, 2006). (Thacker, 11)

Gómez, María Asunción, 'Mirando de cerca "mujer, comedia y pintura" en las obras dramáticas de Lope de Vega y Calderón de la Barca', *Bulletin of the Comediantes*, 49.2 (1997): 273–93. (De Armas)

Gómez Tello, José Luis, '*Fuenteovejuna*' (review), *Primer Plano*, 23 November 1947: 23. (Wheeler)

Góngora, Luis de, *Obras completas*, ed. Juan & Isabel Millé y Giménez, 6th edn (Madrid: Aguilar, 1967). (Samson)

González Echevarría, Roberto, *Celestina's Brood: Continuities of the Baroque in Spanish and Latin American Literatures* (Durham, NC & London: Duke University Press, 1993). (Friedman)

González Martel, Juan Manuel, *Casa Museo Lope de Vega: guía y catálogo* (Madrid: Real Academia Española & Comunidad de Madrid, 1993). (Ruano) (McGrath)

González Palencia, Ángel, 'Pleito entre Lope de Vega y un editor de sus comedias', *Boletín de la Biblioteca Menéndez y Pelayo*, 3 (1921): 17–26. (Reidy)

González Rovira, Javier, 'Estrategias narrativas en *El peregrino en su patria*', in *Lope en 1604*, ed. Xavier Tubau (Lleida: Milenio & Universitat Autònoma de Barcelona, 2004), pp. 137–49. (Samson)

Goody, Jack, ed., *Literacy in Traditional Societies* (Cambridge: Cambridge University Press, 1968). (Coates)

Gracián y Morales, Baltasar, *Agudeza y arte de ingenio*, ed. Eduardo Ovejero y Maury (Madrid: La Rafa, 1929). (Fisher)

———, *El comulgatorio*, in *Obras completas*, ed. Arturo del Hoyo, 2nd edn (Madrid: Aguilar, 1960), pp. 1015–1105. (Fisher)

Granada, Luis de, *Guía de pecadores*, ed. José María Balcells, Clásicos Universales Planeta, 119 (Barcelona: Planeta, 1986). (Mayo)

———, *Obras completas de Fray Luis de Granada: obras castellanas*, ed. Cristóbal Cuevas, 2 vols, Biblioteca Castro (Madrid: Turner & Fundación José Antonio de Castro, 1994–97). (Mayo)

Grieve, Patricia E., 'Point and Counterpoint in Lope de Vega's *Rimas* and *Rimas sacras*', *Hispanic Review*, 60.4 (1992): 413–34. (Fisher)

Gubern, Román, *La censura: función política y ordenamiento jurídico bajo el franquismo (1936–1975)*, Historia, Ciencia, Sociedad, 166 (Barcelona: Ediciones Península, 1981). (Wheeler)

Güell, Monique, ed., *'La Dorotea': Lope de Vega* (Paris: Ellipses, 2001). (Tubau)

Hall, J. B., *Lope de Vega: Fuenteovejuna*, Critical Guides to Spanish Texts, 42 (London: Grant & Cutler, in association with Tamesis, 1985). (Samson & Thacker, 8)

Halstead, Frank G., 'The Attitude of Lope de Vega toward Astrology and Astronomy', *Hispanic Review*, 7.3 (1939): 205–19. (Dixon)

Hartt, Frederick, *History of Italian Renaissance Art: Painting, Sculpture, Architecture*, 4th edn, rev. by David G. Wilkins (New York: Harry N. Abrams, 1994). (De Armas)

Hartzenbusch, Juan Eugenio, 'Cervantes y Lope de Vega en 1605: citas y aplicaciones relativas de estos dos esclarecidos ingenios', *Revista Española*, 1 (mayo de 1862): 169–86. (Samson)

Heiple, Daniel L., 'Lope's Arte poética', in *Renaissance and Golden Age Essays in Honor of D. W. McPheeters*, ed. Bruno M. Damiani, Scripta Humanistica, 14 (Potomac, MD: Scripta Humanistica, 1986), pp. 106–19. (Torres)

Hermenegildo, Alfredo, ed., *El tirano en escena: tragedias del siglo XVI*, Clásicos de Biblioteca Nueva, 39 (Madrid: Biblioteca Nueva, 2002). (Coates)

Hess, Catherine, *Italian Ceramics, Catalogue of the J. Paul Getty Museum Collection* (Los Angeles: Getty Publications, 2002). (Mujica)

Hibbard, Howard, *Michelangelo* (New York: Harper & Row, 1974). (De Armas)

Huarte de San Juan, Juan, *Examen de ingenios para las ciencias*, ed. Guillermo Serés (Madrid: Cátedra, 2005). (Fisher)

Hutcheon, Linda, *A Theory of Parody: The Teachings of Twentieth-Century Art Forms* (New York & London: Methuen, 1985). (Torres)

Infantes, Víctor, 'De *Officinas* y *Polyantheas*: los diccionarios secretos del Siglo de Oro', in *Homenaje a Eugenio Asensio*, ed. Luisa López Grigera & Augustin Redondo (Madrid: Gredos, 1988), pp. 243–57. (Dixon)

Jacobs, Fredrika H., 'Aretino and Michelangelo, Dolce and Titian: Femmina, Masculo, Grazia', *The Art Bulletin*, 82.1 (March 2000): 51–67. (De Armas)

Jacquemond, Richard, 'Translation and Cultural Hegemony: The Case of French-Arabic Translation', in *Rethinking Translation: Discourse, Subjectivity, Ideology*, ed. Lawrence Venuti (London: Routledge, 1992), pp. 139–58. (Johnston)

Jaime, Antoine, *Literatura y cine en España (1975–1995)*, Signo e Imagen, 61 (Madrid: Cátedra, 2000). (Wheeler)

Jameson, A. K., 'Lope de Vega's Knowledge of Classical Literature', *Bulletin Hispanique*, 38 (1936): 444–501. (Dixon)

———, 'The Sources of Lope de Vega's Erudition', *Hispanic Review*, 5.2 (1937): 124–39. (Dixon)

Johnston, David, 'Interview with Laurence Boswell', in *The Spanish Golden Age in English: Perspectives on Performance*, ed. Catherine Boyle & David Johnston (London: Oberon, 2007), pp. 148–54. (Johnston)

———, 'Lope de Vega in English: The Historicised Imagination', in *The Comedia in English*, ed. Susan Paun de García & Donald Larson, Colección Támesis, Serie A: Monografías, 261 (Woodbridge: Tamesis, 2008) (forthcoming). (Johnston)

Jones, R. O., 'Renaissance Butterfly, Mannerist Flea: Tradition and Change in Renaissance Poetry', *Modern Language Notes*, 80.2 (1965): 166–84. (Torres)

Jordan, William B., *Juan van der Hamen y León and the Court of Madrid* (New Haven, CT & London: Yale University Press, 2005). (McGrath)

Jordán de Urríes y de la Colina, Javier, 'El coleccionismo del ilustrado Bernardo Iriarte', *Goya*, nos 319–20 (July–October 2007): 259–80. (McGrath)

Juliá Martínez, Eduardo, 'Lope de Vega en Valencia en 1599', *Boletín de la Real Academia Española*, 3 (1916): 541–59. (Samson)

———, ed., *Poetas dramáticos valencianos*, 2 vols, Biblioteca Selecta de Clásicos Españoles, Serie 2 (Madrid: Real Academia Española, 1929). (Thacker, 7)

Kelly, Stephen, 'Translating Cultures: Suggestions from the Middle English Prose *Brut*', in *Metaphrastes, or, Gained in Translation: Essays and Translations in Honour of Robert H. Jordan*, ed. Margaret Mullett, Belfast Byzantine Texts and Translations, 9 (Belfast: Belfast Byzantine Enterprises, 2004), pp. 91–102. (Johnston)

Kennedy, Dennis, *Foreign Shakespeare: Contemporary Performance* (Cambridge: Cambridge University Press, 1993). (Johnston)

Kennedy, Ruth Lee, 'Attacks on Lope and His Theatre in 1617–1621', in *Hispanic Studies in Honor of Nicholson B. Adams*, ed. John Esten Keller & Karl-Ludwig Selig, University of North Carolina Studies in the Romance Languages and Literatures, 59 (Chapel Hill, NC: University of North Carolina Press, 1966), pp. 57–76. (Rizavi)

———, *Studies in Tirso, I: The Dramatist and his Competitors, 1620–26*, North Carolina Studies in the Romance Languages and Literatures: Essays, 3 (Chapel Hill, NC: University of North Carolina Press, 1974). (Rizavi)

Kenworthy, Patricia, 'Lope de Vega's Drawing of the *Monte* Stage Set', *Bulletin of the Comediantes*, 54.2 (2002): 271–85. (Ruano)

Kirby, Carol Bingham, 'Observaciones preliminares sobre el teatro histórico de Lope de Vega', in *Lope de Vega y los orígenes del teatro español: Actas del I Congreso Internacional sobre Lope de Vega*, ed. Manuel Criado de Val (Madrid: EDI-6, 1981), pp. 329–37. (Coates)

Kirschner, Teresa, 'Sobrevivencia de una comedia: Historia de la difusión de Fuenteovejuna', *Revista Canadiense de Estudios Hispánicos*, 1.3 (1977): 255–71. (Samson & Thacker, 8)

Knight, Alan E., 'The Enacted Narrative: From Bible to Stage in Late Medieval France', *Fifteenth-Century Studies*, 15 (1989): 233–44. (Canning)

Kowal, David Martin, *Ribalta y los ribaltescos: la evolución del estilo barroco en Valencia* (Valencia: Diputación Provincial de Valencia, 1985). (McGrath)

La Barrera, Cayetano Alberto de, *Nueva biografía de Lope de Vega*, 2 vols, Biblioteca de Autores Españoles, 262–63 (Madrid: Atlas, 1973–74). (Ruano) (Samson & Thacker, Introduction)

Lafuente Ferrari, Enrique, *Los retratos de Lope de Vega* (Madrid: Imprenta Helénica, 1935). (McGrath)

Lara Garrido, José, '*El peregrino en su patria* de Lope de Vega desde la poética del romance griego', in *Lope en 1604*, ed. Xavier Tubau (Lleida: Milenio & Universitat Autònoma de Barcelona, 2004), pp. 95–122. (Samson)

Larson, Donald R., '*La dama boba* and the Comic Sense of Life', *Romanische Forschungen*, 85.1 (1973): 41–62. (Thacker, 11)

———, *The Honor Plays of Lope de Vega* (Cambridge, MA & London: Harvard University Press, 1977). (Friedman) (Evans)

Larson, Paul E., '*Fuente Ovejuna*: History, Historiography, and Literary History', *Bulletin of the Comediantes*, 53.2 (2001): 267–90. (Samson & Thacker, 8)

Laspéras, Jean-Michel, *La Nouvelle en Espagne au Siècle d'Or* (Montpellier: Castillet, 1987). (Rizavi)

———, 'Lope de Vega y el novelar: "un género de escritura"', *Bulletin Hispanique*, [102].2 (2000): 411–28. (Rizavi)

———, 'Novelar a dos luces', *Bulletin Hispanique*, [106].1 (2004): 185–202. (Rizavi)

Lázaro Carreter, Fernando, *Lope de Vega: introducción a su vida y obra* (Salamanca: Anaya, 1966). (Coates)

Leavitt, Sturgis E., 'Spanish *Comedias* as Pot Boilers', *PMLA*, 82.2 (1967): 178–84. (Reidy)

Lee, Christina H., 'The Rhetoric of Courtship in Lope de Vega's *Novelas a Marcia Leonarda*', *Bulletin of Spanish Studies*, 80.1 (2003): 13–31. (Rizavi)

Leighton, Charles H., 'La fuente de *La quinta de Florencia*', *Nueva Revista de Filología Hispánica*, 10 (1956): 1–12. (Dixon)

León, Fray Luis de, '*De la muerte, vida, virtudes y milagros de la Santa Madre Teresa de Jesús: libro primero*', in *Obras completas castellanas I*, ed. Félix García (Madrid: Biblioteca de Autores Cristianos, 1991), pp. 921–41. (Mujica)

———, 'La perfecta casada', in *Obras completas castellanas I*, ed. Félix García (Madrid: Biblioteca de Autores Cristianos, 1991), pp. 223–358. (Mujica)

Leoni, Monica, *Outside, Inside, Aside: Dialoguing with the Gracioso in Spanish Golden Age Theatre* (New Orleans, LA: University Press of the South, 2000). (Canning)

Lerner, Isaías, 'Misceláneas y poliantas del Siglo de Oro español', in *Actas del Congreso Internacional sobre Humanismo y Renacimiento*, coord. Maurilio Pérez González (vol. I) & Juan Matas Caballero (vol. II), 2 vols (León: Universidad de León, 1998), II, pp. 71–82. (Dixon)

Lida de Malkiel, María Rosa, *La idea de la fama en la Edad Media castellana* (Mexico City: Fondo de Cultura Económica, 1952). (Coates)

————, *La originalidad artística de 'La Celestina'* (Buenos Aires: Eudeba, 1962). (Tubau)

Lindenberger, Herbert, *Historical Drama: The Relation of Literature and Reality* (Chicago & London: University of Chicago Press, 1975). (Coates)

López Bueno, Begoña, 'Las tribulaciones "literarias" del Lope anciano: una lectura de *La Dorotea*, IV, ii y iii', *Anuario Lope de Vega*, 11 (2005): 145–63. (Tubau)

López Pinciano, Alonso, *Obras completas*, I: *Philosophía antigua poética*, ed. José Rico Verdú, Biblioteca Castro (Madrid: Fundación José Antonio de Castro, 1998). (Thacker, 11)

López Poza, Sagrario, 'Florilegios, polyantheas, repertorios de sentencias y lugares comunes: aproximación bibliográfica', *Criticón*, 49 (1990): 61–76. (Dixon)

López Rubio, José, '*Fuenteovejuna* ovacionada', *Primer Plano*, 23 November 1947: 4. (Wheeler)

Ly, Nadine, '*La Dorotea*: la question du genre', *Les Langues Néo-Latines*, 95, no. 319 (2001): 41–68. (Tubau)

————, 'Mémoire théorique et mémoire de l'âme: la matière de poésie et la poésie dans *La Dorotea* de Lope de Vega', in *Lectures d'une oeuvre: 'La Dorotea' de Lope de Vega*, ed. Nadine Ly (Paris: Éditions du Temps, 2001), pp. 137–224. (Tubau)

McCready, Warren T., '*Empresas* in Lope de Vega's Works', *Hispanic Review*, 25.2 (1957): 79–104. (Dixon)

McGrady, Donald, 'Notes on Jerónima de Burgos in the Life and Work of Lope de Vega', *Hispanic Review*, 40 (1972): 428–41. (Samson & Thacker, Introduction)

McGrath, David, 'Interview with Jonathan Munby', in *The Spanish Golden Age in English: Perspectives on Performance*, ed. Catherine Boyle & David Johnston (London: Oberon, 2007), pp. 133–40. (Johnston)

McKendrick, Melveena, 'Language and Silence in *El castigo sin venganza*', *Bulletin of the Comediantes* 35.1 (1983): 79–95. (Friedman)

————, 'Celebration or Subversion?: *Los comendadores de Córdoba* Reconsidered', *Bulletin of Hispanic Studies,* 61.3 (1984): 352–60. (Evans) (Thacker, 11)

————, 'Honour/Vengeance in the Spanish "Comedia": A Case of Mimetic Transference?', *Modern Language Review,* 79.2 (1984): 313–35. (Evans)

————, 'Lope de Vega's *La victoria de la honra* and *La locura por la honra*: Towards a Reassessment of his Treatment of Conjugal Honour', *Bulletin of Hispanic Studies*, 64.1 (1987): 1–14. (Evans)

————, *Theatre in Spain: 1490–1700* (Cambridge: Cambridge University Press, 1989). (Ruano) (Johnston)

————, *Playing the King: Lope de Vega and the Limits of Conformity*, Colección Támesis, Serie A: Monografías, 182 (Woodbridge: Tamesis, 2000). (De Armas) (Thacker, 7 and 10)

Mañas Martínez, María del Mar, 'Reflexiones sobre *El perro del hortelano* de Pilar Miró', *Dicenda: Cuadernos de Filología Hispánica*, 21 (2003): 139–56. (Wheeler)

Mariana, Juan de, *Historia de España*, in *Obras del padre Juan de Mariana*, [ed. Francisco Pí y Margall], Biblioteca de Autores Españoles, 30–31, 2 vols (Madrid: Rivadeneyra, 1854), I and II, pp. 1–411. (Coates)

————, *Tratado contra los juegos públicos*, in *Obras del padre Juan de Mariana*, [ed. Francisco Pí y Margall], Biblioteca de Autores Españoles, 30–31, 2 vols (Madrid: Rivadeneyra, 1854), II. (De Armas)

Marín, Nicolas, 'Un volumen de cartas de Lope poco conocido', *Cuadernos Bibliográficos*, 32 (1975): 63–75. (Samson & Thacker, Introduction)

Márquez Villanueva, Francisco, 'Literatura, lengua y moral en *La Dorotea*', in his *Lope: vida y valores* (Río Piedras: Universidad de Puerto Rico, 1988), pp. 143–267. (Tubau)

Martín-Estudillo, Luis, 'El sujeto (a)lírico en la poesía española contemporánea y su trasfondo barroco', *Hispanic Review*, 73.3 (2005): 351–70. (Torres)

Martínez Berbel, Juan Antonio, *El mundo mitológico de Lope de Vega: siete comedias mitológicas de inspiración ovidiana*, Publicaciones de la Fundación Universitaria Española, 15 (Madrid: Fundación Universitaria Española, 2003). (Dixon)

Mascia, Mark J., 'To Live Vicariously Through Literature: Lope de Vega and his Alter-Ego in the Sonnets of the *Rimas humanas y divinas del licenciado Tomé de Burguillos*', *Romance Studies*, 19.1 (2001): 1–15. (Torres) (Samson & Thacker, Introduction)

May, T. E., 'Lope de Vega's *El castigo sin venganza*: The Idolatry of the Duke of Ferrara', *Bulletin of Hispanic Studies*, 37.3 (1960): 154–82. (Friedman)

Mayo, Arantza, *La lírica sacra de Lope de Vega y José de Valdivielso*, Biblioteca Áurea Hispánica, 45 ([Pamplona]: Universidad de Navarra; Madrid: Iberoamericana; Frankfurt am Main: Vervuert, 2007). (Mayo)

Menéndez Pelayo, Marcelino, ed., 'Introducción' in Vega y Carpio, Lope Félix de, *La bienaventurada Madre Santa Teresa de Jesús. Obras XII. Comedias de vidas de santos IV*, ed. Marcelino Menéndez Pelayo (Madrid: Biblioteca de Autores Españoles, 1965). (Mujica)

————, *Obras de Lope de Vega*, XVI–XXVIII: *Crónicas y leyendas dramáticas de España*, Biblioteca de Autores Españoles, 195–98, 211–15, 223–25, 233 (Madrid: Atlas, 1966–70). (Coates)

Menéndez Pidal, Ramón, *L'Épopée castillane à travers la littérature espagnole*, trans. Henri Mérimée (Paris: Armand Colin, 1910). (Coates)

————, 'El Rey Rodrigo en la literatura', *Boletín de la Real Academia Española*, 11 (1924): 519–85. (Wheeler)

————, *Reliquias de la poesía épica española: acompañadas de Epopeya y romancero*, *I*, Reliquias de la Épica Hispánica, 1, 2nd edn (Madrid: Gredos, 1980). (Coates)

——, *La épica medieval española: desde sus orígenes hasta su disolución en el romancero*, ed. Diego Catalán & María del Mar de Bustos, Obras de Ramón Menéndez Pidal, 13 (Madrid: Espasa-Calpe, 1992). (Coates)

Mesonero Romanos, Ramón, *El antiguo Madrid: paseos histórico-anecdóticos por las calles y casas de esta villa* (1861), Obras de D. Ramón de Mesonero Romanos, 5–6, 2 vols (Madrid: Renacimiento, 1925). (Ruano)

Middleton, Thomas, *The Urban and Architectural Environment of the 'Corrales' of Madrid: The Corral de la Cruz in 1600* (Ann Arbor, MI: University Microfilms International, 1976). (Ruano)

Milá y Fontanals, Manuel, *De la poesía heroico-popular castellana*, ed. Martín de Riquer & Joaquín Molas (Barcelona: Consejo Superior de Investigaciones Científicas, 1959). (Coates)

Miró, Pilar, 'Síntomas de envidia', *El Mundo*, supplement ('La Esfera'), 25 January 1997: 2. (Wheeler)

Moir, Duncan, 'The Classical Tradition in Spanish Dramatic Theory and Practice in the Seventeenth Century', in *Classical Drama and Its Influence: Essays Presented to H. D. F. Kitto*, ed. M. J. Anderson (New York: Barnes & Noble, 1965), pp. 191–228. (Friedman)

Moll, Jaime, 'Diez años sin licencias para imprimir comedias y novelas en los reinos de Castilla: 1625–1634', *Boletín de la Real Academia Española*, 54 (1974): 97–103. (Reidy) (Tubau)

——, 'La *Tercera parte de las comedias de Lope de Vega y otros auctores*, falsificación sevillana', *Revista de Archivos, Bibliotecas y Museos*, 77.2 (1974): 619–26. (Reidy)

——, '¿Por qué escribió Lope *La Dorotea*?', *1616: Anuario de la Sociedad Española de Literatura General y Comparada*, 2 (1979): 7–11. (Tubau)

——, 'De la continuación de las partes de comedias de Lope de Vega a las partes colectivas', in *Homenaje a Alonso Zamora Vicente*, ed. Pedro Peira et al., 5 vols in 6 (Madrid: Castalia, 1988–96), III.2: *Literatura española de los siglos XVI–XVII* (1992), pp. 199–211. (Reidy)

——, 'Los editores de Lope de Vega', *Edad de Oro*, 14 (1995): 213–22. (Reidy) (Tubau)

Montalbán, Juan Pérez de, *Fama póstuma a la vida y muerte del doctor frey Lope Félix de Vega Carpio y elogios panegíricos a la inmortalidad de su nombre*, ed. Enrico di Pastena, Biblioteca di Studi Ispanici, 3 (Pisa: Edizioni ETS, 2001). (Samson & Thacker, Introduction)

Montero, Manuel, 'Miró: "Despreciamos nuestra cultura"', *El Periódico*, 26 November 1996: 58. (Wheeler)

Montero Reguera, José, '*La Dorotea* como tragedia', in *Silva: studia philologica in honorem Isaías Lerner*, ed. Isabel Lozano-Renieblas & Juan Carlos Mercado (Madrid: Castalia, 2001), pp. 479–85. (Tubau)

Monteser, Francisco de, *El caballero de Olmedo*, in *Comedias burlescas del Siglo de Oro*, ed. Ignacio Arellano et al., Colección Austral, 463 (Madrid: Espasa-Calpe, 1999), pp. 113–88. (Samson & Thacker, 8)

Montesinos, José F., 'Algunas observaciones sobre la figura del donaire en el teatro de Lope de Vega' (1925), in his *Estudios sobre Lope de Vega* (Salamanca: Anaya, 1967), pp. 21–64. (Thacker, 11)

———, 'Las poesías líricas de Lope de Vega' (1925–26), in his *Estudios sobre Lope de Vega* (Salamanca: Anaya, 1967), pp. 129–213. (Tubau)

———, 'Lope, figura del donaire' (1935), in his *Estudios sobre Lope de Vega* (Salamanca: Anaya, 1967), pp. 65–79. (Tubau)

Moore, Jerome Aaron, *The 'Romancero' in the Chronicle-Legend Plays of Lope de Vega*, Publication of the Series in Romance Languages and Literatures, 30 (Philadelphia, PA: University of Pennsylvania Press, 1940). (Coates) (Thacker, 11)

Morby, Edwin S., 'Some Observations on *Tragedia* and *Tragicomedia* in Lope', *Hispanic Review*, 11.3 (1943): 185–209. (Friedman)

———, 'Persistence and Change in the Formation of *La Dorotea*', *Hispanic Review*, 18.2 (1950): 108–25 and 195–217. (Tubau)

———, 'Levinus Lemnius and Leo Suabius in *La Dorotea*', *Hispanic Review*, 20.2 (1952): 108–22. (Dixon)

———, 'A Footnote on Lope de Vega's *barquillas*', *Romance Philology*, 6 (1952–53): 289–93. (Tubau)

———, 'Franz Titelmans in Lope's *Arcadia*', *Modern Language Notes*, 82.2 (1967): 185–97. (Dixon)

———, ed., Lope de Vega, *La Dorotea*, see Vega Carpio, Lope de.

———, 'Constantino Castriota in the *Arcadia*', in *Homage to John M. Hill: in Memoriam*, ed. Walter Poesse (Bloomington, IN: Indiana University, 1968), pp. 201–15. (Dixon)

———, 'Two Notes on *La Arcadia*', *Hispanic Review*, 36.2 (1968): 110–23. (Dixon)

Morley, S. Griswold, 'Lope de Vega's *Peregrino* Lists', *University of California Publications in Modern Philology*, 14.5 (1930): 345–66. (Samson & Thacker, Introduction)

———, 'The Pseudonyms and Literary Disguises of Lope de Vega', *University of California Publications in Modern Philology*, 33.5 (1951): 421–84. (Samson & Thacker, Introduction)

——— & Courtney Bruerton, *The Chronology of Lope de Vega's 'Comedias': With a Discussion of Doubtful Attributions, the Whole Based on a Study of His Strophic Versification* (New York: The Modern Language Association of America, 1940). (Thacker, 7 and 11)

——— & ———, *Cronología de las comedias de Lope de Vega: con un examen de las atribuciones dudosas, basado todo ello en un estudio de su versificación estrófica*, Biblioteca Románica Hispánica, 11 (Madrid: Gredos, 1968). (De Armas) (Dixon) (Evans) (Canning) (Ruano) (Mujica) (Samson)

Morris, C. B., 'Lope de Vega's *El castigo sin venganza* and Poetic Tradition', *Bulletin of Hispanic Studies*, 40.2 (1963): 69–78. (Friedman)

Morrison, Robert R., *Lope de Vega and the 'Comedia de Santos'*, Ibérica, 33 (New York: Peter Lang, 2000). (Dixon) (Thacker, 11) (Canning)

Morros Mestres, Bienvenido, 'El arte de la seducción en *El peregrino en su patria*', *Anuario Lope de Vega*, 6 (2000): 147–62. (Samson)

——, 'El género en *La Dorotea* y la imitación de *La Celestina*', in *'La Dorotea': Lope de Vega*, ed. Monique Güell (Paris: Ellipses, 2001), pp. 93–111. (Tubau)

Moura Sobral, Luís de, 'Josefa de Óbidos and her Use of Prints: Problems of Style and Iconography' in *The Sacred and the Profane: Josefa de Óbidos of Portugal* (Washington, D.C.: The National Museum of Women in the Arts, 1997). (Mujica)

Mujica, Barbara, *Lettered Women: The Correspondence of Teresa de Ávila* (Nashville, TN: Vanderbilt University Press). (Mujica)

Müller-Bochat, Eberhard, 'Técnicas literarias y métodos de meditación en la poesía sagrada del Siglo de Oro', in *Actas del Tercer Congreso Internacional de Hispanistas: celebrado en México D.F. del 26 al 31 de agosto de 1968*, ed. Carlos H. Magis (Mexico City: Colegio de México, 1970), pp. 611–17. (Mayo)

Muñón, Diego, '¿Quién sabe lo que quiere el público?' (review of *El perro del hortelano*), *La Vanguardia*, 26 November 1996: 23. (Wheeler)

Murray, Janet Horowitz, "Lope through the Looking-Glass: Metaphor and Meaning in *El castigo sin venganza*', *Bulletin of Hispanic Studies*, 56.1 (1979): 17–29. (Friedman)

Nader, Helen, ed., *Power and Gender in Renaissance Spain: Eight Women of the Mendoza Family, 1450–1650*, (Urbana, IL: University of Illinois Press, 2004). (Rizavi)

New Catholic Encyclopedia, prepared by an editorial staff at the Catholic University of America, Washington, DC, 17 vols (New York: McGraw-Hill, 1967–79). (Canning)

Nicholl, Charles, *Leonardo da Vinci: The Flights of the Mind* (New York & London: Penguin, 2004). (De Armas)

Novo, Yolanda, *Las 'Rimas sacras' de Lope de Vega: disposición y sentido*, Monografías da Universidade de Santiago de Compostela, 155 (Santiago de Compostela: Universidade de Santiago de Compostela, 1990). (Mayo)

Novoa, Matías de, *Memorias de Matías de Novoa, ayuda de cámara de Felipe IV*, 4 vols (Madrid: Imprenta de Miguel Ginesta, 1878–86). (Samson)

O'Connor, Thomas Austin, 'Culpabilidad, expiación y reconciliación en la versión de *Fuenteovejuna* filmada por Juan Guerrero Zamora', in *Hispanic Essays in Honor of Frank P. Casa*, ed. A. Robert Lauer & Henry W. Sullivan, Ibérica, 20 (New York: Peter Lang, 1997), pp. 122–31. (Wheeler)

——, *Love in the 'Corral': Conjugal Spirituality and Anti-Theatrical Polemic in Early Modern Spain*, Ibérica, 31 (New York: Peter Lang, 2000). (De Armas)

Ocampo, Florián de, *Las quatro partes enteras de la Crónica de España que mandó componer el Sereníssimo rey don Alonso llamado el Sabio [...]: vista y emendada mucha parte de su impresión por el maestro Florian Docampo* (Zamora: Agustín de Paz & Juan Picardo, 1541). (Coates)

Oehrlein, Josef, *El actor en el teatro español del Siglo de Oro*, Literatura y Sociedad, 54 (Madrid: Castalia, 1993). (Ruano)

Oleza, Juan, 'La propuesta teatral del primer Lope de Vega', *Cuadernos de Filología* (Valencia), 3.1–2: *La génesis de la teatralidad barroca* (1981): 153–223. (Thacker, 11)

——, 'Claves románticas para la primera interpretación moderna del teatro de Lope de Vega', *Anuario Lope de Vega*, 1 (1995): 119–35. (Samson & Thacker, Introduction)

——, 'Del primer Lope al *Arte nuevo*', 'Estudio preliminar' to Lope de Vega, *Peribáñez y el comendador de Ocaña*, ed. Donald McGrady, Biblioteca Clásica, 53 (Barcelona: Crítica, 1997), pp. ix–lv. (Thacker, 11) (Tubau)

Osbourne, John, *A Bond Honoured : A Play (from Lope de Vega)* (London: Faber & Faber, 1966). (Johnston)

Ostlund, DeLys, *The Re-Creation of History in the Fernando and Isabel Plays of Lope de Vega*, Ibérica, 18 (New York: Peter Lang, 1997). (Coates)

Osuna, Rafael, '*El peregrino en su patria*, en el ángulo oscuro de Lope', *Revista de Occidente*, n.s., nos 113–14 (August–September 1972): 326–31. (Samson)

——, *La Arcadia de Lope de Vega: génesis, estructura y originalidad*, Anejos del Boletín de la Real Academia Espanola, 26 (Madrid: Real Academia Española, 1972). (Dixon)

——, *Polifemo y el tema de la abundancia natural en Lope de Vega y su tiempo* Teatro del Siglo de Oro: Estudios de Literatura, 37 (Kassel: Reichenberger, 1996). (Dixon)

Owens, J. B., *'By My Absolute Royal Authority': Justice and the Castilian Commonwealth at the Beginning of the First Global Age* (Rochester, NY: University of Rochester Press, 2005). (Samson & Thacker, 8)

Pabst, Walter, *Novellentheorie und Novellendichtung: zur Geschichte ihrer Antinomie in den romanischen Literaturen*, 2nd edn (Heidelberg: Carl Winter, 1967). (Rizavi)

Pacheco, Francisco, *Libro de descripción de verdaderos retratos de ilustres y memorables varones*, ed. Pedro M. Piñero Ramírez & Rogelio Reyes Cano (Seville: Diputación Provincial de Sevilla, 1985). (McGrath)

Palau y Dulcet, Antonio, *Manual del librero hispanoamericano: bibliografia general espanola e hispanoamericana desde la invencion de la imprenta hasta nuestros tiempos con el valor comercial de los impresos descritos*, 28 vols, 2nd edn (Barcelona: Palau Dulcet; Oxford: The Dolphin Book Company, 1948–1977). (Rizavi)

Pardo de Guevara y Valdés, Eduardo, *Don Pedro Fernández de Castro, VII conde de Lemos (1576–1622): estudio histórico* (Santiago de Compostela: Xunta de Galicia, 1997). (Samson)

Parker, A. A., *The Approach to the Spanish Drama of the Golden Age*, Diamante, 6 (London: The Hispanic & Luso-Brazilian Councils, 1957). (Coates)

——, 'Towards a Definition of Calderonian Tragedy', *Bulletin of Hispanic Studies*, 39.4 (1962): 222–37. (Friedman)

Paterson, Alan K. G., 'Stages of History and History on Stage: On Lope de Vega and Historical Drama', in *Spanish Theatre: Studies in Honour of Victor F. Dixon*, ed. Kenneth Adams, Ciaran Cosgrove & James Whiston, Colección Támesis, Serie A: Monografías, 187 (London: Tamesis, 2001), pp. 147–56. (Coates)

Pattison, D. G., *From Legend to Chronicle: The Development of Epic Material in Alphonsine Historiography*, Medium Aevum Monographs, 13 (Oxford: Society for the Study of Mediaeval Languages and Literature, 1983). (Coates)

Pedraza Jiménez, Felipe B., 'El desengaño barroco en las *Rimas de Tomé de Burguillos*', *Anuario de Filología*, 4 (1978): 391–418. (Torres)

——, *Lope de Vega* (Barcelona: Teide, 1990). (Thacker, 11) (Samson & Thacker, Introduction)

——, 'Introducción' to Lope de Vega, *Rimas*, 2 vols (Ciudad Real: Universidad de Castilla-La Mancha, 1993–94), I, pp. 9–119. (Tubau) (Fisher)

——, '*Las bodas entre el alma y el amor divino*: texto, espectáculo y propaganda ideológica', in *La fiesta de Corpus Christi*, ed. Gerardo Fernández Juárez & Fernando Martínez Gil, Estudios, 84 (Cuenca: Universidad Castilla-La Mancha, 2002), pp. 235–51. (Samson)

——, *El universo poético de Lope de Vega*, Colección Arcadia de las Letras, 16 (Madrid: Laberinto, 2003). (Mayo)

Pedrocco, Filippo, *Titian* (New York: Rizzoli, 2000). (De Armas)

Pérez, Luis C. & Federico Sánchez Escribano, *Afirmaciones de Lope de Vega sobre preceptiva dramática: a base de cien comedias*, Anejos de Revista de Literatura, 17 (Madrid: Consejo Superior de Investigaciones Científicas, 1961). (Thacker 7 and 10)

Pérez-Boluda, Adrián, 'Costumbrismo erótico y parodia antipetrarquista en el *Tomé de Burguillos* de Lope de Vega', *Calíope*, 12 (2006): 57–75. (Torres)

Pérez Millán, Juan Antonio, *Pilar Miró: directora de cine*, 2nd edn, expanded and updated (Madrid: Ediciones Calamares, 2007). (Wheeler)

Pérez de Montalbán, *see* Montalbán. (Samson & Thacker, Introduction)

Pérez Pastor, Cristóbal, *Nuevos datos acerca del histrionismo español en los siglos XVI y XVII* (Madrid: Revista Española, 1901). (Ruano)

——, *Documentos para la biografía de D. Pedro Calderón de la Barca* (Madrid: Fortanet, 1905). (Ruano)

——, 'Nuevos datos acerca del histrionismo español en los siglos XVI y XVII (segunda serie)', *Bulletin Hispanique*, 9 (1907): 360–85. (Ruano)

——, Cristóbal. *Noticias y documentos relativos a la historia y literatura española*, I (Memorias de la Real Academia Española, X) (Madrid: Real Academia Española, 1910). (Samson & Thacker, Introduction)

Pérez Sánchez, Alfonso E. *Pintura española de los siglos XVII y XVIII en la Fundación Lázaro Galdiano*, Catálogos de la Fundación Lázaro Galdiano, 9 (Madrid: Fundación Lázaro Galdiano & Fundación Pedro Barrié de la Maza, 2005). (McGrath)

Pérez Sierra, Rafael, 'Versión cinematográfica de *El perro del hortelano*', in *Lope de Vega: comedia urbana y comedia palatina: Actas de las XVIII Jornadas de Teatro Clásico, Almagro, 11, 12 y 13 de julio de 1995*, ed. Felipe B. Pedraza Jiménez & Rafael González Cañal (Almagro: Universidad de Castilla la Mancha, 1996), pp. 107–14. (Wheeler)

Peristiany, J. G., ed., *Honour and Shame: The Values of Mediterranean Society* (London: Weidenfeld & Nicolson, 1965). (Evans)

Perriam, Chris, *Stars and Masculinities in Spanish Cinema: From Banderas to Bardem* (Oxford: Oxford University Press, 2003). (Wheeler)

Petrarca, Francesco, *Canzoniere*, ed. Marco Santagata (Milan: Mondadori, 1996). (Fisher)

Petro, Antonia, 'El chivo expiatorio sustitutorio: *El castigo sin venganza*', *Bulletin of the Comediantes*, 55.1 (2003): 23–46. (Friedman)

Pineda, Juan de, *Diálogos familiares de la agricultura cristiana*, ed. Juan Meseguer Fernández, 5 vols, Biblioteca de Autores Españoles, 161–63, 169–70 (Madrid: Atlas, 1963–64), IV. (De Armas)

Pisos, Cecilia, 'Burguillos y Góngora frente a frente', *Filología*, 26.1–2 (1993): 167–81. (Torres)

Pitt-Rivers, Julian, 'Honour and Social Status', in *Honour and Shame: The Values of Mediterranean Society*, ed. J. G. Peristiany (London: Weidenfeld & Nicolson, 1965), pp. 21–77. (Evans)

Plato, Excerpts from the *Symposium*, *Phaedrus* and *Ion*, in *Classical and Medieval Literary Criticism: Translations and Interpretations*, ed. Alex Preminger et al. (New York: Ungar, 1974), pp. 25–48. (Fisher)

Portús Pérez, Javier, *Pintura y pensamiento en la España de Lope de Vega*, Colección Arte, 55 (Hondarribia: Nerea, 1999). (McGrath) (De Armas) (Dixon)

——, 'Varia fortuna del retrato en España', in *El retrato español: del Greco a Picasso*, ed. Javier Portús Pérez (Madrid: Museo Nacional del Prado, 2004), pp. 18–71. Translated as 'The Varied Fortunes of the Portrait in Spain', in *The Spanish Portrait: From El Greco to Picasso*, ed. Javier Portús Pérez (London: Scala, 2004), pp. 16–67. (McGrath)

Poteet-Bussard, Lavonne C., 'Algunas perspectivas sobre la primera época del teatro de Lope de Vega', in *Lope de Vega y los orígenes del teatro español: Actas del I Congreso Internacional sobre Lope de Vega*, ed. Manuel Criado de Val (Madrid: EDI-6, 1981), pp. 341–54. (Thacker, 11)

Presotto, Marco, *Le commedie autografe di Lope de Vega: catalogo e studio*, Teatro del Siglo de Oro: Bibliografías y Catálogos, 25 (Kassel: Reichenberger, 2000). (Ruano) (Mujica)

Profeti, Maria Grazia, *La collezione 'Diferentes Autores'*, Bibliografías y catálogos, 6 (Kassel: Reichenberger, 1989). ('Further reading')

——, 'Comedias representadas/textos literarios: los problemas ecdóticos', in *Teatro, historia y sociedad: Seminario Internacional sobre el Teatro del Siglo de Oro Español, Asociación Internacional de Teatro Español y Novohispano del Siglo de Oro, Murcia, octubre 1994*, ed. Carmen Hernández

Valcárcel (Murcia: Universidad de Murcia & Universidad Autónoma de Ciudad Juárez, 1996), pp. 207–16. (Reidy)

———, 'Strategie redazionali ed editoriali di Lope de Vega', in her *Nell'officina di Lope*, Secoli d'Oro, 10 (Florencia: Alinea, 1998), pp. 11–44. (Reidy)

———, *Per una bibliografia di Lope de Vega. Opere non drammatiche a stampa*, Bibliografías y catálogos, 35 (Kassel: Reichenberger, 2002). ('Further reading')

Rabell, Carmen R., *Lope de Vega: el arte nuevo de hacer 'novelas'*, Colección Tamesis, Serie A: Monografías, 150 (London: Tamesis, 1992). (Rizavi)

———, *Rewriting the Italian Novella in Counter-Reformation Spain*, Colección Tamesis, Serie A: Monografías, 199 (Woodbridge: Tamesis, 2003). (Rizavi)

Randall, Dale B. J., *The Golden Tapestry: A Critical Survey of Non-Chivalric Spanish Fiction in English Translation (1543–1657)* (Durham, NC: Duke University Press, 1963). (Samson)

Randel, Mary Gaylord, 'Proper Language and Language as Property: The Personal Poetics of Lope's *Rimas*', *Modern Language Notes*, 101.2 (1986): 220–46. (Fisher) (Torres)

Reichenberger, Arnold G., 'The Uniqueness of the *Comedia*', *Hispanic Review*, 27.3 (1959): 303–16. (Johnston)

Rennert, Hugo Albert, *The Life of Lope de Vega, 1562–1635* (1904) (New York: Benjamin Blom, 1968). See also Castro & Rennert. (Ruano)

Retratos de los españoles ilustres, con un epítome de sus vidas (Madrid: Imprenta Real, 1791). (McGrath)

Rico-Avello, Carlos, *Lope de Vega: flaquezas y dolencias* (Madrid: Aguilar, 1973). (Samson & Thacker, Introduction)

Roas, David, 'Lope y la manipulación de la historia: realidad, leyenda, e invención en la *Comedia de Bamba*', *Anuario Lope de Vega*, 1 (1995): 189–208. (Coates)

Robbins, Jeremy, 'Male Dynamics in Calderón's *A secreto agravio, secreta venganza*', *Hispanófila*, 117 (1996): 11–24. (Evans)

Rodríguez Marín, Francisco, 'Lope de Vega y Camila Lucinda', *Boletín de la Real Academia Española* 1.1 (1914): 249–90. (Samson)

Romera-Navarro, M. 'Querellas y rivalidades en las Academias del siglo XVII', *Hispanic Review*, 9.4 (1941): 494–99. (Ruano)

Rosaldo, Renato I., Jr, 'Lope as a Poet of History: History and Ritual in *El testimonio vengado*', in *Perspectivas de la comedia: colección de ensayos sobre el teatro de Lope, G. de Castro, Calderón y otros*, ed. Alva V. Ebersole, Colección Siglo de Oro, 6 (Valencia: Estudios de Hispanófila, 1978), pp. 9–32. (Coates)

Rose, Margaret A., *Parody: Ancient, Modern, and Post-Modern*, Literature, Culture, Theory, 5 (Cambridge: Cambridge University Press, 1993). (Torres)

Rosenthal, Earl, '*Plus Ultra, Non plus Ultra*, and the Columnar Device of Emperor Charles V', *Journal of the Warburg and Courtauld Institutes*, 34 (1971): 204–28. (Rizavi)

Roses-Lozano, Joaquín, 'Algunas consideraciones sobre la leyenda de Bernardo del Carpio en el teatro de Lope de Vega', *Inti: Revista de Literatura Hispánica*, no. 28 (1988): 89–105. (Coates)

Rosskill, Mark W., *Dolce's Aretino and Venetian Art Theory of the Cinquecento*, Monographs on Archaeology and Fine Arts, 15 (New York: New York University Press for the College Art Association of America, 1968). (De Armas)

Rothberg, Irving, 'Algo más sobre Plauto, Terencio y Lope', in *Lope de Vega y los orígenes del teatro español: Actas del I Congreso Internacional sobre Lope de Vega*, ed. Manuel Criado de Val (Madrid: EDI-6, 1981), pp. 61–65. (De Armas)

Rozas, Juan Manuel, 'Burguillos como heterónimo de Lope', *Edad de Oro*, 4 (1985): 139–63. (Torres)

——, *Estudios sobre Lope de Vega*, ed. Jesús Cañas Murillo (Madrid: Cátedra, 1990). (Dixon) (Samson & Thacker, Introduction)

——, 'Lope de Vega y Felipe IV en el "ciclo *de senectute*"', in his *Estudios sobre Lope de Vega* (Madrid: Cátedra, 1990), pp. 73–131. (Tubau)

——, 'Lope contra Pellicer (historia de una guerra literaria)', in his *Estudios sobre Lope de Vega* (Madrid: Cátedra, 1990), pp. 133–68. (Tubau)

——, '"Sacras luzes del cielo": el soneto 161 de Burguillos, un epifonema de sus *Rimas humanas y divinas* y de la obra poética de Lope', ed. Jesús Cañas Murillo, *Anuario de Lope de Vega*, 6 (2000): 229–34. (Torres)

Ruano de la Haza, José María, 'An Early Rehash of Lope's *Peribáñez*', *Bulletin of the Comediantes*, 35.1 (1983): 5–29. (Ruano)

——, 'Noticias para el gobierno de la Sala de Alcaldes de Casa y Corte', *Bulletin of the Comediantes*, 40.1 (1988): 67–74. (Ruano)

——, 'La relación textual entre *El burlador de Sevilla* y *Tan largo me lo fiáis*', in *Tirso de Molina: del Siglo de Oro al siglo XX: actas del Coloquio Internacional, Pamplona, Universidad de Navarra, 15–17 de diciembre 1994*, ed. Ignacio Arellano et al. (Madrid: Revista Estudios, 1995), pp. 283–95. Republished in *Hispanic Essays in Honor of Frank P. Casa*, ed. A. Robert Lauer & Henry W. Sullivan, Ibérica, 20 (New York: Peter Lang, 1997), pp. 173–86. (Ruano)

——, 'Teoría y praxis del personaje teatral áureo: Pedro Crespo, Peribáñez y Rosaura', in *El escritor y la escena, V: estudios sobre teatro español y novohispano de los Siglos de Oro*, ed. Ysla Campbell (Ciudad Juárez: Universidad Autónoma de Ciudad Juárez, 1997), pp. 19–35. (Samson & Thacker, 8)

——, *La puesta en escena en los teatros comerciales del Siglo de Oro*, Literatura y Sociedad, 67 (Madrid: Castalia, 2000). (Ruano)

—— & John J. Allen, *Los teatros comerciales del siglo XVII y la escenificación de la Comedia*, Nueva Biblioteca de Erudición y Crítica, 8 (Madrid: Castalia, 1994). (Ruano)

Rubin, Gayle, 'The Traffic in Women: Notes on the "Political Economy" of Sex', in *Toward an Anthropology of Women*, ed. Rayna R. Reiter (New York: Monthly Review Press, 1975), pp. 157–210. (Evans)

Rubinos, José, *Lope de Vega como poeta religioso: estudio crítico de sus obras épicas y líricas religiosas* (Habana: Cultural, 1935). (Mayo)

Rufo, Juan, *Las seiscientas apotegmas y otras obras en verso*, ed. Alberto Blecua, Clásicos Castellanos, 170 (Madrid: Espasa-Calpe, 1972). (Evans)

Ruiz, Juan, Arcipreste de Hita, *Libro de Buen Amor*, ed. Joan Corominas, Biblioteca Románica Hispánica: Textos, 4 (Madrid: Gredos, 1973). (Fisher)

Ruiz de la Puerta, Fernando, *La cueva de Hércules y el palacio encantado de Toledo*, Biblioteca de Visionarios, Heterodoxos y Marginados, 21 (Madrid: Editora Nacional, 1977). (Coates)

Russell, P. E. & D. M. Rogers, ed., *A Catalogue of Hispanic Manuscripts and Books before 1700 from the Bodleian Library and Oxford College Libraries, Exhibited at the Taylor Institution, 6–11 September* (Oxford: Dolphin Book Co. for Primer Congreso Internacional de Hispanistas, 1962). (Samson)

Sabbatini, Nicolò, *Pratica di fabricar scene e machine ne' teatri* (Ravenna, 1638), ed. Elena Polovedo, Collezione del Centro di Ricerche Teatrali, 1 (Roma: Carlo Bestetti, 1955). (Ruano)

Sage, J. W., 'The Context of Comedy: Lope de Vega's *El perro del hortelano* and Related Plays', in *Studies in Spanish Literature of the Golden Age Presented to Edward M. Wilson*, ed. R. O. Jones, Colección Tamesis, Serie A: Monografías, 30 (London: Tamesis, 1973), pp. 247–66. (Thacker, 11)

———, *Lope de Vega: El caballero de Olmedo*, Critical Guides to Spanish Texts, 6 (London: Grant and Cutler, in association with Tamesis, 1974). (Samson & Thacker, 8)

Salomon, Noël, 'Algunos problemas de sociología de las literaturas de lengua española', in *Creación y público en la literatura española*, ed. J. F. Botrel & S. Salaün, Literatura y Sociedad, 5 (Madrid: Castalia, 1974), pp. 15–39. (Reidy)

Samson, Alexander, 'Anti-Semitism, Class, and Lope de Vega's *El niño inocente de La Guardia*', *Hispanic Research Journal*, 3.2 (2002): 107–22. (Canning)

San Román, Francisco de B., *Lope de Vega, los cómicos toledanos y el poeta sastre: serie de documentos inéditos de los años de 1590 a 1615* (Madrid: Imprenta Góngora, 1935). (Ruano)

Sánchez, Alfonso, '*Fuenteovejuna*' (review), *Informaciones*, 30 November 1972: 31. (Wheeler)

———, '*El mejor alcalde, el rey*' (review), *Informaciones*, 30 April 1974: 37. (Wheeler)

Sánchez-Arjona, José, *Noticias referentes a los anales del teatro en Sevilla desde Lope de Rueda hasta fines del siglo XVII* (Sevilla: E. Rasco, 1898). (Ruano)

Sánchez de Lima, Miguel, *El arte poética en romance castellano* (1580), ed. Rafael de Balbín Lucas, Biblioteca de Antiguos Libros Hispánicos: Serie A, 3 (Madrid: Consejo Superior de Investigaciones Científicas, Instituto 'Nicolás Antonio', 1944). (Fisher)

Sánchez Escribano, Federico & Alberto Porqueras Mayo, ed., *Preceptiva dramática española del Renacimiento y el Barroco*, Biblioteca Románica Hispánica, 4: Textos, 3, 2nd edn (Madrid: Gredos, 1972). (Thacker, 7)

Sánchez Jiménez, Antonio, 'Composición de lugar en las *Rimas sacras* (1614) de Lope de Vega: la influencia ignaciana', *Anuario Lope de Vega*, 10 (2004): 115–28. (Mayo)

———, *Lope pintado por sí mismo: mito e imagen del autor en la poesía de Lope de Vega Carpio*, Colección Tamesis, Serie A: Monografías, 229 (Woodbridge: Tamesis, 2006). (De Armas) (McGrath) (Torres)

Sánchez Martínez, Rafael, 'El requiebro en las *Novelas a Marcia Leonarda*', in *Memoria de la palabra: Actas del VI Congreso de la Asociación Internacional Siglo de Oro, Burgos-La Rioja, 15–19 de julio 2002*, ed. María Luisa Lobato & Francisco Domínguez Matito, 2 vols (Madrid: Iberoamericana; Frankfurt am Main: Vervuert, 2004), II, 1609–18. (Samson)

Sánchez Romeralo, Antonio, ed., *Lope de Vega: el teatro II*, El Escritor y la Crítica, 193 (Madrid: Taurus, 1989). (Samson & Thacker, 8)

Santore, Cathy, 'Danae: The Renaissance Courtesan's Alter Ego', *Zeitschrift fur Kunstgeschichte*, 54.3 (1991): 412–27. (De Armas)

Santos, Jesús María, 'Entrevista con Mario Camus, director cinematográfico', *El Adelanto*, 3 August 1973: 12. (Wheeler)

Santos Coco, Francisco, ed., *Historia silense*, Textos Latinos de la Edad Media Española, Sección Primera: Crónicas, 2 (Madrid: Sucesores de Rivadeneyra, 1921). (Coates)

Schechner, Richard, *Between Theater and Anthropology* (Philadelphia: University of Pennsylvania Press, 1985). (Mujica)

Schwartz Lerner, Lía, 'Tradition and Authority in Lope de Vega's *La Dorotea*', in *Cultural Authority in Golden Age Spain*, ed. Marina S. Brownlee & Hans Ulrich Gumbrecht (Baltimore, MD: The Johns Hopkins University Press, 1995), pp. 3–27. (Tubau)

Sears, Theresa Ann, 'Like Father, Like Son: The Paternal Perverse in Lope's *El castigo sin venganza*', *Bulletin of Hispanic Studies* (Liverpool), 73.2 (1996): 129–42. (Friedman)

Serés, Guillermo, '"A mis soledades voy ...": fuentes remotas y motivos principales', *Anuario Lope de Vega*, 4 (1998): 327–37. (Tubau)

———, 'La poética historia de *El peregrino en su patria*', *Anuario Lope de Vega*, 7 (2001): 89–104. (Samson)

Shakespeare, William, *A Midsummer Night's Dream*, ed. Harold F. Brooks, The Arden Shakespeare (London: Methuen, 1979). (Fisher)

Shaw, Leroy R., *The Playwright and Historical Change: Dramatic Strategies in Brecht, Hauptmann, Kaiser and Wedekind* (Madison, WI & London: University of Wisconsin Press, 1970). (Coates)

Shergold, N. D. & J. E. Varey, ed., *Genealogía, origen y noticias de los comediantes de España*, Fuentes para la Historia del Teatro en España, 2 (London: Tamesis, 1985). (Ruano)

Simón Díaz, José, *Ensayo de una bibliografía de las obras y artículos sobre la vida y escritos de Lope de Vega Carpio* (Madrid: Centro de Estudios sobre Lope de Vega, 1955). (Samson & Thacker, Introduction)

Sinclair, Alison, *The Deceived Husband: A Kleinian Approach to the Literature of Infidelity* (Oxford: Clarendon; New York: Oxford University Press, 1993). (Evans)

Sliwa, Krzysztof, ed., *Cartas, documentos y escrituras del Dr. Frey Lope Félix de Vega Carpio(1562–1635)*, 2 vols (Newark, DE: Juan de la Cuesta, 2007). (Samson & Thacker, Introduction)

Smith, Colin, ed., *Spanish Ballads*, 2nd edn (London: Bristol Classical Press, 1996; repr. 2002). (Coates)

Smith, Paul Julian, *Writing in the Margin: Spanish Literature of the Golden Age* (Oxford: Clarendon, 1988). (Torres)

Sobejano, Gonzalo, 'La digresión en la prosa narrativa de Lope de Vega y en su poesía epistolar', in *Estudios ofrecidos a Emilio Alarcos Llorach: con motivo de sus XXV años de docencia en la Universidad de Oviedo*, 5 vols (Oviedo: Universidad de Oviedo, 1976–83), II (1978), pp. 469–94. (Rizavi)

Sobral, Luís de Moura, *Pintura e poesia na época barroca: a homenagem da Academia dos Singulares a Bento Coelho da Silveira*, Teoria da Arte, 12 (Lisboa: Estampa, 1994). (Mujica)

Sohm, Philip, 'Gendered Style in Italian Art Criticism from Michelangelo to Malvasia', *Renaissance Quarterly*, 48.4 (1995): 759–808. (De Armas)

Soria, Florentino, '*El mejor alcalde, el rey*' (review), *Arriba*, 6 May 1974: 22. (Wheeler)

Spitzer, Leo, '"A mis soledades voy ..."', *Revista de Filología Española*, 23 (1936): 397–400. (Tubau)

Stott, Andrew, *Comedy* (New York and London: Routledge, 2005). (Thacker, 11)

Stroud, Matthew D., '*Los comendadores de Córdoba*: realidad, manierismo y el barroco', in *Lope de Vega y los orígines del teatro español: Actas del I Congreso Internacional sobre Lope de Vega*, ed. Manuel Criado de Val (Madrid: EDI-6, 1981), pp. 425–30. (Evans)

———, 'Rivalry and Violence in *El castigo sin venganza*', in *The Golden Age Comedia: Text, Theory, and Performance*, ed. Charles Ganelin & Howard Mancing (West Lafayette, IN: Purdue University Press, 1994), pp. 37–47. (Friedman)

Subirá, José, *El gremio de representantes españoles y la Cofradía de Nuestra Señora de la Novena*, Biblioteca de Estudios Madrileños, 5 (Madrid: Consejo Superior de Investigaciones Científicas, Instituto de Estudios Madrileños, 1960). (Ruano)

Tanner, Norman P., ed., *Decrees of the Ecumenical Councils*, 2 vols (London: Sheed and Ward, 1990). (Mayo)

Tate, Robert B., 'Mythology in Spanish Historiography of the Middle Ages and the Renaissance', *Hispanic Review*, 22.1 (1954), 1–18. (Coates)

Taylor, Gary, *Reinventing Shakespeare: A Cultural History, from the Restoration to the Present* (New York: Weidenfeld & Nicolson, 1989). (Johnston)

ter Horst, Robert, '"Error pintado": The Oedipal Emblematics of Lope de Vega's *El castigo sin venganza*', in *'Never-Ending Adventure': Studies in Medieval and Early Modern Spanish Literature in Honor of Peter N. Dunn*, ed. Edward H. Friedman & Harlan Sturm, Juan de la Cuesta Hispanic Monographs, 19 (Newark, DE: Juan de la Cuesta, 2002), pp. 279–308. (Friedman)

Terence, *The Comedies*, trans. Palmer Bovie, Constance Carrier & Douglass Parker, ed. Palmer Bovie (Baltimore, MD & London: The Johns Hopkins University Press, 1992). (De Armas)

Teresa of Ávila, Saint, *The Complete Works of Saint Teresa of Jesus*, trans. E. Allison Peers, 3 vols (London: Sheed and Ward, 1946; repr. 1953, 1963, 1975, 1978). (Mujica)

——, *The Collected Works of St. Teresa of Avila*, trans. Kieran Kavanaugh, O.C.D. & Otilio Rodríguez, O.C.D., 3 vols (Washington, DC: Institute of Carmelite Studies, 1976–85). (Mujica)

——, *Epistolario*, ed. Luis Rodríguez Martínez and Teófanes Egido (Madrid: Espiritualidad, 1984). (Mujica)

——, *Libro de las fundaciones* (Buenos Aires: Espasa-Calpe, 1951). (Mujica)

——, *Libro de su vida*, ed. Dámaso Chicharro (Madrid: Cátedra, 1993). (Mujica)

——, *Obras completas*, ed. Tomás Álvarez (Burgos: Monte Carmelo, 1998). (Mujica)

Terni, Elisa Aragone, 'Introduzione', *Vida y muerte de Santa Teresa de Jesús: commedia inedita*, ed. Elisa Terni Aragone, Università degli Studi di Firenze, Publiccazioni dell'Istituto Ispanico (Messina & Florence: Casa editrice D'Anna, 1970), pp. 9–42. (Mujica)

Terry, Arthur, 'Lope de Vega: Re-Writing a Life', in his *Seventeenth-Century Spanish Poetry: The Power of Artifice* (Cambridge: Cambridge University Press, 1993), pp. 94–121. (Torres)

——, *Seventeenth-Century Spanish Poetry: The Power of Artifice* (Cambridge: Cambridge University Press, 1993). (Fisher)

TESO: Teatro Español del Siglo de Oro, CD-ROM database (Madrid: Chadwyck-Healey España, 1998). (Reidy)

Texeira, Pedro, *Topographía de la villa de Madrid* (1656), facsimile edn (Madrid: Ayuntamiento de Madrid, n.d.). (Ruano)

Thacker, Jonathan, 'Lope de Vega's Exemplary Early Comedy, *Los locos de Valencia*', *Bulletin of the Comediantes*, 52.1 (2000): 9–29. (Thacker, 11)

——, *Role-Play and the World as Stage in the 'Comedia'* (Liverpool: Liverpool University Press, 2002). (Evans)

——, 'Lope de Vega, *El cuerdo loco*, and "la más discreta figura de la comedia"', *Bulletin of Hispanic Studies*, 81.4 (2004): 463–78. (Thacker, 11)

——, *A Companion to Golden Age Theatre*, Colección Tamesis, Serie A: Monografías, 235 (Woodbridge: Tamesis, 2007). (Thacker, 7 and 11)

————, 'History of Performance in English', in *The Spanish Golden Age in English: Perspectives on Performance*, ed. Catherine Boyle & David Johnston (London: Oberon, 2007), pp. 15–30. (Johnston)

Thompson, Currie K., 'Unstable Irony in Lope de Vega's *El castigo sin venganza*', *Studies in Philology*, 78.3 (1981): 224–40. (Friedman)

Thompson, Peter E., *The Triumphant Juan Rana: A Gay Actor of the Spanish Golden Age* (Toronto, University of Toronto Press, 2006). (Evans)

Ticknor, George, *History of Spanish Literature*, 3 vols (London: John Murray, 1849). (Canning)

Tietze, Hans, 'An Early Version of Titian's *Danaë*: An Analysis of Titian Replicas', *Arte Veneta*, 8 (1954): 199–208. (De Armas)

Tomillo, A., & C. Pérez Pastor, *Proceso de Lope de Vega por libelos contra unos cómicos* (Madrid: Fortanet, 1901). (Tubau) (Samson & Thacker, Introduction)

Torre, Guillermo de, *La difícil universalidad española*, Biblioteca Románica Hispánica, 7, Campo Abierto, 17 (Madrid: Gredos, 1965). (Johnston)

Torreiro, Mirito, 'A vueltas con el amor' (review of *La dama boba*), *El País*, 24 March 2006: 37. (Wheeler)

Torres, Isabel, 'Interloping Lope: Transformation and Tomé de Burguillos', *Bulletin of Spanish Studies* (forthcoming). (Torres)

Trueblood, Alan S., 'The *Officina* of Ravisius Textor in Lope de Vega's *Dorotea*', *Hispanic Review*, 26.2 (1958): 135–41. (Tubau) (Dixon)

————, 'Plato's *Symposium* and Ficino's Commentary in Lope de Vega's *Dorotea*', *Modern Language Notes*, 73.7 (1958): 506–14. (Tubau)

————, *Experience and Artistic Expression in Lope de Vega: The Making of 'La Dorotea'* (Cambridge, MA: Harvard University Press, 1974). (Tubau) (Torres)

Tubau, Xavier, ed., *Lope en 1604* (Lleida: Milenio & Universitat Autònoma de Barcelona, 2004). (Samson)

————, *Una polémica literaria: Lope de Vega y Diego de Colmenares*, Biblioteca Áurea Hispánica, 42 ([Pamplona]: Universidad de Navarra; Madrid: Iberoamericana; Frankfurt am Main: Vervuert, 2007). (Rizavi) (Tubau)

Valdivielso, José de, *Exposición parafrástica del Psalterio y de los cánticos del Breviario* (Madrid: Viuda de Alonso Martín, 1623). (Mayo)

————, *Romancero espiritual*, ed. J. M. Aguirre, Clásicos Castellanos, 228 (Madrid: Espasa-Calpe, 1984). (Mayo)

Vals, Javi, '*La dama boba*' (review), *Cinemanía*, April 2006: 119. (Wheeler)

Varey, J. E. & N. D. Shergold, *Teatros y comedias en Madrid, 1600–1650: estudio y documentos*, Fuentes para la Historia del Teatro en España, 3 (London: Tamesis, 1971) (*Fuentes III*). (Ruano)

Vega, Lope de, *El acero de Madrid*, ed. Stefano Arata, Clásicos Castalia, 256 (Madrid: Castalia, 2000). (Thacker, 11)

————, *Las almenas de Toro*, in *Obras escogidas de Lope Félix de Vega Carpio*, ed. Federico Carlos Sainz de Robles, 3 vols (Madrid: Aguilar, 1946–55), III (1955), pp. 771–805. (Coates)

————, *Amar sin saber a quién*, ed. Carmen Bravo-Villasante, Biblioteca Anaya, 81 (Salamanca: Anaya, 1967). (Thacker, 11)

————, *Arcadia*, ed. Edwin S. Morby, Clásicos Castalia, 63 (Madrid: Castalia, 1975). (Dixon)

————, *Arte nuevo de hacer comedias*; *La discreta enamorada*, Colección Austral, 842 (Madrid: Espasa-Calpe, 1948). (Thacker, 11)

————, *Arte nuevo de hacer comedias*, ed. Enrique García Santo-Tomás, Letras Hispánicas, 585 (Madrid: Cátedra, 2006). (Thacker 7 and 11) (De Armas) (Samson) (Friedman)

————, *Barlaán y Josafat*, ed. José F. Montesinos, Teatro Antiguo Español: Textos y Estudios, 8 (Madrid: Centro de Estudios Históricos, 1935). (Canning)

———— (attr.), *La bienaventurada Madre Santa Teresa de Jesús. Obras XII. Comedias de vidas de santos IV*, ed. Marcelino Menéndez Pelayo (Madrid: Biblioteca de Autores Españoles, 1965), pp. 248–305.

————, *El caballero de Olmedo*, ed. Francisco Rico, 17th edn (Madrid: Cátedra, 1999). (Samson & Thacker, 8)

————, *El caballero de Olmedo*, ed. Edward H. Friedman, Cervantes & Co., 15 (Newark, DE: Juan de la Cuesta, 2004). (Friedman)

————, *El Caballero de Olmedo*, ed. Anthony John Lappin (Manchester: Manchester University Press, 2006). (Samson & Thacker, 8)

————, *La campana de Aragón*, in *Obras escogidas de Lope Félix de Vega Carpio*, ed. Federico Carlos Sainz de Robles, 3 vols (Madrid: Aguilar, 1946–55), III (1955), pp. 835–72. (Coates)

————, *Cartas*, ed. Nicolás Marín, Clásicos Castalia, 143 (Madrid: Castalia, 1985). (Fisher) (Samson & Thacker, Introduction)

————, *El casamiento en la muerte*, in *Obras de Lope de Vega*, XVII: *Crónicas y leyendas dramáticas de España*, ed. Marcelino Menéndez Pelayo, Biblioteca de Autores Españoles, 196 (Madrid: Atlas, 1966), pp. 49–93. (Coates)

————, *El castigo sin venganza*, ed. C. A. Jones (Oxford: Pergamon Press, 1966). (Friedman)

————, *El castigo sin venganza*, ed. José María Díez Borque, Clásicos Castellanos, n.s., 10 (Madrid: Espasa Calpe, 1987). (Friedman)

————, *El castigo sin venganza*, ed. Antonio Carreño, Letras Hispánicas, 316, 3rd edn (Madrid: Cátedra, 1998). (Friedman)

————, *El castigo sin venganza*, ed. Felipe B. Pedraza Jiménez (Barcelona: Octaedro, 1999). ('Further reading')

————, *El castigo sin venganza*, ed. C. A. Jones (Oxford: Pergamon, 1966). (Evans)

————, *Los cinco misterios dolorosos de la Pasión y muerte de Nuestro Señor Jesucristo con su Sagrada Resurrección*, ed. César Hernández Alonso,

Clásicos Madrileños, 4 (Madrid: Instituto de Estudios Madrileños, 1987). (Mayo)

————, *La Circe, con otras rimas y prosas* (Madrid: Viuda de Alonso Martín, 1624). (Rizavi)

————, *La Circe: poema*, ed. Charles V. Aubrun & Manuel Muñoz Cortés, Chefs-d'Oeuvre des Lettres Hispaniques, 2 (Paris: Centre de Recherches de l'Institut d'Études Hispaniques, 1962). (Rizavi)

————, *Comedias de Lope de Vega* (Lleida: Milenio & Universitat Autònoma de Barcelona, 1997–) (a critical edition in multiple volumes of Lope de Vega's *Partes de comedias*, coordinated by the research group Prolope, under the direction of Alberto Blecua and Guillermo Serés, at the Universitat Autònoma de Barcelona, including fundamental introductions to the editorial history of these collections of plays. *Partes I–VI* have been published as of May 2007). (Reidy)

————, *Los comendadores de Córdoba,* in *Obras de Lope de Vega*, XXIV: *Crónicas y leyendas dramáticas de España*, ed. Marcelino Menéndez Pelayo, Biblioteca de Autores Españoles, 215 (Madrid: Atlas, 1968), pp. 1–60. (Evans)

————, *El conde Fernán González: tragicomedia*, ed. Raymond Marcus, Chefs-d'Oeuvre des Lettres Hispaniques, 4 (Paris: Centre de Recherches de l'Institut d'Études Hispaniques, 1963). (Coates)

————, *El cuerdo loco*, ed. José F. Montesinos, Teatro Antiguo Español: Textos y Estudios, 4 (Madrid: Centro de Estudios Históricos, 1922). (Rizavi)

————, *El cuerdo en su casa*, in *Comedias escogidas de frey Lope Félix de Vega Carpio*, III, ed. Juan Eugenio Hartzenbusch, Biblioteca de Autores Españoles, 41 (Madrid: Rivadeneyra, 1873), pp. 443–64. (Evans)

————, *La dama boba*, ed. Diego Marín, Letras Hispánicas, 50, 9th edn (Madrid: Cátedra, 1985). (Thacker, 11) (Samson)

————, *El divino africano*, in *Obras selectas*, ed. Federico Carlos Sainz de Robles, 3 vols (Mexico City: Aguilar, 1991), III, pp. 205–37. (Canning)

————, *The Dog in the Manger*, trans. and ed. Victor Dixon, Carleton Renaissance Plays in Translation, 21 (Ottawa: Dovehouse Editions Canada, 1990). (Johnston)

————, *The Dog in the Manger*, trans. David Johnston, Absolute Classics (London: Oberon, 2004). (Johnston)

————, *La Dorotea*, ed. Edwin S. Morby (Berkeley, CA: University of California Press; Valencia: Castalia, 1958; 2nd edn, revised, 1968). (Dixon) (Fisher) (Tubau)

————, *La Dorotea*, ed. Edwin S. Morby, Clásicos Castalia, 102 (Madrid: Castalia, 1980). (Tubau) (Rizavi)

————, *La Dorotea*, trans. and ed. Alan S. Trueblood and Edwin Honig (Cambridge, MA and London: Harvard University Press, 1985). ('Further reading')

————, *La Dorotea*, ed. José Manuel Blecua, Letras Hispánicas, 408 (Madrid: Cátedra, 1996). (Reidy)

————, 'Epístola nona: a Don Francisco López de Aguilar', in his *Obras poéticas*, ed. José Manuel Blecua, Clásicos Planeta, 18 (Barcelona: Planeta, 1969), pp. 1311–18. (Fisher)

————, *Epistolario de Lope de Vega Carpio*, ed. Agustín G. de Amezúa, 4 vols (Madrid: Aldus, 1935–43). (Dixon) (Ruano) (Reidy) (Fisher) (Mayo) (Samson & Thacker, Introduction)

————, *La fábula de Perseo, o La bella Andrómeda*, ed. Michael D. McGaha, Teatro del Siglo de Oro: Ediciones Críticas, 6 (Kassel: Reichenberger, 1985). (De Armas)

————, *Las ferias de Madrid*, ed. David Roas, in *Comedias de Lope de Vega: Parte II*, dir. Alberto Blecua & Guillermo Serés, 3 vols (Lleida: Milenio & Universitat Autònoma de Barcelona, 1998), III, pp. 1823–1967. (Thacker, 11)

————, *Las ferias de Madrid*, ed. Donald McGrady, Juan de la Cuesta Hispanic Monographs: Ediciones Críticas, 25 (Newark, DE: Juan de la Cuesta, 2006). (Thacker, 11)

————, *Fiestas de Denia*, ed. M. G. Profeti, with historical notes by B. J. García García, Secoli d'Oro, 41 (Florence: Alinea, 2004). (Samson)

————, *Fiestas en la traslación del Santísimo Sacramento a la Iglesia Mayor de Lerma* (Valencia: José Gasch, 1612). (Mayo)

————, *La Filomena, con otras diversas rimas, prosas y versos* (Madrid: Viuda de Alonso Martín, 1621; Barcelona: Sebastián Cormellas, 1621). (Rizavi)

————, *Fuente Ovejuna*, trans. and ed. Victor Dixon (Warminster: Aris and Phillips, 1989). ('Further reading')

————, *Fuenteovejuna*, ed. Francisco Ruiz Ramón, Clásicos Almar, 23 (Salamanca: Colegio de España, 1991) (Friedman)

————, *Fuente Ovejuna*, ed. Juan María Marín, 16th edn (Madrid: Cátedra, 1995). (Samson & Thacker, 8)

————, *La hermosura de Angélica*, ed. Marcella Trambaioli, Biblioteca Áurea Hispánica, 32 ([Pamplona]: Universidad de Navarra; Madrid: Iberoamericana; Frankfurt am Main: Vervuert, 2005). (Dixon)

————, *Justa poética y alabanzas justas al bienaventurado San Isidro*, in *Obras escogidas de Lope Félix de Vega Carpio*, ed. Federico Carlos Sainz de Robles, 3 vols (Madrid: Aguilar, 1946–55), II (1946), pp. 1569–83. (Fisher)

————, *Laurel de Apolo*, ed. Christian Giaffreda, with an introduction by Maria Grazia Profeti, Secoli d'Oro, 32 (Florence: Alinea, 2002). (Dixon)

————, *Lo fingido verdadero*, in his *Décimasexta parte de las comedias* (Madrid: Viuda de Alonso Martín, 1621), fols 261r–284v. (Canning)

————, *Los locos de Valencia*, ed. Hélène Tropé, Clásicos Castalia, 277 (Madrid: Castalia, 2003). (Thacker, 11)

————, *Lope de Vega: Five Plays*, trans. Jill Booty, with an introduction by R. D. F. Pring-Mill, Mermaid Dramabook, 20 (New York: Hill and Wang, 1961). (Johnston) (Samson & Thacker, 8)

————, *Las mocedades de Bernardo del Carpio*, in *Obras de Lope de Vega*, XVII: *Crónicas y leyendas dramáticas de España*, ed. Marcelino Menéndez Pelayo,

Biblioteca de Autores Españoles, 196 (Madrid: Atlas, 1966), pp. 2–48. (Coates)

————, *La moza de cántaro*, ed. José María Díez Borque, Colección Austral: Literatura, A105 (Madrid: Austral, 1990). (Thacker, 11)

————, *The New Art of Writing Plays*, trans. William T. Brewster, with an introduction by Brander Matthews, Papers on Play-Making, 1 (New York: Printed for the Dramatic Museum of Columbia University, 1914). (De Armas)

————, *Novelas a Marcia Leonarda*, ed. Julia Barella, Biblioteca Júcar, 93 (Madrid: Júcar, 1988). (Evans)

————, *Novelas a Marcia Leonarda*, ed. Antonio Carreño, Letras Hispánicas, 487 (Madrid: Cátedra, 2002). (Rizavi)

————, *Novelas a Marcia Leonarda*, ed. Julia Barella, Clásicos de Biblioteca Nueva, 44 (Madrid: Biblioteca Nueva, 2003). (Samson)

————, *Obras poéticas*, I: *Rimas, Rimas sacras, La Filomena, La Circe, Rimas humanas y divinas del licenciado Tomé de Burguillos*, ed. José Manuel Blecua, Clásicos Planeta, 18 (Barcelona: Planeta, 1969). (Dixon)

————, *El peregrino en su patria*, ed. Juan Bautista Avalle-Arce, Clásicos Castalia, 55 (Madrid: Castalia, 1973). (Reidy) (Samson)

————, *Peribáñez y el comendador de Ocaña*, ed. J. M. Ruano and J. E. Varey (London: Tamesis, 1980). ('Further reading')

————, *Peribáñez y el comendador de Ocaña*, ed. Juan María Marín, Letras Hispánicas, 96, 6th edn (Madrid: Cátedra, 1986). (Samson & Thacker, 8)

————, *El perro del hortelano*, ed. Victor Dixon (London: Tamesis Texts, 1981). (Thacker, 11)

————, *The Pilgrime of Casteele* (London: [Edward Allde for] John Norton, 1621; 2nd edn: Edward Allde for John Norton & Thomas Dewe, 1623). (Samson)

————, *Poesía*, ed. Antonio Carreño, 6 vols, Biblioteca Castro, Obras Completas de Lope de Vega, 36–41 (Madrid: Fundación José Antonio de Castro, 2002–5), IV (2003). (Mayo)

————, *Poesía*, IV: *La Filomena; La Circe*, ed. Antonio Carreño, Biblioteca Castro, Obras Completas de Lope de Vega, 39 (Madrid: Fundación José Antonio de Castro, 2004). (Rizavi)

————, *Poesía selecta*, ed. Antonio Carreño, Letras Hispánicas, 187, 4th edn (Madrid: Cátedra, 2003). (Torres)

————, *Prosa*, I: *Arcadia*; *El peregrino en su patria*, ed. Donald McGrady, Biblioteca Castro, Obras Completas de Lope de Vega, 33 (Madrid: Fundación José Antonio de Castro, 1997). (Rizavi)

————, *La quinta de Florencia*, ed. Debra Collins Ames, Teatro del Siglo de Oro: Ediciones Críticas, 65 ([Valparaiso, IN]: Valparaiso University; Kassel: Reichenberger, 1995). (De Armas)

————, 'Respuesta de Lope de Vega Carpio' (to a 'Papel que escribió un señor destos reinos […] en razón de la nueva poesía'), in his *Obras poéticas*, I, ed. José Manuel Blecua, Clásicos Planeta, 18 (Barcelona: Planeta, 1969), pp. 873–88. (Fisher)

———, 'La respuesta', in his *Obras poéticas*, I, ed. José Manuel Blecua, Clásicos Planeta, 18 (Barcelona: Planeta, 1969), pp. 889–91. (Fisher)

———, *Rimas*, ed. Felipe B. Pedraza Jiménez, 2 vols (Ciudad Real: Universidad de Castilla-La Mancha, 1993–94). (Tubau) (Fisher) (Thacker, 7)

———, *Rimas humanas y otros versos*, ed. Antonio Carreño, Biblioteca Clásica, 52 (Barcelona: Crítica, 1998). (Fisher) (Tubau)

———, *Rimas humanas y divinas del licenciado Tomé de Burguillos y La gatomaquia*, ed. Antonio Carreño, Biblioteca Hispánica, 38 (Salamanca: Almar, 2002). (Fisher)

———, *Rimas humanas y divinas del licenciado Tomé de Burguillos*, ed. Juan Manuel Rozas & Jesús Cañas Murillo, Clásicos Castalia, 280 (Madrid: Castalia, 2004). (Dixon) (Torres)

———, *Rimas sacras*, ed. Antonio Carreño & Antonio Sánchez Jiménez, Biblioteca Áurea Hispánica, 25 ([Pamplona]: Universidad de Navarra; Madrid: Iberoamericana; Frankfurt am Main: Vervuert, 2006). (Mayo)

———, *El robo de Dina*, in *Obras de Lope de Vega*, VIII: *Autos y coloquios*, II [III], ed. Marcelino Menéndez y Pelayo, Biblioteca de Autores Españoles, 159 (Madrid: Atlas, 1963), pp. 7–50. (Canning)

———, *San Nicolás de Tolentino*, in his *Obras selectas*, ed. Federico Carlos Sainz de Robles, 3 vols (Mexico City: Aguilar, 1991), III, pp. 239–74. (Canning)

——— (attr.), *Santa Teresa de Jesús, monja descalza de Nuestra Señora del Carmen*, in *Obras de Lope de Vega*, V: *Comedias de vidas de santos y leyendas piadosas; Comedias pastoriles*, ed. Marcelino Menéndez Pelayo (Madrid: Real Academia Española, 1890), pp. 248–305. (Mujica)

———, *Servir a señor discreto*, ed. Frida Weber de Kurlat, Clásicos Castalia, 68 (Madrid: Castalia, 1975). (Dixon)

———, *Three Major Plays*, trans. Gwynne Edwards (Oxford: Oxford University Press, 1999). (Samson & Thacker, 8)

———, *El último godo*, in *Obras escogidas de Lope Félix de Vega Carpio*, ed. Federico Carlos Sainz de Robles, 3 vols (Madrid: Aguilar, 1946–55), III (1955), pp. 629–59. (Coates)

——— (attr.), *Vida y muerte de Santa Teresa de Jesús: commedia inedita*, ed. Elisa Aragone Terni, Università degli Studi di Firenze, Publiccazioni dell'Istituto Ispanico (Messina & Florence: Casa editrice D'Anna, 1970). (Mujica)

———, *Viuda, casada y doncella*, ed. Ronna S. Feit & Donald McGrady, Juan de la Cuesta Hispanic Monographs: Ediciones Críticas, 24 (Newark, DE: Juan de la Cuesta, 2006). (Thacker, 11)

———, *La viuda valenciana*, ed. Teresa Ferrer Valls, Clásicos Castalia, 263 (Madrid: Castalia, 2001). (De Armas) (Thacker, 11)

Vega, Miguel Ángel, ed., *Textos clásicos de teoría de la traducción* (Madrid: Cátedra, 1994). (Johnston)

Velasco, Sherry M., 'Visualizing Gender on the Page in Convent Literature', in *Women, Texts and Authority in the Early Modern Spanish World*, ed. Marta V. Vicente and Luis R. Corteguera Hampshire (Aldershot: Ashgate, 2003), pp. 127–48. (Mujica)

Venuti, Lawrence, *The Translator's Invisibility: A History of Translation* (London: Routledge, 1995). (Johnston)

Vianna Peres, Lygia Rodríguez, 'El retrato en la expresión barroca del teatro del Siglo de Oro: emblemática y teatralidad', in *Memoria de la palabra: Actas del VI Congreso de la Asociación Internacional Siglo de Oro*, ed. María Luisa Lobato & Francisco Domínguez Matito, 2 vols (Madrid: Iberoamericana; Frankfurt am Main: Vervuert, 2004), II, pp. 1507–22. (Samson & Thacker, 8)

Vila, Juan Diego, 'Lectura e imaginario de la femineidad en *Las Novelas a Marcia Leonarda*', in *Silva: studia philologica in honorem Isaías Lerner*, ed. Isabel Lozano-Renieblas & Juan Carlos Mercado (Madrid: Castalia, 2001), pp. 697–708. (Rizavi)

Vilanova, Antonio, 'El peregrino andante en el *Persiles* de Cervantes' (1949), in his *Erasmo y Cervantes*, Palabra Crítica, 8 (Barcelona: Lumen, 1989), pp. 326–409. (Samson)

Villegas Ruiz, Manuel, *Fuenteovejuna: el drama y la historia* (Baena: Adisur, 1990). (Samson & Thacker, 8)

Virgil, 'Eclogue III', in *Virgil in Two Volumes*, ed. and trans. H. Rushton Fairclough, Loeb Classical Library, revised edn (Cambridge, MA: Harvard University Press; London: Heinemann, 1965), pp. 176–217. (Fisher)

Vitoria, Fray Baltasar de, *El teatro de los dioses de la gentilidad*, 2 parts (Madrid: Imprenta Real, 1676). (Rizavi)

Vocabulario della lingua italiana, ed. Rita Levi-Montalcini (Rome: Instituto della Enciclopedia Italiana, 1994). (Fisher)

Vorágine, Santiago de la (Jacobus de Voragine), *La leyenda dorada*, ed. José Manuel Macías, 2 vols, Alianza Forma, 29–30 (Madrid: Alianza, 1982). (Mayo)

Vossler, Karl, '*Euphrosina*', *Corona*, 8 (1938): 514–33. (Tubau)

Vosters, Simon A., 'Lope de Vega y Titelmans: cómo el Fénix se representaba el universo', *Revista de Literatura*, 21 (1962): 5–33; 'Dos adiciones a mi artículo "Lope de Vega y Titelmans"', *Revista de Literatura*, 22 (1962): 90. (Dixon)

———, 'Lope de Vega y Juan Ravisio Textor: nuevos datos', *Iberoromania*, n.s., 2 (1975): 69–103. (Dixon)

———, *Lope de Vega y la tradición occidental*, 2 vols ([Madrid]: Castalia, 1977): I (*El simbolismo bíblico de Lope de Vega: algunas de sus fuentes*); II (*El manierismo de Lope de Vega y la literatura francesa*). (Dixon)

———, *Rubens y España: estudio artístico-literario sobre la estética del Barroco* (Madrid: Cátedra, 1990). (De Armas)

Wardropper, Bruce W., 'La comedia española del Siglo de Oro', addendum to Elder Olson, *Teoría de la comedia*, Letras e Ideas: Minor, 11 (Barcelona: Ariel, 1978). (Thacker, 11)

――――, 'Civilización y barbarie en *El castigo sin venganza*', in *'El castigo sin venganza' y el teatro de Lope de Vega*, ed. Ricardo Doménech (Madrid: Cátedra & Teatro Español, 1987), pp. 191–205. (Friedman)

Weber, Alison, *Teresa of Avila and the Rhetoric of Femininity* (Princeton, NJ: Princeton University Press, 1990). (Mujica)

Weber de Kurlat, Frida, 'Lope-Lope y Lope-preLope: formación del subcódigo de la comedia de Lope y su época', *Segismundo*, 12, nos 23–24 (1976): 111–31. (Thacker, 11)

Weimer, Christopher B., 'The Politics of Adaptation: *Fuenteovejuna* in Pinochet's Chile', in *Echoes and Inscriptions: Comparative Approaches to Early Modern Spanish Literatures*, ed. Barbara A. Simerka & Christopher B. Weimer (Lewisburg, PA: Bucknell University Press, 2000), pp. 234–49. (Samson & Thacker, 8)

Weiner, Jack, 'Lope de Vega's *Fuenteovejuna* under the Tsars, Commisars and the 2nd Spanish Republic (1931–39)', *Annali Istituto Universitario Orientale, Sezione Romanza*, 24.1 (1982): 167–223. (Samson & Thacker, 8)

Weisinger, Herbert, '*Theatrum Mundi*: Illusion as Reality', in his *The Agony and the Triumph: Papers on the Use and Abuse of Myth* (East Lansing, MI: Michigan State University Press, 1964), pp. 58–70. (Canning)

Wheeler, Duncan, '*We Are Living in a Material World and I Am a Material Girl*: Diana, Countess of Belflor Materialised on the Page, Stage and Screen', *Bulletin of Hispanic Studies*, 84.3 (2007): 267–86. (Wheeler)

――――, 'The Performance History of Golden-Age Drama in Spain (1939–2006)', *Bulletin of the Comediantes*, 60.2 (2008) (forthcoming). (Wheeler)

Whinnom, Keith, 'The Problem of the "Best-Seller" in Spanish Golden-Age Literature', *Bulletin of Hispanic Studies*, 57.3 (1980): 189–98. (Mayo)

Wilder, Thornton, 'New Aids Toward Dating the Early Plays of Lope de Vega' (1952), in his *American Characteristics and Other Essays*, ed. Donald Gallup (Lincoln, NE: Authors Guild Backinprint, 2000), pp. 257–66. (Samson)

Williams, Patrick, *The Great Favourite: The Duke of Lerma and the Court and Government of Philip III of Spain, 1598–1621* (Manchester: Manchester University Press, 2006). (Samson) (Samson & Thacker, Introduction)

Wilson, Christopher, 'Saint Teresa of Ávila's Martyrdom: Images of Her Transverberation in Mexican Colonial Painting', *Anales del Instituto de Investigaciones Estéticas* 74–75 (1999), pp. 211–233. (Mujica)

Wilson, Edward M., & Duncan Moir, *A Literary History of Spain: The Golden Age: Drama, 1492–1700* (London: Ernest Benn, 1971). (Wheeler) (Evans)

Winkel, Marieke de, 'The Artist as Couturier: The Portrayal of Clothing in the Golden Age', in *Dutch Portraits: The Age of Rembrandt and Frans Hals*, ed. Rudi Ekkart & Quentin Buvelot (The Hague: Royal Picture Gallery Mauritshuis; London: National Gallery; Zwolle: Waanders, 2007), pp. 65–73. (McGrath)

Wolf, Kenneth Baxter, ed. and trans., *Conquerors and Chroniclers of Early Medieval Spain*, Translated Texts for Historians, 9, 2nd edn (Liverpool: Liverpool University Press, 1999). (Coates)

Worthen, W. B., *Print and the Poetics of Modern Drama* (Cambridge: Cambridge University Press, 2006). (Johnston)

Wright, Elizabeth R., *Pilgrimage to Patronage: Lope de Vega and the Court of Philip III (1598–1621)* (Lewisburg, PA: Bucknell University Press, 2001). (Rizavi) (Samson & Thacker, Introduction)

Wright, Roger, 'How Old is the Ballad Genre?', *La Corónica*, 14 (1985–86): 251–57. (Coates)

———, ed. and trans., *Spanish Ballads with English Verse Translations* (Warminster: Aris & Phillips, 1987). (Coates)

Ximénez de Rada, Rodrigo, *Historia de rebus Hispanie, sive, Historia Gothica*, ed. Juan Fernández Valverde, Corpus Christianorum: Continuatio Medievalis, 72 (Turnholti: Brepols, 1987). (Coates)

Yarbro-Bejarano, Yvonne, 'Lope's *Novelas a Marcia Leonarda*', *Kentucky Romance Quarterly*, 27.4 (1980): 459–73. (Rizavi)

———, *Feminism and the Honor Plays of Lope de Vega*, Purdue Studies in Romance Literatures, 4 (West Lafayette, IN: Purdue University Press, 1994). (Canning)

Ynduráin, Francisco, *Relección de clásicos*, El Soto: Estudios de Crítica y Filología, 12 (Madrid: Editorial Prensa Española, 1969). (Rizavi)

Yudin, Florence L., 'The *novela corta* as *comedia*: Lope's *Las fortunas de Diana*', *Bulletin of Hispanic Studies*, 45.3 (1968): 181–88. (Rizavi)

Zabaleta, Juan de, *El día de fiesta por la mañana y por la tarde* (1654, 1660), ed. Cristóbal Cuevas García, Clásicos Castalia, 130 (Madrid: Castalia, 1983). (Evans) (Ruano)

Zamora Lucas, Florentino, *Lope de Vega censor de libros: colección de aprobaciones, censuras, elogios y prólogos del Fénix, que se hallan en los preliminares de algunos libros de su tiempo, con notas biográficas de sus autores* (Larache: Boscá, 1941 [1943]). (Dixon)

———, *Lope de Vega: poesías preliminares de libros*, Cuadernos Bibliográficos, 2 (Madrid: Consejo Superior de Investigaciones Científicas, 1961). (Dixon)

Zamora Vicente, Alonso, *Lope de Vega: su vida y su obra*, Biblioteca Románica Hispánica, 7: Campo Abierto, 1 (Madrid: Gredos, 1961). (Samson & Thacker, Introduction)

Zuckerman-Ingber, Alix, *El bien más alto: A Reconsideration of Lope de Vega's Honor Plays*, University of Florida Monographs: Humanities, 56 (Gainesville, FL: University Presses of Florida, 1984). (Evans)

INDEX

Works by Lope de Vega appear directly under title; works by others under author's name.